# Studies in Empirical Philosophy

by

# John Anderson

Challis Professor of Philosophy
In the University of Sydney
1927–1958

with an introduction by

# John Passmore

SYDNEY UNIVERSITY PRESS

SYDNEY UNIVERSITY PRESS
Print on Demand Service
SETIS at the University of Sydney Library
University of Sydney
www.sup.usyd.edu.au

Originally published in Sydney by Angus and Robertson in 1962. New edition by SUP Print on Demand 2005.

The publication of this book is part of the University of Sydney Library's Australian Studies electronic texts initiative. Further details are available at www.sup.usyd.edu.au/oztexts/

© 2005 Sydney University Press
Introduction © 2005 Professor John Passmore. Reproduced with the permission of Professor Passmore and Mrs Passmore.

**Reproduction and Communication for other purposes**
Except as permitted under the Act, no part of this edition may be reproduced, stored in a retrieval system, or communicated in any form or by any means without prior written permission. All requests for reproduction or communication should be made to Sydney University Press at the address below:

Sydney University Press
Fisher Library
University of Sydney
NSW Australia 2006

E-mail: *info@sup.usyd.edu.au*

ISBN 1 920898 17 4

For current information see http://purl.library.usyd.edu.au/sup/1920898174

Typeset by Laserwords Private Limited, Chennai, India
Cover Designed in Australia at the University Publishing Service University of Sydney

# CONTENTS

Foreword     v

John Anderson and Twentieth-Century Philosophy     vii

1   Empiricism (1927)     1

2   Propositions and Judgments (1926)     17

3   The Truth of Propositions (1926)     23

4   The Knower and the Known (1927)     31

5   Realism and Some of its Critics (1930)     50

6   The Non-Existence of Consciousness (1929)     74

7   Mind as Feeling (1934)     84

8   The Place of Hegel in the History of Philosophy (1932)     99

9   Design (1935)     111

10   The *Cogito* of Descartes (1936)     128

11   "Universals" and Occurrences (1929)     146

12   Causality and Logic (1936)     154

13   The Problem of Causality (1938)     158

14   Hypotheticals (1952)     172

15   Relational Arguments (1962)     186

16   Empiricism and Logic (1962)     204

17   Classicism (1960)     239

| | |
|---|---|
| 18 Socrates as an Educator (1931) | 257 |
| 19 Determinism and Ethics (1928) | 271 |
| 20 Utilitarianism (1932) | 288 |
| 21 Realism versus Relativism in Ethics (1933) | 301 |
| 22 The Meaning of Good (1942) | 313 |
| 23 The Nature of Ethics (1943) | 339 |
| 24 Ethics and Advocacy (1944) | 352 |
| 25 The One Good (1945) | 364 |
| 26 Marxist Philosophy (1935) | 369 |
| 27 Marxist Ethics (1937) | 397 |
| 28 The Servile State (1943) | 415 |
| 29 Freudianism and Society (1940) | 430 |
| 30 The Freudian Revolution (1953) | 454 |
| 31 Psychological Moralism (1953) | 459 |
| **Bibliography** | **474** |
| **Index** | **481** |

# FOREWORD

This book is published as part of a commemoration of the work of John Anderson, for more than thirty years Challis Professor of Philosophy in the University of Sydney. Anderson's chief philosophical papers, hitherto printed only in journals, are now brought together and reprinted along with two newly-written papers and an introductory essay by Professor John Passmore, a former student of Anderson's.

The publication of the volume has been made possible by the generosity of a number of contributors to an Anderson Testimonial Fund, and has been considerably assisted by a special grant given by the Australian Humanities Research Council.

Acknowledgments for permission to reprint certain papers, noted in the Bibliography, are made to the Mind Association, the Arostotelian Society, the Australasian Association for Philosophy, and the Australian Humanities Research Council.

A. K. Stout
For the Anderson Testimonial Committee

## NOTE

Many references are made, throughout the text, to the Australasian Journal of Psychology and Philosophy (A.J.P.P.) and to the Australasian Journal of Philosophy (A.J.P.). These are one and the same journal; the name was changed in 1947.

# JOHN ANDERSON AND TWENTIETH-CENTURY PHILOSOPHY

## J. A. Passmore

The University of Glasgow, when John Anderson entered it in 1911, was still an outpost of Absolute Idealism, as represented especially by Sir Henry Jones, friend and pupil of Edward Caird. Anderson's original inclinations were towards physics and mathematics rather than philosophy. (He graduated with first-class honours in the Mathematics and Physics School and in the Philosophy School in 1917.) He was unlikely, then, to be wholly satisfied by Jones's measured rhetoric; and his family tradition of radical politics—his father was a Socialist headmaster—set him in opposition to the solidarist tendencies of Absolute Idealism. Nor was the logic of Jones's colleague, Latta, Idealist in its general assumptions, even if Latta himself was a little more amiably disposed than most Idealists towards traditional formal logic, sufficiently rigorous or sufficiently consistent to satisfy Anderson's demands. Yet, unlike most rebels against Absolute Idealism, Anderson was not prepared to reject its teachings as wholly worthless; he took seriously the Idealist criticisms of Mill; he was not going to swing back in simple reaction from Absolute Idealism to "impressions and ideas", however ingeniously they might be deployed in their new guise as "sense-data".

In the theory of ideas Anderson detected not the true contradictory of Absolute Idealism, but rather a variant development of the same metaphysical impulse: the search for something ultimate, in contrast with which the complex objects of everyday experience are arbitrary constructions, mind-made. The vital issue for Anderson is whether facts are constructions; the question which divided Absolute Idealist and traditional empiricist—whether facts are hacked out of the Absolute or built up out of sensations—was for him of slight importance. Against Absolute Idealist and traditional empiricist alike, Anderson set out to show that there is no reality (whether "higher" or "lower") other than the complex, and complexly interacting, objects of everyday experience. For Anderson as for "the vulgar", when I assert that the book is on the table I am neither imposing abstractions upon Reality nor constructing objects and their interconnections out of simple experiences; I am taking something to be the case, really to be the case. And if there is any doubt whether it is "really the case" that the book is on the table, this is because the book might in fact be on the floor or in the book-case or because what is on the table might not be a book but a cigar-box, not because the book is neither the Absolute nor an elementary perception.

Anderson is not being merely arbitrary when he describes himself as an "empiricist", for all that he has broken so sharply with traditional empiricism. Like, say, Hume and Mill, he sees in experience the only guide to what is the case; like them, he rejects the transcendental and those special modes of cognition which are supposed to lead us to the awareness of the transcendental. But their account of experience, he considers, is metaphysical, "rationalistic". Impressions, ideas, sense-data, function in traditional empiricism as ultimate foundations for, justifications of, our everyday beliefs; whereas for Anderson a belief can be justified only by another belief, a statement that something is the case only by a statement that something else is the case. Justification, explanation, proof, is never "ultimate" in the sense of resting on entities or principles which are transparent, whether they be Cartesian "simple natures", Lockeian simple ideas, Platonic forms, or the axioms of classical rationalism. To believe, to experience, to know, to assert, so Anderson argues, is to take something to be the case and in so doing to run the risk of being mistaken—a risk that no degree of care can wholly rule out. There is no experience prior to, as there is no form of knowledge higher than, taking something to be the case.

In his criticism of traditional empiricism, Anderson shows the influence of William James, whom he closely studied. James rejected the view (which, once more, Absolute Idealists and traditional empiricists had shared) that relations are "the work of the mind", imposed upon an original experience which is itself wholly disconnected. As Hume had expressed the matter: "All our distinct perceptions are distinct existences and the mind never perceives any real connexion among distinct existences". James condemned this account of experience as "vicious intellectualism"; it rests on the supposition, he argued, that if A and B are connected, it is impossible for them also to be distinct, and if distinct, impossible for them to be connected. In fact, James insisted, things are, and are experienced as being, both connected and distinct; and there is no good reason for supposing either that their connectedness is unreal and their distinctness real, or that their distinctness is unreal and their connectedness real. This is essential to Anderson's position. For it is impossible to identify, as he does, "experiencing" and "taking something to be the case", if experience is always of the unrelated. To take something to be the case is to point both to connections and distinctions. "The book is on the table" presupposes the possibility of distinguishing the book and the table from what surrounds them, yet it at the same time links them; unless there are both connections and distinctions in experience no proposition can be a simple statement of what we experience.

Anderson's position on this point may at times remind the reader of Wittgenstein's *Tractatus Logico-Philosophicus*, for which "the world is the totality of facts, not of things". But the parallel extends only thus far: for Anderson as for Wittgenstein the starting point is facts, not elementary entities which are later put together into facts. Anderson, in contrast with the *Tractatus* (a book of which he was not aware when he was working out his own position), rejects both the conception of "the world"—understood as a totality of facts—and the conception of an atomic fact. Furthermore, there is still talk in the *Tractatus* of elementary objects, even if they are supposed only to exist in facts. For Anderson, on the contrary, every fact (which includes every "object") is a complex situation: there are no simples, no atomic facts, no totalities, no objects which cannot be, as it were, expanded into facts. On Anderson's view the statement that "X exists" can always be expressed in the form "some Y are Z", whatever X may be. That is why he describes himself as a "pluralist".

This again can be misleading; traditionally, pluralism has been the theory that there is a plurality of ultimate entities. Anderson's pluralism, on the contrary, is thorough-going: he wholly rejects the view that complexes are built out of simple entities. "Even if the world is infinitely complex", Wittgenstein wrote, "so that every fact consists of an infinite number of atomic facts and every atomic fact is composed of an infinite number of objects, even then there must be simples and atomic facts." When Anderson, on the contrary, asserts infinite complexity he is denying that there are simples; and far from its being the case that there *must* be simples, there cannot, on his view, be simples. The least one can encounter, in his own phrase, is "a thing of a certain sort", something of a certain kind (indeed, of an endless variety of kinds) happening somewhere. "There are only facts", as he writes in "Empiricism", "i.e. occurrences in space and time"; within such a fact we can always distinguish what is happening from where it is happening.

Why cannot there be simples? Because, Anderson would say, the supposition that there are simples is unspeakable—as Plato pointed out in the *Sophist* (252c), the theory of simples is self-refuting. Or, approaching the matter in another way, because the whole point of supposing that there are simples is that the simples are the building blocks out of which complexes are constructed whereas, in fact, complexes cannot be built up out of purely simple ingredients. A table is not brownness, and darkness, and hardness, and smoothness, in the sense of being a logical conjunction of these properties. In general, as soon as we try to say anything whatever about alleged ultimates—and *something* has to be said about them—they turn out to be either entirely empty of content, and hence useless as "foundations", or else to be no more ultimate than what they are supposed to support. So far as it rejects atomism Anderson would be in sympathy with Wittgenstein's *Philosophical Investigations*, but Anderson's spare and dialectical manner of procedure is at the opposite extreme from Wittgenstein's diary-like ruminations. Indeed towards "ordinary language" philosophy of every sort Anderson's hostility has been unmitigated. He has refused in any way to take it seriously; its rise to prominence undoubtedly did a great deal to make him feel disheartened about the prospects for philosophy.

In his criticisms of traditional empiricism, Anderson looked for support to certain of the "new realists", both in Great Britain and the United States. However, many of the self-styled, or by-others-styled, realists were actually phenomenalists. They attempted, as Russell did, to develop more systematically the traditional approach of British empiricism, with Mill and Mach as the immediate starting-point; with such "realists" Anderson certainly did not wish to associate himself. In his eyes, indeed, epistemological questions are always secondary to logical (or, some would say, ontological) questions. A realist theory of knowledge, he thinks, is a particular application of a realist theory of relations, flowing out of the rejection of "constitutive" relations and taking the form of an attack on what Anderson calls "relativism". Opposing the phenomenalist doctrine that the *esse* of what we perceive consists in its being perceived, he argues that what we perceive must have characteristics of its own. Even the assertion: "I am perceiving a red sense-datum", makes a specific claim: the claim to be perceiving a certain sort of object; did "the whole essence" of that object consist in its being perceived, then I should no longer be claiming to perceive it rather than something else, say, a blue sense-datum. Indeed, I should not be claiming to perceive anything at all. I should be entitled to say only: "I am perceiving", for to claim to perceive x would at once distinguish x from the fact that it is perceived, thus denying that the whole essence of x consists in its being perceived. The phenomenalist, that is, gives no account of what is perceived, for it is not such an account to assert that I perceive "perceptions".

To the question: "What do I perceive?" then, the answer: "A perception" will not suffice; and the same is true of such answers as "awareness", or "consciousness" to the question: "What perceives?" Just as what is perceived cannot be constituted by its being perceived, so what perceives cannot be constituted by its perceiving; both perceived and perceiver, according to Anderson, must be complex states of affairs—variously describable occurrences. When the perceiver perceives the perceived this will simply be another complex state of affairs. "Being a book" is being an occurrence of a certain sort; so is "being a book on the table", and so is "someone's perceiving a book on the table".

Of course this, as a purely logical point, still leaves completely open the question what sort of complex thing is perceived and what sort of complex thing perceives. It is still possible in principle that I never perceive anything but complex states of my own mind; but that will not at all be a plausible view, Anderson thinks, once logical confusions are cleared out of the way. Similarly, logic cannot by itself determine what are the distinctive features of mind. It can however, rule out the supposition that mind is wholly constituted by its apprehension of objects, or that it is a mere "consciousness".

Equally, Anderson thought, logic can rule out the supposition that mind has a mode of existence that is somehow "higher" than that of other things; minds, too, must be complex occurrences in space and time. At this point the decisive influence was Alexander's *Space, Time and Deity*, which Anderson heard as Gifford lectures in the University of Glasgow (1916–18). Alexander profoundly stirred Anderson's philosophical imagination; those who heard his lectures on Alexander felt that they were being led into the very heart of Anderson's philosophy.

Of course, as "The Non-Existence of Consciousness" makes clear, Anderson came to be anything but a whole-hearted disciple of Alexander. The crucial thing Anderson derived from Alexander was the doctrine of a single spatio-temporal medium within which everything had a place and a time, whatever its specific characteristics. However, Alexander's Space-Time is both a medium and a stuff; for Anderson, it is a medium only. Alexander, too, had taken over from Lloyd Morgan a theory of emergence (involving a distinction between degrees or levels of complexity) which Anderson wholly rejected. But for Anderson, as for Alexander, there are no "special", no "privileged", entities. All distinctions are distinctions in characteristics, not in status. There is no special realm of "mental entities"; in remembering, in imagining, in expecting, in desiring, we are concerned all the time with independent states of affairs. Any other view, Anderson thought, built impassable boundaries between the mental and the non-mental—barriers which yet, it had to be admitted, constantly were passed through in our everyday dealings with things. His objection to Alexander was that in his theory, too, not all the barriers are down; if, as Alexander had argued, mental processes are "enjoyed" and non-mental processes "contemplated", then it is impossible in principle, Anderson thought, to give any coherent account of our observation of the connection between the two. For that connection itself, by the nature of the case, can neither be contemplated nor enjoyed.

Alexander taught Anderson, however, that knowledge is a way of striving with things rather than a simple reflection of them. Quite as vigorously as Collingwood, Anderson rejected what Collingwood called the "transparency" theory of knowledge and ascribed to his "realist" contemporaries. Knowledge—using this word in its broadest sense to include every case where a proposition is taken to be true—is never, according to Anderson, the bare reception of a given object by an act of awareness. Rather, it is an attempt to come to terms with ourselves (in self-knowledge) or the things around us. The transparency theory, he thought, could give no account of belief, whether true or false, and no account, either, of the selectivity of knowledge, or of error. In any adequate theory of knowledge the knowing mind must be regarded as a complex entity with its own demands, which are partly satisfied by, partly encounter obstacles in, the complex behaviour of other things, including other people and other tendencies within the same mind.

Unlike Alexander, however, Anderson does not adopt a merely conationalist theory of mind; for Anderson the mind is a complex of feelings or passions, these being the things that strive. Such an approach to mind is by no means unique. It is more than suggested by a number of eighteenth-century moralists; it is explicit in Nietzsche when he speaks of mind as "the social structure of instincts and passions"; Anderson was led to it by his reading of McDougall and Freud. But most contemporary philosophers will no doubt regard it as one of the oddest features of Anderson's philosophy; the general philosophical tendency has been to regard passion as lying quite outside the mind with which the epistemologist concerns himself—as something which perhaps ought to be discussed, as Aristotle discusses it, in connection with ethics but ought to be strictly excluded, as merely psychological, from epistemology. (Anderson's Cook-Wilsonian contemporaries were particularly insistent upon this apartheid policy.) If, like Hume, philosophers have argued for the complexity of mind, they have taken it to be a complexity of "perceptions", not of passions. But certainly that will not be a satisfactory view once it is recognised that what Hume refers to as "perceptions" are simply what we perceive, and that what we perceive is not, ordinarily, part of our mind at all. The question then has to be raised afresh: "Of what is the mind a complex?"

Anderson would not be content with the answer suggested by Ryle in *The Concept of Mind*, that, to put it roughly, a person's mind is wholly describable in terms of his actions and dispositions to act. When Anderson speaks of a "motive", he thinks of it as actually being a moving force; the familiar expression "he is moved by curiosity" is to be taken quite literally: curiosity, understood as a complex mental structure distinguishable from, but continuous with, other mental structures, can be the actual agent in our attempts to understand the things around us. Curiosity is not to be thought of as operating upon "the mind" and inducing it to act in a particular way; for "the mind" is nothing but a complex of such complex structures. Thus for Anderson, it is curiosity itself which moves us, and psychology will describe the interplay of such mental structures just as sociology describes social structures. It is to such mental complexes, too, that ethical predicates apply: our motives (not in the sense of our objectives but of our moving forces) are good or evil.

Anderson describes these motives as "tensions"; they are, of course, physical as well as mental structures. Such ways of talking Ryle would no doubt condemn as "para-mechanical". This accusation would not disturb Anderson, but would rather help to confirm him in his belief that he is thinking along sound lines. Anderson's approach is essentially that of a generaliser; he expects to find that methods of approach, principles of explanation, modes of description, which have proved fruitful in one field of inquiry will also prove fruitful in others. Of course, he would freely admit that they might not, in a given case, turn out to be appropriate. What he is looking for, all the same, are modes of description which will be as widely applicable as possible—in opposition to the differentiating approach of so much contemporary philosophy, which seeks to make distinctions rather than to establish connections. Thus if, as McDougall maintains, the influence of mind on mind turns out to be parallel to electrical induction—or, one should rather say, to exemplify the same sort of general relationship as is also to be found in electrical theory—that is exactly what Anderson would expect to be the case.

Certainly, Anderson would wish to reject any account of mind which was wholly dispositional. To assert of any person that, say, he "has a happy disposition", is, on this view, equivalent to asserting that he displays certain characteristics under unspecified, but specifiable, circumstances. Disposition-statements are reducible to categorical statements about the actual behaviour of complex entities. This is connected with Anderson's general logical doctrine that hypothetical assertions are simply a rhetorical variant of categorical assertions. "If..., then..." is used, he would admit, in a variety of ways, but always as a way of asserting that some actual occurrence takes place, or some actual relation holds. Thus, for example, "if he were to come, I should be astonished" asserts an actual connection between the sort of circumstances under which he would come and my being astonished; it might be expressed as: "The arrival of people of his sort at ceremonial occasions always astonishes me".

In general, Anderson's logic, like his psychology, will strike strangely on the ears of his contemporaries. With his mathematical bent, Anderson might have been expected to pick up and develop the Russellian mathematical logic; alternatively, he might have been expected to associate with his pragmatic theory of belief ("We believe what satisfies us") the characteristic pragmatic criticism of formal logic. He did neither of these things. Of course, he was aware of, and was affected by, Russell's work, taking over, for example, Russell's conception of a "propositional function". But it was the traditional formal logic which he chose to expound and to develop, defending it against its critics, whether they were Russellians, pragmatists or idealists.

To put the matter thus, however, is certainly to underestimate Anderson's contributions to logic. For, if his logic is traditional in its allegiance to the "four forms" and its emphasis upon syllogism, no topic in the traditional logic comes out of his hands quite as it entered them. His logic is philosophical, thought through consistently, as the traditional logic of the text-books is not. For example, he brings into the open the existential presuppositions of traditional logic; he rejects both the class interpretation and the substance-attribute interpretation of the proposition; he denies that the validity of a syllogism depends either upon a dictum or on rules about distribution; he sees that to assert that a term is distributed is identical with, not a necessary preliminary to, the recognition that certain forms of syllogism are valid and others fallacious; he develops and generalises the traditional theory of opposition; he describes and systematises a number of forms of non-syllogistic inferences; he considers at length, if he finally rejects, the claims of relational, hypothetical and disjunctive reasoning to be regarded as wholly distinct from syllogism. If his logic is traditional, the tradition is worn with a difference.

What he would with special vehemence oppose is the doctrine, now almost universal, that logic is a calculus. He would not be prepared to grant, for example, that his own logic is simply an alternative version of the traditional predicate calculus. Logic, as Anderson sees it, describes the general structure of facts, including the relationships between facts. What are sometimes regarded as the supreme examples of logical truths, e.g. the principle of identity, are not, on his view, truths at all; they say nothing. But he does not agree with Wittgenstein that all the propositions of logic are tautologies. This is not true, he would say, of a proposition which asserts the validity of a type of syllogism or even the equivalence of "No X are Y" and "No Y are X". Such propositions tell us something; we have to learn that "No X are Y" and "No Y are X", unlike "Some X are not Y" and "Some Y are not X", are equivalent.

Logic, as Anderson conceives it, incorporates what Mr Strawson has recently described as "descriptive metaphysics". It is neither about forms of language, nor about reasoning processes, nor about special-status entities, e.g. universals; it is about the most general features of facts. There are, indeed, no "universals", in the sense that there are no entities which are simply properties. But equally there are no "particulars", in the sense in which logical atomism presumes the existence of particulars. Every proposition, for Anderson, is about things of a certain description and offers a further description of them. Both subject and predicate, indeed, are things of a certain description; but the primary function of the subject, Anderson argues, is to "locate" i.e. to be the centre of reference which a predicate describes. The function of the predicate is, on the other hand, to describe. There are not two classes of entities: pure locations ("particulars" or "substances") and pure descriptions ("universals"). Any entity is both specific and general. It occurs somewhere and somewhen but it also behaves in a regular way and stands in certain relations to other entities; it is of a variety of descriptions. To talk of an "entity", a "fact", an "occurrence", or to describe a proposition as "true", is in each case to say that something happens in a certain place or in certain places.

The logician, it will follow, is already discussing universals, individuals, identity, space-time, causality, when he describes the function of subject and predicate in propositions and the logical relations between propositions. Thus, so Anderson argues in "The

Problem of Causality", to discuss causality is not to describe a special sort of metaphysical entity—a "necessary connection"—but is rather to draw attention to the form of the universal propositions asserted by "A is the cause of B". The logician is always concerned with "what is". He does not deduce an ontology from logic or a logic from ontology; rather, in discussing logic, he is already discussing ontology.

Anderson also rejects the view, now almost universally held, that a mathematical "truth" is "true" only within a calculus, its "truth" consisting in its derivability from a given set of postulates. Mathematical truths, too, are concerned with the general types of relationship holding between facts; and what we take to be a mathematical truth may turn out to be false. Quite generally, on his view, there are no "analytic truths"; if a proposition says anything at all it can be false. And he is not to be persuaded that mathematical propositions "all say the same thing i.e. nothing at all", as Wittgenstein had suggested.

It does not follow, however, that mathematical propositions are "empirical generalisations". Anderson totally rejects Mill's view that universal propositions are generalisations, and the "inductive logic" that goes with it. According to the traditional empiricist doctrine, an immediate experience is always particular, in a sense of "particularity" which prevents it from also being universal; a universal proposition is derived by generalisation from such facts. But this way of regarding universal propositions (as derived by some special sort of inference from experience) depends upon a conception of immediate experience which Anderson completely rejects on the ground that, so conceived, it would allow no such inference. His criticisms of induction are in some respects very like although quite independent of Karl Popper's; but Popper has not wholly broken with the traditional doctrine of immediate experience. When somebody says: "I know by immediate experience that the book is on the table", this is just a way of claiming, according to Anderson, that I found out that the book is on the table by being there with it and looking for myself, as distinct from hearing somebody say that the book was on the table, or deducing that it would be on the table from our knowledge of the habits of the person reading it. It is not a way of saying that I first had "an immediate experience" and then somehow (but how?) inferred from this experience that there is a book on the table. And I can know by experience, Anderson would add, that fire burns, that when two lines meet they make four angles, or that a Boeing 707 has four engines. If, indeed, I could not know this sort of thing by immediate experience, then equally I could not know that a particular thing is a fire, or that there are two lines on the piece of paper, or that what confronts me is a Boeing 707.

In a way, Russell realised this; he saw that Mill's "particular propositions" contained general descriptions and that if immediate experience must be of "pure particulars", then we cannot properly be said to know by immediate experience that, say, "Socrates is dead". But whereas Russell went off in search of what could be known by a completely particularised immediate experience (in formal terms, he looked for a "logically proper" name) and ended in bankruptcy, Anderson denied there can be immediate experience as Russell defined it. There are, on his view, no merely "given" particulars and no "logically proper" names—names, that is, which refer to a thing without being potentially descriptive.

Thus, on Anderson's account of universal propositions, the truth of mathematical propositions can be a "matter of experience" without the conclusion following that their truth depends on the validity of some sort of inductive inference; they, like all other universal propositions, can be derived from other universal propositions, can be tested in experience, can be simply taken to be the case. Of course they might, when taken to be the case, turn out to be false; but so might any finding of ours. I may wrongly take it to be the case that all fires burn, but so, too, I may wrongly take it to be the case that this is a fire, that it burns, that my hand is hurt—or whatever else I can take to be the case.

What, on Anderson's view, does a universal proposition assert? It certainly does not say that there is "a general connection" between being A and being B if by there being such a general connection is meant anything more than the simple fact that all A are B. Nor does it assert that some sort of class relation holds between A and B. For one thing "All A are B" does not unambiguously point to any such relationship between classes—it could be the case either that B includes A or that A and B are coextensive; for another thing, to assert a class relationship is just a way of saying that certain propositions are true. Classes are not entities. Nor, as Bradley and Russell thought, does "All A are B" assert only a hypothetical connection between descriptions. For although "All A's are B" does not assert that "there are A's", it certainly presupposes that there are, and if somebody convinces me that there are no A's I shall not continue to assert that "All A are B".

In a way, Anderson could only reply to those who offer such interpretations of the universal proposition that "All A are B" says what it says; it is just because he thinks that alternative modes of formulation fail to bring out the full force of that proposition, and no more than its full force, that Anderson prefers this—the traditional—way of asserting a universal proposition to any of the alternatives that have been suggested. But "All A are B" is not, of course, about some totality describable as "All A"; it asserts of each and every A, that it is a B. This comes out, Anderson considers, in the fact that we recognise as valid the argument "All A are B, this is an A, therefore this is a B".

Indeed, the validity of such a syllogism is, in a sense, Anderson's starting-point in logic. In such a syllogism, we see exhibited, he thinks, such basic logical facts as that what is a subject in one proposition can be a predicate in another—in opposition to the view that subjects and predicates are names for different classes of entity; that a singular and a universal proposition are of the same general structure, since the logical form of a syllogism will not be disrupted by the replacement of one by the other; that such expressions as "Jones is a man" and "Jones is human" have the same logical form (here once again Anderson is in opposition to most of his contemporaries), since either can appear indifferently as minor premise in an argument in which the major premise refers either to "men" or to "human beings".

"Being a man", "being human", "being a human being", "being a member of the class 'man'", "having the attribute of being human", "being truly describable as human", if Anderson is right, are different ways of offering precisely the same description of something. One mode of speech is, no doubt, more natural than another in a given context; a noun is most often the subject of a sentence, an adjective its predicate. But the logical subject is what we are talking about and the logical predicate, i.e. the description we are offering of it, will be the same whatever of these forms of words we select. (The choice is determined by rhetorical, not logical, considerations.)

Thus, once more, Anderson seeks to generalise, in an age of differentiation. The distinction between singular and universal propositions; between categorical, hypothetical and disjunctive; between the actual, the possible and the necessary; between class-membership and predicative propositions—all of these turn out, if he is right, not to be differences in logical form but only in modes of expression. The logical form of any statement will reveal it to be asserting some matter of fact (whether truly or falsely), to be offering a description, that is, of a certain kind of thing.

What about ethical and aesthetic statements? Here again Anderson begins with an attack on "relativism". Traditional ethics abounds in such conceptions as that whose nature it is to be an end (the "intrinsically desirable"). All such conceptions Anderson at once rejects, on the ground that nothing can have its nature in being an end or in being binding. We do, certainly, have desires, we do, certainly, make demands upon ourselves and upon other people, but we desire something, or we demand of ourselves that we act in a certain way, because the objective or the act has such-and-such characteristics, not because it is its nature to be sought after or to be incumbent upon us.

For Anderson the most important of ethical writings since the Greeks is Moore's *Principia Ethica*. Of course, Anderson wholly rejects the view that good is a non-natural, simple, quality, that "good" is different from "the good" or that there is a "naturalistic fallacy"—except in so far as Moore was attacking relativism under that name. He admits, too, that Moore had by no means freed himself from the presumption that good is an end, however inconsistent this might be with his more general doctrine that to call something "good" is just to characterise it. All the same, Anderson saw in Moore's work a fundamental contribution to what he calls "a positive ethics".

Ethics, of course, must for Anderson be concerned with facts; there are no "values" above facts. To call a mental activity "good" (it will be remembered that, on his view, it is to such activities, to certain "spirits" like the spirit of inquiry, that ethical predicates apply) is to describe it in a way which it is one task of ethics further to elucidate. Not, however, its only task. Ethics is not simply "the analysis of ethical predicates"; it is an inquiry into ethical facts, which may lead us to the conclusion that many conventional ethical judgments are false. Anderson himself tries to show that whatever is good is a form of enterprise, that it is productive, capable of developing in a special way, by means of what he calls "communication". In saying, for example, that human affection is good, Anderson is not asserting that it always ought to be pursued, or that it is obligatory to bring it about; good activities, he thought, are not even the sort of things that we can be obliged or (sensibly) exhorted to pursue. Far from its being the case that good activities are by nature ends, they are, unlike economic goods, the sort of thing that is not ordinarily achieved by being pursued; one does not come to love, or to be courageous, or to develop a spirit of inquiry, by taking these activities as one's objectives, but rather by "catching" them in the course of one's membership of social groups.

When it comes to the other concepts with which ethical theorists have commonly concerned themselves—right, obligation, duty—Anderson's position is quite different. Ethical theorists like Ross, in developing Moore's ideas, had argued that "right", too, ought to be treated as a special sort of quality. Anderson is convinced that it cannot be; that the notion that something ought to be done is, as it were, "written into" the description of an act as obligatory, or as right, or as our duty; and that it certainly cannot be a quality of an act that it ought to be done, whether *prima facie*, as Ross thought, or after consideration. Indeed, he works out what might be described as a "sociological ethics", so far as these expressions are concerned. A form of social organisation, he argues, develops regular habits of action, and these come to be thought of as being obligatory upon those who adhere to such an organisation even when they would prefer to act otherwise. If, then, we describe an act as right, or as our duty, this will be easily understood by those who are involved in the same mode of life. We will think of the act in question as being in some absolute sense our duty, as possessing an intrinsic ought-to-be-doneness; but the theorist can understand why we take one act rather than another to be our duty, not by simple examination of the act in question but by psychological and sociological inquiry.

Indeed, whereas many ethical theorists have seen in duty the central ethical concept and have thought that to act from a sense of duty is to be impelled by the best of all motives, Anderson argues that if we act only because we "feel obliged" to do so, this is a clear indication of the absence of goodness. Where there is goodness, there is free participation, spontaneity (although not in a metaphysical sense—Anderson rejects the metaphysical idea of "free will"), and certainly not a feeling of constraint. A person who lives under the shadow of conscience, in a desperate effort to avoid feelings of guilt, is the very type of the neurotic.

Anderson's most fully worked-out defence of the logic of his procedure is in "The Meaning of Good". If somebody asserts, and somebody else denies, that an expression qualifies rather than relates, the issue cannot be easily settled. Anderson originally directed his argument mainly against those who tried to hold both that good is a quality and that it is its essence to be pursued. Rather different problems arise when the prevailing view is that "good" ought to be analysed much as Anderson analysed "right"—as a way of indicating our adherence to a way of life. Anderson is attempting what is now sometimes called a "rational reconstruction" of ethics; he sees in traditional ethical theory a partly confused, partly enlightening, attempt to draw attention to the characteristics he has himself emphasised. The question for him is not, it should be observed, "whether there is such a thing as the property of goodness", but whether it is possible to discover distinguishing characteristics in certain of the things which have ordinarily been called "good", characteristics sufficient and necessary to mark them off from the morally indifferent and the evil.

In his lectures on ethics, Anderson devoted a good deal of attention to establishing this sort of link between his theories and those of his predecessors. But also he concerned himself with describing the activities he took to be good. Love, courage, the spirit of inquiry, aesthetic creation and appreciation—these too stand in need of "rational reconstruction". Thus Anderson is not prepared to restrict himself to considering "the logic of ethical statements". For him the ethical theorist is discussing forms of human activity—not, primarily, what people say about these activities; it is quite natural for him to appeal for confirmation of his views to writers as diverse as Sorel, Freud, Marx, Joyce, Marshall, Arnold. In this respect, his approach to ethics links him with Continental or American speculation rather than with the general stream of British moral thought.

In aesthetics the story is much the same. There, again, he is looking for the distinguishing characteristics of beautiful objects;

he has been particularly concerned to battle against relativism; he has been influenced not only by professional aestheticians but at least as much by novelists and by critics. Aesthetics, for him, is the direct consideration of works of art (and of nature) with the object of discovering their general characterising properties; and that procedure naturally demands a close attention to the works themselves. So, again unlike most philosophical aestheticians, he has written a number of special literary studies—most notably, perhaps, on Joyce's *Ulysses*—as well as attempting, in *Some Questions in Aesthetics*, to present his general ideas about the character of aesthetic inquiry.

Similarly, too, he does not admit a distinction between political theory and political philosophy, whether the latter is understood as "the application of ethics to politics" or as an investigation of, say, "the vocabulary of politics". The philosopher who takes up the study of politics, he would freely admit, will naturally be particularly concerned with the logical points raised by political theory. At the same time he will have to look concretely at what happens in human society.

Naturally, Anderson rejects both the traditional atomism of British political theory, for which a society is "really" a collection of individuals and the State a deliberate arrangement, and that Absolutism for which there is only "Society", which the State expresses. Human beings, as he sees them, are neither self-originative centres of activity, nor instruments in the development of Absolute Spirit. The subject matter of political theory, like the subject matter of any other theory, will be complex structures which both act and are acted on, which enter into relations with one another and with other things and contain relations within themselves. Once more, this still leaves open the question (which logic by itself cannot settle) what these structures are. Anderson takes them to be such complexes as traditions, social movements of one sort or another, considered as giving rise to and as being themselves shaped by a variety of social institutions, of which the State is only one—although one of particular concern to political theory. Here again, this is not the ordinary starting-point of British philosophers; his views grew out of his reading of Marx and of the political pluralists, especially in the great days of Orage's journal *The New Age*, rather than out of the empiricist tradition, to the individualism of which he is profoundly opposed.

Anderson places great emphasis upon social conflicts, as opposed to the traditional emphasis on social unity. Like Heraclitus he believes that "the hidden harmony is better than the open". Pre-Socratic philosophy, in general, greatly attracts him—he thinks of Burnet's *Early Greek Philosophy* as one of the most philosophically enlightening of all books—but he was particularly fascinated by, and made particularly fascinating, the philosophy of Heraclitus. On Anderson's interpretation of him, Heraclitus taught that a thing's permanence, its stability, as well as its growth and development, had their source in the counter-poising of opposite tendencies, not in the subordination of every force within it to a single objective. This, according to Anderson, is as true of the human mind and of human society as it is of the candle-flame.

Thus we ought not to ask of a social institution: "What end or purpose does it serve?" but rather: "Of what conflicts is it the scene?" That is the way in which we shall come to an understanding of its mode of operation. Anderson is particularly interested in educational institutions and in the struggle within them between what he takes to be the classical tradition (the tradition of critical inquiry) and the utilitarian attempt to use educational institutions for merely vocational training or for "social adjustment". Similarly, in the political institutions of a society—in the State, for example—he sees neither "an expression of the general will" nor the instrument of a particular class, but rather an arena within which conflicts are fought out and compromises reached. Particular social forces could no doubt be dominant within the State at a particular time, but the mere existence of legislative and judicial institutions clearly indicates that their domination is not absolute. To glorify the State, to attempt to subordinate all social activity to its powers, is in his eyes wholly to misunderstand what gives a society vitality—the free play of a variety of traditions, of diverse modes of life, in their conflicts and co-operations with one another.

Similarly, Anderson is opposed to a religious view of things, whether understood as laying down a principle of conduct to which all human activities are to be subordinate, or as determining some goal towards which "the whole Universe" moves. In religion, as in State-worship, he detects a fundamental servility; unlike many critics of Christianity, he is as opposed to what he takes to be its moral standpoint (not in all, but in very many, respects) as to its theological doctrines. So far as it offers consolation, exhorts man to meekness and humility, emphasises individual salvation, Christianity cuts across Anderson's conviction that struggle is unceasing, that every good activity is a form of enterprise, that what is of first importance is the continuance of tradition. Not by subordination to a person, human or divine, he would say, but only by critical participation in forms of productive activity can men be "saved".

If Anderson does not much like being described as an "atheist", this is primarily because of the negative suggestion of that description—as if it were a matter of primary concern to him to deny that God exists. For what Anderson argues against is any conception of a total system, an ultimate end or a final principle of explanation, whether or not it is regarded as being, or as being related to, an omnipotent person. Thus he is as critical of Haeckel as of Aquinas, of the conception of a man-centred, as of a God-centred, scheme of things. Indeed, in so far as some forms of religion emphasise that our life is not of our making, that it goes on, in large part, in independence of our plans, he much prefers them to any form of sentimental humanism. He is as sympathetic to the view that "providence moves in mysterious ways" as he is to Hegel's "the cunning of history", but he is not prepared to admit that providence or history is a supranatural entity with plans of its own.

Similarly, Anderson's determinism and his materialism are each of them of a rather special character. He is not a "reductive materialist" i.e. he does not believe that there is some single entity "matter", of which minds, for example, are a confused appearance. For him minds have distinctive characteristics; they are not only physico-chemical structures, they are also passionate. His determinism, similarly, is not Laplacean; there can be no question for Anderson of "giving a complete description", whether of the present or of the future. It amounts only to this: that whenever a change takes place, it does so under sufficient and necessary conditions. There are genuine novelties, new characteristics appear, but always under determinate conditions. Indeed, we must always, in Heraclitus's phrase, "expect the unexpected"; we cannot make the future safe for ourselves, any more than we can make the world safe for democracy. Struggle, uncertainty, risk, disappointment, are not accidental features of human life, remediable by the exercise of sufficient good will; they arise inevitably out of the general structure of things, including our own structure.

No total scheme, no simple units, no first principles, no ultimate objectives, no modes of being, no necessary truths—these, not the rejection of God, are the fundamental negations of Anderson's philosophy. To put it positively, there is, on his view, a single way of being: the complex activity of a spatio-temporal occurrence, within which discriminations can be made and which is itself discriminable within a wider system. To explain, to prove, is to draw attention to relationships which occur between such occurrences; to assert a proposition is to take something of a certain kind to occur; any proposition can be false; science proceeds by the critical examination of hypotheses; any objective has a variety of characteristics and it can always be pursued as part of a procedure for getting something else.

These are definite and general doctrines. In taking it to be his task as a philosopher to enunciate, and to argue for, propositions of such a kind, Anderson is in total opposition to the view that philosophy is simply analysis, or that its object is purely therapeutic. So far he is an untypical figure in recent British philosophy. Yet he has no sympathy either, for the rhetorical methods of so much contemporary Continental philosophy. Like his Continental contemporaries, he wants to discuss large issues, but critically, analytically. A common presumption of our time is that this cannot be done; in England, that large issues either fall within the province of a particular science, or else are matters of decision, not of argument; on the Continent, that large issues certainly belong to philosophy, but that careful analysis, close criticising, has no place there. Yet there are signs that the tide is turning, in England at least. Many positions which Anderson in the early 'thirties was almost alone in defending, are now at least respectable. In the United States, there has been, indeed, a continuing interest in the critical discussion of large issues as a result of the influence of such philosophers as C. I. Lewis and Morris Cohen. Even within the better sort of "ordinary language" philosophy, I should say, the same interest is clearly exhibited—notwithstanding, sometimes, the explicit pronouncements of its proponents—as it most certainly is in the philosophy of Karl Popper. Their presumptions and their arguments Anderson would certainly wish to challenge, but they belong, at least, to the same controversial tradition. To the presentation and continuance of that tradition, Anderson has hoped to contribute; to its judgment, he submits his case.

# 1
# EMPIRICISM (1927)[1]

## I

There has always been a certain indefiniteness about the nature of the distinctions between the different types of philosophical theory and correspondingly about the meaning of each particular "-ism". It is obviously not an easy matter to describe a whole outlook; an attitude of mind which is felt to cover a wide range of problems cannot readily be communicated without going over all these problems. Thus it is that philosophers who disagree never seem to come to an end of their disagreements, and can hardly even understand one another. But if anything could alleviate such misunderstandings, it would be a resolute attempt to define exactly the issue or issues between different views; and this is a task which is all too seldom undertaken. It is recognised that there is a natural opposition between rationalism and empiricism, but the basis of the opposition commonly remains obscure or is wrongly stated. In briefly discussing the issue and defending empiricism I cannot hope to show exactly how this theory should be distinguished from those which go by the name of realism, naturalism, materialism, pluralism, determinism and positivism. These are all, I should argue, connected with empiricism; it is on an empiricist view, and only so, that they can be maintained. But I take empiricism as central, as giving the best general description of the philosophy which the other terms partially convey, because the issue which it raises and which it disputes with rationalism, is fundamental to logic, being concerned with truth itself. In the discussion of this issue the ways in which more detailed issues should be dealt with, will in some degree appear.

Rationalistic theories of all sorts are distinguished from empiricism by the contention that there are different kinds or degrees of truth and reality. The distinguishing-mark of empiricism as a philosophy is that it denies this, that it maintains that there is only one way of being. The issue has been confused in the past

---

[1] Based on a paper read at the Annual Congress of the A.A.P.P., Sydney, 1927. The part dealing with geometry (Part II) has been greatly expanded.

by a reference to knowledge. It was quite naturally maintained, by those who postulated different ways of being, that in relation to them different ways of knowing are required. Hence empiricism has been connected, in the history of philosophy, with the view that there is only one way of knowing, and particularly that that way is what was called "sense" in contrast to "reason"; or, rather differently, that sense is the only *originator* of knowledge. But fundamentally the issue is logical; the dispute is about ways of being or of truth, not about ways of knowing truths. It is only after it has been assumed that there are other truths than matters of fact, or that there are objects which "transcend" existence, that a special faculty has to be invented to know them.

Thus, although we naturally associate rationalism with the theory of a mental faculty of reason, the discussion of faculties will become pointless if it can be shown that any postulation of different orders of being is illogical. The same criticism will serve whether the differences are said to be of kind or of degree, since the differences of degree are to be determined in relation to a supposed highest degree, which is that of a supremely real object or Absolute. It is because objects of "higher reality" are supposed to transcend *experience* that the opposition to transcendentalism has the name empiricism. But if experience (by which, of course, is to be understood not our having experiences but what we experience) consists of matters of fact, then it enjoins us to reject all ideals or powers or whatever else may be contrasted with facts. Moreover, rationalistic views are contrary to experience, not merely because they set up something additional to facts, but because they set it above facts, because they make it appear that facts are somehow defective, that they are not real enough in themselves but require to be supplemented by explanations, ends or whatnot, before they can be understood or accepted by a mind.

The chief, and I think final, objection to any theory of higher and lower, or complete and incomplete, truth is that it is contrary to the very nature and possibility of discourse; that it is "unspeakable". The empiricist, like Socrates, adopts the attitude of considering things in terms of what can be said about them, i.e., in propositions.[2] And he regards this not as a "second-best", but as the only method of speaking or thinking at all, since every

---

[2] v. i., p. 169.

statement that we make, every belief that we hold, is a proposition. Since, then, the supposed higher and lower objects of experience both take the propositional form, we are concerned with a single way of being; that, namely, which is conveyed when we say that a proposition is *true*. Deviation from this view must take the form of saying either that facts are propositional but ideal explanations are above the propositional form, or that explanations are propositional and what they have to explain are mere data, not yet propositionalised. But in order to indicate data or ideals, we have to make statements. If there were anything either above or below the proposition, it would be beyond speech or understanding. If, for example, there were anything that required explanation before it became intelligible, we could say nothing about it in its unintelligible form; plainly, then, we could not even say that it had such a form. And, in general, it cannot be maintained either that the proposition is our way of understanding things which in themselves are not propositional, or that we have further ways of understanding the proposition which is in itself defective. Whatever "explanation" may be, it must at least be a relation of such a sort that what is explained and what explains it can both be stated and believed, i.e., are both propositions. But if there is no way of getting behind the proposition to something either lower or higher, we must assume that propositions can stand by themselves with nothing to supplement them, that facts need no explanation. Discourse, in fact, depends on the possibility of making separate statements, in regard to each of which the very same question can be asked—"Is it true?"

It follows that the conception of higher truths than those of fact, and that of a total truth to which all "merely particular" truths contribute, have both to be rejected. The latter view is what is currently called idealism, but since it differs from the former only in holding that there is a highest truth instead of a number of higher truths, it can be regarded as a variety of rationalism. The objection to rationalism is just that what is meant by "truth" is what is conveyed in the proposition by the copula "is". And logically there can be no alternative to "being" and "not being"; propositions can only be true or false. There is no question, therefore, of degrees or kinds of truth; of higher and lower orders of discourse, dealing, e.g., respectively with realities and appearances. The very theory that attempts to make such a distinction has to be put forward in the form common to all discourse, it has to lay claim to the "being" signified by the copula, it has to face the direct question, "Is it true?" Thus empiricism regards it as illogical to make such distinctions as that between existence and subsistence, or between the "is" of identity, that of predication and that of membership of a class; and still more obviously illogical to say that there *is* something defective about "is" itself. These are all attempts to get behind the proposition, to maintain—in words!—that we mean more than we can say.

Considering propositions as they occur in discourse, we find that they can be asserted or denied, questioned, proved or disproved. In saying, then, that whatever can be asserted can be significantly denied, i.e., that there are no undeniable truths, and that whatever can be asserted or taken for granted can also be made a subject for inquiry, can be questioned or proved, i.e., that there are no unprovables, we are conveying certain characters of the common "is" of discourse (certain conditions of existence). In particular, there is no question of its indicating "necessity" as something over and above actuality. As related to other propositions any proposition has what we may, if we like, call "contingency"; but at the same time, as distinct from other propositions, as being *a* proposition and therefore requiring separate statement, any proposition has "absoluteness". The forms of assertion, denial and implication being precisely the same in relation to the supposed different kinds of "is", there is no way of establishing the difference. We can *say* that certain truths are of the peculiar "necessary" sort, just as we can say that no truths are "absolute", but in both cases our speech bewrayeth us.

Rejecting in this way the distinction between necessary and other truths, empiricism takes up the position that in discussion or inquiry any proposition can be treated as (*a*) a conclusion to be proved from premises accepted, (*b*) a premise accepted to be used in proving some conclusion, (*c*) a hypothesis to be tested by the observation of the truth or falsity of the conclusions drawn from it, or (*d*) an observation to be used in determining the truth or falsity of conclusions drawn from a hypothesis. And if it be asked how it is determined which of these functions a proposition is to have, the empirical answer is that this is determined in discourse. Discourse depends on what the parties to it *believe*. If you deny what I assert, I may try to prove it by means of other propositions you admit; if we both agree on some propositions, we may set out to see what follows from them; if we are doubtful about any proposition, we may test it by its consequences. In general, discourse is possible when and only when persons come together who (*a*) agree about something, (*b*) either disagree, or wish to inquire, about something else. This position itself implies a common logic of assertion, implication and, I should add, definition. Apart from that logic, actual beliefs and observations are all that can be appealed to, and without them the process could not go on. Each of us (not excluding those who take a false view of logic) directs his inquiries and establishes his conclusions, in greater or less disagreement with others, by means of this mechanism of individual statements and particular inferences. The person who holds that there are higher truths has still to draw lower conclusions from them in the ordinary way (as it is inferred, e.g., from the "moral government of the universe" that a man is not dead after he has died); he who holds that there is a total truth can only advance towards it step by step. We have all to rely on what we find to be the case; unless we could say that a certain thing is *so*, we could not begin to discuss or inquire. And all this implies, I maintain, that science depends entirely on observation, i.e., on finding something to be the case, and on the use of syllogism, either for proof or for testing; or, more generally, on observation in connection with, and in distinction from, anticipation. This means that there is no distinction between empirical and rational science. Since everything that can be asserted can be denied or doubted, since deduction and hypothesis are always possible, all sciences are observational and experimental.

## II

We may take for example the science of geometry which, like other mathematical sciences, has been regarded as "rational". It has been commonly alleged that over and above the truths stated in geometrical theorems there are certain "first principles" of the science which in themselves are unprovable, and that the whole science follows from these principles. Leibniz has given classical expression to this position in the statement (*New Essays on the Understanding*, Bk. IV, Ch. I) that "it is not the figures which make the proof with geometers... It is the universal propositions, i.e., the definitions, the axioms, and the theorems already proved, which make the reasoning, and would maintain it even if there were no figure". The proof of the last-mentioned theorems, of course, comes under the same general statement, and so we find that the whole science depends on axioms and definitions, supposedly identical propositions, i.e., propositions which cannot be significantly denied or conceived to be false. This position Leibniz expresses by saying that these propositions follow from "the principle of contradiction", which therefore has embodied in it the whole of geometry and of rational science. It empowers us to reject all propositions which "involve a contradiction" and to affirm their contradictories—which neglects the fact that if a "proposition" were unintelligible, we should not know what its contradictory was.

The attempt is, in fact, to derive geometry from the notion of incompatibility or of the difference between truth and falsity. But obviously this notion could not provide us with the notion of a triangle or any other matter that geometry treats of. In order to find out that having interior angles together greater or less than two right angles is incompatible with triangularity, we require to have the specific things, triangles, before our minds. Apart from observation we could make no assertion of incompatibility whatever. To say, for example, that black is incompatible with white "because it is black" or "because it is not white" is, in either case, to presume the very thing to be proved. In demonstrating the analytic or necessary character of the proposition we surreptitiously introduce the synthetic relation, the fact. "If triangles were not X", says the rationalist, "they would not be triangles". Why? we ask. The only possible answer is "Because triangles *are* X". The fact is required, and the "principle" adds nothing to it. We agree that in a sense the figures do not make the proof; men had known triangles long before they had raised the question of the sum of their angles. But without the figures there would be no proof, because there would be nothing to talk about. No more need be said to demonstrate the falsity of the view that geometry follows from axioms and definitions.

It is curious that, all the while that geometrical truths were regarded as having an ideal or rational character owing to their derivation from pure identities, application of them was made to physical phenomena. Yet, if they had not been synthetic, if they had not conveyed information which it was quite possible not to have about things of certain types, they could not have been applied at all. It is no answer to this argument to say that all that was required, in relation to the physical facts, was something approximately correct, something good enough for practical purposes. This is to say that geometrical truths could be treated as physical hypotheses; which would have been impossible unless there were definite points of contact between the geometrical and the physical. We could not say "Let us suppose this object to be triangular", if triangularity were a "rational" entity and the object a "natural" one; and we could not go on to say "The object must then have certain other properties, and these do not differ greatly from the properties we observe it to have", unless we could make a direct comparison between the two sets of properties. Even in *supposing* that a physical object has geometrical properties, we imply that there is no difference of order between physical and geometrical objects, that physical objects do fall within the field of geometry. Thus our geometrical hypotheses, or our hypothetical geometry, might actually be falsified by physical facts. If any such contradiction arose, the conclusion would not be that physical facts had failed to come up to geometrical requirements; it would be that our geometry had to be revised. The logic of application is simply the logic of syllogism; and if a geometrical theorem and a physical observation together imply the contradictory of a physical observation, we are as much entitled to question the theorem as to reject the observations. And if careful observation continues to give us the same results, we are bound to deny the theorem. This position will only appear arbitrary and out of harmony with our actual scientific procedure, to one who does not realise that our geometrical theorems are themselves the results of careful observation. But since, whether the conclusion be false or not, a theorem and a fact can together imply nothing unless they have a common term, we are bound to say that the fields of geometry and of physics are not cut off from one another, and that the two sciences are on the same empirical level. This conclusion will apply, however far "rational physics" may be carried. At some point there must be contact between "truths of fact" and "truths of reason"; as is sufficiently established by the fact that we know them both. And that which is capable of implying a fact is equally capable of being falsified by a fact.

It is on the basis of the view that geometry is hypothetical and so, by a curious perversion of the meaning of the term "hypothetical", unaffected by fact, that the various "geometries" have been set up. Thus we are told that we can obtain different geometries according as we assert or deny Euclid's "axiom of parallels". Now no doubt different consequences will follow from the two contradictories, but it is our business to seek for errors in these sets of consequences, in order that we may determine whether the "axiom" is true or not, i.e., whether as a matter of fact two intersecting straight lines can or cannot both be parallel to a third straight line in their plane. It is certainly a merit to have seen that Euclid's axiom can be denied, but what is then demanded will be either a testing of it by its consequences, or a deduction of it (or its contradictory) from propositions which we find to be true, or a direct statement that we find *it* to be true (or false). Instead of this, other propositions have been retained as axioms, and it is made a matter of choice whether we accept the proposition on parallels or not; and thus we have the various "geometries" and "spaces". And this position is even combined with the admission that the geometries which reject the axiom have to define the straight line differently; which is really an admission that Euclid's proposition is true, and incidentally one which could not be made unless there were straight lines which answer to Euclid's description.

Bertrand Russell, in his *Foundations of Geometry*, does not make this admission; but he only avoids it by bringing in (p. 173) a reference to spherical space, in which, while "in general" it is true that there can be only one straight line between two points, in the case of antipodal points this is not so. Since the distance between such pairs bears a special relation to the constitution of the space in which they are, "it is intelligible that, for such special points, the axiom breaks down, and an infinite number of straight lines are possible between them; but unless we had started with assuming the general validity of the axiom, we could never have reached a position in which antipodal points could have been known to be peculiar". Russell appears to use the word "general" in some private and personal sense. The natural conclusion would seem, however, to be that since the axiom is *not* generally valid, we have not reached a position in which antipodal points are known to be peculiar, and so no exception to Euclid's axiom has been discovered. It is also noteworthy that "unless we have started with assuming" Euclid, there would not have been terms in which to describe the "non-Euclidean" geometries and spaces. It appears to be the case that such geometries are only Euclidean geometry with different terminologies. As to the disputed proposition on parallels, it can be proved by assuming that the sum of the interior angles of a triangle is equal to two right angles. As it is employed in Euclid to prove the latter proposition, we are faced with circularity of reasoning. But the proposition on the angles of a triangle can be independently proved, if we assume that direction and difference of direction (angle) mean the same at different points; failing which there can be no question of the *sum* of such angles.

Waiving this point, however, we shall find it profitable to consider Russell's general argument. There are, he says (pp. 200, 201), certain "*a priori* axioms" which are "necessarily true of any form of externality"; but this leaves some of Euclid's "axioms", including the proposition on parallels and that two straight lines can never enclose a space, to be "regarded as empirical laws, derived from the investigation and measurement of our actual space, and true only, as far as [the two mentioned] are concerned, within the limits set by errors of observation". In other words, it is only by observation that we can determine whether our actual space is Euclidean or non-Euclidean. (Russell admits that we have an actual space; no doubt to save the possibility of physical applications. Nowadays this is not considered necessary, and we have the utterly illogical theory of relativity according to which nothing is "actual" and "is" has no meaning.) But there are still the *a priori* axioms (axioms proper) which are not empirical laws but are necessarily true of any form of externality. In considering this position we have to ask how, except by observation of actual externality, we discover what is true of it or what is "deducible from the fact that a science of spatial magnitude is possible (p. 175); how this deduction proceeds, so as to enable us to distinguish what is true of experienced space and what is necessary to any form of externality; how, in fact, we can distinguish in space those characters which make it external from its other characters. Russell wishes to show that there are, or may be, forms of externality which, having certain characters of the form which we have observed, do not have others. But in order to show this he must point to forms which do not have the latter characters. If space is the only form of externality that we know, then all the forms that we know have all the characters of space. In order to distinguish characters which are essential to externality from others which are accidental, we shall have to say that in the case of the former we can "see the connection" and as regards the latter see that there is no connection. In other words, necessary connections between some of its attributes and necessary disconnections between others are among the characters of space. To justify this conclusion it would have to be said that we had grasped by a single act of thought *all* the characters of externality in general and of our actual space in particular. Such a position ignores the possibility of discovery and the nature of deduction.

The question is, then, in what way the view that "all forms of externality are X, Y, Z" but "some possible forms of externality are not A, B, C", i.e., are not Euclidean, can be supported. X, Y, Z, the *a priori* axioms, are supposed to follow from "analysis" of externality. But this analysis can only proceed by simply finding certain characteristics of externality. If analysis were taken to show the necessity of these characteristics, then this necessity in turn would be a characteristic which was simply found. In short, Russell's "deduction", which is supposed to demonstrate necessity, can only start from, and proceed in terms of, observation of actuality. Similarly when he says (p. 62) that "those properties [of the form of externality] which can be deduced from its mere function of rendering experience of interrelated diversity possible, are to be regarded as *a priori*", his position is quite illogical. The properties of interrelated diversity can be discovered only by examining situations which exhibit interrelated diversity; so that not only are the premises and the conclusions of the supposed deductions *identical* (viz., all things which render experience of interrelated diversity possible are X, Y, Z), but nothing is said to show that Euclid's axioms are not equally "*a priori*", since Euclid claims that they indicate properties which he finds in such situations, i.e., in the only interrelated diversity he knows. In fact, the question is solely of "empirical laws". This is partly obscured, not only by the reference to "deduction", but also by the reference to "experience" of interrelated diversity. But all the propositions in question are about what is diverse and interrelated, and nothing about experienc*ing* really enters into the argument.

Russell makes a great point of the "logical consistency" of non-Euclidean systems. Here again he is assuming that he knows "all about" such systems, or that he has the peculiar privilege of declaring what is to be regarded as assailable and what is unassailable. We have to note two distinct senses in which consistency and inconsistency are spoken of. There is inconsistency in fact; two propositions are said to be inconsistent when one, with a fact or a number of facts, implies the falsity of the other, i.e., when the two together, with or without certain facts, imply a false proposition. This cannot be determined by taking the propositions by themselves but only in relation to facts. But two propositions, inconsistent in this sense, may be perfectly consistent in the other sense, viz., that neither by itself implies the falsity of the other. Now consistency in the latter sense is of the very slightest importance as a description of a group of propositions. Limiting ourselves to that group we find no member of it disproved by any other or collection of others. But there is nothing scientific about limiting ourselves to such a group, allowing them to "define" a science. We ought, on the contrary, to bring them into relation with every available fact, so that any real inconsistency will appear. Russell cannot say that both Euclidean and non-Euclidean geometries are consistent in the broader sense; so that the consistency he claims for non-Euclidean geometry is a barren distinction.

We conclude, then, that geometry is, like all others, an empirical or experimental science dealing with things of a certain sort, that there is nothing "*a priori*" about it but that it is concerned throughout with fact. When Russell says (*Principles of Mathematics*, p. 5) that pure mathematics asserts "merely that Euclidean propositions follow from the Euclidean axioms, i.e., it asserts an implication; any space which has such and such properties has also such and such other properties", he is again using "implication" in his characteristically loose way, and he omits to indicate that these facts can be discovered only if we can examine a space having "such and such properties". Geometry, we may say, is concerned with empirical characters and relations of things in space and is a practical science, and Euclidean geometry consists not of "implications" but of propositions (connected to some extent, of course, by argument) which are either true or false. We can say that, if there were no externality, no geometrical propositions would be true, just as we can say that if there were no distinction between truth and falsity, no propositions whatever would be true. But these statements do not help us in the least to discover any proposition, geometrical or other, which is true. To call them, therefore, statements of the *implications* of the form of externality and of the principle of contradiction is the sheerest absurdity. We must rather say that, since these "principles" have no practical consequences, *there are no such principles.* Our sole concern in science is with facts, and we can attach no meaning to the suppositions "if there were no externality" and "if there were no distinction between truth and falsity"; they cannot even be *conceived* to be facts, that is, they cannot be supposed.

## III

We have found that the conditions of discourse and inquiry demand the rejection of "pure" science and the assertion that all sciences deal with facts, in relation to which we assert or deny, prove or suppose. We have found, in other words, that the theory of different ways of being is untenable. But with it falls the theory of different ways of knowing, the distinction between sense and reason. The very slightly empiricist character of the work of those philosophers who are called "the English empiricists" is accounted for by their still making this very unempirical distinction. In maintaining that all our knowledge is derived from sense (a position which, on account of their rationalist preconceptions, they by no means maintained consistently) they took a view of sense which was dependent on its having been regarded as an *inferior* way of knowing. It was supposed to provide isolated data, materials which reason had to shape into, or subordinate to, the coherent system of knowledge which we call science. And Hume, while admitting that no such coherence *could* be imposed upon isolated data, still maintained that the data of sense were isolated, and accordingly could not show how science is possible. The rejoinder of idealists like Green that Hume's position leaves out of account the function of the mind as a relating agency, that it takes as real what has not yet been made real by the work of the mind, is no reply. Hume's argument is precisely that neither mind nor any other agency could possibly perform such work on "distinct existences". And this is the point of departure of the "radical empiricism" of James. Mind is not required to relate things, because things are given as related just as much as they are given as distinguished. Connections and distinctions, in fact, are given together; and those who argue that the work of the mind is required to connect distinct things, might equally well maintain that work had previously been required to distinguish them. Here James is drawing attention to the important fact (important, as well as for other reasons, in view of the persistent misunderstanding of the meaning of empiricism) that there is nothing in the least empirical in the conception of a "distinct existence". It is on the contrary the rationalist conception of "essence" masquerading as a fact of experience.

If, then, there is to be any question of what is given or presented (though it would be better to speak of what is observed), connections must be included. This is in line with the view already set forth that what can be contemplated or enunciated is always in the form of a proposition; in other words, that we always deal with complex states of affairs and never with "simple entities". Any theory which refers to the work of the mind, or to rational factors, as contributing, along with sensible or given factors, to making things intelligible, is self-refuting or "unspeakable". If whatever is intelligible has both connections and distinctions, then in order to speak intelligibly of what is contributed by the mind we shall have to assume that it has both connections and distinctions, and in order to speak intelligibly of what is given by things we shall have to assume that *it* has both connections and distinctions, so that no "work of the mind" is required to make it intelligible. And in the same way, in speaking intelligibly of "knowledge", we are speaking of a certain state of affairs, the mental process which knows, as connected with and distinguished from another state of affairs, the process or situation, mental or non-mental, which is known.

We cannot, then, make any such distinction as between "things as we know them" and "things themselves". Unless the former *are* things themselves, we are not entitled to speak of things (and hence to speak) at all. On the other hand, we are entitled to reject, by reference to things themselves, viz., the things we know, any suggestion of an agency whose operation cannot be detected; which we cannot observe acting on some observed situation and bringing about observable changes therein. As "rational factors", *ex hypothesi*, cannot be seen at work (since they must have worked before anything can be seen; since they are "conditions of the possibility of experience"), not only can we not assert that there are such ideal entities, but we cannot show what they would do, if there were. An agency whose presence cannot be detected is an agency which it is of no advantage to postulate, as Berkeley showed in regard to Locke's "matter". We cannot have a "merely inferential" knowledge of it. We must be able to say: "This is the sort of thing which under certain circumstances will act in such and such a way, and under other circumstances will act in a different way". But if we have never observed it so acting, if we have never been able to distinguish it from its effects on the situation, then the whole content of our knowledge, all that we are in a position to speak about, consists of the circumstances, no longer to be described as effects of "it", at least. The appeal to inference, or to the distinction between "knowledge by acquaintance" and "knowledge by description", is futile. We can say, for example, that any man we happen to meet had parents; we can have an indirect knowledge of their existence, though we have never seen them. But this would not have been possible if we had not at some time known individuals who stood in that relation to some one, and had not thereafter come to believe that all beings of a certain sort have parents. We cannot, then, by inference from what we observe, conclude that there is a mind whose function it is to observe these things, i.e., which is purely instrumental, a pure agency. Unless we have observed minds, we cannot speak of them. Having observed them, and having observed that they are related by "knowledge" to other things, we can also consider how they fall into error. But this criticism of the mind's operation in regard to things cannot take the form of "criticism of the instrument". We cannot, without self-refutation, undertake to criticise the mind's entire knowledge; for it is by our knowledge that we criticise. Criticism, then, can only proceed by our asserting what we find to be the case; we can criticise propositions only by means of propositions, similarly asserted. The distinction of ways of knowing, at least in the form of a distinction among *faculties*, is therefore untenable. We can, of course, distinguish such attitudes as asserting and supposing. But in every case we are dealing with something which is, or may be, found to be the case, and there is no question of seeking for and fostering some superior instrument.

EMPIRICISM (1927)    15

In terms of this theory it must be said that in psychology, and likewise in ethics, our knowledge is observational and propositional. The question is of psychological and ethical facts, and not of an ultimate agency or ultimate standards. These sciences, like all others, are nothing if not empirical and experimental. This does not, of course, mean that minds must be studied in a laboratory; they show some of their characteristics better in *other* social situations. Love, for example, is a very important psychical phenomenon; in fact it may be said that no one can know much about minds who has not taken it into account. But none but the most hardened "experimentalist" will claim that a laboratory is the best place for getting to know its characters and conditions. The main point is that, in order to know minds, we have to observe them and *think* about them. There is no real distinction between thinking and experiment. In each we require some hypothesis, and in each case we test it by reference to what we believe, or find, to be the case, i.e., by whether or not its consequences are in accordance with facts which we know. In holding that in order to know minds we have to look at them, empiricism is not opposed to "introspection", the study of our own minds, though it opposes the supposition that in this peculiar case the process which knows and the process which is known are identical; i.e., it insists on the fact that the study of our own minds takes place by means of observation. But, an empiricist will say, there is no more reason for confining ourselves to "introspection" than for considering only our own bodies in studying physiology.

What has chiefly to be emphasised, however, is that the observation of minds, the knowledge of them in propositions, requires the rejection of the "unitary" view of mind. the conception of it as having only one character and being self-contained in that character. This is a rationalist, "unspeakable" view. If we are to have any dealings with minds, we must be able to consider how they act in different situations, i.e., to consider them as having complex characters and activities, as being divisible and determinate. Psychological science will only be possible if we have a variety of psychological truths, between which, and in each of which, connection and distinction are discernible. And the same applies to ethics. These sciences are historical, they are studies of occurrences and activities, they are concerned with situations in space and time. I have thus, without going into detail, indicated the place in the empiricist scheme of the other anti-rationalist theories I mentioned. The general conclusion is that all the objects of science, including minds and goods, are things occurring in space and time (the only reason for regarding minds as not in space being the rationalistic contention that they are indivisible), and that we can study them by virtue of the fact that we come into spatial and temporal relations with them. And therefore all ideals, ultimates, symbols, agencies and the like are to be rejected, and no such distinction as that of facts and principles, or facts and values, can be maintained. There are only facts, i.e., occurrences in space and time.

# 2
# PROPOSITIONS AND JUDGMENTS (1926)

In his discussion of Bradley's philosophy, Dr Schiller (*Mind*, N.S., 134) argues that the sceptical position which arises from the "refusal to recognise the actual procedures of our thought", is further supported by the systematic substitution of propositions for "genuine judgments". Bradley, he maintains, is sceptical because he ignores the requirement of relevance and insists on merely verbal forms. Thus "the question of absolute truth becomes that of whether the totality of truth can be packed into a single form of words"; and since this is clearly impossible, a sceptical theory, "which denies truth to man to reserve it for the Absolute," is inevitable.

It is not, however, necessary in admitting this conclusion to admit either that the question of relevance enters into the question of the truth of judgments, or that insistence on propositions raises any barrier to truth. Our procedure, in passing judgments on things or in voluntarily selecting certain subjects for consideration, may well be taken to indicate that we do not as a matter of fact seek any "totality of truth" but on the contrary believe, as our ordinary discourse shows—indeed the whole possibility of discourse depends on it—that there are any number of independent truths, each as "absolute" as any truth can be. But all this goes no way towards showing that these independent truths take the form of judgments, as distinct from propositions. What is indicated is that the conception of a "totality of truth" is a confused one—as confused as Dr Schiller, in his discussion in *Mind*, N.S., 130, has shown the conception of an "infinite whole" to be. The impossibility of packing the "totality of truth" into a single form of words is the best reason for rejecting this conception; it could never be a reason for rejecting forms of words.

Dr Schiller's main argument against forms of words is, of course, that no such form could stand the strain of being applied under every conceivable set of conditions and circumstances, whereas, if we restrict ourselves to the judgment which the words conveyed, and which has its application and its proper conditions solely in "its psychical setting and the context in which it arose", falsification is no longer inevitable. Now it seems so clear to me that, when we make a statement, we are trying to convey something which is true independently of us and in distinction from any circumstances (though we admit that it has circumstances), something which equally raises no question of application to different cases or of being menaced by a variety of possibilities, something which just is "literally true", that I have some difficulty in following Dr Schiller's argument and can only hope that I may not be misrepresenting it. It is surely the case that if there is any actual situation whatever which conflicts with the literal truth of a statement, then that statement is false. If "no human truth could stand this strain", then we *should* have to despair of truth. (Of course this position is untenable, since if any proposition is not literally true, its contradictory is literally true.)

It appears that one of the main possibilities that Dr Schiller has in mind, in holding that a form of judgment could not stand the test of all situations "in its verbal integrity", is ambiguity. Now it is perfectly true that the same set of words may be used to convey entirely different things. But, when we recognise this in any given case, it is always by means of words that we proceed to make the further distinctions that are necessary. When I agree with Dr Schiller that "Bradley is sceptical", a third person may take the statement to refer to a different Bradley. The ambiguity may then be removed by saying "F. H. Bradley", adding, if necessary, "author of 'Appearance and Reality'", and so on. A similarly verbal procedure would be adopted, if there were any dubiety about the meaning of "sceptical". But, as it is, we are agreed on the verbal statement "Bradley is sceptical".

What we agree on is not, of course, a form of words. The words cause us to suppose a certain situation or state of affairs, which, treated as a possibility in the question "Is Bradley sceptical?" is treated by those who believe the proposition as actual or as having occurred—as what we call a "matter of fact". Now what else is meant by the truth of the proposition except that the supposed state of affairs *has actually occurred?* But this occurrence is just as independent of our having judged it, as it is of the words in which we state it; on the other hand, it is just as capable of being stated unambiguously in words, as it is of being judged in distinction from anything else. We can misunderstand a statement, but equally we can misinterpret an occurrence; these are the risks we have to take in our reactions to things. But we assume, in the various distinct statements and judgments that we make, that there are various independent occurrences to be known. Now no one will deny that knowledge of actual occurrences *is* conveyed by means of words, that, in fact, discourse is the vehicle of the communication of truth. To supplant verbal forms by psychic settings is therefore to despair of communicable truth and eventually of all objectivity. Thus there is no need to appeal from propositions to judgments, but every reason for not doing so, if scepticism is to be avoided.

A distinction has to be made, in considering the question of context, between the psychical conditions of our thinking and the objective conditions of the occurrence of which we are thinking. No doubt it depends on our state of mind whether we believe a certain proposition or not (and similarly whether we understand a statement made to us). But to explain how we come to think anything does not explain whether it is true or not. Even if the proposition is about ourselves, its truth is not dependent on our believing it. But only on the basis of a confusion between judging and judged could it be supposed, as Dr Schiller appears to do, that all our judgments are about ourselves. He takes as the *meaning* of the judgment "that in view of all the circumstances present to its maker's mind and judged relevant by him, he has judged it best to make his judgment". His judging may imply all this, but what he has judged does not; and it is for what he has judged, and not for his judging, that truth is claimed. If the truth-claim of a judgment "can be disputed only by showing that under these same conditions something better and so truer could have been judged", then, considering that another person's judgment, as well as the same person's judgment at another time, would arise from a different psychic setting and so introduce different conditions, it would appear that a truth-claim could never be disputed. This shows the necessity of considering truth as concerned with what is judged, and not with judging, and so of eliminating the *psychic* context, at least.

If now we consider the objective circumstances or conditions of what is judged, it at once appears that in so describing them we distinguish them from the occurrence which they condition, and justify ourselves in speaking independently of it. Dr Schiller, it may be noted, speaks in this way of the conditions, but a consistent procedure would compel him to go on to consider conditions of conditions and circumstances of circumstances, and so on in the direction of that "totality" which he is anxious to avoid. If "circumstances" are really relevant to an assertion, they are part of what is asserted, and so cease to be circumstances. In short, with whatever other occurrences an occurrence may be *connected*, in asserting it we take it as *distinct* from those others, and thus as something which may be independently known (known even if they are not known); this distinctness (which does not exclude connection) being the ground of our referring to it as an independent occurrence—of our formulating the proposition. On this view it appears that in propositions we are not concerned with application or context, nor are propositions "about" anything.[1] They are simply true or false; and, if true, they are independently or "absolutely" true. To reject this view it would be necessary to show that we do not mean by a "truth" something which actually occurs. We can of course make specific assertions about circumstances, but this merely means that we can refer to a situation or occurrence which can be described as, or which involves, the connection or distinction of a number of occurrences. This will be a description of what it is that we are judging, and not of *its* context.

There is a sense in which we can say that a proposition is *about* something, viz. about the subject of the proposition. Thus "Bradley is sceptical" might be said to be about Bradley. We can say so, because we know Bradley independently of this proposition; i.e. we know other characteristics of his. Such a distinction is necessary, if the proposition is to convey information. But the information which it does convey (which we may sum up as "Bradley's scepticism") is something which equally is distinct from that other knowledge; it is, assuming as I have done that the statement is true, one particular occurrence. And this occurrence, which is what the proposition conveys, is not about anything.

Selection, then, if it is an admissible description of judging, does not consist in taking certain conditions into account as "relevant" and rejecting others as "irrelevant", but in speaking of a certain thing *unconditionally*. We select occurrences, i.e. speak of them independently, because there *are* distinct occurrences; because

[1] v. i., p. 169.

only by speaking of specific things can we speak at all. Hence there is no need to demand a "right" to select. We need only refer to that independence which truth implies. This does not mean that things do not condition one another. But if we say that two things are connected, we imply that they are distinct and can be distinctly spoken of. And when we speak of one such thing, we are perfectly aware that it has connections with, as well as distinctions from, other things, although these do not enter into the statement in question.

Taking "things" roughly in the sense of subjects of possible propositions, it may be said that we can select those things we wish to speak about; but what we say about them will be either true or false. What Dr Schiller calls selecting "from the mass of possible predicates the assertion we judge best to make about" the subject, cannot be construed otherwise than as judging that the predicate *truly* belongs to the subject. Hence the right to select is not logically prior to any question about truth. Our selection of predicates is justified, or not, only in relation to what actually occurs. Our selection of subjects is justified in relation to the fact that there are any number of distinct things. But, as has been said, things though distinct may yet be connected or together. And it may be argued that we may make any combination we like of things, and call it one thing. This is opposed to the view that a thing has a special context, to which alone it belongs. But, as we saw, there is no ground for rejecting the universe as context and still insisting that things have a peculiar context of their own. In treating of any arbitrarily chosen thing we shall still be dealing with a subject which has certain predicates and not others; with specific states of affairs, connections and distinctions, which occur or do not occur. Our choice may be arbitrary; but the occurrence of the chosen thing and its predicates will be quite independent of our choice.

Granted that as a matter of fact things are together and distinct, we are not entitled to limit the possibilities of combination of many things into a "unity", as Dr Schiller does in his criticism (*Mind*, N.S., 130) of Prof. Scott's theory of the "Infinite Whole". We find, on the contrary, that whatever can be spoken of as one thing can also be spoken of as many things, and vice versa. We can speak of a number of MIND, which is composed of many articles, or of a collection of numbers of MIND, which includes that number; and in speaking of such "things" we shall attribute to them predicates which either belong to them or do not. We *can* synthesise two minds, if we can speak of "A's mind and B's mind", though we may find it difficult, and above all uninteresting, to discover predicates of this peculiar thing. Dr Schiller asks, "How can the feelings, desires, idiosyncrasies, delusions, dreams, defects, errors and imaginations of two minds combine into a unity?" But does not drama precisely consist in the combination of the feelings, etc., of several minds into a unity? The point is simply that this unity is not a sort of identity; the components remain distinct. But the combination is also a distinct thing and has its actual predicates. And it is this distinctness that leads us to the rejection of the conception of an "infinite whole", or of "everything" as a possible subject of discourse; just as it leads us to the recognition that, whatever combinations or components our interests may direct us to consider, the truth of the matter is independent of our consideration.

My general contention is, then, that it is by reference to propositions, and not to judgments, that the conception of the "totality of truth" is to be rejected; that, in fact, Dr Schiller's theory is just as sceptical as Bradley's, and that it shares the same defect—viz., the assumption that a thing is infected by its conditions and cannot be considered apart from them. This leads Bradley to the conclusion that the only thing that can really be considered is the unconditioned whole or Absolute; it leads Dr Schiller to seek to take things in connection with their *peculiar* conditions, which are to be found in judgment. In both cases it leads away from the acceptance or rejection of statements or propositions just as they stand; that is away from objective and communicable truth.

# 3
# THE TRUTH OF PROPOSITIONS (1926)

The account of the truth of propositions which I gave (*Mind*, N.S., 138) seems to me not only to have been relevant to Dr Schiller's treatment of the question in his criticism of Bradley, but also substantially to embody the fundamental objections to his theory as restated (*Mind*, N.S., 139) under the heading *Judgments versus Propositions*. I cannot, therefore, hope to avoid repeating, and perhaps labouring, points that I have already made, but it may be possible for me in further discussion to make the issues clearer. Dr Schiller dwells on the difficulties and errors that arise from confusing propositions with judgments, and the sort of truth we can attribute to the one with that which can be claimed for the other. I should agree that it is highly undesirable to confuse propositions and judgments, if by "judgment" is meant *judging*; but, if so, there is no question of the truth of judgments, since, as I said in my previous discussion, it is for what a person judges, and not for his judging, that truth is claimed. On the other hand, if "judgment" is taken to mean *what is judged*, then I should deny that there is any distinction between judgments and propositions, and so any question of different sorts of truth. If to argue along these lines is to raise "the issue of Realism v. Idealism", I do not see that it is irrelevant to the points in Dr Schiller's discussion of Bradley which I was criticising. Since what is judged is commonly not in a psychic setting, "truth in a psychic setting" can hardly be claimed for it.

But I argued further that even if we consider the actual conditions of what is judged, we still cannot claim for it "truth under those conditions" or conditional truth; that, unless we can think of it as having unconditional or unqualified truth, we cannot call it true in any sense. It is not a question of the "formal independence of truth-claims", but of *the claim of independent truth* which we make whenever we assert anything as a matter of fact, i.e., whenever we assert anything at all. I had argued that Dr Schiller's theory was sceptical, because it denied that assertions (things asserted) were to be taken as simple matters of fact, or the reverse, and so implied that no definite assertion could be made. But the point can equally well be put by saying that any theory of the kind is illogical, since it can only be upheld by the making of statements of supposed fact. Now such statements are propositions. It appears to me, therefore, that this line of argument was strictly relevant to the attempt to show that, so far from adherence to propositions being capable of inducing scepticism, scepticism can only be avoided by insisting on claims to unqualified truth and rejecting claims to "truth in a context". If Bradley aimed at both absolute truth and truth under conditions, he would necessarily arrive at a negative result. What I am maintaining, as against Dr Schiller, is that the aiming at truth under conditions must have been responsible for this, and not the aiming at absolute truth.

This "absolute truth" is, of course, just the truth that we claim for what we definitely *believe*. There is no question of truths of which we can be eternally certain, of beliefs which under no conceivable circumstances could we give up. Any proposition whatever can be denied, i.e. can be conceived to be false; and we have all had experience of giving up beliefs which we once confidently held. But *while* we held them, we held them to be absolutely true; we could not *then* imagine that there would be circumstances under which we should give them up, since we took them to hold quite independently of us. Otherwise, we could never have had any need to give them up, nor, if we had come to think differently, should we have thought that we were previously *wrong*. The point is, then, that at any given time there are certain things that we believe and, in so doing, regard as matters of fact. And if there is anything about which we are uncertain, what we are uncertain about is whether or not it is a matter of fact; we do not regard it as a matter of "uncertain fact". Experience has shown us that we make mistakes, but it could not show us anything at all unless we sometimes made no mistake. Thus the mere possibility of contradiction, the general consideration that "we may be wrong", could never lead us to give up a particular belief that we held; only a belief in other propositions which disprove it, could do so. The very fact that contradictory views are held is sufficient to show that some beliefs are true. Now when any belief is true, what is believed (the proposition) is something that has occurred; and when a belief is false, it is still, in being believed, *supposed* to have occurred. To speak, on this basis, of "absolute" truth, while it may be said to add nothing to the notion of occurrence, at least emphasises the fact that we cannot speak of relative or conditional occurrences.

I had contended that to reject this view of the truth of propositions, "it would be necessary to show that we do not mean by 'truth' something which actually occurs". But though this view is equally opposed to "correspondence" and "coherence", Dr Schiller has not dealt with it in arriving at the conclusion that "the sense of 'truth' which a 'proposition' may fitly claim would seem to be either that which is involved in the 'correspondence' or that which is involved in the 'coherence' theory of truth". I shall not attempt to elucidate these "claims", since if it is possible for a proposition to claim to be a matter of fact, there can be no other sense of truth to consider. I still maintain that what is "proposed" or supposed in a proposition is a certain state of affairs, and that whoever believes the proposition takes that state of affairs to have actually occurred—as he indicates by the use of the copula "is". When, for example, I invite anyone to believe that Bradley is sceptical, I ask him to consider the actual Bradley and whether in his works he displays the actual characteristic of scepticism. I might attempt to prove my point by argument, but what I should expect to be proved at the end of the argument would simply be the occurrence (truth or fact) of Bradley's scepticism. In general, then, when a person formulates a proposition, the copula indicates that he thinks something has occurred, and the terms (the different functions of which need not be considered here) indicate *what* he thinks has occurred. In other words, a proposition is something which can be thought to have occurred or not to have occurred. But thinking that something has occurred is simply judgment, in the sense of judging. Thus when we speak of judgment in the sense of what is judged, we are speaking about a proposition; and the proposition or judgment is true, when the supposed situation *has* occurred. There is no question here of how we know this, how we can be "sure of our facts". It is sufficient that we have beliefs, and that this is what they mean; that believing something and believing that it has occurred are the same thing. It still seems to me that this line of argument suffices to dispose of any theory which takes truth to depend on adequacy or relevance, or, in general, to be a matter of degree. We cannot think of situations as more or less occurring or as conditionally occurring. There are, as I said, cases where we assert that A *conditions B*, but then we take this whole situation as an absolute fact. In short, there can be no intermediate stage between absolute occurrence and absolute non-occurrence.

The difficulties about verbal forms and ambiguity, which Dr Schiller again raises, seem to me to go no way towards showing that a true proposition ought to be said at best to "correspond to a fact", instead of to be a fact. If a proposition were merely a form of words, and words had that arbitrariness which he appears to assign to them, I do not see how it could even *correspond* to a fact. And the same can be said, if for "proposition" we substitute "statement". By a statement we mean something *stated* by means of words, and by literal truth and literal falsity we mean that the propositions so stated are either truths conveyed by words or falsehoods conveyed by words. Dr Schiller thinks that if I demand literal truth, I have made for myself a short cut to scepticism, since "literal truth is *at most* only verbal, and, for the purpose of determining real truth, quite inadequate. It is for example bowled over by the slightest hint of ambiguity". Yet we all make statements in words and *believe* them, and hence believe that any one who denies them is wrong; and, as I said in my previous discussion, "no one will deny" (and Dr Schiller has not denied it) "that knowledge of actual occurrences *is* conveyed by means of words". It is not at all necessary for me to maintain that misunderstanding never occurs, but only to point out that understanding occurs and to indicate what sort of thing it is that is then understood. There could not be understanding of statements, unless it were false that a statement "always has, in principle, a *plurality* of meanings". The principle of verbal communication is that the set of words used in making a given statement should have only one meaning. This is the principle that we employ in learning any language, our own included. There are exceptional cases where the same word stands for several distinct sorts of thing, and in these cases, as I pointed out, misunderstanding is commonly removed by the use of *other* words. But for the most part the distinct things we have to know are a certain arrangement of words, an occurrence of a certain character and the fact that those who understand the language think of the latter when they see or hear the former. This may be a state of affairs which has not "passed unobserved by anyone", but it has to be pointed out in order to reinforce my previous contention that misunderstanding of words and misunderstanding of things are on precisely the same footing. Persons may make

THE TRUTH OF PROPOSITIONS (1926)    27

*mistakes* about words, but this does not render it impossible for a language to be understood and thus for literal truths to be believed and communicated.

In denying this, Dr Schiller, though he claims to have made a clear distinction between the truth of propositions and that of judgments, has not really shown what he means by "the 'truth' (in general and in the abstract) of a 'proposition' ", or what is the "verbal meaning" to which formal logicians are supposed to confine themselves. In general and in the abstract any word might mean anything, and thus on a merely verbal basis there could be no such distinction as that between true and false propositions. But formal logicians surely proceed on the basis of the fact that, since we are capable of knowing what words mean, we can believe or disbelieve statements in words, i.e. find them literally true or false. And Dr Schiller himself, when he objects to the assumption "that the mere hearing of a proposition, which once formulated what seemed a truth in the judgment of its first discoverer, will suffice to re-start the same process in any mind that hears it", has implicitly conceded, in the words "seemed a truth", all that they require for their purpose. What was it that it seemed, and what was it that seemed so? It was a *state of affairs* that seemed (was judged) to have occurred. If words do formulate such suppositions and if they ever enable a hearer to make the same supposition, then true and false propositions can be stated and understood without being "verbal". But it does not appear, on Dr Schiller's theory of propositions, how a proposition could ever seem to formulate a truth.

It is equally difficult for him to account for the notion of "seeming true" in terms of his theory of the truth of *judgments*. He wishes to consider "what the actual judgment meant" and to "discount as irrelevant the formal truth-claim made by all judgments true or false". But we cannot leave the claim aside without explaining, as Dr Schiller does not do, what it is that is claimed; and it can hardly be denied that the person judging *means* to make this claim. All that would remain, if it were removed, would be the material, the terms, of the judgment, and they do not by themselves make it a judgment or convey what it means. The truth a judgment claims, then, and the truth it may possibly have, is what is indicated by the copula; viz. occurrence. It is certainly not adequacy to a situation, for if anything was claimed as adequate to a situation, it would be its adequacy that was said to have occurred. This line of argument is in accordance with my previous criticism of "contexts". I pointed out that in his original discussion (*Mind*, N.S., 134, p. 221) Dr Schiller had said that "the judgment means that in view of all the circumstances present to its maker's mind and judged relevant by him, he has judged it best to make his judgment". That is to say, when a man judges that A is B, he has *ipso facto* passed the judgment, "Judging that A is B is the best I can do under the relevant circumstances". The infinite regress involved in attempting to maintain this position is obvious. On the other hand, it is equally obvious that the man is supposed, in the second place, to make a judgment of fact—"Judging that A is B *is* the best", etc. Similar criticisms may be passed on what Dr Schiller now says—"The making of a (*bona fide*) judgment thus *ipso facto* implies its maker's belief that it *was*" (my italics) "the best response to the circumstances which he could conceive". If he can make a judgment of fact in the second place, there is no reason for turning his *original* judgment from a claim to truth in fact into a claim to "truth in a context". Dr Schiller contrasts the discussion of the truth of a judgment, as a question of *value*, with that of its meaning, as a question of *fact*. But if there is such a thing as a matter of fact, surely that and that only is what we mean by truth.

I should therefore maintain that Dr Schiller has not made it clear what he means by the "truth of judgments", any more than by the "truth of propositions". It may be admitted that whether or not we pass a certain judgment will depend on our purposes, and again that there is a distinction between judgments which are relevant to a certain inquiry and those which are not. But this has nothing whatever to do with truth; a relevant judgment may be false, an irrelevant one true. It may be more to the purpose of a certain discussion to consider whether a penny stamp is scarlet or not than whether it is red or not, but this fact will not enable us to determine whether it *is* scarlet. Moreover, if it is scarlet, it is also red, while if it is red, it may not be scarlet. Thus Dr Schiller has said nothing to show that being relevant makes a statement true. He has correspondingly not shown how being "misapplied" could make a "proposition" false. "Even the best and 'truest' form," he says, "will not be applicable to all situations". But the only situation to which it could be supposed to be "applicable" is the situation which, it says, occurs. I can only assume that the question is of implication; that, for example, we should "misapply" the proposition "All men are mortal", if we proceeded from it to believe that "All chessmen are mortal". But what this meant would be that we supplied a minor premise "All chessmen are men", which is false, and which is therefore capable of leading to false conclusions. It does not, accordingly, appear either that a true proposition can by itself imply false conclusions, or that one proposition can be an "application" of another.

This raises the question of distinctness and connectedness, what a proposition or group of propositions implies being something distinct from itself, though connected with it. Dr Schiller, in his criticism of my remarks on selection, takes no account of my statements that things which are connected are at the same time distinct, and that a number of distinct things may be taken together as constituting one thing (as articles of furniture constitute a suite) without being any less distinguishable. Had he done so, he could hardly have referred to my "assumptions that there is only one way of selecting and that its objects are all distinct and lying about waiting to be recognised". I gave definite examples of different ways of selecting and of the embodiment of one thing in another (though the two are still different things). And I pointed out that though "the truth of the matter is independent of our consideration", our interests may lead us to consider various combinations and components of things. I cannot therefore consider myself entirely responsible for the obscurity which Dr Schiller finds in my argument. I repeat that unless we can speak of things independently, speak of them, that is, as simply occurring and not as "conditionally occurring", we cannot make intelligible statements (or have beliefs) at all. The fact that there are conditions under which a state of affairs occurs, does not make it occur conditionally; it occurs and can be known to occur even if its conditions are not known. As before, I can know that Bradley was sceptical without knowing under what conditions he became so, or under what conditions in general scepticism arises.

What I was primarily considering, in discussing "selection", was whether knowing a distinct state of affairs in the above way could be so described; whether, as I said, selection "is an admissible description of judging". And I concluded that we might be said to select occurrences, in that our interests and purposes led us to consider certain occurrences and not others. What I denied was that our selection of a predicate for a selected subject could possibly be prior to any question of truth, since predicating one term of another is stating what we suppose to be true; and that we required a "right" to select, since, though we may choose or select certain objects of interest to us, we do not choose to select. Before it can be said that we exercise a right to select, it would have to be shown what would happen if we did not; but this could not be shown—knowledge of what was "neither one thing nor another" being quite inconceivable. *Prima facie*, then, the practice of speaking about distinct things stands in *no* need of justification. There is no distinct thing called "the real" which can be spoken of as a "continuum", and which requires to be broken up before any other thing can be spoken of. Unless things were first of all distinguished, we could never "find from experience that great masses of reality are in fact irrelevant to our purposes and may safely be neglected"; hence this cannot be given as a *reason* for selecting. We can certainly "select wrongly" in that we may take things to be distinct which are not so, or things not to be distinct which are so, but we cannot consider whether we are entitled to make distinctions or not, since any sort of thinking involves distinction. In accordance with this view it should be said that truth is to be sought not in concentration upon "parts", but in consideration of things or description of occurrences.

I have tried to show the importance of the fact that such descriptions are either true or false. I admit that we want to know *whether* they are true or false, but we cannot come to a conclusion in any given case by considering "rights" or statements of logical theory; we can only do so by observation or, in general, by reference to propositions which we believe. And the nature of belief requires the rejection of any theory of distinct *sorts* or different *degrees* of truth; truth being simply what is represented by the copula "is" in the proposition. Any such theory, or any view which attributes different meanings to "is", is inherently sceptical or illogical, since only by the use of the unambiguous "is" of occurrence (as I have shown in relation to Dr Schiller's view, in particular) could the theory be formulated at all. We must think of propositions, therefore, as capable of being unconditionally true; a consistent adherence to the treatment of them as merely verbal forms would not allow of any enunciation of belief, that is, of any "judgment".

# 4
# THE KNOWER AND THE KNOWN (1927)

We are accustomed to think of Realism and Idealism as conflicting views about knowledge. In this paper I shall be concerned partly to bring forward arguments in support of the realist view of knowledge, but even more to indicate what I take to be important consequences, in regard not only to mind and knowledge but to philosophy in general, of accepting that position. While it may be conceded to Professor Montague that "the point at issue between realism and idealism should not be confused with the [point] at issue between empiricism and rationalism",[1] in that the former has specially to do with knowledge while the latter has not, there are reasons, which I think conclusive, for holding that a realist can only be an empiricist. The question of the nature of relations is at any rate one issue between rationalists and empiricists, and, as the authors of *The New Realism* have shown, the basis of a realistic theory of knowledge can only be a certain theory of relations; which enables us to draw definite conclusions from the contention that knowledge is a relation. Thus, according to Professor Montague, "Realism holds that things known may continue to exist unaltered when they are not known, or that things may pass in and out of the cognitive relation without prejudice to their reality, or that the existence of a thing is not correlated with or dependent upon the fact that anybody experiences it, perceives it, conceives it, or is in any way aware of it."[1] And Professor Marvin makes the theory of relations here indicated still more explicit. "In the proposition 'the term $a$ is in the relation R to the term $b$', $a$R in no degree constitutes $b$, nor does R$b$ constitute $a$, nor does R constitute either $a$ or $b$."[1] Knowledge being taken as a relation, it is thus asserted that, when I know this paper, "I know" in no way constitutes this paper, nor does "know this paper" in any way constitute me, nor does "know" in any way constitute either me or this paper.

The view that knowledge is a relation implies that knower and known are two different things or that, in knowledge, the knower

[1] *Program and First Platform of Six Realists; The New Realism*, Appendix, pp. 473,4.

is not the known. It is indeed admitted on any view that there is a distinction between them, and if knowledge were not then called a relation, it would only be because relations were held to be comparatively unreal; but those who would say this would say the same about distinctions. The realist is thus found to be maintaining that distinctions are absolutely real. According to the opposing view, distinctions are "distinctions within identities", and any relation is a "form of identity". If a thing is *really* related in a certain way, the relation in question belongs to its "nature", and since that to which it is related is thus not essentially separate from it, a certain "identity of nature" holds between the two. But this theory of natures or essences is precisely rationalism, and the realist, in denying that *a*R*b* asserts or implies any identity between *a* and *b*, is taking up an empiricist position.

He does not, of course, deny that there is a certain "identity" in the case, viz., the identity of *a*R*b* as a given situation or state of affairs. When it is argued that the distinction between subject and object must be "a distinction within an identity", the reason alleged is that there is no subject without an object and no object without a subject. But this merely means that any "subject-object" relation has two terms; it could not for a moment show that knower and known are not two different things, or that anything is to be regarded as *in itself* either a subject or an object. Hume points out that the facts that it takes a man to be a husband and that every husband has a wife do not imply that every man has a wife; similarly, to assert that it takes a mind to know or a thing to be known does not imply that every mind knows or every thing is known. But of more importance here is the fact that while we speak of a certain marriage, and agree that there is no husband without a wife and no wife without a husband, we find husband and wife in any marriage to be two different persons. The one *is not* the other. Those who argue that knower and known are in some way identical because they are in a *certain* relation, have also to maintain that any two different things are in some way identical, since any difference is a certain difference or since "A is different from B" is a certain state of affairs. So that when we say that A is not B, we are somehow also saying that A is B and B is A. On this basis discourse would be impossible.

It is thus seen to be logically necessary to hold that, in knowledge, "the knower is not the known". It follows that to tell us *what a man knows* is not to give a description of that man (to state some character or quality which he has), any more than to tell us *who knows it* is to give a description of a thing. The fact that a man does know certain things may enable us to infer that he is a man of a certain character, but this inference would not be possible unless we had previously come to believe that only persons of that character knew these things, i.e., unless we had had previous opportunities of observing that character independently. But again, since knowledge is a relation, to tell us *that a man knows* is not to give a description of him, any more than to say *that a thing is known* is to say what sort of thing it is. We may believe that only beings of a certain sort do know, but that depends on our having recognised their character independently of their knowing. And, in general, in saying of any two related things that they are distinct, we must suppose each to have some character, or certain qualities, of its own. We must distinguish complete statements like "X is a man" from incomplete statements like "X is a husband". The latter is, of course, used roughly to convey the fact that X has those characteristics which will be found in the first term whenever there is a true statement of the form "X is the husband of Y". But those characteristics are understood to be discoverable by observing X alone, while we could not in that way find out what was meant by his being a husband.

Arguing then, as realists, that no thing or quality of a thing is constituted by the thing's relations, we have to assert that nothing is constituted by knowing and nothing by being known. The notion of "that whose nature it is to know" is expressed in the term "consciousness"; the notion of "that whose nature it is to be known" in the term "idea". Realism is therefore concerned to reject these terms, as involving the attempt to take relations as qualities. If the term "conscious being" merely meant that sort of thing which can know, and "idea" that which can be known, they might be used in incomplete statements similar to "X is a husband". But we must have some notion of what sorts of things these are, since we could never have supposed that nothing knew something or something knew nothing. Thus we must know what sort of thing a mind is, independently of terms like "consciousness" or "state of consciousness"; and we must be able to describe things independently of their being known or of their being known in some particular way, so that "sensa", for example, cannot be a proper name for any species of things. A strictly realist theory must dispense with all expressions of these sorts, in order to be consistent with its empirical starting-point and logical basis.

# I

(*a*) The theory of "ideas" as entities "whose nature it is to be known" (or which are "essentially known") is most explicitly formulated by Berkeley. To think of what is known as having a nature independent of its being known is, he says, to be guilty of "abstraction". This error consists in thinking separately of things which cannot exist separately. Thus we cannot truly know any object without knowing "all about" it (its "whole nature"); for if we only knew something about it, we should be separating that something from other somethings which in fact are also about it. In terms of this theory, if a thing really is known, we cannot think of it otherwise than as known, or we should not be thinking of *it*. "Can there", asks Berkeley, "be a nicer strain of abstraction than to distinguish the existence of sensible objects from their being perceived, so as to conceive them existing unperceived?"

It is, of course, impossible to maintain a view of this kind consistently, since strictly in accordance with it we could make no statements at all. That Berkeley does not do so is shown when he says, "It is not in my power to frame an idea of a body extended and moved, but I must withal give it some colour or other sensible quality." He really ought to maintain, in the case of a coloured body which is extended and moved, that its being coloured and its being extended and its being moved and its being a body all mean precisely the same thing; in which case his argument is stultified. But otherwise he is admitting that we can conceive the thing as having any one of these characters, that we can truly assert something about it without saying "all about" it. He does in fact admit that, though it may be true of an object A that it is given to us by God as a sign of B, we can know A without knowing this fact. It may equally well be that we may know a thing which is known, without knowing that it is known. There is no reason for denying this, if its being known is only *something* about it. And the alternative, which Berkeley would have to follow, is that, since we can only conceive separately what may exist separately, the separate statement that a thing is known implies that nothing else can be said of it but that it is known. There could not then be a number of different known things; there would simply be the essence "known". Indeed, since what I know must be "known by me" and there is nothing else that it must be, all that I can ever know is the single essence "known by me".

The only sort of assertion that we could make in starting from such an essence as "known" would be the identity "The known is known"; and only by means of abstraction (passing from a whole nature to a supposed part of it) could any consequences appear to follow from such a statement. Now Berkeley does start from an identity, stated negatively, viz., "What is perceived cannot be unperceived"; which is merely an expression of the essence "perceived". But he proceeds from this, as the first quotation shows, to draw the conclusion that what is perceived cannot be *conceived to be unperceived.* Now the only guarantee of this conclusion is the fact that the thing is perceived; and if this is a guarantee, it must be because the thing is perceived to be perceived. (Here the notion of "idea" emerges, in the form of the "percept"; the conceiving of "concepts" and the sensing of "sensa" are suppositions of the same type.) What is perceived to be perceived cannot be taken (there is no special force in "conceived" here) to be unperceived. The obtaining of the given conclusion from the identity thus depends on the substitution of "perceived to be perceived" for "perceived". And the plausibility of the conclusion itself depends on ambiguity; it is plausible as meaning that we cannot conceive or suppose that "what is perceived is unperceived", but not in the required sense that things which are perceived cannot be supposed not to be perceived and must be supposed to be perceived. This cannot be admitted, since the various things that are said to be perceived cannot have their whole nature constituted by being perceived.

The fact, then, that we can make such statements as that red, or something red, is perceived, is sufficient to dispose of Berkeley's theory that what is known must be known as known. It would, on the contrary, be true to say that we know things as independent of being known, since we can only know them as existing and having characters of their own. Berkeley's theory, it should be noted, is not dependent on the use of the term "perception";

it could be maintained in exactly the same way that "whatever is apprehended cannot be unapprehended", without any reference to modes of apprehension. So that his criticism of Locke, who had first admitted the "essentially apprehended" and then presumed a further knowledge of independent things, is quite sound. The criticism applicable to both is that we never know "ideas", but always independent things.

(*b*) Descartes's demonstration that there is something "whose nature it is to know", or, as he puts it, "whose whole essence consists in thinking" (i.e., "consciousness"), proceeds in a similar fashion to Berkeley's substantiation of "ideas"; in fact, it may be said that Berkeley has simply applied to the known the principle of Descartes's argument about the knower. The latter is complicated by the fact that what guarantees the essential knowingness of a knower is the knower himself; but the same mechanism of essence, identity and ambiguity can be discerned. The assumption is that we cannot suppose ourselves, in knowing, not to know, i.e., we cannot suppose that when we know, we do not know; but it is employed as if it meant that we cannot, in knowing, suppose ourselves not to know. Or, putting the argument positively, we must suppose ourselves, in knowing, to know; hence we must, in knowing, suppose ourselves to know (or, in thinking, think that we think). By means of identity and ambiguity, therefore, Descartes arrives at the conclusion that we always know ourselves as knowing, and never know ourselves as anything else; because we *can* suppose ourselves, though knowing, not to have that other character. The method, once more, is that what can be conceived separately from a certain thing is not of its essence but is a different thing, while what cannot be conceived separately is of its essence. And the strict consequence would be that no positive (non-identical) assertion could be made, since we could only make it by specifying a distinct part of a "whole nature".

The view that in knowing we know ourselves knowing, that we know as knowing or consciously know, is thus seen to be as ill-founded as the view that we know things as known. The identity "the known is known" does not imply that it is the same thing to know X and to know that X is known; nor does the identity "I know what I know" imply that I must know *that I know it*, or know anything about myself at all, in knowing it. Descartes, having taken his knowledge as a subject to be considered, cannot in the same argument doubt that he knows; but a man who knows need not have taken up this position, and might quite well doubt that he knew, or that he doubted, or that there was such a being as himself. The conclusion that a person could not know without knowing his knowing, as we have seen, depends on ambiguity, and the conclusion that he could not know himself without knowing his knowing depends on the assumption that he must know "all about" anything he knows. This theory being logically untenable, there is no ground whatever for supposing that we must know minds as "conscious" or for treating their knowing otherwise than as a relation to other things which is not part of their own "character". We have no more right to talk of a "conscious state" than of an "on state" or an "above state". And we may take it as possible that anything which knows may at another time not know, just as things which are known may at another time not be known.

It is not in the least implied that minds are not known, but only that they are to be known as having certain qualities. "The knower is not the known" has sometimes been taken to mean that the knower is not known; hence the doctrine of the transcendental ego. Alternatively, the distinction is taken to imply that the knower can only be known as knowing, i.e., known *in a different way* from things which are known as known. But all that is implied is that the relation has order; it is not asymmetrical, but at least it is "non-symmetrical". When A knows B, B need not know A; and even if B does know A, this is a different state of affairs from A knowing B. Just as, in the relation of parenthood, "the parent is not the child" and yet is always the child of someone else, so, when I know a thing, someone else may know me and he may know my *knowing the thing*. Only if there are cases of this kind can it be possible for us to talk about "knowledge". But the person's knowledge of my relation to the thing is distinct from his knowledge of my qualities.

As regards my knowledge of myself, this will have to be accounted for by saying that a certain process in my mind knows another, or knows myself, but without knowing *itself.* We can only know ourselves, in fact, as certain very familiar *objects.* And if it is urged that the process which knows does nevertheless belong to myself, the answer must be that what we know consists not of things simply but of states of affairs (or propositions). Suppose, then, that I know that I am angry, the "object" may be roughly expressed by saying that within a certain contour anger is occurring; and the fact that the process which knows it also occurs within the contour is not to the purpose, since we do not require to know "all" that occurs within the contour. That which knows a given occurrence is a different occurrence; it is not my anger which knows my anger. Detailed discussion of how we come to use the term "I" would be out of place here. It is enough to point out that on the realist theory the conception of a mind as a "unity" or indivisible whole cannot be sustained; according to that conception neither I nor anyone else could know *anything about* my mind.

## II

According to realism, I have argued, we never know "ideas" but always independent things, or rather states of affairs. It seems to me to follow that such expressions as appearances or data, and as concepts, percepts or sensa have no place in realist theory. If, e.g., there is a peculiar way of knowing called "sensing", it will only be on the assumption that relations somehow constitute their terms that we can use the term "sensa" to describe a class of things or a way of being. If, on the other hand, any class of things can properly be described as "sensa", to speak of knowing them as "sensing" is to make the same sort of assumption, and is no more justifiable than to speak of knowing trees as "treeing". I should maintain that there is no such thing as either sensing or sensa, since "the sensa which I sense" are taken to be those things, my knowing which depends on where and how I am, and since this (*a*) does not describe the things, (*b*) is true of all my knowing.

For Berkeley the things we know are "essentially related to our minds" and thus have a "relative existence", as our ideas. The theory of sensa is likewise a theory of "relative existence", in someone's or some "sense-field", and of "that whose nature it is to have certain relations". Dr Broad's theory, in this connection, does not, I think, differ greatly from other theories of sensa. Sensa are shown to be private and non-physical because of their *dependence* on certain conditions. Dr Broad does not commit himself to the view that sensa are mind-dependent. "The facts are on the whole much better explained by supposing that the sensa which a man senses are partly dependent on the position, internal states and structure of his body". But certain examples, though they "do not suggest for a moment that sensa are existentially mind-dependent...do strongly suggest that they are to some extent qualitatively mind-dependent".[2] Now dependence is presumably a relation, and if a certain existence or a certain quality depends on something, this does not justify us, rejecting as we do the theory of constitutive relations, in describing it as a "dependent existence" or a "dependent quality". The existence or quality, though it might not have been but for that other thing, is independent in the sense of being distinct and having a character of its own. If Dr Broad's explanations were correct, we should have to say that a certain thing now exists because my body was in a certain position, etc., and has certain qualities because my mind was in a certain condition. Granted all that, the thing now exists and has these qualities, and no reason has been shown for calling it private or non-physical.

Whether the explanations should be accepted is made exceedingly doubtful by noting the ambiguity of the statement that "the sensa which a man senses" are dependent on his body. This may merely mean that what is dependent is "the fact that he senses these sensa", i.e., his sensing them, i.e., his standing in a certain relation to them. That this should be dependent on where he is could occasion no surprise to commonsense, and would justify no statement about the dependence of the "sensa" themselves. The fundamental criticism is, however, that what exists because of me nonetheless *exists*, apart from or independently of me. The houses which would not have existed, had not men planned and built them (i.e., but for their minds and bodies), are physical and are not private to these men; they stand for other men to see them and may remain when no one perceives them at all. The argument from dependence commits us to the Berkeleian theory of "relative existence"; as does also the notion of a special "sense-field" in which a given sensum occurs. Dr Broad regards it as a merit of his sensum theory that it does not require the assumption of an absolute Space-Time. But "absolute" Space-Time is simply that in which things "absolutely" exist, and realism is committed to the rejection of "relative existence", and so of "relativity".

It may now be asked what reasons there are for supposing "sensible objects", which differ from physical objects, and which

[2] *Scientific Thought*, pp. 259, 261.

are brought about and affected by persons to a greater degree than the latter. In arguing that there can be no adequate reason for such a supposition, I shall consider mainly the question of "sensible" shapes and sizes. Dr Broad explains "the notion of sensible appearance", in regard, particularly, to shape, as follows: "We know that when we lay a penny down on a table and view it from different positions, it generally looks more or less elliptical in shape. The eccentricity of these various appearances varies as we move about, and so does the direction of their major axes. . . . It is a fact that we do believe [that there is a single physical object... which appears to us in all these different ways]. It is an equally certain fact that the penny does look different as we move about."[3] There then arises a difficulty about the relation between the round penny and an "elliptical appearance", or something "appearing elliptical". As regards the latter alternative (which Dr Broad rejects and which he connects with the theories of Professor Dawes Hicks and Professor Moore), it seems to me necessary to point out that "appearing" is a relation, viz., that of being known or apprehended. So that what is apprehended in this case is that "something is elliptical", and, since this interpretation does not allow us to speak of "an appearance", the precise belief would seem to be that the penny is elliptical; a belief which is simply false. Now there are cases in which such a false belief is held, but in many cases it is not, so that it may be questioned whether anything "appears elliptical". In any case, "appearing elliptical" does not state a relation between *the penny* and us, except when we are wrong.

"Appearing elliptical" at least involves apprehension of a state of affairs, but, according to Dr Broad, the "elliptical appearance" is apprehended without judgment, though it is apprehended as existing. This compromise is as unacceptable as that of Berkeley. We have something whose "whole nature" is apprehended (since an appearance is exactly what appears to a person), and then it is supposed to exist. As before, its nature and its existence must mean the same thing, and it must be perfectly indescribable. A similar point emerges in connection with the "different appearances" mentioned. Unless we think of a physical object as something which has to be known in its "whole nature", there

[3] *op. cit.*, p. 235.

is no reason why it should not have different appearances, i.e., why different characteristics of it should not be observable from different standpoints.[4] And it cannot be denied that when we do know a physical object, we know a variety of distinct things about it. The recognition that, whenever we know, we know existences and that to know existences is to know states of affairs in which complex things occur, is sufficient to dispose of the theory of "appearances".

Thus an "elliptical appearance", in respect of the penny, can only mean a false belief. I have said that in many cases this false belief is not held; what visibly appears to us is the round penny (or the penny's being round), even though the round surface is not at right angles to the line of vision. The assumption underlying the whole theory of differing shapes and sizes, seen from different directions and distances, is that we look out at, or there visually appears to us, a plane projection of the visual field. It is quite certain that a penny may be so placed that its projection on a plane perpendicular to the line of vision is elliptical; it is equally certain that the further a penny is beyond such a plane, the smaller its projection on the plane will be, and that it may be so near the plane that its projection is larger than that of the moon. But if, as is the case, it is not true that, when we look out, we either look at or see things arranged in a plane, if we do see things at various distances and at various angles to one another—in short, in three dimensions—then the contention that a thing looks smaller as it retreats, or that a round disc looks elliptical when it is oblique, is robbed of its force. Since we see things in three dimensions, there is no reason why we should attribute to a thing itself the shape of its projection on a plane perpendicular to the line of vision, or see that shape at all.

In cases where there is said to be an "elliptical appearance", there really is something elliptical, viz. (assuming the surface affected to be plane and perpendicular, or sufficiently near the perpendicular, to the line of vision), that part of the surface of the retina on which the rays of light from the object fall. As we are not looking at the retina, this does not affect the question directly. But

---

[4] This seems to be a much more important feature of Professor Dawes Hicks's theory than any point about "looking elliptical"; he rejects the distinction between sensible objects and physical objects precisely because physical objects are complex. Cf. "The Basis of Critical Realism", *Proc. Arist. Soc.*, 1916–17, p. 342.

it is sometimes assumed (on a theory similar to Berkeley's) that the retina is affected in precisely the same way, no matter how far the light has travelled; that consequently we cannot distinguish distances by sight, so that any part of a visual object, or field, must "visually appear" to be at the same distance as any other part. (What distance this could be is quite obscure.) It is, however, perfectly conceivable that rays from different distances should affect the retina differently; even though "the picture imprinted on the retina" remained the same, the effects might differ in other respects. The fact is that we do see things at different distances, and if it is alleged that this must be due to something not given by vision, the answer is (*a*) that what it is due to is quite irrelevant, (*b*) that the objection involves the attempt to maintain that we cannot see what we actually do see.

But, though reference to the retina is irrelevant, there may still be something elliptical to be considered. We commonly see things against a background, and if that background were perpendicular to the line of vision, the shape of the part of the background concealed by the thing would be that of the thing's projection on a perpendicular plane. In this way an oblique penny may conceal an elliptical part of the wall of a room—and this also happens in cases where we are looking obliquely at the wall. Now we are just as capable of observing that an elliptical part of the wall is concealed as of observing the round penny; and the concealed elliptical part is just as much a physical object as the penny. In such a case, on a casual glance, we may fail to distinguish the distances of wall and penny, and suppose that the penny is elliptical. There is something elliptical in the same direction as the penny, something moreover of which we only see the shape, and there is a consequent possibility of our attributing that shape to the seen penny. If, however, something in the appearance of the object suggests that it is a penny, then we doubt the supposition we have made, and by stricter attention observe that the penny is not in the plane of the wall but is oblique and round. The previous mistake may be described by saying that we had "displaced" the elliptical shape from the wall to the penny, just as we might displace the red colour of red spectacles to the things we saw through them. Also, the fact that we know that the penny is round need not prevent us from making the mistake; it would only require to be two different processes which had the two beliefs, and we should attribute "knowledge" to that process which was able to overcome the other when they came into conflict.

It is possible for us, then, correctly to distinguish something elliptical from something round, the two being physical objects occupying different places; whereas, if we could only distinguish things in accordance with their projections, almost all our observations would be mistaken. It may be said that we can judge or discriminate best the shapes of surfaces which are perpendicular to the line of vision.[5] But though we could less easily distinguish a circle and a nearly circular ellipse if they were lying obliquely to our vision, that would not prove that we see their projections. We may tend to err by assuming that the easier conditions are fulfilled, but it is possible, when we are presented with an oblique circle, to "see it circular". Again, we can judge sizes best when the things compared are close together; but we *can* see a distant tree larger than a man near at hand, who, if he stepped aside, would conceal the tree, and the relative sizes of the projections only appear to us in terms of concealed portions of a common background. Improvement in discrimination is possible, and may come about with the aid of other senses, as well as through the movements of the observed things and of ourselves in observing them. But it could never begin if we saw a flat picture.

I have considered at length the case of "elliptical appearance" in order to show the kind of mistake that is possible (though not necessary), and the possibility of correcting it by means of other judgments. I regard the general theory that I have advanced, as showing that an account along similar lines could be given of more difficult cases. In general, it cannot be maintained that in this (or any other) sort of apprehension, judgment, i.e., apprehension of states of affairs or situations, is not involved, since (*a*) it is always something that appears elliptical or smaller; we do not apprehend "ellipticity" or "smallness" by itself; (*b*) that something is always taken to be in some particular place. Any such judgment will be either correct or mistaken; but correction will only occur by means of judgments of the same order. At no time in the process of making our observations more precise, i.e., *of discovering new*

---

[5] According to James, it is because getting things into a perpendicular position gives us the best means of recognising them by shape, that we call the shapes projected under these circumstances the "real shapes" of the things. Cf. *Principles of Psychology*, vol. II, pp. 237–240.

*distinctions and connections, as well as previous errors* (and it is just in these ways that, on any view, we extend our knowledge of physical objects), do we suppose that we are not observing the things themselves and their actual shapes and sizes: at no time do we distinguish a "datum" or "sensum" from a thing. There is no thing or quality, then, which we can suppose ourselves to know "all about"; discrimination and association are always possible—whereas a "datum" could enter into no proposition. The same considerations are applicable to all the so-called sensa. The artist comes to discriminate and know colours better; and we can apprehend by sight many other qualities besides colour. What we see, like what we apprehend in any other way, is always complex, always a state of affairs; and the physical object is no more to be supposed to lack the "secondary qualities" than to lack the shapes which we see.

## III

The fundamental reason for rejecting the term "consciousness", or "awareness", is that, like "sensum", it involves the notion of "relative existence". This is brought out very clearly in the account given by Professor Dawes Hicks (*l.c.*, p. 319) of the theory of Meinong. "With the doubtful exception of certain feelings and desires, he lays it down as a characteristic feature of the psychical, in contradistinction to the non-psychical, that it is directed upon something...A physical event can be described in and for itself. Not so a mental event. To speak of an act of awareness simply would be to speak of that which is never met with. Awareness in and for itself has no existence, and, indeed, no meaning; a 'something' of which there is awareness is its indispensable correlative." The natural conclusion would seem to be not that a mental event cannot be described in and for itself, but that it might possibly be described as feeling or desire, and that, however described, it may have the relation "awareness" to something else. Yet we find so realistic a thinker as Professor Alexander declaring that consciousness is the sole quality of mental acts, and denying that the unconscious, i.e., any process which does not know, is ever mental.

That he is really setting up mind as "that whose nature it is to know" is made quite clear in the account which he gives of experience.⁶ He begins, realistically enough, by asserting that "any experience whatever may be analysed into two distinct elements and their relation to one another". But, he continues: "The two elements which are the terms of the relation are, on the one hand the act of mind *or the awareness*, and on the other the object *of which it is aware*; the relation between them is that they are together or compresent in the world *which is thus so far experienced*". (My italics.) Awareness, then, means both the relation itself and one of the terms.⁷ It is as if we should say that the terms of the relation, paternity, are on the one hand the father or the paternity, and on the other the child of whom he is the father. But the last phrase italicised shows the identity of Professor Alexander's argument with that of Descartes. In each case an account is to be given of knowing or experience, and in each case it is assumed that what is found, by the observer of the experience, to be involved in it is experienced by the person having the experience; e.g., all that I know about your knowing must be known by you in knowing. This is what James calls "the psychologist's fallacy". Certainly, the two terms are required for the experience, but this does not mean that both are experienced.

If they were, the distinction of *-ing* and *-ed* would disappear. Yet Professor Alexander actually uses this distinction to support the view that "the two terms are differently experienced. The one is experienced, that is, is present in the experience, as the act of experiencing, the other as that which is experienced." In other words, the one knowingly knows, or is known as knowing; the other is known as known. And to complete the parallel with Descartes, we have the statement that "my awareness and my being aware of it are identical". Now, no doubt, if an experience is experienced or known (though there is no more reason for saying that this must be so, than for saying that a marriage must be married), the knower must be known as knowing and the known as known. But this gives no ground for saying that in any experience the knower

---

⁶ *Space, Time and Deity*, vol. I, pp. 11, 12.
⁷ Professor Alexander refers in this connection to Professor Moore's "Refutation of Idealism". There Professor Moore certainly speaks of the awareness as having the relation "knowing" to its object; but in "The Status of Sense-Data" he speaks of *something* which has that relation, and by a mental act he appears to mean apprehending, i.e., the relation which the something has to the object, and not the something itself. Cf. *Philosophical Studies*, pp. 24,5 and 174,5.

knows his own knowing, or that there are two ways of knowing, enjoyment and contemplation, such that the mind "experiences itself differently from [the physical things which are objects to it]. It *is* itself and *refers to* them".[8] No such identification of the character of a thing and the relation of knowing, or experiencing, is possible. It merely makes "knowing" ambiguous, and resurrects the notion of "that which knows itself". For mind to *be* itself is not to know at all; and thus no definite meaning can be found in the terms "enjoyment" and the "quality of consciousness".

Unless, then, mind can be contemplated by mind and found to have certain qualities, we cannot know minds at all or speak of their knowing. It is precisely the Cartesian type of theory that leads James to argue, since he finds that only one term is experienced (is *-ed*) in an experience, that consciousness does not exist. But, if so, no satisfactory account of the terms "knower" and "known" can be given; James's theory of intersection would make them interchangeable. It has to be admitted, in fact, that we do observe situations of the sort "A knows B" (whenever, e.g., we take part in a discussion). And this implies that we know A, as well as B, as having a distinctive character, and not simply as knowing. Such characters of mind are found whenever we say that anyone is angry or pleased or afraid. It is, of course, argued that these characters are "attitudes" to things, i.e., involve relations; that anger, e.g., is always anger *at* something. Now anger, or any other feeling, has always an occasion, and a man, in being angry, may know what the occasion of his anger is. But he need not do so; it is admitted that a man may not know "what he is angry at". To say, in the face of this fact, that he cannot be angry without being angry at something, clearly depends on mere prejudice in favour of a theory of mind as essentially knowing. We have, then, empirical grounds for distinguishing between what a mind is and what it experiences; and we see that it is possible both that a mental process should know without being known and that it should be known without knowing (and, for that matter, that it should neither know nor be known).

This view is supported by the Freudian theory of the "unconscious". The term seems often to mean processes which are not known, instead of processes which do not know. But what is

---

[8] Vol II, p. 89. Italics in text.

really meant is that the "object" of the process in question is not known. How, then, can it be said to have an object? It has to be remembered that Freud speaks of unconscious processes as "wishes". Now a "conscious" wish is *for* a certain state of affairs or occurrence; that is its "objective". To complete the theory, then, we have to identify objects with objectives, things known with things sought. This, it seems to me, is what is done by Professor Alexander in his "Foundations and Sketch-plan of a Conational Psychology".[9] Thus he treats *judgment* as simply the theoretical form (i.e., the form in which the reaction does not directly affect the thing known) of *will*, and *will* as having as its object the state of affairs it is striving to bring about. "In all practical volition the *cognitum* is a proposition." "This proposition states the so-called end of the volition and states that end as attained.... The object in question is not necessarily conceived as future. It is the business of the act of will to secure its future existence. What is as a matter of fact future is thus made actual and present" (pp. 265,6). And Professor Alexander holds (p. 245) that "theoretical and practical conation cannot be divided sharply."

In terms of a theory of this kind, we may say that an unconscious process has a tendency to bring about some state of affairs but has not done so; and we may be able to find out what it would bring about if it were not obstructed or "repressed" (just as we can find out that a person would do something if he were not prevented), and so to describe it as an "unconscious wish" for that state of affairs. But still this is not its character, and it is important to observe that we can know ourselves or other minds as of a certain emotional constitution, whatever this brings about and knows. It is possible that all mental processes are of the nature of wishes, but in order to specify any one such wish we require to know what it is, as well as what it is *for*. We may know that a man is in a rage, while his rage has not yet found anything on which to vent itself; and a repressed wish, while it does not attain its objective, can be known to exist and to have definite effects on other processes.

The theory of the wish itself indicates that knowing is not an inseparable feature of mental processes, but at the same time it enables us to give an account of knowing which is in accordance with the plurality of these processes and supplies an answer to

---

[9] *British Journal of Psychology*, December, 1911.

certain difficulties. According to the realist theory "the known" consists of independent things in space. But, it may be asked, if what I know when I look at a chair is just something out there, which would be the same whether I looked at it or not (as I certainly take for granted in looking at it), how is it that I *know* that chair and not other things; how is it again that I know certain characters of the chair and not others; when all these things and characters are equally *out there*? Must not those objects which I "select" be attached to my mind in some special way, which does not affect those equally present things which I do not know? On this basis, Professor Alexander's description of knowledge as "compresence" might be criticised, for, though he means by "compresence" presence in the same *motion*, it is a fact that we often recognise things to have been present which we did not notice at the time. The answer to the question depends partly on what has been said regarding the "whole nature" of things, i.e., on taking things in propositions or states of affairs, there being distinguishable states of affairs in any situation whatever. In saying that specific features of our minds "select" specific features of our surroundings, we are only saying what can be said of any two things that come into relation. We can point out, for example, that the Earth and Moon move in relation to one another in terms of their *masses*, and that all other qualities of either can be neglected. If this mutual selection of masses is said to be our abstraction from the total situation, the answer is that no other type of relation could be stated or conceived; that we know things only as having specific characters and as occupying Space and Time. But the selection which we call "knowing" is made more precise if we can say that we *pursue* states of the things that surround us and they *satisfy* processes in our minds. It is still being stated in terms of the relations of two complex things, and leaves "subject" and "object" perfectly distinct and independent. And it is precisely in terms of the complexity of knower and known that an account can be given of error, which cannot be done on the "whole nature" theory. It is required that both knower and known should be changeable and should have internal distinctions.

In short, the foundation of the realist position is logical, and if this logic is not impugned, then, whatever the difficulties of any special problem, it must be capable of being worked out in accordance with that logical basis. A theory of "sensa" or of "consciousness" could not be accepted merely because it enabled us to give a simple account of some limited range of facts. It would sooner or later be found to conflict with a logic of propositions; while that logic itself assists us to give a definite theory of the nature of "subjects" and of any particular class of "objects".

# 5
# REALISM AND SOME OF ITS CRITICS (1930)[1]

"I am convinced that some of the principles on which Realism bases itself and some of the arguments by which it buttresses itself are so palpably unsound as to cause wonder why admittedly competent minds have accepted them." So says Professor A. C. Fox in leading up to his discussion and rejection of "the cardinal principle of Realism", particularly as formulated and supported in my paper, "The Knower and the Known" (*Proc. Arist. Soc.*, Vol. XXVII). Professor Fox's treatment of this "cardinal principle" is, as I shall attempt to show, far from being thorough, but it is gratifying to find an approach being made to the discussion of the central issues.

It is indeed the case that there is no mind so competent that it never falls into fallacy and inconsistency, and the realist and the idealist, humanly prone though they are to wonder how any sensible person can hold the view they oppose, can advance matters only by discussing specific issues. As I pointed out in discussing the philosophy of Alexander ("The Non-Existence of Consciousness"; *A.J.P.P.*, Vol. VII, No. 1[2]), we cannot define Realism by what any particular realist says, for it is perfectly possible for him to make some quite unrealistic errors—as Alexander, I argued, has done, although "in his doctrine of Space-Time he has laid the foundation of a thorough-going realism as a logic of events". Similarly I do not hold Idealism responsible for all that appears in the articles referred to, but shall endeavour in discussing these articles to keep the main issues clear.

Nevertheless, the fact that discussion is advanced by consideration only of *the issue itself*, and not of the minds of persons who

---
[1] The criticisms referred to are those contained in the following contributions to the *A.J.P.P.*: Vol. VII, No. 3. E. V. Miller, "The World of Truth and the World of Enjoyment". Vol. VII, No. 3. W. A. Merrylees, "Participation (II): The Logical Significance of Participation". Vol. VII, No. 4. A. C.Fox, "An Examination of Realism". Vol. VIII, No. 1. E. Morris Miller, "The Beginnings of Philosophy in Australia and the Work of Henry Laurie (II)". Vol. VIII, No. 1. T. A. Hunter, "Theory and Practice in Morals: A Rejoinder".
[2] v. i., p. 60.

hold views about it, is evidence of the truth of the realistic position. For Idealism, which makes the settling of every issue depend on the settling of every other, no issue can ever be settled—and thus Idealism itself cannot be upheld. All actual argument implies the independent issue or individually true proposition, and this is the same sort of independence as the realist finds in the terms of the relation, "knowledge". On this issue there can be no compromise; the realist and the idealist simply cannot recognise each other's competence. Speaking as a realist, I find myself bound to assert that Idealism, so far from being competent philosophy, is not philosophy at all. But this does not prevent me from recognising that an adherent of Idealism may be acquainted with many philosophical truths, while an adherent of Realism, such as myself, may fall into many philosophical errors.

## I. REALISM *VERSUS* MONISM

Realism appears first, then, as a pluralistic doctrine or theory of independence; and this brings it into conflict with the monistic doctrine properly called Idealism, which denies independence to everything but the "Absolute" or one true Being. It is this question of independence which is the "cardinal" issue, and on which, though it may be convenient to discuss it with special reference to the question of knowledge, the settling of the dispute about knowledge really turns. This is what I tried to make clear in the paper I read to the Aristotelian Society, but it does not appear at all clearly in Professor Fox's "examination" of my argument. The following summary of what I said may therefore help readers to come to a conclusion.

Logically we are bound to recognise real differences (as opposed to the idealist doctrine of the "merely relative" nature of differences), since otherwise we could not distinguish between affirmative and negative propositions, or indeed make statements at all. If "when we say that A is not B, we are somehow also saying that A is B and B is A... discourse [will] be impossible". But to recognise real differences, or, what comes to the same, different real things, is not to say that these things are unrelated. On the contrary, any relation has two terms, or holds between different things; and if these things are not "really" different, then there are not really two terms and there is really no relation. Hence there is no argument from relatedness to monism, quite the reverse.

Thus the recognition of the "subject-object" relation, or relation between knower and known, implies that each of these is an independent thing, or thing with an existence and characters of its own, and that it cannot be properly described in terms of the other thing or of the relation between them. This point I expressed (following Marvin; "The New Realism", p. 473) by saying that the thing which is known, or the "object", is not *constituted* by the knower or by being known, nor is the thing which knows, or "subject", constituted by knowing or by the known. In other words, we cannot define the nature or character or constitution or "what is it" of a thing by saying what relations it has or what it is related to. Hence I concluded that we must reject the notions of "that whose nature it is to know", or *consciousness*, and "that whose nature it is to be known", or *idea*. The rejection of the theory of constitutive relations leads therefore to a criticism of those "realists" who inconsistently permit themselves to speak about consciousness or ideas, as well as of idealists.

It is as a consequence, then, of a consideration of relations that I put forward the statement, quoted by Professor Fox, that "nothing is constituted by knowing and nothing by being known". To say that X has the relation R, or has the relation R to A (where R might, for instance, be *knowing* or *being known*), is not to say what sort of thing X is, and, if the above were all the information we had about X, we should not know X at all. The fact that we can in many cases come to a conclusion about X's character, when we are told that it has a certain relation, is due, I argued, to our having the *additional* information that only things of that character have that relation; but, as I said, we could not have this information unless we could distinguish the character from the relation. For example, we know that only men can be husbands. And it is owing to our having this additional information that we find ourselves, when we are told that X is a husband, knowing some of his own qualities. So far from attempting to meet these contentions Professor Fox does not even mention the question of relations in his criticism of my views.

On the question of being "constituted by knowing", I contended that to say that A knows or that A knows X is not to give a description of A, and that, unless such an independent description is possible, there is no relation. Professor Fox thinks this is "obviously" false. "That Einstein knows (or believes he knows) certain things is precisely what makes him Einstein; and that I do not nor ever can know these things in the same manner is what hinders me from becoming the same sort of person." It should be obvious from my exposition that I do not deny, but assert, that only beings of a certain sort have certain relations to other things, e.g., know certain mathematical theorems. But to say that they have these relations is not in the least to tell us what beings they are. We should never succeed in identifying Einstein if all that we knew of him was that he had certain beliefs; we could never find out what beings are mathematically gifted unless we could observe their qualities, as well as their relations to mathematical facts.

In fact, unless things had qualities of their own, there would be nothing to have relations to other things. What I have in effect maintained is that even those who support other views, do unwittingly concede, in the language they employ, the distinction between relations which hold between two things and qualities which belong to a thing itself. Professor Fox passes over this distinction when he says that "to possess human knowledge is (partly) identical with being a man". All that the phrase "human knowledge" conveys is that there are certain things that only men know, but it does not tell us at all what men *are*. They do not possess the things they know as *qualities*; yet if the relation were part of what a man is, the things related to him would also have to be part of what he is. This is the doctrine that Berkeley tried, and failed, to maintain. It is contradicted by the admission of the distinction in the first place, e.g., between Einstein and the "certain things" which he believes. *He* is not his relation to these things.

What the idealist has, in fact, to show is that there is no real distinction, and the answer is that in that case there is no real relation. But we may also criticise the arguments used to show that the distinction is "unreal" or "not ultimate". It is urged, as I pointed out in the paper referred to, that "there is no subject without an object, and no object without a subject. But this merely means that any 'subject-object' relation has two terms; it could not for a moment show that knower and known are not two different things, or that anything is to be regarded as *in itself* either a subject or an object." It was here that I introduced Hume's "husband and wife" analogy, the point being that, although there is no husband without a wife and no wife without a husband, husband and wife are two different persons, just as cause and effect are two different things.

This, as I stated, is the importance of the analogy for my argument. But I introduced in a subsidiary way the point that was important for Hume. Although "every effect has a cause" and though it would be agreed that effects are events, this *does not prove*, Hume says, that every *event* has a cause, any more than it follows, from the facts that every husband has a wife and that husbands are men, that every *man* has a wife. Similarly, I argued, though every subject has an object, and even if it be granted that subjects or knowers are always minds, it is not proved that all minds know or that anything that can properly be called *mental* must have an object. Professor Fox translates this argument into the form that "we may believe a being to be a man in order that he may be a husband, but may not believe him to be a husband in order to be a man", and thus loses the reference to *implication*, and makes the question only whether men (as he says, instead of minds) do in fact all know something or other. This I should not think of denying, but what I did, in accordance with the Freudian theory, deny in a later part of the paper is that every mental process knows. Professor Fox, however, does not refer at all to what I said was the important point, namely, that knower and known are different things; so that even if minds were always knowing, this constant relation would not constitute them, any more than causes are constituted by having effects or husbands by having wives.

On the question of being "constituted by being known", Professor Fox proceeds more cautiously. He does not say, "That the moon is known by certain minds is precisely what makes it the moon", though it is clear that he would desire finally to come to this conclusion. For a beginning he argues that the moon's being known by me (or my knowing the moon) *contributes* to making it the moon that it is, because, in knowing it, I affect and alter it. "I assume", says Professor Fox, "that affecting and altering are modes of constituting, and if we can establish these minor modes, the way will be opened (should we desire to pursue it) to a demonstration that the literal constituting of things by some mind is a pre-condition of their knowledge by any mind." The assumption, in fact, begs the question. Of course, there is just as strong reason for taking "altering" to be a constitutive relation as for holding that view about "knowing"; but no more. "X is altered by me" can no more be a statement of X's own qualities than "X is known by me". That things should literally *be* some mind, in order that a mind may know them, and that a thing should be me (or I should constitute it) in so far as I affect it, are alike consequences that would follow from the view that to be related to a thing is somehow to be it; but on this view, as I said, discourse would be impossible.

In fact, the treatment of relations as forms of identity was definitely exploded by Hume, whose argument on causality is applicable to any other case. If there were in A a "power to produce B", then *B* would be in A, and no production would take place. Similarly, as Berkeley saw, if there were in me a knowledge of the moon, then the moon would be in me, and, as Berkeley did not see, no relation of knowledge would hold. There is, as I argued, an identity in the case, namely, the particular state of affairs, "A causes B", or "I know the moon", or "Jack is married to Jill". But this is not the slightest ground for identifying A with B, me with the moon, or Jack with Jill; nor, again, for regarding my identity or that of the moon as in any way *inferior* to that of my knowledge of the moon, or constituted by it. And the theory of *partial* identity is only an attempt to hold to the doctrine of identification while avoiding some of its consequences.

The case of Berkeley is instructive here. He argues that it is of the *nature* of whatever I know, to be known, but he concedes that such an "object" need not be known by me but may have its constitution kept up by other minds. But if I can know that which, however it is constituted, exists independently of my knowledge of it, the basis of the contention that there must be some other mind in whose knowledge it consists is removed. Either I can know things which, in spite of this relation, I do nothing to constitute (and Berkeley is compelled to admit this in the case of other minds and laws of nature), or I can know nothing but what I am—indeed, there is no difference at all between knower and known, and so there is no knowledge. More broadly, if the knowledge, say, of the moon by various minds were precisely what made it the moon, there would be nothing for these minds to know; the position would be that the minds know that the minds know that... To stop the regress, we have to say that they know *the moon*, and that it is *not* constituted by their knowing it. If I say, "The moon is made of green cheese", that is a significant, though false, statement; but if I say, "The moon is made of someone's knowing it", the unanswerable question arises, "What is it?"

This is aside from the question whether the moon is made *by* someone, or whether I can make a bit of it. As I have already pointed out, causality is on the same footing as other relations (the cause is *not* the effect), and the fact that I can cause or affect things does not imply that I "constitute" them. In the paper referred to, I said that "what exists because of me nonetheless *exists*, apart from or independently of me. The houses which would not have existed, had not men planned and built them (i.e., but for their minds and bodies), are physical and are not private to these men; they stand for other men to see them, and may remain when no one perceives them at all."

Professor Fox's argument on alteration is therefore beside the point. If, when we know a thing, we alter it, that means that we cause it to have a character which it did not have before; i.e., its having that character now is an independent fact, and so is its not having that character before. Again, whether we say that "the moon terminates at the confines of its bodily mass" or that "the moon does not terminate at the confines of its bodily mass", the fact remains that one of these propositions is true; and the moon's so terminating or not so terminating (whichever it does) is an independent fact, in the assertion of which nothing whatever is said about us or our knowing or our altering. It may be noted in passing that if we could not know the moon if it terminated at the confines of its bodily mass, it would follow at once that we could not know that bodily mass, which certainly has these confines. Yet apparently we talk about it; just as we talk about confines and differences in general, in spite of idealists.

Idealism, then, stands or falls with the doctrine of constitutive relations, and I have tried to show that it falls because that doctrine cannot even be consistently stated, because it is contrary to the fact of independence which we have all in some measure to recognise in our discussions. And this is not, as the idealist imagines, to take our modes of recognition as the determinant of fact; on the contrary, to do so would be to recognise *them* and we can recognise them only as facts, i.e., as having that independence of which we would illogically deprive other things. The doctrine of "principles of understanding", or of "the world as intelligible", defeats itself.

If it is held, in a Kantian manner, that existence in Space and Time and subjection to categories are our ways of regarding things, the answer is that either things are *not* under these conditions and so our principles are principles of error—and in that case, moreover, we are wrong even about there being such principles, and in fact know nothing at all—or things are under those conditions, and, while we are right in thinking so, their being so is an independent fact. And this fact, which we do not constitute, we do not even cause; because that would imply that there was a time when things were not under these conditions, which, *ex hypothesi*, we cannot even imagine to have been the case. That is to say, we believe that everything that is acted upon is subject to these conditions; we recognise that that is *so*.

This is the answer to Professor Morris Miller who, in his exposition of "The Work of Henry Laurie", takes exception to those who argue that what we know exists independently. "What we know, Laurie would reply, we know in relation; and what relates and recognises relations can only be the mind." No realist will deny that what recognises relations, or anything else, can only be a recogniser, and, if it is only minds that are recognisers, that a mind must do so in the case of relations. But what is it that the mind recognises? That certain things are related in a certain way. Now, if they are not, the recogniser is simply mistaken. Otherwise, they are themselves, or independently, related in that way. And, similarly, if what we were recognising was a relation between us and things, we should recognise it, as well as the things, as having independent existence.

As I have argued, this independence would not be affected even if we ourselves had brought about all the relations we know; we should have brought about nothing, unless the relations proceeded to exist independently. But we all do distinguish between relations we cause (as when we drop a book on the floor) and relations we do not cause (such as the order of the words in the book), and, as I have shown, this distinction gives us no ground for supposing that the latter are caused by other minds. In fact, the idealist says nothing to show that the mind is responsible for the relations it knows, except that it recognises them; and thus Professor Morris Miller's "relates and recognises relations" is merely an attempt to have things both ways—to identify, while appearing to distinguish, the conditions of relation and the conditions of the recognition of relation.

The same confusion appears in Professor Fox's reference to vision. "In general, the moon would remain invisible were there no visual mechanism in the universe. But the fully constituted moon is a visible moon, so that the seeing of it does something even to constitute it." On the contrary, when we speak of the moon's being as it is, we are referring to *what is seen*, i.e., to the actual characteristics of the moon, and not at all to anyone's getting to know them or to how he does so. Similarly, when Professor Morris Miller says that we cannot "even affirm the independence of what is real apart from the mind which is called on to assert the fact of the 'independence', and which cannot do so out of nothing" (i.e., apparently must do so out of its own resources), the sufficient answer is that there is here a confusion between the conditions of *our asserting X* and the conditions of X itself.

It may be added that it is the idealist who makes the mind "nothing", by identifying it with its relations of assertion, just as he makes things nonentities by identifying them with their being asserted. That "the object for us can only exist as related to the experiencing mind" seems plausible only because "existing for us" is a common loose expression for "being known by us to exist"; and this is then translated into "being known by us to exist for us". As I pointed out in "The Knower and the Known", out of the identity, "What is known to us is known to us", idealists construct the highly disputable assertion, "What is known to us is *known as being known to us*". No evidence but the identity is ever offered for this view, but, even if it were true, *being known to us* would be different from *being known as being known to us*, and likewise from *being*. The "irrational use of abstraction", which Professor Morris Miller deprecates, is simply the attempt to get idealists to realise what they are saying, and not "overcome" distinctions by smothering them in ambiguous phrases.

Such ambiguities lie at the root of all monistic theories, i.e., all theories which deny independence, or the "ultimate reality" of differences. The realist answer (stated similarly in "The Non-Existence of Consciousness"[3]) is that, if we say that differences

---

[3] v. i., p. 61.

are comparatively unreal, then "the comparative unreality of differences" is ultimately real. Yet it is not *the* ultimately real or Absolute; it must be an aspect or expression of the Absolute. But, in taking this view, we are admitting that it is *really different* from other aspects or expressions. Again, when we say that the Absolute *is* self-subsistent and its aspects *are* relatively existent, we are recognising the independent existence of "the self-subsistence of the Absolute" and "the relative existence of the aspects"; i.e., we are recognising, in spite of ourselves, a *single way of being*. It is seen, therefore, that Monism is not only a false doctrine but an incoherent one; that it implies a division, which it cannot sustain, between "higher" and "lower" orders of being, i.e., that it is dualistic or rationalistic. The realist has to supplement his assertion of real difference or independence with a rejection of the false distinction of any other way of being from existence, since only among existents can there be real relations.

## II. REALISM *VERSUS* DUALISM

Realism thus appears in the second place as an empiricist doctrine, or theory of existence as the single way of being; and this brings it into conflict with any theory of "ultimate" or unhistorical entities—things of "higher" reality, because they are above change. As already noted, Monism is merely one particular resort of the rationalistic dualist; the unbridgeable gulf between the "higher" and the "lower" remains, whether we postulate *many* "ultimates" or only One. The *locus classicus* of the idealist-rationalist entanglement is Plato's *Parmenides*, where we are shown the illogicality of both hypotheses, "that there are many" and "that there is one"—the obvious solution being that there are *none*, i.e., no "ultimates"; which was the conclusion already reached by Gorgias.

The point is that the believer in ultimate or eternal entities is logically bound to deny historical things altogether. This was the position taken up from the beginning by the Eleatics in their criticism of the Pythagoreans. That which has not "real being", really has not being; i.e., it is nothing at all. Or again, if the "higher" is *the reality of* the "lower", then there is really only the "higher". It was easy for the Eleatics, then, to show that the

Pythagoreans could give no account of history in terms of what they regarded as the real; if the real is unhistorical, the historical is unreal. But the sole reality or Absolute of the Eleatics is in no better case; as soon as they say anything about it whatever, they represent it as having "aspects" which are only relatively to it and are nothing in themselves; so that, by the same argument as before, there are no aspects, and there is no One. The second and longer part of the *Parmenides* shows the overthrow of Eleaticism by means of the same logic as the Eleatics had used against the Pythagoreans; but this is because it is a commonsense logic, a logic of events, that logic, in fact, which is involved in all discussion and criticism. Thus, as soon as the monist says anything at all, he can be refuted; and, of course, if he says nothing, there is no Monism to refute. But he has a dialectical advantage over the ordinary rationalist, who says a great deal, and openly employs the distinction between the real real and the somewhat real.

What the *Parmenides* shows, then, is that all doctrines of "ultimates" fall together, because they all have to admit the "relative" but can give no coherent account either of its relation to, or of its distinction from, the "ultimate". If this relation or distinction is ultimate, then both its terms must be ultimate, and if it is not, then there is, "ultimately", no relation or distinction. Thus the refutation, in the first part of the dialogue, of the reconstructed Pythagoreanism of Socrates is itself sufficient to establish the doctrine of a single way of being, the being of historical things which are related and distinguished, come to be and cease to be. And if the arguments of Parmenides against Socrates can be made good, we may credit Plato with holding a realistic and empirical theory, though he may not have worked it out so consistently as did the earliest critic of Pythagoreanism, Heraclitus.

The Eleatic criticism of rationalism is equivalent to the rejection of constitutive relations. The early Pythagoreans had held that the real was certain units, and that empirical things were simply *arrangements* of these units, so that the reality of a thing was simply the units which constituted it. And the Eleatic arguments, which found their clearest form in Zeno's paradoxes, were to the effect that this derivation from the real admitted the reality of something other than the real. Later Pythagorean theory recognised as ultimate certain *forms*, or types of constitution of things, the things themselves having their reality in being (or in so far as they were) of the nature of the forms. This relation, expressed by Socrates as "participation" of things in forms, is supposed to overcome the logical objections to different ways of being, but actually the later statement of the theory is just as vulnerable, and by the same line of reasoning, as the earlier. The important feature of the theory of Socrates (as we find it expounded particularly in the *Phaedo*) is that he introduced a definite reference to the proposition, but, as this did not lead him to reject the doctrine of different orders of being, a propositional criticism of his "higher realities" was still required.

As I have argued, a relation can hold only between two things, each having characters of its own, i.e., between two independent existents, not between an "ultimate" and a "relative", or, for that matter, between two "ultimates"—and it is this which gives point to the Monism of Parmenides, as to that of Spinoza. It is here that I come into conflict with Mr W. A. Merrylees, who recognises "the teleological nature of reality", and accepts participation as "that relation between anything and its ideal (and between that and its ideal until we reach the first principle) in virtue of which it is intelligible". In other words, Mr Merrylees holds the Socratic theory that things are constituted by what they tend towards or strive after, that a thing has reality to the extent to which it approximates to its reality or perfection. Not only does he hold this, but he regards the theory as *Plato's*, and he considers that it is supported, instead of being disposed of, in the *Parmenides*. In replying previously (" 'Universals' and Occurrences"; *A.J.P.P.*, Vol. VII, No. 2[4]) to Mr Merrylees's criticisms of realism, I asked what he made of the *Parmenides*. This appeared in his article (which had, in fact, been written earlier) in the following number; he regards it as a logical failure on the part of the Eleatics to weaken Socraticism and to maintain their own position. What I require to show, then, is that the "participation" theory is really overthrown.

The discussion begins from the type of "contradiction" brought out by Zeno in his paradoxes. How can the same things be both like and unlike, as they must be if there are many of them? The importance of this question is that to answer it properly is to give an account of the distinctions and relations which hold

[4] v. i., p. 115.

among things themselves, and to show that to go *beyond* them for explanations, besides being inadequate, is unnecessary. But as Socrates tries to evade the difficulty by means of his explanatory "forms", a demonstration of the inadequacy of his theory has to be made. And this is what Parmenides undertakes.

Mr Merrylees expresses no dissatisfaction with the argument of Socrates on likeness and unlikeness, or, in general, to show that "though one idea cannot be or become its opposite, nevertheless the same subject may participate in opposite ideas"; but, indeed, to recognise its weakness is to recognise the weakness of the whole Socratic theory. To say that the form of unlikeness "is the opposite of likeness", and that, while no one "could prove the absolute like to become unlike, or the absolute unlike to become like... there is nothing extraordinary in showing that the things which only partake of likeness or unlikeness experience both", is to take all the meaning from the term "opposite". If *like* means "having qualities in common with", and unlike "not having qualities in common with", then no two things can be at the same time like and unlike. If, on the other hand, *unlike* merely means "having qualities not shared by", then any two things whatever are both like and unlike. But, in that case also, there is no point in saying that likeness and unlikeness are "opposites", and that, for that reason, they cannot participate in one another.

Thus Socrates has said nothing to show that, if there is such a thing as participation by one form in another, likeness cannot partake of unlikeness. Obviously it might be said that likeness is unlike some other relation, e.g., paternity. The real point is that to say that two "forms" are really opposites is equivalent to saying that no thing can "partake" of both at the same time. Incidentally, the example is a good one as showing the tendency of Socrates to confuse a relation, such as likeness, with a quality of a single thing; just as he confuses the quality *good* with the relation *being pursued*, and, in general, any quality a thing has with the thing's *striving after* an "ideal" of that kind.

It is this which gives point to the doubts of Socrates as to whether all things have forms, and Mr Merrylees misses the point in saying that, in the mild rebuke of Parmenides, "Plato is expressing his own view—that there is an idea of whatever can be thought". Why should Socrates, youthful as he was, have had any doubts on the subject? Entirely from the nature of the theory of forms; from the ridiculousness of saying, for example, that a particular piece of mud is striving after the ideal of perfect muddiness. As Burnet suggests, the theory of ideals appears plausible only when there does seem to be some important end to be attained. But even then the criticism still remains, and this is what the "third man" or "two world" argument enforces, that the particular and the ideal must each be regarded as having characters of its own, if the one is to be related in any way to the other.

Thus whether we take the case of mud or any other, whether or not we admit that certain things are *themselves* "just muddy", we have to admit that they are just something, or else they are just nothing. The latter is, of course, the Eleatic view which Socrates wished to avoid. And it is only natural that Parmenides should demonstrate his critic's failure. If the particulars have not their character in themselves, they cannot have it out of themselves as an end to strive for, for there is no "they" to have it. This is the objection to the contention in the *Phaedo* that any actual pair of things that we call "equal" are not *just equal*, but are only "nearly equal". If so, then they are *just* "nearly equal", and not "nearly nearly equal"; and there is no earthly reason for saying that their reality consists in an equality which they do not have, and not in an approximate equality which they do have. To quote my previous reply to Mr Merrylees: "In short, as the *Parmenides* shows, we can maintain the doctrine of ideals only by describing things in terms which do not apply to them, but all the time we are using terms which do apply to them, and so are contradicting the doctrine of ideals."

Socrates would seem to be employing the same device when he says, in the passage quoted, that things which "only partake of" likeness or unlikeness may partake of both; suggesting, i.e., that the things may be *not quite like* and *not quite unlike*. But this, besides implying that for idealists the things are "advancing in all directions", still indicates that the things are to be understood as having characters of their own, just as definite as anything they could be supposed to strive after. Thus, as Parmenides insists in his final argument, if we are to talk about the things at all, we must do so in terms of the characters they really have (in the "sensible world"), and any reference to characters they "ought to" but do not have (to "forms in the intelligible world") is quite irrelevant. So, in respect of relations, if the things have any real relation, whether we call it "participation" or anything else, it also will be in the sensible world, and so will what is thus related to the things.

Naturally, Parmenides is not satisfied with this empirical conclusion, since he does not believe in the sensible world. But this merely means that for him the conclusion would be that we are *not* to talk about the things or "many". Nothing can have (or partake of) being, since if it is being, there is no relation, and if it is not being, there is nothing to have the relation. What the later part of the dialogue shows, however, is that even Parmenides cannot help talking about things, if he talks at all. And the upshot is that the Eleatic and the Pythagorean-Socratic theories of ideal being are shown to be alike untenable. This proof can only be of an empirical character, but that does not hinder it from being historically true to Eleaticism. It has not been observed that the paradoxes of Zeno, for example, bring out not the "self-contradiction" of Pythagorean theories but a contradiction between their rationalist assumptions and their empirical assumptions; and that this contradiction is demonstrated empirically, however little this may accord with the conclusions Zeno wished to establish. As already noted, the use of the Eleatic method to destroy Eleatic philosophy is credited to Gorgias, and even Parmenides may quite well have been acquainted with his work.

The correct conclusion, then, is the empirical one, that there are no "higher" entities, but everything that concerns particulars is on their own level of existence. Mr Merrylees considers that the plausibility of Parmenides's criticism of the Socratic attempt to bridge the gulf between "higher" and "lower" depends on the choice of a metaphor. The real point is that, no matter how we describe the relation, the description must be such that we can recognise as a single situation "a thing partaking of a form", and this situation can only have a neutral sort of being (neither "higher" nor "lower") which must likewise be that of its constituents. And all the proposed relations are intelligible only as perceptible relations between perceptible things, i.e., historical relations between historical things. We all know what is meant by "having a share of", as when the owl and the panther were sharing a pie; we can see the partakers and the partaken of, and we can see the partaking going on. Similarly, when one thing "comes under" another, or "is copied from" another; we have often come across such complex, existing states of affairs. But none of these experiences helps us to understand the *real* "participation"; it is something unspeakable—and so is not even something, and not even unspeakable.

Socrates himself puts forms and particulars on the same level, when he admits that they may both "come under" forms, and even under the same forms. We get such examples of this, in the *Phaedo*, as "Fire is hot" and "This body is hot" (as I pointed out in " 'Universals' and Occurrences"). And we get the answer to it, in the *Parmenides*, in the infinite regress of forms. Mr Merrylees meets this argument, according to which, he says, "the idea is (1) a character common to many things which we discover by comparing these things, (2) a character which, when found, can in the same way itself be compared with these things, thereby revealing a further character common to itself and these", by saying that "Plato's real point" is, that while (l) may be true in a sense, (2) is not. "The idea is of a different order to the things compared, and cannot in any sense be regarded as another thing alongside these with which they can be compared."

This can only mean that, in spite of Socrates, things and a form cannot both come under the same form, and, as already suggested in the statement that participation is "that relation between anything and its ideal (and between that and its ideal until we come to the first principle) in virtue of which it is intelligible", that a thing cannot come under more than one form. So that, if this body is fiery, then, even if fire is hot, this body is not hot; and, if we go on to the "first principle", this body is not *real*—a conclusion which would have pleased Parmenides. Again, for one thing to be different from another, it must have a different character; so that every thing has its peculiar "ideal", and every ideal has *its* ideal—and when do we ever come to the "first principle"? On the other hand, granting that a thing's ideal *is the* explanation of that thing, we have to go, in explaining anything, right to the "first principle", the "self-explanatory", and we can recognise no distinction between anything and anything else; there is only the self-subsistent One—another conclusion which would have pleased Parmenides.

Thus the refutation of Eleaticism, in the second part of the dialogue, is more than sufficient for the refutation of Socraticism, which appears separately in the first part. It has therefore to be recognised that "This body is fiery", "This body is hot" and "Fire is hot" are propositions all of the same order, and their terms are all of the same order. So far from the recognition of "forms" settling problems such as that of the like and the unlike, it renders them insoluble; they can be solved only by sticking to things, and recognising that they are *sorts of things*, i.e., historical situations or occurrences. We have to reject the distinction between being and becoming, and recognise, with Heraclitus, that whatever is, is in process and whatever is in process, is. Thus the realistic rejection of "constitutive relations" develops into the empirical recognition of a singe way of being, that, namely, of observable things—*existence*; and the position finally appears as that of a positive and pluralistic logic of events. It was fitting that, in the development of such a logic as far as Plato was able to carry it, honourable mention should be made of the names of Parmenides, Zeno and Socrates, since they had all contributed to the working out of the propositional method, though none of them had seen its incompatibility with "ultimates" and all of them had opposed the Heraclitean theory of a single historical order.

## III. REALISM *VERSUS* RELATIVISM

Realism appears finally as a positivist doctrine, a logic of propositions or events; and this brings it into conflict with every theory of degrees of truth and reality. It will have been seen that there are natural affinities between the different rationalistic theories; indeed, as Burnet has shown, the Eleatic was simply a heretical Pythagorean. It is characteristic of the instability of the whole position that the extremes between which rationalism fluctuates are the Eleatic doctrine of the One as the sole reality and the doctrine of the super-Eleatic, Gorgias, who held that "there is nothing" (absolute) but all is "relative". The inconsistency of this Sophistic position, involving, as it does, a hidden Absolute which appears obscurely as Opinion, does not prevent Relativism from being the most prevalent of "philosophic" views.

The realist answer is that there is something absolute, namely, *facts*; that even the relativist doctrine itself implies that "the relativity of all" is an absolute fact—not absolute in the sense of being above history, but absolutely historical; so that the doctrine cannot be maintained. Socrates understood that the task of philosophy is to save science from degenerating into scepticism, but he was unable to carry out this task because he was not a realist. The scientist, in so far as he recognises facts and a pluralistic order of events, is in a stronger position than the teleologist. But when he falls short in his logic, divides matters of certainty from matters of uncertainty and makes "probability" the guide of life, when, in fact, in the Pythagorean manner, he separates the rational from the irrational and appears as an unconscious teleologist, his errors are far more difficult to root out. In our own day scientific agnosticism has achieved apotheosis in the doctrine of Relativity.

Rationalist fluctuations are due simply to this, that the rationalist cannot state his doctrine at all without introducing a certain amount of empirical fact, "irrational" as he may call it, and steps have to be taken to conceal the conflict of this fact with the "ultimates", whatever they may be. And until the recognition of a logic of events has prompted us entirely to "remove hypotheses" of degrees of reality and treat things on a common level, we are prone to fall into dualistic errors and, while imagining that we are conducting a straightforward inquiry, to *remove appearances*, i.e., deny facts, instead of "saving" them. It is only from the division of the rational from the irrational that "theories of knowledge" have grown up, and that illogical considerations of "certainty" and "probability" have replaced the sole basis of scientific progress, the formulation of propositions which we believe to be true.

The position of Mr E. V. Miller is not that of extreme relativism; like most modern scientific theories, it comes fairly close to the doctrines of the semi-Pythagorean Atomists. In particular, it adopts the notion of "data" or of "that whose nature it is to be *given* to some mind"—a notion which can no more be supported than that of any other constitutive relation. But, as we have seen in connection with Socrates, there is no limit to the multiplication of "ultimates" and "relatives", once we have made the fatal division, and Mr Miller's "ultimates", which he calls "enjoyments", are quite unable to make contact with "the world of truth".

Mr Miller develops his views from a criticism of Realism, as I expounded it in "The Non-Existence of Consciousness". Pure realism, he considers, suffers shipwreck "on the rock of the distinction of truth from error". As a mere theory of propositions, it provides no criterion of truth. Thus, in any dispute, "the contestants can never get away from propositions, and as there is nothing in the system [i.e., the system of propositions] to cause us to regard one proposition as better than another—no ultimates, as Professor Anderson says—they can never get away from doubt, or even mitigate it in the slightest degree". It may be said, however, that this is not true of actual discussion. Though there may be cases in which B goes on denying every premise that A brings forward, it does happen occasionally that A gets back to a proposition which B admits, and which settles the dispute in favour of A.

But, supposing that this does not happen, does this mean that "they can never get away from doubt"? Not at all. As Mr Miller has put it, "A makes a statement which he believes to be true, but B doubts it; what can A do to show that he is right?" A began, it appears, not by doubting but by believing; and, though he has failed to make B believe, this does not give A any reason for ceasing to believe. And, of course, if he *had* convinced B, that would not be an additional reason for believing. "A supported proposition", I agree, "is not less doubtful than any other", since it is supported only by other propositions. But this is merely to say that inference is not the only way of getting to know, that, in fact, it is impossible except on a basis of observation or belief. But what we believe, as Mr Miller has said, we believe to be true—without asking for any "criterion". And when we doubt, we doubt whether a proposition is true; we do not believe that the proposition is "doubtful".

The realist position is, then, that there is no criterion of truth, nothing *by believing which* we believe something else. If the criterion is a proposition, we have not "got away from propositions", and we still require a criterion to apply to *it*. If it is not, it cannot settle any dispute. Mr Miller's solution is that certain propositions have "original truth". They are those "thought-objects" which are the "original counterparts" of an "enjoyment". Whenever an enjoyment occurs, there is given, in the world of contemplation, a thought-object which, as corresponding to the enjoyment, is true. But these counterparts, which as original are sensed, may later be recollected and manipulated so as to give any number of propositions, which not being original cannot be true, though they may have true consequences, and thus be more or less "probable" or "reliable". The enjoyments, on the other hand, cannot be contemplated at all; they cannot appear in propositions, since they are not thought-objects, and, as relations are thought-objects, enjoyments cannot even be related to thought-objects.

The main realistic objections to this theory may be briefly stated. If enjoyments cannot be related to thought-objects, they cannot have them as "counterparts". If, as Mr Miller says, he believes in the existence of enjoyments, he is formulating the proposition, "Enjoyments are existing things". But, more important still, "original truths" cannot settle disputes in the way required, because people disagree just as vehemently about what is immediately in front of them (what they "sense") as about anything else. If, in the Sophistic manner, each man's "data" are held to be "true for him", still that will not give a point of agreement for the settlement of a difference; and it will be impossible to show how such a datum could ever be a verification of a speculative proposition, because the verifying and verified propositions require to have some terms *the same*. And finally, unless we could find implication as a relation among propositions, i.e., unless implication were a sensible fact, we should never know how to infer.

It appears, then, that we are entitled to recognise neither degrees of truth nor anything outside "the world of truth", and, if we did, it would bring us no nearer "certainty". The theory of "enjoyment" falls with the monistic theory of "consciousness". Realists will not deny that there is a relation between what a person believes and the state of his mind; but they maintain (*a*) that this implies that "states of mind" can themselves be discussed and contemplated; (*b*) that "the fact that I believe X" is not a criterion of the truth of X, nor is "what caused me to believe it", unless this happened to be inference, at all relevant to the proof of it; (*c*) that the only propositions that anyone will accept as deciding an issue are such as he himself believes, or regards as facts. If science advances it is because one or more persons believe truths, and not because any authoritative criterion, any "ultimate", is discovered. The absence of agreement about facts would in no way suggest a possibility of agreement about "ultimates". And, indeed, the existence of science implies nothing as to general agreement, but only that somebody *knows*; and what he knows consists of true propositions.

It is most of all in ethics that these scientific requirements are repudiated, and that disagreement and the absence of a "criterion" are taken to imply that there are no independent facts, or that the facts cannot be discovered. But this is a quite incoherent view, as has been shown most particularly by Socrates, in his criticism of Sophistic theories, and by G. E. Moore. Disagreement implies no "doubtfulness", but is possible only if each disputant believes something to be definitely the case. If subsequent consideration leads him to believe that it is *not* the case, he is still in the position of asserting something to be an independent fact. And if he is doubtful about the matter, this does not affect any other person who has a definite belief about it. Only if believing X implied (as it does not) believing that everybody believes X, would disagreement have the required effect. Thus if anyone passes a "moral judgment", he is asserting the occurrence of a certain moral situation. Yet (as I pointed out in "Determinism and Ethics"; *A.J.P.P.*, Vol. VI, No. 4[5]) there are theorists who find it possible to say that the moral judgments which we pass are the "data of ethics"; that is to say, that ethics has to begin by studying our judging, our acts of "approval" and "disapproval", instead of with what we judge to be facts. It is further supposed that we promote, or advocate the promotion of, what we approve. And thus the field of ethics is defined by our attitudes of approving, promoting, advocating, etc., and what we take up these attitudes to comes in only relatively.

Having thus, as strongly as I could, repudiated ethical (or any other) relativism, I am surprised to find Professor T. A. Hunter regarding my more recent criticism of it as an "inconsistency" on my part. I have certainly at the same time attacked any theory of an absolute or ultimate, since "ultimates" and "relatives" hang together; but I have always maintained that true, ethical or other, propositions are absolute, or independent, facts—in other words, that they are actual occurrences. Professor Hunter does not escape Absolutism by saying that "all goods are relative"; he merely omits to state what his absolute is, i.e., to what they are relative, while his language implies that the things he is speaking of are *actually* or *absolutely* both good and relative. In fact, his ethical absolute turns out to be no other than the old Sophistic "convention" (νόμος) or, as he puts it, "a code to act upon". It is the more surprising that he praises Socrates (who developed his ethical views in criticism of the Sophists) for bringing morality to earth, and neglects the real exponents of a "practical morality".

The fact that Socrates upheld the relativity of goods to "The Good", did not prevent him from presenting some very forcible

[5] v. i., p. 216.

criticism of "codes", and this realistic work was his real contribution to ethics. It appears notably, as I pointed out in my comments (*A.J.P.P.*, Vol. VII, No. 4) on Professor Hunter's original article ("Theory and Practice in Morals"; *A.J.P.P.*, Vol. VII, No. 1), in the *Euthyphro* and in Book I of the *Republic*. The argument is that, even if we could divide good acts into religious and social, we cannot say that good religious acts are those which please the gods, because that does not tell us *which* those are, and because "pleasing" is only a confused way of saying "being regarded as *good* by"; and similarly we cannot say that good social acts are those which benefit people, because this also does not tell us which those are, and because "benefiting" means "doing good to". In each case a qualitative distinction is required, and in each case there is a covert reference to the quality *good*. These, as I indicated, are the fundamental objections to the popular notion of "rendering services".

These considerations also apply to Professor Hunter's theory of the "divergence" between theory and practice in morals. There are, it appears, codes and codes; codes to act on and codes only to advocate. A person's moral practice is the code he acts on, while his moral theory is the code he advocates; and there is divergence if he does not act on what he advocates. Now we should all doubtless agree that people have habits or ways of behaving, and the realist is at liberty to say that some of these ways of behaving are good and others are bad. Not so the relativist; for him they can only be recognised or not recognised, i.e., supported or opposed. Where, then, does morality come in? On this view, it would seem that the activities of molecules are as moral as those of men; they interact, they aid or hinder one another. What is the difference?

The difference, it appears, is that people do not merely do or refrain from doing certain things, but certain things are "done" and others are "not done". Or, as Professor Hunter, in his absolutist way, puts it, men act on "principles". This is nothing but a dualistic attempt to introduce a peculiar kind of causality, the *teleological*, into human affairs. But, even so, it fails to account for the "divergence". If the code a man formulates is a statement of the principles he acts on, and if his actual principles of action are different, he is simply mistaken, or else he is lying—in any case, the *code* is merely false. But Professor Hunter will not accept this interpretation. For him, therefore, the code is not a statement of the principles on which its formulator acts, but is a declaration of what is *the thing to do* or what are the principles *to* act on. We see, then, that there is no divergence whatever, if the man does not "act up to" his code, because his actions are not a code; but secondly, and more important, that the supposed relation "to" conceals a qualitative distinction between "the thing to do" and "the thing not to do". And this confusedly apprehended quality is *goodness*; the thing to do is the thing which it is good to do, i.e., that the doing of which is good, i.e., a good activity. This, then, is a moral fact, which the relativist only obscures and distorts with his "codes" and his "principles".

Now, granted that activities may be good or bad, they still have the ordinary causal relations; they support and oppose one another. In "Determinism and Ethics" I adopted the Socratic view that goods always support one another and oppose bads, while bads may support or oppose other bads. But, as I said, all this cannot be found out merely by observing relations of support and opposition between human activities. On the contrary, unless we take *qualities* into account, we cannot distinguish an ethical struggle from a merely physical one. The failure to recognise qualities is incidentally the main defect of the utilitarian doctrine of "the greatest good of the greatest number", or the greatest possible mutual support But even when we do recognise qualities and can thus appreciate the ethical struggle, the carrying on of that struggle is not, I stated, the same as our investigating it. "People in general do not think very much about the goodness of their activities. They are simply to be found trying to make discoveries or to produce works of art, exhibiting love or courage, or, on the other hand, imposing obligations on themselves or others, because they are made that way, i.e., because their character, in relation to their history, has so developed. And these are the conditions, and not any metaphysical 'freedom' "—and equally, I should add, not any metaphysical "utility"—"on which, if at all, further development is possible."

That is my answer to Professor Hunter's queries, "how we are to decide whether an activity is good, bad or indifferent, and why we take the trouble to study the moral facts", and again to the question, "if, as Professor Anderson admits, we must study moral facts, must we not come to some conclusions, and, if we do, may not these conclusions influence or direct conduct?" I have never admitted that "we" must study moral facts; if anyone is of an inquiring turn of mind and is specially interested in ethics, he *will* do so; and, of course, his interest in the subject may be stimulated by other people's. Regarding the investigatory activity as good, whether it is directed to ethics or any other subject, I conclude that it will assist other goods; but I could not conclude, without circularity, that that is its "purpose". We learn about goods, as about other things, by observing them; and we can be assisted by what other people tell us about them and their distinctions from and relations to other things. For example, I recognise a qualitative distinction between investigation and obscurantism, and I say that the former is good, and the latter is bad. And by this I do not mean either that I am an investigator or that I think that other people, who are not that way inclined, "ought to" investigate. But I certainly do not cease to recognise the distinction because someone else does not recognise it. I could do so only if I became acquainted with other facts which implied that there was no distinction of the sort I had attempted to draw.

\*

For Realism, then, as against all the "ultimates", facts are good enough. It does away with the philosophy of good intentions, of "service" to the idol of social utility or any other, and establishes philosophy as logic, the logic of events. It rejects as unphilosophic the "saving of hypotheses" of discontinuity, whether the hypothesis is only a little one or is the great One. And, rid of "meanings" and "purposes" and other products of "vicious intellectualism", it proposes as the formal solution of any problem *the interaction of complex things.*

# 6
# THE NON-EXISTENCE OF CONSCIOUSNESS
(1929)

In spite of the important advances towards realism which have been made in recent philosophical work, there has not yet been established anything which could be described as a realist school. This is due to the fact that the realist position has been insufficiently worked out, so that we have many competing mixtures of realism and idealism with, as is natural, no clear criterion for deciding among them. Such difficulties invariably arise when any important innovation in theory is made; it is impossible to recognise immediately all that it implies, and many views, which harmonise only with the position that has been abandoned, are still taken as a matter of course. Hence, it happens that the real value of the discovery is often lost, and that backslidings are almost as common as conversions. A particularly sustained effort is required to remove all the germs of idealism, so deeply has it penetrated into the systems and traditions which make up "modern philosophy".

These statements can best be supported by reference to the work of Professor Alexander, who has given the fullest and most logical statement of realism yet presented,[1] but with such concessions to idealism as have rendered it practically ineffective, greatest interest, as was only to be expected, having been taken in the idealistic elements in his theory, and particularly in the notion of "emergence" which he did not even initiate. It is singularly unfortunate that he should have preferred an attitude of conciliation to the denunciation of false doctrine. The result has not been to make his general position any more attractive or even intelligible to his opponents, while those who might support it must very often fail in the task of disentangling his genuine contribution to philosophy from the forced interpretations and special pleas by which his

---

[1] *Space, Time and Deity*. By S. Alexander. London: Macmillan and Co., Ltd. First Edition, 1920. Reprinted, with new preface, 1927.

statements on consciousness and perspectives, on truth and goodness, are supported and reconciled with it. When the separation is made, it will appear that in his doctrine of Space-Time he has laid the foundation of a thoroughgoing realism as a logic of events. But the greatest obstacle to this consummation is to be found in his theory of consciousness.

This theory is anti-realist and is, in fact, Cartesian; and history has shown how Cartesianism leads on to absolute idealism. To get rid of idealism we have to go back upon all sophisticated "modern" views and recapture the Greek directness. We have to banish mind from philosophy, and in so doing make incidentally possible a positive account of mind itself. The position from which realism in these days has taken its departure, and with which the name is most closely associated, is that we are able to know what *exists independently*. It follows that the study of anything is not, on account of its being a study, at the same time a study of mind, and that the study of mind must be a definite, particular undertaking; or, as Alexander himself puts it (Introduction, Vol. I, p. 7), "that minds are existences in a world of existences and alongside of them". Yet he contends that this statement would be accepted by absolute idealism (though "with qualifications"), and he adopts the very view of the study of mind which realism would lead us to reject. This indecision is due to insufficiently close analysis of the nature of idealism.

The essence of absolute idealism, he says, "consists not so much in its idealism as in its faith that the truth is the whole, in comparison with which all finites are incomplete and therefore false. With the omission of the concluding phrase, 'and therefore false', the proposition might be accepted by other doctrines than idealism." But the faith that the truth is the whole, or that there is such a thing as *the* truth or *the* whole, is precisely idealism. The denial of independent existence to things which are related to mind is only an example, though historically an important one, of the denial of independent existence to things in general in relation to the Absolute or the ideal. Certainly, if we call this ideal "mind", it is not what we ordinarily mean by mind, in speaking of our relations with things of that character; but so much the worse, idealists will say, for what we ordinarily mean by mind. When any search is made for an ultimate, a standard, an unconditioned or rather self-conditioned condition of things (and the search for the ultimate is idealism or metaphysics), then, in place of the independently existing, we have, on the one hand, the self-subsistent as the basis of things, and, on the other hand, the relative existence of things to that basis. So that, consistently with its initial assertion in regard to knowledge, realism must deny any sort of ultimate. In particular, it must deny "universals", which is one of the points on which realism has hitherto failed. It (i.e., as misrepresented by its sponsors) has been rationalistic instead of empirical, and Alexander, though he sets out to be empirical, is very often rationalistic.

The history of Greek philosophy shows with the greatest clearness the inevitable passage from rationalism to idealism, the coalescence of the many ultimates into the One. It shows with equal clearness the untenability of the latter view, its fatal admissions even in *denying* the many. In brief, the notions of "relative existence" and "self-subsistence" are both confused; if "all finites are incomplete", then the incompleteness of any one is a complete or absolute fact, and yet it is not "the whole"; and there must be a distinction between the Absolute's sustaining itself and the self which is thus sustained.[2] If theory is to be possible, then, we must be realists; and that involves us in a denial of monism, or of a Being which is the whole, a "universe", and in the assertion of a single way of being (as contrasted with "being ultimately" and "being relatively") which the many things which we thus recognise have. This is just that independent existence of which realism speaks; more particularly, it is occurring or happening or being in Space and Time. That is the real fruit of Alexander's teaching, divested of his concessions to monism and to its offspring, "consciousness".

It would be unnecessary, then, for Alexander even to propose to treat the independent existence of things, as contrasted with their existence "in experience", as a hypothesis, if he began by demonstrating that otherwise we could not have theory at all. But his statement (p. 8) that "all philosophies are concerned with experience as a whole" is not even consistent with his hypothesis, and the finding of minds *alongside of* other existing things is, if "it is experienced differently from them", a sheer impossibility. The analysis of experience which he proceeds to give (pp. 11,12)

---

[2] v. s., pp. 47,8.

exhibits all the confusions from which idealist arguments have ever suffered, and for that reason is worth quoting in full.

"Any experience whatever may be analysed into two distinct elements and their relation to one another. The two elements which are the terms of the relation are, on the one hand, the act of mind or the awareness, and, on the other, the object of which it is aware; the relation between them is that they are together or compresent in the world which is thus so far experienced. As an example which presents the least difficulty take the perception of a tree or a table. This situation consists of the act of mind which is the perceiving; the object which is so much of the thing called tree as is perceived, the aspect of it which is peculiar to that perception, let us say the appearance of the tree under these circumstances of the perception; and the togetherness or compresence which connects these two distinct existences (the act of mind and the object) into the total situation called the experience. But the two terms are differently experienced. The one is experienced, that is, is present in the experience, as the act of experiencing, the other as that which is experienced. To use Mr Lloyd Morgan's happy notation, the one is an *-ing*, the other an *-ed*. The act of mind is the experiencing, the appearance, tree, is that upon which it is directed, that of which it is aware. The word 'of' indicates the relation between these two relatively distinct existences. The difference between the two ways in which the terms are experienced is expressed in language by the difference between the cognate and the objective accusative. I am aware of my awareness as I strike a stroke or wave a farewell. My awareness and my being aware of it are identical. I experience the tree as I strike a man or wave a flag. I am my mind and am conscious *of* the object. Consciousness is another general name for acts of mind, which, in their relation to other existences, are said to be conscious of them as objects of consciousness."

In this passage Alexander begins by confusing one of the terms of the relation with the relation itself. When we speak of "the object of which an act of mind is aware", then clearly the relation between the act of mind and the object is expressed by the words "aware of" and not by "of" alone. Instead of "the act of mind which is the perceiving", we should read "which *does* the perceiving" or "which has the relation 'perceiving'" to whatever is perceived. We might just as well identify the tree, as Berkeley does, with its being perceived, as identify the act of mind with its perceiving. As it is, we have said nothing about the act of mind except that it has a certain relation; we are not entitled to say that all acts of mind have this relation and so to repudiate, as Alexander later does on no other basis than this, the Freudian "unconscious"; we have found no general name for acts of mind (and no relational term, awareness, consciousness or other, could be such a general name) except acts of mind. It should be noted, moreover, that when the relation, reduced to "of", is expressed as togetherness in some situation, it is symmetrical; that is, either term may be called the knower and the other the known, as in James's theory of "intersection"—which is certainly not what either James or Alexander intends or adheres to. The unfortunate feature of this contention of Alexander's is that, when he comes to deal with the actual spatio-temporal relation of togetherness, he imports into it certain of the peculiar characteristics of knowledge, and so is developed the theory of perspectives, which opens the way to relativity; just as the idealists begin by treating mind as an absolute, and end by treating the Absolute as having some of the real characters of mind, and so make "the universe" progress, and logic along with it.

Alexander goes on to make the perfectly gratuitous assumption that both terms in "the total situation called the experience" are experienced (the question of the way in which the relation between them is experienced is dealt with later and raises fresh difficulties), that whatever is "present in an experience" must somehow be experienced. The *-ing*, it appears, is *-ed*, but, of course, it is *-ed* in a different way from that in which the *-ed* is *-ed*! It ought to be clear, without any argument, that what is experienced or known in any experience is the object; that is what we mean by the object. It is, indeed, possible that that which knows that object, or again the relation between the two, may *also* be known, i.e., may also be an object, but there is nothing in the first thing's being known to show that this must be so; and where it is so, the second thing's being known will be a *different* experience. To assert that mind can be experienced only by and in its experiencing something else at least wants proof. But no proof can be given without making the surrender to idealism completely apparent, if it is not already apparent in the phrase "My awareness and my being aware of it are identical." When mind is treated as essentially "subject", things

THE NON-EXISTENCE OF CONSCIOUSNESS (1929)    79

must be treated as essentially objects, i.e., as having their existence in their relation to mind. It is necessary, therefore, to deny that the two terms are differently experienced, when it happens, as it need not, that that which knows is known or experienced at all; and so to deny that "I am aware of my awareness" is analogous to "I strike a stroke", which is merely an extended way of saying "I strike". The difference is that if I am to talk of my awareness, then I must be aware of it, must have it as an object to which terms can be applied. If Alexander were correct in supposing that only my awareness of X can be aware of my awareness of X (and why should anyone suppose this?), the term awareness would never have been employed. But if what we experienced were always a situation in which knower and known were together, if that were what every bit of the world that we came across was like, then the idealist conclusion that the world is a system of knowings would be irresistible.

The names which Alexander proceeds to give to the different ways of experiencing (which naturally follow from the different ways of being experienced, "that is", as Alexander falsely puts it, of being present in an experience) are enjoyment and contemplation. "The mind enjoys itself and contemplates its objects." The realist position is, then, that there is no such thing as enjoyment or self-sustaining knowledge ("consciousness"), but that if minds are known, as they are, they are contemplated, and if relations of contemplation are known, as they are, they are contemplated. Curiously enough (or naturally enough, if we think of his realism as striving to break down the barriers which his unrealistic adherence to Descartes and Spinoza has erected), Alexander admits that these things *can* be contemplated, but only by beings at a higher level than ourselves, "angels". Psychology is then possible by anticipation of the angel's view. But how can we anticipate or know anything about the angel's view, since all that we know is at a lower level than ourselves? And how can the angel help being *wrong*? "What the angel sees as the compresence of two objects I experience as the compresence of an enjoyed mind and a contemplated non-mental object" (p. 20). The angel sees a thing of a peculiar quality, a mind, but he cannot see its self-relation, its experiencing itself by being itself. The realistic angel would, in fact, repudiate knowing by being; he would maintain that if we could only *be* ourselves, then we could not know ourselves at all.

Alexander, indeed, appears to think that in introducing this idealist conception of enjoyment or knowing by being, he is preserving realism. Certainly, in relation to the position that knowledge is a relation between two different things, my knowing myself presents a difficulty; but not my knowing other persons, and therefore the contemplation of mind in general. But to one who treats of *acts* of mind, who regards things as events, there should be no difficulty. Whereas every argument against the self-contemplation of a mind is an argument against the self-enjoyment of an act of mind, the fact that there are many acts of mind shows how it is possible for a man to know his own mind; one act can know another, or any group of others, or the general system of events which is the mind within which it falls, without being required to know itself. For in knowing that mind which it calls "I", it does not know all about it; it knows it only as certain particular events or acts. The same applies to our knowledge in general; we do not deem it impossible to learn more about a thing or event than we observed at first. The knowing event, then, might quite easily be one of the unknown characters of the known event.

There is thus no ground for Alexander's statement (p. 17) that only on his view "can we realise that experience declares mind and things to be fellow-members of one world though of unequal rank". It is true that "to be an experiencer of the experienced is the very fact of co-membership in the same world," in other words, that we are related to the things we know, but being related is quite different from knowing or "realising" that we are related. To be able to say "I know a tree", we must be able to have this before our minds as a single fact, not as broken up into an enjoyed and a contemplated element, which could neither be enjoyed as united nor contemplated as united. If we can contemplate minds and things together, then we are in a position to find, and have found, their "co-membership". Yet Alexander argues that "we miss this truth only because we regard the mind as contemplating itself. If we do so, the acts of mind are placed on the level of external things, become ideas of reflection in the phrase of Locke; and thus we think of mind as something over and above the continuum of enjoyments, and invent an entity superior both to things and to passing mental states." If we did, we should certainly be quite unrealistic. But the argument has cogency only on the assumption that thinking of mind is equivalent to thinking of mind's thinking of mind—which is precisely what those who adhered to contemplation and rejected enjoyment would deny.

The question now arises, What of introspection, if it is the case that I cannot contemplate my own mind since I am it? "Introspection is in fact merely experiencing our mental state, just as in observation of external things the object is contemplated. The accompanying expression in words is extorted from us, in the one case by the object, in the other case by our mental condition. Now, except in refinement and purpose, there is no difference in kind between the feeling expressed in the ejaculation of disgust and the reflective psychological analysis of that emotion. Replace the interjection Ugh! by a whole apparatus of elaborated speech; instead of the vague experience of disgust, let us have the elements of the emotion standing out distinct in enjoyment, and we have the full-blown introspection of disgust" (p. 18). Now enjoyment, we may remember, is simply the mental act being itself. Thus at any time disgust is itself, and its elements are themselves, so that at any time we have "the full-blown introspection of disgust". The fact cannot be concealed that "standing out" means being contemplated or observed. But if we adhered to Alexander's expressed theory, we could not possibly determine when an expression was extorted from us by the object and when by our own mental condition. "The contemplation of a contemplated object is, of course, the enjoyment which is together with that object or is aware of it" (p. 12). Thus if we applied *any* of our expressions to the object, we should apply all. But the fact is that we sometimes speak about our own minds and sometimes about other things; that is, our own minds are sometimes objects to us. Alexander has failed to establish that "my own mind is never an object to myself in the sense in which the tree or table is. Only an *-ing* or an enjoyment may exist in my mind either in a blurred or subtly dissected form." Once more the *-ing* is an *-ed*; but to say blurring and dissecting would be to admit that the introspection is extrospection or contemplation, not identity. The argument reaches its climax in the statement (p. 19) that "if I could make my mind an object as well as the tree, I could not regard my mind, which thus takes in its own acts and things in one view, as something which subsists somehow beside the tree". That is, because my mind is doing something, therefore I can't do it! No, these are not arguments which establish the existence of a mind whose character is consciousness and whose consciousness is self-consciousness; they are the consequences of that *assumption*, they are its *reductio ad absurdum*.

There remains to be considered the question of the experiencing of the relation between the two terms in an experience. It also is experienced; in short, the whole experience, just because it is an experience, must be experienced.[3] The togetherness of the *-ing* and the *-ed* is "the fact of their belonging together in their respective characters in the situation. But since the one term is an enjoyment and the other a contemplation, and the relation relates the terms, how, it may be asked, is the togetherness experienced? Is it an *-ing* or an *-ed*? Now from the angel's point of view I am together with the horse I see and the horse together with me, we are together both. But when we ask how, in the knowing relation, the togetherness is *experienced*, we ask the question from the point of view of the being which has the experience, that is, the mind. Thus the mind in enjoying itself enjoys its togetherness with the horse. It does not contemplate the horse's togetherness with itself, the mind." We are not permitted, then, before asking how the togetherness is experienced, to ask *whether* it is or not. To know a horse is somehow to know that I know it. But in knowing this, I know the "I know" (i.e., the *-ing* and the relation) by enjoyment and the "it" by contemplation, but neither by enjoyment nor by contemplation can I know that "I know it". This simply will not serve; we should have to enjoy the horse as well, in order to have before our minds "I know the horse" as a single proposition—as we do have it. Or else, we should have to contemplate our minds and their relations of knowing; thus alone could we avoid subsisting for ever on our own enjoyments. Here, again, the distinction breaks down, as Berkeley's theory of notions and ideas breaks down, when he is called on to explain how it is possible to know that "I produced this image". The facts are too much for enjoyments and notions alike.

It is not surprising, in view of the interweaving of opposite strains in his thinking, that Alexander found it impossible to make alterations in his work on the occasion of this new impression. Any serious alteration would have led on to many others. The excision, of which I have tried to show the necessity, of the notion of

---

[3] As I have argued in another place, we might with equal reason say that a marriage must be married (v. s., p. 38).

THE NON-EXISTENCE OF CONSCIOUSNESS (1929)   83

"enjoyment" would leave few parts of the argument unaffected. It would certainly leave little of the Introduction beyond the contention that mind can be contemplated; and the admission that there are not different ways of knowing would render nugatory a large part of the discussion of knowing in Book III. But the fundamental theory of mind would be substantially the same, since Alexander has for the most part accommodatingly taken the angel's view; parallelism would be as decisively rejected, and the view, again emphasised in the new Preface, that mental processes are those brain-processes which have the quality, consciousness, would, with the recognition that there is no such quality and that the quality of mind is still to seek, give the clue, as before, to the understanding of the spatio-temporal theory, viz., that all things belong to the single order of *events or propositions*. In such a reconstruction Space-Time would be shorn of the monistic features attached to it, and taken consistently, not as the stuff of which things are made, but, in its other formulation, as the medium in which things are. And with a positive theory of events and of mind would go a positive theory of truth and goodness. The relative theories with which Alexander presents us are imbued with that spirit of conciliation which was the stock-in-trade of his idealist teachers, and which makes this work only a mighty fragment to those who are not prepared to carry out its reconstruction in a different spirit.

# 7
# MIND AS FEELING (1934)[1]

Traditionally mind is regarded as having characteristics of three fundamental kinds—cognitive, conative and affective—knowing, striving and feeling. This division is understood in two main ways. According to modern idealistic theory, cognition, conation and feeling are complementary *aspects* of all mental process, each implying the others and the three together constituting what we mean by mentality; and this is perhaps the most widespread view of the matter. At the same time we find in contemporary thought as well as in earlier theories the conception of the cognitive, the conative and the affective as different *sets* of mental processes. This is the view implied by Hume, for example, when he says that reason is no motive to action; reason is regarded as purely cognitive and passive, as having no conative or active character, and similarly as having no affective character.

It may be said, in fact, that all English thinkers of the eighteenth century were in difficulties as to the distinction and relation between reason and the passions—with the possible exception of Shaftesbury, who, recognising affections towards affections as well as affections towards outside things, made possible an account of mind as a system of affections. To Butler, on the other hand (and here his views are similar to those of Socrates and Aristotle), there could not be system unless there was a specially systematising affection, one which informed man as to his nature or showed him how he could live up to it. Now Butler, like his Greek predecessors, is unable to maintain a distinction between reflective principles and passions or to show what these principles are; this comes out in the ambiguous position of benevolence in his theory, and in his difficulty in distinguishing the operations of conscience and of self-love. He fails, in fact, to show that any of our motives (tendencies to action) are anything but passionate or how the object of a reflective principle could have any relation to the object of a passion—such a relation, in particular, that the two

[1] A paper read to the Sydney branch of the A.A.P.P. in April, 1931.

tendencies could conflict. Similarly, Hume cannot consistently uphold the existence of a reason which is not operative (i.e., which is not already among our actions and capable of affecting others), and which has not particular objects that it pursues in preference to other things and therefore passionately.

Berkeley, again, leaves the passions of the mind in a somewhat ambiguous position in his theory. They are, according to his first division, one main class of "ideas"; but he immediately goes on to argue that the mind is something over and above ideas (which it may "have"), that it is something of which we cannot have an idea but can only have a "notion", since it is essentially active and ideas are passive. But this means that the "ideas" he calls *passions* are no more intimately related to the mind (no more "its") than any other ideas; or, if he is going to adhere to the view that passions are in some special way mental, he must abandon the doctrine of the mental as an agent, but not an object, of ordinary cognition. The fact that he goes no further into the question of the passions, is a sign of the weakness of his position.

## COGNITION

The above preliminary survey indicates that the upholders of the "aspect" theory have a certain advantage over those who believe in separate processes of cognition, processes of conation and processes of feeling. But in the end, in consideration of criticisms of a realistic character, we find that both these theories have to be rejected.

Modern realism is founded on the contention that knowledge is a relation, i.e., that it holds between two things and so cannot be a part of the "nature" of either. The main realist attack has been directed against the conception of what is *characterised by being known*, or the "idea". Realism has denied that what we know need be in any way mental or in any way dependent on the mind which knows it (though realists have not perhaps seen clearly enough that the very term "idea" requires to be dispensed with). And it has thus also attacked the doctrine of the absolute idealists that *we are what we know*, that the whole field of which we are aware ("our world") is equivalent to our consciousness and to our very selves. It has maintained, on the contrary, that what we know is part of an independently existing order of things, that the existence of a mind is one thing, and the existence of a field of things known by that mind quite another.

But the further implications of realism have not been so clearly grasped by realists in general, viz., that it has equally to reject what is *characterised by knowing*, or "consciousness"; that it has to say that what knows, as well as what is known, must have a character of its own and cannot be defined by its relation to something else. It has also to reject the whole "self-consciousness" theory of the idealists, who, in upholding the rationalist conception of the knowledge relation as belonging to the "nature" of the things related, brought the whole relation (and both terms of it) within the mind and tried to make a special character out of this internal distinction and relation—tried to make it *generate* the system which it characterised. This self-sustaining mind must be denied if we take relations seriously, and the rejection of the view that we are what we know must be accompanied by the rejection of the view that *we know what we are*.

This does not mean that we cannot have knowledge of our minds (apart from the knowledge we can have of other minds); it means that we are not bound to know all that goes on in our minds. This side of the realist position has been most developed by psycho-analysts and has been neglected by the leading realists themselves. It clearly opens up the field of psychological inquiry, which is narrowed down by the assumption that we always know what we are doing. Unfortunately much of the old cognitionalist psychology still appears in the work of the psycho-analysts, and this is exemplified in the treatment of the *unconscious* (which we should naturally take as the unknowing) as consisting of processes of which we are not aware (the unknown)—the confusion being concealed in the expression "unbewusst". When the necessary distinction is kept clear, we can see that it is possible for a mental process (having a character of its own; having, at least, "mentality", whatever that may turn out to be) *not* to have the relation of knowing or not to have that of being known or not to have either relation. It is evidently the other view that wants proof. And if we reject the notion of "self-consciousness" (as an attempt to turn a relation into a quality), we clearly cannot argue that a mental process, by somehow "knowing itself", is bound to be at once conscious (knowing) and known.

MIND AS FEELING (1934) 87

Rejection of cognitionalism, then, i.e., of the definition of a process by its relation of knowing, carries with it rejection of the theory of the three *types* of psychic process. There can be no merely cognitive process, no "reason" such as Hume assumes, no "intellect", etc.—just as there can be no sensations, percepts, concepts, or other entities defined by the fact that, or the manner in which, they are known. But it also involves rejection of the three *aspect* theory, because we cannot call a relation an "aspect" in the same sense as a quality, and we are also entitled now to give credence to the evidence which would indicate that some mental processes *do not* know.

## CONATION

So much for cognitionalism. What of conation or striving? Is it more fitted than cognition to be an actual description of mental processes? It seems clear that, on the contrary, striving is also a relation, implying a striver and a striven for. Of course, if we regard conation as simply meaning *activity*, then it is just another word for process, and is not a means of distinguishing minds from any other existing things. Taking conation as striving, however, we find in the first instance that the conational theory of mind—exemplified in Alexander's "Foundations and Sketch-Plan of a Conational Psychology"[2] and again in Freud's recognition of the characteristic mental process as a *wish*; suggested, also, in the general position of the pragmatists—certainly marks an advance on the cognitional theory. This is particularly so in respect of the theory of knowledge itself (including the theory of error).

Cognitionalism upholds the doctrine of "ideas", i.e., things characterised by being known, and thus involves us either in the coherence theory of truth or (when certain realist assumptions are implicitly made; when it is assumed that we *somehow* know, beyond "ideas", what they represent) in the correspondence theory. The former theory fails because it, like any other, cannot be consistently unrealistic. If we rightly or wrongly regard a certain idea as cohering with other ideas, we are recognising the existence of actual relations among ideas and are therefore treating them

[2] *British Journal of Psychology*, Dec. 1911.

as independently existing things. On the other hand, if to *have* an idea is to know all about it, if there is nothing more in it than we know, since, as Berkeley and Hume make out, "our idea" is just what we know, then we cannot be wrong about it; and the supposed relations, of coherence and incoherence, are either just ideas among others, or else are outside the region of ideas altogether, and in neither case do we have the adjustment or maladjustment which the theory requires.

The main error of this view—an error which appears also in the correspondence theory and in many other philosophical doctrines—lies in the assumption that there is a kind of knowledge which cannot be mistaken as contrasted with that which can; that, e.g., minds can receive "data" about which there is no dubiety, and can then "interpret" them in various ways which may possibly be mistaken. A sufficient objection to such theories is that they imply a kind of knowledge which both can and cannot be mistaken. Thus the recognition of the fact that "A is an interpretation of the datum B" must be at once the work of the fallible and of the infallible faculty. To avoid this difficulty we have to say that the fallible faculty can also be acquainted with "data", which must therefore be matters of as much dubiety as "interpretations". In short, the indubitable cannot be brought into relation with the "doubtful", i.e., with any real issue, and the solution is that there is *no* infallible kind of knowledge.

This appears again in connection with the correspondence theory. Merely to have an idea which is *like* an outside thing is not on the face of it any better than having an idea which is *unlike* an outside thing; and the latter is not on the face of it *error*. Error arises only if we think the unlike is like, i.e., if we make a direct comparison between "ideas" and outside things; and this comparison is on exactly the same footing as a comparison between one outside thing and another. Thus the question of "ideas" does not arise at all in the general treatment of error, and it can arise in particular cases only if an "idea" is a certain sort of thing, existing perhaps in a special location (e.g., in a mind), but having the same type of independent existence, being on the same logical footing, as a thing existing in some other location (e.g., in a tree). The correspondence and coherence theories alike fail, then, because they cannot avoid admitting, at some point, the realist contention that we are dealing all the time with independent things—with what exists, whatever its location and character may be.

The doctrine of striving, on the other hand, permits us to distinguish cases where we are mistaken from cases where we are not. We are right, it may be said, when we get what we strive for and wrong when we do not. Error, at least, is comparable to missing one's mark (mis-taking); and here the Freudian theory of errors as satisfactions of (unacknowledged) wishes is important. We are in error when we treat A, which is not B, as if it were B; when we mistakenly *use* it as a B—e.g., when we treat a red danger signal as if it were a green safety signal, or treat as a friend a man who will actually deceive us. This clearly implies a certain knowledge of both A and B, i.e., error is impossible without knowledge; knowledge is primary, error secondary—but, of course, that is actually the case. It is to be noted that we are sometimes undeceived and sometimes not. The fact that we do not always find out afterwards what mistakes we have made, and the fact that we do not always know what we are doing or what our actions will lead to, are among the obstacles to a thorough discussion of error.

Error, then, is exemplified in misuse of things (using a pruning-knife to cut down a gum-tree or a sledge-hammer to crush a wasp), and arises in our striving, with the means at our disposal, to satisfy our wishes; or, as I should put it, in our motives themselves, our tendencies or mental tensions, striving to find an object, to find outlet or release. *We believe what eases our minds,*[3] whether it is true or false. Freud's theory of the wish and Alexander's identification of the theoretical and the practical (treating judging, e.g., as Descartes also does, as a form of willing) have prepared the way for this development of psychological theory, in spite of incidental cognitionalist confusions. The theory of the mental tension appears also in James's account of the "active gap" in our "consciousness" when we are striving to recall a forgotten name. And if we take all knowledge as discovery,[4] then we have a general

---
[3] See Addendum.
[4] This is the important point about knowledge, even in cases where it is also *recovery*, i.e., where we have already had that knowledge and are now "recalling" it. The doctrine of reminiscence, in implying that *all* knowledge is recovery, involves an infinite regress. But the value of Socrates's doctrine lies just in his pointing out, as against the Sophistic "instructors", that knowledge is not a passive *taking in*. This recognition of

recognition of tension; and that is known or found, we may say, which releases the tension and sets our minds at rest—or, at least, a part of our minds; we have, of course, many quests, not only successively but at any given time.

This conational view is also in accordance with the whole modern doctrine of *interests*, as guiding our lives and constituting our mental character (though acceptance of that doctrine has to be distinguished from the adoption of any special theory of "instinct"). Even those who speak of "intellect" have still to recognise "intellectual interests", a "passion for truth" and the like. But when all has been said that can be said on the conational side, we find that we have still not learned what are the qualities of mental processes themselves, what it is that may be in tension or relaxed. Striving, like knowing, is a relation, and the mental quality (mentality) is still to seek.


FEELING


This brings us to the third element in the original classification—feeling (affect, emotion). And this, I think, enables us to solve our difficulties; it gives us a basis for a general descriptive account of mind, i.e., we can recognise "affects" as real *qualities* of mental processes (or, what comes to the same thing, as real mental processes), whatever relations, knowing, striving or other, they may have to other things.

McDougall (in *Social Psychology*) does something to suggest this view, but he makes a very unsound division of mental process into a cognitive (leading up, afferent) part, an emotional (central) part, and a conative (efferent) part—as if the process as a whole could have the relations of knowing and striving only by having a knowing part, etc., and as if the central part were not as definitely related to outside things as afferent and efferent nervous processes are. In this division, in fact, we find traces of cognitionalism and

activity in knowing involves the rejection of the "storehouse" theory of knowledge (the conception of the mind as a receptacle into which so much knowledge can be packed), which, along with the correspondence theory, is thoroughly disposed of in the *Theaetetus*. The doctrine of reminiscence is a curious mixture of the two opposing views—*discovery* of the characters of particulars, and a *storing* of the knowledge of forms.

also of physiologism, i.e., of the kind of view which expresses mental facts in terms of the physiological processes to which they are related (as knowledge is called "sensory" because it is related to sense-organs)—though the rejection of physiologism does not imply that mental processes are not themselves physiological. Nevertheless, for McDougall, the central and most distinctively mental part of the process is emotional; and so, if it is mind that we regard as having the relations of knowing and striving, we may go on to express the position by saying that emotions (or feelings) know, emotions strive and, in general, interact with other things.

Interacting is, of course, something that all things can do; and it may be that the relations which we can in the end recognise as knowing and striving are not peculiar to mind at all (cf. Alexander's account of knowing as "compresence"), and that we have thought otherwise solely because we have thought *into* the mind's relations something of its own emotional quality. It is enough, however, for our present purpose that an emotional thing can have these relations; and from this point of view we should reject the cognitionalist formula of Freud about "an idea becoming charged with affect" and speak instead of *a feeling finding an object.*

Such expressions sound harsh, but only to ears attuned to cognitionalism. The real confusion comes from the opposite quarter, in the recognition of "reason", "intellect", "sensation" and so forth—as when McDougall, after making the instincts the native mental forces, introduces a complicating factor of reason,[5] instead of recognising that what reasons is simply a complex of the emotional activities he has already dealt with, and not a new faculty springing from nowhere. Once we have rejected "constitutive relations", once we have seen that what knows and reasons *must* have qualities of its own, we can say that emotion is as likely to know as anything else; we cannot reject it as a possible knower merely because it is a quality, since we should be thrust back on the supposition of something which *consists* in its relations.

The objection that feeling also is a relation comes from the same cognitionalist source. On the theory of mind as feeling it is not denied but asserted that feelings *have* relations and hence that we can be angry at, afraid of, pleased with, something or other

[5] See *Social Psychology*, Supplementary Chapter I (in fifth and subsequent editions).

(this being to say that we are angry, knowing something, or that our anger has an object, i.e., knows something, etc.). But to have a relation is not to *be* a relation. The term "feeling" has certainly been employed to signify some sort of "immediate experience" (*erlebnis*) in which knower and known are one. This appears in Alexander's use of the term "enjoyment", and also in the use of the term "feeling" ("sensation" being sometimes substituted) by such thinkers as Bradley, but especially by James, who, in his *Principles of Psychology*, speaks of feelings of red, of green, etc., and again of feelings of and, but, etc. Such views fall with the rejection of relativism (the belief in constitutive relations), whilst at the same time they testify to a certain recognition of the "inwardness" of feeling. What should be admitted is that feelings (e.g., anger and fear) are qualitatively different from one another, though they still have the general feeling-quality in common. It will not surprise us then to find that, besides having similar relations to outside things, they also have different relations to these things, e.g., that they have different objects, that one seeks what another avoids, etc.

The thorough-going rejection of cognitionalist doctrine involves the recognition of the following facts: (*a*) that a mental process may exist in us without our knowing it (as when we find out afterwards that we were angry or afraid); (*b*) that a mental process may exist without knowing (as in what are called "nameless fears"); (*c*) that nothing mental is simple or passive, but that we have a vast complication of tendencies (tensions) which pass through one another, and become variously organised, in pursuits and aversions, strivings and capitulations, sentiments and interests of all descriptions; that "intellectual pursuits" are thus operations of the *love of truth* (the inquiring spirit), developing from original scattered curiosities—for we have no reason to suppose that all curiosities are parts of *one* curiosity, all angers the work of a single faculty of Anger, etc. We thus have a conception of mind as a society or economy of impulses or activities of an emotional character. This conception of our "motives", conscious or unconscious, as emotions will, I am convinced, give coherence to psycho-analytic doctrine, and, though this is a point of less immediate importance, will be found to work in with the physiological examination of those brain processes (in their relation to bodily processes in general) which are "the seat of" the emotions, i.e., which are the mind.

MIND AS FEELING (1934) 93

We may here refer to the James-Lange theory (which is, of course, of a cognitionalist character) of emotions as "sensations of certain bodily processes". In the first place, "organic sensations", regarded as objects, are *the organic processes themselves* and thus are distinct from the special class of emotional or mental activities, even though the latter are also organic; e.g., if we mean by hunger what is going on in the stomach, it is not mental. On the other hand, if by "organic sensation" we mean *what knows* the organic process in question, then we have still to be informed where and what that knower is—what *qualities* it has. It is not, of course, the case that we are sorry because we weep, etc., but it may quite well be the case that, on a given occasion, we *find out* that we are sorry by noticing that we are weeping, find out that we are afraid by noting the condition of our breathing, and so on. We are not, as has been seen, bound to know directly what is going on in our mind, and in such cases we may discover it inferentially. But this inference depends on the previous observation of a connection between the two, between the (central) emotional process of sorrow and the (peripheral) process of weeping; which implies that we have a direct acquaintance with both terms of this relation.

The same circumstance, that we are not bound to know what is in our mind, accounts for the fact that many emotions have no names or are named only from their objects (e.g., as "love of" something), these objects, which the emotions themselves are interested in, being naturally what is known when they are operating, and attention, by other emotions, being directed to the former emotions only rarely—e.g., when they are obstructed. Progress in psychology may therefore be made by the actual *discovery* of the emotional character of sentiments or motives, i.e., of what is in our minds, as contrasted with what is *before* our minds, when we engage in certain pursuits.

These, however, are matters of detail. The main points are: (1) that knowing and striving, as relations, cannot be the *character* ("mentality") of the mental; (2) that feelings, as qualitative (a point which is illustrated by the qualitative distinctions among feelings), are capable of characterising the mental—as well as of having relations to other things; (3) that we must assume that they do, that feeling is mentality, unless we are going to suppose that some entirely unsuspected character of mind has yet to come to light; but (*a*) as we have seen, there are multifarious suggestions that feeling is already, if only confusedly, recognised as the mental quality;[6] and (*b*) we do recognise and speak of *minds* and therefore we must already have recognised some mental quality. To say that we know mind only as "that whereby" certain effects are produced or arrangements made is to say that we do not know mind at all—for how, except by observation, do we know *what* sort of thing would have these effects or that there *is* a thing, of some peculiar kind, to have them? In fact the rejection of the belief in constitutive relations implies that to know a thing is to know some of its qualities. We are thus in a position to say that mind is feeling, and that it is such feelings that *have* objects.

Having this basis, we can go on to discuss how feelings develop and interact, how they are affected by the bodily organisation in general, and how by things outside the body, including feelings in other minds—in which connection McDougall's theory of "sympathetic induction" is of interest—and for this discussion we shall also have to take into account how they affect these other things. This discussion (including, of course, an account of what various feelings there are) will be psychology.

## ADDENDUM

Some further remarks on the connection between belief and behaviour may help to remove difficulties in regard to what has been said about conation. It was contended that on the view that it is certain interests that know, certain feelings operating so as to secure "outlet" or relaxation of tension, an account can be given of error and other difficulties which the ordinary theories of knowledge cannot meet. In terms of the formula that we believe what eases our minds, it appears that we shall refuse to accept situations which we find intolerable. Now this attitude of opposition to situations which occasion us uneasiness or distress can operate in various ways according to personal as well as external factors (the breadth of our interests, the difficulty of the situation, etc.). The simplest case is that in which our uneasiness

---

[6] Cf. also Stekel's view that nothing in the dream is true except the emotion. Dreams are one important ground of opposition to the behaviourist view that the difference, say, between anger and fear is just the difference between facing up and cowering or running away, i.e., that there is no difference of emotional quality.

expresses itself simply by removing the obstacle, so that uneasiness ceases, i.e., we are satisfied with what is the case, and there is no question of error. But, since error does occur, we require a more general formulation of the position, covering all cases.

It may be said, then, that there is in general a *tendency* to remove obstacles; or it may be enough to say that there is striving. Now, in terms of the conational theory outlined, what is striven for will be identical with what is believed. As Alexander points out, if we will that a certain person should leave the room, then the situation we have before our minds as occurring is just *that person being out of the room*; the object of our judgment is identical with the objective of our willing. The success of the judging, the "click" of conviction, the "satisfaction that" the event is so, is identical with the success of the willing and the relaxation of tension.

Obviously there may be complications in the case; while having as our object the person's absence, we may recognise that he is not yet gone. But, in the first place, we can have opposing interests and thus opposing judgments. And, secondly, we can recognise phases in a situation; we can find the person's presence temporarily tolerable (and therefore admissible as a fact) because it is a stage in the process leading up to his absence, when we shall be quite satisfied. In other words, we can distinguish a main objective from subordinate objectives which are means to it or preliminary conditions of it, and on the theoretical side this is expressed by saying that we recognise not merely single situations but implications (or, more generally, the passage of one situation into another), this being the state of affairs to which the term *thinking* is ordinarily attached, just as *conduct* is commonly taken as the carrying of a line of action through a series of stages.

The general position is, then, that we regard what we want as brought about, and if our action (or simply our situation) is such as to bring it about—if we get what we want—then we have a true belief. In certain cases, however, our action is unsuccessful; and then, though there are various possibilities according to the variety and development of our interests or demands, our primary tendency, Alexander contends (in line with the views of the Freudian school, particularly as expressed by Freud himself and by Ferenczi), is to regard the wished-for result as brought about. That is to say, we obtain a certain satisfaction or release of tension under a condition of hallucination or illusion. Such a condition, it is to be observed, is not logically different from error in general. To suppose that it is is to suppose some objective situation of a simpler type than the proposition (hallucination being conceived, e.g., as a "datum" which does not "correspond to" reality).

One possible way of obtaining ease of mind or release of tension, then, is the false belief that the object has been achieved; but the fact that it has not may result in a continuance or re-establishment of tension. We know that this is not bound to be the case; there are people who retain false beliefs throughout their lives or at least are never disabused of certain errors—indeed, this could be said of any of us. But still there are cases where our satisfaction proves evanescent, where we are undeceived, and the demand for the thing itself, for "real" as opposed to "hallucinatory" satisfaction, is reinstated. In such cases the object may eventually be obtained or we may secure some substitute for it—in any case, the tension has to be diminished in some fashion, or the position really would be intolerable.

This process of finding substitutive satisfaction has been dealt with in detail by Freud and his followers. The point to be emphasised here is that it is just the process of developing a theory of things, so far as we do develop a theory; and it may be incidentally observed that the distinction of "illusion" from "reality", i.e., the recognition that we are capable of falling into error, is a considerable theoretical step. But, as Freud has also shown, unsatisfied tendencies may remain in a state of subdued tension, of repression, in which they do not secure outlet but, on the one hand, draw away energy from the operation of the interests in general, leaving the person comparatively inactive, and, on the other hand, interfere with the other interests, altering the direction of their activity, and thus precipitating (a) those confusions and mistakes which Freud deals with under the heading "Psycho-Pathology of Everyday Life", and (b) the *dream* form of hallucination. We can distinguish, then, a number of different types of reaction to a unsatisfactory situation—there is simple hallucination; there are various forms of self-deception and confusion, whereby we contrive to hold contradictory beliefs at the same time; there are various methods of substituting one object for another; and finally there is the possibility of such a rearrangement of tensions (i.e., such a development of the mind) that repression and dissatisfaction are overcome—though we may admit that this development will never go so far as to enable *all* our tendencies to find outlet.

In line with these distinctions, we may distinguish from simple error various forms of "interpretation" of the things we deal with—as when it is said that we interpret the unfamiliar in terms of the familiar. Here, on the one hand, we can have that dictation to Nature, or looking for simple solutions, of which Heraclitus accused the Pythagoreans, and which is bound to land us in error; but we can also have simple insistence on special uses of certain things, emphasis on some aspects of them at the expense of others—a preference which need not in itself amount to misuse or confusion. Granted that we have interests and that it is these interests that operate on things and give us our knowledge, then it is naturally the case that we select certain characters of things for special attention and neglect others, and thus that we select those most familiar or easy to deal with or most satisfactory to us. This selectiveness is in fact the condition alike of error and of discovery.

Now in this connection Heraclitus upholds the replacing of desire by understanding, and similarly Freud speaks of passing from the pleasure-principle to the reality-principle, getting an interest in things as they are as contrasted with what we should want them to be. Clearly we must be wary of over-stressing such a transition, since understanding, or adherence to the reality-principle, is still the operation of an interest, and desire (or what follows the pleasure-principle) even in the first instance finds things to be the case, whether correctly or incorrectly. It is not a question, then, of a theoretical interest coming out of a non-theoretical interest. We may admit that peculiarly scientific interests can be developed, but we shall still have to say that, as interests, they have special objects, and that there are special conditions of their finding outlet. It is therefore not surprising that we find throughout the history of scientific inquiry a recurrence of that dictation to Nature (as contrasted with "expecting the unexpected") which Heraclitus condemned in the Pythagoreans.

Of course, inquiry, confused or otherwise, expresses itself in saying that something is the case, and such an assertion must be met in the first instance by showing that it is not the case; only after that has been done can we go on to the question of how the particular inquirer came to prefer his erroneous view. But, while that is the *form* of argument, of refutation or proof, the carrying out of arguments or inquiries is still the work of our wants or interests, and the notion of a "dispassionate reason" rests on a confusion between the *objectivity* of the issue (i.e., the simple contrast between truth and falsity, occurrence and non-occurrence) and the activity of the inquirer into that issue. And along with the notion of dispassionate reason we must reject the notion of "reasonable conduct", or conduct enjoined by reason. The most that can be meant by reasonable conduct is *the thing that is to be done*, i.e., what is demanded by certain interests; and, since this will obviously differ from what is demanded by other interests, we see that "what is to be done" is a relative expression and that there can be no absolute "duty". It appears, then, that the clearing away of cognitionalist confusions is also of advantage to the ethical inquirer—as it must be to any inquirer whose field includes any part of human behaviour.

# 8
# THE PLACE OF HEGEL IN THE HISTORY OF PHILOSOPHY (1932)[1]

Hegel, one might say ironically, died a hundred years ago and yet the world still goes on—or, more pointedly, philosophy still goes on, though it was to have culminated in the Hegelian system. Nevertheless, there is some ground for raising the question whether it does go on. No such philosophical *system* as Hegel's has appeared since his time. On any important philosophical or scientific question there is what may be recognised as a Hegelian view, and as much cannot be said of the position of any subsequent philosopher—or, for that matter, of any earlier one.

The position of Plato is peculiar. It has been maintained that Plato had no philosophical system and would not have recognised the necessity of system. But we have to remember the historical interest of Plato's works, his desire, in particular, to expound in detail the position of Socrates, as well as his view that philosophical publications should consist not in the presentation of results but in the raising of problems, in such a way as to stimulate the reader's own thinking. These facts being understood, we cannot suppose that the pupil of Socrates did not recognise the value of coherence, the need for a philosophy, and we can gather much from the later dialogues as to what that philosophy was.

Plato's objection to the publication of a finished philosophy would apply to Hegel. Many of the latter's extant works were not, of course, published by himself. But he did aim at completeness, at a comprehensive treatment of the totality of things, and the defects of this outlook appear notably in his work. It has the particular effect of fostering pretended solutions of problems—solutions which are mere re-statements of the problem or of the fact that there is a problem, as in the well-known formula of "identity in difference". The development of a "metaphysical" terminology

[1] An address delivered to the Sydney branch of the A.A.P.P. on the occasion of the centenary of the death of Hegel. (G. W. F. Hegel, 27th August, 1770, to 14th November, 1831.)

in which we appear to be saying something when we are not, is clearly a hindrance to philosophical discovery. And the fact that philosophy is made to cover all questions leads not merely to such "vague generalities" but to forced and absurd interpretations of things, such as are seen at their worst in the work of some of Hegel's disciples[2] but are present also in his own work. Every historical thing has to have logical necessity, just as every earlier theory has to contribute something to the Hegelian summing up of reality.

Nevertheless, the appearance of a distinctively Hegelian solution of any problem is in accordance with the need for finding a philosophical solution of any philosophical problem; and it cannot be said that any subsequent philosopher (granted that Alexander approaches this requirement, and that a working out of his position would provide a more coherent philosophy than the Hegelian) comes up to Hegel in this respect. The most comprehensive philosophical theories that have been presented in the last century are those of the Hegelians, particularly of the English Hegelians or semi-Hegelians, like Green, Bradley and Bosanquet; in spite of their fine phrases and their mystification, the "literary" philosophers of the idealist school have shown a philosophical tenacity much greater than anything exhibited by theorists professing a "scientific" exactitude.

To get a philosophy comparable in range to Hegel's and capable of disposing of it, we have to take account of *many* recent developments—of the work of William James, of English Realism and especially of Alexander, of the Freudian psycho-analysis, and of Burnet's work on Greek philosophy. And even here a certain Hegelian influence has to be recognised. In spite of his forcing the Greek philosophers to fit into his scheme of logically successive outlooks, Hegel has done much to stimulate interest in

[2] Cf. Croce: *What is Living and What is Dead of the Philosophy of Hegel?*, p. 208. "Who will narrate in all their wealth of amusing details the lamentable fortunes of the dialectic method at the hands of Hegel's disciples? One of them dialecticised spirit as the masculine principle, nature as the feminine, and history as the matrimonial union. Another found in the Oriental world the category of being; in the classical world the category of essence; and in the modern world the category of the concept. For yet another, antiquity was the kingdom of art; the modern world that of philosophy; the future was to be the kingdom of morality. And in the ancient world Athens was made to correspond with dynamic electricity, Sparta with static electricity, Macedonia with electro-magnetism, Persia with light, Rome with expansive and absorbent heat."

Greek philosophy; and this, along with his attention to logic, has helped to discredit the pragmatic or utilitarian attitude which had largely dominated modern philosophy till his time, and which is as evident in Kant's "regulative principles" as in the various attempts to determine the limits of possible knowledge. Moreover, his insistence on a single logic had some influence on the development of that positivism (or naturalism) which has affected the work of James and Alexander and, one might add, Freud. Apart, however, from the adumbrations of a realist philosophy in the above-mentioned movements, Hegelianism has been opposed mainly by the resurrection of old views—Cartesian rationalism or English "empiricism", as in Mill's rehash of Berkeley and Hume. Hegel had sufficiently demonstrated the "inadequacy" (the illogical or incoherent character) of these positions, and much subsequent work, so far from exhibiting any advance on his views, has depended on a mere ignoring of the points he made.

Hegel is right, then, in maintaining, in opposition to eclecticism or pragmatism, that philosophy should be systematic. But its systematic character should appear in the form of a single logic, not in the form of "totality", of a pretended *solution of all problems*. He is right, also, in maintaining that this logic should be historical, if we take this to mean that it is the theory of things as historical; but it should not itself be considered as advancing, however the study of it may do so. It is the theory of what things are at any time; and, granted that philosophical progress may be made, the nature of philosophical problems remains the same now as it was in 500 B.C. It is only if modern philosophers have discovered truths which ancient philosophers failed to discover, that modern philosophy can be said to have made any advance on ancient philosophy. To substitute for a logic of things as developing a developing logic is to do away with the object of philosophical study and fall into scepticism; for logic can only develop illogically. The *pretended* object of philosophical study which remains for the devotees of a progressive logic—the totality, the "Absolute", the historical-unhistorical—merely exemplifies this scepticism, for its "phases" have to be taken at random; there is nothing to show that any phase is a phase of *its*, that any history is *its* history.[3]

---

[3] This point has practical demonstration in the case of those "historical materialists" who, while on the one hand they are quite empirically concerned with a historical

To overcome scepticism, then, to have philosophy, we must recognise that there is no universal history, no one-track development. Our attention being drawn to history, the weaknesses of Hegel's position enable us to see that it is *not* a single process, not the progressive unfolding of the Absolute. We find likewise that the history of philosophical theory is not a progress from lower to higher outlooks. There is retrogression (i.e., the recrudescence of errors) just as much as progress, and we cannot say that there will be a time when we do not require to go back to earlier problems, that earlier views can be "taken up" into a higher system as Hegel thought preceding philosophies could be into his, that philosophy can culminate. Truths, we say, can be discovered but they can also be forgotten. Indeed the doctrine of "outlooks" (of a general point of view which can cover or embody each particular view we have) rests on inability to grasp the independence of truths and is part of the illogicality of the Hegelian totalism.

Any period in the history of philosophy will afford illustrations of these points. In Greek philosophy there is the notable case of Heraclitus, who, in spite of his exposure of Pythagorean rationalism, exercised a very slight influence on later thought in comparison with the Pythagoreans. Again, Aristotle's "advance" on Plato consisted largely in a vulgarisation of his doctrines. So in modern philosophy (the passage to which raises the further question of periods which were philosophically null) there is no steady advance, but commonly a man's successors, even when they arrive at a better position on one point, get into a worse position on others. Berkeley successfully exposed Locke's representationism (though this did not prevent either Berkeley himself or his successors from falling into representationist errors), but wrongly

treatment of a definite thing, *society*, are idealistic enough to make social history a part of the history of a postulated Absolute. Naturally they are unable to show what part it is or to supply the cosmic background. But, like the more orthodox Hegelians, they derive from the doctrine of the Absolute support for treating everything else as relative, and thus from the supposition of a developing logic, an ascending series of categories, they import into social theory the conception of special categories, a special logic, for each social phase and social class. This results in a particular form of *ignoratio elenchi*, viz., the acceptance or rejection of arguments according to the "ideology" on which they are based. In practice it induces *faith* or concentration on "the one thing needful"; but the force thus gained is counteracted by the weakness of sectarianism, and this has to be overcome (as far as it can be) by various alliances, on a basis of "immediate demands", with people who accept a commonsense logic.

opposed Locke's recognition of the existence of things independently of their being known. Hume refuted Berkeley's theory of spirit, but went back to an acceptance of "rational science" in his doctrine of relations of ideas. Kant corrected Hume's theory of spatial and temporal discontinuity and strikingly developed his theory of causality, but at the same time deviated into a confused doctrine of moral causation. Hegel, in turn, while rightly attacking the Kantian dualism, was equally if less obviously dualistic in his conception of a reconciliation or transcendence of differences in Spirit, and lost, in a flood of categories and teleological bathos, what was positive even in Kant's phenomenalist conception of science.

To say that all these were necessary errors is to say that Kant, e.g., can be criticised only from the Hegelian point of view (or if we select someone else, say Fichte, as exemplifying the next "moment" in thought, only from the Fichtean point of view), which is simply not the case. We can understand Kant's position, and, for that matter, Hegel's criticism of Kant's position, only by considering what are the questions at issue, i.e., only by investigating certain logical problems and seeing whether Kant was right or wrong about them. In considering these questions we are not concerned with whether Hegel ever lived or not; and even if it was he who had shown us how to criticise Kant, he could have done so only by showing where Kant was wrong, i.e., by leading us not to the adoption of an "outlook" but to the recognition of certain truths—not *Hegelian* truths but objective facts.

This is not to say that the study of historical connections, of the influence of one man's theory on another's, is not a good thing. But one of its merits is just that it enables us to get over "illusions of progress". Not the least of the reasons for studying the Greek philosophers is that they are far clearer on many questions than modern philosophers, that they avoid many modern errors, and especially that they are not, like the moderns, obsessed with "the problem of knowledge"—that they do not set out to discover (i.e., to know!) how, or how much, we can know, before they are prepared to know anything. This "criticism of the instrument" amounts to scientific defeatism, and the instrumental view of mind has both prevented a knowledge of minds themselves and hampered direct inquiry into logical and other scientific problems.

Now it is part of the value of Hegel's work that he attacked such utilitarian conceptions, that in his theory of "the thought in things" he recognised that minds and what they know are subject to the same logic. But he was sufficiently infected by the doctrines he opposed to recognise an initial opposition which had to be overcome, a transcendence of differences and a resultant unity. On this theory, then, in place of the logical recognition of distinctions, relation (e.g., between a mind and something it knows) was illogically treated as union, as precluding or overcoming distinction. Differences had then to be reinstated as aspects of or moments in the whole, each expressing the whole in a certain degree or with a certain intensity, though it could not be shown how they did so, any more than the nature of the passage from one moment to the next could be demonstrated. (A similar point arises in connection with Leibniz's theory of perception and appetition.) The recognition of the interaction of distinct things, of things as complex and active, of history, requires the rejection of transcendence and expression, of the Absolute and its aspects, of the philosophy of Spirit or of Matter.

It is in laying the foundations of a logic of things as historical that Kant is important, and in relation to this part of Kant's theory Hegel can be regarded only as reactionary. He undoubtedly brought out some of Kant's inconsistencies, but he came down on the wrong side, and his influence was such as to close the main path that Kant had opened up. Kant showed, as against Locke, that the objects of science are just the objects of observation, that "matter" (that which is treated of in physics) is what we perceive and not something behind it. He showed as against sensationalism (a rationalist doctrine miscalled "empiricism") that connections and distinctions among things are known *along with* things. And he thus showed how science could be other than a matter of guesswork, as, on the doctrine of Berkeley (more consistent than the other upholders of "ideas"), it would have been.

Nevertheless, and even apart from occasional concessions to this very doctrine of ideas, Kant was sufficiently imbued with the assumptions of his predecessors to take that field of science (things in Space and Time, with the characters and relations which this implies) as only a result of the application of the conditions of knowledge to certain postulated material. The objects of physical science, found by us in a historical medium, are merely "phenomena" and not things themselves. It may be pointed out in criticism that, as soon as we try to think of a relation between things themselves and phenomena (or between mind and the phenomena it knows), we have to think of it as spatio-temporal; in talking of things themselves at all, we are bringing them under the categories which are said to govern phenomenal existence. Hence the solution of the Kantian division in reality is just that the objects of observation *are* things themselves, and that we ourselves are also such things, existing under the same spatio-temporal conditions as other things, and, under these conditions, entering into relations with them (being *in the same situation* as they are) whereby we can know them. Such an empirical development of Kantianism, while showing how positive science is possible and what is the field of a positive logic, incidentally does away with the peculiar "problem of knowledge". Historical situations in which A knows X will be possible objects of study on the same footing as other historical situations.

Hegel, however, did not make this philosophical advance but side-tracked it. He "did away with" the difficulty of a divided reality by taking the different types of reality as moments within a spiritual whole, different aspects of a unity, reconciled within that unity. Thus the division is retained and at the same time "overcome"; Hegel takes the typically idealist line of having things both ways. In support of the "union of the diverse" it is argued quite properly that there can be no object without a subject and no subject without an object. This is to say that, whenever knowledge occurs, there is both something which knows and something which is known. But that does not imply that these are not distinct things, that they are aspects of a totality, mental or otherwise; it does not imply that a non-mental thing need be an object (need be known), or that mind (or anything capable of knowing) cannot be an object. There is, then, no "union" in the matter and no question of "aspects".

Hegel, like Berkeley, certainly did good work in attacking representationism, i.e., the view that the mind has "ideas" which symbolise "outside things". But his solution, like Berkeley's, is itself representational; each factor in a situation becomes an aspect or expression of the whole, is the situation "raised to a certain power" though not completed. Hence thought, instead of being regarded as a relation, is regarded as a certain essence or spirit which can be expressed, with different degrees of adequacy, (*a*) in minds, which can think and which are thus "thought at the subjective level", and (*b*) in things which can be thought and are thus "objective thought" (or objective mind). Expressing the whole, these forms of thought at the same time, and on that account, express one another; they are "powers" of one another and of the whole. Now this doctrine is clearly otiose or "metaphysical", because, in order to say *what* power of Spirit anything is, we have to state it in its own character (e.g., Space will be the *spatial* power of Spirit). At the same time, in making things "signify" one another, it denies independence, and leads to just such a division between immediate data and meanings as is found in the most crudely representationist theory.

While it may be said, then, that the doctrine of "objective mind" permits, up to a point, of the study of things in their own character and thus of the development of positive science, it does so to a less extent than Kant's doctrine, since Space and Time are put on the same footing as any quality of things, viz., as powers of mind; and the demand for an underlying "spiritual significance" of every event, and for "spiritual necessity" linking events, can only have the effect of bringing science down to the level of theology or guesswork (ἠικασία). This is an outstanding defect of the Hegelian philosophy—that every new historical fact alters logic by introducing a new "logical moment" or category, and since each problem is that of understanding reality "from a certain point of view", we have no means of making any problem precise.[4]

A secondary, though serious, defect of the doctrine of objective mind is its implication that minds are not specific things, the distinction between the mental and the non-mental being the one which suffers most in the attempted removal or transcendence of all distinctions. This incidentally renders obscure the description

---

[4] Hegel's demand for a "criticism of categories" is, it may be said, in accordance with sound logic. But such criticism should take the form of a *rejection* of unsound, relative conceptions (striking examples of which are found in ethical theory in the notions of "right", "happiness" and the like), and not of the relegation of a defective conception to a supposed "level of reality" to which it is "adequate". In the same way Berkeley is thoroughly philosophical in rejecting the relative conception of matter as *that whereby* we have our ideas, but is unphilosophical in retaining the relativist conception of "our ideas".

of the Absolute as mental. Indeed the illogical character of any Monism comes out in any attempt to describe the One, to show how it can have aspects at all, let alone the particular aspects it is said to have—how, so to speak, there can be a distinction without a difference. Thus, confusions as to mind apart, the illogicality of the Hegelian position is most clearly seen in the general conception of the reconciliation of opposites, or of questions to which the answer is *both yes and no*. A sufficient rejoinder to such attempts to have things both ways is that "No" means "*Not* Yes", as is indicated by the fact that we can intelligibly say that the answer is *not* both yes and no. The person who says "No" to Hegelianism is not at the same time saying "Yes". In fact, exposition of the Hegelian philosophy brings it under the conditions of discussion, in which issues have to be settled one way or the other, and permits its playing fast and loose with logic to be shown up.

It may be asked, then, why so clearly illogical a doctrine as the denial of direct negation should have been so influential. It could not influence the development of science except to retard it, but the fact that it has retarded science and especially psychological science still wants explanation. The answer is that Hegelianism has to be met, that it can be met only by the abandonment of all idealistic or totalistic notions, and that this requires the abandonment of any form of rationalism. The impossibility of an aggregation of elements or "whole natures" is shown in the Hegelian criticism of associationist psychology, as it was originally shown in the Eleatic criticism of the Pythagorean units. So long, we may say, as any "ultimate" is recognised, whether it be a purpose, an essence or a totality, real distinctions, the existence of independent things, cannot be. And this is borne out by the prevalence in the sciences, not only of rationalistic and teleological or instrumental conceptions, but of conceptions of "the whole", of Nature and the like. Thus, whatever professions of "starting from the facts" may be made, the transcendence of differences is still the chosen and hopeless task.

The only serious answer, then, to the assertion that the universe is spiritual, is that there is not a universe. If all things were aspects of the One, the One could just as much, though just as little, be called mental as anything else. Hence any doctrine of "the physical universe", any "materialistic monism", can no more provide an answer to Hegel than any form of atomism can. Only a thoroughly pluralistic doctrine, a logic which, in its application to psychology, will eliminate the totalistic conception of The Mind, can meet and overturn the position of Hegel. And such a doctrine has not yet been set up by Hegel's successors and critics. The "positive philosophy" of Comte showed the possibility of it, but Comte was still teleologist enough to take a merely instrumental view of mind and to recognise stages in a universal history. Strains of rationalism are also observable in the work of the various writers previously mentioned, even though, by taking what is valuable in each, we can construct a coherent anti-idealist position.

These considerations emphasise the necessity of abandoning the vulgar, optimistic doctrine of progress and recognising that things, including philosophy, can regress; though, this being admitted, it may still be found that, in the development of certain things, progress has been made. We have to recognise *accident*, i.e., the fact that there is no formula, no "principle", which covers all things; that there is no totality or system of things. And this recognition at once supports a life of "responsibility and adventure" and leads to scientific discovery. We are unscientific if we take the Hegelian view that the end is present in the beginning; the doctrine of potentialities, while it denies real development, enables us only to parade our wisdom after the event. But we are equally unscientific if we say that the beginning is present in the end, that a thing is what it comes out of, instead of what it has it in it to become. We are giving no account of mind if we say that it is an "epiphenomenon" or a mere "property" of matter; we do not solve psychological problems by the simple assertion that thought is a function of the brain. *What* property, *what* function, is the question. If we are going to solve problems on a basis of identity, we may indifferently make our identification in one direction or the other. Evolutionary rationalism of this kind is sufficiently met by the Hegelian demonstration that mind must be something, even if Hegel wrongly takes it as something teleological (something with a reconciling mission) and himself upholds a philosophy of identity and a one-track development.

What is required for the emancipation of psychological science, in particular, from identity-mongering is the abandonment of the notion of "thought", as something either to be contrasted or to be identified with things. Our thoughts are just our dealings with things; and this pragmatic view, developed to some extent by

James and at least suggested by Marx, enables us, setting things on the level of historical facts, to stress that in which scientific objectivity is to be found, viz., the proposition. "The thought in things" can usefully mean not any ultimate or cosmic significance, not any evolutionary purpose, but only their propositional and consequently assertible character. Whether *we* assert or recognise any particular fact or not depends on our character and our historical situation, i.e., depends on our being here and such, while it is there and so. The recognition of a single logic of events, of complex things interacting in Space and Time, disposes at once of the logic and of the psychology of "thought".

For an answer to Hegel, then, we have to drop epistemology—the intrusion of mind into logic and of a false logic into psychology—and return to the Greek consideration of *things*, as Burnet, no less than the English realists, assists us to do; we have to develop a positive theory of mind as feeling and as multiple, on the lines suggested by Freud; we have to be empirical, like James, and to recognise Space and Time as the conditions of existence, as is done by Alexander, largely under the influence of Kant. Doing this we can reject significance and purpose and any single "stuff" of reality, whether matter or spirit. We find such notions, in whatever form they appear, to be on the same level of romanticism as Hegelian formulae like "the end is present in the beginning", "the truth is the whole", or "the real is the rational"—i.e., they are all solutions *on a higher plane* than the problem, and so are denials of the problem. Romanticism, whether it seeks to uplift or to reach profundity, is always of this intellectually defeatist character.

Certain main points, which, of course, could be more fully and exactly treated, emerge from this brief consideration of Hegel's place in the history of philosophy. We find that only a pluralistic logic of events can provide a logical answer to idealism, and that rationalism, in science and philosophy, opens the way to monism and this again to scepticism—theology, defeatism, leaving things in the hands of higher powers. We find, further, that history is not progress, that the history of speculation, in particular, is not a progressive discovery of truths and removal of errors, an outstanding illustration being that the idealistic errors of Kant, akin as they are to the errors erected by Hegel into a system, did not prevent him from utilising empirical material and working out a logic of events which was not developed but only obscured by Hegel. It may also be pointed out that the most widely prevalent contemporary philosophies are varieties of representationism Scepticism Theology, more or less similar to Locke's, in spite of the decisive refutations of Locke's view that have been formulated by philosophic thinkers from Berkeley onwards. This failure to progress in philosophy indicates that it is not sufficient for a rejection of representationism to have gone through the stage of Hegelianism, nor is it necessary, as we see from a consideration of the commonsense realism of the Greeks.

But the denial of the doctrine of progress does not prevent us from recognising the occurrence of discoveries and other good things. So the baneful effects of the anti-logic of Hegel, his encouragement of mystification in the doctrine of reconciliation of opposites and the cult of profundity, his provision of a sounding and worthless terminology for the theologically-minded and the literary moralisers, his detrimental influence, in opposition to precision and to independence of thought and action, on culture in general—all this should not keep us from seeing that inquiry has here and there been stimulated by his attempt at finding a single logic and his insistence on the historical treatment of things, and even by his merely drawing attention to the work of his predecessors. But to say, in the face of all the obscurities and confusions he introduced, that he represents a "necessary stage" in the history of philosophy, is to be wise, like Hegel himself (or like "the owl of Minerva"), after the event; it is to be, like him, opposed to precision, to the investigation of *the independent issue*, the proposition; it is, in fact, to be unscientific and unhistorical.

The philosophy of aspects is not an aspect of philosophy, though philosophers may learn much from studying it and may see more clearly, in considering its influence, what is and what is not a refutation of it. And this will help them to see that philosophy is not "the history of philosophy" but is a certain subject to be studied, that the philosopher's business is the enunciation and demonstration of philosophic truths, and that these truths do not progress.

# 9
# DESIGN (1935)

In the Introduction to his just published edition of Hume's *Dialogues concerning Natural Religion*,[1] Professor Kemp Smith remarks (p. 38) that the *Dialogues* have a "unique place in philosophical literature. They are unique in two respects. As Leslie Stephen has pointed out, they were the first work in our literature to subject the argument from design to a passionless and searching criticism. And secondly, Hume's destructive criticism of the argument—allowing for the limitations... under which it was formulated—was final and complete. For a couple of generations, theologians, especially in Britain, may have continued on the old lines, as if the *Dialogues* had never been written. But in the altered outlook of present-day theology, these older ways of argument have in large measure ceased to be approved, and Hume's indictment of them is now but seldom challenged." Kemp Smith admits that the argument from design, in the form in which Hume[2] criticised it, not only "persisted into the nineteenth century in the writings of Paley" and others, but "survives in popular and semi-popular forms to the present day" (p. 36). He appears to think, then, that these uncritical conceptions, like those of popularisers of the Jeans type, carry no great weight not merely among philosophers but even among the more serious theologians. This is a view which, while I have no great acquaintance with present-day theology, I should be very much inclined to question. For, apart from the mere ignoring of Hume, there is also the tendency to substitute for the criticised doctrine other doctrines which are open to the very same type of criticism. And both these reactions are facilitated by Hume's "scepticism", i.e., by his failure to work out a *logic*.

Arguments like that of design, in fact, cannot be thoroughly gone into until attention is directed not merely to the illogicality

---

[1] Clarendon Press, 1935.
[2] I share the view, and shall assume it in this article, that, allowing for dialogue form and the social conditions, which, as Kemp Smith shows, prevented complete candour, Philo presents Hume's own position. Kemp Smith's demonstration, it seems to me, should put any other interpretation of the *Dialogues* finally out of court.

of the proofs offered but to the illogicality of what they are supposed to prove. And, whatever suggestions Hume may make towards a thorough-going solution, he cannot arrive at it and force subsequent attention to it, because of the defects in his philosophical outlook—because, like the other "English empiricists", he was rationalistically concerned with "ideas" (that whose nature it is to be perceived) and not with propositions (what is the case). So long as any admission of "natures" is made, dualism is inevitable; and even if the term "design" is abandoned, some comparable and equally confused way in which the nature may "express" itself must be retained. Hence, while Hume could point empirically to many of the difficulties of the theory of design, not only could he not prevent it from raising its head again, but his own rationalist preconceptions were an influence towards its doing so. Similarly, it may be remarked in passing, it is because of its rationalism, its retention of "principles" and the like, that the realist movement set going by Moore and Russell has failed—failed, i.e., to work out a realist *philosophy*. To reap the full benefits of Hume's work, then—and the same applies to the work of the later movement—it is necessary to follow up the questions raised, to cut away rationalist conceptions and so to arrive at a logical position.

That progress has been made in this direction by philosophers (whatever may be said about theologians and pseudo-philosophical scientists) is due not merely to Hume's work but to the fact that Kant, as Kemp Smith points out (p. 39), incorporated Hume's main criticisms in his "Transcendental Dialectic". But, whatever stimulus Kant may have given to logic, he remains a dualist, and theories which do not go beyond Kant's position can be criticised in Philo's manner, even if not with his precise arguments. One of the most important points made by Kant is that the physico-theological argument, as he calls it, is not an argument *a posteriori* or from experience, but has as much of an *a priori* or ontological character as any of the others, that it depends on the conception of that which is ultimate or establishes itself. It should be emphasised here that ontological arguments are not confined to proofs of the existence of God or of something described as *the* Absolute, but are the means of establishing all ultimates, even in nominally pluralistic theories. It is really in the ontological fashion that the Pythagoreans set up their units or Socrates his forms or that anyone sets up *that which is by its own nature*. It seems indeed to be shown by the Eleatic criticism of the Pythagoreans, and similarly by Spinoza's criticism of Descartes, that there cannot be more than one ultimate, but the more important question is whether there can be one at all. And until it has been shown that there cannot, until the very conception of "ultimacy" has been rejected, until it has been demonstrated not merely that certain arguments are unsound but that their supposed conclusions are untenable, the position has not been worked out and the same types of error recur. Thus not only can we say that Kant argues ontologically in his theory of the good will, i.e., that which establishes itself by willing itself (just as in the conception of consciousness, by theorists from Descartes onwards, as that which establishes itself by thinking itself); we must also note that the very conception of the "thing-in-itself" involves an ontological argument—for what is an argument but a recognition of dependence?—and that the only solution is not a problematical recognition but the rejection of *that which is in itself.*

This is connected with the inseparability of cosmological and ontological arguments. Kant shows that the cosmological argument depends on the ontological, that that on which all other things depend can only be that which establishes itself. But, equally, that which establishes itself has to be taken as that on which other things depend, because in its very conception there is the distinction between its character of establishing and its character of being established; and, while the latter now appears, like a created cosmos, as having "dependent existence", the same problem as before breaks out in regard to the "self-subsistence" or self-supporting character of the former, the same distinction has to be made between its supporting and its being supported, and so on indefinitely. There is likewise no logical division between cosmological and physico-theological or teleological arguments, because in each case we have the dualism of ways of being, that which has its being in supporting and that which has its being in being supported. The only way to escape from the vicious circle, in which dualism collapses into monism and monism explodes into dualism, is to adopt a pluralist position in which variously characterised and related things are recognised as existing in the same way (spatio-temporally)—a single logic of existence replacing conceptions of "self-subsistence", "relative existence" and any other flights of rationalistic fancy.

It is worth noting that all theories of higher and lower realities are stated in terms of the common reality we all know—and, indeed, can be stated in no other way. Thus, as Berkeley points out in criticism of Locke, we are all acquainted with the way in which one thing supports another, we know the empirical relation of supporting, but we are not acquainted with the way in which "matter", in the Lockian theory, supports accidents. Locke had to use an ordinary term, at the same time suggesting that it was to be understood in an extraordinary sense; but he could not even begin to tell us what that sense is, how the "supporting" of accidents by matters differs from the supporting that we know. Thus the common relation gives us no help in the understanding of the metaphysical one, but the use of the common word tends to confuse our minds and makes us *imagine* that we have understood something. The force of Berkeley's criticism here is not weakened by the fact that his position is open to the same objections, that he utilised our acquaintance with dependence as an actual relation between actual and distinct things, in order to make it apparently intelligible to us that certain things have "dependent existence". In so doing, in separating the active from the passive, the effective from the effected, he takes up a position logically indistinguishable from that of Cleanthes (and, of course, closely resembling it in detail; Berkeley, we may say, was a notable participant in that movement in eighteenth century thought which Cleanthes represents in the *Dialogues*), but in his criticism of Locke he did some of the work of Philo.

What Philo does, in fact, is to lay bare just such empirical material as the rationalists use in their arguments, and to show that it will not bear the metaphysical doctrines erected on it. All that his criticism lacks is development in the direction of a thorough-going empiricist logic, which would show that his declension to scepticism is uncalled for. For the sharpening of the logical issues, then, we may take as our point of departure the famous passage (Part II) in which Cleanthes sets forth the main theme of the discussion. "Look round the world: Contemplate the whole and every part of it: You will find it to be nothing but one great machine, subdivided into an infinite number of lesser machines, which again admit of subdivisions, to a degree beyond what human senses and faculties can trace and explain. All these various machines, and even their most minute parts, are adjusted to each other with an accuracy, which ravishes into admiration all men, who have ever contemplated them. The curious adapting of means to ends, throughout all nature, resembles exactly, though it much exceeds, the productions of human contrivance; of human design, thought, wisdom, and intelligence. Since therefore the effects resemble each other, we are led to infer, by all the rules of analogy, that the causes also resemble; and that the Author of nature is somewhat similar to the mind of man; though possessed of much larger faculties, proportioned to the grandeur of the work, which he has executed. By this argument *a posteriori*, and by this argument alone, do we prove at once the existence of a Deity, and his similarity to human mind and intelligence."

The weakness of analogy, the question-begging character of the reference to *the* Author of nature, are obvious points of criticism here. But a more important line of attack is that which proceeds from the fatal admission of Cleanthes that there is nothing which does not bear the same marks as are borne by the productions of human contrivance, i.e., that what he regards as marks of contrivance are conditions of existence. If we could distinguish the contrived from the uncontrived, then we might be able to discover certain marks of the former; but if everything bears certain marks, then, naturally, human contrivances will do so, but this will be no argument in support of the view that they are marks *of contrivance.* As far as human operations are concerned, the materials worked upon, the things not humanly contrived, will bear the marks in question just as much as the things produced or humanly contrived. Accordingly, the alleged *a posteriori* argument from the special mode of operation of human contrivance, conceived as the *introduction* of marks of design, disappears, and we are left with an *a priori* argument, of the cosmological type, to the effect that everything in nature, whether it is worked upon by human minds or not, is necessarily dependent on some creator or source or has a *subordinate* form of existence. Such a position is involved, indeed, in this very use of the term "nature" (generally, in our day, with a capital). Now, as we have seen, even an *a priori* position has to make use of empirical material; we could never entertain the conception of dependence as a peculiar form of existence (i.e., as a qualification of the *copula*), unless we were acquainted with it as a character of actual situations—unless we had had experience of the occasioning of one thing by another, whether the latter is a mind or not. But there is nothing in this experience to warrant the conception of dependent existence; on the contrary, we are concerned with whether or not the one thing is *actually* dependent on the other—and not with whether it is *dependently* dependent, and so on indefinitely, as we should have to assert if we took it to have this peculiar mode of being.

Logically, then, even if there are marks of design, this is only a matter of a particular relation between different sorts of particular things, which are all alike "actual" or, as I should prefer to put it, spatio-temporal. But Cleanthes is quite correct in taking the adjustment he refers to as characteristic of things in general, i.e., anything we like to take has characteristic ways of working, one phase of which leads on to another, and acts differently in different situations. Accordingly, since adjustment is found alike in the things we ordinarily call machines and in those we do not, there is no ground for tracing the adjustment of the former to the fact of their being machines and thence concluding that the latter also are machines produced by some non-human contriver; just as there is no ground for Berkeley's argument that those of our "ideas" which we do not control must be controlled by some other mind, but a mere assumption, in spite of appearances to the contrary, that control or efficacy is always mental, so that working on mind must be working by mind. There is then, no special "working" character of mind and no special "wrought" character of machines or other things. According to the admissions of Cleanthes—and if he does not make them, his argument cannot proceed—human contrivance consists not in making things work together, since they already do so, but in making things work together in a certain way, i.e., in making certain "workings" or activities, which simply means *making certain things*.

Human contrivance also involves the working of things on minds, but that is a matter to which I shall return. Meanwhile, it may be of some interest to consider another incidental point. If human contrivance consists of making things which worked together in a certain way work together in a different way, then we have human interference with God's arrangements; in other words, Cleanthes, in starting from human contrivers, has no argument for a single contriver but must admit a multiplicity of competing contrivers. The alternative is to take human beings also as contrivances of the original contriver, and not as contrivers at all. A similar dilemma faces Berkeley in his theory of "the conduct of life" and of our knowledge of other finite minds. Unless the conduct of life consists merely in imagining what we like, without the slightest effect on the sensations that are forced on our minds, Berkeley must admit that we can operate on God's ideas, i.e., that we can give him new ideas just as he can give us. And, again, unless other minds can alter God's ideas, we cannot have the slightest reason for taking any particular sensation as indicative of the operation of another mind, but only as coming direct from God. Finally, as in the case of Cleanthes, Berkeley either has to admit that we are simply some of God's ideas and have no "agency" whatever, or has to recognise a thoroughgoing interaction and abandon his doctrine of the "active" over against the "passive".

To return to the main argument, human contrivance means that human beings, by "thinking" and other operations, produce certain things, and it may well be that *only* human beings produce things of certain sorts. In that case, if we see such a thing, we can infer that a human being made it; but the inference depends not on our finding in the thing a peculiarly designed or contrived character, but, as Philo points out, on our knowledge of the fact that things of that kind *are* made by men. We have all seen men going through a series of operations culminating in the existence of a house, and we have never seen a house coming into existence in any other way. It is on this account that, when we come across a house which we did not see being built, we conclude that somebody built it, and not because we see a contrived character in it. But, if Cleanthes were right in finding contrivance in everything, then we should be just as ready to conclude that a house or a ship which we did not see constructed had been made by the contriver of things in general and that no man had a hand in its construction, as to draw the conclusion that we do. Moreover, if Cleanthes were right, he would have no need of any analogy; he could argue straight to a designer from the designed character of anything he liked to consider, without having to refer to human performances. The fact is that there is no designed or contrived character, that contrivance is a relation between different things and not a character of either by itself. Knowing such relations (e.g., all houses are made by men) we can draw inferences—we can infer the human contrivance of some things, the mouse or bird contrivance of other things, and so on—but never contrivance by *the* contriver, and always on the basis of experience of things of the sort A contriving things of the sort B.

The fact that Philo does not enforce the *logical* issues, does not insist, e.g., that "the adjustment of means to ends" signifies merely that when something happens to a thing it does something else, accounts for his being able at the conclusion of the argument to put forward the modified, and, as he admits, useless, assertion "that the cause or causes of the order in the universe probably bear some remote analogy to human intelligence". Nevertheless, his suggestion that what is really required is revelation may quite well not be ironical, but, taken in conjunction with his earlier argument, may rather indicate that Hume had some conception of the weakness of relativism, the impossibility of characterising a thing by its relations or of taking the character of a thing *in itself* as testifying to the character of a related thing. This, indeed, is the very point that Hume made in regard to causality in the *Treatise*; but only the abandonment of his rationalistic theories of "ideas", "relations of ideas", and, still more important, spatial and temporal *units*, would have enabled him to bring these questions to a decisive issue.

Cleanthes, at any rate, does not and cannot explain why what he takes to be provable is not also observable, just as, when we see a house and infer that men built it, we also believe that someone saw them build it. He wishes to argue to the existence of something with which we are not acquainted and whose modes of operation we therefore do not know, on the ground that these (unknown) modes of operation are the only thing that will account for the existence of something with which we are acquainted; and a good deal of Philo's "scepticism" is just the bringing out of the sceptical character of this position. The particular contention that a greater contrivance implies a greater contriver is one which, as Philo suggests, we are not in any way bound to accept; for if by a greater contriver we merely mean one who makes a greater contrivance, we have not indicated any characteristic of his which we can call his greatness and which can distinguish him from lesser contrivers—and if we try to specify such a characteristic, if, e.g., we make it a matter of physical size, then, while it is still a question of experienced connections, of *finding* a bigger thing making a bigger thing, we must admit many contrary cases of a physically smaller cause having a physically more extensive effect. Only its vagueness can protect such a contention, which is still an attempt to find in the effect a positive characterisation of the cause.

Equal difficulty is found in the attempt to characterise the cause negatively from the effect. Cleanthes argues—all machines are designed by minds (which we have seen to be a mere assumption, if all that is meant by a machine is something which has characteristic modes of operation under various conditions); the universe is a machine not designed by a human mind; therefore, the universe is designed by a non-human mind (and, as above, since the universe is greater than any human contrivance, this non-human mind must be greater than any human mind). Now, leaving aside for the present the questions arising in connection with the conception of "the universe", we may object to the above argument that, unless we had independent evidence of the existence of a non-human mind, or if human minds were the only minds we knew, the acceptance of the second premise would lead us to cast doubt on the first. In other words, we should require to have some acquaintance with non-human minds before this argument would produce conviction, and consequently we cannot take it as a proof of the existence of a non-human mind or a means whereby we could be led for the first time to suppose a non-human mind to exist.

This criticism has a certain similarity to Alexander's criticism of the view that we argue to the existence of minds other than our own by analogy, i.e., that, since we know that certain bodily processes are associated with certain of our own mental processes, then, when we find such bodily processes not associated with our own mental processes, we assume that they are associated with some other mental processes and thus recognise the existence of other minds. Alexander's contention is that such bodily behaviour could not give us the conception of "another mind", and that, if we were not independently acquainted with other minds, we should simply take it that the bodily behaviour in question was not associated with any mind. Apart, however, from the special difficulties in which Alexander is involved by his conceptions of our "assurance" of other minds and "enjoyment" of our own, it may be pointed out that if we *are* acquainted with our own minds, then we may, as Moore puts it, reasonably suppose a similar mind to exist in similar observed conditions. So that, even if inference is not the only or the regular way in which we learn of the existence of other minds, it may be (and is) one of the ways. But it cannot be the way in which we learn of the existence of a special type of mind, with which we are not otherwise acquainted. Or, if the last statement is one which must be received with caution, at least we do not so learn of a type of mind (or of anything else) with which we *cannot* be otherwise acquainted.

The caution referred to is enjoined by the following considerations: we may believe that things of the sort A come into existence by the contrivance of minds or mental processes of the sort a, B by b, C by c, and so forth. Then if we come across a thing of the sort ABC, we are thereby led to suppose the existence of a mental process of the sort abc, even if we have no direct acquaintance with such a process. There would still, of course, be the possibility of our being mistaken about some of our premises, and we might retain a lingering doubt about the existence of the mentality in question until we had observed it; but at least we were led to conceive it by that evidence. Even so, we think of its contrivance of ABC as a particular contrivance going on at a particular time, just as we found the contrivances of A, of B and of C to be in the first place. It is another matter entirely when it is a question of Contrivance as a whole; in that case there is not even the remotest analogy with human contrivance, there is no reason for calling the assumed "higher" operation contrivance at all.

As we saw, if we take positive account of human contrivance, we find that it is a relation between human minds and other things, and that both exist in the same way, not that one "exists contrivingly" and the other "exists contrivedly". The question is then just to find what things human beings do contrive, and this raises no question of any contrivance of other things by other beings. Equally, there is no question of "marks of contrivance". But if, like Cleanthes, we take as marks of contrivance working in certain regular ways, having a certain harmony of parts, and so on, i.e., having a certain character or "constitution", then we must take the things we call contrivers as also contrived; the workings of the mind are of the same "contrived" character as the workings of any other thing. But to say in this way that all contrivers are contrived is not to argue for the existence of one great contriver who is not contrived; it is to argue against it. On the other hand, if we say that contrivers are not contrived, then we cannot take regular working, etc., as marks of contrivance, because they also have these marks, and so we have no ground for calling the ordinary "works of Nature" contrivances, and the argument of Cleanthes has not even a beginning.

There are, of course, additional difficulties in the way of the conception of an original contriver of the whole of "creation", but in the first place there is the same difficulty, viz., that if we are to say anything about this contriver at all, we must regard him as having characteristic ways of working, as being of the same logical order as his alleged "creation", as being a set of interacting situations—and, apart from the question of this set being itself situated or environed, we are already committed in those admissions to the rejection of an *origin* of things and to the treatment of the emergence of further situations in the same way as we treat developing situations now, viz., as exhibiting certain forms of action and interaction (though indeed this emergence and the implied pre-existence already constitute an environment). It seems of minor importance then to point out that there can be no contrivance of a "universe" or totality of things, because the contriver would have to be included in the totality of things; and if things constituted "one great machine", he would be part of the machine and not its maker. Alternatively, things would not constitute one great machine, but the least we could think about would be *the contriver contriving contrivances*—in which case, of course, there would be no *argument* to a contriver. Even that, however, does not provide an escape; but (as in the case of Berkeley's similar minimum of *a mind having ideas*) the different elements in this complex situation must be taken as all existing in the same way and none as having "higher" being than another. So that, as in the case of human contrivance, we have a particular relation between particular things—or else we have nothing at all.

We see, then, that Cleanthes, in speaking of the contriver of the universe, is not seriously thinking of the latter as a universe or totality. But it is no more possible, even if we could separate things active from things passive, to think of a totality of created things (or "Creation", as it is called) than to think of a totality of things in general. Indeed it is a mere phrase, without any experience or serious argument to justify it, because if we do think of something we call Creation or The World, we can think of it only as certain things acting in certain ways—just as, if we thought of a creator, we could only think of him as acting in certain ways, and so could not make the logical distinction which the theory requires. But, speaking simply of the things Cleanthes calls machines, things to which we do not attribute any power of contriving, we do not find that they make up one great machine; we do not find any total situation or any way of working which is that of the whole. There is no object of which we can say, "That is the world with all its parts and characters adjusted to each other"; there is no observable situation of all things working together—for good or for anything else. On the contrary, in any observation, while we find adjustment or ways of working, they are always ways of working of particular things; and, even so, these are not all the ways of working of the things, apart from the influence of the other things with which they may come in contact. Thus there is no formula or law which will cover every action of any group of things, however large or small, that we like to take, and there is no question of one great machine or one total way of working.

The facts of complexity and interaction have a further bearing on the notion of a machine. As we have noted, contrivance is a relation between distinct and independent things—independent in the sense that, though a house, e.g., would not have existed but for the operations of men (and in that sense of dependence human beings are also dependent on inanimate things), it now does exist in the same way as they do, we can know it even though we know nothing about them, and we can interact with it in the same way as we interact with them. It is important to observe, then, that, apart from the fact that we can only operate on given materials, there is nothing which is a mere contrivance; anything that we contrive always has (without reference to *mistakes* we may make about it) characters which we did not anticipate. In the same way, of course, as against voluntarism, there are always characters of our voluntary actions which we were not aware of when we willed them, so that they are not simply "our decisions". To say, then, that there is something more than we "contrived" about the things we have made is to recognise that they are independent things and to do away with any logical division between contrivers and contrived, and so with any conception of a totality of the contrived—or, for that matter, of a totality of any kind, as contrasted with the interaction of independent things. And to say that, while this may be the case with human contrivances, there is nothing about God's contrivances, or God's creation, of which he was not aware when he created it, is to destroy the analogy between God's contrivance and our contrivance, and to make the mere assumption that there could be a contriver who knew everything about his contrivances. There certainly could be nothing about his contrivances to prove that he did—though, if he did, he would know something, i.e., there would be two distinct terms to the relation of knowledge, and so there would still be independent existence of the contrived. But a more important point here is that, if God knew "all about" his contrivances, they would not be things at all but "natures", and the question of the contriving of things would be quite untouched.

Connected with this question is the further point raised by Philo that the order and contrivance put into the world by God implies a pre-existing order and contrivance of God's ideas. It is not a sound objection to Philo's argument here to say that the theory of ideas is false; because, if we admit that certain beings contrive a certain order or arrangement of things, we have to admit a certain order or arrangement in them, whatever it is an arrangement of. Thus, in order to *intend* to create an ordered world, God would have to have a certain arrangement of intentions or gestures towards what he was going to create; and, if these expressions are criticised as merely statements of relations, there is still implied a certain order of the related things, i.e., of the things which intend as well as of the things which are intended. Consequently, rejecting the theory of ideas (or simply saying that the only positive sense that can be given to "our ideas" is our demands), we can still say that Philo's line of argument is sound, that complexity and order in the contrived imply complexity and order in the contriver, and so, if order requires a contriver, the contriver must have a contriver. And it is not open to Cleanthes to say that, just as he need not, in knowing a causal relation, inquire into the cause of the cause, so he need not concern himself with how God came to be; because it is only by having a general contriver that we can have a general contrivance or "Creation"—though, as we have seen, we cannot have it even then. The point also arises here as before, from the complexity of God's contriving, that any of his acts of contriving takes place among others, i.e., in an environment, and, even if we could limit that environment, that limited environment would be "the universe", so that the universe would not be created by any act of contriving. We note, further, that, while Philo has not succeeded in working out a logical position, he has raised some of the most serious logical questions.

It is in view of some of these difficulties that Cleanthes goes back on his previous position and says, since it is on the analogy of men that he is arguing, that he is prepared to accept a theory of many gods operating as various men do, i.e., to treat "God" as finite, imperfect, many, just as men are. He would be quite satisfied, he says, so long as it was still admitted that there is design everywhere. But actually, on that view, he would be dropping his theory of the world as a total machine and substituting for it a theory of various single contrivances, which then would interact in a perfectly natural manner, without any question of all these interactions being contrived—though, as has been indicated, this would be the case even on the hypothesis of a single contriver. Thus there would *not* be design everywhere; and, incidentally, on his "pluralistic" theory, Cleanthes could give no reason for rejecting the view that anything we have not seen being made by men was nevertheless made by some man or body of men in the past ("Once a warrior, very angry", etc.); in other words, his position becomes manifest as one of pure guesswork or mythology. He has no escape, then, from the truly pluralistic position that even a designed thing is an independent thing, something which has its own existence and ways of acting—the alternative being that the designed has not its own ways of acting, since *designing* is the only way of acting, and hence that the designed does not exist, and consequently designing does not either.

The fact that we cannot think of a totality of things is brought out again when Demea, as the more consistent logician, refuses to make the admission that Cleanthes had made; for we find that Demea can give no account whatever of his all-causing deity, that his position is really a sceptical one, because he has to say that we can know only of the existence of God, or that we must postulate his existence, without knowing anything of his nature, which is in fact incomprehensible to us. This is so, of course, if he has a "nature". But that is only to say that doctrines of "natures" or of the incomprehensible are quite otiose, that they give us no assistance whatever in knowing things—indeed they are hindrances. The point is that, if we know nothing of God's character, then we do not know what it is that is said to exist, and consequently Demea's position is a perfectly empty one. But so is the main position of

Cleanthes, and it is no accident that, in the discussion of evil, he falls back on "incomprehensibility". It is indeed quite a common type of argument to try to make out that God's goodness is of a higher order than ours and that we cannot fully comprehend his purpose or we should recognise that all men reckon evil has a place in the grand design, and meanwhile we have to take it as a matter of faith. This simply means that the postulation of a total and perfect design is to induce us to reject the knowledge that we actually possess. Descartes argues in a similar manner in comparing the perfection of deity with the imperfection of men and the errors they fall into on account of their limited intelligence. Now one definite objection to all such arguments concerning our limited intelligence is that it is our limited intelligence that is putting forward these arguments, and if there is any dubiety about our ability to understand these matters, then there is equal dubiety about the arguments themselves. But there is no reason whatever for scepticism or "suspense of judgment" so long as we have beliefs, i.e., so long as we find things having definite characters and acting in definite ways; and we always do.

It is curious that Philo should propose suspense of judgment (end of Part VIII) immediately after he has come nearest to presenting a position which would completely dispose of that of Cleanthes. "In all instances which we have ever seen, thought has no influence upon matter, except where that matter is so conjoined with it, as to have an equal reciprocal influence upon it. No animal can move immediately any thing but the members of its own body; and indeed, the equality of action and reaction seems to be an universal law of nature." Here, in spite of the rationalistic theory of equality (and the theory of ideas appears in the same passage), we have an approach to the recognition of interaction as a condition of existence, so that even a contriver is seen to be influenced by his material—just as Socrates, in his attempt to show that the mind "rules" the body, cannot get over the fact that, in order to do so, it must act in certain ways on the *occasion* of certain bodily conditions. Earlier in the same Part, Philo has recognised the fact "that matter is, and always has been in continual agitation, as far as human experience or tradition reaches". But, in going on to consider the hypothesis of a material cosmogony, he considers it possible that matter may exist for a time in a "disorderly" state, after which it may or may not achieve "order"—as if there could be any existence at any time except that of sorts of things, as if "chaos" itself, if it had any meaning, could mean anything but certain things going on in certain ways, i.e., a certain "order". The position is, as indeed we otherwise know, that Hume has not freed himself from dualism, from the doctrine of kinds of existence; yet it is remarkable how little further pressing of the argument of Philo would enable him to do so.

Philo's scepticism, however, his deficiency in logic, comes out most clearly in the well-known passage in Part VII, where he says: "In this little corner of the world alone, there are four principles, *reason, instinct, generation, vegetation*, which are similar to each other, and are the causes of similar effects. What a number of other principles may we naturally suppose in the immense extent and variety of the universe, could we travel from planet to planet and from system to system, in order to examine each part of this mighty fabric? Any one of these four principles above mentioned (and a hundred others which lie open to our conjecture) may afford us a theory, by which to judge of the origin of the world; and it is a palpable and egregious partiality, to confine our view entirely to that principle, by which our own minds operate." The hypothesis of Part VIII, then, is the conjecture of a fifth principle of explanation, that of motion or agitation. But, in the light of the above passage, it is clear why Hume did not see how near he then was to the mark; for, although the question is plainly one of the conditions of existence in general (somewhat confused, no doubt, by the reference to an *origin*), he does not see that these conditions will govern alike the various forms of operation he mentions, that they are not "principles" but particular proceedings of particular things. Philo's question reminds one of the supposition that in certain parts of the "universe" two and two may not be four; indeed, it is even worse, since it is a logical question that is at issue, since we cannot travel away from logic, however distant a system we go to, but the very supposition of such a system is a supposition of complex and interacting things.

Certainly, he quite correctly says (Part VIII) that: "Every event, before experience, is equally difficult and incomprehensible; and every event, after experience, is equally easy and intelligible." Certainly, again, Hume, recognising that the effect always differs from the cause, could have no logical difficulty in supposing, e.g., that minds arise from the non-mental. We have to remember also that the theory of Cleanthes is the theme of the *Dialogues*, and that Philo is more concerned with weakening the position of Cleanthes than with presenting a position of his own. Nevertheless, design has not been thoroughly dealt with until such a position has been worked out; but that would require the removal of the defects of Hume's theory of causality and more particularly recognition of spatio-temporal continuity and rejection of the theory of spatial and temporal units.

Once that is done, the removal of the dualism of active and passive presents no difficulty. For although, "before experience", we could suppose these classes to be exclusive or again to intersect, so that, in addition to things which are active and passive, there are active things which are not passive and passive things which are not active, in actual experience we find only interaction, things which act and are acted on. Apart from a rationalistic theory of "natures" (as presented, e.g., by Berkeley) we find no basis for the conception of separate classes of agents and patients, arrangers of phenomena and phenomena to be arranged, designers and the designed. We do not require to go beyond the facts themselves, and of course we cannot logically do so, to obtain an answer to the question how things came to be arranged as they are. The answer to the question how any particular arrangement arose is that it issued from a certain other arrangement, and there is no question of any total arrangement demanding (and being unable to receive) explanation by something more than total, viz., the arrangement of its arranger and itself. Anticipation, as far as it goes, is only one particular relation of the general type in question, and the anticipator is not pure "force" but also "matter", i.e., also acted upon, even in his anticipating, just as the anticipated also acts. This pluralistic conclusion is the upshot of Philo's argument or, at least, it is that alone which would make his position consistent; and it is a positive, not a sceptical conclusion.

# 10
# THE *COGITO* OF DESCARTES (1936)[1]

The *cogito ergo sum* of Descartes has been variously regarded by subsequent philosophers, and much discussion has been given to such questions as whether it is an inference or not, and, if it is, what conclusion is drawn from what premise (or premises) and whether the inference is valid or invalid. As we shall see, the difficulties here are largely due to rationalistic confusion as to what inference is; but they can best be resolved by an examination of the line of argument by which the formula itself is arrived at, and an exhibition of the confusions which that argument involves. It can thus be shown that the *cogito* as it appears in Descartes (i.e., as a "principle" or an "intuition" or a "rational certainty") is utterly without foundation, and that, as a consequence, certain conceptions which have quite a wide currency among present-day philosophers—particularly the conceptions of "subject" and the "subjective"—must likewise be abandoned.

First of all, however, we may observe that Descartes's own presentation of the case would naturally give rise to divergent interpretations, the point being that he *has* no consistent view, that he exhibits the instability which is characteristic of rationalism. Thus it might be said that, in spite of its containing *ergo*, the *cogito* cannot be taken as an inference, since Descartes specifically refers to it as a *proposition* which he has discovered to be true, and uses it to illustrate the general conditions under which a proposition can be true and certain. Again, it might seem fairly easy, even if the *cogito* were taken as an inference, to dismiss that interpretation of it according to which it proceeds from an activity to a substance which has that activity (*cogito ergo ego*, so to speak). For, as Gilson emphasises in the notes to his edition of the *Discourse*, the Latin text reads *Ego cogito, ergo sum, sive existo*, so that the *ego* is in the premise, if premise it be. Moreover, as Descartes immediately goes on to determine the substance as one "whose whole essence or nature

---

[1] The reference is particularly to the *Discourse on Method*, Part IV. Quotations are from Veitch's translation.

consists in thinking", this would seem to reduce the "inference" to *cogito ergo cogito*. Nevertheless, remembering that rationalism is a philosophy of essences or identities, we may consider that the reduction of inference to identity is what Descartes's argument really amounts to, and that the conception of "substance" is only one of the devices by which the emptiness of the position is concealed. A more detailed explanation will, I think, bear out these points.

Descartes, as we have noted, wished to establish the *cogito* as a true and certain proposition, as contrasted with propositions which may or may not be true but at least can be doubted. He had decided, in the search for truth, "to reject as absolutely false all opinions in regard to which I could suppose the least ground for doubt, in order to ascertain whether after that there remained aught in my belief that was wholly indubitable". On this basis he found he could reject the evidence of the senses, the reasonings of geometry, and, indeed, all the objects that ever entered his mind. "But immediately upon this I observed that, whilst I thus wished to think that all was false, it was absolutely necessary that I, who thus thought, should be somewhat." This result he formulates as the *cogito* ("I think, hence I am"); this is what remains in his belief that is wholly indubitable.

The mechanism of the doubting process, then, is the recognition of something in our belief, some proposition that we entertain, which it is possible to consider false. Thus we can say "I think that grass is green, but I may be wrong" or "I think that the sum of the angles of a triangle is equal to two right angles, but I may be wrong"; these doubts are quite *possible*, i.e., they contain no internal contradiction. But we cannot say "I think that I think, but I may be wrong", because even in being wrong we should be thinking, and thus there *is* contradiction in supposing that we are wrong in this case. It is worth noting that, in following Descartes's own version of the procedure of doubting, we have arrived simply at *I think* as that which is not subject to doubt. As Descartes indicates, it is "I, who thus thought" that must be something, and this something (as previously pointed out) is "a substance whose whole essence or nature consists only in thinking"; so that what must be something is only *my thinking*—or, if we care to press the argument further, only *thinking*. Waiving the latter point, we must insist that the formula that Descartes has been able to reject as involving contradiction is "I think that *cogito*, but I may be wrong" and not "I think that *cogito ergo sum*, but I may be wrong".

The rejection of views on the ground of the contradictions they involve is, of course, a regular part of rationalistic or identity-philosophy, and always depends on ambiguity or confusion of some kind. Descartes's confusions can be more clearly exposed if we emphasise the differences between the concluding doubts which, in the above examples, have been expressed by the same formula, "I may be wrong". The question, we have noted, is one of possibility and necessity. Thus doubting that grass is green, or considering that our belief to that effect is not certain, may be expressed as "I think that grass is green, but it is possible that grass is not green". The corresponding attempt to doubt that we think would take the form "I think that I think, but it is possible that I do not think". And the argument is that, whereas there is no contradiction in the first case and thus it is possible to accept the contradictory of "Grass is green", there is a contradiction involved in the second case and thus it is not possible to accept the contradictory of "I think". In other words, to deny that "I think" is self-refuting, and "I think" is certain or, as it is sometimes put, "follows from the principle of contradiction". Actually, of course, nothing follows from the principle of contradiction, and no proposition is "self-contradictory". It may here be remarked that those who contend that a "self-contradictory" proposition must be rejected as false, and thus its contradictory accepted as true and certain, do not observe that, since it is its own contradictory, its contradictory also must be false. But, while it is important to observe that there is confusion in any postulation of "rational" or self-evident truths, our immediate concern is with the confusions underlying the *cogito* in particular.

Returning, then, to our last formulation of the Cartesian doubt, and putting in brackets the proposition to be examined in each case, we have "I think (that grass is green), but it is possible that grass is not green"; "I think (that I think), but it is possible that I do not think". The latter formula is rejected as absurd, and it is asserted, on the contrary, that "I think (that I think), and it is *not* possible that I do not think", i.e., it is necessary that I think. Now, as regards the rejected formula, the point is that its absurdity depends not on the second, bracketed "I think", but on the *first*, and the second, which was the one to be examined

THE *COGITO* OF DESCARTES (1936) 131

and established, has not been examined at all. This is clearly seen if we put something else in the brackets; if we say "I think (that grass is green), but it is possible that I do not think", the absurdity remains exactly as before. On the other hand, if we retain the second "I think" and substitute something else for the first, if we say, for example, "It is said (that I think), but it is possible that I do not think", there is now no absurdity. It appears, then, that the bracketed part has nothing to do with the rejection of the formula, and that the contradiction on which Descartes's "demonstration" depends is that which is involved in saying "I think, but it is possible that I do not think"—a contradiction which would appear equally in the assertion, "Grass is green, but it is possible that grass is not green".

Thus it is not the case that the proposition "I think" has been subjected to the doubting process and has withstood the test and emerged as indubitable. It is the first "I think", the one that is common to all the formulae and stands outside the brackets, that remains at the end of the process; and it remains merely *asserted*, as it was to begin with. Descartes, as he has told us, has set out to examine his thoughts, and, in saying that he is doing so, he implies that he has thoughts or does think. We take this as a piece of information that he possesses, something he believes or has found to be the case, just as he might find that grass is green. Formally the two beliefs are equally capable of being contradicted; the proposition "I am not thinking" is no more absurd (even if it be false) than the proposition "Grass is not green". But it is possible that in actual fact we do not contradict or doubt either of the original propositions, that we regard them both as pieces of correct information; and if Descartes really doubts or disbelieves that grass is green, it is only because of other beliefs that he holds. In any case, whatever may be the beliefs and doubts of any particular person, no distinction at all has been indicated between propositions dubitable and indubitable in themselves, between mere contingencies and "first principles".

It may be noted, incidentally, that at best the proposition "I, Descartes, think" would be certain only for Descartes, that anyone else might doubt it freely, so that Descartes would not on his own showing have established any proposition that was certain in itself. That is why he has to go on from *his* self-certainty to *the* self-certain (the "perfect being"); he has to set up a universal (or essential) Essence in order to support the conception of himself as a particular essence, viz., a thinking essence. On the other hand, he has to import his essence theory into some empirical field in order to appear to have anything definite to say; a vague, general rationalism, in the form, say, that ultimately there must be a "reason" for everything, would not have the force of the *cogito*—and, of course, would not have the same mischievous effect on the empirical study of mind.

The method, however, is the same in either case; "perfection" and *cogito* are alike made to appear to be self-establishing (even if the latter has afterwards to be additionally established by the former), and this can only be done by means of some sort of equivocation, the removal of which shows that nothing at all has been established. In the case we have considered, when the second "I think" is removed as irrelevant, we are left with identity masquerading as inference; we are left with "I think, and it is not possible that I do not think" or "I think, and it is necessary that I think"—in other words, we are left, after all, with *cogito ergo cogito*, and we then see that the *ergo cogito* is superfluous, and that the first *cogito* is not established but merely asserted. More generally, it can be said that the very notion of "certainties" or "necessary truths" is an attempted amalgamation of truth and implication, a uniting of a proposition with a relation between propositions in the supposition that it has that relation to itself—just as the theory of "ideas" attempts to unite being true and being believed in the supposition of something whose truth resides in its being believed. The conception of "that which establishes itself by *thinking* itself" is, then, only a special case of the general confusion of character and relation. And it is on the same logical footing as that which, as we may put it, establishes itself by establishing itself—the necessary being which must exist (or necessarily is) *because* it is a necessary being.

This last conception may be further elucidated by the consideration, hitherto deferred, of the use of *sum* in the Cartesian formula. Why, it may be asked, does not Descartes confine himself to the "I think" which his method proves, if it proves anything? As his own further argument shows, nothing else that can be attributed to his *ego* can stand the test; it is on that account that he is said to be a thinking essence and nothing more. And that is why such formulae as "I walk, therefore I am" are not accepted as alternatives to the *cogito.* Logically, as far as *sum* is concerned, there *is* no difference between the two cases; "I am walking" implies "I am" no more and no less than "I am thinking" does. In actually distinguishing them, in saying that my walking does not imply existence whereas my thinking does, Descartes is saying that the latter supposition is bound to be *true*, while the former is not. And the only support for this contention is to be found in the non-contradiction of "I think that I walk, but it is possible that I do not walk", i.e., as we have seen, in the non-contradiction of "I think, but it is possible that I do not walk". This, of course, is no more reason for describing my walking as doubtful than is "I walk, but it is possible that I do not think" for describing my thinking as doubtful. But while the fact that my walking is not my thinking is the sole reason for doubting that I walk, and the identity that my thinking is my thinking is the sole reason for asserting that I think, while, in fact, *sum* is equally irrelevant to what is rejected and to what is accepted in accordance with the "method", its inclusion in the latter has the advantage of making it appear something more than an identity, and at the same time conveys its "acceptability".

*Sum*, then, in the first instance, appears in the formula to convey the notion of truth, of a truth which is *added* to the "content", and which, as added by means of *ergo*, appears further as a necessary or guaranteed truth, though nothing has been said or can be said to justify such a notion. The addition, moreover, helps to conceal the fact that truth is already conveyed by the copula of *any* assertion; so that to assert "I am walking" is to assert the truth of "I am walking", and, though this can be questioned, the question is as to the truth of "I am walking" or the truth of "I am not walking", and nothing can be added to the belief in one or the other. There are various propositions which we believe and the contradictories of which we disbelieve; but the *sum* is introduced to make it appear that we can do something more than believing. In the second place it is introduced to give some particularity, some positive character, to the doctrine which is being developed, by emphasising the *ego* as distinct from the *cogitans* or the *cogitatio*. Actually it is impossible on Descartes's theory to distinguish one cogitator or cogitation from another. When he says that he is a substance whose whole essence consists in thinking, he annuls any possible distinction between himself and another thinking substance; yet he is compelled to say so, because his thinking is the one thing that fulfils his conditions of indubitability or "essentiality". The *sum*, then, is a means of smuggling in distinctions, of which, strictly speaking, an essence or "identity" theory can make nothing. In the same way, Socrates falls into inconsistencies when he attempts to distinguish one man from another and, at the same time, to make manhood the essence of all of them. But the fact that we are immediately aware of such distinctions tends to make us, in accepting them, overlook their incompatibility with whatever rationalistic suppositions are in question.

Thirdly, the use of *sum* in the formula is a step towards the establishment of *the* perfect or necessary. In reducing an empirical fact to an essence, Descartes has amalgamated subject and predicate; the fact of "my thinking" is equated to the fact (existence) of "myself". But so long as the distinction remains between existence and what exists, so long as the copula appears even in the distorted form of an attribute, there is a danger of the re-establishment of the distinction between subject and predicate, i.e., of the recognition of facts ("brute" facts, as the phrase goes) which simply have to be learned, instead of being spun out of some essence or "explained" by a "reason". Consistently with this recognition, of course, anything that can be called an explanation is simply a relation among facts and is itself a "brute" fact. To save the Cartesian doctrine of "transparency", then, that which is to be seen through has to be further reduced; the step has to be taken of amalgamating subject and existence, finding something whose essence "comprises" existence. And so we have the verbalism of the ontological argument, the very emptiness of which gives it plausibility, while leaving those who accept it free to fill it out with any material that they prefer—to choose which of two opposite conditions they will call a "perfection" and regard as sustained by *the* perfect. The very fact that there is nothing there makes the essential existence of the essentially existing all the more "transparent" to uncritical minds. And, while there is no *logical* passage from this to minor transparencies, while Descartes is involved in fresh equivocations in trying to show how there can be any essence but Essence, how, in particular, there can be an *ego*, his principle device, as has been suggested, is already present in the notion of "perfection". The *sum*, then, has served its purpose in the fabrication of this rationalistic edifice, both by its identification of an actual thing with an essence and by its treatment of truth as an attribute.

The foregoing argument, if it be sound, shows that criticism of Descartes must be on grounds of logic, and the persistence of rationalistic confusions of the functions of subject, predicate and copula (as in the distinction of an "is" of existence from the "is" of predication, and so forth) shows that such criticism is not of merely historical interest. But it is on the psychological side that Descartes has been specially influential; and, though criticism of rationalistic psychology must still be logical (i.e., must be criticism of rationalism), it is important to bring out the particular ways in which mental events are confused and obscured by Cartesian assumptions. In the first instance, however, it should be observed that those who have followed Descartes in this matter have not in general repeated his argument, that many of them, indeed, have so disguised the introduction of the *cogito* into their theories that they appear to be anti-Cartesian. Thus Berkeley, in the second paragraph of his *Principles*, remarks that "besides all that endless variety of ideas or objects of knowledge, there is likewise something which knows or perceives them, and exercises divers operations, as willing, imagining, remembering about them"; and here the *cogito* is introduced by the use of the simple word *besides*. Again, Hume, in spite of his criticism, later in the *Treatise*, of those philosophers "who imagine we are every moment intimately conscious of what we call our *self*", has assumed the *cogito* from the very beginning in speaking of the objects of our knowledge as "perceptions of the human mind"; i.e., he has assumed, like Berkeley, that they are known *as known* and thus as relative to something else which is on a different footing. And Reid, while in the Introduction to his *Inquiry* he raises explicit objections to the *cogito*, implicitly accepts it, in the same place, in putting forward a doctrine of *inner knowledge* (when he says, e.g., that a man's own mind "is the only subject he can look into"), a doctrine which he adheres to throughout. In all these views, "subject" is set over against "object", self-knowledge against other-knowledge, and thus the Cartesian confusion persists.

The problem naturally arises of relating these two forms of knowledge, and it is just as insoluble as the general problem of relating two essences. We may take for example the way in which Berkeley completes his statement of the position in the paragraph referred to. "This perceiving, active being is what I call *mind, spirit, soul,* or *myself.* By which words I do not denote any one of my ideas, but a thing entirely distinct from them, *wherein they exist,* or, which is the same thing, whereby they are perceived; for the existence of an idea consists in being perceived." (Italics in text.) The minor problem of *how we know* the relation between the thinking essence and a thought essence is one that Berkeley cannot solve. For when he says "I see the table", and since he holds that the table is known by way of "ideas" and the "I" by a "notion" (another form in which he introduces the *cogito*), then, whether the "see" is to be known by way of "idea" or "notion", he cannot say that the whole situation "I see the table" can be known in either way—not, at least, without undermining his whole distinction—and so cannot take it to be known at all. Alexander is placed in a similar difficulty in his Cartesian theory of "enjoyment", since, on his assumptions, "I contemplate the table" can be known neither by enjoyment nor by contemplation—so that he can arrive at a consistent position only by giving up Cartesianism and admitting that there is no knowledge but contemplation.

The more important question, however, is that of the occurrence of the relation itself. For Berkeley, "I" exist in knowing, and the table exists in being known; but the whole situation "I see the table" cannot exist in knowing and cannot exist in being known—it cannot exist as "subject" or as "object". That is to say, with the retention of the essence doctrine, it cannot exist at all. On the other hand, if it does exist, then both "I" and the table exist in that situation, and therefore do not exist, respectively, "in knowing" and "in being known". The difficulty is not met by any "supra-relational" theory, any doctrine of the "relativity" of relations or of objects as "aspects" (or expressions of the essence) of a subject. Any such theory depends for its very statement on the assertion of relations. If the "identity behind the diversity" is not to be the empty "essentially essential", if it is really to be diversely "expressed", then the various expressions are variously related to one another and to that "of" which they are expressions—in fact, we have a set of interrelated situations, no one of which can be "higher" or more essential than any other, since, as we have seen, its superiority would then have no way, higher or lower, of existing. The case can be met only by a logic of situations, which treats mental situations, and non-mental situations, and situations embracing the mental and the non-mental, as all of the same order, none having any peculiar "inwardness" or "outwardness". If we care to put it so, we can call each of them "inward", as having its own character, and "outward", as being distinct from other things. Externality is, of course, a symmetrical relation; when people say that certain things are external to them (or are "in the external world"), they imply that they are external to the things. Thus, if we could take existing in the external world simply to mean existing under conditions of externality, we could say that the mental exists in the external world. And in treating A, B, and A knows B, as alike situations, we are confronted with no greater difficulty than in treating thunder, lightning, and thunder follows lightning, as alike situations—remembering always that situations interpenetrate and exist in wider situations.

Any question of mentality, then, is a question of fact; if we know the mental, we know it as a certain sort of thing, distinct from and related to other sorts of things. And that means that we know it not "inwardly" but outwardly, that it is one of the things which, when we recognise that they are known, we call "objects". If that is not so, if it is a question not of our knowing mentality as a particular sort of thing but of our knowing "mentally", if, in other words, being mental is not a distinguishing-mark of what is known on one occasion rather than another, then it is equally not a distinguishing-mark of what knows but is just another expression for existing. The term "mental", in short, would simply have to be dropped; that is the upshot of Idealism. However, we do speak of the mental, and we do say that minds know, and we think, in saying so, that both the relation and the thing related are different from other things and other relations (e.g., that trees grow). And here as elsewhere, in our knowledge of minds as in our knowledge of trees, it is a question of the assertion of propositions any one of which can be significantly denied, i.e., of the raising of issues which are settled, in each case, by what we believe to be true. We may directly observe the truth in question, or, when we do not (and even sometimes when we do, viz., when other people disagree with us), we may draw inferences from what we have observed (or from what is agreed on). This is the method of settling issues whether in the mental or in the non-mental field, whether the subject is admittedly one of controversy or is allegedly one of "certainty".

Here, incidentally, we may remark on how the procedure of actual inquiry differs from the Cartesian "method". There is, it must be emphasised, no such thing as absolute doubt; there is no question of adopting an attitude of doubting in general or of finding a proposition to be doubtful in itself. We doubt only in relation to what we believe, i.e., to what we do not doubt. If we are doubtful whether A is B, this is possible only if we have some knowledge of both A and B. Descartes himself cannot express his doubts except in terms of what he does not doubt. As we have seen, he assumes from the beginning, as a matter of information, that he thinks; and every word he uses in working out his argument implies something that he does not doubt. It is only because there are certain things that he believes, without doubting, that he can arrive at the view that his senses sometimes deceive him; and there is no question of his thinking that "all is false", since, if a proposition is false, its contradictory is true. Doubt arises, then, only in particular cases, and is settled not by what is indubitable but by what is believed. Propositions are not doubtful or certain; we doubt and are certain—and sometimes when we are certain, we are wrong. Thus we may hold with assurance certain propositions about ourselves or our minds; alternatively, we may be doubtful about them, or we may have our assertions challenged. Such an issue can be settled only by observation and inference from observations. And, in particular, the class of propositions (variously placed and dated) "I am thinking" has among its members some that have been doubted and none that could not be made a matter of controversy. As we have seen, it is only the mechanism of identity and ambiguity that makes this appear to be an exceptional case.

It may be argued, of course, that, even if the matter *is* a controversial one, even if we can make mistakes about the "subject" as we can about "objects", that is no reason for confusing the two—that there can be an empirical inquiry into the facts of the "subjective" life. What we have to remember here is that the "subjectivists" are dealing, however confusedly, with certain actualities. In the same way, Descartes started with knowledge of his thinking as a fact, and it was this fact that he erected into an essence or certainty; this explains how some who would reject the ontological argument, are still prepared to accept the *cogito*, though actually without the general notion of that which is in itself there would be no special notion of that which thinks itself. So, the familiar arguments regarding "subject" and "object" start from the fact that in the situation of knowledge there are the two things, what knows and what is known, and thus that we are falsifying the situation if we confuse the two, just as we should do if, in the relation of eating, we confused the eater with the eaten. But, erroneous as this would be, and while it is possible that an eater should never be eaten, it also happens that some eaters are eaten. Now, when the subjectivists say that we are falsifying a "subject" if we represent it as an object, they are saying that what knows can never be known. And while, if they adhered to that, they would have to say that there can be no theory of what knows, they make confusion worse confounded by holding that the knower is *always* known—only not known as an object, but known in its true character as knower; in other words, known by the inner or identical knowledge of the *cogito*.

The virulent rationalism of this doctrine is evident. It is only on the assumption of a knowing *essence* that it could be supposed that, if X knows, to know X is to know that it knows. Further, it is only if knowing is the "whole nature" of what knows that it can be argued that the very same thing which had an object could not be an object in another relationship. Eater and eaten are distinct, yet what eats may be eaten. Above and below are distinct, yet what is above something is always below something else. The "domain" and the "converse domain" of a relation can have any relation from co-extension to exclusion; we can determine the matter only empirically in each case, and we do constantly make such statements as that we know X and X knows Y. Indeed, in saying these things, we profess to have knowledge of what knows and what is known by a single act and in a single situation, i.e., as objects occurring within a more extensive object, and the bare assertion that "the knower is not the known" casts not the slightest doubt on these contentions. The weakness of the theory of "subject" appears finally in the treatment of a *relation*, knowing, as the "nature" of what knows. Certainly, as Leibniz saw, if we are going to have a theory of natures, we shall have to bring its relations within each nature—but he himself could explain away some relations only by bringing in others, and it is, as we have noted, on the question of relations that rationalism most conspicuously breaks down. As regards knowledge, then, there is nothing in the subjectivist argument (and likewise nothing in experience) to confute the views that, if something knows, it need not be known, that, if it is known, it need not be known that it knows, and that, if it is known and even known to know, it is what we call an "object"—or, what is more important, it is a situation or occurrence, differing in quality from other things that know and from things that do not know, just as they differ from one another.

Thus there is no question of setting mind apart from objects, of giving it a special way of being known (any more than of existing), viz., "in itself"; the only questions are whether minds are known and, if so, what is known about them, what situations they are found to exist in, what other things they are distinguished from and connected with. The theory of "subject", denying that minds are anything in particular, leads straight to the denial of mind altogether in the doctrine of behaviourism. Now behaviourism is to be commended in that it insists on dealing with what is observed and rejecting the "inner light". Those who hold that there are two sources of psychological knowledge, "introspection" of ourselves and observation of the behaviour of others (and of ourselves also, since this forms the link between the other two), are in as untenable a position as we have seen Berkeley's to be; they can establish no connection between the "introspected" and the observed—or else they are supposing such a combination of inner and outer knowledge as simply annuls the distinction. But, since the behaviourists do not realise that minds are observed just as other things are, they have to treat the mental as simply a name for certain sequences, so that, whereas in the ordinary course of things A is observed to be followed by B, in the "mental" course of things C and not B is found to follow. On this view, "mind" means a magical setting aside of the course of nature. The only scientific attitude is to admit a difference not in the types of sequence, but in the antecedent conditions in the two cases, and to try to discover what that difference is. And this is something that we quite frequently do; we have indeed a wide knowledge of mental qualities (kinds of emotion); the only thing we are not acquainted with is mental "inwardness".

It is worth emphasising that knowledge of mind is obtained as much by observation of other people's minds as by observation of our own. The knowledge of other minds presents insuperable difficulties for the subjectivist. Unless it is to be said that we are "members of one another" (i.e., unless we are to adopt the "aspect" theory, the theory of one ultimate Subject, which culminates in the denial of all distinctions), it must be admitted that we cannot have inner knowledge of another "subject", and yet, according to subjectivism, we should be falsifying it in knowing it as an object. Alexander's attempt to get over the difficulty by his theory of "assurance" merely adds to the original problem of relating the enjoyed to the contemplated an equally insoluble problem of relating the "assured" to either. The theory is so far valuable, however, in that "assurance" is taken to be a form of direct knowledge; what is required to complete the argument is the rejection of the conception of "subject" (in the form, in this particular case, of the "enjoyed") or of "self"—as if a mind itself and a stone itself were not alike just a mind and a stone. Once this is done, it can no more be contended that, as physiologists, we are interested in other minds only in a secondary and subsidiary way, and that our own minds remain as the essential subject of our inquiries and the test of all the rest, than that, as psychologists, we are primarily concerned with own bodies and only secondarily with others. On the contrary, much of our knowledge of ourselves is arrived at through our knowledge of others, and, while we can make mistakes in either connection, we are at least (as Marx has pointed out) not in the habit of taking a man's own estimate of himself as likely, on account of its "intimacy", to be the best we can obtain—least of all, as being "certain", though on the subjectivist theory it would have to be.

As already indicated, the question of the knowledge of mind has been especially confused by the taking of a relation, thinking, as the mind's "nature"; and this applies equally to the question of the conditions under which minds exist. Thus the doctrine of psycho-physical parallelism is vitiated from the start by the fact that what is supposed to run parallel to brain processes is "thought", and this, in the usual sense of what is thought, is commonly not mental at all. There is, of course, the additional objection that parallelism (like correspondence) merely suggests a relation without stating what the relation is—just as the contention that "thought is a function of the brain" is defective in not stating *what* function it is. Nevertheless, none but subjectivist objections have ever been urged to the view that it is certain brain processes that think and also that it is certain brain processes that are mental (emotional), i.e., that in the parallelist theory the psychical has been put on the wrong side. The main *logical* point is that, when we say "A is parallel to B", we are asserting the existence of a situation of the same order as any that can be said to exist in either of the "parallel series" and so are failing to keep the series separate. But this does not prevent but rather assists the putting forward of the psychological position that, in the case of what is thought, the "parallelism" between it and brain processes is just the *cognitive* relation, i.e., that they know or think it, and that, in the case of what thinks (assuming this to be mental), the "parallelism" is just *predication*, i.e., that certain brain processes *are* mental. As has been said, the only objections to this commonsense view are based on the doctrine of "subject", which is also responsible for the widespread belief that what is mental must think—a belief which has had a retarding influence on the acceptance of the important contributions of Freud and his followers to psychology.

In this connection we may consider the arguments of Feuerbach (as outlined by Sidney Hook[2]) against "absolute materialism"—all the more because it is principally with this form of materialism, and with some justice, according to Hook, in view of his later work, that the name of Feuerbach is associated. "To say that thought is a material activity is as senseless as to say that gravitation has a taste or smell, for according to Feuerbach a proposition has meaning only when the predicate is of the same generic kind (*Gattung*) as the subject." Here we have a direct, but easily answered, attack on a situational logic. There is no such thing as gravitation in general, there is only what gravitates; and it is *not* senseless to say that what gravitates has a taste or smell. Any difficulty there is in calling thought a material activity is due to the fact that thought is a relation, just as there would be difficulty in saying that "on" or "after" was a material activity. But there is no difficulty at all, when A is on B, in saying that A is a material activity, and B is too, and while it might be false to say that *A's being on B* is a material activity, it would not be senseless. In other words, A, B, and A's being on B are alike situations, which we have to observe to see what characters they respectively have and what they have not. Similarly, there is nothing senseless in saying that what thinks is a material activity or that what is thought is a material activity or

---

[2] Article on "Feuerbach" in the *Modern Monthly* (New York) for December, 1935; section on "Critique of Absolute Materialism", pp. 366–370. [Reprinted in Hook's *From Hegel to Marx* (Gollancz, 1936), pp. 238,9.]

THE *COGITO* OF DESCARTES (1936)   143

even (though it may not be true) that A's thinking B is a material activity. We can settle such questions not on the basis of forms of predication (ways of being, characterisation of a thing in its own "categories"), which, as we have seen, can never be related, but only on the basis of observation—assuming, in this particular case, that we know what quality "materiality" is.

"To call thinking a function of the brain", says Feuerbach, "is to say nothing about *what* thinking is.... Such a characterisation does not characterise.... Thought must be something *more* than, something quite *different* from, a mere activity of the brain". (Italics in Hook's text.) We have seen that there is a certain amount of force in the objection to the "function" formula; and, even if we say that the brain thinks, it is true that we are not then saying what thinking is, just as, when we say that A is on B, we are not saying what "being on" is—though we may know it perfectly well. But certainly we cannot know relations without having some knowledge of the things related, and thus it is false to say that "it is only in terms of thought that the nature of thinking can be understood". This contention is plausible only because "thought" is commonly used to mean both terms of the relation as well as the relation itself. If we adhere strictly to Feuerbach's description of thought as the *product* of thinking, we cannot admit that anything is to be understood by understanding something else that it is related to, whether the relation be "producing" or any other.

Again, Feuerbach takes up an equivocal position in the matters of the "more" and the "different". If thought *is not* a brain-activity, there is no point in saying that it is "more" than a "mere" brain-activity. If it comes to that, any brain-activity is more than a mere brain-activity, any X is more than a mere X, i.e., it is not the "nature", X. In other words, any brain process differs from other brain processes, and any mental process, if it is a brain process, will differ from other mental processes, from other brain processes, and from other processes of whatever kind—while at the same time there will be respects in which it does not differ from such other processes. Thus there is no question of "mereness" (except for rationalists); there is only the question whether mental processes actually are brain processes, and Feuerbach has said nothing to show that they are not.

It is Feuerbach, indeed, who is treating mentality as "mere", or treating it merely as producing "ideas". It is not true that "the clue to our mentality is *what* we think", though it is certainly *a* clue, granted that we already have some knowledge of mentality and its relations. There can be no objection to the "study of ideas" (i.e., of our demands), a study which will involve us in a broader consideration of the movements in which we are caught up, and which greatly affect our mentality. It has always to be remembered that minds exist under conditions, and that we cannot study them without taking account of some of these conditions. Actually, this is just what Feuerbach seems to neglect; at least, although he holds that without body there can be no mind, the proposal to treat of mind in its own terms leads logically not, as Hook says, to a *relative* autonomy of thought but to an unconditioned or self-conditioned mental sphere—in fact, it leaves us with nothing more or less than the *cogito*. Rejecting rationalism, however, recognising the interconnection of situations, we have still to insist on the *distinction*, as well as the connection, between mind and its surroundings—and also, of course, on the fact that it conditions or affects them just as they affect it. This is a matter which has been inadequately grasped in the Marxist movement; the interest in mentality has been almost entirely subordinated to an interest in the larger social movements into which minds enter. And, while this has occasioned many mistakes in regard to these movements themselves, it is itself facilitated by the *cogito*, from which no Marxist thinkers have shaken themselves free. For, when mind is treated as a bare identity, it is natural that anything else will be discussed rather than mind—on this assumption, indeed, there is nothing to discuss.

It will be seen, then, that acceptance of the *cogito* has been an abiding fetter on the observation of minds, and that its decisive rejection is a condition of any considerable progress in psychological science. It has been observed that there is no logical difference between observation of mental processes in oneself and observation of them in others; the ordinary person does both, and it would appear that the psychologist advances most rapidly when he develops both. Certainly there are difficulties, constant possibilities of error, involved in the observation of minds; we regularly make mistakes both about ourselves and about other people, and even the trained analyst, though he has found out many of the mistakes to avoid, is obviously not infallible. But this brings us at once to the point that there are difficulties in the observation of anything; and the way to meet them is just to follow out the general conditions of inquiry—particularly, the forming of hypotheses and the testing of them by what we *can* observe. Acceptance of the *cogito*, however, places insuperable difficulties in the way of psychological science; and, in so far as it has been accepted, i.e., granted that even those who have accepted it have inevitably reverted from time to time to commonsense views and that only so have discoveries been made, it has been a tremendous hindrance to inquiry.

Much could be said about the psychological basis of the doctrine itself—about the fetishism which lies at the root of all rationalism, about the motives which lead men to seek the "safe and certain", about the very close connection between the notion of "salvation" and that of the *ego*. Much could be said, again, about its social connections, about the appearance of the *cogito* in a period of rising individualism, and so forth. But, interesting as these questions may be, they are at any rate subsequent to its logical rebuttal. And, considering it simply from that point of view, we can still describe it as one of the greatest impositions in the history of human thinking.

# 11
# "UNIVERSALS" AND OCCURRENCES (1929)

"To deny the universal is to make discourse impossible; both to deny the universal and still to discourse is to contradict oneself." The position I uphold against this view would be expressed, with all the clarity I desire, by the substitution of "assert" for "deny". I can thus bring my argument with Mr Merrylees to a sharper issue than was possible in the general references to idealism in the two articles referred to,[1] although I think that they contained answers to many of the difficulties that have now been raised.

What prevents Mr Merrylees from seeing some of the implications of those arguments is just his obsession with "universals" (the universal being something which is *a* universal, and yet is not particular) and, in connection therewith, with "reality" (i.e., that which is everything but is not anything). Such is the force of this obsession that he actually refers for support to Plato's *Sophist*—a dialogue which, in conjunction with the *Parmenides* and the *Theaetetus*, affords the most decisive refutation of idealist logic that has ever been presented. It is perhaps natural that Mr Merrylees makes no reference to the *Parmenides*; he must find it exceedingly difficult to reconcile that dialogue with his assumption that the theories of the *Sophist* and the *Phaedo* are identical. I shall endeavour to weaken that assumption by playing Parmenides to his Socrates.

To begin with, he professes to agree with me in standing by the proposition, but considers that my objection to kinds of truth amounts to no more than the familiar truth that "to judge is to assert that reality is so and so". It amounts, in fact, to something very different. Mr Merrylees has committed himself straightaway to kinds of assertion, and his upholding of the proposition consists in reducing it to a term—of another proposition! It should be evident that if we are able to assert that reality is so and so, then we are equally able to assert "so and so" without the reality. On the other hand, if the latter assertion requires interpretation, so does

---

[1] John Anderson, "Empiricism" (*A.J.P.P.*, Vol. V., No. 4) and "Determinism and Ethics" (*A.J.P.P.*, Vol. VI, No. 4)—commented on by W. A. Merrylees, in Discussion, "Some Features of Professor Anderson's Logic" (*A.J.P.P.*, Vol. VII, No. 2).

the former. If, to take the familiar Bosanquettian formulation, "A is B" means "Reality is such that A is B", then that again means "Reality is such that Reality is such that A is B"; and so on. This infinite regress, like others which I have employed in the articles in question, is merely a way of indicating an initial contradiction; it serves to emphasise the fact that if we can understand and accept the second proposition without further "reference", the same applies to the first. *Is* A B? The "reference to reality" can have no other effect than to obscure this clear issue.

And just as it is impossible to introduce "Reality" into the proposition, so it is impossible to introduce any of the "universals" of which Mr Merrylees speaks. A particular good, we are told, is "the Good in one of its particular expressions or embodiments". To say that "X is good", then, means that "X is a particular expression or embodiment of the Good", or, more briefly, that "X is expressive of the Good". It follows that this, being interpreted, means that "X is expressive of the Expressive of the Good"; and so on. Is it not clear that we can understand the interpretation only if we could have understood the original proposition without it? And is it not equally clear that the introduction of "the Good" *is* an attempt to get behind the proposition, since there is nothing about "the Good" in the original statement? In brief, if Mr Merrylees interprets propositions in this way, he can, like Socrates, be confronted with a "third man" (and a fourth man and a fifth man) for whom there is no room in his theory. And, since he professes to find support in the *Sophist*, will he tell us that "Theaetetus is sitting" means that Theaetetus is an expression or embodiment of the Sedentary?

The fact indicated by such infinite regresses is that the theory of forms or universals—as expounded by Socrates in the *Phaedo*, and refuted by Parmenides in the *Parmenides*—suffers from a fundamental contradiction. "The Good", we are told, is not a particular. What, then, is so "the" about it? Is it not, in accordance with this theory, not only *a particular universal* (and even if that is denied of "the Good", even if it is distinguished from other universals as the universal universal, is not its distinction from them a particularisation of it?) but actually the only thing which is particularly or specifically good? "No particular expresses the universal completely, the universal is, as Plato", i.e., Socrates in the *Phaedo*, "pointed out in regard to the idea of equality, an ideal which is not completely realised in any particular". And such ideals, Mr Merrylees goes on to say, are "essential to discourse". What has discourse to say to this? Obviously that ideals are *particular* essentials of discourse! Again, Socrates, in his discourse, says that two sticks are imperfectly equal. The form of equality, then, is not in question here. The sticks embody or express "imperfect equality", and they embody it *perfectly*. In short, as the *Parmenides* shows, we can maintain the doctrine of ideals only by describing things in terms which do not apply to them, but all the time we are using terms which do apply to them, and so are contradicting the doctrine of ideals.

It is, then, not the denial of universals, but the assertion of them, that contradicts discourse; there is nothing in the proposition about "the Good" or any other such entity. There is admittedly a distinction between subject and predicate, but this is a difference of function, not of kind; and granted that the function of the predicate is to characterise or describe, the very same term can also have the function of indicating, i.e., can be the subject of another proposition. Thus, every term, as a possible description of something else, has universality or characterises, and, as a possible indication of something else, has particularity or locates. In describing things as "particulars" I merely meant to emphasise this function of locating, and not to deny to them the capacity for characterising. That even Socrates in the *Phaedo* is unable to maintain a distinction between particulars and universals is easily shown. "Those things which are possessed by the number three must not only be three in number, but must also be odd." Socrates, i.e., is introducing syllogism, an example of which would be, "The Graces are three; three is odd, therefore the Graces are odd". Now in one of the premises here three is a "particular", an instance of oddness; in the other it is a "universal", a character of the Graces. And, unless it is precisely the same term, there is no argument. We can go on, as Socrates does, to say that odd is not even; we might also say "These are the Graces". But, apart from the question whether every term may have either function, the fact that any one term can function in these two ways is sufficient to dispose of the doctrine of "universals".

Mr Merrylees, in face of this difficulty, would apparently maintain that in the proposition we have *two* universals, or "a connection of contents". But the question is—*What* connection? Both terms, no doubt, are capable of being predicates, but in the actual proposition only one is. Subject and predicate, then, must have different functions; "sugar is soluble" and "soluble is sugar" are different statements. Now in describing the former by saying that "solubility" is located in, or that it characterises, sugar, we are not suggesting (and cannot do so without departing from the standpoint of the proposition) that there is such a thing as the Soluble, or as solubility in general. We can explain the use of an "abstract term" like solubility by saying that it is a contraction for "being soluble", i.e., for propositions of the form "X is soluble", however X may be specified in any particular case; or, again, it may be taken to mean the fact that there *are* soluble things, that certain things have certain characters, just as the term "man" means, if we adopt for the sake of argument the conventional definition, the fact that some animals are rational. In these ways we keep to the proposition; but, in speaking of "the Soluble", we should be taking the predicate apart from its function in the proposition.

In terms of occurrence, on the other hand, we can distinguish the functions of subject, predicate and copula; the subject is the region within which the occurrence takes place, the predicate is the sort of occurrence it is, and the copula is its occurring. This theory is not, like the doctrine of "universals", an attempt to get behind the proposition, because, instead of giving a special explanation of individual elements, it deals with the proposition as a whole—as a complex arrangement, S is P. In taking *is* as occurrence, i.e., as involving Space and Time, we are taking it as it appears in the proposition, in relation to a subject and a predicate, and indicating by its position both their connection and the difference of their functions. If we adopt the Bosanquettian position that there is no difference, both being "contents" and all relations being "ultimately" symmetrical, then we are putting ourselves at odds with discourse. Something must be made of the copula. In this connection, the formula of Mr Merrylees, "If sugar, then soluble", is simply not a proposition at all. We can see what it means only by bringing back the copula. That meaning would be better expressed by "Where sugar, there soluble", or, again, by "Sugar acts solubly", but these expressions are not really additions to, or improvements on, what is conveyed by "Sugar *is* soluble".

In choosing this example Mr Merrylees has overlooked the necessity of distinguishing between the question of universal propositions ("connections of contents") and that of "potentialities". I cannot here discuss the latter question fully. But I see little or no difficulty in saying that "Sugar is soluble" does mean that all lots of sugar which are introduced into a solvent *are* dissolved. Mr Merrylees prefers to say that it means that sugar is "of such a nature" that the above occurrence takes place, or would take place if the introduction in question had first occurred. The most, I think, that can be made of this reference to "natures" is that the proposition really stands for two "propositions": (1) All things of the character X, which are introduced into a solvent, are dissolved; (2) all lots of sugar are X. Obviously, until X is specified, these are not propositions. But it may quite well be that, when we say that sugar is soluble, we have in mind some vague notion of a character which would fulfil these conditions. Taking X as this character, then, I grant that the second proposition does not say that introduction into a solvent has taken place. But the first one does, and, in addition, the second asserts the occurrence of the "X-ness" of sugar, i.e., of sugar's being X. It is not, I agree, a question of "evidence", but of the fact. And it would appear that, in calling the fact a "connection of contents" and in specifying this connection as a "hypothetical" one, Mr Merrylees is really confusing between the propositions "All lots of sugar are X" and "All lots of sugar, which are introduced into a solvent, are dissolved". This confusion is responsible for the suggestion that there is a "hypothetical" reference to dissolving. But when these two propositions, as well as proposition (1), have been clearly stated, we can see that they are all different, but that nothing has been said to show that they are not all occurrences. And so with "potentiality" in general; if there is in any substance something that we can call a potentiality of its, then its having that potentiality *occurs*; if not, the reference to potentiality is a mere confusion.

Leaving aside potentialities, then, and taking the proposition "Sugar is sweet", which would be as much entitled to be called a "connection of contents" as the proposition previously employed, we can hardly avoid asserting that the sweetness of sugar occurs in space and time. In fact, this is merely an emphatic way of saying that sugar *is* sweet, comparable to saying that the sweetness of sugar is a *fact* or that any proposition is *true*; this method of statement indicating that the occurrence stated in the proposition may also be a term in another proposition; e.g., the sweetness of sugar (or sugar's being sweet) is a source of pleasure to many persons. Similarly, having said that "This is red", we can go on to make statements of which "this red" (or this red thing) is the subject. Mr Merrylees seems to think that this is a particularly good example of a "particular". But, as I have pointed out, "sugar" in the proposition mentioned and "this" in "This is read" are also particulars, i.e., subjects. And, being subjects, they can be predicates. Mr Merrylees appears to hold that there *are* "particulars", even though they cannot be known apart from propositions, just as he holds that there are "universals". Now it would certainly seem that expressions like "this" are commonly applied only to subjects. But that is because they contain, besides a certain term, the sign of quantity which goes with the subject; the same term could be predicate, but it would not take the sign of quantity with it. (The theory of quantification of the predicate, it may be noted, resembles that of connection of contents in failing to distinguish the functions of subject and predicate.) Briefly, then, "this" means "the thing indicated", "thing indicated" can be a predicate, and "the" is a sign of quantity like "all" and "some", and is in fact equivalent to "all". It is from confusion between the function a term has in a proposition (there being various signs of what that function may be) and the term itself that the doctrine of "universals" (and of "particulars" conceived in opposition to "universals") arises.

The point which Mr Merrylees most insists on, however, is not that a term may have different functions, but that it may have the same function, in different propositions. There are many true propositions of the form "X is good", and, if we say that all these propositions have *the same predicate*, we have to explain what exactly this "predicate" is, that occurs in all these different places. Now it may be noted, in the first place, that this question would not arise at all unless the various things really had the character in question; if they only had something *like* it, then the peculiar character of each would occur once only. Accordingly we do not require to introduce repetition in order to understand a thing's being of a certain sort; a single proposition tells us that, and we have no occasion to think of the "sort" as a peculiar kind of "recurrent" entity. But there is no more difficulty about having propositions which tell us that other things are of that sort than about having propositions which tell us that that thing is of other sorts or has other characters. Any occurrence is the occurrence of a certain sort of thing; that is already indicated in the inter-relation of the constituents of any one proposition.

But there is nothing whatever in propositions with the same predicate to indicate that the various subjects are "members of a system", which is "pervaded" by that "universal". The Parmenidean objections to this position have already been indicated. Here it may simply be said that the propositions "X is good" and "Y is good" justify no inference whatever as to a relation between X and Y. The fact that various things are good is no proof that the history of any one has anything to do with the history of any other, or that they are in any way *collected*. That Mr Merrylees means more by "belonging to a system" than "having a common predicate" appears from his treatment of desires which "are all members of the system of Desire"; the fact that "our actual desires conflict with one another" *means* "that they are imperfect realisations of the universal". What becomes of the proposition now? There is certainly nothing in the attribution of the same character to different things to tell us that they cannot conflict. The argument seems to be—if two men quarrel, they are not both "perfect" (i.e., good) men; therefore, they are not both *perfectly* human. Now, apart from the fact that goodness is just as specific a character as humanity, we have here again the "third (or perfect) man". These Socratic shifts will not serve. Nor will the dragging in of self-realisation by expressing the universal of "my desires" as "myself", and by saying that the subject *is* an "attempt to realise" the universal, and thus introducing a new universal which again the particular has to attempt to realise. It is interesting to notice that the attempt to get behind the proposition is made for the sake of that orderliness which Socrates mistook for goodness, but it adds nothing to the logical refutation.

Much could be said in criticism of Mr Merrylees's concluding attack on the realist position, but I propose only to touch on a few points. The fundamental idealist fallacy comes out in the statement that if we do ascribe certain characters to things (and Mr Merrylees admits that we do), "we can do so only *in virtue of* our sensations". It may be true that we know certain things only when our mind is affected in a certain way, but it does not follow that we know that mental effect, still less that it is through knowing it that we know things. Knowledge of things is knowledge of knowledge of things—another infinite regress. The real point is that, when we ascribe certain characters to things, they may *have* these characters, in which case we are right, or they may not, in which case we are wrong; but, in either case, their having some characters is just as much a matter of absolute fact as *our* having characters. Why should we say that the water is hot "on the strength of" any sensation? If it is the sensation that it is hot, we have no occasion to speak of the water at all. On the other hand, if we do distinguish the water and the sensation, we can do so only by recognising each to have characters of its own.

Further, Mr Merrylees gives no reason for assuming that the same thing cannot have both the qualities, hot and cold. But even if it were admitted that hot is not a quality but a relation, meaning, for example, "hotter than my hand", it would be impossible to say *what* was hotter without recognising some of its qualities; and not the slightest reason is or could be advanced for saying that all supposed qualities are in the same position, so that green would mean "greener than my eye", etc. The general weakness of the argument is clearly indicated in the monstrous concluding fallacy—primary qualities exist in relation to secondary qualities, secondary qualities are characters of our attitudes, therefore primary qualities also are characters of our attitudes. The argument is not stated precisely in that way, but that is what it means. The ingenuity of Mr Merrylees fails to conceal the fact that we do talk about things, and that, unless we could distinguish them from our attitudes, there would be nothing for us to take up an attitude to. Our taking up the attitude is one occurrence, the thing attended to is another; and the fact that we know it and discourse about it does not entitle us to say that we, any more than "reality", are such that it is. For this, as before, implies that we can attribute an independent meaning to the statement that "it is".

## 12
# CAUSALITY AND LOGIC (1936)

The refutation of indeterminism is rendered difficult, or, at least, deficient in persuasiveness, by the fact that, like all rationalist theories, it necessarily embodies a certain amount of empirical fact. Thus the indeterminist will meet accusations of ignoring facts by saying, "But I have *also* admitted that that is so"; he will adopt such devices as the "in so far as", so that any demonstration of causal necessity will hold of things only in so far as they are necessitated, and will leave it possible for them to proceed quite otherwise in so far as they are free. While, however, it would be too laborious to pursue the indeterminist through all the shifts by which he tries to defend his position, the consideration of some of them may help to bring out the main issues. When, for example, in supporting man's freedom, he "also" admits necessitation in nature, he prompts the determinist to bring up the important point that there is no distinction whatever between man and nature (and hence no question of a false or forced analogy between the two), that "nature" means no more and no less than *what is*, and that a theory of the conditions of existence, embodying a general theory of causality, will apply indifferently to men and any other existing things.

It is to be noted, at least, that, in default of the presentation of such a general theory, any discussion of supposed peculiarities of human causality is quite beside the mark. Moreover, this general theory will not be affected by the appeal to special cases in the attempt to find a "negative instance". The determinist may quite well admit that he *does not know* the determining cause of a particular mental event; but this will no more lead him to doubt the truth of determinism than a similar ignorance in the case of a non-mental event would do. In fact, if causal necessitation were an "unproved and unprovable assumption" in respect of mental events, it would be equally so in respect of other events. It is not surprising that indeterminists should avoid this extreme position, the unscientific and mythological character of which is only too apparent. But without giving some ground for belief in causal

CAUSALITY AND LOGIC (1936)    155

necessitation in "nature", they cannot show that this ground is *lacking* in the case of man; and if they do give such a ground, it will be seen to cover the case of any "humanity" with which we are acquainted—apart from the point, previously noted, that humanity is in any case included in the subject-matter of logic ("what is") and comes under the logical theory of causality.

Something may be said here about the kind of "proof" that is possible on a point of logic. As regards direct argument, one may attempt to show, in the manner of Alexander (largely following Kant), that a thing *as spatio-temporal* exhibits a certain character, e.g., that it occupies a definite place in a regular sequence of a certain type. To speak of a thing, it may be said, is to speak of certain "ways of working", the continuance and the development of which are, of course, affected by the other ways of working by which the thing is surrounded. It would be argued, in this way, that it is a condition of a thing's existence that it determines and is determined by other things, and that to investigate or "give an account of" it involves consideration of such determinations. Thus, to give an account of any actual thing that could be called "initiative" would be to exhibit certain regularities, to present it, in the common phrase, as "subject to laws", including those which "govern" its relations to other sorts of things which, in any particular instance, may or may not be present. In other words, discounting metaphysical notions of "governing" and restricting ourselves to a positive account of interrelated ways of working, we should treat the occurrence of "initiative" in the human mind in exactly the same logical way as we should treat the occurrence of magnetism in a pin.

The above remarks suggest a less direct treatment of logical problems, viz., by considering what is involved in the recognition of a thing as a subject of investigation—more generally, in the very possibility of "discourse". This is, of course, the traditional approach (the "Socratic" approach) to logic; it leads up to and does not abrogate the consideration of what is involved in the recognition of the thing as existing; it is only in terms of existence that we can, in the end, criticise discourse. But this way of expressing the matter brings out the point that, in rejecting a particular logical theory, we should be able to show that the exponent of it not merely has a false view of existence but implicitly, in his own statement of the case, admits the view that we are upholding against him (as when a person *argues* against objective implication or *denies* objective truth). A particularly important instance is that of the demonstration, by the upholder of a spatio-temporal logic, of the fact that those who argue that certain things (e.g., minds) are *not* spatio-temporal, cannot avoid implying that they are. Again, indirect "proof" of a logical position may take the form of showing that our opponent's view involves him in insoluble problems—though this amounts to the same as contradicting the possibility of discourse. At any rate, while bringing out the insoluble problems of indeterminism is not the most rigorous proof of determinism, it may well be the most effective and would seem to be an essential preliminary.

The question of complete indeterminism need scarcely be argued here; it will perhaps be admitted that such a position cannot consistently give any description of anything—not even that of being "undetermined". The position confronting us is that which upholds determination and also indetermination. And this position can be met by the regular arguments against any attempt to divide reality into "realms" (in effect, to have more than one logic or theory of being)—and particularly, as I have indicated in a number of papers, by the demonstration of the impossibility of finding any *relation* between the different realms; so that there will be a "universe" of complete determination and *another* "universe" of complete indetermination. If it were true, as Dr Loughnan says,[1] that "the doctrine of free will has nothing to say about the realm of physical science, neither explicitly nor by logical implication", this would mean that free will had no physical effects, that it "subsisted" in entire separation from the physical—and so, apart from other difficulties, we should be back, on the side of the free, at complete indetermination: in fact, nonentity.

But if it is contended that the free acts on the determined (if the usual "interactionist" position is taken up), then the upshot is that there is no determination, no "law", anywhere. For any physical "uniformity" is to the effect that a certain set of physical antecedents gives place to a certain set of physical consequents; but, with the intervention of a free agent, the very same set of

---

[1] "Determinism and Responsibility", by H. B. Loughnan; *A.J.P.P.*, September, 1936, p. 217.

physical antecedents will have a different set of physical consequents. It is surely clear that if, with no physical difference in the antecedents, there is a different physical sequence, then there can be no physical uniformity. This is simply an illustration of the impossibility of combining the free and the determined in any situation. For the determinist, of course, there is no difficulty. For, while in any case he holds the mental to be physical, the recognition of the occurrence of a certain sequence *except when* some other factor intervenes is a commonplace of the theory of physical interactions. To deny "interactionism" (interaction between different realms or levels of reality) is not to deny interaction. To state, e.g., that two substances combine in a certain way except when a third substance is present is still to state a uniformity, and leaves it possible to determine the "uniform" action of the third substance. But, as has been shown, the operation of a *non*-uniform factor would destroy all uniformities.

The argument is not affected by the adoption of a theory of a partly determined and partly free mind or, again, a theory of what we may call "inclining" but not necessitating causes. In the former case, the same problem as before arises in connection with the relation of the mind's free activities to other activities, mental or non-mental, and the additional difficulty of the same thing's having free and unfree parts is scarcely worth considering. In the latter case, the difficulty is the same; for, if we have a condition which is necessary but not sufficient for a certain result and this result nevertheless occurs, we simply have an arbitrary and occult factor contributing the remaining part of what is necessary—and, as before, this really means giving up uniformity. Either, in fact, we have necessary and sufficient conditions all the way, or we have something "causa sui", which, mysteriously, is *also* the cause of something else—and it is no more possible to connect the self-causing with the other-causing of such an entity than to connect the determined and the undetermined in general.

In conclusion, it may be said that the selection of mind as a bearer of freedom is not due to any special interest in mind. Those who are interested in mind's workings will naturally take up a determinist position. The indeterminists are those with an axe to grind, with certain "values" to defend, with the view that certain things *ought to be* or *are to be done*. Theoretical concern with what is the case is, it seems to me, coextensive with determinism.

13
# THE PROBLEM OF CAUSALITY (1938)

Causality resembles the other main issues of logical investigation in that it presents the mind with puzzles. Hume's question, "Why a cause is always necessary", and the question why the same cause should always have the same effect, are examples of difficulties which have recurred throughout the history of thought. This is not to say that such difficulties cannot be got over; it merely indicates at once the importance of an exact logic and the tendency of the human mind to depart from or fail to reach exactness. It will be argued here that by the use of certain logical considerations (and particularly by emphasis on the notion of a *field*) the outstanding difficulties can be removed and a straightforward theory of causality developed.

We may take our departure from the question, often asked, why it is not just as natural and defensible to think that the same phenomenon has different causes, or the same agent different effects, on the various occasions of its occurrence, as to suppose an invariable order of events. The preliminary answer (allowing for distinctions to be developed later) is that, on the assumption of variability, we could not say that there was any causal connection at all. We could, of course, point out some succession of phenomena in any given case; but we could not say that the later phenomenon in question was any more "the successor" of the earlier one than anything whatever that occurred at the later time—and similarly with the notion of a "predecessor". It may be that, when X occurs, we rightly anticipate Y, but, since this anticipation may also be rightly made in the absence of X, we have no right to say that it was X, and not some other factor W, that was the occasion of Y's appearance in the former case. In fact, we have no right to say that anything is "the occasion of" anything else.

According to Mill, in the consideration of Plurality of Causes as a case actually occurring in nature, "there is required no peculiar method. When an effect is really producible by two or more causes, the process for detecting them is in no way different from that by which we discover single causes" (*System of Logic*, Bk. III,

Ch. X, § 3). But the process of "discovering single causes", as he has expounded it, is one of excluding the irrelevant, by the consideration that that in the absence of which the phenomenon occurs, and that in the presence of which the phenomenon does not occur, is not its cause. The admission of "plurality" involves the abandonment of this position, and it would appear that any one of the "two or more causes" could just as easily be broken up—so that we are left with no method of discovery or even of elimination.

The point is that, in distinguishing the relevant from the irrelevant, that is to say, the necessary from the unnecessary, we are concerned with *general* conditions (necessity being equivalent to universality), and, if we do not find a general condition of a given occurrence, we are not answering the question that has been raised. If it were not a general question, a question of "sorts of things" and not of "mere particulars", we should have no right to speak of the irrelevant or, as already suggested, of a "connection". But it always is a general question. When we ask, for example, what causes this fire, it is not its being *this* but its being *fire* that we are seeking to account for. There might, indeed, be a special question of what causes fire here rather than anywhere else—it will be seen, as the discussion develops, that there is a particular sense in which "plurality" must be admitted—but, even so, it is fire, a certain sort of thing, that is the effect in question, and, if any distinction is to be made among conditions of its production, it will be a distinction between different *kinds* of conditions. It *is* natural, then, that, to the question what causes a certain sort of thing, the answer should be "a certain sort of thing"; it appears that what we are all the time seeking to establish is a general connection, that is to say, a universal proposition, to assert which is to assert that something happens invariably.

It is a curious but commonly unremarked feature of Mill's logic that, while, in what he calls Induction, he professes to have a method of arguing from particulars to generals, he is all the time working with generals. His exposition of his methods depends upon the assumption that it is possible to enumerate the features of a situation—and, as these features are, of course, general, the situation composed by a finite number of them would also be general. This is a difficulty of a kind which is bound to arise on any theory of induction, and is only one of the difficulties of

Mill's theory in particular. But it brings out the fact that, since we can never say that we have completely analysed a situation (every factor in it being complex, every feature having itself features), Mill's methods can at most indicate how we can verify a hypothesis previously entertained and not how we can establish a conclusion. It is illogical to speak, as Mill does, of a number of situations having *only one* feature in common or of our varying only one factor when we are experimenting. If, for example, a chemist introduces hydrogen into some mixture, it is not "pure" hydrogen, hydrogen as such, that he introduces, but a particular sample of hydrogen, differing in some respects from other samples. And while, in actual fact, these differences may be irrelevant to the result obtained, this is not *proved* by the introduction, however careful the experimenter may have been; there is only a verification of a postulated general connection between a certain kind of antecedent (the entry of hydrogen) and a certain kind of consequent (whatever it may be). But, it may be remarked, on the theory of variability referred to at the outset, there would not even be verification; the position would be one of sheer guesswork—a position not relieved by the appeal to "probabilities" (the fashionable substitute for the "occult powers" of the primitive superstition or the good and bad luck of ordinary speech) in place of connections of kind.

The inconsistency in which we have seen Mill to be involved in connection with "plurality", turns on whether a cause is a necessary as well as a sufficient condition of an event's taking place. In expounding his methods Mill implies that it is; thus, in his exposition of the Method of Agreement (l.c., ch. VIII, § 1), he says that "b and c are not effects of A, for they were not produced by it in the second experiment", i.e., it is not sufficient for them; while the "phenomenon a cannot have been the effect of B or C, since it was produced where they were not", i.e., they were not necessary for it. The theory of Plurality of Causes implies that a cause is only a *sufficient* condition of "its effect", for, if it were necessary as well, this would imply that, in what we call bringing an effect about in different ways, we had, in introducing a second sufficient factor, also introduced the first sufficient factor, even though we were unaware of having done so—so that the event really comes about in the same way in every case.

Now it may be argued that we are frequently aware of different sufficient conditions of a certain type of event, without taking any or all of them to be necessary. To quote an example given by Mill in the chapter first cited: "One set of observations or experiments shows that the sun is a cause of heat, another that friction is a source of it, another that percussion, another that electricity, another that chemical action is such a source." Leaving aside for the present the possibility that different questions are at issue in the different cases, we may note that on no theory will it be denied that there are various sufficient conditions of an event (indeed, on the theory of the infinite complexity of things, there will be various *necessary and sufficient* conditions of anything, these all being necessary and sufficient for one another). But this is not to say that sufficiency is all that is required for causality, or that there is not a question of finding a necessary feature which is common to all the sufficient conditions. That question arises at once from the consideration of relevance. If it were merely the case that, when A is given, X follows, and that it follows likewise in the presence of B and in that of C, then A, B and C might have nothing to do with its occurrence.

The point here is not the possibility of error, the absence of conclusive proof. Generals require generals for their premises, necessity and sufficiency can be inferred only from assertions of necessity and sufficiency, and a causal connection can be proved only from causal connections already known. Where we do not have such knowledge but have only formed a hypothesis (e.g., that X always follows A), then we may get verification of it, but verification is not proof and is quite consistent with the falsity of the verified proposition. But, granting that verification may be all we are looking for, the question is what *sort* of hypothesis we have formed in suggesting a causal connection; and it is clear that we are at least distinguishing conditions under which something occurs from conditions under which it does not. If X occurred in any case, then it would be idle to say that it was conditioned in turn by A, B and C, merely because it ensued upon each of these. But if it did so ensue, and if A, B and C covered all cases, i.e., if, in A's absence, B or C was bound to be present, then X *would* occur in any case. It appears, then, that, even in enumerating sufficient conditions, we take them to be restricted in scope; we assume that a certain set of them (say, for the sake of simplicity, three as above) cover all cases of X's occurrence. That means that the expression "A or B or C" gives a necessary and sufficient condition of the occurrence of X. It may be, of course, that we do not look for such a set, that we are content with the knowledge that certain things are sufficient; it may be again that we should regard "A or B or C" as a cumbrous and unsatisfactory solution of our problem, and that, as already suggested, we should look for some common feature of the three that would meet the case. But the important point is that, to whatever extent we may actually prosecute out inquiries, in the mere assertion of sufficiency the problem of finding a necessary *and* sufficient condition is already posed, and, if we deny that there need be such a condition, we make the very use of the term "condition" pointless.

If, then, it be contended, in accordance with Mill's first position, that by a cause we mean a necessary and sufficient condition (more particularly, a necessary and sufficient *precedent* condition), it will appear that a hypothesis of causality really involves *two* universal propositions, and, it may be said, requires a double verification. This is what is implied in Mill's account of the simplest use of the Direct Method of Difference, where we first observe the absence of the factor in question as well as of the phenomenon it is supposed to cause, this verifying the supposition that the factor is necessary, and then observe the phenomenon ensuing upon the introduction of the factor, this verifying the supposition that it is sufficient. It should be observed, however, that, strictly speaking, the same observations verify both suppositions; the observation of A and B in conjunction verifies the supposition that A is sufficient for B and also the supposition that B is sufficient for A or, what comes to the same thing, A is necessary for B (the time-factor being neglected here for the sake of brevity). But the point about the double verification is that it informs us of the existence of "negative instances". The difference between the suggestion that the presence of B entails the presence of A and the suggestion that the absence of A entails the absence of B is, it may be said, that the latter lays it down that A *is* sometimes absent; and, accordingly, a verification of its absence is of importance. But, again, in strict logic, this is not correct. Unless A is just any condition whatever—in which case to refer to it as a "factor" is quite off the mark—it will be a differentiating condition; it will be sometimes present and sometimes absent. In logical form, if A is something specific (and, if it is not, no assertion is being made), the assertion "All B are A" is equivalent to the assertion

THE PROBLEM OF CAUSALITY (1938) 163

"All non-A are non-B", each being the contrapositive of the other. What is brought out by the consideration that there may not be "negative instances" is that we are concerned not with relations between A and B in general but with their relations within certain limits or in a certain "field"; and it is the consideration of the "field" that enables us to make the theory of causality precise and to clear up the difficulties in which Mill and others are involved.

For, while a verification of a proposition is necessarily a verification of any equivalent proposition and the two contrapositives formulated above *are* equivalent (or imply one another), the case is different when it is a question of a "virtual contrapositive" or "contraposition" within a field. An instance in which A and B are jointly present in the field X verifies the supposition that the presence of A entails the presence of B in the field and also the supposition that the presence of B entails the presence of A. But before we translate the latter assertion into the assertion that the absence of A entails the absence of B from the field, we have to be assured that A ever is absent from the field, and this assurance is given by the "negative instances". If, however, we knew in advance that A is sometimes absent from the field, we could make the transition in question without having to examine these instances. That is, granted that some X are not A, we can pass from "All X which are B are A" to "All X which are non-A are non-B", and we can go through the reverse process granted that some X are B; so that, in cases where we know that examples of two terms and their opposites are all to be found within a field, we can speak of propositions like the above pair as "virtual contrapositives", remembering that they are not strictly contrapositives and are not strictly equivalent. We can now see what is meant by speaking of a necessary and sufficient condition of a certain type of occurrence within a certain field; and, assuming it to be a precedent condition, then it is what we call a "cause". In other words, if there is any force in the line of argument so far pursued, a cause is always a cause within a field.

On this theory the difficulties of "plurality" disappear. A may be necessary and sufficient for the occurrence of B within the field X, and yet not be necessary or sufficient for its occurrence within the field Y. And the fact that A cannot, as we say, make a Y become B, is nothing against its having that effect on an X and suggests no variability in the causation of B in the field X. Thus, what makes me angry may leave you quite indifferent, but this does not mean that there are not perfectly definite conditions of the occurrence of anger in me. Further, it does not mean that there are not definite conditions of the occurrence of anger in *men*; for what is necessary and sufficient for its occurrence in this wider field must be necessary and sufficient for its occurrence in me, and in you, as part of the field, but what is necessary and sufficient for its occurrence in me may not be necessary and sufficient for its occurrence in other men. We could inquire, again, into the conditions of its occurrence in the still wider field of *animals*. That is to say, we can have many different problems, but no one of them is definite, and only confusion can result, if we have not begun by specifying (a) the field, (b) the phenomenon which may or may not occur within the field (e.g., anger in me) and of whose occurrence we are seeking to determine the conditions.

The inquiry into causes, in fact, is only a special case (involving, as mentioned above, a time-factor) of the solution of problems in general. In trying to determine when a phenomenon is present, and when it is absent, in a given field, we are endeavouring to divide a *genus* (the field) into two species, one of which has a certain *property*, while the other has the opposite. We are asking what distinguishes the cases in which a G is P from the cases in which a G is not P; that is, in terms of the doctrine of predicables, we are looking for a *difference* (or *differentia*) which will solve the problem posed by the variable property in the genus (e.g., by the appearance and non-appearance of anger among men). And we have solved it, or at least proposed a solution, when we say that (a) all G which are D are P, and (b) all G which are non-D are non-P—that is, that D is a necessary and sufficient condition of the occurrence of P in the field G. In other words, we have a problem when we know that a G may or may not be P, and we have a solution when we can use D as a criterion determining absolutely whether it is or not.

Now it is important to observe that "necessary and sufficient" is a symmetrical relation (if A is necessary and sufficient for B, B is necessary and sufficient for A), this arising from the fact that "necessary" and "sufficient" are converse relations (if A is necessary for B, B is sufficient for A, and *vice versa*); and the same applies to a necessary and sufficient condition within a field. For the two propositions, all G which are D are P and all G which are non-D are non-P, assure us that D, P and their opposites all occur in G, so that we are entitled to pass to the "virtual contrapositives", all G which are non-P are non-D and all G which are P are D, where D appears as the property and P as the difference. This reversibility, of course, raises no logical difficulty, and the fact that either may be taken as a criterion of the other is met in practice by our selecting the more readily observable or controllable, granted that we already know the solution, and, prior to that, by our starting from a specific problem wherein something is taken as the property, and the difference is what we are looking for. It is, however, a point to be remembered in view of rationalist attempts to represent some properties or conditions as "more fundamental" than others.

In the theory of causality this rationalism takes the form of representing the cause as superior in reality or logical standing to the effect. But, when a cause is taken as a necessary and sufficient precedent condition of the occurrence of a phenomenon (its "effect") in a certain field, then it follows that the effect is a necessary and sufficient *subsequent* condition of the occurrence (or operation) of the cause in the field. So that, granting the temporal priority of the cause, there is no question of any logical priority; and while, if our causal beliefs are true, we can with certainty, given the cause, infer that the effect will occur, we can with equal force infer, given the effect, that the cause has occurred. In this way, the cause is no more a "reason" for the effect than the effect is for the cause. But, before we can be satisfied with this solution, we have to consider a difficulty in the very conception of a "necessary and sufficient precedent condition", a difficulty which may appear to force us to recognise a difference in status between causes and effects.

This is that, if condition A exists for a time, however short, during which condition B does not exist (and, otherwise, A does not *precede* B—and, if both came into existence at the same time, there would be no reason for calling one cause and the other effect), then A is not sufficient for B; a lapse of time, at least, is also required. And this will appear all the more strikingly when it is observed that causing, conceived as above, must be a transitive relation (one such that if A has it to B and B to C, A has it to C), since both "necessity and sufficiency" and precedence are transitive relations; so that, if we find a number of terms in a causal series, the first can be said to *cause* the last, in exactly the same sense as the last but one does. The difficulty might be met by saying that the lapse of time should be included in the statement of the condition, that having been A for some time, or having been subject to A some time ago, should be taken as the occasion of an X's being B. Or, again, it may be said that, in using the very phrase "precedent condition" in this connection, we are signifying a condition of an X's *going to be* B, and that A may be sufficient for that, even if it is not at all times indicative of B's *presence* in the field X.

This brings us to an essential point of distinction between the consideration of causal relations and that of relations of properties; in the latter case, we are concerned with establishing conditions under which an X is B or under which it is not B, whereas in the former case our inquiry is into conditions under which an X *becomes* B. It is this that marks the distinction between the direct and the indirect method of difference, in Mill's theory—in the direct method (or, at least, in what Mill admits to be the principal type of its application) a factor is introduced and a certain change ensues; in the indirect method (also called the joint method of agreement and difference) we have only observation of the joint presence and joint absence of two properties, but no indication of the temporal priority of either to the other—if there were, that would involve the *entry* of a factor and the use of the direct method. It appears, then, that the indirect method, which, like the rest of Mill's methods, gives only verification and not proof, can at most verify a hypothesis of *difference*, i.e., of a criterion for distinguishing, within a genus, that species which has a certain property from that which has not. In the case of the direct method, on the other hand, the position is that a member of the genus (or part of the field) *acquires* a character which it previously had not; and it is this acquisition, or, more exactly, the thing's now having the character, that we speak of as an effect. For example, when something makes me blush, it is "my blushing now" that is said to be the effect of its operation, and not my transition from non-blushing to blushing, though it has to be understood that I was not blushing before.

Thus the effect, in ordinary usage, corresponds to the "formal cause" in the Aristotelian classification—at any rate, to the acquisition by the "material cause" (which, here, is the field or the relevant part of the field) of the form or character in question. And, "the matter having the form" being actually the effect, we are left with the "efficient cause" as the cause proper—which is still in accordance with ordinary usage. From this point of view, the field is what is "acted upon", and the contention that a cause is a cause in a field amounts to the assertion that any "causal law" embodies the statement both of what acts and of what is acted upon, so that the fact that something acts differently on different things implies no "exception" to law or variation in it—nor does the fact that it may act differently on the same thing at different times, for this merely indicates that the thing acted on has changed in some respects, i.e., has ceased to be a member of a certain genus and become a member of another. Nevertheless, we see that the above way of speaking puts cause and effect in different positions, since the effect characterises some member of the genus, whereas the cause, if not necessarily outside the genus (since members of the same genus do interact), at least may be so and is certainly outside the member affected, though the two enter into the same situation.

Such a difference of relation to the field does not, of course, imply any difference in logical standing, any division of reality into agents and patients; whatever we call the cause and whatever we call the effect are alike situations, and any situation can have "efficacy" in that it can be the sufficient (as well as necessary) condition of another situation. Thus, when something makes me angry, my anger (the effect) may cause amusement in someone else. The difficulty which arises is not whether the same thing can be a cause and an effect, but whether it can be a cause and an effect within the same field. It has, in any case, to be emphasised, in the consideration of causality as a transitive relation, that the same field should be in question throughout—otherwise, the argument to prove that a cause of a cause of a thing is a cause of the thing itself has an ambiguous middle. But, if the effect is regarded as characterising a member of the genus (or field) and the cause is not, it would appear that this ambiguity is always present, that there is no such thing as a "causal chain" (or transitive causality). It is quite certain that this expression is often used very loosely of cases where neither necessity nor sufficiency carries over from one link to the next.

At the same time, we commonly recognise *stages* in the development of certain kinds of things, i.e., we find them to have a regular succession of properties. But we do not say, in such cases, that the earlier stages cause the later. And this is so not merely when, as in the case of the "chains" which are not really linked, it is possible to have the succession interfered with, e.g., in the "ages of man", where the prior stage of youth is necessary but not sufficient for the attainment of age. We still do not use the term "cause" even when we know that the later development is unavoidable; we know that whatever is alive is going to die, but we do not say that being alive is the cause of death. When, in fact, we proceed to give a causal account of the development of anything, it is by considering the interactions of the minor systems which it comprises—in addition, of course, to its interactions with other systems. If, therefore, we say that an effect is a property (or a thing's having a property) while a cause is not but is an outside thing (a thing situated in such-and-such a way towards the first thing), we are not raising any obstacles to investigation. On the contrary, we have the advantage, in regarding causation as external action, of rejecting any rationalist doctrine of development from internal resources or by "unfolding of potentialities"; and, in discarding "causal chains", we are recognising that there is no unilinear form of development but interaction at all points.

Further working out of the theory here outlined would undoubtedly lead on to fresh problems; the attempt to give a thorough treatment of any of the main questions of logic involves us sooner or later in the others. But it has at least been indicated how the theory of the "field", without departing violently from common conceptions, enables us to combine scientific rigour with recognition of the actual plurality of things. And it provides a solution of all those minor puzzles in which Mill, in his discussion of the subject, becomes entangled. In regard to the "invariable sequence" of day and night, for example, Mill argues soundly enough that neither is an unconditional antecedent of the other; but, lacking the conception of the field, he is unable to clear up the question altogether. To make it more precise, we have to observe that the distinction, as regards any selected portion of the earth's surface, is between its being illuminated (by the sun) and its not being illuminated. Calling the region X and "being illuminated" B, we see that the assertion that night is the cause of day amounts to saying that X's not being B is the cause of its being B; in other words, the assertion is that a certain change's not having taken place is the cause of its taking place. Obviously, to become B, X must have been non-B; but this is not an account of the conditions of the change. To speak of sequence at all is to imply the occurrence of some change, and, if the passage from non-B to B were called an "invariable sequence", *every* sequence would be invariable. Once we have made our problem precise, however, there is no difficulty about the answer. Taking "regions of the earth's surface" as the field, we find that the cause of the acquisition of the illuminated character (and, similarly, of the unilluminated character) is the rotation of the earth in relation to the sun's rays; or, if we include the rotation in the specification of the field, we have simply the sun's rays as the cause. Any number of problems can be raised in regard to any natural phenomenon, but, once we have specified field and property, we know, at any rate, the *form* that an unambiguous answer will take, and we shall not be misled into taking the problem, or part of it, as its own solution.

It is, again, through failure to specify the field that Mill falls into confusion on the distinction between cause and conditions, and wishes to treat "the whole of the antecedents" as "the real cause". Thus, when people say that the eating of a certain dish was the cause of a person's death, Mill thinks they are leaving out of account such conditions as "a particular bodily constitution, a particular state of health, and perhaps even a certain state of the atmosphere" (l.c., ch. V, § 3); whereas it is obvious that some of these conditions should be taken not as part of the cause operating but as part of the field operated upon, since no one supposes that the eating of that dish is the cause of death in general. It is likewise failure to specify the problem, or confusion between different problems, that leads Mill into difficulties (l.c., ch. VI) regarding "exceptions" to the principle of Composition of Causes, according to which "the joint effect of causes is the sum of their separate effects". The real question is whether what has been taken to be the effect of a factor A occurs or not when a factor C is also operating—if it does not, then A is not sufficient for its supposed effect; if it does, the fact that C is also operating is beside the point. In the special case in which the causal hypotheses are stated in quantitative terms, the test of them is still whether the quantity specified *occurs or not* in the given instances. And, finally, the theory of "intermixture of effects" is open to similar objections to those which have already been urged against "plurality of causes".

Mill's main error, however, lies in the assumption, which he holds in common with other rationalists, that a situation or "phenomenon" can be analysed into a number of simple factors—that science, indeed, consists in the reduction of facts to their simple laws of connection. The recognition of the infinite complexity of things, on the other hand, leads us to see that there will be many different laws "governing" the same process, that everything goes on in various, though interrelated, ways. And just as, on this view, there will be many "differences, each solving the problem of a certain variation within a genus, so, even allowing for the distinction that has been drawn between the two cases, there will be many causes of the acquisition of a character by a certain sort of thing, since any situation which is said to have this effect will be a complex of interrelated ways of working. Since, in fact, to have a character is itself to have a complex way of working, there will be no line of demarcation between the inquiry into differences and the inquiry into causes (and no distinction between classificatory and historical or developmental science), but the former will involve recognition of causal action within a thing (of the thing as a system), this being never unconnected with causal action without.

It will seem curious to some minds that one should say that there can be *many* necessary and sufficient conditions of any situation, since to say that something is sufficient is understood to mean that nothing else is necessary. But there is no real difficulty here. The recognition of equality of sides is sufficient to distinguish equilateral from other triangles, and yet the recognition of equality of angles is an equally sound basis of discrimination. That is to say, the *recognition* of equality of sides is not required for our distinguishing the species of triangles, but the species must *have* that difference even when we use another criterion. Difficulty arises only on the assumption of simple characters or factors, as when Mill speaks of "the only" difference between two sets of circumstances. But, as we have observed, any specific difference is itself complex, and the fact that there are many ways of specifying it (since it has many ways of working) does not involve it in ambiguity or lead to the denial of "invariability" in the form of universal truths. It is, of course, possible for us to make mistakes in regard to universal connections, just as in regard to particular "collocations"; but it is not possible for us to think at all without believing in some "laws". Errors can be corrected by the testing of beliefs, though even so it is by other beliefs that we test any given one. It is only the attempt to reduce them to "elements" or rest them on "ultimates" that makes error inevitable.

# 14
# HYPOTHETICALS (1952)

The view that hypotheticals (or, more broadly, conditionals) are a peculiar *species* of propositions illustrates the inferior way of treating logic—that which, instead of bringing everything under logic, subordinates logic to something else; specifically, to forms of speech, i.e., ultimately, to types of human procedure and relationship. Thus, in classifying propositions, one can go to forms of speech, to the ways in which things are said, or one can go to the sorts of things that can be *meant*; in other words, to the sorts of things that can be.

The former method is, at best, eclectic; no classification could possibly cover all the forms of speech, all the varieties of communication. But all possible forms of speech must fall under forms of being; anything that can be said, or, perhaps better, that can be conveyed, must have some "logical form"—and the first task of logic is to find the types of logical form, even if "putting into logical form" is rendered difficult in particular cases by the confusion of the speaker's thought or by the multifarious purposes which people try to serve by what they say. In other words, the logician's task is to cut through forms of speech to real content; and the main aid to his doing so is absorption in the philosophical tradition. But such absorption depends, again, on his rejection of eclecticism, rejection, in particular, of an external view of philosophers as exponents of this or that ("ideas", "transcendental unity", etc.); it depends on his own sense of what is vital in their work, of what is the connecting philosophic *theme.*

In stating this theme as that of objectivism versus subjectivism, of the issue versus the purpose, of truth versus satisfaction, I should have to say that this alone "makes sense" of the course of philosophical inquiry, but also that that "sense" would emerge from a series of studies (*digging out* the contributions to an objective view of things, to a positive conception of truth, made by various philosophers—or, in the first instance, merely becoming capable of *seeing* such issues) and would not be a simple finding or a simple inference from "the philosophical data".

Nevertheless, I should say that not a great deal of reflection is required to see the force of the contention that "finding the logical form" of any utterance is finding what it purports to convey as truth, as objective, as "the case", and of the further contention that it is by considering what can be true, or what can be (what is the form of) an issue, a question of truth or falsity, that we determine what *are* the logical forms. Now the issue in its broadest form (the issue as such) is expressed as "Is it so or not?"—and it is from this that we find what are the forms of propositions and that they are all "categorical"; that they are, in fact, the A, E, I and O forms of the text-books. It is conceivable, of course, that there could be differences of *notation* not implying any real departure from this classification. But it should be understood that even if the argument to which I am proceeding, an attempted demonstration of "the four forms" as the only logical forms, were open to decisive objections, some argument of this *kind* is essential to logic—the alternative, as I said, being eclecticism, the employment of an unformulated and uncriticised method of selection, the adoption of an unstated "logic" amounting in fact to the subjection of logic to non-logical considerations.

The form of the issue, "Is it *so* or not?" indicates that there is no question of kinds of truth (truth in practice, necessary truth, conditional truth, etc.) or, as I have alternatively put it, that there is only one copula, "the unambiguous 'is' of occurrence" or of *being the case*. But to say that this alone is the form of the proposition, that everything else belongs to its material or is part of *what* is the case, would be misleading if it were taken to signify that there is only one propositional form. The fact that a proposition is, or "raises", an issue already implies the distinction of quality (affirmative and negative); what has further to be brought out is that it implies also the distinction of quantity (universal and particular). The demonstration of this depends on the order of terms in the proposition, on the distinction between subject and predicate, on the expansion of "Is it so?" into "Is *what how?*" or "Is what thing of what character?". The same point can be expressed by saying that "X is Y" is a different proposition (raises a different issue) from "Y is X", even if, whenever there is one such issue, there is also the other; that subject and predicate have different "functions", roughly expressible as "locating" and "describing". It should still be noted, however, that any term can have either function (whatever can locate can describe or be located, whatever can describe can locate or be described) so that the expressions "things" and "characters" are merely indicative of the functions, respectively, of subject and predicate, and are not indicative of different classes of entities.[1]

Over and above outright denial of this distinction of functions, we do of course find writers on logic slipping away from it, slipping into *symmetrical* expressions of the import of the proposition (e.g., "connection of contents"). But the necessity of the distinction can be seen from considerations of *implication*—from the difference, for instance, between the two arguments "X is Y, Z is X, therefore Z is Y" and "Y is X, Z is X, therefore Z is Y". The recognition of the validity of the former and the invalidity of the latter argument depends on the recognition of the distinction of quantity, the distinction, here, between "All X are Y" and "Some X are Y". (Alternatively, the distinction can be approached from considerations of *contradiction*, from the fact that "X is Y" and "X is not Y" present not a single issue but two issues—or permit a confusion of issues which can be cleared up only by the distinction of quantity.) Broadly, the argument is that the distinction of quality requires the distinction of subject and predicate, and this requires the distinction of quantity; and thus we have the four forms, A, E, I and O (XaY, XeY, XiY, XoY), each of which raises a single issue and, of course, presents a settlement of it. These "categorical" forms, then, are *the only* logical forms, the only forms in which we can assert that *something is so*; and thus the logical form of "hypotheticals" (and similarly with "modals", etc.) must be found among the four forms.

It may be urged in criticism of the above argument that the distinction in validity of the two inferential forms cited depended on the assumption of a certain interpretation of the proposition or on the preference of a type of proposition to another equally admissible; that, if the propositions in question were identities, both arguments would be valid. My contention, against any doctrine of a distinction among copulas, of different "is"-es, including, e.g., "the 'is' of identity", is that it is impossible to *make* such a distinction except by means of an unambiguous copula or absolute "is", that any real distinction that was in question would be a distinction

[1] v. i., p. 170.

in the materials, not the forms, of propositions. Thus if we profess to be able to distinguish the identity of X and Y from any other relationship that might hold between these terms, we should have to express it by saying not "X is Y" but "X is identical with Y"; and here we have the ordinary "predicative" form (distinct terms with distinct functions, the predicate "applying to" the subject), we have the predicate "identical with Y" attached to the subject X by the ordinary copula ("the 'is' of predication"). But we do not in fact require such terms as "identical with Y"; what is ordinarily meant by identity, what alone at any rate would have any relevance to the treatment of the two arguments as valid, is coextension, and this is formally a pair of propositions, XaY and YaX, each of which is in the predicative form—and, even if we found it convenient to group them together, we should still, in considering their consequences, have to distinguish consequences of XaY from consequences of YaX and recognise where validity would be lost by substituting one for the other.

Similar objections apply to another prevalent doctrine of symmetricality—to the recognition of an "'is' of existence" and the doctrine that any proposition (or any "categorical proposition") asserts either existence or non-existence. If "X is", meaning "X exists", is a real issue, then the question is whether X has or has not the character "existing"—which would be a "categorical" question. But to say that there is such an issue is to profess to distinguish a class of existing things from a class of non-existing things, and on the face of it there is not the latter class; it is to profess to find the predicate "non-existing" in a subject which, if *it* were to be found, would not be non-existing. Thus, like the identity theory, the "existence, non-existence" theory of import, whether of all or only of some propositions, is not a consistent departure from the predicative theory, from the logic of the four forms; it cannot consistently treat "existing" as the only predicate or as a predicate at all, and yet it cannot escape from this interpretation. And when, for example, it treats XiY as "XY exist", it cannot, except by returning to a predicative logic, explain what "XY" means; viz., things which *are* X and also *are* Y, or simply *being* X and also *being* Y.

Returning, then, to the necessity of treating "hypotheticals" under the four forms and not as requiring any extension of our classification, we find the question complicated by different *uses* of the "if—then" formula; to show how this supposedly special form fits into a categorical logic, we have to distinguish (A) the hypothetical as a relation between terms, (B) the hypothetical as a relation between propositions, (C) the hypothetical as a relation between "functions".

A. In the simplest case of the use of the hypothetical form, it represents, or would have as its "logical form" the A or universal affirmative proposition. The matter can be approached from consideration of the "location" formula suggested above—the interpretation of "X is Y" as "X is a *place* where Y is". Clearly, this could not be taken as an alternative to ordinary predication; it is simply a way of bringing out certain of its features. Now, according to my previous argument, any term can function as a predicate, so that X can describe or be placed as well as placing; in other words, X is not a "pure place" but is, like Y, a descriptive term, and thus we could express "X is Y" by "What is of the description X is (also) of the description Y" (a formula which, as before, raises the question of quantity). But equally we could, from the point of view of location, express "X is Y" by "Where X is, Y is" or, more briefly, "Where X, there Y"; and this in turn could be given the hypothetical form "If X, then Y". Thus we might have "If man, then mortal" as an alternative to "Where man, there mortal".

Clearly, however, these are short-hand expressions; in the hypothetical form, in particular, "if man" needs completion, and do does "then mortal". Hence we encounter such expanded formulae as "If anything is a man, it is mortal" and "If x is a man, x is mortal". But these are still not formulae in which we can rest; the vagueness of "anything" and the suggestion in "x" of a gap that *could* be filled in one way or another drive us back to the categorical form "All men are mortal" as what is positively said. It might be argued that the hypothetical formula conveys not merely the A proposition but also the possibility of its being the major premise in a number of Barbara syllogisms; but this would equally be conveyed by formulating the A proposition as "Anything that is man is mortal", i.e., by reminding ourselves that the subject of the proposition is also a predicate, and this "capacity" of the A proposition (for being a major) need not be taken as anything additional to the proposition itself.

The logical form, then, of "If X, then Y" or "If anything is X, it is Y" is simply XaY. And the suggestion, as against this, that the hypothetical form covers the possibility that in fact nothing is X is met by the contention, supported above, that there are no "non-existent" terms. A formula containing a "non-existent" term is meaningless; that is to say, there is a set of words or, more exactly, of marks or noises, but there is no proposition, no issue. This, however, may be somewhat hard to see in the case of complex terms; to say "If anything is XZ, it is Y" (or even, categorically, XZaY) would quite commonly be taken to have a meaning when X, Y and Z all exist even if XZ does not. And while, strictly, there is no sense in saying that XZ locates Y when XZ itself has no location—any more than in saying that "X" is Y when there is no "X"—the *appearance* of sense may arise from confusion with something that does have sense, viz., "If any X is Z, it is Y", which, besides conveying ZaY in the same way as if "anything" were substituted for "any X", also suggests *arguments* containing the three "existing" terms, X, Y and Z (e.g., XaZ, ZaY, therefore XaY), and thus made up of intelligible propositions, whether they are true or not.

B. This brings us to the second use of the "if—then" formula, viz., for relations of implication among propositions. When the propositions p and q are presented in the relationship "if p, then q" (hereafter, for brevity, "if p, q"), there are the two cases (a) where what is meant is that p itself implies q, (b) where what is meant is that p and some other proposition r, which is "understood" or taken for granted, together imply q. The latter usage is quite common; people often say such things as "If Socrates is a man, he is mortal", where the passage from "Socrates is a man" to "Socrates is mortal" depends on the assumption that all men are mortal. The relationship in this case, then, is that of the premises of a syllogism to its conclusion; the suggested syllogism is the full "logical form" of "If Socrates is a man, he is mortal". But the other usage is also encountered; it is exemplified in Swinburne's "If thunder can be without lightning, lightning can be without thunder", where the form is that of immediate inference even though in fact the inference is fallacious, being the conversion of an O proposition, the inference of YoX from XoY.

In either case, however, we are concerned with inference or implication, and it is here that we find the relevance of the terminology of "antecedent and consequent"; if q in "if p, q" is taken to be consequent upon or to follow from p, p and q must be regarded as propositions, whether or not "if p, q" is also so regarded. This use of the hypothetical form may be connected again with the "method of hypothesis" and its consideration of "consequences", though there is much confusion in accounts of this method, as may be seen from Burnet's discussion (*Greek Philosophy, Part I*, ch. IX, pp. 162,3). For if τα συμβαίνοντα of p are the things which are *contingent on* p, then they are not its consequences but have it as a consequence; the humanity of Socrates is contingent on his mortality, not the other way round. If, on the other hand, it *is* a question of what follows from p, it must be observed that to arrive at a true consequence of p is not to prove p true, any more than to arrive at a construction which we can carry out, and which must be carried out if construction C is to be carried out, establishes our ability to carry out C; hence we are not entitled to say, at the conclusion of our drawing of consequences, that "what was to be demonstrated" has been demonstrated or that "what was to be done" has been done. Confusion in such expositions has, of course, been fostered by the fact that the principal field of their application was geometry, in which the relations studied are frequently symmetrical, so that moving in the wrong direction could be overlooked.

But, admitting the existence of such confusions, the fact remains that we can consider consequences, can consider what follows from p or "what would be true if p were true". Commonly, however, we bring under this head not just immediate inferences from p but propositions which follow from p together with other premises, premises which are taken for granted, are regarded as true by the person or persons engaged in finding p's consequences. This is important in regard to the "falsification of hypotheses" by finding false consequences. We reject a hypothesis when we find to be false something that "would be true if the hypothesis were true". But if we happen to be mistaken in believing the premise we have combined with p, then we are mistaken in believing the conclusion to be (or, at least, we have not found it to be) a "consequence" of p, something that would be true if p were true, and so we have not falsified p by its consequences.

A more important point here, however, is that of "the consequences of false propositions"; whether we can strictly say that false propositions have any consequences, any more than "non-existing" terms have predicates. We do not, in fact, have to say so.

Taking the simplest case of falsification, that of the hypothesis XaY which we have combined with the proposition ZaX, accepted as true, in the syllogism "XaY, ZaX, therefore ZaY", ZaY then being found to be false, the position is that we have found or believe to be true the two propositions ZoY and ZaX, and that these as the premises of a syllogism imply XoY, which is the contradictory of XaY. The falsification of a proposition, then, is the implication of its contradictory by true propositions; and the syllogism with true premises can be taken as the strict logical form of the argument, a "real implication" to which we have been led by consideration of actual types of connection among propositions, even if this consideration included a "hypothetical" procedure, the setting out of things we were uncertain of as well as things we were certain of.

Taking it, then, that the question of hypotheticals in this second usage is that of relations of implication among propositions, we have particularly to note that it is not a question of our proceedings or attitudes. These are, of course, subject to logic (there can be logical consideration of them), but logic is not subject to them; they do not affect the characters and relations of issues. Thus we can be more or less sure about something, we can "suppose" as well as assert; but this does not entitle us to distinguish *propositions* as certain and uncertain or to recognise "supposals" as forms additional to the forms of assertion. It is from this point of view that we can attack the conventional doctrine of the "mixed hypothetical syllogism", whose form is "if p, q; p, therefore q"; viz. as an argument with two premises and a conclusion. Since p is a premise and q the conclusion, p and q are propositions; hence "if p, q" is a relation between propositions, and, as it can only be the relation of implication, we have, in what is described as a "syllogism", merely stated the same implication twice. It would be possible to distinguish between "if p, q" and "p, therefore q" only in terms of our attitudes, i.e. according as we are sure of p and infer q or merely consider, from the formal relationship, that being sure of p would lead us to infer q; but logic is not affected by our taking up one attitude or the other—the logical question is that of implication.

On this showing, the so-called major premise has nothing to do with the inferring of q; "p, therefore q" is the whole argument—or, if an additional premise r is "understood", we still have a "categorical" and not a "hypothetical" argument. If, as against this, it is argued that "if p, q" is the assertion of the formal relationship and that the further *actual* assertion of p is required for the inferring of q, the answer is (a) that, in that case, the "major premise" will be concerned not with p and q but with a type of relationship, so that the connection between the "premises" will not be as represented—an illustration being "Any A proposition implies the I proposition with terms in the opposite order; XaY, therefore YiX", (b) that this "major premise" is the principle or, more exactly, the form of the inference of YiX from XaY alone. In short, if p and q come into the "major", we have the same implication twice, and, if they do not, we have it once—"p, therefore q".

C. These considerations lead on to the third usage mentioned above. Although reason has been found for rejecting the usual presentation of the "mixed" form, this is not all that is to be said about that form or about the hypothetical form in general. It is commonly understood that, while the "major premise" in the mixed form lays down a general connection or connection of kinds, the "minor" refers to a particular case; and that means that the given form is misleading, that the two "p's" (and similarly the two "q's") are not the same. The determination of the difference may be approached by asking *of what* the special case is a case. It cannot be a case of a proposition (a proposition does not have different cases or instances), and, particularly, we cannot talk about cases of the *truth* of a proposition and cases of its falsity (since a proposition is just true or just false). Nevertheless, this is a common way of rendering the matter; the formulation would be "All cases of the truth of p are cases of the truth of q; this (special case) is a case of the truth of p, therefore, this is a case of the truth of q", and the argument, if we accepted such terms, would be an ordinary categorical syllogism.

We have to ask, then, what is there which might be confusedly taken as a proposition and yet which could have cases. And the answer is, a "propositional function"—a formula, containing a variable or variables, such that, when a "value" is given to each variable, we have a proposition. In other words, a propositional function "represents" (is the form of, is what is common to) a *class* of propositions. Thus "x is a man", where x is variable, is a function whose values, corresponding to the values of x, are propositions ("Socrates is a man", etc.), some of which are true and some of which are false. We have then the distinction between a type of case and cases of that type, and we can see how p could be understood in one premise as "p in general" and in the other as "a case of p", how readily, even if confusedly, "x is a man" and "Socrates is a man" could be represented by the same symbol.

It is still the case that the strict form of "If x is a man, x is mortal; Socrates is a man, therefore Socrates is mortal" is just the categorical syllogism "All men are mortal, Socrates is a man", etc. And recognition of the major in its hypothetical form, recognition of such relationships as that between "being a man" and "being mortal", would not give us the third usage; we might speak of the relationship as one between "possibilities", realised in some cases and not in others, but we should still not have got beyond the first usage, that of the "relationship between terms", or proposition. In fact the third usage, even in the more complicated form I am about to consider, can always be brought back to the first (a connection of "possibilities" *is* a connection of terms); but the complications are of some interest and are, I should say, one main occasion of adherence to the belief in a peculiar "hypothetical form".

The question, then, is not just of possibilities, and their realisations and non-realisations, in general—of the occurrence and the non-occurrence of a certain character in this place and that—but of possibilities within a *field*, of a region or genus of things within which various possibilities are variously realised, of a *limited* range of "values", of the filling of the gap (turning the function into a proposition) by things of a particular kind. Such fields are often left unstated ("understood"), and, while this permits a special hypothetical form to be used, (a) full statement, making the implicit explicit, would still be categorical, (b) the absence of full statement opens the way to ambiguity and thus to the drawing of unwarranted conclusions. If, for example, in a "pure hypothetical syllogism", the field understood in one premise differed from that understood in the other, then we should have an apparently valid argument, "if p, q; if q, r; therefore, if p, r", whereas full statement of the premises would show that they had no common term and that the conclusion (whatever *its* field) did not follow; taking F and G as the two fields, we should have the unconnected premises "All F such that p are F such that q" and "All G such that q are G such that r"; where "F such that p" are members (of the field or genus F) in which the possibility p is fulfilled, etc.

The reference to a field renders intelligible "cases" of truth and falsity; the confused notion of cases in which a *proposition* is true and cases in which it is false is replaced by that of instances in a field, or members of a genus, which fulfil a possibility and instances or members which do not, so that it is *different* propositions which are true, and which are false, in the various cases. An example may make the position clearer. Such an assertion as "If the barometer is falling, bad weather is coming" is typical of the "major premises" of hypothetical arguments—and the argument might be completed by "the barometer is falling, therefore bad weather is coming". The "minor" here is understood to refer to some particular case; but it is not indicated *what* the case is (there is merely the suggestion of "now" or "in this case") or what it is a case of. Two conditions of exact statement of the argument, then, would be (a) the specification of the "field" or class of cases, (b) the specification of the particular case.

These specifications are frequently difficult. But we may suggest as the field in the above example "atmospheric conditions" or perhaps more exactly "atmospheric pressures" or perhaps more exactly again "pressure-regions". Thus the question would be of *pressures such that,* or *"pressure-regions" in which,* the barometer is falling, etc., and the minor premise would refer to "this" pressure-region (where the speakers are) or to the pressure "here"—the argument would then be "All P such that (or in which) condition A is fulfilled are P such that condition B is fulfilled; this P is a P such that condition A is fulfilled; therefore, this P is a P such that condition B is fulfilled". But, while this is an ordinary syllogism, the less exact hypothetical form is one which readily arises when we are confronted with diverse possibilities (p and non-p, q and non-q) and with connections among such possibilities (say, between p and q). The field may be left unstated for the sake of brevity, though, as previously noted, the omission makes for ambiguity and bad argument; but it frequently happens that we notice a sequence or concomitance of conditions without being able to specify the field (or without having more than a rough notion of it), so that in seeking and finding such specification we are actually *advancing* in knowledge. Thus where reference to pressures is lacking (in the mind, say, of the uninstructed child) the connections between the barometer and the weather would be magical rather than scientific connections; the specification of the field brings out the point that there is a real continuity, a *series* of connections, with which we can become more and more fully acquainted. (It may be remarked in passing that one reason why the doctrine of "material implication" is a philosophical blind-alley is just its ignoring of such connection; implication then becomes quite arbitrary or "magical"—divorced from inquiry.)

An important point about the "field", and one of special significance for hypothetical argument, is that it complicates the question of negative cases. If we were concerned with possibilities in general, we could represent "if p, q" by PaQ (where P is "cases in which p is fulfilled", etc.) and could then recognise its equivalence to "if not q, not p", represented by $\overline{Q}a\overline{P}$ (all non-Q are non-P), since PaQ and $\overline{Q}a\overline{P}$ are equivalents (in fact, contrapositives) of one another. But when we are concerned with possibilities in a field, the categorical forms are PFaQF and $\overline{Q}Fa\overline{P}F$, which are not equivalent and are not contrapositives but "virtual contrapositives" of one another (a terminology used in my article, "The Problem of Causality"; *A.J.P.P.*, August, 1938; pp. 133-5[2]); the point being that PFaQF does not assure us that any F are not Q (that $\overline{Q}F$ "exists"). Hence the recognised equivalence, the regular substitution of "if not q, not p" for "if p, q", the recognition of "denying the consequent" as having the same validity as "affirming the antecedent", depend on the assumption that the opposite possibilities (non-fulfilment as well as fulfilment) all exist within the field.

Of course if there were no field, we should be back either at the first, simple usage, at "if—then" as a rough way of expressing the A proposition, or, if p and q were propositions, at the second usage, where, if an argument of the form "p, therefore q" is valid, an argument of the form "not q, therefore not p" is also valid, and if "p, r, therefore q" is valid, "not q, r, therefore not p" is valid. Even in the third usage, where there *is* a field, the "hypothetical form" is only a convenient short-hand; but in using it we have to consider the *conditions* of its use, and one of the most important is that of the existence of the opposite possibilities in the field. Where that assumption is justified, "virtual contraposition" is

[2] v. s., p. 130.

justified, and so the regular transformation of "if p, q" into "if not q, not p", and vice versa, is justified.

Another limitation on the use of "conditionals" is to be found in the question of contradiction and particularly in the fact that the contradictory of a hypothetical is not a hypothetical. We can, if we so desire, find a form for such a contradictory, by means of the equivalence of hypotheticals and disjunctives, and the relation between disjunctives and conjunctives. The matter can best be approached from the side of disjunctive and conjunctive *terms*; and here I would contend that there is nothing to be said for the view that the alternatives of a disjunction are exclusive. "Either" means "not neither"; the opposite of being either P or Q is being neither P nor Q, and thus the opposite of the disjunctive term "P or Q" is the conjunctive term $\overline{PQ}$ (not P *and* not Q). "Not both" is quite a different thing, even if it should hold at the same time; it could be true of any X that it is not neither P nor Q *and* that it is not both P and Q, but these would still be different truths, and there would in general be other subjects of which only one of these things could truly be said (i.e., unless P and $\overline{Q}$ were coextensive). So, in the case of disjunctive *propositions* (the disjunction of functions or possibilities), "p or q" would be a different proposition from "not p or not q" and would not imply it, though both might hold; it would be equivalent to the hypothetical "if not p, q", and it would not be equivalent to or even imply the hypothetical "if p, not q". It could, on the analogy of the conjunctive opposite of a disjunctive *term*, be contradicted by $\overline{pq}$ (not p *and* not q), a conjunction of possibilities, the non-fulfilment of p along with the non-fulfilment of q; and the equivalent hypothetical would be contradicted by the same conjunction. Or, starting from the hypothetical "if p, q", we should contradict it by $p\overline{q}$ (p and not q).

The adoption of such a notion, however, would be cumbrous and also confusing. Full statement of the contradictory of a hypothetical, i.e. statement with specification of the field, would be in the form of a particular proposition (I or O); but, in the shorthand formulation, we could not distinguish it from the "particular case", also unspecified, of the minor premise. Thus, contradicting "If the barometer is falling, bad weather is coming" by "The barometer is falling and bad weather is not coming", we should have a statement which would be understood as one to be supplemented by "now" or "under *these* circumstances"—and thus as *not* the simple contradictory of the given statement, as not a particular but a universal proposition. To get an unambiguous notation we might, if we wanted to avoid going back to categoricals, introduce *modal* expressions; we might give "if (or when) p, it is possible that not q" as the contradictory of "if (or when) p, it is necessary that q". I do not think, indeed, that consistency could be reached even in this manner; the opening part of my argument shows for what general reasons I should regard "modals" as reducible to "categoricals", as having A, E, I and O as their strict forms; a detailed reduction would involve complications similar to those we have encountered with "hypotheticals", but no real difficulties.[3] But what I am concerned with here are hypotheticals or, more broadly, conditionals, and I think I have said enough to show that a logic of conditionals can have no consistent notation, that it cannot cope with many of the problems, carry out many of the operations, which present no difficulties to a categorical logic, and that, as regards the operations to which it is in some measure adequate, their strict form is still the categorical.

As I contended earlier, there must, if there is to be logic, be a limited number of "logical forms", and there will be the problem of finding *some* argument which shows what they are. There will, if this problem is solved, be the further problem of carrying out the "reduction" of forms which superficially appear to escape the basic classification. I do not think anyone will deny certain *analogies* between hypothetical and categorical forms; the question, then, is whether there is any real distinction. My contention has been that there is not, that hypotheticals are rough devices for dealing with matters that can be covered in an exact way by a categorical logic, a logic which recognises *only* A, E, I and O propositions, their features and relations.

---

[3] Modality is discussed in some detail in "Empiricism and Logic" (v. i., pp. 175-7).

15
# RELATIONAL ARGUMENTS (1962)

Opponents of a predicative logic have commonly maintained that there are valid arguments of the form ArB, BrC ∴ ArC (arguments holding wherever the relation r is transitive; such validity, in fact, being what is meant by calling a relation transitive) which cannot be presented in ordinary predicative form, particularly in syllogistic form, but depend on principles other than the syllogistic. It may be admitted at once that there is no question of the putting forward of a "principle", the transitiveness of r, as a major premise, the specific terms involved appearing in the minor premise and a syllogistic conclusion then being drawn; to which, however, it should be added that the "principle" of the syllogism (what is conveyed in the "dictum") is equally not a premise but is the *form* of valid syllogism (or, putting it at its minimum, the form of the Barbara syllogism) and that in any argument of this form the conclusion follows from the *premises* (an X-Y conclusion from X-Z and Y-Z premises) without any superadded principle—it being just by the direct recognition of the implication of a given conclusion by given premises that we recognise the validity of a certain form of argument (recognise the "principle"). There is, however, no question of the validity of *any* argument of the form ArB, BrC ∴ ArC, and in order to distinguish valid from invalid "relational arguments", or relations which are transitive from those which are not, we have to get a more detailed formulation of both. When we do this, I would argue, when we get a distinction between the valid and the invalid which can be "read off", a distinction, i.e., which is determinable simply from the form and not at all from the material of the arguments, this can only be in terms of a predicative logic; and I shall endeavour to show that in a number of types of argument which have been taken to be striking *exceptions* to the syllogistic character of demonstrative reasoning, the formal distinction must actually be made in syllogistic terms—that the distinction is between valid and invalid *syllogisms*.

The standpoint of predicative logic involves an immediate questioning of the view that relational assertions (or relational propositions) are the constituents of relational arguments and are to be definitely distinguished from "subject-predicate" assertions. The line of criticism of this view is the same as I have followed in the article "Hypotheticals". Any assertion whatever is an attempt to settle an issue, to give a decisive answer to the question "Is it so or not?" Whatever is called a relational assertion is open to formal contradiction and thus is properly stated, can only be unambiguously stated, in one of the four forms—in a proposition with a subject and a predicate and (besides the sign of quantity) the affirmative or negative copula—in exactly the same way as the assertion of the possession of a quality. We ask "*Is* A greater then B or is it not?" just as we ask "*Is* A red or is it not?", and no use of symbols (A > B, A ≮ B; or, in general, ArB, ArB) can alter the fact that what is being asserted or denied is that something is so, and that only the *is* and *is not* (more properly, *are* and *are not*) really indicate the formal character of contradiction, whereas the > and the r run together or confuse between *formal assertion* and material features of what is being asserted, between the copula and something that belongs to the terms, between the notion of occurring or not occurring and the notion of *what* it is that occurs.

When these are clearly distinguished, we are faced, in the "relational" assertion just as much as in the "qualitative" assertion, with the independence of terms, the fact that subject and predicate are distinct and that the latter can be as significantly denied as it can be asserted of the former, and likewise with the "convertibility" of terms, the fact that any predicate can function as a subject and any subject as a predicate; and this, as before, leads on to quantification. Thus as the converse of "A is greater than B" we have to give "Some (things) greater than B are A"; similarly, the converse of "A is not to the left of B" will be "No (things) to the left of B are A", and *its* converse will be "No A are (things) to the left of B", which thus appears as a stricter form of the original assertion. In the same way "A is greater than B" will be replaced by "All A are (things) greater than B", and, in general, assertion and denial of the occurrence of relations will take place in the four forms. But what must specially be emphasised, besides the need for quantification, is the fact that "a relation" is not a term, that there is no sense in any such formula as "A is *greater than*"; and since, as has been noted, the presentation of "*is* greater than" (perhaps in the form "exceeds") as the relation simply amalgamates *being so* with some specific thing that is said to be so, the conclusion we are led to is that "the relation" falls not between the logical terms (subject and predicate) but *within* one (or both) of them—as is indicated in the formula "All A are *things* greater than B", where the term "things greater than B" does not indicate any concrete quality of such things but indicates that they must have some concrete qualities if they are to have the relation; to which it may be added that some qualities must be *recognised* if any relation the things have is to be considered.

On this understanding, on this doctrine of the four forms and the unambiguous copula, the strict form of "relational statements" is the predicative form and the strict form of "relational arguments" may quite well be syllogistic form and will at any rate be one whose validity can be determined quite independently of the *matter* or terms. It is still to be understood that syllogism is not the only form of demonstrative reasoning, though it is by far the most important; we can have, without any departure from admittedly qualitative assertions, the non-syllogistic forms of conjunctive argument (combinations of predicates) and disjunctive argument (combination of subjects)—e.g., (1) AaX, AaY ∴ AaXY (All A are both X and Y); (2) AaX, BaX ∴ (A or B) aX (What ever is either A or B is X). Both these arguments differ from syllogism in the particular point that the two premises can be inferred in turn from the conclusion, and hence it might be argued that no real inference is involved; but this is not uniformly the case with such arguments (e.g., the premises of the conjunctive argument AaX, AiY ∴ AiXY cannot be inferred from the conclusion, though AiX, AiY can). It should be noted, moreover, that even in the conjunctive argument first given neither of the premises by itself implies that the conjunctive term XY is a real term (that XiY), so that a certain inferential discovery has been made; and, equally, neither premise in the given disjunctive argument implies that (A or B) is a real term, since it does not imply that the opposite, $\overline{AB}$, is a real term, and, unless it is (or if "everything" is A or B), saying that any given thing is A or B is not settling any real issue, is not distinguishing that thing from anything else.

The special importance of disjunctive argument, or of the conclusion to which it leads, is that it presents us with the notion of a plurality of things (terms) that have a common character and thus with the notion of "class", or, more broadly, that the disjunctive term, A or B, adds to the notion of *quality*, of a predicate which A singly or B singly may possess, the notion of *juxtaposition*, of the possession of a quality by A and B even if neither qualifies the other and thus of their falling within a common expanse or range in which they can still be distinguished. These notions make possible the recognition, within a predicative logic, of distinctions of extent or amount and of the distinctions among class-relations, particularly the relations of co-extension and inclusion, in terms of which arguments involving quantitative relations can be presented. (It might be observed that disjunction points directly to these two class-relations, since **A or B** includes B, except where AaB, and includes A, except where BaA, and in the exceptional cases the relation is co-extension.) Intersection and exclusion, in which there is no question of transitiveness, do not enter into these arguments; but if quantitative equality can be presented in the form of co-extension of classes, and quantitative inequality in the form of the inclusion of one class in another, then quantitative arguments can proceed by means of ordinary predicative assertions and, in particular, syllogistically.

The initial step is the representation of A = B by AaB, BaA (A and B are co-extensive classes), even if A in these two propositions had to be understood as "measurable by the quantity A" and similarly with B—the meaning of "measurable by" is a point I shall take up later—and the representation of A > B by AoB, BaA (the class A includes the class B); it will hardly be denied on any view that the co-extension of classes is at least *comparable* to equality in amount, and class-inclusion to excess or deficiency in amount. The predicative form which can thus be given to quantitative arguments can be carried over to a considerable number of relational arguments (including, as observed above, many which have been taken as beyond the scope of predicative and syllogistic logic, as demonstrating its inadequacy) and indeed, I should further hold, to all in which formal criteria, irrespective of any material consideration, can be found for validity—this being, of course, the condition under which objective validity can be intelligibly spoken of.

The position is, then, that two quantitative or extended things, two things of some *amount*, are equal when and only when anything measurable by the one is measurable by the other. Thus, when A and B are equal quantities, what I am also calling A and B are equal classes, in that anything measurable by A is measurable by B and vice versa; and thus A = B can be represented by the two propositions AaB, BaA. The *transitiveness* of equality is then exhibited in a pair of syllogisms. Replacing A = B and B = C by AaB, BaA and BaC, CaB, we have the two Barbara syllogisms AaB, BaC ∴ AaC and BaA, CaB ∴ CaA, the conclusions AaC, CaA being, on the view presented, the logical form of A = C. We thus see that the so-called axiom "Things which are equal to the same thing are equal to one another" is just an assertion of the validity of the Barbara syllogism and is not an additional premise; or, more exactly, the "axiom" is the *form* of the two AAA arguments, and it is from A = B and B = C, and not from any "axiom", that A = C is proved. We may note also that the treatment of equational reasoning as syllogistic reasoning gets rid of any doctrine of an "equational logic" in contrast to the ordinary predicative logic—an outstanding defect of such a supposedly *special* logic (and likewise of the view of logic as essentially equational) being that it cannot cope with ordinary logical relations, notably *contradiction*, since the contradictory of an assertion of equality is not an assertion of equality (" 'A = B' is false" is not an equation), whereas the contradictory of a predicative assertion is a predicative assertion and any particular case of co-extension that happens to arise can be presented in a pair of predicative assertions and suggests no logical "realm" distinct from that of the four forms.

The two syllogisms which indicate the transitiveness of equality also bring out the fact that it is a symmetrical or reversible relation (as co-extension is). In the case of *unequal* quantities we recognise that one quantity is greater than the other, and this is presented in argument by means of the class-relation of inclusion, which is a transitive but *asymmetrical* relation (as "greater than" is). Using, as before, the same symbol for the term (whose extension is the "class") and the quantity, we represent A > B by BaA, AoB (which, as before, might be presented in the alternative formulation as "All things measurable by B are measurable by A" and "Some things measurable by A are not measurable by B"—assertions capable of precisely the same syllogistic use as BaA, AoB). And, with this representation, we can exhibit the transitiveness of the asymmetrical relation "greater than" (and similarly of "less than") as definitely as that of the symmetrical relation "equal to" was exhibited above; though there are complications in the case of inequality or class-inclusion which do not appear in the case of equality or co-extension.

Thus we can argue syllogistically from the premises BaA, AoB and CaB, BoC to the conclusions CaA, AoC (from A > B and B > C to A > C) with the same validity as we can argue from BaA, AaB and CaB, BaC to the conclusions CaA, AaC. In the latter case, however, we use all the premises in arriving at the required conclusion, whereas in the case of inclusion, while we have to use both of the A premises, we need use only one of the O premises. We argue to the conclusion CaA from the premises CaB, BaA, but to prove AoC we may use either BaA, BoC (OAO, third figure) or AoB, CaB (AOO, second figure). In the former case we do not use AoB as a premise and, in fact, we could use the OAO argument even if AaB—i.e., since BaA, even if A and B were equal. Similarly in the second case, where BoC is not used, we could get the required conclusion even if B and C were equal. The common way of expressing this in mathematical reasonings is to say (first case) that if A *is greater than or equal to* B (A ≥ B) and B is greater than C, then A is greater than C; similarly (second case) if A > B and B ≥ C, A > C. An alternative way of expressing "greater than or equal to" is "not less than". Thus when we prove CaA, AoC from BaA, CaB, BoC, we are treating BaA as simply asserting that A is not less than B, and when we get the same conclusions from BaA, AoB, CaB, the last of these is expressible as "B is not less than C". Now it appears strange that "A is less than B" (AaB, BoA) should be contradicted simply by the denial of the O proposition; but the point is that terms quantitatively comparable belong to a single scale or range, so that, if any two do not coincide, one must include the other (one quantity must be higher in the scale than the other) and thus there will always be one true A proposition having them as terms and such a position as AoB, BoA (or again AeB) could not arise. I do not here argue the question whether there must be some scale on which any two quantities or measurable things can be compared; but, in any argument concerning things all of which are quantitatively comparable, the relation "not less than" (and similarly "not greater than") is conveyed by a single proposition.

Thus, in the argument BaA, CaB, BoC ∴ CaA, AoC, the premises leave it an open question whether AaB or AoB; indeed, the single proposition BaA does this—there is no question of this proposition's sometimes *meaning* co-extension and sometimes *meaning* inclusion, no question of qualifying the copula in the manner suggested by such confused and confusing conceptions as "the *is* of identity" or "the *is* of inclusion in a class". The making of such distinctions is an error of the same type as that of importing some of the material of an assertion into the formal sign of something's being asserted; and their pointlessness becomes clear when it is noted that co-extension, and similarly inclusion, can be quite directly and unambiguously presented by the assertion of a *number* of propositions, each with the unambiguous copula of occurrence or "being so". Thus, while BaA never means BaA *and* AaB and never means BaA *and* AoB, the possibility of presenting either situation in two propositions leaves BaA itself quite unambiguous. The point is reinforced by the consideration that "not less than" leaves "not greater than" an open question, and that to take each as conveyed by an A proposition leaves it possible that both propositions, BaA and AaB, are true—so that the truth of both, the co-extension or equality of A and B, is equally expressible by "A is not less than *and* not greater than B". When we understand the A proposition in this way, we get a further type of quantitative argument involving A propositions alone; $A \geq B, B \geq C \therefore A \geq C$ (or A is not less than B and B is not less than C, therefore A is not less than C) takes the form of the Barbara syllogism BaA, CaB $\therefore$ CaA, where no decision is involved as to the truth of falsity of the propositions AaB, BaC, AaC, and it is perfectly possible that the argument $B \geq A, C \geq B \therefore C \geq A$ has true premises and thus (being valid) establishes its conclusion, C is not less than A.

One important point in connection with all this is the clear understanding of what a class-relation (or a relation between the extensions of two terms, an "extensive relation") actually is. There is no question of the enumeration of "individual instances"; for, if we say that any subject is a predicate (or has subjects), there will be no limit to the list of instances, no question of "setting it out in full", any more than there will be a question of setting out in full a term's intension, of enumerating its properties, if every predicate is a subject or has further predicates. This is what gives the extension-intension rule, similarly to quantitative arguments, no application to the cases of intersection and exclusion where any quantitative comparison would have to rely on the (impossible) full count. It applies only to co-extension, where it can be said that two terms having the same subjects have the same predicates, and inclusion where the term that has more subjects has fewer predicates (general properties) —A's "having more subjects" than B being conveyed in the two propositions BaA and AoB (there are no B that are not A, there are A that are not B); while, strictly, "having the same subjects" must be brought down to what is conveyed by AaB, BaA, since a term is not one of its own subjects. Arguments involving quantitative comparison, then, will take one of the syllogistic forms presented above.

What I should further maintain is that any type of relational argument in which formal validity (the only kind of validity) can be distinguished from formal invalidity can be set out in the same way as quantitative arguments; and that it is not merely a question of one form of argument being "akin" or analogous to another, but that to see that some relation is transitive and symmetrical, to see that some relation is transitive and asymmetrical, to see that some relation is transitive and "non-symmetrical" (that B may or may not have it to A when A has it to B), is to recognise the existence of some class-relation of co-extension or of inclusion or (in the "non-symmetrical" case) of *either co-extension or inclusion.* I select for special consideration the transitive and asymmetrical relation "to the right of" which, for some reason, has been taken as an outstanding example of non-syllogistic arguments that have as great and as obvious cogency as syllogism; and my contention here will be that the relations "to the right of", "to the left of" and "level with" not only *can* be treated in the same way as "greater than", "less than" and "equal to", that is, as indicating relations of inclusion and co-extension so that arguments involving them will appear in syllogistic form, but that *only* in this treatment is their cogency, their formal character, definitely brought out—in other words, that syllogistic argument is their strict logical form.

The first point to be noted with regard to the relation "to the right of" (and similarly with any other relation of spatial direction) is that it is meaningless except with reference to (*a*) some field which the things related occupy (most commonly, some field of vision) and (*b*) some point *from which* the field is to be taken or before which the field is spread out, so that rotations or turnings round the point in one or other direction can be considered. If that point is not kept constant, if some other point before which the field is spread out could be taken instead, then A, which was first of all said to be to the right of B, could just as easily be said to be to the left of B. The question, then, when the relation is spoken of with any settled meaning, is of comparisons between turnings round a point O ("origin" or observer), within a field "in front of" it, in a rightward (or, similarly, in a leftward) direction; and A is to the right of B when and only when the turning to the direction of A, perhaps from a postulated "extreme left" position or simply "from the left" if it were maintained that the extremities of such a field could never be precisely marked, *is greater than* the turning to the direction of B. Thus we are back at the question of unequal quantities and hence at the question of class-inclusion, and we can have exactly the same sorts of syllogisms conveying the transitiveness of "to the right of" as we have in the case of the transitiveness of "greater than", with the very same complications, or special arguments, involving "not to the left of" as we have in the case of "not less than". We say that A is further to the right than B (that, as it might be put, A has "greater rightwardness") in the given field and from the given origin or point of view in the same way as we say that A is of greater quantity than B, and we can have arguments concerning the interrelation of *several* things in different directions from O in the same forms as the arguments concerning several things of different quantities or amounts. The position is roughly illustrated in the following diagram—

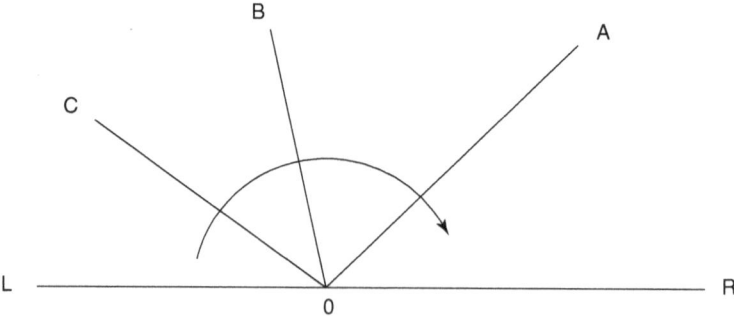

where the upward direction from the line LOR represents the outward direction (towards the field) from the origin.

Leaving aside for the moment the question of the precise terms to be used in the relevant syllogisms, we see that the relation "to the right of" involves a relation of greater and less, and that in this special case we shall be able as before (a) to exhibit the transitiveness of the relation (to bring out the validity of the argument "A is to the right of B, B is to the right of C ∴ A is to the right of C") in the form of two valid syllogisms, one in the AAA form and one with an O premise and an O conclusion, (b) to distinguish the cases in which the two different O premises are used and thus to distinguish the arguments (equally valid) "A is not to the left of B (it is either to the right of it or *level with it*, i.e., in the same direction from the origin), B is to the right of C ∴ A is to the right of C" and "A is to the right of B, B is not to the left of C ∴ A is to the right of C", (c) to recognise the valid AAA syllogism expressed more loosely in the argument "A is not to the left of B, B is not to the left of C ∴ A is not to the left of C", (d) to recognise that the truth of the premises here is quite compatible with the truth of "A is not to the right of B, B is not to the right of C", and thus recognise a possible argument of the same form as that of "A = B, B = C ∴ A = C"—an argument roughly expressible as "A is level with (or in the same direction as) B, B is level with C ∴ A is level with C"; where "in the same direction as" is a particular example of being of the same quantity as, the quantities in this case being *turnings*. Thus we find, in addition to the transitiveness of "to the right of" (and "to the left of"), that of "not to the left of" (and "not to the right of") and that of "neither to the right of nor to the left of" (or "level with"); so that the argument involving the transitiveness of "to the right of" is only one example of a whole class of "angular" arguments, the distinction and the interconnection of which are brought out by their presentation in syllogistic form.

To see in what terms these arguments may be set out syllogistically (or in strict form) we can consider swings or turnings from left and observe that any such swings which pass through A must pass through B, whereas those that pass through B need not pass through A; or we can say, in terms of positions and directions, that to be beyond A in a rightward swing is to be beyond B, while to be beyond B is not necessarily to be beyond A. Putting this more concretely in terms of *things* beyond or not beyond a given thing in a rightward swing, we come to the pair of assertions "All things to the right of A are (things) to the right of B" and "Some things to the right of B are not (things) to the right of A"; that is to say, to a relation of inclusion. Adopting for brevity the notion RA for "things to the right of A", etc., we can present the types of argument above referred to in the form of syllogisms with the following premises and conclusions:-

(a) $R_1aR_1$, $R_1oR_1$; $R_1aR_1$, $R_1oR_1$ ∴ $R_1aR_1$, $R_1oR_1$ (the transitiveness of "to the right of");

(b) $R_1aR_1$, $R_1aR_1$ $R_1oR_1$, ∴ $R_1aR_1$, $R_1oR_1$ (the case where A is given as "not to the left of" B) and $R_1aR_1$, $R_1oR_1$, $R_1aR_1$ ∴ $R_1aR_1$, $R_1oR_1$ (the case where B is given as "not to the left of" C);

(c) $R_1aR_1$, $R_1aR_1$ ∴ $R_1aR_1$ (the transitiveness of "not to the left of");

(d) $R_1aR_1$, $R_1aR_1$ ∴ $R_1aR_1$ *and* $R_1aR_1$, $R_1aR_1$ ∴ $R_1aR_1$ (the transitiveness of "neither to the right of nor to the left of").

In cases (a), (b) and (c) we can get similar syllogistic arguments for leftward as contrasted with rightward turnings by simply substituting left for right and right for left; but it should be noticed that there is no need to introduce an LA notation, since the formal statement of "A is to the right of B" ($R_1aR_1$, $R_1oR_1$) will also serve for "B is to the left of A", and the same form serves for "B is not to the right of A" as for "A is not to the left of B".

The fact that we can argue on leftward turnings by using "rightward" symbols raises the question whether we can treat the two assertions, "A is to the right of B" and "B is to the left of A", as saying exactly the same thing—as asserting the very same *proposition* in different words. We can certainly treat them as equivalent (so that whatever, other than the two themselves, is a consequence of one is a consequence of the other, and either is a consequence of whatever, with the same proviso, the other is a consequence of) and thus substituting either for the other in an argument will not affect its validity though it might affect the rapidity with which the implication could be grasped. The point of this equivalence is that the relation in question is a relation of "right and left" (comparable to "north and south", "above and below", "before and after"), that it is impossible to recognise either "rightward" or "leftward" without recognising *both*. But if these considerations justified the denial of any difference between the two assertions, the same would apply to any pair of "equivalent" assertions; and this, in the case of XeY and YeX (which, on certain views, would each be rendered by "XY do not exist"), would lead to the rejection of the distinction between *subject and predicate* (between location and description) which is essential to logical form, even with the recognition of the "convertibility" of terms, and which would still be required by the "existence, non-existence" theorists if there was to be any sense in asserting or denying "existent" of this or that subject, or, for that matter, if there was to be any meaning in XY (things which *are* X and *are* Y—a conjunctive term giving two descriptions of something, or being a combination of predicates, even when it is used as a subject, just as a disjunctive term gives two locations or is a combination of subjects). Thus the necessary distinction of subject and predicate shows that "No cows are horses" and "No horses are cows" are different assertions even though they imply one another; the assertion that cows lack the equine character can be put in conjunction with the recognition of the characters cows do possess, as well as raising the question of how they are connected with and distinguished from other non-equine things, and thus has a quite different place in discourse and investigation from that of the assertion that horses lack the bovine character.

Equivalence, then, does not mean identity; and the necessity of thinking right and left together, of seeing their interconnection, is nothing against seeing their opposition but indeed depends on this. The *irreversibility* of each of the relations "to the right of" and "to the left of" reinforces the point that, in spite of the equivalence referred to, quite different questions arise concerning things to the left of A from those concerning things to the right of B. Alexander (*Space, Time and Deity*, Vol. I; first edition, p. 243), discussing, with special reference to north and south, such differences in the "sense" or direction of relations, says that when "the same situation is expressed in two different senses by interchanging the terms (Edinburgh is north of London, London is south of Edinburgh), the difference is not indeed a merely verbal one, though perilously near to it, but a difference of aspect or description, what Aristotle expressed by saying that the two things *are* the same but not in their *being*" (italics in text). It is not at all clear what would be meant by being "perilously near to" a merely verbal difference without being precisely there, nor what, in the Aristotelian reference, is being attributed to the two things other than their *being and not being* the same. The point is that, taking it that we have two different assertions, we can indicate the difference quite clearly on the predicative view (any assertion having subject and predicate with different "functions"); in the one case, the subject is Edinburgh, and the predicate applied to it, in spite of being only a "relational description", enables us to classify it with other things north of London, to say "All (E. or A or B...) are north of L.", while in the other case the subject is London and we can similarly proceed to the assertion that "All (L. or X or Y...) are south of E."; and here it might incidentally be noted that some things north of London are not south of Edinburgh and some things south of Edinburgh are not north of London. Thus the two assertions Alexander has difficulty in differentiating not only have different subjects (in fact they have *no* common terms) but raise the quite distinct questions of what is north of London and what is south of Edinburgh. Understanding of the north-south range still shows the two assertions to be equivalent; but, to see how this is so, we have to see that, if a "relational assertion" has a subject, it must have a predicate—that, unless this is so, we can give no account of the possibility of contradicting such an assertion or of the form of the arguments (implications) in which it is involved.

It might be contended that if we identify "A is to the right of B" with "All things to the right of A are to the right of B" *and* "Some things to the right of B are not to the right of A", and particularly if we take the former of these propositions to be part of what it signifies, we are assuming, not demonstrating, the transitiveness of "to the right of", and that it is pointless to go on to any syllogistic argument in which this is brought out. And a similar point might be made about the interpretation of A > B as the inclusion of the class of things "measurable by" B in the class of things "measurable by" A: viz., that "measurable by" has to be understood as "not greater than", in that anything not greater than A can be *marked off* on A, if it is not precisely equal to A which would thus still give its measure; so that the assertions in which A > B was presented in syllogistic argument would have to be understood as "All things not-greater-than B are not-greater-than A" and "Some things not-greater-than A are not not-greater-than B" or, taking the equivalent contrapositives, "All things greater than A are greater than B" and "Some things greater than B are not greater than A"—where, as before, it could be contended that the former of these propositions conveyed the transitiveness of "greater than" and that nothing was contributed to the understanding of the relation by the syllogistic arguments in which this proposition was a premise. (The same types of relation would hold and the same problems would arise if "Measurable by" were taken as meaning "not *less* than"—i.e., if a thing were taken to be "measured" as so many unit measures, together with a marked off part of a unit if the units did not fit exactly. The question would still be one of class-inclusion and its transitiveness, etc.)

But such considerations would be an *objection* to the view here taken of the way in which the arguments can be precisely formulated only if, e.g., the two propositions which, in such arguments, represent "A is to the right of B" were taken as explaining what is meant by "to the right of"—which, since "to the right of" is contained in them, would be obviously circular. What can be said, in the first place, is that the two propositions ($R_1aR_1$, $R_1oR_1$) are true *when and only when* A is to the right of B, so that, in using them as syllogistic premises, we can formally exhibit what does follow from "A is to the right of B". But we are aware of this "when and only when" relationship, we can carry out the "transformation" in question, we can understand and recognise its justification, only in being aware of a continuous range, a field of things in various "angular" relations, apart from which "to the right of" would have no meaning and, incidentally, in recognising which we recognise what extends beyond as well as what falls between the things compared; in order to speak of A's being to the right of B, we have to be aware of a greater stretch to A than to B from the left and a smaller stretch from A than from B to the right, and thus there is no impropriety, no deviating from or passing beyond what we are observing from the outset, in speaking of "things to the right of A".

Being acquainted, then, with such a range (field of vision or whatever it may be) we can see how to present "angular relations" (involving greater and smaller turnings) as examples of inclusion and co-extension, and we can make clear in syllogistic argument the inter-connection of a set of such relations. As we saw, the transitiveness of "to the right of" is only one member of a whole class of connections which are formally presented in syllogisms and which are all involved in the recognition of a range of directions from an origin. It should still be noted that what we are doing in such arguments is not *to establish transitiveness* (even though in establishing the particular conclusion we come to—say, A is to the right of C—we *exhibit* the transitiveness of "to the right of"; and similarly with the rest of the class referred to) and that, unless we could *observe* this transitiveness as a feature of the situation in which A, B, C, etc., are (of the whole field or range), we could never argue in the way we do; our distinction between transitive and non-transitive relations, between valid and invalid arguments, would be quite arbitrary unless we were able to *see*, to take in a single view, the validity of the whole process and unless we had some way of setting it out so that formal criteria for determining the distinction were apparent. The syllogistic form shows us more clearly not only how a given conclusion is established but what relations are transitive and what are not.

These considerations, of course, apply to syllogism in general and not just to the cases ("angular arguments") we have been specially considering; unless we can observe in one situation the whole "syllogistic principle", unless we can see as a fact the force of the syllogistic argument, i.e., the implication of the conclusion by the two premises, any assertion we make of the validity of some forms and the invalidity of others will be quite arbitrary. If we obtained our belief in the validity of the Barbara syllogism, for example, from something other than observation, we could never *apply* this belief to what we observe; we could never say "This is an example of that sort of interrelation of propositions (situations)" unless we could observe that interrelation as a single situation, observe, that is to say, the *implication* which holds in any Barbara syllogism. We could still say that the syllogism BaC, AaB ∴ AaC assumes and does not demonstrate what we may roughly call "the transitiveness of the relation a" (having as a property); what it demonstrates is AaC. But we could not see that it does, unless we could see *BaC and AaB implying AaC,* just as much as we can see the truth of any of these three propositions. The position is similar, then, with any argument, like the "angular" arguments, which involves a continuous range; it is no objection to a particular way of setting out such an argument that it implies that we can *see* transitiveness, that we can observe it within the observed complex situation, since, if we could not, we could not see the force of the argument or set it out in any way.

Since the treatment I have given of "angular" arguments depends simply on the recognition of a continuous range, it would appear that the same treatment would be applicable to any transitive relation, with the same complications when it is asymmetrical—that arguments involving it would start from class-relations of co-extension and inclusion and would take the same syllogistic forms, supplemented in some cases perhaps by conjunctive and disjunctive arguments. In the simplest case of transitive asymmetrical relation, that of *before and after*—simplest because the question is just of continuity, because there is no range more special than Time itself and no peculiar "origin" or point of view—the main type of relation, "A is before B", will again be presented formally as inclusion, i.e., by the two propositions "All things before A are before B" and "Some things before B are not before A", while "B is *not after* C" (B is either before or simultaneous with C) will take the form of a single A proposition, "All things before B are before C", which can be taken along with the previous two propositions or with other "not after" assertions, just as in the "not to the left of" examples.

The case of *north and south*, previously referred to, is one in which the range has definite extremities, so that, if we were to say "The North Pole is north of Greenland", we could not present this as "All *things north of the North Pole* are..." ", etc. It might be suggested, however, that, when we are comparing the latitudes of two things, we are concerned with which of them is further from the North Pole (or, similarly, from the South Pole), and that we treat the extremes not as things within the range but, like an "origin", as part of the *background* or the "terms of reference" of the relation. At the very least, we have to *distinguish*, where there are specific limits, the recognition of differences within a continuous range from the recognition of such limits, and what confronts us, in our consideration of transitiveness or continuous transition in a range, is the shading off of a specific segment into an indefinitely extended background. This shading off, with non-specification of extremes, is also to be found, as suggested earlier, in *right and left* judgments, so that, even though we always recognise a "beyond" and could not make a specific comparison without doing so, our definite reference is always to things (or positions) within the range. The distinction between the question of limits and that of internal comparisons is emphasised by the fact that where, as with *before and after*, there is no question of such limits, the types of "transitive" argument are the same as where there are limits; and it is of some relevance to observe, in the case of *north and south*, that distinctions and relations of this sort were recognised before there was any question of extreme points.

Such special considerations are secondary to the general contention that recognition of implication requires recognition of the *formal validity* which may be seen in syllogism and in other arguments (conjunctive and disjunctive) set out in strictly predicative form. But it is interesting to note that the question of ranges and of "shading off" also has a certain application to syllogism in general. I have spoken of "the transitiveness of the relation a", i.e., of the A proposition—though a proposition is not strictly a relation; and the point to be observed here is that, in asserting XaY (as, indeed, in using the terms X and Y at all), we always have the sense of a background—of further subjects of which X is a predicate or locations of which it is a description, of further predicates of which Y is a subject or descriptions of which it is a location. We have, in other words, a sense of an indefinitely continued range of extensions and intensions; we have, in knowing any proposition, a background of possible syllogisms, of lines of further inquiry and discovery. This is nothing against the definiteness of any given proposition or of any given syllogism; though recognition of further possibilities may at times make us uncertain of our "grasp" of some sort of thing with which we had supposed ourselves well-acquainted, it is only in so far as we have definite knowledge that we can take any step in inquiry or distinguish one line of inquiry from another. But the recognition of such "lines" is recognition of some range or ranges, exhibiting what may be roughly called the transitiveness of "qualifying" and of "being qualified by"; though this does not mark off "qualitative syllogisms" from "relational syllogisms", since it is only on the predicative view of the proposition, on the three-term view of the syllogism, that validity in syllogistic reasoning can be recognised.

This assimilation of relational and qualitative arguments does not mean a breaking down of the distinction between relations and qualities. It is, I have suggested, from a qualitative starting-point, specifically from seeing that a given predicate has many subjects, that we pass to the question of relations, by way of the observation of juxtapositions or differences of place within a certain region or range. But it should be emphasised on the other side that even the distinguishing of various predicates of a given subject proceeds by finding the place of each quality in a set of "exchanges" or interactions between it and its surroundings (other subjects). Thus the question of ranges or lines of connection arises in regard to any issue whatever, whether it is primarily a qualitative or a relational one. The point is that we are always confronted simultaneously with questions of relations and questions of qualities, that relations and qualities are linked in the recognition, as in the existence, of any situation, any complex state of affairs, and that there is nothing less, and nothing more, than a complex (spatio-temporal) situation that we can be confronted with in dealing with any material, i.e., in any recognition of or search for connections and distinctions. The attempt to have separate *relational* and *qualitative* logics can only lead to confusion and insoluble problems; what this attempt misses is the fact that any object (any known thing and any existing thing) is a complex situation involving both relations and qualities, so that there will always be connections to be found between any object and any other object, between any and any other problem or line of investigation.

# 16
# EMPIRICISM AND LOGIC (1962)

In my article "Empiricism" (*A.J.P.P.*, December, 1927)[1] I presented it as a mark of empiricism that it rejects any doctrine of different kinds or degrees of truth and reality and maintains that there is only one way of being (describable as "being a matter of fact" or simply "being so" or "being the case"). I argued that, in the distinction between empiricism and *rationalism* (with its division between facts and principles, between actual things and their "grounds" or "explanations"), the question of ways of *knowing* is a quite secondary matter, though the denial of distinct ways of knowing has still to be recognised as a feature of the empiricist position. It is, in fact, quite illuminating, of the particular question of knowledge as well as of the general question of reality, to present the matter from the side of knowledge and take empiricism as the doctrine that whatever we know we *learn*—in other words, that to know something is to come into active relations, to enter into "transactions", with it—a position which at once rules out any rationalist notion of ultimates or principles above the facts, any suggestion of "that whereby" things exist, as something distinct from the things themselves, since, unless we were *acquainted* with it, had acquired empirical knowledge of it, we could never infer it from what we are acquainted with or assign it any way of operating on objects of our acquaintance.

More broadly, it might be said that we cannot uphold any doctrine of kinds of reality, since to do so we should have to know the distinction or the relation between any two such kinds, and that is something we could not know except as a single situation—which would mean that we knew it as of a single reality, so that the doctrine of *distinct* kinds of reality would be automatically abandoned. It is in this way that empiricism is seen as a doctrine of what is real as situations, and that therewith goes the denial that anything can be *known* except as situations, which is to say except as spatio-temporal and except in *propositional* form.

[1] v. s., p. 3.

I have argued at the end of the preceding paper, "Relational Arguments" that, important as the distinction is between qualities and relations (impossible as it is to regard, e.g., "A is after B" or "A is beside B" as a *description* of A), the fact remains that to find a situation is to find a tissue of qualities and relations, a "nest" of situations or propositions. Thus there is no question of *separate regions* of the existent or the knowable, but the question is always of complex and interrelated states of affairs; and recognition of this makes it possible to have a coherent view of the acquisition of knowledge of any subject-matter, in a way that cannot be done on a rationalist or "separatist" position.

It is remarkable that Locke, Berkeley and Hume, so widely regarded as the founders of modern empiricism, should take their departure from just such a rationalist doctrine of simple and separate entities—the "ultimates" by reference to which any actual state of affairs is to be explained. It is no less remarkable that these entities should be called "particulars" when, as "whole natures", as "nothing but" yellow or a shade of yellow, etc., they would appear rather to be "universals", to be merely descriptive, and to say that their simple nature was of a *non*-descriptive character would be to say that they were indescribable—and indistinguishable. But, it being on a situational or propositional view of things that such a division, or *any* belief in simples, would be denied, it is *not* remarkable that the "British empiricists" are unable to give any coherent account of complexity—of propositions or of relations. (Of course, from an atomistic starting-point, the most that propositions could be would be relations—of juxtaposition, etc.)

The position can perhaps be best illustrated from the work of Berkeley. Of the three he is the most openly committed to "natures", particularly to the treatment of the "idea" as that whose nature it is to be perceived—the logical outcome of which is the impossibility of distinguishing one idea from another. Yet he is definitely more empiricist than Locke and Hume in taking the truths of mathematics to be as "matter of fact" as those of any other subject, taking them as something that has to be *learned* just as anything else has, and in standing out the most decisively against the treatment of what we are acquainted with as "standing for" (presenting us with knowledge of) something we are not acquainted with at all. Nevertheless, in spite of all his empiricist strivings, he gets himself into a complete impasse in his attempts to deal with situations.

The failure of Berkeley's attempt to account for "the objects of human knowledge" in terms of atomic "ideas" already emerges in § 1 of the *Principles* when, having spoken of the ideas furnished to the mind by the various *senses* (what these are being not itself explicable in terms of simple ideas), he goes on to say that "as several of these [ideas] are observed to accompany each other, they come to be marked by one name, and so to be reputed as one thing. Thus, for example, a certain colour, taste, smell, figure, and consistence having been observed to go together, are accounted one distinct thing, signified by the name *apple*. Other collections of ideas constitute a stone, a tree, a book and the like sensible things; which, as they are pleasing or disagreeable, excite the passions of love, hatred, joy, grief, and so forth". Concomitance is only one of the relations which Berkeley "annexes" to his supposedly ultimate objects of knowledge, yet it is clear that to *observe* such going together is to have as an object (cognitum) a single and at the same time complex situation, and, if an "idea" can be found in such a situation, knowing it is not the same as *separating* it from all that is not of its nature. If it were, "going together" would at best be another separate object or piece of content, and there would be no such situation as "the going together *of* A, B, C and D"; but, if it is not, the knowing of various qualities in various complex situations shows neither the necessity nor the possibility of any such separability (or of any absolute "original") of any one of them—it brings out no meaning, in fact, in the notion of taking one of them by itself, taking it in any other way than in a complex situation.

This, of course, would be a spatio-temporal situation, for the fact that various contents were *near in time* to one another (though even that would be unintelligible on a doctrine of distinct atoms of information) would give us no reason for regarding them as making up "one distinct thing" or total content, but *spatial* togetherness would also be a condition of any such "unification". Over and above that, however, it should be noted that Berkeley's concomitants are descriptive terms and their concomitance would be a *conjunction* or addition of descriptions, so that their "unification" would be not merely of a spatial and temporal but of a *predicative* character. This point is reinforced by the fact that

Berkeley's argument gives us no suggestion of any purely "particular" idea but only of classes or *kinds* of ideas (colours, tastes, smells, etc.) so that such ideas would differ in various ways from others of the same kind and, as thus complex, would not be ultimate units but would themselves be situational or propositional. Thus our recognition of distinct complex things is not accounted for at all by "collections of ideas" (of separate, unitary pieces of content) but is intelligible only as a recognition of complex situations, of situations within situations (in which terms alone "concomitance" can be understood), of interpenetration as well as juxtaposition—in other words, of infinite complexity (with no least and no greatest situation) in place of the "simplicity" which cannot be squared with any complexity or combination.

It may also be noted that Berkeley, in the final sentence quoted, admits situations in which collections of ideas are related, in the way of "exciting", to mental situations (those of the passions and operations of the mind)—something that is possible only if objects of observation are "on the same level" of reality as mental operations, instead of having the one *dependent* and the other *independent* existence. This is to say that the empiricist position in which any coherent account of observation must issue has also to be a realist position, that the rejection of any doctrine of ultimates and derivatives carries with it the rejection of any doctrine of "ideas", of existence relatively to minds as much as (or as one case of) existence relatively to what is "self-existent". But of course Berkeley does not recognise this; and, in spite of the soundness of much of his criticism of "representationism", of any view of an observed content as deputising to our minds for an unobservable content, he himself is not free from representationism, as no one can be who recognises the "idea" (that whose relationship to what knows it is inherent in its own content) in any shape or form. And an essential point here is that, if we find in our minds "a collection of ideas", what we find (the combination of A, B, C and D) is just as much a matter of fact, something that just is *so* and not something that "is dependently so", as any situation that could be found "existing absolutely", in minds or out of them.

The untenability of any doctrine of "dependent existence", then, whether the dependence is supposed to be on the mind which is aware of the "existence" or on anything else, is a particular case of the impossibility in any coherent theory of admitting realities of different kinds or orders. The incoherence of Berkeley's anti-realist position, which is a part of his anti-empiricist position, appears most strikingly in §§ 30 and 31 of the *Principles*—headed, in Lindsay's text, "Laws of Nature" and "Knowledge of them necessary for the conduct of worldly affairs". We are told (§ 30) that laws of nature are "*the set rules or established methods, wherein the mind we depend on excites in us the ideas of sense*", and that we learn these laws by experience "which teaches us that such and such ideas are attended with such and such other ideas, in the ordinary course of things". And again it is said (§ 31) that knowledge of such laws "gives us a sort of foresight, which enables us to regulate our actions for the benefit of life. And without this we should be eternally at a loss: we could not know how to act on any thing that might procure us the least pleasure, or remove the least pain of sense. That food nourishes, sleep refreshes, and fire warms us; that to sow in the seed-time is the way to reap in the harvest, and, in general, that to obtain such and such ends, such and such means are conducive, all this we know, *not by discovering any necessary connexion between our ideas*, but only by the observation of the settled laws of nature, without which we should be all in uncertainty and confusion, and a grown man no more know how to manage himself in the affairs of life than an infant just born" (Berkeley's italics in both the above places).

Now Berkeley is anti-representationist in so far as he maintains that "our ideas" (the objects of our observation or experience) are actual things and not merely ways in which some of the features of an unobservable "matter" are conveyed to us, but in so far as he takes them as relative to our minds he is not treating them as actual and is forced into representationism in order that our knowledge may be taken as in any way confronting us with the actual. As ideas of ours, our successive sensations are dependent on us, but their regularities, as instituted by God for our guidance, are quite independent of us, so that our knowledge of "laws of nature" is knowledge of objective facts. And the only support Berkeley can give for the adhibiting of objectivity to part of what we experience is that our sensations are not under our control (an objective fact of which it seems we are directly aware) whereas our "images" or reproductions of sensations are (another fact, independent of our knowing it, which we can discover); so that Berkeley's position is a hotch-potch of realism and representationism, an unavoidable result so long as "ideas" (entities of a different order of reality from minds or agents) are retained.

Further confusion is disclosed by a more thorough consideration of what can be meant by "the conduct of worldly affairs", by the regulation of our actions through attention to "laws of nature" such as that food nourishes and fire warms. Such utilisation of our knowledge involves the securing of results that we desire and the avoidance of others that we object to, and this avoidance can only mean that, on having a sensation that is normally the sign of another sensation, we act so as not to get that second sensation, so as to avoid the experience which the first "signified". But that is to say that we actually falsify the supposed regularity which we were said to be using as a guide—that, e.g., we get the visual sensation of a fire and then do not get the tactual or cutaneous sensation of being warmed or perhaps burned; in other words, the conduct of life, as an avoidance of certain sensations, would mean a contravening of the "laws of nature". In fact, however, when we make such avoidances, we do not think there has been any interference with natural regularities; we believe that fire, food, etc., operate as they always did, even if some of their effects are not sensed by us. And this belief is possible only because we distinguish our perceptions or sensations of things (the fact that on certain occasions certain things are perceived by us) from the things themselves, only because we do not identify the effects of fire, e.g., with the "sensations" which ensue upon a "sensation" of fire, only because we distinguish our knowing of a sequence (though this knowing too is an objective fact) from the occurrence of that sequence—only, i.e., because we take a realist view. But if we did not take that realist view, we should have to abandon the recognition of regularities that Berkeley speaks of and thus to deny any possibility of the conduct of life through knowledge of them.

The conduct of life, however, does not involve only that there are ways of working of things we observe, independently of whether we observe them or not; it also involves *our working on them*—our eliminating certain things and so the effects they have been producing, our instituting certain things, as contrasted with merely seeing signs of their approach. Now on Berkeley's view that our sensations are not under our control and that all we can control is the reproduction of them in imagination, the conduct of life would be restricted to such imaginative exercise while the sequence of sensations proceeded regardless, and we should not be making any use of our knowledge of the laws of such sequence. But, even if it were supposed that we could do so, i.e., that we could take such action as to avoid some sensations and secure others, it is not apparent how such securing and avoidance could make us any less "at a loss" than we should otherwise be. For, on the doctrine of active mind and passive ideas, our sensations would merely *confront* us, like images on a screen, and it would not make the slightest difference to us whether one or another was there; we could have, say, the sensation of extreme cold, or again that of gentle warmth, or again that of burning (even what is called the burning of our flesh), but which of these was present would not matter to our *minds*.

Thus, when Berkeley speaks of food nourishing, sleep refreshing and fire warming *us*, he should mean only that they are signs of other *ideas*, of the sort, no doubt, that we call "organic sensations" but having, on the doctrine of ideas, no more intimate relation to the percipient than ideas we do not so describe. But the notion of "the conduct of life" implies that these objects do affect our very selves, that they are not mere data but things that make a difference to our activities. Berkeley to some extent obscures this position by talking of our being affected by pleasure and pain; if this means only our having *perceptions* of pleasure and pain, this will still not bring us any nearer to the active mind (the perceptions would still make no difference to it), but if, as seems to be the case, pleasure and pain are to be taken as features of mental processes, then their being procured by the securing of some sensations and the avoidance of others can only mean the operation of what is sensed itself on the mental. In any case, unless the sensible has direct effects on *us*, there can be no conduct of life by means of recognition of its regularities. But, if there is direct interaction between minds and what they perceive, that means that minds themselves come within the range of laws of nature, that they and not just what they contemplate are parts of the natural realm, that there are regular sequences between, e.g., the provision of food and fire and various types of mental occurrence; and without this interconnection, without continuous processes between the mental and the non-mental, there would be no such thing as "affairs of life", no relevance of "laws of nature" to the sequence (if such there could be) of mental activities.

Even Berkeley's account of the conduct of life, then, is unintelligible except in terms of interaction between minds and things they observe (which, of course, include minds), i.e., except as implying the unintelligibility of any assignment of different sorts of reality to the mental and the non-mental, except as recognising both (besides the relations between them) as equally matter-of-fact, in precisely the same sense situational or propositional—a sense which is *realist*, recognising independence, the existence of many distinct things in any situation, and *empiricist*, recognising a single level, on which only situations can and situations always do connect situations. But, while consideration of his inconsistencies leads to the showing up of any attempted separation of mind and nature, Berkeley remains sunk in them just because of his rationalism, his doctrine of natures or elementary entities, the discontinuity between which is set aside by the postulation of impossible leaps, such as he himself has shown Locke's representationism to be. For, in spite of all his efforts to find real connections between minds and what they contemplate, he also, as we have seen, makes the representationist leap; it is something he is forced to do by the doctrine of "ideas", which must be taken as at once "in" minds and "of" things, leaving us with the insoluble problems which arise on any doctrine of relative existence.

Dualism, disconnections, ambiguities and insoluble problems, can, of course, be brought out just as readily in the theories of Locke and Hume as in that of Berkeley. The point is that on the supposition of elementary ideas it is impossible alike to have any knowledge of them singly and to have knowledge of any relations among them; we cannot know the absolutely separate but equally we cannot know the togetherness of a number of separates—as argued above, we can know only the togetherness of complex and situated things (things having situations within them and situations around them and themselves being situations). Thus when Locke speaks of our knowledge of "agreement" among ideas, he is (apart from allowing the symmetrical relation "agreement" to do duty for the A proposition which is not, as such, reversible) making possible knowledge of what is in the realm of ideas by recognising the occurrence there of complex states of affairs, but, first, is thereby leaving no room for their supposed elementary constituents and, secondly, is taking all point from the notion of a realm of ideas, since what we know is that A does objectively or as a matter of fact *agree* with B (assuming that agreement can have a definite meaning here) and there is no conceivable point in saying that that fact *further* agrees with or "corresponds to" something "in reality"—it is already "in reality" in being a fact.

In line with the general argument against dualism, the distinction between an "inner" and an "outer" reality (between mind and "the external world", as the phrase goes) is one of which no account can be given, since there will be no reality for that distinction to have. In more detail, to say that anything is external to mind is to say that it is part of a situation which includes mind, and thus to say that it does not constitute a "world" but is just such and such situations related to (in common situations with) other situations; again, to say that A is external to B is to say that B is external to A and thus, just as much as A, exists under conditions of externality (and this may remind us of the fact that what is external to any mind *includes minds*); and, finally, to note (as has been done above) that what is called "inner" reality contains complex states of affairs is to indicate that it has within itself relations of externality and thus that there can be no "world" (apart from the objections to that notion itself) to distinguish from an "external" one—there will be only variously qualified situations (mental and otherwise) variously disposed spatially towards one another. But if there could be separate kinds of reality, "inner" and "outer", there could be no *relations* between them, and when we look closely at supposed relations like "correspondence" or "agreement", we find nothing that can consistently be meant by them.

We cannot say that X "corresponds to" a fact unless, as I have indicated, X is already a fact, and then how it could be regarded as "standing for" (or being "of") some other fact is not apparent. We cannot even say that X *corresponds to something unspecified* without implying our awareness of this whole situation, but there is no suggestion in that that this object of our awareness stands for or corresponds to something else. We cannot say that knowledge of X (something "inner") "claims to be" knowledge of Y (something "outer"); if this claim were supposed to reside in some *resemblance* between X and Y (a resemblance which, on the doctrine of "the external world", we could not know—though, if we could, our knowledge would be directly of X's resembling Y and not of anything that *that* could be supposed to "correspond to"), the claim could be made with much more force that knowledge of X is knowledge of Z, another "idea", the resemblance of which to X we could, on the doctrine of an "inner" reality, be aware of. Or, putting it in terms of "agreement with reality", we can say that X agrees with Y only if the knowing of X is the very same thing as the knowing of Y (if X and Y are the very same state of affairs); we cannot maintain a *dual* theory of knowledge and say that knowledge of the situation X is "somehow" at the same time knowledge of a *different* situation Y. The only solution is to reject the whole doctrine of "inner" and "outer" and to maintain the realist doctrine of a direct knowledge of propositions, of mental as of non-mental states of affairs, which are variously related but none of which can be said to *mediate* others to our minds.

The force of this propositional or situational realism is commonly concealed by the treatment of the *proposition* as a tertium quid or mediator, something *by which* we can assert facts but which is *distinct* from the facts as well as from us. This, however, is as untenable a view as the doctrine of correspondence, of which indeed it is just a variety. When we assert the proposition "All men are mortal", *what* we are asserting is the actual mortality of men, and to call the assertion of the proposition merely a *means* to the asserting of the fact is to say that we have *no* way of asserting the fact, just as we have no way of specifying the "reality" with which certain ideas of ours are supposed to "agree" unless those "ideas" (what we know) *are* the reality. I have spoken in a misleading way on this matter in "Empiricism" *A.J.P.P.*, December 1927, p. 242),[2] i.e., as if I regarded the proposition as a tertium quid, in saying: "The empiricist, like Socrates, adopts the attitude of considering things in terms of what can be said about them, i.e., in propositions"—when I certainly did not think that there was any other way of considering them, that "things" could be other than propositional (or situational) in their content. I had indeed said earlier (in my discussion paper, "Propositions and Judgments"; *Mind*, vol. xxxv, N.S., No. 138, p. 239)[3] that propositions are not "about" anything (i.e., that, as above, the proposition which is commonly said to "assert a fact" just is that fact). I there allowed a loose sense in which a proposition could be said to be "about" its subject; which is connected with my formulation (arrived at

[2] v. s., p. 4.
[3] v. s., p. 17.

very much earlier, but presented in "Hypotheticals", *A.J.P.*, May, 1952, p. 3)[4] of the "function" of the subject of the proposition as *location*, as giving a "point of reference" at which we can check the truth of the proposition, in contrast to the predicate's function of *description*. The fact that any term can have either function (is both locative and descriptive) brings out the fact that the *term* also is situational in its content, but to be presented with a single state of affairs that we can consider we have to be presented with a proposition; it is a single issue, not a group of issues, and is not "about" any other issue.

The distinction of functions is important (as I have argued in "Hypotheticals", pp. 3–5)[5] in the criticism of certain views of the import of the proposition or of possible propositional forms, and also in the consideration of "the false proposition" which has been taken to involve a fatal objection to non-representationist views. The position is, just as in the case of "correspondence", that if a "false proposition" were simply a certain contemplated content, it would not *be* false; it would be a state of affairs that we found to occur—and not, as in the similar case of "ideas", specifically "in our minds", but just as *constituted* in a certain way. What could be considered false would be the "claim" of this content to represent or reproduce a *different* state of affairs, which is to say *another* proposition; but this is a claim which is not made and could not be made, any more than the "claim" of "ideas" to "correspond to" (or agree with) "reality" can be made. The question, then, is not of the occurrence of a state of affairs with the attribute "falsity" (any more than of a state of affairs characterisable as "not corresponding to reality"); what is meant by the occurrence of a "false proposition" is explained, by reference to the distinction of subject and predicate, as *someone's mistaking* X for Y (taking X to be Y when it is not)—the question of this threefold relationship not being one that the person who is mistaken intends to raise, and not arising when he is *not* mistaken, when he is presenting the single situation X is Y.

This predicament is made possible, in the first place, not merely by our knowing X and Y in other propositions but by the fact that they are themselves complex or situational, that the content of a

[4] v. s., p. 138.
[5] v. s., pp. 138–40.

term can be set out in propositions, as when we define A as BC and thus identify its content with that of the proposition BiC (the position is really more complicated—the I is only one of a *group* of propositions making up the definition); secondly, by the fact that there are different formal possibilities of the "propositional connection" of two terms, that, e.g., knowing situations of the A and of the O forms we can *consider whether* XaY or XoY is true, without, for the time, being able to decide (though, when we do decide that XaY and thus call XoY "a false proposition", this, as said above, does not mean that we are recognising a "false situation" but the logical form of "O is false" is A or, as it is commonly put, is "the truth of the contradictory"); and, thirdly, as I have argued in some detail in "Mind as Feeling" (*A.J.P.P.*, June, 1934),[6] by the fact that knowing is a matter of learning or finding out, that we may be seeking or demanding the occurrence of the predicate Y in the subject X, wishing to introduce, or simply desiring that there should be, this character in a place which we otherwise identify—in particular, by other predicates. No coherent position can be got by dividing the class "propositions" into two species, "the true" and "the false" (the species of "what is" and the species "what is not")—there is no parallel between this and the division of animals, say, into the male and the female—and the treatment of every proposition as a subject of inquiry and dispute (of seeking and mistaking) is *opposed* to the treatment of the proposition as a tertium quid, which would make any discovery, any *outcome* of discussion or inquiry, impossible.

The rejection of the "tertium quid" view leaves us with a propositional view of reality, which, without fully canvassing the matter here, I have been indicating reasons for identifying with a situational or *spatio-temporal* view. My general thesis has been that there cannot be separate kinds or realms of reality, and I take the separation of the situational or propositional from the non-situational or non-propositional to be an example of this—though a case might be made out for taking it as the true content of all such separations. I have contended that the rejection of "separatism" of this kind is characteristic of empiricism, even as a doctrine of knowledge, i.e., of the conditions of our becoming acquainted with things, though this is secondary to the characterisation of

[6] v. s., pp. 72 and 76–8.

*what* we are acquainted with as situational, as "complex and interrelated states of affairs". Another way of putting the matter is that empiricism is the doctrine of the continuity of things—a continuity which would be broken if we could admit different kinds of reality, notably elemental or ultimate as against secondary or derivative being. Professor Gilbert Ryle who, in an article entitled "Logic and Professor Anderson" (*A.J.P.*, December 1950), criticises my position as set out in a number of *A.J.P.P.* articles, and particularly endeavours to show the inadequacy of my situational view of things, seems to me to fall conspicuously into errors of discontinuity, of dualism or division in reality.

Ryle takes me to have carried out with some success "deflationist" arguments against "ultimates" and "levels of reality" but considers that in the views I advance, particularly, of mathematics, of good and of implication, I am telling just as "impossible stories" (p. 142) as those I have detected in the work of Plato, Locke and other philosophers. My contention is that in these views ("stories") I am pursuing the same empiricist line (rejection of divisions in reality) as I do in my "deflating" generally, and that the exposure of such divisions is all that "deflating" can mean. Thus my position on implication (cf. what I have said above in "Relational Arguments") is that we have to recognise implication among propositions in the same way and by the same acts as we recognise the propositions themselves, i.e., in a continuous situation with them; that the alternative is a complete *disconnection* between the observed facts and what is supposed to relate them, and thus a quite arbitrary view of what implies what and of what implication is; that only on a view which rejects such divisions, which will not put implication outside the continuum of situations—only on an empiricist view, denying that implication is a special, a "rational", kind of fact—could it ever be *learned* that p implies q or that r and s imply t. In the same way, it is a condition of our getting to know mathematical truths, and of their having any relation to, any continuity with, other truths—a condition, e.g., as I mentioned in "Empiricism" of the mathematical having any "application" to the physical—that they should be discovered in the same situations and by the same experiences as those other truths; and, if this were never so, mathematical truths would have to belong to a different realm of reality from physical truths, and presumably from what is true of ourselves, so that they could never be learned. Similarly on good, a question to which I shall return, I have attacked doctrines of a dualistic kind, and it is not hard to find dualism in the doctrines that Ryle sets against mine.

It is particularly where he touches on categories that Ryle shows the "separatist" or atomistic character of his thinking. He accuses me (quite wrongly) of having such an "exiguous logical alphabet" that I recognise only two categories where Aristotle recognised ten in line with his earlier contention (p. 143) that I have a logical dichotomy "Quality or relation?", whatever is not a question of one being a question of the other. I think it could easily be maintained that questions of both quality and relation are features of the questions raised under any other category (pretty obviously, e.g., both arise in questions of causality or the continuance of one situation into another); but the vital point is that, while a question of the occurrence of a relation is not a question of the occurrence of a quality, it is only by seeing these different types of question together (as they must be seen in any concrete inquiry) that they can be thoroughly understood. Ryle does not specifically say that he takes questions of quality and questions of relation (and so on with whatever other categories he recognises) to belong to different regions of inquiry; but he gives no sign of seeing that the logician is concerned not with a miscellaneous bunch of types of question which can be raised about this subject or that, but with a group of types of question which have a *common ground*, which hang together in any inquiry and thus apply to any subject-matter. This, I would say, is the ground of Space and Time (or of being situational) in terms of which the universal application and the interlocking of logical questions appear. It is because questions in all the categories are spatio-temporal, because they all arise within any region or "contour", to use Alexander's expression, that they are not *discontinuous* with one another but all form part of a common inquiry (not, of course, an inquiry into everything but inquiry into any specific subject, it being remembered that subjects are not cut off from one another but each of them embraces relations among subjects). Apart from such a common ground, there would be no such thing as logic, no sort of connection between one inquiry and another, and thus no inquiry.

Now just as there are not separate *regions* of relational facts and qualitative facts but all situations embody both (recognising a situation might indeed be equated with recognising both qualities and relations), so there are no separate regions of the universal and the particular, but any situation exhibits both particularity and generality. This is indicated by the fact that any proposition has both a subject and a predicate or is both locative and descriptive; but here the "convertibility" of terms has to be remembered—there is no such thing as the purely locative or the purely descriptive, there are not two classes of terms, subjects and predicates. Thus, over and above the fact that Ryle's division between universal and particular "statements" would prevent there being *any* connection between universality and particularity, we find that he uses "particular" in the confused sense of something "unique" or "individual", thus making "a particular" something indescribable and not realising that there is no such thing as "a particular" but only "a particular X", i.e., some subject of which X is a predicate but which can itself be a predicate and thus is a descriptive or "general" term. Thus there is not the antithesis he postulates, and takes me to be possibly conceding (p. 145), between "at least one sort of general proposition" and "*a report of* [why this?] a *particular* spatio-temporal situation" (my italics), since this situation also has generality.[7]

Since I take A, E, I and O propositions to be equally situational and do not admit Ryle's "particulars", I do not admit that there is any ground in my "Problem of Causality" (*A.J.P.P.*, August, 1938)[8] for the suggestion that I might have abandoned the identification of propositions and situations, nor do I admit that there is any "affinity" (p. 142) between my "spatio-temporal

---

[7] Ryle's belief in absolute particulars may be compared with the doctrine of *momentary occurrences* which he puts forward (pp. 148,9) in correcting my "patently wrong" view of knowing. He thinks that we, e.g., *learn* things at moments, but that we *know* things "from the time we learn them till the time we forget them or die." In fact it would be from the *identifying* of knowing with learning that we should take it to have duration, since any occurrence is temporally as well as spatially extended. As far as usage is concerned, it could with complete propriety be said that contemplating takes time and contemplating is knowing, while *having* contemplated is not knowing. We know things while we continue to exercise our minds on them, while we continue to grapple with the questions they raise. Of course, there is a quite widespread assumption of the *storehouse* view of knowledge (of any piece of knowledge as being tucked away in some mental compartment) and language is used so as to support that view; but it is one of philosophy's tasks to *correct* common assumptions and usages, not to follow them. In the same way, we may note the confusion consequent on the grammatical distinction of nouns, verbs, adjectives and adverbs, when the content in each case is that of *going on in certain concrete ways*.
[8] v. s., p. 127.

situations" and "the atomic facts once patronised by Russell and Wittgenstein". That their "completely elementary propositions assert that named particulars have specified qualities or else stand in specified relation to other named particulars" is nothing to me, since, as I have indicated, I reject "pure particulars" and take any term to be general or have instances; otherwise, it *could not* be named or have qualities or have relations—thus, there is for me no question of anything atomic or elementary. The representationism bound up with this doctrine of particularity is brought out when Ryle says (pp. 142,3) that "Russell and Wittgenstein did not suppose that all or most or perhaps any of the assertions that we actually make are atomic statements. They are, rather, cheques drawn against these solid coins." What appears here is that any supposed "solid coin" is merely a postulated "that whereby" cheques are validated, but there is nothing to show that anything validates them or why one rather than another could be said to be validated. Ryle does not commit himself to the Russell-Wittgenstein view he presents, but a similar representationist weakness is seen in his reference (p. 145) to a "report" of a spatio-temporal situation, where the question would be what was the difference between the report and what was reported, just as, when he asks (p. 144) whether "John is not at home" *describes* the same situation as "John is at the theatre", we are left with the question of the difference between what is said to describe and what is said to be described. The terminology of "reports" is also used as if it supported the mere dogmatism of the following (p. 146): "Certainly universal statements are not reports of other-worldly states of affairs; but nor are they reports of this-worldly states of affairs. For we report states of affairs in the idiom of—reports of states of affairs. And this is not the idiom of universal statements." In each case we say that something *is so*, and that can be alternatively expressed by saying that something *is a state of affairs*. I have argued that unless what is asserted in a "statement" of a "particular" spatio-temporal situation is not logically different from, is on precisely the same footing as, a universal "statement", the two must be taken to be completely disconnected (even though this could not be *consistently* maintained); and Ryle's reply in terms of "idioms" amounts to no more cogent refutation of my view than that some people do not believe it.

What I have denied, then, and continue to deny, is that universal propositions raise any special problem for our knowledge; they are matters of direct experience, objects of *observation*, situations, just as particular propositions in the strict sense (the contradictories of universal propositions) are—and the attempt to get round this by any doctrine of "the pure particular", "the uniquely individual fact", is a clear failure. The supposed "harshness" of the observational view cannot be escaped from by the substitution of "the verification of hypotheses", since, apart from direct experience of universal truths, we should not know what the universal form signified (*what* was being asserted, recognised as actual, when we said that XaY or XeY); moreover, since *any* proposition can be verified or found to have true consequences (since some propositions recognised as true can always be found to follow from the combination of the hypothesis with other propositions recognised as true, i.e., since there are always propositions which "would be true if the hypothesis were true" and which *are* true), verification, applying equally to any proposition and its contradictory, can never settle any question (or be *proof*—cannot, that is to say, bring us any nearer to belief in the truth of a universal (or of any other) proposition.

Again, the setting up of a universal proposition by way of "convention" would (apart from other objections) give us no assurance of anything that was not "by convention", and any proposition called "axiomatic" would either be a matter of fact or have no bearing on matters of fact. Ryle gives no indication of how my view of mathematics constitutes an "impossible story" (and gives no answer to the arguments in the second part of "Empiricism"), but a passing reference to "analytic propositions" and the use of "modal" expressions make me think that his objections would be couched in terms of the analytic and the necessary. I repeat from "Empiricism" that there are no analytic propositions, that any proposition is an issue or has a contradictory and that it is only by experience that we find how the two terms "combine", that to say something "could not conceivably be otherwise" is to say we could never find it out—or, more exactly, that no proposition has been advanced at all, though we may be deceived into thinking that one has. With the rejection of "analytic propositions" would go rejection of the notion of "analysis", as in "What is the analysis of X?"—either in the meaning of what are X's "ultimate constituents" (which never could be discovered, and any suggested list of which could never add up to a situation but would remain so many "natures") or in the meaning of what compartment or division of reality does X belong to, with which other things would it fit and from which would it be quite disconnected (with the same problem as before concerning relations or distinctions among such divisions).

The doctrine of "necessary truths", or, in general, of "modal" distinctions among propositions, is subject to the objections I have advanced in "Hypotheticals" to any attempt to go beyond the four forms. The main relevant consideration is that of contradiction (Is it so or not?), though there are important connected questions of implication. And the position is that any doctrine of kinds of truth (of *ways* of being so, and not just of *being* so) is opposed to the recognition of a "straight issue", of what precisely is or is not so. The attempt is to introduce some qualification into the copula instead of restricting it to the terms, to carry over something of the material of the proposition into the form. But any such "qualification of the copula" is *exposed* by reference to contradiction; on Berkeley's doctrine of independent or mental reality, as contrasted with the dependent reality of ideas, where we should have to say that some mental process *is independently* A and some idea *is dependently* B, the only way in which we could *see the difference* between the "two copulae" would be by seeing it as a *material* difference, a difference of concrete character, and we could deny the first assertion only by saying that the process *is not* independently A, not by saying that it *is independently* not A. It would then appear that we had been asserting a *conjunction* of characters, asserting that the process is independent and is A, and, assuming that we could state positively what the character of "independence" is, we should be back at a straight issue with the unambiguous copula of occurrence or being the case.

In the case of "modals" the similar question whether X *is or is not* necessarily Y will dispose of the special copula "is necessarily" (or "must be"); at the same time, the precise issue will certainly not be a conjunctive one—whether X is Y *and* is a necessary being or has the characteristic of being necessary—and the same will be the case with possibility. Being necessarily Y is taken to be a special way of being Y, the necessity is taken to "contaminate" the Y-ness and not just to accompany it (though whatever was thought on this point would not prevent there being the straight issue whether X is Y or not) because the question is in fact not one of material but one of form. Before taking up that point in detail, however, we may note the curious position of *actuality* as a form of modality, viz., that there is no difference between X's being actually Y and X's being Y; that the use of "actually" (like that of "as a matter of fact") merely "gives emphasis" to the statement that X is Y, by which is meant that it conveys or suggests some additional assertion to the effect "I want you to take particular note of this"—which, however, does not affect the question of X's being Y. If, then, modal questions were material ones, we could give the emphasis in any case, and say that X's being Y was *actually* necessary or *actually* possible, and overthrow "modality" as a special sort of *logical* question. But if modal questions are formal ones, then the exclusion of any effect of modality on the copula leaves open only the treatment of it as a question of quantity, and this, while it does not affect the "categorical" character of the assertions in question, is in fact the line which is taken by non-qualifiers of the copula.

On this line, the strict form of a statement of "necessity" is that of a universal proposition and that of a statement of "possibility" is a particular proposition, so that the distinction between "X is necessarily Y" and "X is possibly Y" is that between XaY and XiY. So, to contradict "X is necessarily Y" by "X is possibly not Y", to identify the latter with "X *is not* necessarily Y", is simply to contradict XaY by XoY. Accepting this "equivalence", we often find it convenient in ordinary speech to use "modal" expressions—to ask "Must A be B or need not A be B?", "Can A be B or cannot A be B?"—without thinking that we have raised anything other than questions of fact, which would be more strictly presented in the four forms. If, on the other hand, the question were of distinct *fields* of necessity and of possibility (contrasted with the field of the actual), the contrast would be material, and logical relations among the types of assertions would be inexplicable. If we said that the contradictory of "X is necessarily Y" is "X is *not necessarily* Y", we could not call this an assertion in the realm of necessity, for what is asserted *has not* the character of necessity. And if we tried to set up special rules (cutting across the boundaries we had erected) such as that the contradictory of a statement of necessity is a statement of possibility (that "X is necessarily Y"

EMPIRICISM AND LOGIC (1962)            223

and "X is possibly not Y" are contradictories, and so are "X is possibly Y" and "X is necessarily not Y"), we could know the right way to do it only by getting away from "fields" (or similarly from different "manners" or "ways" of being true) and getting back to a "categorical" issue, an issue with the *unambiguous copula* which merely indicates that there *is* an issue, a question whether *something* is so or not, with no indication or suggestion of what that something is.

But, over and above this general use of "modals" to convey the distinction of quantity (*cannot* could be said to convey a distinction of both quality and quantity, but that is just *can not*), there are special uses connected with arguments and with knowledge, though having some affinities with the general use. Sometimes, when we say something is necessarily so or must be so, we mean that we know it is so—which is simply a question of fact. (There may be a suggestion that, as the phrase goes, "there is no possible doubt of it", but that is never strictly correct, and, suggesting something of a rationalist kind, cannot be said to raise a positive issue.) We also have factual statements of the form that something is possibly so or may be so, meaning that we *do not know* that it is not so (e.g., the assertion "Plato *may* have written the *Menexenus*", meaning "I do not know that Plato *did not* write the *Menexenus*"), and similarly we have statements to the effect that something is possibly not so. These renderings of "must be", "may be" statements differ from the previously considered universal-particular renderings in the fact that they introduce terms not in the given formula, but they do present "categorically" types of issue that are raised in apparently modal form.

Again, the question of necessity and possibility may be that of proof or the absence of proof. When we say, All men are mortal and Socrates is a man, hence Socrates *must be* mortal, our "must be" means that we are saying not merely that Socrates *is* mortal but that the proposition, Socrates is mortal, is *proved* (is implied by propositions we believe to be true)—two distinct assertions but both asserting that something is a fact or just is so; though, taking the "hence" (or "therefore") as indicative of following or being proved, we should have to call the replacement of "is" by "must be" superfluous. Still, the point of this repetition, the thing that is being emphasised, is that proof is relative to premises, that it is *by the given data* that X is Y is established. Correspondingly, we have the use of "may be" as meaning *is not proved not to be*, the equation of possible with not disproved, just as of necessary with proved—always with references to premises taken to be true. If we said, Socrates is a man and Socrates is mortal but all men *may not* be mortal (or it is *possible* that not all men are mortal), our meaning would be that the proposition, Some men are not mortal, is not disproved by the given information—or, on these premises, All men are mortal *is not proved.* This is what we mean by saying that All men are mortal is possibly not so or its contradictory is possibly so. But in such cases of *not therefore not* (possibly), just as in the case of *therefore* (necessarily), we are concerned with fact or "actuality" and there is no question of special kinds of copula; even though the statements have not always been put in precise logical form, we are clearly not going beyond the ordinary predicative logic, the logic of unqualified fact.

"Possibly not" may also be used in a less definite way than as meaning the non-implication of a proposition (say, All men are mortal) by a given set of propositions we accept; we might mean its non-implication by any information we possess, i.e., merely our inability to prove it. Thus we say "Possibly some men are not mortal" to convey that we are unable to prove that all men are mortal. This comes closer to the first of the special meanings mentioned; where "p is possibly true" (or "p is possible", though this is not specifying any character of the proposition p itself) means "I do not know that p is not true". But neither of these meanings (I do not know or I cannot show) is of any importance to inquiry as compared with "I cannot prove from propositions specified"—the fact of *non-implication* of some propositions by others. The general point remains that none of the uses I have distinguished raise anything but positive questions, questions of fact, though all are distinct from what I called "the general use"—the A or O issue and the E or I issue with the original terms.

Another case in which the question of "necessity" arises is that of imperatives. It is sometimes maintained that an imperative is not an "indicative" statement in that it cannot be contradicted, but obviously it can. When A says to B "Go away", B quite often replies "I will not", where he is clearly rejecting what A has said. Now B replies by making a statement about himself, so that he is taking A's "command" as a statement about himself (B)—thus the conflict of assertions can be presented fairly accurately as

EMPIRICISM AND LOGIC (1962)   225

"You (B) are departing (or about to depart)", "I (B) am not departing (or about to depart)". But what complicates the case, what enables it to be passed off as not a conflict of assertions, is the suggestion of "necessity"; of course, *your going is necessary* (or is required) can be replied to by the statement that *your going is not necessary* (or is not required), but this raises the point that "X is necessary" has no meaning (that nothing has "necessity" as one of its own characters or belongs to a class of "necessary things"), that indeed any such formula has to be *filled out* if there is to be a real issue, that until the question has been answered "necessary for what?" (or necessitated by what?), nothing on which there can be opposing views has been presented. When, however, the statement *is* completed, when it is said that your going is required for X (that unless you go, there will not be X—or will not be X here), this, firstly, is a straight question of fact and, secondly, does not convey that you *must* go (the "absolute necessity" of your going), which the imperative form is intended to impress on your mind. Thus we can say that, while the positive content of the imperative form is no more than an asserted fact, it also embodies the logical confusion of maintaining that the assertion *cannot be denied*, that it is not really an issue but is above question. And the same can be said of the "must" form (you must go, etc.); this is just another way of making out that there is no real issue, that the matter is *settled* beyond the possibility of question (Cf. "Socrates must be mortal.")

Of course, the matter of *your going* may be settled (in the sense that you *are* going) but this does not settle its "necessity"; and again its "necessity" can be settled only as its necessitation by X, which is not "absolute" (or inherent) necessity. But, however we might expand the statement (your going is necessitated by my desire, or by the promotion of certain things we are agreed to promote—any such expansion giving us something we could argue about), the absence of the expansion that would make it a positive issue conveys an "absolute necessity", the impossibility of contesting (denying the existence or imminence of) what is "commanded". There is the *suggestion* of some reason for the doing of "what is to be done"; you are going (because I tell you), you are going (because it is the right—or required—thing to do), etc.; but, in general, the suggestion is quite vague (you are going—just because!), in order that the pretence may be kept up that there is something (some ground or reason) that lifts "what is to be done" above discussion, something that establishes its necessity or "requisiteness", when nothing more of a reason has been given than "You are going because you are going". (It is pretty clear that the same would apply to much that is put forward as "modal" necessity.) Thus, while the real content is only *you are going* (a disputable matter), the special "imperative" form introduces logical confusion—inserts a "necessity" that is not in, but is above, the facts and that has to be excised if a definite *issue* is to emerge. (The issue, "Go", "No, I won't", might have been expressed more accurately as "You are going *voluntarily*", "I am not going *voluntarily*", but this would not affect the above discussion. The important point is that "Your going is imperative" looks like an issue, like something that someone might positively assert, but is not—though if anything *could* be meant by something's being "absolutely imperative", this would be a positive issue and would not be a special kind of issue.)

The same question has been very prominent in what has passed as *ethical* theory, particularly in the conception of the "categorically" imperative, what is "required in itself", not by or for something else; and here we have a further logical quirk in the notion of "obligation" or of what "ought to be"—of something which is necessary, or must be, and yet need not be. While, then, we have still the objections to dualism, the impossibility of finding any relation or distinction between ordinary states of affairs and what is supposed to "hold" in a different way, we can see what ambiguities, confusions, and, indeed, contradictions arise when such "ethical theorists" try still to maintain a footing in ordinary (historical) reality, to make their "ethics", their absolute imperatives or obligations, still have some bearing on actual living—be imperative or obligatory *on something*. It is still true that they cannot do so, cannot cross the barrier between things that "are real in different ways", cannot find any connection, e.g., between "judgments of value" and "judgments of fact" unless the former are just judgments of fact, the finding of whatever is meant by "value" in certain actual things (itself being an actual thing), and the upshot of their theoretical entanglements is just to encourage the view that there can be no science of ethics, that there is no subject-matter which such a science could consider.

The position is illustrated in what is said by Ryle on p. 141: "Like, for example, some members and followers of the Vienna Circle, Anderson begins by denying that ethical predicates stand for transcendent properties. But while they drew the consequence that ethical predicates do not stand for qualities or relations at all, but are merely emotive or hortatory expressions, Anderson draws the consequence that they stand for empirically ascertainable qualities or relations. Where they said that ethical pronouncements cannot express propositions, since they cannot, in principle, be verified or falsified by observation or experiment, Anderson says that they do express propositions, or describe spatio-temporal situations, and therefore that they are empirically verifiable or falsifiable." This presentation of the case is vitiated by the use of a representationist terminology to which I at least have never subscribed; what I have said is that what are "pronounced" in ethical matters *are* propositions, *are* spatio-temporal situations (granted that those who amalgamate relation and quality or confuse form and matter, as in the notion of "necessity", have to have these disentangled before the positive content of their "pronouncements" can appear); and the whole vocabulary of "expression" is simply a means of passing back and forward between what pronounces and what is pronounced. Even what are being called "emotive and hortatory expressions", even interjections or exclamations, are means of communication, of presenting issues—though certainly in the incomplete form which is a regular time-saving device in social life, and which often occasions misunderstanding; at any rate, where people live in close contact, such "expressions" can convey a great deal not only about a person's emotions (say, of gratification or displeasure) but about the things he is gratified or displeased with. If this were not the case, what are called interjections would be mere noises and not, as they regularly are, part of a body of human communications. But what the "exclamationists" ignore are the facts (a) that, while something of a person's emotions may often be observed in his making a statement, they need not be part of *what he is stating* at all—he may be, while communicating it in an abbreviated manner, pointing to something that is *not* a state of himself, (b) that if the only reason for taking it that an objective *ethical* issue has not been raised is that the speaker's emotions are exhibited, or perhaps just concerned, in the making of his pronouncement, then it would be a reason for rejecting the possibility of raising issues altogether, because a person's emotions are concerned, and are quite often exhibited, in the making of pronouncements in any field at all; e.g., on mathematical issues, on which many people feel very strongly.

But no other reason has been brought out by Ryle in the passage quoted above. It is certainly not apparent how anyone could draw either of the "consequences" that Ryle mentions from the premise that ethical predicates do not "stand for" transcendent properties, and I in particular have not made the inference I am said to have made. I would strenuously deny that we ever start with predicates and then look for subjects for them, whether or not this can be called looking for "what they stand for" (that we ever have, so to speak, a bunch of predicates in search of a subject); what we start with is propositions, which already have subjects as well as predicates. And, that being so, we simply find something to be *true* and are not in the predicament of having to look for "verifications" of it—for something that would in turn have to be verified (*ad infinitum*) if propositions *needed* verification. In fact, what can verify and what can be verified are propositions of the same order (apart from which they could not be connected by the relation "verifying" or any other); and any proposition can have either function, can be checked against other propositions or be directly found, so that there is no question of passing over to "verifiers" from a separate sphere of findings or issues, no question of what in a particular case is a testing proposition being any more empirical than the one that is being tested.

We are not, then, looking for a subject "ethics"; we have ethical beliefs, which can test as much as be tested, which in any case are part of our direct experience. Of course, we can see how sophistical or "propaganda" devices (e.g., the confusions I initially adverted to) have flourished in the ethical field; but for anyone to say that ethics is "positively all deception" is simply to empty out his past experience. But this is something that no one can thoroughly do; and that is why there is also deception in "anti-ethical" theories, why their proponents are always smuggling in what they profess to have thrown out. Part of the deception, of course, part of the "analytic" myth, is of an egoistic character (what do *I* find when I set my analysis-machine rumbling?), and this is opposed to the fact that language and inquiry are inherent in social life, are at all stages part of communication—which is the main reason why any doctrine of "the fresh start" falsifies the facts, including procedures of the primitivist himself. It is not in the least the case that pronouncements on "the good life" (or on good activities generally) have as their empirical content emotions of the speaker or that their content need have as part of it anything at all that is going on in him.

We get to know good activities, then, learn their locations and descriptions, by coming in contact with them, by entering into activities which *embrace* them as well as other people's activities—by there being continuous processes of which all these are parts. And this is the case with our knowledge in general—which makes impossible a recognition of different levels or "types" of reality. Yet Ryle actually presents a theory of types as a way of *getting out of* logical difficulties; he introduces the *fresh* obstacle to knowledge of postulating types of questions that can have no relation to one another (new dualisms, new divisions in reality). "When Russell came across the contradiction of the class of all classes that are not members of themselves, and then found the parallel contradictions of 'the Liar' etc., he was forced to look for a solution in some sort of theory of Logical Types" (p. 150). And the solution according to Ryle lies in distinguishing "sentences" which do not "express" propositions at all from those which do, the "nonsensical" from the "significant"; i.e., those whose constituents belong to different compartments of reality from those which fit wholly into one box. It is, of course, not difficult to see that words can be strung together without conveying anything (e.g., "I am telling a lie"), but there is in this no suggestion of divisions (or higher or lower regions) in reality. And "the contradiction" depends simply on confused views of the notion of "class"; the class X is just the various things which are X (distributively), what Russell calls "the class as many", and the question whether this is or is not a member of the class X is the "question" whether or not the X'es are X, i.e., no question at all. To suggest that there is a problem Russell has to introduce the conception of "the class as one" and ask whether *it* is a member of "the class as many"—but this "class as one" is just the various things which are X *taken collectively*, or *the collection of X'es*, and this is not the same thing (it is not a "class" at all), which means that there is no such thing as "the class as one" and the question of what is or is not "a member of itself" simply does not arise.

The details, of course, do not seriously matter; a "real contradiction" is just a confusion; but to say that a contradiction can have a "solution" is, in any case, to say that there is not a contradiction at all, and no special "logical" conceptions have to be invoked to deal with it. There is nothing here to suggest a distinction between science as concerned with what makes [!] (significant) statements true or else false and philosophy as concerned with what makes [!] statements significant or nonsensical—or to support the further representationism of taking science as talking about "the world", while philosophy talks about talk about "the world", when all that the introduction of "the world" means is that science asserts propositions, says that something is the case, uses the copula *are*—and there is nothing else that talk about *talk* (about no matter what) can do; it can only talk about states of affairs. There is no basis except different "orders of being" on which we could suppose that it *could* do anything else. The question of meaninglessness is not a question of uniting different categories, since the whole point about categories, as contrasted with qualities, is that they apply to *all* material; it is solely in terms of concrete reality that we can speak of things which do not go together—the common case being that of the use of the term XY when XeY (e.g., in XYaZ); and even though XYaZ has no subject or point of reference and so cannot be raising an issue, the consideration of whether it does or not can be an important feature of inquiry, whereas any suggestion of types of inquiry that do not mix (or fields of reality that cannot interpenetrate) can give no stimulus to inquiry. The belief in such divorced realities is only a device for protecting particular views, as, for example, the belief in immortality is protected by the contention that it is "meaningless" to say that a mental process is material (has weight or other such features of material processes)—such a division among regions of reality standing in the way of any coherent theory of mind and body. The division is supported by illogicality (particularly, the relativism of "that whose nature it is to know") and thus the question of meaninglessness is shifted to that of "logical exclusion" from that of *material* exclusion, in considering which, in terms of our experience, we can easily see that it does not apply in this case but the mental *is* bodily. It is only, in short, when we distinguish realms of reality (qualify the copula) that we get involved in logical impasses—not when we *deny* such distinctions.

Professor Ryle, then, cannot draw a distinction between science and philosophy in the way he proposes; philosophy, when it "talks", must talk of states of affairs, because there is nothing else to talk of, and if "significance" were not a state of affairs, it would just be—insignificant. I have argued above that recognition of meaninglessness is recognition of concrete fact ("findings of science"), and I would still maintain (from the remarks Ryle quotes, on p. 139, from my review of C. A. Campbell's "Scepticism and Construction": *A.J.P.P.*, June, 1935) that the philosopher "has true statements to make about the very things any special scientist is examining", that "what is called 'method' is not something different from 'findings' " (that what we call *method*, or, more exactly, *knowing* method, is knowing that any subject we examine has causes, has genera, etc., as a matter of actual fact), and that it is not true that philosophy has its own province, *the province of the ultimate*—on which last special point, of course, Ryle is not disagreeing with me. For, if Campbell's view were true, philosophy from its peculiar realm could not impinge in any way on the other realm, and there would be no such thing as the philosophical criticism of science, no appeal that could be made from findings here and now to findings "in the ultimate". But, in combining the first of the above remarks of mine with the statement that *philosophy is science*, I spoke in a very loose and misleading way, for there is nothing in that statement to show that science cannot just as readily criticise philosophy as philosophy can criticise science, nothing to show, indeed, what criticism could be other than one scientist's finding out that another was mistaken. I do not think, in spite of my carelessness in expression, that that was ever my real position, or that I had any doubt at the time that it was philosophy that could criticise science and that such criticism was what was properly called "method"—though holding then as now that for the criticism to have any *impact*, the two sorts of inquiry would have to be directed to the same field.

What would have influenced my apparent assimilation of philosophy to science (not so much besides as incidentally to my repudiation of "the ultimate") is that each of them is concerned with situational reality, with the spatio-temporal field, with things as they in a single sense are. What distinguishes them is that philosophy is concerned with the forms of situations or occurrences, science with their material; but it is only as forms of such material, as material with such forms, that they can be known. But this means that, if the work of inquiry is to be carried on, it must be *at once* scientific and philosophic, that if, in particular, the scientist is not philosophic, he will fall into confusions, he will rebuff philosophic criticism—he will lack a theory of categories, of sorts of problem, of "method"—especially he will be carried away by practical interests, by the interest in producing something or implementing a programme instead of in finding something out.

Burnet is dealing with this problem (not always quite clearly) when he presents the account given in the *Republic* of the work Dialectic does, in showing the defects of the special sciences, as "destroying the hypotheses", e.g., the hypothesis of three distinct kinds of angles (cf. *Greek Philosophy: Thales to Plato*, p. 229—I take this to mean that an angle is a *turning*, and that, considering a continuous turning round a centre, we shall not be disposed to break up the class of angles into the usual species distinguished in the theory of triangles); and the position is made even plainer (p. 323) when Burnet refers to Aristotle's objection to the assimilation of geometry to arithmetic, the proof of geometrical by arithmetical propositions, on the ground that "the proper hypotheses of each science must be left undisturbed. Aristotle's principle here could be described as that of *saving* hypotheses instead of destroying (or removing) them; it is one by which realms of reality are separated, and the question in each case is what is "true on these assumptions", not just what is true—which makes it impossible to *examine* the assumptions by reference to findings in the fields they are supposed to mark off, as must be possible if they have consequences in their specific fields.[9] We can thus connect the opposition between (a) separate fields and restriction

---

[9] C. A. Campbell, in the work referred to, follows the fairly common line of saying that science depends "upon presuppositions which it is not its business to examine". It is, however, absurd to say that an investigator should not be ready to consider *anything* that has a bearing on what is true in his field (if the difference between p's truth and p's falsity makes a difference to the truth or falsity of q, a mathematical proposition, the mathematician who has not considered the question of p has no business enunciating q), though this could never include the "ultimate" in the sense of the unquestionable (since if p is relevant to the *q or not q* question, q is relevant to the *p or not p* question). That is to say that there is never any question of fixed presuppositions, but only of either suppositions (hypotheses) or direct findings, in the investigation of any group of facts. If there really were mathematical presuppositions unquestioned by mathematicians, that would merely amount to an unnecessary decision to restrict mathematical inquiry. It may be noted, where there is no question of realms of reality but the question is only

of inquiry and (b) unrestricted inquiry into a single field of reality (space and time, interrelated situations with no smallest and no largest) with an opposition between (a) saving hypotheses and removing appearances (e.g., ethical facts)—which is rationalism, and (b) saving appearances and removing hypotheses—which is empiricism. Hypotheses requiring removal are exemplified in axioms of science and elements of things, as well as the general mass of entities supposed to exist or be true in special ways, like normative truths, epiphenomena and sensa.

It is this rationalism, this separatism, this breaking up of reality into sundered sections, that is the mark of the scientist who is not a philosopher, who instead presumes to teach the philosophers (it being mostly scientists who have given the lead to contemporary "philosophic" schools) his own rationalism, his own devotion to ultimates and unquestionables, his own "analysis" (what are the elementary constituents of this?), on the basis of his own practicalism—of what he takes to be absolute ends. It is just because of its *concrete* concerns that the scientist takes his science to be more capable of criticising philosophy than philosophy is of criticising it, and thus we find a variety of "philosophies" (doctrines of the conditions of inquiry and even of the conditions of social life) which, in accordance with the concrete interests of their authors, lay down the law for technical philosophy, knowing next to nothing of philosophy's history, cling to subjectivism (or the personal outlook) in ignorance of the case either for or against realism or objectivism, and, finally, with their "practical" resources, intimidate the professional philosophers into showing less and less interest in the philosophical tradition and more and more subservience to "science". Thus with what is esteemed to be the scientific progress of the twentieth century has gone philosophical retrogression. A certain practicalism or instrumentalism has, of course, been characteristic of modern philosophy in general; this is illustrated in the categories employed by Locke which are merely a set of devices by which men can arrange their material and are not exhibited as belonging to it or as having any

---

of formal procedures, that there are two ways of removing or destroying a hypothesis: (1) by showing that it has consequences which are false; it then, being false itself, is discarded as a possible explanation of things: (2) by showing that it is a consequence of true premises; it then, being true, is discarded as a hypothesis (a suggested explanation of things) and is set up as a *finding* in the field.

common ground. This view was considerably corrected by Kant's criticism (followed up in some directions by Hegel's), and the correction was carried further by Alexander. There can be little doubt, however, that the failure of such criticisms to stick was due to the steadily larger and more influential groups who devoted themselves to inquiry but had little knowledge of the history of critical thought and treated "method" rather in a mechanical than in a logical way.

Professor Ryle speaks of what logic *tells me*, with the suggestion that I am laying claim to some private communication or even special revelation. What I maintain is that there can be no logic unless it is in the facts, unless their logical characters are found in any facts (or situations) of which we are aware. And what I take myself to be informed of by what might be called my "logical sense" is the *continuity* of things or their *coherence*, their "making sense" because they have a common ground, their negating all "breaks in reality", all doctrines of units or realms—and there seems to me to be no doubt that there is a divergence of view here, that the issue arises anywhere and that to offer a settlement of it is to offer a view of the interlocking of questions or of categories. It would, of course, be maintained by the empiricist logician that no one can offer a *consistent* "separatist" answer to logical questions, but the primary point is that logical questions arise wherever *any* questions arise. It is obvious that the history of philosophy offers a very great stimulus to thinking on these questions (as I myself have been greatly stimulated on the general continuity-discontinuity question by the work of Burnet on the pre-Socratics and on Plato's later dialogues, as well as by Alexander's work on "Space-Time"), it is obvious, too, that great stimulus is afforded by the work of *separatist* thinkers like Descartes and Locke; but the stimulation is possible in either case just because all the time we are confronted by, or rather immersed in, what may roughly be called "the world", i.e., things which extend around, within and through us. That is something we must always be considering, as part of our consideration of any special situations whatever, and that is how we come to have a "logic"—to see (as I should say), if we are consistent, the errors of dualism, the absence of any breaks in reality, along with special problems of how things intermingle. I have suggested that *lack* of consistency in these matters is contingent on pursuit of special aims and objects; but the main point is that we cannot have a piecemeal logic, that logic is concerned with the *running together* of questions of all sorts ("in all the categories") and that to be confused on this matter is to be hazy in one's "logical (or philosophical) sense". This I have also described as a sense of *form*; and it is because form is not additional *matter*, but is characteristic of any matter that may be in question, that one can speak of logic (or philosophy) as governing or directing science, and not the other way round—just as it is *taking* it the other way round, making matter do duty for form, making science do duty for philosophy, that has produced the intellectual chaos of the present day.

This sort of "materialism" is well illustrated in Marxism, a leading strain in which is the treatment of social revolution as the common measure of terrestrial events—a role that could be filled only by something *formal*. I have myself severely criticised this aspect of Marxian thought, but I was so incompletely emancipated by Marxism or proletarianism at the time of writing "Marxist Philosophy" (*A.J.P.P.*, March, 1935) that I concluded the article by saying that the realist philosopher might find his activity to be part of a producers' movement, so that he would "see his intellectual levelling as an integral part of social levelling".[10] The intellectual worker might quite well be said to be engaged in "levelling" in so far as he was denying "higher realities", but to say that there are not different levels of existence has no connection whatever with being opposed to social privileges and distinctions—there is no reason why seeking to induce people to abolish such distinctions should form part of a common campaign with seeking to persuade them to reject "higher entities"; indeed the social egalitarian is for the most part highly superstitious, though preferring to call his presiding spirits by fashionable names like "progress".[11]

---

[10] v. i., p. 313.
[11] It seems to me that Plato's later philosophy was affected by the same error as is exhibited in my article, though my argument goes the other way round: i.e., that, instead of arguing from the "necessity" of logical equality to that of social equality, he argued from the "necessity" of social inequality to that of logical inequality, that his residual rationalism, his continued adherence to a hierarchical logic, his inability to take the last steps to empiricism (in spite of his contributions to empiricism in the development of a propositional logic and in an approach, at least, to the theory of *being* as the copula and not as a concrete entity or term) could be accounted for by the belief that to support "egalitarian logic" was to support egalitarian society and thus to wreck cultural life.

It is apparent, of course, that there is in all this a confusion in the meanings of "supporting" and "opposing" as, first, trying to bring about and trying to prevent and, second, trying to prove and trying to disprove. And it seems clear also that such confusion between practical and theoretical questions (connected with which is the sheer superstition of the view that any practice *follows* from theory, that finding p to be true could in any way require us to *do* X) or between material and formal questions is one main reason why there could not *be* co-operation of intellectuals with proletarians, who, in spite of Sorel, do not exhibit the producers' mentality (the condition of co-operation) but are concerned with being better off, with reform, with *making* society go in the right way—a meliorism and a voluntarism that are opposed to the work of the student of society, to any intellectual grasp of his subject. I have remarked in "The Freudian Revolution" (*A.J.P.*, August, 1953, p. 102)[12] that the only revolution properly so called is an intellectual revolution, "a revolution in ideas", not any re-arrangement of externals. This is what the work of the intellectual producer (or the realist or empiricist philosopher, I would say, as in my article) resides in; not "social levelling" or any other "practical" undertaking but simply making discoveries—rejecting conventional or customary associations, like that of "benefiting" with all social activities, or, more broadly, that of theory and practice, and being concerned simply with following an intellectual tradition within an intellectual institution. It is the custody of such traditions and institutions that requires privileges or "charters", and the work of egalitarianism in breaking these down is one of the major causes of injury to intellectual activity in our present period. It is true, of course, that social equality is merely a mirage, but devotion to it has still much to contribute to the destruction of culture. Culture, on the other hand, is concerned with the maintaining of boundaries, with *opposition* to levelling, to the treatment of everyone as of the same standing in any cultural field, and, in the intellectual field particularly, with the search for what is the case as opposed to what can be secured, with the discovery of the laws according to which society works as against *ignoring* such laws and proposing to make society go according to personal decisions.

---

[12] v. i., pp., 359.

EMPIRICISM AND LOGIC (1962) 237

It is interesting to note how badly "the ethics of the producers" (G. Sorel, *Reflections on Violence*, Ch. VIII, esp. § V)[13] fits the workers of to-day, though it possibly fitted better those of the early century—how opposed current attitudes are to what Sorel took to be the outstanding features of a producers' ethic, the chief "heroic values" of proletarian life; viz., initiative, emulation, care for exactitude and rejection of the notion of "reward". These "values", as I say in "Marxist Ethics", are typical of *disinterested* activity and may still be found in intellectual institutions, which have not yet been completely eaten up by utilitarianism (interestedness) and egalitarianism, expressed in care for the careers of "individuals" as against the advancement of learning. We may recall here the remark of de Tocqueville that democracies are not interested in questions of *form* (it is only custodians of traditions that would be so)—their outlook, in other words, is materialistic. The same, in general, may be said of scientists, those, i.e., who are not also philosophers; they also are not concerned with form, or, in substituting for questions of form questions of technical procedures or devices, they are really giving to the material or subject-matter of their science functions it is unable to carry out, they are using it to set aside the exact studies that can be made of formal questions and that can bring out issues which would otherwise be missed.

It is thus that philosophers, as far as they still carry out their own studies and do not, as has happened so much of late, submit to the direction of scientists dialectically untrained, can themselves offer guidance which would remove "hypotheses" or blockages in the lines of scientific study; it is thus that logic, even while asserting the equal reality of all existing things, can claim that it "stands above" the sciences, that it "governs" the various concrete fields of investigation in a way in which science could not govern *logic*—since it is by common forms, and not by special materials, that investigation can be directed. It is to be understood, of course, that the scientist who sets himself up as a master of method though he has engaged in no systematic study of philosophy will always be found to be *borrowing* from philosophy, to be using scraps from Locke, Hume and so on, in fixing up his rickety apparatus.

[13] See my discussion of Sorel's theory in "Marxist Ethics" (*A.J.P.P.*, June, 1937, pp. 115-7): v. i., pp. 325-7.

But the objections to this procedure, to the light-minded way in which scientists will tell us that we must deny the existence of causality or must take a phenomenalist view of it or must always proceed by "induction" because we can only start with "particulars", the objections, more generally, to the substitution of human devices whereby material may be manipulated for forms that are embedded in it—the intellectual *mess* of all this—can be plainly seen. What can also be seen is the extent to which it has all been furthered by the fashionable philosophy of our day.

# 17
# CLASSICISM (1960)

To claim educational pre-eminence for the classics, or simply to present classicism as an important view of culture, would commonly in these times be met with ridicule or indifference, since neither the notion of culture nor the classical outlook is now accorded any great respect even in reputedly educated circles. At the outset of the intense struggles, which have occupied the past century or more, over the nature and organisation of education, the conception of it as "liberal" and hence classical was widespread and apparently well-entrenched. But the position has changed so radically that nowadays it is rare to find any greater concession made to liberal study, either in the narrower sense of concentration on the "classical tongues" or in the broader sense of attention to the major productions of humane letters, than that it is a harmless eccentricity which may still for a time occupy its small corner. What is of special educational importance, it is widely maintained, is study of the sciences; for, while liberal study had at no time an intrinsically greater capacity for developing the mind, it has under present conditions a very much slighter power of bringing us to a serious grappling with our vital problems. And this is in line with the view which prevails among professional educationists who, even though the main emphasis is not always on science, conceive education as the preparation of the pupil for the problems of the real world in which he is to live, and on that principle dismiss the upholder of tradition as a follower of phantasies.

It is open to the traditionalists to reply that preparation for grappling with what is contemporary does not necessarily involve concentration on the *study* of what is contemporary and that the setting aside of tradition, of "the best that has been thought and said" on major human problems, may well be the way to miss their solution. But first it may be pointed out that the classical and the utilitarian views of education are distinguished as employing intrinsic and extrinsic criteria, the one considering education in its own character, as the development of thinking or criticism, the other considering it in its contribution to something else, subordinating it in this way to the non-educational and running the greatest risk of distorting its character. For clearly there can be no subject or field of study which is utilitarian in itself, whose character resides in what it produces or helps to produce, and this applies as much to science as to any other study; its intrinsic character, taken as the search for laws, the study of the ways of working of actual things, has no reference to the turning of its findings to "practical" account. But there can be no doubt that science as currently understood is concerned with the production of results, with the making of physical translations and transformations, and that, in the view of many scientific practitioners, science even enjoins us to produce this result rather than that.

In so far as science is regarded in this way, it is assimilated to the theology which at one time it seemed destined to replace; it also is supplementing consideration of what is the case by injunctions to us to seek the means by which we may be saved. A topical example of such salvationist thinking is to be found in agitations for peace, in which, leaving aside any attempt to determine the objective conditions either of the occurrence of international conflicts themselves or of the discovery of the truth concerning them, it is assumed that anything that is "undesirable" can, by a sufficiency of protests or "appeals to reason", be eliminated. The implication is that there are no natural laws in the social or political sphere—for, if there were, there would be certain things which, under given conditions, could not be eliminated, since they were necessary consequences of those conditions. But it is in no way scientific to suppose that there is any field of occurrences not marked by regularities, and it is scarcely less naive to represent the social field as one in which there are a few simple truths which can be grasped without intensive study and which are already sufficiently recognised. The maintaining of such views holds out no prospect of assistance to the settlement of matters of practical urgency; it operates merely as an obstacle to *inquiry* into social affairs in general and international affairs in particular. It is still important to note that the belief, increasingly popular since the days of Spencer and Huxley, that science can prescribe practical policies, rests on the assumption that society itself is not a subject of science. But this in turn carries the implication that science has nothing to contribute to society's development.

The connection between the trend to a more and more "scientific" education and the conception of education as having to be directed beyond itself to social usefulness, to "serving the community" in non-educational ways, falls within the same chapter of ideas. Such external direction, however weak its theoretical foundation, is an inescapable contemporary phenomenon, and it is responsible not only for the steady fall in educational standards, the slighter and slighter *literacy* of the supposedly educated, but for what may fairly be called the growing industrialisation of educational institutions. This is exhibited not merely in their directing students to industry and thus engaging in the provision of the techniques which industry requires, but in their becoming themselves more and more technological, applying techniques of teaching, overcoming "wastage", learning how to turn out the maximum number of technicians—and losing scholarship in the process. This external view of the function of *Universities* in particular is one of the leading notes of the Murray report, however it may be blended with pious phrases in the older mode. Thus, to the Committee's contention (*Report of the Committee on Australian Universities*, 1957, p. 120—"Summary and Conclusions") that "the universities are or should be the guardians of intellectual standards and intellectual integrity in the community", it can be retorted that they cannot be such guardians if their work is subordinated to *other* standards, if they are serving a postulated unity of interests ("the community") of which the intellectual interest is only a part. Nothing short of a rejection of this imaginary "common good" (something that satisfies every interest and every person) can maintain at their proper intellectual level institutions whose work is criticism or the examination of all assumptions. The carrying out of this work requires them to recognise that they are one of a number of *competing* social forces and that what, for example, is industry's gain is quite commonly education's loss.

The conception of education as an industry, then, with its raw materials, machines, machine-minders and turned-out goods, is opposed to the conception of it as conversion, a turning round of the mind, or, as Arnold has it in his definition of culture (*Culture and Anarchy*, Preface), the turning of "a stream of fresh and free thought upon our stock notions and habits". It is true that Arnold himself is still somewhat bemused by the stock notion of "the common good", but, at least, in "The Function of Criticism at the present time" (*Essays in Criticism*, First Series, I) he allows that the "mass of mankind will never have any ardent zeal for seeing things as they are", and that men will be content for the most part to rest their practice on very inadequate ideas. "For", as he puts it even more forcibly on an earlier page, "what is at present the bane of criticism in this country? It is that practical considerations cling to it and stifle it. It subserves interests not its own. Our organs of criticism are organs of men and parties having practical ends to serve, and with them those practical ends are the first thing and the play of mind the second; so much play of mind as is compatible with the prosecution of those practical ends is all that is wanted."

Concentration on what serves one's purposes, satisfaction with the "just as good" or the "good enough to get there", exists even more strikingly and influentially in public life at present than it did in Arnold's time, and it has penetrated more and more deeply into education, promoting shoddy thinking and slipshod language in the name of social equality and amelioration and other "inadequate ideas" which have less and less critical intelligence applied to them. It is not surprising, in particular, that pupils should be turned out with a poor sense of the English language, when their teachers are concerned to propagate and benefit by the whole range of meliorist and utilitarian ideas and, in their satisfaction with what "gets across" in this way, feel no impulse towards the largeness of view and precision of thought which would require its remoulding and which would stimulate sensitive expression. The "practical end" of taking one's place in the community, of securing more or less useful and remunerative occupation, overshadows critical thinking; and, to draw more fully on Arnold's terminology, the function of education at the present time is substantially that of turning the populace into Philistines.

Incidentally, Arnold's notion of "practical ends" is a somewhat loose and uncritical one. To take anything as an end is presumably to regard it as capable of actually coming about—of coming about, as we say, "in practice". It is not apparent, on this basis, how practical ends could be distinguished from any other ends. A distinction might be attempted in terms of the common antithesis of practice and theory, and practical outcomes of human activity might then be taken as those which were not theoretical—not, that is to say, as states which could not be *objects* of thought but as states which had no *thinking* embodied in them. Much of what is actually produced by contemporary education may well be of this unthinking character, but where thinking, as contrasted with conformity and intellectual vacuity, does emerge from the process, it can hardly be dismissed as unpractical—it may have distinctly more social force than much that passes as practical. Arnold would have been speaking more to the purpose if, instead of distinguishing types of ends, he had distinguished between concentration on ends, on definite objects to be secured, and the carrying on of certain activities (in particular, the activity of inquiry) without regard to any such programme; but this is a conception at which he does not arrive.

In fact, while Arnold's contribution to the understanding of these questions is considerable, he makes in a number of places undue concessions to practice and fails in critical elucidation of its character. This is notably so in his discussion of "Hellenism and Hebraism" (*Culture and Anarchy*, Ch. IV) when he contrasts the uppermost Hellenic idea, "to see things as they really are", with the uppermost Hebraic idea of "conduct and obedience", or, in his alternative formulation, "spontaneity of consciousness" with "strictness of conscience", and treats the two not as antagonistic but as complementary sides of culture. Apart from the fairly obvious objection that conscience has an adverse effect on the free play of intellect (if, indeed, it does not *spring* from intellectual narrowness), Arnold does not explain why conduct is not just one of the things to be seen as they are, or how it can be regarded as raising any distinct *type* of problem. Certainly, in *Literature and Dogma* (Ch. I), he distinguishes speculative problems concerning human character or activity from "practical" problems, the merely theoretical difficulty of finding what happens from the difficulty of *doing* "what we very well know ought to be done", i.e., in his view, the "difficulty of religion" which "extends to rightness in the whole range of what we call *conduct*; in three-fourths, therefore, at the very lowest computation, of human life". But he definitely does not mean that such problems are solved *ambulando*, that it just so happens that we sometimes do what "ought" to be done, whatever we might know or think about it; the question is always of the solution of a speculative problem, of finding out that something *is the case*—e.g., that doing what is right is contingent on the acceptance of a certain kind of guidance—though it still might be argued, in this connection, that "right" and "ought" are stock notions we should have to dispense with if our speculation on conduct went any distance. Perhaps it is some sense of the weakness of his doctrine of conduct that leads Arnold into the bathos of his concluding observation in the section of his argument to which I am referring: "And so, when we are asked, what is the object of religion?—let us reply: *Conduct.* And when we are asked further, what is conduct?—let us answer: *Three-fourths of life.*"

But however strongly all this may point to the conclusion that no account can be given of culture as a conjunction of Hellenism and Hebraism, this would be nothing against the account of it as Hellenism itself, i.e., "seeing things as they are"—adopting the objective as against the subjective outlook—turning critical intelligence on all subjects, including (and perhaps especially) the subject of human activities. Such an account, of course, would not imply that Greek civilisation, even in its "classical" period (the period of the flourishing of objectivism, criticism, intellectual detachment), was objectivist through and through. It is, indeed, part of the classicist position to see that this cannot be the case, to see, as in the notable example of Socrates,[1] that culture exists in the struggle with superstition and backwardness. Socrates upheld the objective treatment of all subjects—and specifically of the subjects, such as religion, ethics, aesthetics, in which subjectivism still seeks a refuge; he combated subjectivism alike in the form of Sophistic conventionalism ("Man is the measure of all things") and in that of Athenian democratism ("The people are the measure of all things"). Remarkably enough, it is largely from the force of his criticisms that his opponents retain a place in the history of civilisation. And what these criticisms bring out is the difference between the reality and the pretence of knowledge, whether the pretenders were reputedly learned men or, like his prosecutors, men who thought that knowledge—of morals in particular—came from immersion in civic life and did not require or admit of formal scrutiny and the raising of difficulties. Here for the first time in the history of thought we encounter the notion of "practical truth", of knowledge without study, of assertions that cannot be challenged

---

[1] On the Socratic philosophy I very largely follow the views of John Burnet, whose work on Socrates and on Greek philosophy generally, neglected though it is in these days, seems to me to make a remarkable contribution both to classicism and to philosophy, and whose wholeness of view provides a striking contrast to the piecemeal "philosophies" which are now in vogue.

because they are backed by the process of living. The position is illustrated again in the case of the contemporary evangelical who, in saying "He's real to me", imagines that he has provided a sanction for certain lines of action, though engaging in them has no demonstrable connection with the postulated sanctioning figure. It is this "practical" jumping over of problems that Socrates was especially concerned to expose. And, as he predicted, even the practical expedient of slaying him furnished no escape from the difficulties he had raised.

But neither the position nor the influence of Socrates can be described as exclusively objectivist. That there is in his doctrines a streak of romanticism or mysticism (even though this can often be treated as merely a trimming round a realist or empiricist core) is clear enough from his belief in "ultimates", entities standing above the actual movement of things. This is in striking contrast with the thorough-going objectivism of his predecessor, Heraclitus, who was unremitting in his attack on subjectivist illusions, on the operation of desire or the imagining of things as we should like them to be, as opposed to the operation of understanding or the finding of things (including our own activities) as they positively are, with no granting of a privileged position in reality to gods, men or molecules, with conflict everywhere and nothing above the battle. His criticism was directed especially against the school of Pythagoreans (whence much of it could in turn have been directed against Socrates) — against their little absolutes or atomic realities; against their distortion of their material from a desire for simplicity, for the tidy and complete solution; against the division of the unhistorical from the historical, of the exact from the inexact. This last point recalls Arnold's distinction (again in Ch. I of *Literature and Dogma*) between "a term of science or exact knowledge" and "a term of poetry and eloquence" —and here the Heraclitean or objectivist position is that no line can be drawn between these, that there can be no defensible claim to knowledge of distinct things which have no common measures, which do not exist in the same situations and enter into joint transactions. And, in particular, there is the implication that we can no more have quantity without quality than we can have quality without quantity or otherwise than as spatio-temporal process.

But while Heraclitus had this sense of the interlocking of all materials and all problems, he had by no means worked out a critical apparatus (a doctrine of types of problem and forms of solution in any inquiry) in the way that Socrates, followed by Plato, did. And thus for a general conception of the objectivist outlook, of classicism on its basic *philosophical* side, of the "judgment" which applies to all subjects and the "literalism" which is always ruinous to inquiry, we have to go to both these sources; they together set up the model of philosophical Hellenism, and, even though the other contributors to the thought of the period did not reach the same level, these would suffice to make it a classical period—a period in which disinterestedness stands out from the wrangle of special interests as it does not do in culturally lower times.

It is in so far as it has followed the Greek model that modern philosophy has also had a classical character, though it has had to fight against an even more debilitating modernism (or "up-to-dateness") than that of the Sophists. This modernism comes out strikingly in the work of the two thinkers who have been commonly regarded as the founders of modern philosophy—Bacon and Descartes. We need not perhaps take very seriously Descartes's reported remarks that he was proud of having forgotten the Greek which he had learned as a boy, and that Latin, lauded as "the language of Cicero", was just as much the language of Cicero's serving-maid—though it might be observed in passing that an infusion of the Hellenic spirit may persist beyond the recalling of Greek words, and that it is not true that "the same language" is used by the learned and the vulgar, that, on the contrary, it is pre-eminently in *letters* that a language has its characteristic existence.[2] What is more to the purpose in both thinkers is their practicalism and progressivism, illustrated in Bacon's view that the "end of the sciences is their usefulness to the human race" and that to "increase knowledge is to extend the dominion of man over nature, and so to increase his comfort and happiness, so far as these depend on external circumstances" (Bury, *The Idea of Progress*, p. 58), and in the view of Descartes (Bury, p. 67) that the intellectual advance consequent on his own discoveries "would

---

[2] Many of the errors of our day are linked with the delusion that a "spoken language" means what is spoken by the unlearned mass (which, as Arnold has indicated, is too much concerned with immediate "practical" objects to trouble about the finer distinctions and connections embodied in learned speech and writing) and that resistance to the incorporation of vulgar locutions in the recognised language is mere pedantry and archaism.

have far-reaching effects on the condition of mankind" and in his first proposed title for the *Discourse on Method*, "The Project of a Universal Science which can elevate our Nature to its highest degree of Perfection."

Adamson (*History of Logic*, p. 85) says that to both Bacon and Descartes "the scholastic logic presented itself as the essence of a thoroughly false and futile method of knowledge.... Both thinkers were animated by the spirit of reformation in science, and both emphasise the practical end of all speculation. For both, therefore, logic, which to neither is of high value, appeared to be a species of practical science, a generalised statement of the mode in which intellect acquires new knowledge, in which the mind proceeds from known to unknown." This degradation of the subject, logic, to the status of an instrument or set of devices is typical of the practicalist or instrumentalist outlook (though it still cannot show how deviser and devised can enter into common situations or, as the phrase goes, "exist in the same world"). and it may be compared to recent views of scientific method (which is actually logic, considered in terms of types of questions that can arise in inquiry) as simply the procedures of scientists. The matter is illustrated again in the contempt of the two thinkers for syllogism (in fact, the commonest as well as the most fruitful form of demonstrative reasoning) and its replacement by the Baconian "induction" and the Cartesian "intuition". But "induction", where it is not syllogism disguised, is at best fallacious reasoning and at worst mere guesswork—though it is interestingly related to that great region of modern science (reminiscent of Pythagorean doctrine) in which ignorance is treated as a kind of knowledge, uncertainty as a kind of certainty. And "intuition", again where it is not disguised syllogism, is merely knowledge divorced from any possibility of its being acquired by a mind, i.e., knowing without learning.

The anti-classicism of Descartes comes out not merely in his antipathy to history and tradition, but in his proposing, as the ground of the distinction of men from animals, an abstract rationality in place of the concrete and many-sided culture (language and literature, law, investigation, etc.) which really does distinguish them. This lack of concreteness is characteristic of the whole modernist position; it is bound up with that opposition to quality or distinction which is a recurrent feature of modern thought (in the social as in other spheres), and one expression of which is proof by identities and not by concrete facts. It comes out in Descartes's epistemological approach to philosophy which proved so influential in later thought and which gives the question of our power of comprehending actualities priority to that of actualities themselves. This, however, can readily be seen to be a quite confused position; for knowledge of our cognitive powers does not set us on the way to detailed knowledge of the actual unless they also are actual, and, if they are, they have no higher standing as objects of cognition than other cognisable things. The difficulty is merely evaded by Descartes in his doctrine of self-knowledge (his *cogito ergo sum*), since, on the one hand, there is still no logical passage from self-knowledge to knowledge of other things, and, on the other hand, knowledge of a real self would have to be of its concrete characters and not of mere dispositions or capacities. The Cartesian *cogito*, then, is rooted in ambiguity; it derives such plausibility as it has from its assigning all the parts in a complex relationship to the same thing. But it does so at the cost of content; the certainty it can be taken to give us is not the certainty of any particular thing but, at most, the certainty of "certainty itself". Its certainty, in other words, is indistinguishable from its emptiness.

This criticism of the *cogito* is moderately familiar; what is not so commonly recognised is that criticism of the same sort applies to those other prominent features of modernist doctrine, its utilitarianism and its progressivism—that their plausibility also is grounded in their lack of content. Ordinarily, to call anything useful is to say that it brings about something else—more specifically, perhaps, brings about something wanted—but since there is no limit to the range of things that people want, since anything might be wanted by someone, the effective meaning of useful is just *having effects*, and this covers anything whatever. On this interpretation, it would be idle for a person to say that he supports "utility", for he would not be supporting any distinguishable thing. But the utilitarian does not want to say that he supports the indefinite going on of things; he wants to affirm the existence of definite stopping-places; he wants to recognise, beyond the mere relation of producing or bringing about, "absolute utilities"—things which have their usefulness in themselves or as part of their own character. And here again we have a quite empty conception—the conception of the attainment of "attainment" or the satisfaction in "satisfaction" and not in any concrete thing.

In the same way, "progress" can only mean the going on of what goes on, or the futurity of the future, unless the question is of the progress not of "things in general" but of a distinct class of things, things of some specific quality. And, even working with a rough-and-ready conception of the "flourishing" of such a class, we can never find more than risings and fallings (the strengthening of such things at certain times and places, matched by their weakening at other times and places) and thus can find no reason for belief in a law of their progress, let alone a law of universal progress. Such beliefs rest on belief in a "scheme of things", but a scheme which is always fragmentarily conceived and gives no ground on which it may be demonstrated that one form of activity rather than another is bound to thrive. And an even more serious defect of progressivist doctrines is that they are doctrines of betterment, i.e., of higher and lower *degrees* of goodness; and this, if goodness is a quality, is unintelligible, and, if it is not, is a measurement of things on an unknown scale and brings us back to the verbiage of "evolutionary ethics", according to which the later is, of its very nature, the better—in other words, to the peddling of identities in the guise of information. It may be added that doctrines like utilitarianism and progressivism whose special concern is the future are not merely anti-classical but are opposed to study, since the past is a field of study which can be constantly opened up, while the future is a field of conjecture or phantasy. It is in this way that pessimism or the sense of a steady cultural decline has greater affinity to learning than the optimistic belief in continual advance; it points to concrete models and to the great difficulty of maintaining standards, as against the facile belief that they will automatically rise. All these considerations bring out the emptiness of the modernist outlook, as contrasted with the fullness of the historical and classical.

The Cartesian doctrine of "matter" is likewise lacking in content; the doctrine that extension is the essence of the material affirms the sameness of all things and eliminates all quality and distinction (carrying egalitarianism right through the universe!); it is a doctrine that could be founded only on a fallacious working with identities, and yet it is still treated by most scientists not as absurd but as commonplace, the real distinguishing-marks of things being set aside as "secondary" or illusory. It is needless to dwell on the writhings of the intellect by which Descartes tries to straddle the gulf between mind and matter, and bring pure thought and pure extension into relation; it is enough to say that, while only historical actualities (alike material and moving) can be so related, it is the empty abstractions which have penetrated modern thought. Nevertheless, this penetration has emphasised the fundamental weaknesses of the Cartesian antithesis of thought and extension, active and passive, user and used—for it emerges in the writings of the eighteenth century, above all in the work of La Mettrie, that anything we concretely call *man* is as much subject to external influences (as capable of being *used*) as anything we call *matter*, and so would go over into the passive side of reality if there were such a side; yet this is combined, among these "old materialists", with belief in a class of men who are *users*, a section of society, as Marx puts it, set above society in general, and concerned (however inexplicably and however, on the original premises, hopelessly) to raise the social level.

This theoretical instability comes out in a specially grotesque way in Owen's "A New View of Society", where, for example, in the Third Essay, he passes directly from the doctrine of external determination ("the character of man is, without a single exception, always formed for him.... Man, therefore, never did, nor is it possible that he ever can, form his own character") to a call to action, to the question whether the "substantial advantages" of the application of rational principles *should* be longer withheld from the mass of mankind and the assertion that it is "by the full and complete disclosure of these principles that the destruction of ignorance and misery is to be effected, and the reign of reason, intelligence, and happiness is to be firmly established". It is against such confusions, and with particular regard to how they affect education, that Marx directs the third of his Theses on Feuerbach, arguing that it is impossible to divide society into active and passive sections (whether conceived, implausibly enough, as *helpers and helped* or in any other manner), that there is no-one who is merely a victim of circumstances and no-one who is completely a master of circumstances, that there is interaction at all points. Or at least this last is the natural conclusion of the Thesis, but it is somewhat obscured and confused through Marx's obsession with the revolutionary re-making of society and the conflictless Utopia which he expects to see emerging.

Leaving aside, however, Marx's own inconsistencies and admitting the full force of his attack on Owen, we have still to recognise that it is meliorist ideas of the Owenite type that now prevail in public life and especially in the educational field. It is education above all that is overwhelmed by the flood of devotees of "the fresh start", by those eloquent advocates of reform, satirised by Arnold (once more in *The Function of Criticism*), who are prepared to remodel all institutions on "first principles", to the accompaniment of declamations like: "Away with the notion of proceeding by any other course than the course dear to the Philistines; let us have a social movement, let us organise and combine a party to pursue truth and new thought, let us call it *the liberal party*, and let us all stick to each other and back each other up. Let us have no nonsense about independent criticism, and intellectual delicacy, and the few and the many. Don't let us trouble ourselves about foreign thought; we shall invent the whole thing for ourselves as we go along." This, even though the names have changed,[3] is true to the character of current meliorism—improvisation, vague "principles" (like "development of personality") instead of a knowledge of and immersion in traditions, the overcoming of any intellectual resistance by the sheer weight of ignorance.

But of course, there is less resistance than there was; the custodians of learning, shaken by the movement of the times, have to a quite considerable extent succumbed to modernism—or, at the best, are no longer masters of the case against it. One reason for this decline in critical power is that it is no longer expected of those who embark on a higher course of humane studies that they will give some serious attention to philosophy; accordingly, they are free to fall into as flagrant errors as Owen's and not even to have heard of the standard arguments against voluntarism or against utilitarianism and the whole sickly apparatus of welfare. Men with so narrowly specialised a training (even if it is called humane) do not understand that, if social conditions depend on the voluntary decisions which are made from time to time, there can be nothing properly called social or historical *theory* but merely

---

[3] That is, if *labour party* were taken as more appropriate to the current situation than *liberal party*; but it might be asked whether they are not all reformers together, nowadays.

*annals*, records of the various decisions made by various persons at various times—a source from which little in the way of critical thinking can spring. In the same way, they are ill-prepared for recognition of the serious intellectual decline, the loss of a sense of quality or distinction, involved in the reduction of ethics to a consideration of questions of distribution, of balanced shares in a single "welfare fund"—as opposed to questions of qualitatively different forms of activity or ways of life which, whatever adjustments they may on occasion come to, can never be brought to a common denominator and will always be involved in conflicts.

It will still be the case that classicism, where it survives, will not give way to the *fears* which have encroached more and more on the academic domain—fear of the prevailing ideas, fear of *criticising* democracy and reform, fear of giving offence to the multitude; for, as Socrates says in the *Crito*, though "the many can kill us", that is no reason for setting their opinions on a level with the opinions of the wise, for believing, though they have a certain power over life and death, that they have any power over truth. There is no question here of putting forward classicism as a remedy for the ills of the time, of formulating slogans like "Clear your mind of the cant of welfare and betterment" or "Take arms against the sea of reforms". The classicist recognises the natural opposition between disinterestedness and interestedness, between concern with the ways of working of things themselves and concern with what we can get out of them. He will certainly note the special weakness of the objective outlook at the present time; he may even decide that our modern intellectual age, dating from the Renaissance, is on the verge of collapse and that a new barbarism is imminent; he can hardly fail to note the resemblance between current conditions and the decline of classical Greece, with the replacement of the solid thinking of the preceding time by a woolly-minded cosmopolitanism and humanitarianism. Whatever his conclusion on this point, he will continue, as a classicist, to work "against the stream", as culture in all ages has had to work or (using the Hegelian terminology) as "objective mind" has constantly had to struggle with the entanglements of "bourgeois society", i.e., the economic system. He will indeed observe the more and more direct *attacks* on culture, the constant pressure, on the part of those who want to make society "go in the way it should", towards making learned institutions follow the same path,

CLASSICISM (1960) 253

however much learning may thus be sacrificed. But the observation of this and other trends of a subjectivist and superstitious kind will be made in the course of exposing them and thus, as far as can still be done, bringing out the contrasting character of objectivism, of "seeing things as they are".

One important point here is the interrelatedness of the various departments of culture, and particularly the interlocking of cultural *studies*. I have spoken mainly of philosophy not just because it is my own subject of study but because I regard it as having a central place in any cultural system. If any other subject is to have a general apparatus of criticism, it can have it only by drawing upon philosophy—that is, on major contributions to the theory of objective reality and of the types of question that can be raised concerning any objective reality or actual subject. Thus the historian has to concern himself with questions of sequence and causality, the literary critic has to go into questions of form or structure, these being in either case primarily matters of logic. Each of them has his special lines of criticism; but, when we examine these, we find that they lead us in the same direction. The historian has his scrutiny of documents and weighing of testimony, but here not only is he confronted immediately with simple logical questions of the soundness or unsoundness of the inferences they present, or of the coherence of their materials, but he has to take account of types of human error and illusion, of obstacles to discovery, which can be elucidated only by reference to logic, to types of actual situations. The student of literature has, in turn, to have such knowledge of illusions as will enable him to understand the struggles of a character in their toils; he has, in addition, to see how such illusions import themselves into literary criticism itself, emerging in "interpretations" (commonly of a romanticist or expressionist kind) which stand in the way of an objective view of the work.

In fact, what is broadly called "judgment" (embracing knowledge of the basic types of objective issue and of the major types of human error) is operative in *all* criticism, and this is why all investigators in the cultural field are engaging in philosophy, even though they may not realise it—and why, again, the fact that it can no longer be taken for granted that a scholar in any field has undertaken some formal philosophical study, is indicative of cultural decline. The type of criticism, of exposure of error, most characteristic of classical or objectivist philosophy is that expressed by Plato in the phrase "removing hypotheses", where the sort of supposition most injurious to thought and requiring most urgently to be got rid of is that which sets up distinct realms of being or of truth. The earliest object of critical attack here (though curiously it flourishes to this day) was on the scientific side, in such suppositions as that mathematical truth is of a different kind from physical truth—which would have the absurd consequence that no mathematical observation could be made on physical things. But the absurdity is no less when it is asserted (as it quite commonly is) that the figures and scenes of literature are the "stuff of fancy", belonging to a different realm from that of ordinary things—which would mean that no critical comment whatever could be made on them, that literary theory would be contentless. The doctrine of "realms" or "worlds" is itself a phantasy (as Heraclitus was the first to point out); and the supposed hard-headedness of believers in an "external world" (as contrasted with an inner world of thought) is simply theoretical muddlement. And here special mention may be made of Hegel as a classical figure in the modern period, who, in spite of some contamination by modernist doctrines, steadily opposed the breaking up of reality into separate realms, for whom philosophy was intertwined not merely with the broad history of thought but with history in general, who greatly stimulated philosophical interest in the work of the Greeks and who gave a great impetus to the development of objective aesthetics, objective ethics and objective social theory—of an objective view of the whole of culture.

His influence was considerable in the period I have referred to, in which it could be assumed that any scholar had studied philosophy, but also that any philosopher had engaged in a range of "humane" studies and would retain these interests throughout his philosophical work, so that his philosophy would be in some measure both historical and literary, and its being so would be essential to his full development of critical judgment.[4] No-one could then have passed off as philosophy the technical exercises

---

[4] Reference may again be made to the work of Burnet in Greek philosophy, with its striking combination of philosophical and historical insight—bringing home to us the way in which knowledge of philosophy can help us to determine the course of philosophical thought and the views of individual thinkers, while knowledge of the

which now pre-empt the field, and which mark the latest stage in the twentieth century "surrender to science". It should be understood that, in the cultivation of the fields of inquiry that have come to be known as "scientific", there is no less need for the exercise of "judgment", for the recognition of logical categories or the formal distinction among types of problem, for the removal of hypotheses of division in reality, than there is in the pursuit of any other inquiry; it is as speculative and critical, not as "technical", that work in these fields would be truly scientific. But in fact what we find there is the multiplication of divisions and specialisations, the identification of "method" not with logic but with the use of technical devices, the substitution of a mechanical for a critical apparatus. And it is this narrow, specialising and instrumentalist attitude that has infected the most influential schools of philosophy at the moment, leading them largely to ignore the history of philosophy, the "classics" of the subject which could provide them with an outlook at once broader and more critical.

The classics of philosophy, as of any other cultural subject, are those works which so fully expound and illustrate objective principles or expose subjective illusions that they have critical application in any age and do not depend on passing fashions. And this can be said particularly of the Greek classics, without which it would be impossible to see the foundation of the main departments of Western thought (politics being an outstanding example), and which are still drawn upon, though in an eclectic manner, even by those who boast of "starting afresh". But what, for our present predicament, classical studies in the narrower sense most strikingly bring out is the interdependence of the classical works in all departments of culture, so that the liberally educated man, whatever his leading interest, will range in his studies over the whole classical field. Indeed, the most insidious foe to classicism and the objective outlook is the specialism which cuts some departments of culture off from the rest and is therefore antagonistic to that solid core of philosophical criticism which is

doctrines of individual thinkers and their historical connections can help us to arrive at philosophical truths (to learn philosophy). This conjunct operation of critical factors, leading to fresh discovery and to comprehensiveness of view, illustrates the general principle that the coherent position, the position that "makes sense", is the one on which all lines of criticism converge.

corrective of any attempt to have one set of critical principles for one subject and a separate set for another, with intellectual chaos where they come into collision. Classicism, in short, stands for the unity of culture against all forms of subjectivism and interestedness, and for the unity, the common principles, of criticism against specialism and *ad hoc* devices—and it is these unities that I take the very existence of this Council[5] to symbolise.

---

[5] The Australian Humanities Research Council, to which, in the first instance, this paper was addressed (12th November, 1959).

# 18
# SOCRATES AS AN EDUCATOR (1931)

## I. SOCRATES AND PLATO

The manner of his life, and still more the manner of his death, have made Socrates an outstanding figure in the history of European thought and morals. That his doctrine has not till recently been adequately understood is due to the fact that he wrote nothing and that his views, fully and clearly as they are expounded in Plato's dialogues, have been taken to be Plato's own. Owing especially to the work of the late Professor John Burnet during his occupancy (1892 to 1926) of the chair of Greek in the University of St. Andrews, it is now possible for us not only to recognise the Greek philosophers as the founders of modern science, but to distinguish and appreciate the contributions of Socrates and Plato to science and general culture.

The supreme importance of Plato is not diminished by the recognition, which his own dialogues enable us to make, of the extent of his indebtedness to Socrates. The marking off of the earlier dialogues as thoroughly Socratic permits of a more careful scrutiny of the later dialogues in which the doctrines of Socrates are either criticised or not referred to at all. It is from these, and most of all from the *Laws*, that, according to Burnet, Plato's position and influence are to be truly estimated. In his posthumously published work, *Platonism* (originally delivered as lectures in the University of California in 1926), Burnet actually claims for Plato a decisive influence on Roman law. "It is not, in my opinion, too much to say that what we call Roman Law is not so much Roman as Hellenistic, and that it has its origin in the *Laws* of Plato."

The explanation of this apparently extravagant claim is simple. The Academy, which Plato founded, was not only an institute for scientific research but a school for training rulers and legislators, and it sent out such legislators to a considerable number of Greek states, both during and after Plato's time. Their influence would naturally be in accordance with Plato's ideas of sound politics, and the fact that he spent his last years in drawing up the legislative scheme which is set forth in the *Laws*, shows that he wished the work to be carried on on the same lines. When, at a later date, these Hellenic states came under Roman domination, it was found that the original civic law of Rome was inapplicable to them, and the adaptable Romans solved the difficulty by developing a new system which embodied much of the Academic legislation of the conquered states. It was this system which spread throughout the Empire, while the older Roman law was confined to Rome itself and "became of less and less importance as time went on". This, Burnet contends, is the explanation of the extraordinary similarities between Plato's dialogue and what we now call Roman Law.

The educational proposals of the *Laws* are particularly important, as Burnet had previously pointed out in his *Greek Philosophy from Thales to Plato*, for the estimation of Plato's originality and influence. Burnet lays special emphasis on the scheme of *higher* education elaborated in the dialogue. "We may easily miss the significance of Plato's proposals as to the education of boys and girls from the age of ten onwards. We must remember that in his day there were no regular schools for young people of that age. They were taken to one teacher for music-lessons and to another to be taught Homer, and there was no idea of coordinating all these things in a single building under a single direction with a regular staff of teachers. By founding the Academy Plato had invented the university, and now he has invented the secondary school. In consequence we find such schools everywhere in the Hellenistic period, and the Romans adopted it with other things. That is the origin of the medieval grammar school and of all that has come out of it since."

This recognition of the practical genius of Plato was not possible to those who regarded the *Republic* as the fine flower of Platonism, and neglected the later dialogues. It may indeed be said that it was at no time a reasonable view that Plato, in order to defend the memory of his master, Socrates, should have written dialogues attributing to him views that he never held. There would have been no reverence or even decent feeling about that. But it was only after the dialogues had been fairly definitely dated that Burnet could satisfactorily show, first, that all the dialogues up to the *Republic* expound a common philosophy, secondly, that, if this is not the philosophy of Socrates, we know next to nothing about his views, since all the alternative versions depend upon material arbitrarily selected from Plato's account, and, finally, that the later dialogues in which, with one explicable exception, Socrates plays no prominent part, expound a *different* philosophy, which is led up to by criticism of the Socratic.

The difference is equally marked in the sphere of education and politics, and in the *Timaeus* we have a definite reference to the shortcomings of Socrates in this regard. The point is, as Burnet puts it, that Socrates "could paint the picture of an ideal state but could not make the figures move. He is made to confess that he could not, for instance, represent his state as engaged in the struggle for existence with other states; to do that men are required who by nature and training have a gift for practical politics as well as for philosophy." In a word, Socrates was deficient in the historical sense. He imagined, as the earlier dialogues show, that all social and political problems can be solved on purely ethical grounds, by direct reference to what is good. Plato, on the other hand, saw the impossibility of making progress by the application of an unreal standard of perfection, and the necessity of working with existing political forces. The life and teaching of Socrates showed him, as nothing else could, the opportunism of both the leading Athenian parties and the consequent political bankruptcy of Athens. But he did not despair of the political development of other Greek states, and though his efforts were unsuccessful at the time, they were not, as we have seen, without a considerable later influence.

## II. EDUCATION AND POLITICS

The uncompromising attitude of Socrates rendered it inevitable that he should come into conflict with the Athenian state, though it was not until Athens was definitely on the decline that his teaching was regarded as a serious danger. Even if the democrats had not suspected that there was an actual connection between Socrates and the aristocratic party, his criticism of the existing form of government, threatened as it was both from within and from without, might well have been regarded as profitable only to their enemies.

This is the natural objection to any unhistorical political doctrine, anarchistic or theocratic, which appeals to an ideal "rule of right". The theory of rigid guardianship expounded in the *Republic* and the practical deification of Law in the *Crito* might be taken as decisive indications of the opposition of Socrates to anarchism. But, though there may be a difference in ethical conceptions, there is remarkably little practical or logical difference between the anarchistic and the theocratic positions. All our social and political difficulties will be solved, for the one, if we are governed by the spirit of equality and refrain entirely from oppression, for the other, if we are governed by the representatives of God and refrain entirely from disobedience. Neither view can give us any idea of how such conditions can be satisfied or even approached, how we can promote equality or recognise God's representatives. But each implies that the existing temporal power does not exemplify the rule of right, that it holds its position by oppression or usurpation. And thus both tend to support, and especially to be regarded by the ruling body as supporting, those political forces which are "in opposition" but are striving to secure domination.[1]

We can see, therefore, that it was natural for the democratic rulers to desire to suppress Socrates. But this is not to say that that desire was to their credit, or that severe criticism of their regime was not called for. Certainly "Be guided by what is good" is inadequate as a solution of political problems, but a scientific consideration of what sort of life is a good one (and, for that matter, of what constitutes oppression) is not politically and socially valueless. What gave particular force to the Socratic criticism was that the political ideas of the democrats were themselves quite unhistorical. The worshipful Athenian people, the sacred tradition of the city, were just as ideally conceived and reverenced as any metaphysical "Good" could be. The demonstration of the hollowness of these pretensions may have been historically inadequate and politically negative, but, as far as it went, it was logically sound. And the disinterestedness of Socrates's criticism of the democracy and its leaders, as well as of those professional educators who were called Sophists, made it doubly strong. To teach the youth to accept the customs of the city in which they lived may have been an essential part of the theory and practice of "getting on", but it implied the

---

[1] For the sake of simplicity I have passed over the case in which the existing temporal power is itself regarded as representing God. But it is worth noting that such pretensions commonly provoke a religious opposition.

SOCRATES AS AN EDUCATOR (1931) 261

existence of interested motives which such teachers were unwilling to reveal.

This fact alone gave Socrates an enormous dialectical advantage, and it was further increased, at his trial, by the existence of a political amnesty. In consequence the real charge of fostering aristocratic sentiments could not be brought, and the teaching of Socrates had to be attacked on religious grounds. Socrates pointed out in his defence that his accusers could give only the vaguest account of what his teaching really was, and he strongly denied that he was a teacher at all, in the sense in which they used the term. "If you have heard", he says to the judges, "that I undertake to educate men, and exact money from them for so doing, that is not true; though I think it would be a fine thing to be able to educate men, as Gorgias of Leontini, and Prodicus of Ceos, and Hippias of Elis do." In fact, if what these Sophists give is education, then Socrates is no educator, and he cannot be rightly accused of corrupting the youth by the inculcation of false doctrines, for he has never given doctrinal instruction to anyone.

But Socrates did not deny, but rather gloried in the fact, that he had striven by example and precept to inculcate the spirit of criticism, to encourage the questioning of received opinions and traditions; and nothing that the Athenians could do, he declared, would prevent his pursuing this task while he lived. "The unexamined life is not worth living"; to lead such a life is to be in the lowest state of ignorance, ignorant even of one's own ignorance. And therefore he would not cease to call upon the Athenians to give an account of their lives, as the facts of life would compel them to do even if they got rid of him.

The Socratic education begins, then, with the awakening of the mind to the need for criticism, to the uncertainty of the principles by which it supposed itself to be guided. This was utterly opposed to the doctrines of the democrats. What education meant for them is seen in the *Apology*, where Meletus, the leading accuser, describes Socrates as the sole perverter of the youth, while everyone else improves them; and again in the *Meno*, where Anytus, the democratic leader (who was really responsible for the prosecution, but kept in the background because the issue was nominally not political but religious), warns Socrates not to be so free with his criticisms of Athenians and their ways. According to these good patriots, to be educated meant simply to become a good Athenian, and that was brought about by enjoying the society of the respectable citizens of Athens.

Now the position of Socrates is simply that this uncritical acceptance of tradition, this acquiring of Athenian virtue, is no education at all. There is no virtue in being an Athenian, no peculiar and superior Athenian brand of goodness, but goodness is the same wherever it occurs, and what passes as good at Athens may not be really good at all. It requires the most careful scrutiny, and until this process of examination has begun, education has not begun. To see the full force of this criticism, we may substitute Australia for Athens, and imagine Socrates saying, "You think there is some virtue in being Australian, and that a good Australian is better than a good Greek or Italian, but what you call goodness is just your own ignorance." Clearly such talk would be infuriating, clearly also it would be very hard to answer; for it would only be by way of afterthought, as a mere "rationalisation", that any suggestion as to what the local virtue consisted in, could be made.

## III. KNOWLEDGE AND OPINION

For Socrates, then, what is fundamental to true education is not tradition but criticism. Tradition itself invites criticism, because it represents certain things as worth while but is unable to give any account of their value. Thus the aim of education is to give an account of things, to find out *the reason why*, and thus put knowledge in the place of opinion. Opinion is all that we get from tradition, all that we get from politicians and Sophists, all that the public, "the great Sophist", is concerned with. For all these what is current is correct. But what is current is a shifting and uncertain thing, it is not "tied down by the chain of the cause" (the reason why), and so may leave us in the lurch just when we are surest of it. Opinion may be right but only by accident, and without criticism, without the discovery of reasons, we cannot say whether it is right or wrong. We cannot even say whether we understand a received opinion in the same sense as does its promulgator, or whether, when we apply a tradition to a new case, we are not misinterpreting it. The only test is popular clamour, and that is the least steadfast thing of all.

SOCRATES AS AN EDUCATOR (1931) 263

Thus opinions and traditions change, and change without reason, and yet we continue to follow them. If we want to know what we are doing and thus have real guidance in our lives, we must get a grasp of sound principles; and such principles will be upheld for their own sake, and not because they have been handed on to us. Indeed, for the reasons given, they cannot be handed on but must be arrived at by a man's own thinking. Such thinking may, however, be stimulated by opinions and particularly by questions. Thus we find Socrates, in the *Theaetetus*, claiming the power of bringing men's thoughts to birth by means of this process of questioning, and this is the process of education as far as the educator is concerned. But the really important process is that which goes on in the mind of the pupil, and that is thinking or learning. If the aim of education is to be fulfilled, the Sophistic method of *instruction* must be avoided, and the dialectic method, in which the pupil is led to form his own hypotheses and test them, adopted. Instruction, by discouraging the critical exercise of the pupil's intelligence, prevents the real acquisition of knowledge.

This theory is worked out in connection with the doctrine of reminiscence as expounded in the *Meno* and the *Phaedo*. Under the stimulus of objects of opinion we recall those criteria or standards which alone give the former their meaning, and with which we were directly acquainted in a previous state. Divesting this view of its mythical character, we may say that the question is of finding certain self-explanatory principles, in the light of which we can estimate the transient objects of ordinary life, and thus have settled and organised knowledge. The systematic character of a man's thinking is the test of his progress from opinion to knowledge, as the orderly character of his actions is the test of his progress towards goodness.

Now this implies the ascription, in the Socratic theory, of a certain relative value to opinions and traditions. They may stimulate our search for what is of settled value and thus for an organised way of life. But in themselves they are inadequate, they cannot in the proper sense of the word be *learned*, because they have not been taken up into a self-explanatory system. The first point that Socrates always makes in his criticism of opinions and traditions is their mutually contradictory character. They imply a diversity of principle which is necessarily bad, weak and miserable; the only strong and happy life is the single-minded pursuit of the good.

Here we have one of the weak points of the Socratic position, since it implies that all men should function alike. But this does not invalidate the characterisation of education as *the finding of a way of life*, as contrasted with the mere acquisition of a number of arts or accomplishments. As tradition may have a relative value, so may the development of a particular aptitude, but it must be made a part of an organised way of life.

We can see from this that Plato's scheme of secondary education owed something to the fundamental conceptions of Socrates. It is also of interest to notice that Socrates, in his criticism of the Sophistic training in accomplishments, was cutting at the root of the modern psychological theory of abilities. Abilities, taken by themselves instead of as part of the general activity of the individual, are falsified and misdirected. The determination of a "vocation" on the basis of a classification of aptitudes may rightly be called an *external* method of procedure, since the classification can be arrived at only by reference to the occupations that are offered. Thus our modern Sophists, as G. K. Chesterton points out, try to discover what job a man is fit for, instead of asking what way of life is fitting for the man; they "temper the shorn lamb to the wind". Similarly, the eugenists desire to breed men for special characteristics, which they consider would be an improvement on existing characteristics, without giving any critical consideration to the notion of improvement or of goodness. "What's Wrong with the World", as Chesterton puts it in his book with that title, "is that we do not ask what is right". We proceed on the basis of notions of improvement, efficiency and fitness, we advocate special tasks, without inquiring what work is really worth doing.

What Socrates stood for, then, against the advocates of "up-to-date" methods of efficiency and specialisation, was coordination or integration of activities. Guidance, he admitted, is possible and desirable, but it must take place in a common and continuous life, and not by any isolated "test" of capacities, and it must aim at the greatest possible coordination of activities, and not at the isolation and development of some special activity. It is for this reason that the teacher, who has lived and worked with the pupil, is the best judge of what he can do. But to be a judge he requires above all to inquire into what is best, to ask *the reason why*, and not take it for granted that existing demands (opinions) must be satisfied; and in pursuance of this policy he will also encourage the pupil to ask the reason why. In this way real guidance and a really coordinated life are possible. And, if we discount the Socratic over-emphasis on ethics, we can still derive from his theories a recognition of the necessity of considering every way of life in its full social and political context. The Socratic view thus finds an interesting modern parallel in the slogan of Lenin, "Every cook a politician!"

It is true that in the ideal state portrayed in the *Republic* real political understanding is supposed to be confined to the ruling caste. This is due to the way in which Socrates divided knowledge from opinion, to his contention that the former is concerned with special objects, the forms or standards, instead of simply involving a more critical treatment of the same objects. But this can largely be corrected by means of his own theory of logical coordination. The method Socrates adopts, however, is to allow a certain relative value to opinion and consequently to a life which, though not itself inspired by understanding, obeys the dictates of understanding. In fact, preliminary education precisely takes the form of learning to go about things in the right way, and only after that can we enter on a course of higher education and get to know what makes such actions right.

## IV. THE PLACE OF DIALECTIC IN EDUCATION

The final working out of the educational theory of Socrates is thus to be found in the first and second schemes of education elaborated in the *Republic*. The early training of the guardians (which is all the training given to those who are not fitted for higher study) produces right opinion, or ability and willingness to follow the dictates of those who have knowledge, but does not produce knowledge. Or, to employ the distinction drawn in the *Phaedo*, it cannot give true or "philosophic" goodness, but only "popular" (or civic) goodness. "The former", as Burnet puts it, "depends on intellect, the latter on habit. It is the former alone that is teachable; for it alone is knowledge, and nothing can be taught but knowledge. The latter is only good at all in so far as it participates in the former. Apart from that it is a shifting and uncertain thing." That is to say, the early education must be directed by those who have had the later education, and not by those who can themselves lay claim to no more than opinion. There is a logical difficulty in that, if the goodness acquired in the early training really "participates in" (i.e., partakes of the nature of) true goodness, it cannot be a mere matter of habituation but must partake of critical activity as well. The concessions which Socrates makes to "opinion" are really due to his anti-historical bias, and weaken, instead of strengthening, his critical case. What should be recognised (as Socrates himself has enabled us more clearly to do) are the different factors of guidance and originality, but these should both be present at any stage in the process of education.

The unhistorical character of the theory of early training in right habits appears in the complementary assumptions of a purely imitative faculty in the pupils, their original tendencies being neglected, and of the existence of "wise and good" educators, whose simple business it is to set up proper models of behaviour, and who are not themselves learning in the educative process. The *Ethics* of Aristotle is based on the same assumptions (being largely derived from the *Republic*), and thus passes over the critical problems of ethics and education. "Conditions of soul", Aristotle says, "arise from activities of like character to the conditions." We become good by doing the right thing, i.e., the thing the good man would do under the same circumstances; and therefore he must be there in the first place to tell us what to do, so that we may acquire the habit.

The alternative to this guidance is that we should be subject to the misguiding influence of pleasures and pains. "It is pleasure that makes us do what is bad, and pain that makes us abstain from what is right. That is why we require to be trained from our earliest youth, as Plato has it, to feel pleasure and pain at the right things. True education is just that." In his "Aristotle on Education" Burnet goes so far as to say of this that it "is the best account of the training of character that has ever been given and should be engraved on the heart of every educator". What it lacks, however, is any explanation of *how* the training takes place, how the affection comes to be transferred from one thing to another—unless the assumption of a general tendency to demand what we have become accustomed to (by having it constantly thrust upon us) is to pass for an explanation. Whereas

SOCRATES AS AN EDUCATOR (1931)    267

Plato, in the *Laws*, goes on to take the child's spontaneous activities as of fundamental importance for any training he is to receive, the more rationalistic Socrates and Aristotle appear to regard him as a mere seeking and avoiding mechanism, whose development is determined by what he is allowed to get (or compelled to take).

The theory of habituation, then, is defective precisely in that it neglects the spontaneity of thought which had been emphasised by Socrates in his criticism of opinion or "what is accepted by all right-thinking men". We may therefore expect to find a correlative defect in his account of that spontaneity or of higher education. We have seen that the fundamental weakness of his philosophy is its unhistorical character, and this finds its logical expression in the attribution of true reality to certain unchanging "forms", or ideals, everything changeable being relatively unreal. It is in terms of these forms, Socrates holds, that it is possible to "give an account" of things. This raises the question of what account can be given of the forms themselves. They cannot each be self-explanatory, or they would be quite unrelated and would not form a system of reality. Accordingly the system itself, or, more precisely, its principle of organisation, has to be taken as the one self-explanatory entity; and this is what Socrates calls "the form of the Good". It is the one self-sustaining or truly spontaneous thing; and what we call spontaneity in ourselves or in other things is dependent upon it, and exhibits the degree of our or their harmony with it.

But when Socrates is asked to give an account of this "Good" itself, he can do so only in vague metaphor. This must be so; for if it is explained only by itself, clearly *we* cannot explain it. But in that case all that we are saying, when we postulate its existence, is that there is "something, we know not what", which is the ultimate explanation of reality. Obviously, in assuming that there is such a thing, we are not entitled to call it good, nor can we derive from what is unknown to us any assurance that some historical thing is good or is better than another. Hence in making his moral distinctions, in saying what should be studied and what should not, Socrates, just like the Sophists, is falling back on opinion. He, too, gives an "explanation" which is no explanation; he, too, has to depend upon "what is accepted by all right-thinking men"—only, his right-thinkers are not the same as those of Protagoras and other Sophists.

To show that Socrates was also infected by the Sophistry he criticised is not, however, to take away all value from his criticism or from his theory of higher education. It more especially explains the weakness of his scheme of early education, its moralistic character—particularly exemplified in the unaesthetic treatment of art, which is considered to be purely imitative and to have its value, positive or negative, solely according as it is or is not a good model for the pupils in turn to imitate. This view of art and education is typical of the *mechanical*, or "external", conceptions which Socrates elsewhere condemned, and which are condemned in the working out of that Dialectic which he regarded as the culmination of higher education.

The theory of Dialectic itself implies that there can be no set of habits which are entirely in accordance with sound thinking and living, and therefore that habituation cannot be a sound method by itself; for Dialectic requires the unlearning of much that has been previously learned. It may be said, in fact, that there is an element of unlearning in all learning; we acquire new reactions to things by developing and altering old ones. The mind is never a *tabula rasa*, and therefore never merely imitative; but, as Plato recognised in the *Laws*, we have certain tendencies to begin with, and it is only by their exercise that we learn. We learn, that is, by trial and error, or, as in the Socratic theory of criticism expounded in the *Phaedo*, by the formation and testing of hypotheses.

What makes guidance necessary is our tendency to stick to established modes of reaction, in spite of confusions and errors. As education advances, the process of removing confusions becomes more of a deliberate act on the part of the learner. But, whatever be the degree of assistance rendered, the process of clarification involves the breaking up of fixed ideas, the rejection of hypotheses which have hardened into prejudices. Thus "clearing the mind of cant" is a characteristic of the educative process in general; and Dialectic is simply the theory of the kind of hypotheses it is necessary to reject—those, namely, which would make the prosecution of inquiry impossible, being set above our scrutiny. The most prevalent form of this cant is the "disabling" of criticism, the treatment of the critic as an ill-disposed person, one who is not worth attending to, *because he criticises*. Such evasion of the issue is described by the educated as "illogical", but the pointing out of fallacies of this kind is a very small part of what is involved in Logic or Dialectic. Its full import can be grasped only when we consider it in relation to the most advanced studies, i.e., to the sciences.

The special scientist, Socrates contends, uses hypotheses which he does not criticise and of which, in fact, he cannot "give an account". They are taken as defining his field of study, and within that field, or using those assumptions, he prosecutes his inquiries and arrives at his conclusions. Thus the mathematician arrives at "mathematical truths". But actually there is no mathematical truth, any more than there is an Athenian truth. Fields of study are not cut off from one another but mingle just as peoples do. And to treat each as a separate "world" is to fall into contradictions. It is the business of Dialectic to show that the supposed "indemonstrables" and "indefinables" of the sciences are not indemonstrable or indefinable, but are subject to investigation. Thus all hypotheses implying a division in reality require to be "destroyed" (or removed).

What this involves is that there is a single logic which applies to all the sciences, a single way of being which all their objects have; we cannot divide reality into higher and lower orders, for the difference and the relation between them would alike be indefinable and indemonstrable. Thus any "science" which affects to discover powers or faculties which "make things what they are", or to apply "laws" to "phenomena", is guilty of logical error. The Socratic theory of forms itself calls for dialectic criticism. And though Socrates maintains the possibility of finding the "reason" of these forms in a single ultimate principle, the very assumption of this principle involves a separation (between the ultimate and the relative) which requires to be removed. The application of logic to "reasons" leads to the conclusion, already obscurely apprehended by the first Ionian philosophers, that any explanation must be on the same level as the thing explained, so that the former in turn can be explained in a similar way.

But the discovery of the illogicalities in the theory of Socrates does not affect the fact that he has given a valuable account of the conditions of scientific inquiry. And on this basis we get an important development of his criticism of specialisation. Every scientist should be a dialectician, critical of hypotheses and recognising the continuity of things, since otherwise he will make mistakes in his science and be unable to correct them. In the same way, such activities as teaching and politics should not be regarded as trades or specialities. Every teacher should be an investigator, every politician a thinker. And, since the distinction between the different types of goodness falls to the ground along with the supposition of an unchanging reality behind history, the logical extension of the argument is, as already indicated, that every citizen should be a politician. No one else can do his thinking for him; and the least thinking will lead him to reject the political and social guidance of "experts" who have no social or political theory. It will readily be seen, for example, that such Sophistic cures for social ills as the encouragement of the "efficient" and the elimination of the "unfit" are based on no coordinated or logical view of society, and thus are merely prejudices to be removed.

But this is because society is viewed unhistorically, as a mere field for personal agreements and disagreements, and not as a developing thing. Socrates is wrong in assuming that social issues can be decided on the basis of a general principle of consistency or coordination, and his democratic opponents could rightly say that his proposals must really have had a more special source, must have arisen, that is, from a definite attitude on particular social questions. In general, we can criticise only by reference to beliefs which we definitely hold; otherwise there would be nothing to say for or against any disputed view. And unless this feature of logical criticism is recognised, the Socratic insistence on logic, the setting of criticism against instruction, is misleading. So long as we do not set anything above criticism, we can make progress; but we do so not by having any kind of higher knowledge, but by having opinions and acting on them, that is, by reacting on things which are as historical as ourselves. To have an opinion or belief is to hold something to be true, to be an actual fact, and we cannot make more of it than that; so that there is no place for the Socratic "knowledge". When this necessary correction is borne in mind, the position of Socrates can still be seen to be of real value in pointing the way to the discovery of educational and political truths—namely, by critical activity in science and politics.

# 19
# DETERMINISM AND ETHICS (1928)

## I. ETHICS, POSITIVE OR NORMATIVE

In maintaining that human behaviour is naturally conditioned, that there is no difference between the kind of causality which conduct exhibits and that exhibited in any other case, determinism implies that the distinctions commonly drawn between normative and positive science, and between freedom and necessity, are unreal. This is not to say, as is sometimes supposed, either that we can have such a knowledge of a person's character and environment as will enable us to predict his whole history, or that his environment alone determines what his history will be. It would be absurd to make any such claim in regard to minds, when we find, in dealing with other things, that both character and environment have to be taken into account—indeed, if this were not so, we should have in turn to consider the environment, and not the character, of the environing things, and so on indefinitely—and that, in the investigation of both, new and unexpected factors are continually being revealed. Such discovery, however, is possible only if we can say that in certain situations things of a particular sort behave in a certain way; and this kind of description, which implies neither "freedom" nor subordination to "standards", is the only way of expressing knowledge of human or any other behaviour. It is no more possible to uphold a theory of different kinds of causality than consistently to believe in different kinds of truth or reality.

Those who distinguish positive from normative science contend that, while the former can tell us "what is", it cannot tell us "what ought to be". In order to know that, we require to invoke "norms"; standards or ideals to which things may conform more or less closely, but which are in some sense *above* these things. Such norms, it is said, appear in practice, where we must have ends to which our actions are directed. And while natural science can tell us as much about the connections of things as will enable us to select means to ends, it cannot determine the ends themselves. It supplies us, not with the absolute or categorical commands of morality, but only with hypothetical commands. Medical science, for example, can say that if we desire health, we should not deprive ourselves of fresh air, but we have to go beyond medical science to find out whether health *ought* to be desired. Now action which is determined by pursuit of an absolute end is thereby subject to a different sort of causality from that which prevails among things which have not ends; it is "free" action.

The illogicality of this theory appears at once from its conception of the different sorts of reality which attach to norms and to the things which come under these norms, or from its attempt to distinguish values from facts. If the statement that something "ought to be" has any meaning, it can only be that the thing *is*, positively, obligatory; that this is a matter of fact. When such a statement is taken to be true, it can be dealt with by means of the ordinary logical mechanism of assertion and denial, proof and testing of hypotheses, definition and division—and in no other way. If we accept the term "obligatory", then we shall say that certain things are or are not obligatory, just as we may say that they are or are not red. But if we set out to show that they "are" in different senses, we can do so only by using propositions in relation to which an exactly similar operation will be required. The consequent impossibility of making any definite assertion would be fatal to *any* science, "normative" or positive.

To get over this difficulty it has been suggested that all science is really normative, that "physical science" is only that part of Science which deals with means, and is thus a mere abstraction from the fundamental consideration of ends. But how is this abstraction possible? Suppose it were granted that medical science deals with means (a fairly plausible assumption), what are they, and how can it deal with them so as to be of any use to us in conduct? They must have characters of their own, they must exist, or they cannot be studied. And, however strenuously it may be asserted that in this existence they are only "relative", it must be admitted that they *absolutely* lead to the desired ends, if we are to get any advantage from knowing them. And, finally, this end that they lead to must have certain physical characteristics, if physical science is to tell us how to get to it. It appears, then, that medical and ethical science may consider the same things, but will concentrate on different features of them. This is a commonplace of scientific investigation, and does not justify the attempt to take those features, in which ethics is specially interested, apart from the rest, and as an end to which the rest are a means. Incidentally, we should then have two sorts of "means to end" relation; fresh air would promote health in quite a different way from that in which health promoted goodness. Yet both relations would be determined in exactly the same way—by seeing what *followed* from certain conditions.

To avoid these inconsistencies we must maintain that it is possible to find physical occurrences without moral characteristics, and also to find physical occurrences with moral characteristics— which, of course, need have nothing to do with ends. If the value of anything were something *above* its occurrence, it would be unaffected by whether the thing occurred or not, and thus the occurrence itself would have no value, i.e., the value would not, strictly speaking, be *of* anything, and, being quite apart from events, certainly could not be chosen as an end. On the other hand if there is anything in the occurrence itself which could be regarded as its "conformity to a standard", then this character is what we mean by the thing's value and we do not require to look beyond the thing itself in order to know an ethical truth. The alternative is that value is a mere label which might be arbitrarily attached to anything.

It will, of course, be said that nothing ever happens which quite comes up to our ideals. But, in the first place, this comparison could not be made unless our ideals were at least *thought of* as happening, i.e., as natural. And while we can and do think of goods which may occur in the future, the same applies to the subject-matter of any science. There is nothing *logically* peculiar about the future; what we think of as existing then, we think of as existing in the same sense as what exists now. And the characters we attribute to future occurrences are those which we have already found in similar occurrences. Allowing, then, that we can suppose that something better will exist than anything that has so far existed, we conceive its *goodness* to be of the same sort as that of things already in existence. But, in the second place, suppositions of this kind are for the most part false and useless; the imagined situation would very often not be particularly good; and if we say "better but not possible", either we mean that it is not possible here but has occurred somewhere else and been observed to be better, or we are speaking about the non-existent and cannot significantly call "it" better or worse than what exists.

## II. THE "MORAL JUDGMENT"

This general position is not affected by the conception of ethics as the science of moral *judgments*; on the contrary, it shows that that conception is wrong. The suggestion is that the data of ethics are acts of approval or preferences, and that, while it is possible to deal positively with the conditions under which we come to approve of this or that, there remains the question of the "validity" of our approval, a question which cannot be treated in the same positive fashion. But when we consider what is meant by validity in this case, we find that it simply means the *truth* of the judgments we pass. Now, admittedly, the truth of a belief is a different matter from how we come to hold it, but the one question is just as positive as the other. In a moral judgment, as in any other, something is judged or asserted, i.e., some situation is said to have occurred; and moral judgments can be distinguished from others only in virtue of some peculiarity of these situations, such that we can describe them as *moral* situations. It would be absurd to say that, although such situations are asserted, ethics cannot take account of them but must begin with our approval; apart from them it would be impossible to say what "our approval" meant. No one but the most recalcitrant relativist would dream of saying that the data of physics are "physical judgments", instead of physical facts, yet the one view is as reasonable as the other.

If, then, we all pass moral judgments, this means that we all suppose that there are moral facts, which, naturally, are the data of ethics. And if any such judgment is to be criticised, this must be done by means of other judgments of a similar kind, i.e., by showing that the supposed situation contradicts the true moral facts; otherwise we have a mere *argumentum ad hominem*. It is just through this sort of confusion between our attitudes to things and their own characters, that it has been supposed that ethics has to do with ends. It is possible for us to pursue something which is good,[1] but this could not be significantly said if goodness meant being pursued, or even being worthy to be pursued, by us. How we are affected by good things, and likewise how we know them, are questions which, though a moralist may be interested in

---

[1] In later writings this is denied; cf. John Anderson, "Logic and Ethics" (*A.J.P.P.*, May, 1939, p.56): "it is not by being aimed at that goodness comes about".

them, cannot constitute ethical inquiry. Statements such as "This is good" are made, and they must be met or supported in just such ways as would be employed in dealing with the statement "This is sulphur". G. E. Moore's theory of "intuition" simply amounts to saying that we find certain ethical propositions to be true; this does not mean, as is evident from other such findings, that they cannot be logically criticised or proved. Intuition, then, means observation, the direct acquisition of positive knowledge, allowing, of course, that people are as apt to make mistakes about moral facts as about physical facts in general.

The illogicality of the theory of the "moral judgment" becomes still clearer if we consider the detailed accounts that are given of approval of the right things, and consequent or concomitant pursuit of the true end. The passing of moral judgments is supposed to be the work of some peculiar faculty or mental power, which approves or disapproves of the ends chosen by other faculties or powers. The more rationalistic form of this theory is that there is a special moral faculty, conscience or sense of obligation, which issues its edicts, while particular inclinations or reflective faculties (like Butler's "self-love") engage in the pursuit of ends which may or may not be in accordance with these edicts. Taking the more idealistic view, we have to think of the whole self as pursuing an ultimate end ("self-realisation") in relation to which alone any special end is to be approved or even understood. In the latter case we have a more definite conception of control on the part of the central power; but even in the former case we can hardly think of approving as going on in the same mind without any effect on actual choice. So that while there is a *prima facie* distinction between the theory of a difference of kind between the approving faculty and the pursuing faculties, and that of a difference of degree between the whole self pursuing the good and functions of the self pursuing aspects or elements of the good, there is in both cases a conception of an ultimate judge and of subordinate functions which it criticises. Thus if we can rule out the supposition of a peculiarly *critical* faculty, we shall have disposed of both "conscience" and the "whole self" as candidates for that office.

Now I have no desire to deny that judgments are passed in the course of our activities and pursuits, of which they may even be said to be expressions. But it does not follow that these judgments are about the activities themselves, or that, since we judge in choosing, our judgment must take any such form as "I am choosing what I ought to choose", or, by generalisation, "This ought to be chosen by anyone similarly situated". There is nothing whatever, in the fact that we find things out in the course of our pursuits, to show that we find out anything about our pursuits, let alone that they have "norms"; and although in our active life we sometimes discover moral truths, we also discover other truths, in which, for the most part, we are much more interested.

The position is that a *motive*[2] (i.e., whatever it is in us that acts; feelings, as I should contend) tends to bring about some state of affairs, or *objective*, and that, if it is not obstructed in its action, we believe (or, as I should say, the motive believes) that that state of affairs has occurred, i.e., a certain *proposition* is held to be true. If this terminology of motives and objectives be adopted, the position that I am criticising is that there is a peculiarly critical motive which judges all other motives by comparing their objectives with its, or that there is a total motive which dominates all partial motives by subordinating their objectives to its; the ultimate objective in both cases being "the good". (Of course, by confusion between what a mental activity is and what it knows, the objective is wrongly called the motive, in many theories.) Whether "the good" is conceived as an abstract or as a concrete universal, the criticism of the theory of an ultimate objective and a fundamental motive is not greatly affected; and, as has been indicated, the two theories do not remain so distinct as they set out to be. They are simply different ways of trying to meet the difficulties involved in setting up a moral *authority*.

The fundamental objection to any theory which distinguishes a universal motive seeking a universal objective from particular motives seeking particular objectives is that all motives and objectives are particular. What we seek can only be some state of affairs. To call it a norm or an ideal is merely an excuse for leaving it indefinite. And, in the same way, aiming at the norm would have to be as much the work of an *inclination* as is sport or drunkenness. The ideal, if it is to be capable of being stated and thought about, must be specific, and thus that which pursues it will be only a part

---

[2] This expression is defective precisely because it is used antithetically to "objective". We have no title to assume that a human or, in particular, a mental activity must "find outlet" in some direction or must be "directed on" the production of some external situation. It might still be held that *good* activities did always have "objectives".

or "aspect" of the self. In short, the notion of a total or supreme good is incompatible with the recognition of ethical propositions, i.e., of situations in which good occurs.

The distinction between conscience and inclinations, as worked out, for example, by Butler, comes to something like this. An inclination pursues a certain thing, and it will pursue this thing irrespective of whether it is good or not; it is incapable of exercising criticism or judgment, since it has a "particular" aim. Conscience, on the other hand, works by means of judgment; it directs pursuit of things *because they are good*; or, judging that a thing is good—a proposition—it approves the inclination that pursues that thing—simply as a thing. But there is no logical distinction between things and propositions. Things are known only by their characters, and so the objective in each case is a complex situation, not any "simple" entity. Hence, any motive that can seek, can judge; and the reverse also holds, each motive being interested in situations of a certain sort. Our object-seeking activities (passions or inclinations) govern our judgments; and there is no logical basis for supposing the existence of a non-passionate judge or "rational" faculty, over and above our activities themselves, which is peculiarly critical of them, or to which they should be referred. The fact that judgments are made by passions does not mean, as already indicated, that they are *about* passions, and it does not mean that they are false. They can be shown to be false only by having other judgments, equally definite, brought against them.

It is, indeed, to be observed that there could be no conflict between conscience and inclinations, if their objectives were of different orders. But if all objectives are of the propositional order, having both particularity and universality in that a certain thing is taken to be of a certain sort, then we can have contradiction and conflict. In fact we can connect the interaction, the mutual opposition or support, of motives with the similar relations between the propositions which are believed. That is, we can explain reasoning without calling in "reason". This reason, which is supposed to guide our activities or to subsume them in itself, is in a quite untenable position. For the guiding or subsuming is surely an activity of ours. So that either we have activities which reason cannot control, or it will guide its own guiding, subsume its own subsuming—and so on.

Criticism, then, is not a special function, but can be undertaken by any motives that can conflict. It is not only in *moral* science, as the history of rationalist thought amply shows, that the attempt has been made to set up authoritative principles. But, when we consider the actual procedure of science, we find that there is no such thing as abstract criticism, but only criticism in terms of certain tenets. Thus what we currently mean by "reasonable" is not transcending particularity but conforming to certain specific standards, viz., to the objectives of the motives which speak as "we" at a given time. And as reasonable means assisting, or at least not hindering, these objectives, unreasonable means obstructing or conflicting with them. The dominant motives are as particular as the subordinate ones, and it is easily seen from the facts of everyday life that it is not always the same motive that criticises. The attempt to get round these facts by means of the notion of a *developing* conscience or self makes the fatal admission that the motive in question *is* a particular one. Actually, then, we find that our motives change and that different motives are dominant at different times. And the theory of a moral authority is simply an attempt to induce conformity to the motives dominant in certain minds, by elevating them to a transempirical level. This attempt owes some of its success to the tendency to seek safety and certainty, which is also, of course, a particular motive with a definite history.

## III. THE FACTS OF THE "MORAL LIFE"

The above criticism of the normative or authoritarian theory shows to some extent what account a positive theory will give of what are called the facts of the moral life, but some further statement and clarification of the positive issues is required. The facts referred to are most specifically those of choice, deliberation, responsibility and exhortation, or, more generally, inducement, to goodness. And, as already indicated, the consideration of them must be based on the fact that we and others have various motives, and that these motives interact and influence one another in a variety of ways.

Simple choice is simply object-finding, i.e., the finding by a motive of an object whereby it gains outlet or expression. This is the process of satisfaction of desire. We are to think of the motive as being in a state of tension, which ceases when the object is achieved. This is the condition of knowledge in general; what we know is what solves our problems or eases our minds. But the case is not always so simple; there may be no immediate solution, and we may go through a process of *deliberation*, which is regarded as the distinguishing-mark of "moral" choice. Now deliberation arises from a certain opposition of motives. And these opposed motives, in struggling to find outlet, excite other motives which assist them, until one set overcomes the other and acts.[3] Or, again, certain parts of the opposed motives may find common outlet, while other parts are repressed. In either case we have the opposition of two complex tendencies, and a final movement arising from some solution of the opposition. The situation is comparable to that represented by a chemical equation, where the interaction of two compounds results in the formation of a new substance and, in general, of a certain "residue". (This, incidentally, is the true "mental chemistry", and not any theory of derivation from elements.) The various "ideas" called up in the course of deliberation are the objectives of the motives that rise to the assistance of the original motives, but it is these motives themselves, in conjunction with the original ones, that enable a certain action to take place; the "ideas" are not in any sense causes of the action. Deliberation, then, exemplifies the conflict and the complication of motives in the course of human activity. There is no pure reason here, no total self or ultimate end.

In exhortation and inducement we have a similar situation, where some of the conflicting and assisting motives are in one mind and some in another. It may, of course, be said that the motives of the one person cause some of the other's motives to become active, and that the latter then goes through a process of deliberation, the point of difference from the previous case being that he has been *induced* to deliberate. But even this explanation admits of interaction between different persons' motives as well as among a single person's. The general position is, then, that we wish another person to act in a certain way, which we may or may not call "good". And apart from the possibility of our seeking to show our power over him, the point will be that the objective we

---

[3] This view was largely suggested to me by S. Alexander's "Foundations and Sketch-Plan of a Conational Psychology," *British Journal of Psychology*, December, 1911 (cf. especially pp. 256,7). Other parts of my argument have also been influenced by his views.

prescribe for him is one of our own, that it satisfies one of our motives. Now what we appeal to or exert influence on in him may be the same motive, so that our action consists in producing a situation in which it is free to act; the conveying of information being a case in point. Or it may be a different motive, in which case we may procure conformity but not the same sort of act as we should perform in pursuing the objective in question. And thus his objective is also different (for example, he may be seeking to avoid unpleasantness), though similar to ours in certain respects. Appeals to persons to be moral in their own interests illustrate this confusion of motives.

The two extremes, then, between which all types of exhortation and inducement are to be found are compulsion and assistance between similar motives in different persons. Accepting McDougall's theory, in respect of the latter, that the activity of a given motive in one person may "sympathetically induce" the operation of the same motive in another, we have to add that this may happen not merely when the motive is dormant or has been temporarily overcome by other motives, but also when it has not previously been active; so that all the varieties of education are accounted for. But it has particularly to be noted that this theory applies to motives of any sort. We have not discovered any method of inducement peculiar to good motives; though it may be maintained that in all other cases there is an element of compulsion. However this may be, it has been found possible to give a positive description of the processes without taking goodness into account, and it remains possible that goodness may be discovered as a positive feature of some of them.

All these methods of influence are likewise to be found in operation among the different motives of a single mind. It is on this basis that a positive account of responsibility is to be given. Responsibility is not the charge that is put upon reason to control inclinations, or on the self to be itself. It is the fact that all our actions arise from motives which we have, and which are in some interactive relation with the motives speaking as "we", even when they are disclaimed by the latter. Of course, they interact with all sorts of things, including other people's minds. But they are in peculiar relations to the other processes which belong to the same mind. Now clearly, if we avoid the confusion between what a thing is and what it knows, we cannot accept the statement, "I did not know

DETERMINISM AND ETHICS (1928) 281

I was doing this", as a justification for the conclusion, "It was not I who did this". To put it otherwise, our motives are complex, and so are our objectives; so that what we vaguely or indirectly pursue has to be taken along with what we directly and definitely pursue; we are equally responsible for both. "Repression" is characteristic of the refusal to accept responsibility; it is the forcing of a motive to find an outlet which "we", the repressing motives, will not observe. But recognition by us cannot be the test of responsibility; we should, in fact, commonly be said to be responsible for this recognition itself, though we might not recognise it. So that the term "responsibility" really stands for such relations as hold between any two activities of one mind.

Similarly, we may speak of effort or endeavour, without requiring to add anything about its being "moral", as characteristic of a motive struggling against obstructions. We have, in short, to think of our motives as striving to find outlet, of various *tendencies* in mind. But this is just as positive a conception as pressure in physics. The main point is the treatment of our various motives as "passions" (that is, as having qualities of their own and not merely relations) and as complex, as opposed to the theory of a variety of simple inclinations which cannot undergo mixture and separation, but pursue different individual objects, and of simple reason which can control them all because it has a universal and single aim, "the good". In place of this scheme of an "identity-motive" and "difference-motives", actual experience presents us with differentiation and integration, variation and adjustment, complication and development. In brief, *the interaction of complex motives* will account for all the facts of "moral psychology".

## IV. GOOD AND BAD ACTIVITIES

If we take the facts which have been considered as constituting the field of ethics, it will appear that the logic of moral events is the same as that of any other events. But even if moral theory has something further to consider than the facts referred to, the natural assumption, in view of what has been said, will be that it differs from psychological theory, not in method, but only in paying special attention to certain things. This will be obviously so, if we find that goodness is a character of certain motives or mental activities. These will be the special object of ethical study, and it will be primarily concerned with what these are and what characters they display, and only subsequently with how they are produced or hindered. It has been shown that there is no room for the assumption of some ideal to which deliberation and inducement lead on, since these processes simply indicate the interaction of specific motives having specific objectives.

The crucial question is whether it is objectives or motives that are to be regarded as good or bad. Now those who take the former view always regard the goodness or badness of objectives as connected with our pursuit of them. It would thus appear that the terms correspond to the arbitrary "reasonable" and "unreasonable" that we have already considered. The question of the character of the objectives themselves will be the important one. Now some objectives are mental and some are not, but it is commonly supposed that goodness and badness have some special connection with mind. It appears to me that objectives are generally called "good" only by confusion with the goodness of the motives which pursue them. Thus the facts which induce Moore to call *beauty* good and many thinkers to say the same of *truth*, seem to me to be accounted for by taking the love of beauty and the love of truth as good. And the unjustified assumption that what a motive pursues must be felt to be better than it, explains these errors. I consider, therefore, that it is the operations of certain motives that are properly called good or bad. By taking this view we are in a position to avoid the ethical dualism of many theories, in which "goodness" is attributed alike to motives and to objectives, but really in different senses. And we are prepared to find that what goods aim at is ethically much more important than what aims at them.

In speaking of the operation of a motive, we require to make a distinction. We may think of its activity as what has been described as "finding outlet", a release of tension taking place when some object is achieved. Or we may consider it as active, when it is not in a state of tension, but is simply occurring within the mind; contributing, in the current terminology, to "feeling-tone". It may be that there is always some degree of tension, if the motive is present at all, and that at other times we simply have a tendency, i.e., that the processes then present in the mind are of such a character that, when certain circumstances arise, the motive will again appear. In any case it would seem that it is when they are in a state of tension that motives assist or resist one another, and also that it is in such cases of intense activity that goodness is to be found. Taking assistance, then, as meaning that a certain motive brings about circumstances in which another will act, resistance that it brings about circumstances which prevent another from acting, and recognising that these relations are facts of experience, we may consider the view that assistance is a mark of good motives, and resistance of bad motives.

This is substantially the view put forward by Socrates in *Republic*, I. He makes it clear, of course, that this distinction is not to be taken as a simple and final criterion, by pointing out that, while goods assist one another, they oppose bads; whereas bads oppose both goods and one another. There is no question, then, of founding ethics on abstract attitudes of assistance and resistance (although as Socrates develops the argument, this point is considerably obscured), any more than on abstract attitudes of altruism and egoism. The position may be expressed by saying that a good motive will always assist another of the same kind, so that that particular good can be communicated to an indefinite extent within the field of human activities. Love of truth, for example, will indefinitely communicate the spirit of discovery, and will assist the development and operation of that spirit whenever it appears and with whatever materials it may deal; a true investigator in any field will always encourage investigation in that or any other field. We do not, of course, *define* goodness by means of that relation, but if we decide, as I think we may, that it is common and peculiar to goods, then we can employ it as a criterion in particular cases. The same facts will show that a good motive will sustain itself in a particular mind by providing the materials for its continued operation, as one discovery leads on to another and the solution of one problem to the formulation of a new problem.

Bad motives, on the other hand, can never get rid of an element of resistance and repression, and, though they may co-operate to a certain limited extent, will eventually be found in opposition, and will always involve a certain friction. Hate, it may be said, breeds hate; but it also fights with hate and tries to destroy it, and in the individual it exhausts itself. So ignorance, though it may breed ignorance, fights with ignorance, and obscurantism defeats its own end. The degree of co-operation possible to motives which are not good is represented in the State sketched by Glaucon in *Republic*, II. Here the assistance is of an external or extrinsic sort, the utilisation of common means to diverse ends, as contrasted with participation in common activities in which the distinction between means and ends is unimportant. We note in the compromise referred to (which is, of course, a fact of common experience) the absence of a common spirit and the recurrence of friction, and also, as Glaucon points out, the element of repression in that some demands are given up in order that others may have a *sure* satisfaction.

That such a state of affairs occurs is not to say that it is not bad. On the other hand, though we may never find a mind or a community which is wholly free from resistance and repression, which, as we say, is "given up" to good activities, this will not prevent us from recognising particular goods and the assistance among them. This assistance, along with the opposition between evils, is no ground for optimism. We have to take account of the conditions of the original appearance of goods and evils, we have to remember that "it is hard to *become* good", and that it is possible for goods to be simply annihilated by evils or by natural conditions generally. But the fact that a good once established both communicates itself and assists other goods, as scientific discovery assists artistic appreciation and creation, is not merely a reason for the continuance of the struggle against evils; it is itself the continuation of the struggle.

We may further illustrate the operation of assistance by reference to the process described by Freud as "transference". Freud is referring primarily to "pathological" cases, but we may consider the matter more broadly. What occurs in transference is that one person, e.g., the patient, makes use of the powers of mind of another person, e.g., the analyst; "identifies" himself with the latter, adopts his views and his ways of dealing with situations. In this way the patient's previously pent-up motives find outlet. But the same may take place within one person's mind, when a conflict is resolved and a new type of activity emerges by the aid of certain abiding motives or sentiments. This is the process of "sublimation", where one motive finds for another a means of expression, provides it with a language, puts its own "ideas" before it as objectives. This is also the process of education. It may be argued, then, that all good motives have this power of transference or conversion, whereby from hitherto dissociated material a new motive is formed which can co-operate with the good motive. Goodness is associative, evil is dissociative; goods have a common language, evils have not. And since, where there is division, each of the opposing forces finds some sort of outlet, it is just under such conditions that we get dualistic ethical systems, like that of "natural" and "moral" good, interest and duty.

## V. THE FRAUD OF MORALISM

Accepting this view, we should regard "obligation" as signifying not merely a false theory of ethics, but also evil motives. Moralism, the doctrine of conscience and "moral necessity", exemplifies the natural causality of repressing motives. There *are* acts which are performed under a sense of obligation, but what they exhibit is not communication but compulsion. Freud has informed us of the elaborate performances which compulsion-neurotics feel bound to go through. They are simply "the thing to do"; they are "right" but not good, forced, not spontaneous. The spontaneous action of a motive seeking its objective cannot be induced by compulsion. Compulsion can only induce conformity. And the motives which will incline a man to conform, to do a thing because he is obliged, are, speaking generally, fear and that desire for self-abasement which, in sexual theory, is called "masochism".

The development of motives has been traced to action in the same or in another person's mind. *Good* motives may be said more specifically to arise through sympathetic induction, or through the spontaneous development of a person's natural capacities. There are certain good motives which we do not expect to find in children, and which appear "as they grow older". That is to say, they are not definitely results of education, except in so far as the child may be said to educate himself. But it is for the most part impossible to lay down exact limits of the operation of these two factors; each may be taken to operate in some degree in the development of all good motives. Compulsion, on the other hand, has no part in this process, except as one of the *obstructions* by reaction against which capacities may develop.

It may be said, then, that the appeal addressed to a person in terms of obligation is either unnecessary, since, if he has the appropriate motive, it will require no external inducement to seek its objective, or useless, since, if he has not the motive, the type of action produced must differ from that commanded. However it may appear to the moraliser, his appeals are prompted by particular motives in his own mind and take effect on particular motives in the other person's mind. It has been admitted that, by means of assistance and transference, new motives may be generated, but this is through natural operations on the motives already present. When one person has interrelated activities A, B and C, and lives in intimate relation with a person who has the activities A and B, the latter will develop C, if he is capable of doing so. In all these cases we have perfectly natural action, moralistic or obligatory action being one particular case. But, since people have different capacities, there is no question of laying down rules for men. The only practical question is what goods a particular person can realise, what good motives can be induced in him. This induction or communication does not require to be commanded, since good motives *will* persistently communicate themselves; and, similarly, response cannot be commanded.

We see, then, how a positive ethics is possible; we see that motives act in accordance with their nature, that communication occurs, and that the study of communicating and non-communicating motives must be thoroughly deterministic. Vague notions of ideals are simply covers for that domination which is the real object of the exponents of "the moral law". The safeguarding of morality, the discovery of "incentives" to goodness, are, as expressions of ethical dualism or "heteronomy", unscientific, and, as repressive operations, bad.

There is, in fact, no moral safeguard. Goodness is *supported* by those good activities already in existence, which encourage the development of other good activities. But in so doing they meet with obstructions, and there is nothing in the nature of things to show that good will overcome evil. Why, then, should we be moral? What inducement to goodness have we? None, except those good motives which we possess and which operate naturally in relation to circumstances—which, of course, they, like all other things, are capable of altering. The ends, by which they are supposed to be dominated, are what they know about their surroundings, and, knowing, affect. The theory of "ideals", like that of "ideas", rests on failure to observe that what we are commonly said to "have in mind" in any situation is some external fact, and that what we really have in mind are certain motives which act "automatically"; and that the interaction of our motives with one another and with outside things is what determines all our actions and whether good or evil will come about.

It is particularly to be noted that the motive which leads us to have an ethical theory is not of primary importance to the discussion of ethical theory. We may certainly consider whether a motive of this kind is good or not, but this implies a direct consideration of good and bad situations. And, in considering the good activities of a person, we are not bound to consider whether he has an ethical theory or not. People in general do not think very much about the goodness of their activities. They are simply to be found trying to make discoveries or to produce works of art, exhibiting love or courage, or, on the other hand, imposing obligations on themselves or others, because they are made that way, i.e., because their character, in relation to their history, has so developed. And these are the conditions, and not any metaphysical "freedom", on which, if at all, further development is possible.

# UTILITARIANISM (1932)[1]

While we cannot regard Bentham as having founded utilitarianism as an ethical doctrine, we may rightly describe him as the founder of modern utilitarian theory. In his hands utilitarianism became a tolerably coherent position and one which exercised a definite influence on economics and on legislation. There was, indeed, no department of public life which it did not affect and into which Bentham himself did not carry it, as is seen from the record of his multifarious controversies on public matters. As Bain puts it (*James Mill: A Biography*, p. 144), "Bentham had an extraordinarily ambitious mind; Aristotle was not more bent on being universally re-constructive. He aspired to remodel the whole of human knowledge; while it is very doubtful if his attainments were up to the level of his own time." There would, however, have been nothing absurd about this aspiration, if Bentham had actually discovered a universal touchstone, a means of systematising all human activities; and this he thought he possessed in the principle of utility.

Utilitarian conceptions, as has been suggested, were present in the work of previous moralists; indeed, they occupied a prominent place in leading theories, as well as in common notions of morality. Ethical theories, from the time of Socrates onwards, were largely concerned with ends, and "the moral end" was commonly conceived as some sort of general good or public interest. The question of the relation of this interest to private interests, in the form, for example, of a sum or average of the latter, appears already in the theory expounded by Glaucon in *Republic*, II, and reappears throughout the history of moral and legal speculation. The notion that society is based on the striking of such an average is, of course, exposed in the *Republic* itself, the main point being that the making of this arrangement, or any other "social contract", implies the pre-existence of society, and that the upholding of an average interest merely puts a premium upon cunning, since,

---

[1] Based on an address delivered to the Sydney branch of the A.A.P.P. on the occasion of the centenary of the death of Jeremy Bentham (6th June, 1832).

if private interest is the motive at work in this compromise, no unity, no public interest, has been established.

It appears, then, that we can account for common activities only by rejecting the whole theory of interests and particularly of "self-interest", only by recognising, as Butler does, the disinterestedness of our affections. Yet we find Butler taking the view that "happiness" (the object of "self-love") is an important object of human activities; and this utilitarian strain appears in the work of the eighteenth century British moralists generally and even in the "formalistic" ethics of Kant. At the same time it is felt that virtue or rectitude is not to be accounted for on a utilitarian basis, and hence we are presented with various mixtures of intuitionism and utilitarianism. Bentham at least has the credit of trying to destroy this ethical dualism or "heteronomy", this divided allegiance to virtue and to happiness.

Intuitionism is criticised by Bentham, as one of the principles adverse to that of utility, under the heading of "The Arbitrary Principle; or the Principle of Sympathy and Antipathy" (*Principles of Legislation*, ch. III). His criticism is important as bringing out the fictions and "vague generalities" by which moralistic theories are supported. "The various systems that have been formed concerning the standard of right and wrong, may all be reduced to the principle of sympathy and antipathy. One account may serve for all of them. They consist all of them in so many contrivances for avoiding the obligation of appealing to any external standard, and for prevailing upon the reader to accept of the author's sentiment or opinion as a reason for itself" (*Introduction to the Principles of Morals and Legislation*, ch. II). It is clear enough that in appeals to moral sense or understanding or to the "fitness of things", in determining rectitude, we have "the negation of all principle" or, better, the absence of all science; and the like applies to the philosopher "who says there is no harm in any thing in the world but in telling a lie; and that if, for example, you were to murder your own father, this would only be a particular way of saying he was not your father. Of course, when this philosopher sees any thing he does not like, he says it is a particular way of telling a lie. It is saying that the act ought to be done, or may be done, when, *in truth*, it ought not to be done."

But though Bentham has shown that in these cases assertion masquerades as proof, it is not shown that his own theory is in any better a position. "What one expects to find in a principle", he says, "is something that points out some external consideration as a means of warranting and guiding the internal sentiments of approbation and disapprobation." In other words, it has to be a means of making us like something that we did not previously like, or *vice versa*. But such a change can be "warranted" or "guided" only by reference to something we like all the time, and not to any "external" considerations. When Bentham says (*Introduction*. ch. I) that the principle of utility is "that principle which approves or disapproves of every action whatsoever, according to the tendency which it appears to have to augment or diminish the happiness of the party whose interest is in question", he is not getting away from "internal sentiments" but is taking one internal sentiment as a guide to all others; and the guide he offers turns out to be as arbitrary as the objection to lying.

It may, of course, be contended, as is done by Sidgwick, that utilitarianism, even if it is reduced to a form of intuitionism, is still defensible in that form; that Bentham is still right in maintaining that utility provides a common measure of objects of approbation or pursuit, and not merely a common measure but a motive-force—that it is a "practical principle". But actually this is not the case. "Pleasure", as Bentham's catalogue of pleasures shows, turns out to be no more definite than "object of approval"; it is merely *that which we like or want*, and an enumeration of wanted things gives us no common measure, and no means of estimating different possible acts by reference to a *sum* of pleasures or excess of pleasure over pain (i.e., how much more we get of what we want than of what we would like to avoid). Certainly, there can be an adjustment between different demands of a particular person, just as there can be between demands of different persons. But we cannot bring all demands to a single "market", and, in order to see what demands will be effective, we have to take account of the whole interplay of social forces; and as far as "quantity of pleasure" is concerned, measurement can be made only after the event. To estimate the keenness of a demand we have to see how far people are prepared to go to get it satisfied; we have to let competing demands *fight it out*.

Pleasure, then, is neither a common measure nor a motive-force; as that which pleases us it is itself a "vague generality" or fiction, on the same footing as that which our moral sense approves. And, failing as a common measure, it is no more successful than the latter (e.g., in the hands of Butler) in building up a public interest out of personal preferences; though a certain "sanction" may be given to the objects of particular demands by making them *appear* to be resultants of the requirements of members of society in general. Such "common public necessities" are satirised by Chesterton in *The Napoleon of Notting Hill*, where King Auberon contends that "Herbert Spencer refrained from theft for the same reason that he refrained from wearing feathers in his hair", not because of any public-spiritedness but "because he was an English gentleman with different tastes".

The view expressed by Chesterton that "you cannot argue with the choice of the soul" is, of course, in accordance with the "arbitrary principle" which Bentham regards as opposed to any exactness in ethical science. But Bentham himself has provided nothing more exact; we could only say, in respect of "pleasures", that the outcome of the pressure of various demands will be the result of the operation of these demands, that the "market" will settle itself. But there are definite social forces, which are not measurable as amounts of a common stuff but which differ qualitatively, and which fight out the social issues. We can consider what they are and how they are situated, and get an estimate of their tendency, but we have to recognise their distinct characters. Thus Chesterton, though he also seems to make it a matter of awaiting the event, is substantially correct in recognising "the choice of the soul", i.e., that there are certain things we are prepared to work and fight for. Choice may indeed be influenced, by argument or otherwise, but, if it is influenced by appeal to "our interest" or to "everyone's interest", this is a process of deception, since strictly we are only appealed to to want what we want. Bentham's "principle", that is to say, is just as arbitrary, just as opposed to scientific measurement, as are the various conceptions of the intuitionists.

Bentham substantially admits this in his account (*Introduction*, ch. IV) of the balancing of pleasures and pains, i.e., of the estimation, addition, and comparison of the sums, of the degrees of *wantedness* of the various objects brought about and prevented by a particular act. "It is not to be expected", he says, "that this process should be strictly pursued previously to every moral judgment, or to every legislative or judicial operation. It may, however, be always kept in view; and as near as the process actually pursued on these occasions approaches to it, so near will such process approach to the character of an exact one." But if this has not been done and we still have passed a moral judgment, it appears that a moral judgment is not a judgment about the "general tendency" of the act in question and therefore cannot be made more exact by stating that general tendency, even supposing that this could be done. Thus Bentham not only, like other moralists, confuses between what is good and what is chosen or wanted, but also, again like other moralists, tries to secure the choosing of certain lines of action by making people suppose that these are what they really, or more exactly, want; and so is imposed the notion of a public interest which it is everyone's interest to foster.[2]

But, whatever deception the use of this vague notion may occasion, it is clear that ordinary choice takes no account of general tendencies. Bentham, then, has to find some connection between general tendencies and immediate demands, between public and private interest, between his "principle" and actual practice. He has to find some means of making his common measure work, and also has to show how we come to pass "moral judgments" at all, instead of simply seeking "pleasure" (i.e., doing what we do and wanting what we want). The theory of *sanctions* is Bentham's attempt to bridge the gap. Sanctions are pleasures and pains considered as efficient causes or means (*Introduction*, ch. III), and through their operation private interests can be made to subserve public interest, i.e., people can be made to demand (or accept) what has a certain general tendency, what, in particular, produces pleasures as ends.

[2] We learn something about the origin of Bentham's theory from the following extracts from his common-place book (*Works*, Bowrings Edition, Vol. X, pp. 70, 79; quoted by Sidgwick, *Methods of Ethics*, p. 88). Helvetius, he says, had "established a standard of rectitude for actions", viz., that "a sort of action is a right one, when the tendency of it is to augment the mass of happiness in the community". "By an early pamphlet of Priestley's, light was added to the warmth. In the phrase, 'the greatest happiness of the greatest number', I then saw delineated, for the first time, a plain as well as a true standard of whatever is right or wrong in human conduct, whether in the field of morals or of politics." The standard, as we have seen, is neither plain nor true. But it is plain that from the beginning Bentham was concerned with establishing a standard of *rectitude*, i.e., a line or lines of action which can be demanded of persons, and that the promulgation of the "greatest happiness" principle is a means of getting such demands accepted.

Now apart from the question of public interest, the general position here is that demands can change, that pleasures can be annexed to pleasures or pains to pleasures, so that what was demanded before comes to be demanded more or less. In the latter case we find that something we like carries with it something we dislike, and thus we may stop demanding it. This is only to say that there can be *conflict* among a person's demands just as there can be between the demands of different persons. There is no evidence in all this that demands can be brought to a common basis, but the opposite is implied. Certainly there must be some upshot of any particular conflict, one demand can defeat another, but this is because they are for different things; and to say that the one which, in the event, is seen to have had greater *force* is thereby shown to be for greater pleasure, is simply to rob the term "pleasure" of all meaning (except one in which it would apply to all physical activities, and planets, e.g., would move "for pleasure").

There can indeed be deliberation regarding objects sought, but there is no general calculus of wants. When we aim at bringing something about, we can consider the obstacles to its attainment and the ways of getting round them; we may be confronted, in the process, with things we do not want or cannot do, and we may accordingly give up that particular aim. Such actual or contemplated struggles have quantitative features but are not reducible to calculable amounts of a single currency, "welfare" or "pleasure". Even in calculations on a monetary basis it is qualitative considerations that settle the matter. A man may say to himself, "If I buy this book, I cannot go to the theatre or cannot have a bottle of wine with my dinner", but it is simply not the case that he estimates what he will get out of the book as quantitatively comparable with what he will get from the other sources of enjoyment. The "utility" of the objects is determined by his decision, and does not determine it. Demands, of course, go in groups; the securing of one thing enhances or diminishes the "value" of another (i.e., what a man is prepared to do to get it). But there is still no total market; there are no exchange rates for all objects of desire.

It follows at once from this that the function of the legislator, who establishes the "political sanction", cannot be conceived as that of a universal calculator or seeker of "general welfare".

Bentham, it may be noted, merely *assumes* that there are some whose interest is the general interest, and that such persons may be legislating. From what has been said it appears that there is no general interest, and that the legislator is simply a person who has certain demands of his own and certain special ways of getting them satisfied; in particular, that of annexing "pains" or penalties to any opposition to his demands. The people legislated for may of course resist the imposition of these penalties; and the intelligent legislator will try to calculate what resistance he will meet with and whether it will be so great as to defeat his proposals. This is a calculation of the same type as that which arises in any attempt to meet difficulties and satisfy demands. It may quite well be in the legislator's "interest", i.e., it may advance his schemes, to put about the notion of public welfare and the supposition that he is acting with that object in view; he may even put it in that way to himself, but it is not so.

Bentham errs, then, in putting the legislator, as a supervisor and re-adjuster of pleasures and pains, on a different level from any other agent; he errs also in distinguishing the moral, political and religious sanctions from the physical or natural sanction. The operations of "public opinion", of legislation and of a man's own beliefs are just as natural as those of any non-human agency. The type of question—if you want to get or avoid A, you must accept or forego B—is exactly the same in each case. Certainly a man may mistakenly hold a view of this kind, but this, as Bentham admits, applies to all the sanctions. In particular, qualifications ("so long as this type of government persists", and the like) may be overlooked; breadth of outlook, formulation of new demands, extension of struggle, are relevant here—but they are relevant to all the cases Bentham mentions, and they are all "natural" factors. The question is not, then, how pleasures and pains may be *made* to operate by some special functionary, but how demands do operate in relation to one another and to existing supplies. This question can be treated only in terms of social movements and struggles, and not as a matter of annexing pleasures and pains to "natural" pleasures and pains so as to secure a maximum of pleasure (or any other result).

It is to be noted that while such a movement will have its successes and its difficulties, it need not have any special activity of calculation. It is quite possible for men to promote specific objects without knowing that they are doing so. This is especially important in relation to moral theory because of the assumption that the question of goodness is linked with that of promotion. But the moral theorist, in determining what is good, is not confronted with any question of a motive for producing it. Only after he has determined where goodness is to be found, can he consider how it is caused; and not only is this independent of any consideration of how *he* can cause it, but he may find that goods do not come about by people wanting them. The political theorist, on the other hand, has certainly to take account of the operation of demands and calculations, but still his own theory is not to be regarded as a political calculation, as a consideration of how a certain movement can set about attaining its objects, what tactics it can adopt, how it can overcome opposition. It is just through confusion on this point, and on the function of the moral theorist, that Bentham is able to set up his conception of public interest (the object of demands in general or of a general social movement) and to take it as setting a standard of "approval". But there is nothing in his theory of utility to show that there is a common interest, and there is nothing in his theory of political sanction to show that such an interest can be created.

As we have seen, Bentham assumes that the legislator is one who finds his own greatest happiness in the greatest happiness of the greatest number. Now his function of annexing penalties to acts implies that the persons for whom he is legislating find their greatest happiness elsewhere and that, by altering the balance of pleasures and pains, he can bring their demands at least nearer to his own. But in thus altering the greatest happiness in individuals he is altering the greatest happiness of the greatest number, and his own calculations will have to be begun over again. It is clear that the real work of the legislator is to make people want "the right thing", i.e., as far as possible to enforce his own demands, and that "the greatest happiness of the greatest number" is a fiction, a vague generality, which renders the enforcement easier. And Bentham himself, when he comes to defend any institution or activity, does so not in terms of "pleasure" but on other grounds.

The appeal is most frequently made to considerations of public *order.* This, indeed, is closely connected with the "greatest happiness", for, if this means the least possible conflict of demands, it may be identified with the greatest possible orderliness. But, whereas "pleasure" can be passed off as something that everyone wants, the existence of social order does not show what objects are attained in the given society and whose demands they satisfy. If it is assumed that the legislator acts in everyone's interest, the desirability of order will follow. But if that assumption is not made, the attempt to show how order is or may be produced does not appear as an application of utilitarian principles, but they rather appear as cloaks for an unexamined order. In speaking (*Principles of the Penal Code*, ch. V) of "seditious disturbances", Bentham advises that the magistrate should speak in the name not of the king but of justice. "Every favour, everything which bears the character of pure beneficence, ought to be presented as the personal act of the father of his people. All rigorous proceedings—those of severe benevolence—ought to be attributed to nobody. Let the hand that acts be veiled. Throw the responsibility upon some creature of reason, some animated abstraction; such as *Justice*, daughter of necessity and mother of peace, whom men ought to fear, but whom they cannot hate, and who ought always to possess their supremest homage." Advice of this kind very strongly suggests that the legislator is taken as upholding a special interest and not any "general interest".

This comes out still more clearly in Bentham's discussion of property (*Principles of the Civil Code*, Part I, chs. VIII–X). That there can be no property without law, he contends, is one of the advantages of law. "Property and law are born together, and die together. Before laws were made there was no property; take away laws, and property ceases." That is not to say that if we take away property, law ceases; which is what Bentham is trying to prove. He goes on to say that "as regards property, security consists in receiving no check, no shock, no derangement to the expectation founded on the laws, of enjoying such and such a portion of good. The legislator owes the greatest respect to this expectation which he has himself produced. When he does not contradict it, he does what is essential to the happiness of society; when he disturbs it, he always produces a proportionate sum of evil." Apart, however, from the fact that people dislike losing their property (and this tells us nothing about society), the only evil Bentham can find to result from attacks on property is "deadening of industry", and here again he assumes, as in the case of law, that because industry has gone along with property, it cannot go without it.

To the objection that "perhaps the laws of property are good for those who have property and oppressive to those who have none", Bentham answers that poverty is the primitive condition of the human race, and that the poor in civilised society are at least better off than men in the natural state. "All participate more or less in the pleasures, the advantages, and the resources of civilised society. The industry and the labour of the poor place them among the candidates of fortune. And have they not the pleasures of acquisition? Does not hope mix with their labour? Is the security which the law gives of no importance to them?... All things considered, the protection of the laws may contribute as much to the happiness of the cottage as to the security of the palace." Argument of this kind to show that the poor man, although he "obtains nothing, except by painful labour", is better off than he would be in a state of nature, is not of a sort to establish any connection between property and "the greatest good of the greatest number".

Bentham's further argument makes his position still clearer. "It is astonishing that a writer so judicious as Beccaria has interposed, in a work dictated by the soundest philosophy, a doubt subversive of social order. *The right of property*, he says, *is a terrible right, which perhaps is not necessary.* Tyrannical and sanguinary laws have been founded upon that right; it has been frightfully abused; but the right itself presents only ideas of pleasure, abundance, and security. It is that right which has vanquished the natural aversion to labour; which has given to man the empire of the earth; which has brought to an end the migratory life of nations; which has produced the love of country and a regard for posterity. Men universally desire to enjoy speedily—to enjoy without labour. It is that desire which is terrible; since it arms all who have not against all who have. The law which restrains that desire is the noblest triumph of humanity over itself."

In brief, social order is equivalent to the maintenance of property, and the legislator's business is to uphold the interests of the propertied class. In his discussion (*Civil Code*, Part III, ch. I) of the relations between master and servant, and with special reference to apprenticeship, Bentham says that "competition will best regulate the price of [their] mutual services, as of all other objects of commerce; and here, as elsewhere, industry should find its just reward". But most governments show a "mania for regulation" and intermeddle with businesses that they do not understand. Governments, then, should not interfere with anything that can be settled by the operation of the property system, but they should interfere with anything that would unsettle that system; they should protect property. Thus it is a matter of serving certain interests, enabling them to work freely, "hindering hindrances" to them. And the "greatest happiness" principle merely dictates the apologetic method of emphasising (or inventing) advantages produced by these interests in any particular quarter and explaining away disadvantages (things objected to by the recipient).

The vagueness inherent in utilitarian arguments is shown in Bentham's statement of "the language of reason and plain sense" on "natural and imprescriptible rights" ("Critical Examination of the Declaration of Rights"; *Works*, Bowring's Edition, Vol. II). "In proportion as it is *right* or *proper*, i.e., advantageous to the society in question, that this or that right—a right to this or that effect—should be established and maintained, in that same proportion it is *wrong* that it should be abrogated: but as there is no *right* which ought not to be maintained so long as it is upon the whole advantageous to the society that it should be maintained, so there is no right which, when the abolition of it is advantageous to society, should not be abolished. To know whether it would be more for the advantage of society that this or that right should be maintained or abolished, the time at which the question about maintaining or abolishing is proposed, must be given, and the circumstances under which it is proposed to maintain or abolish it; the right itself must be specifically described, not jumbled with an indistinguishable heap of others, under any such vague general terms as property, liberty and the like." Here we have the utilitarian pretence at precision; but not only are we supposed to settle the issue on the basis of the "vague general" notion of what is "upon the whole advantageous to the society", but the questions of what are the general conditions of social life and what is the relation to them of government, are completely obscured.

Rights, according to Bentham, are legal rights, and it is "simple nonsense" to talk about natural rights. "We know what it is for men to live without government—and living without government, to live without rights; we know what it is for men to live without government, for we see instances of such a way of life—as we see it in many savage nations, or rather races of mankind; for instance, among the savages of New South Wales, whose way of living is so well known to us: no habit of obedience, and thence no government—no government, and thence no laws—no laws, and thence no such thing as rights—no security—no property:—liberty, as against regular control, the control of laws and government—perfect; but as against all irregular control, the mandates of stronger individuals, none." It is this, however, that is "simple nonsense". Rights can certainly be established by government. But government is simply the operation of a certain set of demands. And so long as we have demands that can be made good, demands that force a recognition of them and gain satisfaction—and this is so in any community—we have rights. Natural rights, then, will be demands which have to be made good if society is to exist. And whether or not there are such abiding rights, there are at least rights independent of law; and though Bentham thinks it monstrous to think of "what the law, the supreme legislature of the country, acknowledged as such, *can not do!*" this is because he does not realise that law is based upon forms of social organisation, the development of which can only to a limited extent be centrally controlled.

The general position is that utilitarian theory neither *explains* nor gives any *force* to legislation (or to any other "moral" or social activity), except the force of deception. It is impossible to legislate for "pleasure". When we talk about utility, about things being useful, we mean that they are *means* to something that we want; but to call it "pleasure" because we want it is absurd. It is absurd also to discuss politics without discussing *interests*, in the form of social movements. There are, then, two ways of supporting such a movement. One is a defence of a certain way of life; and, though this way of life might possibly be legislatively defended, we cannot assume in advance either that legislation exists to maintain it or that it needs legislative defence; the question is whether it enables demands to be made good. The other is a defence of order, welfare, public necessity and the like; and this means a defence of a way of life which is not specified.

The theoretical weakness of intuitionism has been noted; but there is still "the choice of the soul", i.e., there are movements along definite lines, seeking and finding definite objects. The attempt to get over the conflicts thus engendered by reducing these objects to quantities of an indefinite object, "pleasure", will not serve. To say that "quantity of pleasure being equal, pushpin is as good as poetry" (though, indeed, this is in accordance with the eighteenth century estimation of poetry by its "pleasing" character) is to be guilty of moral stupidity. It will be admitted that there is a greater demand for horse-racing than for poetry, for circuses, political and otherwise, than for education. But this fact by itself gives no guidance to the moralist or the legislator, and will not weigh in the slightest degree with those who *want* education, who belong to a scientific or aesthetic *movement*.

What Bentham has done is to clear away a good deal of the moralising, the vague generality, that has surrounded legislative procedure. He has exposed weak talk about "sympathy" or about "eternal laws", and has come nearer than his predecessors to showing the actual operation of demands. But he still retains a vague generality of his own ("pleasure") to cover up the crudity of certain demands; he wrongly supposes a "moral" function to the legislator, a supra-scientific position of *making* things go right and of proving *by compulsion* the soundness of his institution; and he wrongly identifies the demanded with the good. As against this, it must be said that the good, where it exists, has to fight with the evil, however the latter may be entrenched, whatever demands it may make and however much it may be demanded.

The unhistorical character of utilitarianism, then, appears in its concealment of ethical and political struggles, and this is further exemplified in the utilitarian treatment of all psychological and social questions. To the homogeneity of objectives corresponds a homogeneity of motives, and thus all human conduct takes the form of a "reasonable" pursuit of pleasure, limited only by lack of knowledge. It is now fairly well recognised, as against this eighteenth century rationalism, that history cannot be brought under the formula of progressive enlightenment and that culture is misconceived as calculation. But it is not so clearly understood that there is no faculty of "reason" which can guide the passions, but that thinking is an activity of the passions themselves. Only the grasping of this point, however, the recognition of the diverse sentiments arising under different conditions of social life and of their reaction on social conditions, can enable us to root out the last vestiges of utilitarianism and to develop a positive theory of human affairs.

# 21
# REALISM VERSUS RELATIVISM IN ETHICS
(1933)[1]

It is a condition of progress in any science that relativist confusions should be removed; it is also the case that, prior to the development of theory in any particular field, relativist views prevail. This is exemplified in the fact that popular views on all subjects are deeply imbued with relativism—a fact recognised by Socrates when, in the course of his attack on the relativism of the Sophists, he called the public "the great Sophist". On the other hand, however primitive the current conceptions of any subject may be, they are always to some extent realistic; they deal with certain real things. These things, then, being treated in a relativist fashion, are actually taken as confirming the relativist notions with which they have been associated. The development of science thus requires a criticism of popular misconceptions, and the work of disentangling reality from fiction is all the harder, the more deeply the confusion has become embedded in popular thought, and (a substantially equivalent condition) the nearer the subject lies to the centre of our interests and the more it is played upon by our hopes and fears. Now this is particularly the case in regard to human affairs themselves, and it is on this account that the sciences of man and society have made so little progress, and have been so entangled in relativism, as compared with the sciences dealing with non-human material.

The beginning of modern science with the Milesians was bound up with the rejection of mythology, the rejection of the explanation of natural events by non-natural "powers", supposed to lie behind these events and occasion them. What is thus rejected is relativism, i.e., the conception of something whose nature it is to have a certain relation—in this case, *that whereby* an event happens; its hidden cause or hidden meaning. It is necessary for science to

[1] An address delivered in the University of Sydney on 22nd August, 1932, at a joint meeting of the Australasian Association of Psychology and Philosophy, and Section J of the Australian and New Zealand Association for the Advancement of Science.

reject such conceptions, because if, e.g., we know something only as that which caused an event, then we do not know what it is itself, and therefore we do not know what causes the event or even that anything causes it. Certainly it is possible for us to know that an event has a cause without knowing what that cause is, but this is only because we have previously had experience of one event causing another, i.e., of causation as a natural or historical relation between natural or historical things. Extension of knowledge is possible, then, if we view things naturalistically and reject all conceptions of mysterious powers, of ultimates and higher realities.

This applies as much to ethics as to any other science. If there is to be any ethical science, then ethical ultimates or powers, moral agencies above the historical facts, must be rejected. If we are to say significantly that ethics deals with goods, we must be able to exhibit goods as going on, as definitely located activities, just as we exhibit moving bodies or growing plants. This, as has been said, may be a difficult undertaking; disinterested inquiry, the exact determination of issues, the consideration of just what goods are and how they operate, may more easily give way to prejudice than in the case of subjects which touch our interests less nearly. But it is still possible, and recognition of relativism as a foe to science advances the possibility.

The most obstinate confusion obstructing the growth of ethical knowledge lies in the assumption that ethics teaches us how to live or what to live for, that it instructs us in our duty or in the approach to the moral end. It may, indeed, be admitted that, having studied ethics, we shall be able to do things that we did not do before. But this applies as much to the study of mathematics or physics as to the study of ethics; it is a consequence of the fact that studying is a part of our behaviour and influences other parts of our behaviour. It cannot on that account be said that what is studied is our behaviour, and that mathematics, e.g., instructs us in our mathematical duty and shows how to reach the mathematical end (how, for instance, to reach infinity). Knowing mathematical facts, we can do certain things; knowing ethical facts, we can do certain other things. It is thus possible to speak of "applied mathematics" and "applied ethics". But if we are going to call the latter "application" our moral behaviour, we may equally well call the former our mathematical behaviour.

Now it may here be said that our behaviour, and in particular our studying, has ethical characteristics. Of course that is so—though it has also mathematical characteristics. But this is not to say that in ethics we are studying how to behave; nor is it the case that, if in the course of our ethical inquiry we find out that study, including ethical study, is a good thing, this means that there is any study which studies itself. What we are doing as ethical theorists is to discuss certain activities and state their characteristics, to examine certain propositions and see whether they are true or false. What we shall do, once we make up our minds on the matter, is another question entirely; and, as was indicated, our mathematical beliefs affect our conduct just as our ethical beliefs do.

Ethical realities, then, are concealed, the statement of true ethical propositions is hindered, by the confusion of the assertion of such propositions with the adoption of a policy. The confusion works in both directions. When we say that something is good, we are supposed to be stating a programme of action for ourselves or for others; when we adopt a certain line of action, we are supposed to be assuming or indicating by example that that line of action is good. In line with this confusion are to be found such expressions as the desirable, the serviceable or the justifiable. They are all relativist, in that they imply the existence of that whose goodness consists in our pursuing it or saying it is to be pursued. And they all obscure the fact that the possibility of a policy, of the "application" of knowledge, depends on the fact that, when we want something and find that it goes along with or is led up to by something else, we can, by producing the latter, get what we want. Whether what we want is good or not is a question still undetermined. But the relativist confusion leads to its being taken as good, and thus to the obscuring of the objects of particular policies.

Now the leading moral theories, up till quite recently, have all had such relativist confusions embedded in them. They all assume certain higher moral powers *whereby* historical events can have moral characteristics in a secondary sense, just as the metaphysician assumes an ultimate reality whereby historical appearances can have a subordinate reality and be graciously permitted to appear. The main relativist conceptions to be considered are those of "obligation" and "end". The obligatory is that which is essentially demanded of us or that whose nature it is to command our obedience. The end is that whose nature it is to be pursued or which is the goal of striving. Upholders of the former, more rationalistic conception admit that we may refrain from doing our duty but its binding force remains. The more idealistic exponents of the end consider that every striving takes us, however slightly, towards the goal, just as every belief has some degree of truth. The main point is that in either case historical behaviour is alleged to be judged by reference to an unhistorical standard.

Socrates, in the *Republic*, upholds this teleological relativism; yet we find him, in the *Euthyphro*, refuting Euthypro's moralistic relativism; and the logic of the matter is the same in either case. If the obligatory (whether it is a question of "religious duty" or any other) is *what we are to obey* and the end is *what we are to pursue*, then nothing at all has been said as to what these things themselves are; we do not know what to obey or to follow. If, on the other hand, we are not fobbed off with relativist conceptions but are given some specific commands or objectives, then we find them to be just as definite historical events as the things they are related to. In a word, when relativism is removed, we are left with simple historical relations of commanding and seeking—A wants X; B is commanded by C to do Y—and what is moral or good about X or Y does not appear. Nor does it appear that there is any question of what A or B "is to do" or would be "justified" in doing or would have "reason" to do. We are simply presented with the wants of persons and the interaction of these wants.

At the same time, the use of these relativist or transcendental notions, necessarily vague as they are, makes it possible to advance certain unspecified demands, which would be opposed if mental confusion were removed. Socrates and Kant, each with his conception of some unconditioned moral power or moral reality as in some way governing historical existence, argued fallaciously, in the name of logical consistency, to the obligatoriness or virtuous character of certain forms of behaviour. Only moral scepticism can follow from the conception of an end not definitely known but "progressively determined" by our action, or of a pure will which wills itself; any action is as "justified" as any other on such a basis. But the mystical sanction which appears to have been given to the conduct taken as orderly or as universalisable, can easily impose on the simple-minded. The line of criticism here is to say—this action is not required by "the good" or by the "moral law", because there is no such thing; by whom is it demanded, then, and what is his policy? It is not surprising that the Athenians looked for Socrates's political affiliations, when he claimed to take the pure moral stand.

While, then, it is absurd to say that we study ethics as a means of determining what to do, it is equally absurd to say that there is any such question as "What am I to do?" The question of what conduct can be "defended" or what conduct is "reasonable" under certain circumstances is a question in pseudo-ethics. Conduct will be defended by a particular person if it is or leads to what he wants; if there are persons who want good, then the goodness of certain conduct will be accepted by them as a "reason" for it. But it is not the case that policies in general have anything to do with goodness, and it has yet to be established that goodness has anything to do with policy. And any such point can be established only if it shown that what is good is not "the defensible" or "the reasonable" but some definite historical activity, a *force*, in the sense of something which can act, though also capable of being acted upon.

The task of the ethical theorist, then, will be to find goods and consider their ways of working, and in this connection he may well find how they are promoted and how prevented. His study will thus be a thoroughly deterministic one. The relative notions of good or right as the commanded or advised or wanted are connected with the metaphysical conception of human freedom—a conception which, with its division of reality into higher and lower orders, agents and instruments, is rooted in mythology and has played havoc with all the anthropological sciences. The suggestion is that things go on in their historical way until at some point "we" step in and alter their direction for the better—or the worse. To accept a view of this kind would be to give up all science; for we should never know what agent ("that which can use") might be operating on what instrument ("that which can be used") at any time, and we could assert no "law of nature". But, of course, to assert the operation of any agent is to have found that agent as a historical entity and one just as subject to influence, and having as determinate ways of working, as anything he could act on.

We do not, in fact, step out of the movement of things, ask "What am I to do?" and, having obtained an answer, step in again. All our actions, all our questionings and answerings, are part of the movement of things; and if we can work on things, things can work on us—if they can be our "vehicles", we also can be vehicles;

social and other forces can work through us. It is in respect of our existing activities, and not of any abstract "reasonableness", that we ask what is to be done; indeed, it is our activities themselves that, as they proceed, raise and deal with such problems, for there is no unhistorical "I" apart from our activities. As already noted, then, ethical inquiry or, similarly, social inquiry may be one of our activities; it may exemplify the working of a social force through us or of a good force in us; but *what is inquired into* is how social forces or good forces do work, and not what is to be done. What is done, whether it is good or not, will be determined by the forces that exist.

Ethical theory, then, is not a policy. It consists of propositions to the effect that such and such things are good and that they work in such and such ways. But, of course, a student of ethics may have a policy. Investigation itself is a force or form of activity, into the working of which persons are drawn and as working in which they make demands and alter their previous demands. The operation of demands can also be studied. We can consider what is accepted and what is rejected by a certain community, by various social organisations or by persons—in studying the life-history of anything, we have to consider what it opposes and what supports or is supported by it. But this is enough to show that there is no question of any "moral rectitude" or any connection with goodness in the matter. It is, of course, possible to take "right", as Moore suggests, to mean that which supports or leads up to good. But to say of such a thing that it has this effect is sufficiently plain, and avoids the relativism of "the commanded"—as Moore himself does not do when he speaks of certain actions as our duty. Historically considered, obligation can only mean constraint or compulsion, and this, it will be admitted, at least *frequently* prevents instead of promoting goods. It is better, therefore, to drop the term "right" from ethical theory, and it is necessary emphatically to reject the view that goodness has anything to do with obeying commandments.

At the same time it is of some ethical interest to consider the basis of the conception of rectitude, more especially as it can be urged that it was from a consideration of moral codes, of the recognised and the forbidden, that ethical theory, such as it has been, arose. Certainly we find Socrates, who may be taken as the first considerable ethical theorist, criticising the Sophistic and popular reliance on codes, pointing out their inconsistencies, attacking the relativist view that the code of each city determines what is right there. But he does so only to set up an ideal code, a supposedly consistent hierarchy of virtues, regarded, no doubt, as dependent on "the good" but certainly neither deduced by him nor deducible from the formal possibility of goodness or of an end. A consideration of the development of the conception of rectitude may at least help to show how it came to pass as an ethical conception.

In considering how there came to be *mores* in a community, we must start from the fact that that community is a historical force or set of activities. Now there are relations of support and opposition between any activity whatever and others surrounding it; and likewise we can say that any historical thing has its characteristic ways of working, ways which are variously affected by its historical situation. To say, then, that a society exists is to say that it proceeds along certain lines and that there are conditions favourable and conditions unfavourable to its continuance. Thus *mores* are, in the first instance, forms of social operation, the engendering of certain states of things and prevention of others. These may be called the demands or requirements of the society. But when the demands come to be formulated by members of the society (and this takes place through conflict among the demands of members), we have *mores* in the second instance—*recognition* of what is required and what is forbidden—we have especially the operation of taboo. So there develop from customary tasks and customary constraints the notions of right and wrong. It is to be noted, of course, that, just as certain organisms and certain organisations do not survive, so *mores* need not have survival value. They are simply ways of working of that particular community in its particular environment; and a community may perish—or again it may change its *mores*, and such variations may have survival value or they may not. Customs, then, ways of social working, must exist if a society is to exist; but they are not to be understood in the "purposive" fashion, and they raise, of themselves, no question of goodness. Also there is no question of a total social morality; it is seen that there are conflicting demands, conflicting activities, conflicting forms of organisation, within the society; and the upshot of such a conflict may be that what was generally recognised or sanctioned ceases to be so.

If, now, in any society, good and bad activities are going on, they will be supported and opposed by other existing activities; and it may be that what passes as "right" is actually opposed to good activities, and that which passes as "wrong" supports them. It will scarcely be denied that this has been true of some societies. But the point is obscured by the teleological conception of "social welfare" as that which right conduct promotes and by the solidarist conception of a total communal morality, a general virtue which gradually develops and brings welfare nearer and nearer—though again it will hardly be denied that changes in *mores* take place under the influence of "wrong" activities. It appears, then, that the solidarist view does not hold, and that the description of certain events as "right" and "wrong" gives no "reason" for taking either side. Social forces work themselves out historically; goods act in their characteristic way and make their demands, even when they happen to be forbidden or opposed by the main social forces. If this were not so, we could only say that there are no goods, no objects of ethical study, but merely relations of support and opposition—relations such as can be found in any field whatever.

The question for ethics is thus to exhibit the working of forces of a specific kind, not to call for approval or support for them. It may indeed be contended that they support themselves and fight against opposition; and if it is said that persons do "advocate" them, it may be answered that this advocacy is the work of the good activities themselves in and through these persons. At any rate, to have a soundly realistic science of ethics, we have to discover goods as certain real things, just as real as we are, and not "expressions of our attitudes" or any other relativist fiction. The first important attempt to develop such a science was made by Moore in his *Principia Ethica.* Moore endeavoured to found an objective theory of goodness, and he contended that certain definite things were in themselves good aesthetic enjoyment and personal affection being great goods, and knowledge a good of less importance. It has to be acknowledged, however, that there is a great deal of relativism in Moore's theory; as we have already seen, he recognises duty, and his doctrine that good is an indefinable and non-natural object is connected with the conception of good as an end and as having higher reality than other things. At the same time, in accordance with his theory of the intuition of this entity, good would be a mere label or expression of an attitude, and not an independent force.

The question of what, on the realist understanding, are actual goods may be approached by considering what have been called goods. The use of the term "good" even relativistically for what is wanted shows that some recognition was taken to be given to goodness; and the antithesis between good and bad, as contrasted with that between right and wrong, shows that a qualitative distinction was, however vaguely, recognised, and not a mere distinction between relations of support and opposition—though, indeed, there was bound to be a qualitative distinction between the sort of thing supported and the sort of thing opposed, but not necessarily, as we have seen, the ethical distinction.

Now one of the things that have been most widely recognised as good is investigation, and the fact that confused reasons have been given for this view is no indication of its falsity. Ethical theorists, being themselves investigators, might be regarded as suspect in this matter; but since this suspicion, while leading to ethical scepticism, would itself imply some consideration of ethical matters, it cannot be seriously entertained. Investigation appears also as a means to goodness or, rather, to goodness misconceived as order, in the theories of Socrates and Aristotle, and this, it might be suggested, would lead to their attaching an undue importance to it. But if we pass over Aristotle's unsound distinction between goodness of character and goodness of intellect—unsound because to have a good character is simply to be good and this, for all Aristotle has shown, may involve intellectual activity, and because, even if to have a good intellect means only to be good at thinking, this still leaves it possible that intellectual proficiency is ethically good—we find that he regards the speculative life as the "highest happiness" or greatest good, and even as divine. In so describing it, he is distinguishing it from the human goodness with which he had previously been concerned. But this human goodness is simply that for which it is possible to legislate, and, in considering legislation for goodness before considering what is good, Aristotle is really substituting *order* for goodness, and even that problem cannot be solved on a merely legislative basis and without reference to the kind of order or system that is in question.

In suggesting, however, that the speculative life cannot be legislated for, Aristotle is bringing out the point that it legislates for itself or, as he puts it, that it is of all activities the most self-sufficient, as well as being capable of the most continuous exercise. This is connected with the common recognition of goods as "existing for their own sake" (as in Moore's conception of "intrinsic value") and of goodness as being exercised "disinterestedly". Divesting these conceptions of their metaphysical accretions, and not considering goods as existing unconditionally or as "self-subsistent", we find, as marks of investigation and as possible marks of any good, that it is a human activity which communicates itself (investigation giving rise to investigation), which is possible under all conditions (there being no situation which is not a subject for investigation), and which produces the materials for its own continuance (with the reservation that it can be destroyed by opposing activities).

We thus have a distinction between productive or ethical goods and economic goods or goods of consumption, a distinction connected with that commonly made between disinterestedness and interestedness, and with that drawn by Sorel (in *Reflections on Violence*) between the ethic of the producer and the ethic of the consumer. The latter is that which attempts to treat all goods as objects of want and all actions as interested; it is the doctrine of utilitarianism. It may be answered briefly by referring to Butler's theory of the disinterestedness of our passions, the fact that they do not act by calculation, and still more to the consideration that we cannot treat investigation and all other human activities as mere objects of want, because it is our activities themselves that want—a position which has its economic counterpart in the fact that, however demands may operate and though there may nominally be a price for everything, actual exchanges depend upon appropriations and other preconditions of demand. It may also be said that it is the conception of good as the wanted that leads to the view that not all goods are human activities, Moore, e.g., referring to the operation of our preferences in order to prove that natural beauty is good, and being anxious, incidentally, to show that goods have no common quality but their goodness, in order to save his theory of the indefinability of good.

The conception of the productiveness of goods leads to the view that production is itself a good; it fulfils the conditions mentioned in the case of investigation, and it also assists and is assisted by investigation. Indeed, we find investigation flourishing where production is developing, and the assistance given by science to production is equally well marked. Similar considerations apply to aesthetic creation and appreciation; in fact the distinction between these forms of activity is hard to draw; the artist and the investigator are producers of a sort, the producer is in some measure an artist and an investigator. But as we broadly distinguish between Science, Art and Industry within a social culture, so we may broadly distinguish scientific, artistic and productive activity. The recognition of them all as productive is in accordance with the Marxist conception of society as organisation for production, of production as socially fundamental. And this would suggest that there had been goodness, as we certainly can say there has been disinterestedness, in all society—a fact which would help to explain the lip-service rendered to goodness by ethical relativists, which would show, indeed, that a real subject was being dealt with, even though it was maltreated as a matter of commands and wants.

The finding of interrelated goods within the various cultural fields does not, however, support the hypothesis of social solidarity, of a gradually emerging and progressively defined social welfare. On the contrary, we have to recognise that what is good in social culture has had to fight and still has to fight for its existence; that science is faced not merely by open obscurantism but by obscurantism and scepticism masquerading as science; that waste passes for industry, and that luxury is paraded as art. Goods, as social forces, as forms of organisation, are engaged in struggle, and develop ways of working in that struggle. It is such ways of working that constitute a "morality" or code of rules, but, of course, only as the morality of certain forces and in opposition to other *mores*. It is such a morality that Sorel calls "the ethic of the producer"; he recognises as the characteristics developed by the working-class in the course of its struggle, and in opposition to bourgeois morality, the qualities of initiative, emulation, care for exactitude and rejection of the notion of "reward". Such *mores* form part of Marxists call proletarian ideology—that is to say, a general outlook on social questions, a set of attitudes which hang together, being ways of working of the productive activity. It would be urged that bourgeois ideology, being rooted in consumption, is at once less coherent and less socially necessary—indeed, that it is, at the present stage, anti-social; opposed to the continuance of organisation for production and thus to the continuance of the conditions of the possibility of goods.

It will be seen that this theory explains how it is possible both to confuse and to distinguish between morals and ethics, between the required (for some way of living) and the good (which is itself a way of living). But, apart from detailed considerations of social history, the theory of goods as historical forces enables us to dispense with the conceptions of end and right, and with all the confusions they carry in their train; in particular, with such problems as that of the moral faculty or of the "inducement" to goodness. Goods are found to be forces operating through persons, developing their own methods, fighting with the evils of interestedness or consumptiveness. We find, too, that we can describe them as working freely, not in the metaphysical sense, but as showing initiative as contrasted with compulsion and repression. No more than they are uncaused are they lawless, but they have their own ways of working, securing their continuance, establishing solidarity among those who participate in them. It is, of course, possible for goods to be destroyed, by natural accident or social opposition, but while they exist they go on propagating themselves.

It is not denied, then, on the basis either of the deterministic working of goods or of the struggle between goods and bads, that "moral appeal" or persuasion is possible. But there are limits to persuasion and discussion. It can take place only under definite conditions, viz., where there are common ways of living, common demands arising from communicating activities; and under these conditions it does take place. There is no appeal to a metaphysical conscience or to a metaphysical welfare, though people are deluded into thinking that there is. Indeed we see, in connection with the notions of welfare, that economists as well as moralists fall into relativist confusions. The historical and deterministic treatment of goods is, in fact, only one example of the removal of metaphysics from science, the establishment of all scientific objects on a single level of investigation. And in thus upholding a logic of events, realist ethics helps to free philosophy from the confused ethics in which metaphysics is rooted—from the conception of "higher realities", that is to say, preferred delusions.

# THE MEANING OF GOOD (1942)

Discussing in *Principia Ethica* (ch. I, § 5) the question how "good" is to be defined, G. E. Moore considers it "impossible that, till the answer to this question be known, anyone should know *what is evidence* for any ethical judgment whatsoever... the main object of Ethics, as a systematic science, is to give correct *reasons* for thinking that this or that is good, and unless this question be answered, such reasons cannot be given" (italics in text; so in all subsequent quotations). It may be questioned, indeed, whether the giving of reasons depends on definitions; but at least we may argue that one of the main obstacles to the development of ethical science has been the difficulty of getting formal proof of ethical propositions—and perhaps we should add that the difficulty has been increased by acceptance of the doctrine that Moore goes on to uphold, that good is indefinable.

A question that confronts the ethical inquirer at the outset is whether there is a single sense of "good" or, allowing that there are several, whether one can be selected as fundamental to ethics—whether, in fact, there is such a subject as ethics. No one can deny the existence of "moralities" or codes, bodies of rules "recognised" (and backed, to varying extents, by "sanctions") in societies or groups. But the use of such expressions as "legal ethics" and "medical ethics" gives us no ground for believing in ethics in general; the description of adherence to a given code as "good" and breach of it as "bad" is quite compatible with the denial of any absolute goodness or badness. In such cases, it may be argued, the group is concerned to maintain certain types of activity and takes as good whatever is favourable to them and as bad whatever is unfavourable (or, it might be said more broadly, the group takes as good and bad, respectively, what it supports and what it opposes); but such attitudes vary from group to group, and lend no colour to the treatment of things as good or bad in themselves.

Now this position of "ethical relativism" is quite widely accepted. According to it, we may say, "ethical" statements are incomplete;

they signify *relations* one term of which has not been stated. Such abbreviations are common features of discourse and are obviously convenient. Equally obviously, they can lead to a great deal of confusion when the term "understood" by one party to a discussion is not the term "understood" by the other—and it is not only in the "ethical" field that such confusions occur. In this way people may be led to think that they are in agreement when they are not or to think that they are in disagreement when they are not. Thus (as Moore particularly stresses in his other book, *Ethics*) if the unstated term in any person's moral judgments is *his own* feelings, if his attaching a moral predicate to a certain subject means that *he* has certain feelings in relation to that subject, it would appear that two persons could never pass contradictory moral judgments. One might *say* "X is right" (or "Y is good"), and the other might say "X is not right" (or "Y is not good"), but they would be dealing with different issues. Each person would have his own moral terminology, and the apparent contradiction would imply no real contradiction *in any one terminology* of the common belief (shared by Moore) that the same action cannot be both right and wrong or the same thing both good and bad. It will still be possible, moreover, to translate any of the assertions into a common terminology; and if you say "X is the object (or occasion) of certain feelings *in me*", there will be no logical objection, whatever objection there might be on the score of politeness, to my contradicting you, to my believing that X *is not* your sort of right or your sort of good.

But if there can be definite disagreement once the relation in which X is supposed to stand ("pleasing you", let us say) has been clearly stated, this does not explain, it may be said, how *confusion* can ever arise, how I could ever imagine that "X is not right", in my terminology, contradicts "X is right", in yours. And, indeed, one may doubt whether confusion would ever arise if the omitted term were merely the feelings of the speaker. But the fact that people really think they are contradicting one another when they say "X is right" and "X is not right", certainly gives us no ground for attributing rightness to X in itself, for denying that a relation to something unspecified is involved. The point can be illustrated from a set of cases, viz., gustatory differences, in which the primary reference is to the state or attitude of the speaker. A says "Oysters are nice"; B replies "No, they are nasty". Here B is not denying that A *likes* oysters, but he takes A to have asserted more than that, to have implied, at least, that oysters are a *proper* object of liking—and this B denies. He is contending, in other words, that A is wrongly constituted, "abnormal"; he is appealing to a set of normal likings which A's particular taste contravenes. It is possible, of course, that A was merely expressing his own taste (though in that case he might have been expected to say "I like oysters"); if so, B was not really contradicting him. But it is also possible that A and B were expressing opposite views of the relation of a given taste to the "normal".

We can now see how there can be confusion of issues, even though no question of what X is in itself (its qualities as contrasted with its relations) is involved—from the fact, namely, that many different terms may be "understood" in such judgments. And not only is there this variety of reference, but a particular reference, what it is that sets the standard we are upholding in a given case, may be far from definite. In general, as already suggested, the reference is to some institution or "movement"; the question is what forms of activity support or are supported by it. But social movements are not cut off from one another, and even the most well-marked movement has not a thoroughly worked out code but (like the most completely "codified" legal system) has its contradictions and unsolved problems; its policy, moreover, can change, and likewise the individual can change his adherences. Thus the judgments of A or B can have considerable uncertainty of reference, and even comparative certainty of reference does not imply a corresponding certainty of judgment. But this very uncertainty will make men *more* inclined to use an expression like "right" in an unqualified way; however vaguely the matter presents itself to them, they feel the pressure of "codes" and the urgency of adherence, and they are impelled to communicate this urgency to others without being able to indicate any precise ground for it.

Also, perhaps, without being willing—there is a dialectical advantage in ignoring the multiplicity of movements (or sources of norms); when we tell a person that some action is simply "right", we represent it as favouring what he recognises as well as what we recognise, and, even if he remains uncertain about this, we at least confuse his mind so long as he has made no formal search for the missing terms. A common way out of the difficulty is, of course, to set up "society" as the single, ultimate determinant of what is correct or proper in behaviour. But it is not very hard to see that this is an evasion, that unqualified "social necessity" is on the same footing as unqualified "right", that it is a means of concealing the *opposition* of forms of social organisation, that the delineation of a general "movement of society", and the derivation from it of "norms" of behaviour, have not been carried out. It is one thing to recognise, as an outstanding feature of political life, the establishment of working arrangements among divergent movements; it is another thing to allow a postulated social unity to dictate to the social facts, to argue, as Idealists do, that there *must be* a unity "behind" the differences. To adopt this position is, theoretically, to abandon the problem of finding the "justification" of any specific form of action and, practically, to pass off some particular movement as "the whole" and so protect it from criticism.

These considerations apply to Moore's discussion (*Ethics*, chs. III and IV) of "the objectivity of moral judgments". With reference to the view that each man's judgment of rightness is a judgment about *his own* feelings towards the given action (so that the judgments of two different men would never contradict one another), Moore maintains (p. 102) that, if we look at the question fairly, we must admit that such contradiction sometimes takes place, "that both men may use the word 'right' to denote *exactly the same* predicate, and that the one may really be thinking that the action in question really has this predicate, while the other is thinking that it has *not* got it". How we go about "looking at a question fairly" is not indicated; but, if we allow that the two men could be referring to the same movement, it is clear enough that they could differ as to its "requirements"—though it is another question whether the point of their difference should be referred to as a "predicate" of the action. It is also possible, however, that they are referring to different movements; and it is on account of his ignoring of the multiplicity of movements that Moore's treatment of the question of a *social* reference fails.

Considering first the view that judgments of rightness are really concerned with the feelings prevailing in the society to which the person judging belongs, and noting that this would make contradiction on such matters between members of different societies impossible, Moore admits that it would be possible, on this view, for members of the same society to differ about the rightness of an act. But, he argues (p. 111), there is a fatal "psychological" objection to the view. "For, whatever feeling or feelings we take as the ones about which he is supposed to be judging, it is quite certain that a man may think an action to be right, even when he does *not* think that the members of his society have in general the required feeling (or absence of feeling) towards it." To admit this, however, is not to get rid of the social reference. A man may consider, e.g., that he is acting rightly in going on strike, although most members of the society in which he lives are opposed to his action, but he may still take its rightness to consist in the fact that it serves a particular "cause" or movement. And similarly, even if we accept Moore's objection (pp. 142, 143) to the theory, which he thinks is often assumed without being expressly stated, "that to call an action right or wrong is the same thing as to say that an absolute majority of all mankind have some particular feeling (or absence of feeling) towards actions of that kind"—the objection, namely, "that it is quite certain, as a matter of fact, that a man may have no doubt that an action is right, even when he *does* doubt whether an absolute majority of all mankind have a particular feeling (or absence of feeling) towards it, no matter what feeling we take"—we can still take the man's judgment of the act as involving reference to a movement, perhaps a movement which is not limited to any particular society or age but can be regarded as running through human history, but at least a movement which is not identical with that history as a whole and which may at all times be a minority movement.

To say that Moore has failed to prove that judgments of the rightness of actions are not assertions of the requirements of some way of living (or of the policy of those who live in that way) is not, of course, to say that they do assert such requirements. And even if the expression "right" were commonly employed in that sense, it might have another sense which did not involve varying references. But the question would still be whether it involved *some* reference, whether it signified a relation to an unstated term (which might be the same in every instance) or signified a quality, something which really belonged to some subject *itself*. The latter position will hardly be maintained; it is apparent that, in any usage, to say that an action is right is to say that it "is to be done", and that this raises the question *on what consideration* it is to be done. Now, as we have seen, this consideration may be a particular movement, i.e., it is the movement that "calls for" the action—but this is really to say no more than that the action does (or would, if performed) further the movement. Or it may be said more generally that the rightness of the action is its furthering *something*—something that can be agreed upon by the people who use the word "right"—but that, if no such thing were agreed upon or assumed to be agreed upon, the word would never be used.

Here it may be objected that justice is not being done to the conception of what "is to be done" or, more exactly, what "ought" to be done, that the question can always be asked, in regard to my action in furthering anything, "Ought I to further that?" But the assertion that I ought to perform some action, or that the action is binding on me, requires supplementation; it has still to be shown on what consideration it is binding. The notion of that which is unconditionally binding on me falls with every other notion of "that whose nature it is to have a certain relation", viz., in that it treats a relation as if it were a quality. And if it is argued that the consideration in question is goodness, then it is my duty to promote what is good, the answer is that the assertion that certain actions promote good still gives no meaning to the contention that it is "my duty" to perform them—no meaning other than that they do promote good.

It could still be held that good is the unstated but constant term in judgments of rightness—such at least as are relevant to the science of ethics. And Moore follows this line in maintaining that the right action (the one which, in his view, it is my duty to perform) under given circumstances is that which, of all the actions "possible" to me in the circumstances, would have the best total consequences. But, apart from the peculiar difficulties of this formulation (the conceptions of "possible" actions and of a *scale* of goodness, the fact that the impossibility of calculating "total" consequences leaves us, as in the previously mentioned cases of unqualified right and unqualified social necessity, with the choice between uncertainty and dogmatism), it may be remarked in general (*a*) that it has not been shown that the promotion of goodness is not the furthering of a social movement, (*b*) that good might be treated as simply one example of an unstated term (something which can be furthered), the stating of which would render definite an issue of "right and wrong", (c) that good also is commonly treated as a term of varying reference.

In this connection it was said earlier that people might take as good what is favourable to certain types of activity, without its being implied that anything is good in itself. But if so, it may be asked, what do they take it as? Is it merely meant that they take what is favourable as *favourable*? The point would be that they use "good" (like "right") as an abbreviation, the term of reference (what is favoured) being "understood". Now there is no doubt that the expression has relational uses; and all that Moore, in particular, maintains is (p. 162) that "to call a thing 'good' does not *always* mean merely that some mental attitude is taken up towards it"—or, he would argue similarly, that it contributes to some social movement. But his account of an alternative usage is unfortunate for his case. He appeals to judgments of "intrinsic value", to the judgment concerning a particular state of things "that it would be worth while—would be 'a good thing'—that that state of things should exist, *even if nothing else were to exist besides*, either at the same time or afterwards. We do not, of course, so constantly make judgments of this kind, as we do some other judgments about the goodness of things. But we certainly *can* make them, and it seems quite clear that we mean *something* by them. We *can* consider with regard to any particular state of things whether it would be worth while that it should exist, even if there were absolutely nothing else in the Universe besides; whether, for instance, it would have been worth while that the Universe, as it has existed up till now, should have existed, even if absolutely nothing were to follow, but its existence were to be cut short at the present moment: we *can* consider whether the existence of such a Universe would have been better than nothing, or whether it would have been just as good that nothing at all should ever have existed" (pp. 162, 163).

The contention that it is not the same thing to say that somebody is pleased at the idea of X or desires X for its own sake and to say that it would be "worth while" that X alone should exist, is one that few would contest. But the usage "it is good that" cuts across the conception of "intrinsic" goodness, of a thing's being good *in itself*. We say "This is red" or "This is spherical"; but it would be nonsense to say "It is red that this, and this alone, should exist" or "It is spherical that this, and this alone, should exist". The assertions "This is good" and "It is good that this should exist", are intelligible (and compatible) *only* if we take a relational view of goodness—only if they have some such meaning as "This is demanded (or commanded)", and "It is demanded (or commanded) that this should exist". If, on the other hand, we regard good as a quality, as characteristic of a thing without further reference, then "It is good that this should exist" has no meaning. And, in this connection, the question what we should think of the thing if it made up the "Universe" is quite pointless; the sole issue is whether it has this particular quality, no matter what other things exist—though certainly it would not have any quality, it would not exist at all, except in an environment.

In fact, Moore's "large" way of treating the matter enables him to dodge the question "quality or relation?"; it enables him vaguely to suggest relations, without committing himself to the view that they are inherent in goodness. Thus, in spite of his rejection of the identification of being good with being desired, he speaks (p. 237) of a thing's goodness as a "reason for preferring" it, and, as we shall see, a similar confusion runs through *Principia Ethica*. And, on the face of it, to call a thing "worth while" is to say that it has some relation. But, if so, this may be, for all Moore shows, the relation of being the object of a certain mental attitude. It may be true, he is prepared to concede (*Ethics*, p. 166), "that there really is some very special feeling of such a nature that any man who knows that he himself or anybody else really feels it towards any state of things cannot doubt that the state of things in question is intrinsically good". And if any one should maintain that when we call a thing intrinsically good we mean merely that *this special feeling* is felt towards it, "the only obvious argument" Moore can find against that view "is that it is surely plain that, even if the special feeling in question had *not* been felt by any one towards the given state of things, yet the state of things *would* have been intrinsically good". Now, if "intrinsically" means "qualitatively", the obvious and conclusive argument is that a quality is not a relation; but if it can have some relational meaning instead (or as well), then Moore's point is not "plain" at all. And his subsequent, less obvious argument from considerations of "duty" falls with that conception. There are, then, still the two possibilities (*a*) that good is a quality, (*b*) that "X is good" asserts a relation, one term of which is "understood"—leaving it an open question whether the missing term is "feelings" or something else.

It is important to observe that a person who denies that there is any quality, goodness, and asserts that "good" signifies a relation to something, e.g. to feelings, even to the feelings of the speaker, is not thereby denying the "objectivity" of moral judgments. (Presumably the class of judgments containing abbreviations like good and right could still be distinguished as *moral* judgments.) The question whether X causes pleasure in me is (assuming that an unambiguous meaning can be given to "pleasure") just as objective, just as much a question of fact, as the question whether X is red. Briefly, relations are as objective as qualities. Thus the economist can make objective statements about "goods" (commodities) while recognising that, to be a commodity, a thing has to be demanded by a person, that nothing is a commodity *in itself.* It has, no doubt, been argued that certain things are of necessity commodities—the "necessaries of life", the things that everybody demands or, at least, requires. But this further point does not prevent our using the conception of objects demanded, and recognising that the things a person demands, though other people do not, are "goods" in exactly the same sense as are objects of general demand. Again, many economists speak of "welfare"; they treat certain things as the *proper* objects of demand. But this can only mean either that these things, whether they are demanded or not, have some quality, or that the economists (and others) demand that people should demand these things. And these questions—the question of the demand for "goods" in some qualitative sense, and the question of demands for demands—can be fruitfully considered only if the initial, relational usage is quite clearly maintained, only if we are able to speak, with no presumption as to its own character or further conditions, of *that which someone or other demands.*

It is here, however, that not only economists but ethical theorists fall into the most serious confusion. The outstanding characteristic of traditional ethics is the passage from the demanded to the *ultimately* demanded (that for the sake of which anything else is demanded) and the identification of the supposed "final end" with the good. The position can be illustrated from Moore's criticism, with special reference to Mill's *Utilitarianism,* of the Hedonistic principle "that pleasure is the only thing at which we ought to aim, the only thing that is good as an end and for its own sake" (*Principia Ethica*, § 39). This is the view commonly described as "ethical hedonism" and distinguished from the view, "psychological hedonism", that pleasure is the only thing at which we do aim, the only thing that is an end; and one main point in Moore's argument is that Mill confuses these two views, that he derives "ethical" conclusions from "psychological" premises. But the position cannot be cleared up until the notions of "ought" and "good as end" are abandoned; their retention renders ineffective a considerable part of Moore's criticism of hedonistic doctrine.

Mill, says Moore, "has already told us (p. 6)[1] that 'Questions of ultimate ends are not amenable to direct proof. Whatever can be proved to be good, must be so by being shown to be a means to something *admitted to be good without proof*' [Moore's italics]. With this I perfectly agree: indeed the chief object of my first chapter was to show that this is so. Anything which is good as an end must be admitted to be good without proof." Now we should all agree that proof is from premises, i.e., from something which, as far as the given argument is concerned, is not proved—and, though a proof of it might be annexed, the *chain* of argument would take its departure from what we had not proved but simply believed. (This is not the place to contest the view that proof starts from the "self-evident"; but even those who believe this are not denying that the argument starts from something taken to be true and not derived from other propositions.) Thus, if we are proving something to be good, we must have a premise that *asserts* that something is good; we could argue that X is good because X is Y and Y is good, or because X is Y and Y is Z and Z is good, etc.—in any case, the assertion that anything of a certain sort is good is either a premise or derivable from a premise; i.e., "admitting something to be good without proof" is essential to the argument.

But we cannot agree with Mill and Moore in their further characterisation of the argument. What is required, in addition to the admission in question, is the assertion (or a number of assertions which imply) that X is of a given sort; to say that X is a *means* to something of that sort is entirely irrelevant to the proof of the required conclusion. We might say, indeed, that "Y is good"

---

[1] The paging in Moore's references is the same as that in the ninth edition of *Utilitarianism* (Longmans, 1885).

and "X is a means to Y" prove something, viz., that X is a means to something good; but how can this be taken to prove that X is good, let alone to be typical of the method by which *anything* can be proved to be good? If X were a means to Y and Y were red, we should not take this as giving any sort of proof that X was red. It is only on a relational view of goodness that the question of means to ends comes into the matter, only if, e.g., being good signifies being demanded that this "character" could be regarded as transferable from a given thing to what brings that thing about. Even so, of course, the proof would not be adequate if our information were merely that X brings about Y; given that Y is demanded, X would have to be taken as not only a means but the only means to Y if the passing on of the character of being demanded from Y to X was to be justified. Still, under these conditions, consideration of means would be relevant, though proof without reference to means (syllogistic proof from the premises that any Y is demanded and X *is* Y) would also be possible.

It may be contended that the above argument passes over the distinction, on which Moore insists, between being an end simply and being good as an end, or the distinction, which (§ 40) he accuses Mill of concealing in his use of the expression "desirable", between that which can be desired and that which ought to be desired or which it is good to desire. But the question is what Moore's "ethical" expressions can possibly mean—what can be meant by saying that X is good as an end or is that which it is good to desire. Is it meant, in the former case, that X is good *and* is chosen? If so, consideration of its being chosen is quite distinct from consideration of its being good—and this whether its goodness is a quality or another relation (for the presumption is that it is not the same relation, that being good as an end is different from merely being an end). Again, if it is meant that X merely *may be* chosen and that this would be a good choice, then to say that choosing X would be choosing a good thing adds nothing to the characterisation of X as good and gives no justification for the carrying over of "goodness" from the chosen to the choosing. And this would be so even if it were always by being chosen that good things come about.

Moore, then, can give no meaning to "good as an end", and the same applies to his notion of the "desirable". This can scarcely mean that which is good *when it is desired*, for, as before, whether its goodness is a quality or a relation other than that of being desired, it would presumably be good even when it was not desired—or if we held (curious as this might appear) that the sort of thing in question was always desired throughout its existence or as long as it remained good, still its being good would be different from its being desired and speaking of its goodness separately would obviate confusion. If, on the other hand, the "desirable" means that the desiring of which is good, then we are attributing goodness not to certain things chosen, but to relations of choosing—or we might attribute it to that which chooses—but in neither case would any connection have been indicated between goodness and the character of the things chosen, so that *they* could be called "desirable". In other words, unless goodness simply means choosing certain things (which then would not themselves be called "good"), the fact that what is good chooses, or is the choice of, something will be beside the point.

There would be no difficulty in taking a consistent view, of course, if the matter were considered relationally—as a question, say, of support or advocacy. Thus the "desirable" might be taken as that which is advocated by certain people (or is in harmony with a certain movement) or as that the desiring of which is so advocated; and there would be a ready passage from either of these meanings to the other. Something like this, I would suggest, is the ordinary usage; the assertion that X is desirable always invites the question—desirable for the sake of what? But Moore, in upholding the *absolutely* desirable or the notion of "good as an end", is running together relational and non-relational notions. He is falling into the sort of confusion he himself refers to as "the naturalistic fallacy", exemplified in what he takes as Mill's dual use of "desirable" and again in "evolutionary ethics" which at once identifies and distinguishes the good and the product of evolution, maintaining that "good" means neither more nor less than what evolution produces and yet that the product of evolution *is good*. Certainly, Moore holds that some ends are not good; but he cannot distinguish good and bad ends except by their qualities—in which case their being ends has nothing to do with the matter—and thus, when he takes "finality" as essential to goodness, he can be accused of identifying, as well as distinguishing, being good and being an end. Incidentally, whatever may be said of his later argument to show that we desire other things than pleasure, he cannot be said, in the passage above referred to, to have convicted Mill of any blunder based on a misunderstanding of "desirable"; for, if the only thing that can be an end is pleasure, it is equally the only thing that can be a *good* end.

In fine, Moore does treat good as the ultimate object of demand, as that for the sake of which anything else is demanded; for if he should change this to that for the sake of which anything else is *properly* demanded, in other words, that the bringing about or production of which is "proper production", the only meaning he could give to this expression would be *production of good*—and thus he would be saying that good is that the production of which is production of good, which is quite uninformative and, in particular, indicates no connection between production (or the employment of means to ends) and good. But he also wants to treat good as qualitative. And it is this predicament that is at the basis of his doctrine (developed in the first chapter of *Principia Ethica*) of the "indefinability" of good.

In the first place, we may say, it has to be taken as indefinable, there is nothing we can set out as its character, because there is *no* ultimate object of demand. But, secondly, there can be nothing common and peculiar to it, because that could be taken as a reason for demanding it (something common but not peculiar to good could not be such a reason, for it would equally be a reason for demanding what is not good), and, being that for the sake of which some person demanded "good", this "reason", or something to which it in turn was subordinate, would really be the person's standard or ultimate end; i.e., it, and not the thing first called so, would really be the person's "good". To put the matter otherwise, Moore has *implicitly* defined good as that which is ultimately demanded (or desired), but he cannot make this explicit without exposing himself to criticism on the score of the irreducible multiplicity of demands—and, as already said, he has a sense of good as a quality. In fact, in his notion of good he *amalgamates* quality and relation (this being the procedure which, in my view, is properly described as "relativism") and so cannot give either a relational or a qualitative account of it—hence its "indefinability".

This view is borne out by his treatment of good as peculiarly a predicate. In the passage first quoted (§ 5) he considers the assertion that this or that is good as the sort of thing that ethics would seek to establish. One would think that ethics, regarded as specially concerned with good, would try to discover predicates as well as subjects of it, how it operates as well as where it occurs. But it cannot stand as a distinct subject if it is really conceived relationally, if in its use "as a predicate" it is an abbreviation the expansion of which would introduce a hitherto unstated term, if it is not an operating thing at all but a way in which one thing stands to another. Not being prepared to undertake (or even admit the possibility of) this expansion, Moore has to fall back on "intuition", the arbitrary attribution of goodness to certain subjects, with no possibility of discussion. But such attribution, if it cannot be expanded, can never convey an absolute obligation on persons to endeavour to bring such subjects into existence; on the other hand, any actual expansion would still not impose an *absolute* obligation, would not show that anything is obligatory in itself but would merely present something that some persons would be inclined, and others disinclined, to promote. It is more convenient, if there are objects one wishes above all to promote, dogmatically to call them good and let it be "understood" that a certain obligatoriness attaches to them on that account.

Moore supports his position (§ 9) by distinguishing between good and *the* good (that which is good), the latter of which he believes to be definable though the former is not. "I suppose it may be granted that 'good' is an adjective. Well 'the good', 'that which is good', must therefore be the substantive to which the adjective 'good' will apply: it must be the whole of that to which the adjective will apply, and the adjective must *always* truly apply to it. But if it is that to which the adjective will apply, it must be something different from that adjective itself; and the whole of that something different, whatever it is, will be our definition of *the good*." Now, Moore says, "many people appear to think that, if we say 'Pleasure and intelligence are good', or [and?] if we say 'Only pleasure and intelligence are good', we are defining 'good' ". But this is not his own view; whatever definition of the substantive may be found, the adjective, he considers, remains undefined. "It may be true that all things which are good are *also* something else... And it is a fact, that Ethics aims at discovering what are those other properties belonging to all things which are good. But far too many philosophers have thought that when they named those other properties they were actually defining good; that these properties, in fact, were simply not 'other', but absolutely and entirely the same with goodness" (§ 10). And it is this view that Moore proposes to call "the naturalistic fallacy".

In dealing with these contentions, we need not dwell on the fact that they would make *any* term indefinable—so that Moore must be simply wrong about the meaning of definition. The essential point is that the adjective does not "apply" to the substantive ("that which is good is good" is not a proposition), is not predicable of it as one term is predicable of another, but adjective and substantive are the very same term, and when we define the substantive we are defining the adjective. The adjectival form is ordinarily an indication that the term is being used as a predicate, and, when we use it as a subject, we find it more natural to employ the substantive form; but such usages involve no *logical* distinction. Thus "Some animals are men" is the very same assertion as "Some animals are human", and though, in converting the second form, we commonly say "Some human *beings* are animals", we could say, without alteration of content, "Some human are animals", or "Some human are animal". Again, we could derive the syllogistic conclusion "Socrates is mortal" from the premises "Socrates is human" and "All men are mortal", or "Socrates is a man" and "All human are mortal", as easily as from those we ordinarily employ; in fact, it is a question of different formulations of the same premises, not of different premises. The whole point of syllogistic arguments is that the same term may function as a predicate ("adjectivally") and as a subject ("substantively"), that it characterises other terms and is characterised by other terms.

Equally, a term is *defined* by other terms. If "rational animals" were a correct definition of "men", that would mean that we could substitute "rational animals" for "men" in every true proposition in which "men" occurs as subject or as predicate and the resulting propositions would be true. But they would be different propositions from those we started with. In defining A as B, or, more strictly, as BC, we are not proposing never to use the term A again but always to use the term BC instead; we are setting forth a complex relationship among certain sorts of things, A, B and C. Thus there may be some force in Moore's opposition to those who say that good means "nothing but" something or other, e.g., nothing but the object of desire. But the main question in this particular case would be whether good is to be taken qualitatively or relationally. If in the former way, it cannot be described as nothing but the possessor of a relation to something else (it would have to have some other description, or there would be nothing to be so related), whether the proposed "total" description is called a definition or not. If in the latter way, the correct expansion of an abbreviation can certainly not be called a definition, but at least it makes for understanding of the matters talked about.

It is true, as Moore goes on to say (§ 11), that such an explanation of a usage cannot direct us to act in one way rather than another. But it is no less true that the recognition of a quality cannot so direct us. Thus, when he says of people who explain how the word "good" is used, that "in so far as they tell us how we ought to act, their teaching is truly ethical, as they mean it to be", but that it is absurd of them to offer the usage as a reason for acting as they recommend, he is showing that he himself has no clear conception of ethics or of goodness. The point is connected with his assertion that good is not a "natural" object, and with his consequent description of theories which identify good with some natural object as committing the *naturalistic* fallacy (though the same "fallacy" is committed, he considers, if good is treated as "absolutely and entirely the same" as anything whatever). For we can take as natural having a certain quality, and we can take as natural being in a certain relation, but we cannot take as natural that in which being in a certain relation and being of a certain quality are merged. But this is not because it is "non-natural" (perhaps, supernatural); it is because it is nothing at all. The description of good as non-natural, like the description of it as indefinable, is a way of avoiding the clearing up of the ambiguities in Moore's conception of it.

A parallel case is found in the discussion between Socrates and Thrasymachus in *Republic*, Book I. Thrasymachus demands of Socrates after he has demolished the definition of justice which Polemarchus has tried to uphold, that he should give his own definition of it; "and don't dare to tell me that it is the obligatory, or the expedient, or the profitable, or the lucrative, or the advantageous, but make your answer precise and accurate, for I will not have any rubbish of that kind from you" (Lindsay's translation). The point would seem to be that, if we give an "ethical" definition of any ethical term, we have what is really no more than an identity ("the worth while is worth while", say), whereas if we give a "non-ethical" definition of it (if we define it as a "natural object"), we seem to be destroying ethics; hence moralists like Socrates (and Moore) are unwilling to define such terms.

But what we are destroying, if we point definitely to some existing thing as the subject of ethics, if we take good as a merely descriptive term, is its mandatory character. "Goods are just those things" does not direct us to act in any way but it permits us to investigate *their* ways of working, and so ethical science can go on. But "the good is the mandatory" tells us nothing at all; it invites the rejoinder of Thrasymachus, implied in his definition of justice as "what is advantageous to the stronger" (or "the interest of the stronger": Jowett), that such a relation among persons as the command of a ruler to his subjects is all that we can positively mean by an *imperative*. This is something we can observe, it is a type of situation in interaction with which we can develop a theory of it, whatever qualities that which is imposed by command may have. Similarly, we could study things qualitatively describable as good, whatever relations they might have. But an imperative quality is something we could never observe or study; it has to be left in obscurity because it is basically ambiguous—though we may still consider that the postulation of such a "non-natural" entity covers the pushing of certain quite natural objects.

The remainder of Moore's first chapter raises a few further points, which may be briefly dealt with. His distinction (introduced in § 15) between the two types of ethical judgments, those which take something to be "good in itself" and those which take something to be "good as a means", suggests that carrying over of a character from end to means which has already been criticised. Here it may be said that judgments of the former type, which take a "unique property" as attaching to something, would also have to take it as attaching *in a unique way* if it is a non-natural property of a natural object. In fact, it is impossible to see how Moore's "intuitions" would work, how an unobservable predicate could be found to attach to one observable subject rather than another, or how we could ever know that it was the same thing that had some natural property and had the non-natural property. But if we are able to take a thing and its ethical and non-ethical properties in the same view, there is no question of "intuition" (except in the sense of observation), and good is found in things in the same way as red or yellow may be found—the alternative being that it does not "attach" to them.

The point is reinforced by consideration of judgments of the second type, "that the thing in question is *a cause or necessary condition* for the existence of other things to which this unique property does attach". For a thing is not a means to good unless it brings about not merely things which have the property but the property itself, unless good comes into existence through the operation of the thing in question. (It may, of course, already exist elsewhere, but the thing has caused it to exist in a given place.) Otherwise, the existence (or subsistence) of good is quite indifferent to that of the things to which it is said to attach, and in that case there is no sense in saying that it attaches to them. But if a natural thing, in its natural operation, can bring about the result, good, there is no sense in saying that this is not a natural result, no way of distinguishing its natural results from its non-natural results; in each case it produces something somewhere. And it should be noticed that what is in question here is not the theory of universals; it may, indeed, have some relevance to the case, but Moore admits that there are natural properties (e.g., yellow), and he is not entitled to treat some properties in terms of one theory of universals and others in terms of another, to make out that there are peculiarly "subsistent" properties. The conclusion to which he is forced, then, is that good is natural.

His doctrine of organic wholes (introduced in § 18) is of importance only as a confirmation of his relativism. "*The value of a whole must not be assumed to be the same as the sum of the values of its parts*"; it can be greater or less. Moore is speaking here of "intrinsic value", of the "unique property" also referred to in the phrase "good in itself". Thus he is recognising *degrees* of goodness—as he also does in taking the right act to be that which has the *best* total consequences. Now, such recognition presents no difficulties if good is taken relationally, if, in particular, the good is identified with the wanted. For clearly there can be degrees of "wantedness"; we can want one thing more than we want another. Thus we could speak of a thing as "better" than something else or as "the best" of a number of things, using the same sort of abbreviation as we do in calling it "good", i.e., without specifying who it is that does the wanting—though, while we can speak of a thing as a "good" (commodity) if it is wanted by any one at all, specification is more urgent in the case of degrees since different people have different preferences or, as we may put it, since there are different rates of exchange on different markets. The very use of the term "value" suggests that the question is an economic one—remembering always that there is no place, in strict economic science, for the conception of "intrinsic" value.

But if good is taken qualitatively, there can be no question of degrees; if two things have a certain quality, one of them cannot have it "more", in a higher degree, than the other has it. This is a point on which there is a great deal of confusion, and in common speech we constantly make such assertions as "Gum leaves are not so green as grass". Now one possible meaning of this assertion is that, while grass is green, gum-leaves are not green but have certain resemblances in colour to what is green—more generally, that various colours can be said more or less nearly to "approach" a given colour. But, whatever may be meant by "approaching", this will not entitle us to speak of degrees of possession of a given colour. Alternatively, it may be meant that each is of some shade of green but one shade is more "typically" green than the other. But in whatever way the type may be determined, if both shades are really shades *of green*, one is not more possessed of greenness than the other. In other words, if it is in greenness that they agree, it is not in greenness that they differ; and any contrary view would simply involve the use of "greenness" in different senses. Again, we often speak of a thing as "partly green", but this would seem to mean that parts of it are (unambiguously) green and other parts are (unambiguously) not green—and in any case the thing itself is *not* green; it has a green part but it has not a part of greenness. More could be said on this question, but it will always be found, I would argue, that the notion of degrees of any quality is a confused one—that the question of a thing's possession of the quality is confused with the question of its possession of other qualities (or of certain relations) as well.

The persistence of the belief in degrees of goodness, then, is due to the fact that it is not taken qualitatively, or not only so, that it is taken as jointly qualitative and relational. But that means that it is taken in an inconsistent fashion. This inconsistency is present in the very notion of "intrinsic value", i.e., something which is such *in itself* that it requires to be valued (by some other being); for, even if it could be significantly said that the thing "calls for" valuation (this, incidentally, being regularly taken to mean that it calls for support, not merely for recognition of it as of a certain character), that would not be what the thing is in itself. Two consistent attitudes can be adopted. One is to deny that good is a quality, to take a purely relational view of it, e.g., that it is the demanded. In that case we can work out a positive theory of it, while recognising different degrees of "demandedness" (or relative strengths of demands). Equally we can have a positive theory of authority while recognising that some things exercise greater authority over us than others but denying that anything is authoritative in itself. The other is to take good simply as a quality, to recognise goods as things existing in certain places and going on in certain ways. On this view, though not on the other, there will be a distinct science of ethics, but it too will be a positive or natural science. This, however, will be no reason for confusing it with other natural sciences, e.g., the science of the operation of our demands.

It is true, no doubt, that those who recognise such a quality and such a science will have in the end to give some explanation of the confusions that constantly arise, of the fact that the expression "goods" which they use qualitatively is used relationally in economics, of the fact that "justice" has jointly or alternately a political and an ethical meaning—on the one hand, social procedure according to recognised rules and, on the other hand, a *good* way of proceeding. But what they will have to do in the first place is to explain their own usage—and to point out what, in accordance with it, they take as the most serious errors of other thinkers.

Thus they will accuse Socrates, in the *Republic*, of confusing between political and ethical "justice", between the system of rules laid down in a given society—this being always a compromise, a working arrangement among divergent movements, and varying from time to time as well as from society to society—and the modes of operation of goods, limited always by a hostile environment but incapable of existing *except* in the struggle with difficulties. They will accuse him of obscuring the relation between the two (obscuring, e.g., the concrete question how far the operation of goods is necessary for any sort of social cohesion) by erecting an imaginary system in which political and ethical justice are one, in which goodness dominates and the "rules" of its operation are in no way contravened. And they will observe that all this is facilitated by the taking up of a preceptual attitude, the attribution of a mandatory character to goodness, that the questions of how societies work and how goods work are amalgamated in the notion of how societies *ought* to work. They will say, then, that progress in ethics and allied studies depends on the rejection of "mandatoriness", which can only arbitrarily be attached to any line of action. Not that they will accuse Socrates, or again Moore, of mere advocacy—but until, in the work of such thinkers, the recognition of goodness as a quality of certain human activities is disentangled from the advocacy, discussion will not be materially advanced and ethics will remain a free field for any one who thinks he can tell people what to do.

It is in fact a standing obstacle to the acceptance of ethics as a positive science that people simply will not be persuaded that, when we say "X is good", we are not urging them to promote X or to exhibit activities of the character X—that there is no more advocacy in our statement than in the statement "X is red". When they demand proof of such a statement, what they really want us to give them is some reason for supporting X—a reason which, of course, could be given only by connecting X with something (no matter what its nature might be) which they actually support, and thus a reason having nothing to do with the qualitative characterisation of things. Such people, on the other hand, as recognise that it is a quality that is in question will see that formal proof of its belonging to X depends on its being known to belong to something else which may be predicated of X. And proof of this kind will be of no use to those who have still to be persuaded that there is "such a thing" as the quality, good. It has already been observed that there is no question of a mere quality, that good, on the view under consideration, would have to be taken as a "sort of thing" (or term) which could be either subject or predicate. The question is, then, how any one who does not yet admit it, can be brought to see that there is the sort of thing that another person calls "good".

First of all, there is the possibility that he *is* acquainted with the sort of thing (or, putting it extensively, with the class of things) in question but calls it something else, so that all he is brought to do is to alter his usage. But he would not do that if he thought that calling it "good" was an idiosyncrasy of the person trying to persuade him, but only if he considered that it came fairly close to a common usage or perhaps more particularly to a learned usage, that many views of good were concerned with something closely connected with the given sort of thing and, indeed, might be represented as not fully successful attempts to clarify the conception of it. And this leads on to the second possibility, that it is something of which he himself has not a clear conception, something he "implicitly" recognises but has only partially disentangled from other sorts of things (or qualities). Persuading him in such a case would largely consist of showing him that, by drawing lines of distinction where it was proposed that he should do so, he could clear up many uncertainties, could give coherence to his own and other people's views and usages, could, as before, represent them as attempts to grapple with what the suggested position clearly sets forth. It may be said, in fact, that this is a regular feature of criticism and the development of knowledge, and that it must be involved in the establishment of a positive theory of good—that no one who has not some acquaintance with the field (whatever his confusions may be) is going to understand, let alone accept, a view of it. The essential point is that there are degrees of clarity and confusion.

It must not be thought, however, that it is solely (perhaps even mainly) by formal argument that confusion is dissipated. Here we may consider how in general we come to distinguish a quality, recognise a sort of thing, "use a term". What is in question here is not the use of *words*, but can be illustrated by reference to the use of words; the learning of a language exemplifies the characteristics of learning in general. For, while the use of a word may be described as arbitrary in the sense that what we call "green", for example, could conceivably have been (is, in fact, in a language other than English) referred to by some other word, we are not using it as a word unless we refer by means of it to a particular sort of thing. And this implies that we are directly acquainted with that sort of thing or with things of that sort, i.e., with situations. Further, we have to be acquainted with the word as a noise of a certain sort; and the "reference" of this to the other sort of thing is a further situation with which we become acquainted.

As has been pointed out by J. B. Watson, the principle of the learning of a language is that "the word brings the thing", this being a particular example of the way in which one sort of thing signifies another (as black clouds mean rain or fire means heat).

We learn, that is to say, by having desires and expectations and having them satisfied. Of course, we are often disappointed; but it is in trying to overcome disappointments that we learn to make finer discriminations. So we may make mistakes in the use of language, i.e., in the usages of the persons from whom we learn it; a situation being complex, we may "mean" one feature of it when they "mean" another. And there are other reasons why the word does not always bring the thing. But if it had not, in the first instance, led to the presentation of something we recognised and if it did not later elicit certain reactions (forms of communication) from other people, we should never learn the language. The essential point is that it is in our operations (involving, for the most part, co-operation, and marked by fulfilled and unfulfilled expectations) upon the situations in which we find ourselves, that we learn and, incidentally, correct our errors (as far as we do correct them), i.e., our failures to get the expected response from things or from persons.

This means that we can acquire a knowledge of good, in particular, only as something upon which we can act and which can act on us—only as something "natural", present in our environment. Unless good is one description of certain things, helping us to recognise them just as their being green might do, we can have and communicate no knowledge of it—assuming, that is, that it is not something relational; but, if it were, our knowledge of it would still depend on our encountering such relations in the situations that confronted us. The treatment of it as "non-natural", not open to ordinary observation, is due, as we have seen, to the running together of incompatible meanings; and on that view we could never have become acquainted with it. It will be urged, in this connection, that the expressions "good" and "bad" come to us as *hortatory* terms, that the initial meaning of "X is good" is "I want you to do (or to promote) X", while that of "Y is bad" is "I want you not to do (or to avoid) Y". These, of course, would be perfectly natural meanings; we regularly encounter facts of these types in our mature experience. But it may be questioned whether the notion of exhortation can be clearly grasped in early experience, and consideration of what is then conveyed may lead to a modification of the relational view.

The position adopted by members of the Freudian school is of importance here. The child, they consider, being urged to do what is "good" and to avoid what is "bad", finds that the doing of the acts described as "bad" leads to the withdrawal from him of his parents' affection, while the doing of the acts described as "good" involves its retention or restoration. Thus "bad" brings or means for him loss of love, and "good" means love. The general effect of the parents' exhortations, then, is to attach the notion of "goodness" to something of which the child has direct experience—which is, indeed, the main form of his communication with others. It may be contended that the admonitions the child receives are of such a mixed character that he can draw no clear line between what is good and what is not. But, the answer is, unless he can draw some line, the admonitions will have no meaning for him and he will never be "morally trained"; and he has his own experience, of love and the loss of it, to draw upon. Thus, while the mixture of admonitions and, later, of social pressures (and this would vary in different cases) may be responsible for some abiding confusion on the subject of goodness, he has his own way of meeting the situation; according to the Freudians, he divides the parental figure into a "good" and a "bad" parent—the latter being the original of the "wicked step-parent" of the legends.

The "ethical" distinction he adopts can thus correspond very closely to a real difference of quality, and so can be the beginning of a positive theory. It is another question how far the theory will develop, whether the distinction will become more or less clear-cut as time goes on, whether similar differences will be observed in other cases—i.e., whether love will be taken as the only good (the view that the Freudians themselves tend to adopt) or merely as the first recognised or first strongly operative good. And here I would suggest that the distinction between thoroughgoing communication (co-operation) and repression is of considerable importance, that, while this may seem on the face of it to be a distinction between relations, there are distinctive qualities that go with them, that a quality, goodness, is involved in communication itself, whether it be the communication of love, the communication of knowledge, or any other. On this view, good is not merely something that we discover but is that by which we discover things—or, if inquiry is taken as one particular good, it at least communicates with other goods and they assist its operations (a view which I have maintained, in slightly different terms, in an earlier article: "Determinism and Ethics", *A.J.P.P.*, December, 1928).[2]

On this view, too, the consideration of social movements is of considerable importance for ethics and may assist the recognition of good as a quality. It may be recognised first that there are qualitative differences among ways of life, and secondly that a way of life is not something that we adopt, by a voluntary decision, but something that adopts us, takes us as a vehicle, kindles a certain "spirit" in us. Thus the scientific spirit, the spirit of inquiry, may be said to be kindled in us by the scientific movement, by a social phenomenon which no individual or set of individuals could have planned and which, in operating through an individual, never completely absorbs him but strengthens the communicating, as against the divisive, tendencies in him. The other ingredients in culture, like art and industry, are also generative of a communicating spirit and of institutions in which it may be expressed, and this, it may be said, is what prevents the taking of "culture" in a non-qualitative sense, as merely what is established among a group of human beings at any given time. So with "progress"; it cannot be taken simply as the approach to any desired object, for it implies a continuing tradition and the working further, without arriving at any *end*, along the line of that tradition, being thus opposed alike to stagnation and to mere innovation. And only certain activities can proceed in this way, as science, e.g., goes from solutions to further problems.

Progress, then, is not the achievement of "greater good" but is a characteristic of goods; goods are "progressive" in that they continually grapple with new problems on the basis of their previous history. They are the continuing features of social life, the "causes" to which men can devote themselves. The position may be summed up in Croce's description of history as the story of liberty or, as we may put it, liberty as the subject of history. Liberty resides in "causes", and they alone have a history because they alone continue as long as there is society. We may thus approach a *definition* of good. Goods, we may say, are those mental activities, or those social activities, which are "free" or enterprising, which exhibit the spirit of enterprise. It might be better to come down on the mental side. The main point is that ethics penetrates both

[2] v. s., pp. 223–6.

the psychological and the sociological field, but is nevertheless a distinct and positive inquiry. And the recognition of a class of things to be inquired into is more immediately important than a formal definition of good. But definition has its own scientific importance, and it should be understood that there is nothing "indefinable" about good, whether we actually succeed in defining it or not.

That many people would be unconvinced, by the above outline of a view, of the existence of a natural quality, good, is obvious; but others may see that it is something with which they have long been in certain ways acquainted. It may be seen, too, that certain popular "moral" conceptions can be accounted for as approaches to what I have taken to be ethical facts—that "happiness", e.g., may be understood not as the receiving of what we want, so that we want no more, but as the continuance of an activity, securing its material as it goes along; that "freedom" may be taken not in the metaphysical sense of release from causation but as a power of devoting oneself to what transcends oneself (a social movement or "cause"); that even "duty" may be considered as expressing the fact that individuals may fall away from movements and be painfully brought back. The vital point is the rejection of "good as end", of the notion that goods come about by being wanted. This, the individualistic or "consumer's" view, is the main obstacle to the development of a positive science (i.e., a science) of ethics.

That there should be such an obstacle is not surprising. For the goodness of inquiry implies the goodness of ethical inquiry. And, in recognising that goods themselves operate in us and out of us, we have also to recognise that they encounter obstacles both in us and out of us. We cannot, in other words, make the world safe for goodness; it exists and develops in struggle with evils. But it is important also to observe, in rejecting the doctrine of conscious intention (or "planning" of good), that good can exist without consciousness of good, that a person can engage in good activities without being an ethical theorist.

# 23
# THE NATURE OF ETHICS (1943)[1]

In my article, "The Meaning of Good", I maintained (as I have done in other articles) that, if there is to be a science of ethics, it must be a positive science. I hold, in fact, that there is no such thing as a "normative" science, and I endeavoured, in examining the particular views of Moore, to advance considerations that would support that general position. It seems to me that the prevalence of the "normative" view is one main reason why ethics as a science has not progressed. And, while it would be foolish to expect that that view will ever disappear, progress may still be made through the setting of diverse views in clear opposition to one another—a process which involves the specifying of the crucial issues. It may even be argued that the "normative" outlook affects all science, not merely as an external obstacle, but as something inherent in the scientist's own thinking—so that his progress as a scientist will involve his detection of his own "norms", the conceptions which he imposes on the facts. Atomism, in my view, is a case in point; the belief in ultimate units has been a hindrance to the progress alike of physical and of social science, and the bringing of this way of thinking into the light of day, the treatment of it as a matter of controversy, assists in the growth of a body of positive knowledge. There may be reasons why the human sciences will always lag, but the clarification of issues and the opening up of lines of inquiry, through a "criticism of categories", takes place in them as well as in other fields. It is still important to observe that there will never be general agreement in any field, that on the subject-matter of every science there is a greater amount of confused than of clear thinking—and that no one is exempt from confusion.

Now the special importance of Moore's work is that he brings these questions into sharp relief in the field of ethics. He has come nearer than any of his predecessors to a positive theory, not simply by his insistence on the objectivity of goodness but by his setting

[1] Reply to A. D. Hope, "The Meaning of Good" (*A.J.P.P.*, June, 1943), which commented critically on "The Meaning of Good" (above).

forth of propositions in which it is attributed to various "natural" things, i.e., by his recognition of *species* of goods. The Socratic doctrine of "the unity of virtue" is dictated by the conception of goodness as mandatory (though Socrates also, as I suggested, has some sense of its *qualitative* character), and the adoption of a "pluralist" view is a considerable step towards emancipation from moralism and the establishment of a thoroughly naturalistic ethics. And here, too, Moore's criticism of "metaphysical ethics" is important, and Socrates is again typical of the adherents of the mandatory in treating the nature of goodness as bound up with the nature of reality. But precisely because Moore is only half-emancipated, because he still treats good as calling for support, as requiring of us that we should act in certain ways, he becomes involved in logical difficulties; and, in attempting to straighten out these entanglements, we are forced to recognise the opposing strains in his thinking and are sharply confronted with fundamental ethical problems. That disentanglement will ensue only on the adoption of a completely naturalistic position is not a conclusion to which everyone so confronted will come, but, if even a few do so, the study of Moore's ethical position will have contributed to such progress as is possible in ethical studies in general.

To make this sort of point I had to insist on the logical difficulties, and in doing so I paid less attention than I should have done under other circumstances to the nature of Moore's contribution to positive ethical theory—and even to the force of his criticism of certain relativisic views. Detailed discussion of these matters would be necessary in any thorough exposition of *Moore's* theory. But, even within the limits of the subject I was considering, I emphasised his qualitative treatment of good as the naturalistic strain (and a very powerful one) in his thinking. And here I should like to make it clear that I do not think there are two ways in which a naturalistic theory of ethics can be developed. In my view (as I indicated in discussing alternative treatments of good), if judgments of goodness are reduced to judgments of the existence of certain relations, then the theory of these relations is not ethics; it might, as I suggested, be economics or it might be some other branch of social or of psychological science, but the distinctive science of ethics would disappear. I do not consider, however, that it is possible to get rid of ethics. When I said in the passage in question that "Two consistent attitudes can be adopted", I was speaking loosely; I meant that one could correct the inconsistency involved in a conception which amalgamated quality and relation, by concentrating either on a qualitative meaning or on a relational meaning. Now, as I said there and elsewhere, there can be a positive theory of relations; but such a theory cannot avoid giving some account of the related things—in fact, it will not go far unless it correlates difference of relation with difference of quality, and the recognition of some particular qualities may be specially illuminating for it. The theorist of human relations, then, has to take account of human qualities and may go seriously wrong through ignoring certain of them—and inconsistency always goes with error. He might retain formal consistency by sticking to a few initial assertions, but it is otherwise when he *develops* a theory; and if, as I believe, there is a quality "goodness" in certain human activities, its presence or absence will make a difference to some human relations, and passing it over will occasion inconsistencies in the theory of these relations.

This sort of consideration would be relevant to a great part of Mr A. D. Hope's argument. But, before getting to grips with his views, I would point out that a naturalistic theory of a relational kind is the sort of theory that has regularly confronted normative theories, an unreservedly qualitative view having been scarcely represented in the history of the subject. Hence, if we take good to *be* a quality, we must regard normative theories, whatever their logical confusions, as having played a most important part in these controversies—as having, in their erection of an "absolute standard", kept alive the sense of an absolute *quality*. Logical confusion will carry with it empirical error, but a real subject will still be adumbrated. Thus though it is only in Moore that the tension of the opposing strains approaches bursting-point (this being one reason why his doctrines are watered down by such thinkers as Ross), we can find in the generality of moralists, though in varying degrees, traces of a positive and non-mandatory view. Even so extreme a moralist as Kant may be said to convey some notion of qualitative goodness (of that which just is good, without further reference), though he confuses the conception of what, in this sense, is unconditionally good with the illogical conception of a good which does not, like everything else, exist under conditions: for to say that an X exists *only when* a Y exists is not to say that X is "relative" to Y or that Y has a "part" in

X-ness. Criticism of Kant, then, might lead in the same direction as criticism of Moore; having seen the illogicality of the notion of an absolute imperative, we might come to consider, independently of imperatives, the quality from which the "absoluteness" takes its significance. Hegel's criticism has something of this force, but it certainly does not eliminate "metaphysics" or the cult of the absolute. And the fact that Moore's work has as background a very considerable development of positive theory in the intervening period, may help to account for its "explosive" force.

The essential point is that normative theories amalgamate different subjects, but the ruling out of one of them is not a solution. And it seems to me that much of Hope's argument depends on the simple *assumption* of the truth of a relational view. I do not think it is true, at any rate, that I gave no reason for rejecting such a view of goodness. What sort of reason *can* be given except by pointing to a quality, which is the quality in question? And how can one prove that it *is* the quality in question except by showing that it is one of the things that recognised moralists have talked about? Of course, the critic may say that he can detect no such quality, and in that case discussion comes to an end, unless one can show that various things he says imply that he does recognise such a quality. And, since it is impossible to carry out a personal analysis of all critics, we are brought back again to a sifting of "recognised" theories. That is the main way in which discussion can fruitfully proceed, but it requires all the time an acquaintance with specific sorts of things; and my endeavour to draw readers' attention to a kind of thing with which they had been long acquainted, and my suggestion that that was the sort of thing with whose characteristics moralists were struggling, were at least relevant to the disproof of a relational theory of goodness, though, as I said, I only gave the outline of an argument. It should be noted, of course, that on a qualitative theory goods will *have* relations, and the consideration of their relations may be of great importance for ethical theory; but to hold that it is does not in any way involve relativism. Similarly, it may be held that only those who live in a certain way can have a clear conception of goodness; but that would not in the least imply that their ethics was simply propaganda for their way of living.

Now in the outline referred to (the concluding part of my article) I drew specific attention to the fact that, allowing that children become acquainted quite early with something they can positively call good, this positive information comes to them so mixed up with admonitions that they have the greatest difficulty in arriving at a clear view of the matter later on. I do not, indeed, agree with the Freudians in their estimate of the importance of the family-situation; I consider that social forces, working through and beyond it, are mainly concerned in imposing compulsions on the child (cf. "Freudianism and Society", *A.J.P.P.*, June, 1940).[2] But at least I have given some indication of how, on my view, goodness comes to be regarded as authoritative, and thus, over and above the formal objections to relativism, of how Moore can uphold a mandatory ethic. It is the confusion of the relation of command with the quality of goodness that leads to Moore's doctrine of the "indefinability" of good (since definition would force him to clear the matter up) and hence to his belief in ethical intuition. The important point here is not the operation of authority in the mind (on which question I should have thought the Freudian view, whatever weight we attach to it, was fairly familiar), but the attribution of authority to *goodness*. Of course, if there is no such positive thing as goodness, the more complicated question does not arise. But I think I am justified in saying that, in making it simply a question of the establishment of authoritative, unquestionable or "intuitive" judgments, Hope has ignored a great deal of my argument. If he had considered the possibility of regarding Moore as amalgamating authority and goodness, as mixing up two distinct but quite real subjects, and had found reason for rejecting it, he might properly have gone on to a consideration of the psychical determinants of judgments of the "authoritative or good". As it is, seeing that "intuition" involves authority, he has concluded that an account of the setting up of authority is all that is called for—thus begging the question of the existence of a second subject, and of special reasons why good should be cast for the authoritative part.

Apart from this, Hope is to a large extent knocking at open doors. No one denies that there are relational meanings of "good", nor, I think, does anyone deny that there are *causes* of our accepting something as mandatory (or "to be done"), though many might think that these causes are to be discovered in a consideration of social movements rather than in an analysis

[2] v. i., p. 356

of mind. These points leave Moore's theory unaffected, and it is in other ways much stronger than would appear from Hope's account of it. I cannot see the point of his contention that our knowledge of intuition is not, for Moore, intuitive, and I am unable to find, in *Principia Ethica*, § 12, any appeal to observation "for confirmation of the difference between our way of knowing 'good' and knowing yellow"; what I find, on the contrary, is the contention that, even if there were *no* difference between the modes of being (and presumably also between the modes of cognition) of these two entities, even if good were *natural*, it would still be fallacious to identify either of them with the subjects of which it is predicated—in other words, that, apart from all question of ways of knowing, a proposition is not an identity. I do not think Moore gives any account at all of how we are aware of intuition as a cognitive procedure; he has not even much to say about "intuitions" (objects of intuition), and my remarks on the subject were a rather "free" rendering of his position, emphasising the consequences of *any* distinction between ways of knowing or between ways of being. Perhaps the clearest presentation of his view is to be found in § 36, where he says that in the work of hedonists prior to Sidgwick "we find no clear and consistent recognition of the fact that their fundamental proposition involves the assumption that a certain unique predicate can be directly seen to belong to pleasure alone among existents; they do not emphasise, as they could hardly have failed to have done had they perceived it, how utterly independent of all other truths this truth must be". And, while I think the criticisms I offered would apply well enough to that, it should in any case be clear that the position is devised to support the attribution of a certain "status" to good and that not even Moore would imagine that he had observed himself discovering this or going through any other process prior to being *struck* by the "ethical" fact.

But, apart from the question of "status", is there any real problem here? If Moore "can give no account of how he comes to recognise goodness", can he, and would he want to, give an account of how he comes to recognise anything else? If he "apparently has an immediate and vivid apprehension of goodness as a quality", how does this differ from the case of his apprehension of yellow? I hesitate to believe that Hope is maintaining a representational theory of knowledge, making out that there is some internal entity which "mediates" between us and yellow, and enables us to know it; such a theory does not even show how we "come to recognise" the internal entity, let alone how that would help us to know the external one. But, if that is not the position, the most that can be meant by "how we come to know" anything is the conditions which must be present when we do know it. The prime condition, of course, is that it confronts us, and, apart from the difficulties involved in the conception of the "non-natural", Moore could say that there is no more difficulty in our knowing the goodness of something which confronts us and *is* good than in our knowing the yellowness of something which confronts us and is yellow. There are further conditions in each case (illustrated by my suggestion above that only participants in a certain way of living might be capable of knowing good), there are variations in powers of observation and discrimination; but, no matter how fully we state any such set of conditions, they will never show "how" we know the thing in question, in the sense of showing what enables them to enable us to know it or of "constituting" its cognisability. What we have is just that, when one thing happens, another thing happens.

Thus, if the influence of the "Super-ego" is one condition of the passing of an ethical judgment, this would not affect the discussion of such judgments themselves. Hope does in fact admit, as one possibility, that the Super-ego may simply cause the mind to observe good as a (real) quality of things. But that admission takes all point from the question "how we come to know" goodness and from the whole presentation of the Freudian theory of mental structure, and brings us back to the question of what we do find in the facts. It is not very clear what Hope means by the alternative suggestion that "this quality of good" is "only a rationalisation by the Ego of its attitude to conflicting demands in the Unconscious mind: what Freud calls 'projection' ". The Ego, let us say, submits to demands of the sort A and resists demands of the sort B; is the position, then, that when it finds another Ego submitting to A or resisting B, it calls that action "good" (and calls resistance to A or submission to B "bad")? If so, what is the force of the expression "rationalisation"? "Doing what I do is good"—that, whether it is tenable or not, seems a quite straightforward position, but it is in no sense a *defence* of "what I do" unless "good" has an independent meaning. And, if prior to "projection", I call my own actions good, no special mechanism seems to be required to lead me to give the same description to similar actions by other people—but, in calling my own actions good, I certainly do not mean simply that they are my own actions. Or if, finally, goodness is ascribed to acts in obedience to some internal monitor ("Superego" or "conscience"), to speak of "rationalisation" seems in no way to show what is gained by the avoidance of a directly relational terminology—and, indeed, this cannot be explained unless some non-relational (qualitative) factor is being smuggled in, and in that case there must *be* such a factor. This is not to deny that the conceptions of goodness and badness have become associated with *authority*, but at least it casts doubt on the rejection of a qualitative meaning for them, and it indicates that the doctrine of "rationalisation" is no way of reducing what I have taken to be two subjects (commonly confused) to one.

Detailed criticism of the Freudian theory of mind would be out of place here, but something may usefully be said on Hope's considerable misrepresentation of Moore's psychological position and its connection with his ethics. There is not, I should say, the slightest justification for attributing to Moore a unitary view of mind. Whatever may be the objections to the "method of isolation", i.e., to the determination of a thing's "value" by considering whether it would be worth while that it alone existed (and I indicated some of them in my article), the very fact that Moore asks us to imagine a mind wholly occupied by one passion shows that he thinks of it as being ordinarily occupied by many different passions; and even if he treats states of mind as states of *consciousness*, so that "conflicting motives when they occur conflict in consciousness", this would scarcely be treating the mind as "a single conscious unit". It would seem rather to be Hope who believes in the unity of consciousness, so that to save mental plurality he has to bring in the unconscious; at any rate, that Moore can speak of "a defiant hatred of evil dispositions in ourselves" (§ 131) shows that the doctrine of mental unity is not his. Now if knowledge of conscious states is to be called "introspection", Moore will certainly rely on introspection for knowledge of mind—but so will Freud, up to a point. But what Moore is appealing to, in applying his "method of isolation" in § 125, is "intuition"; and that means in practice (leaving out of account the objections to some features of his view) an appeal to our considered judgment, to what we can see, with special reference to ethical characters, in the situation we are examining, *no matter how our knowledge was acquired*. And when he refers to the difficulty of determining the nature of the cognition by the presence of which "the pleasures of lust" are to be defined, he is certainly treating lust as a state of consciousness and his problem is to determine what is its object, i.e., what it is that the lustful person enjoys; but the difficulty may well be due precisely to "suspicion that introspection might have interests to promote", to unwillingness to accept the lustful person's word in the matter.

Hope's most serious distortion of Moore's meaning, however, occurs in his statement that in the final chapter (§ 113) "it is the value of the *consciousness* of beauty or of good which forms the fundamental truth of Moral Philosophy". The words "or of good" are a sheer importation; they convey the suggestion (borne out in Hope's further argument), the quite unjustified suggestion, that Moore confuses between consciousness as a feature of goods and consciousness as the judge of goods, that he treats consciousness as of supreme ethical importance because it makes ethical discoveries—a suggestion quite opposed to Moore's "objectivism". The fundamental truth of Moral Philosophy is for Moore, that aesthetic enjoyment and personal affection are "by far the most valuable things that we know or can imagine". He refers to them, of course, as "states of consciousness"—on any view, they *involve* consciousness. In connection with the former he mentions that he differs from Sidgwick in holding that the mere existence of beauty is good but agrees with him in taking its value to be negligible in comparison with that of "consciousness of beauty" (in other words, "aesthetic enjoyment", or in one word, *appreciation*). It is a question, then, not of the general thesis that consciousness is the key to goodness, but of the quite specific contention that appreciation is good. And if we reject (as I contended that we must) the doctrine of degrees of goodness, we may still think Moore has made a useful contribution to ethics in recognising appreciation and love as specific goods, things having goodness as a character. Again we might disagree with his view that certain non-mental things are good, while holding with him that those mental things which are good are conscious. This would have nothing to do with the fact that inquiry into ethics is a conscious procedure; at the same time it would not be rendered dubious by the mere fact that some mental processes are *unconscious*, or that they have an influence on our conscious behaviour. We are acquainted with the specific thing, aesthetic appreciation, and that means that we find specific characters in it.

This leads me to a brief consideration of Hope's remarks on "fictions". Apparently, for him, "aesthetic appreciation" would be an elliptical way of referring to the fact that somebody feels or thinks aesthetically, and it would not be appreciation that proceeded in any way but an appreciator. In putting forward this view Hope seems to have forgotten his earlier pluralism, to have replaced it by a doctrine of the unitary "person" who alone can do things. It would be a very curious account of mental qualities and mental history that could be erected on this basis. In my article I took for granted the plurality of mental entities (sentiments, passions or whatever they may be called) for which I have argued elsewhere—the existence of a society of "motives", having distinct characters and a certain capacity for independent action. I do not propose to traverse that ground again in this discussion but would observe that my view gains considerable corroboration from the work of Freud. A little may be said, however, on the question of "activities". When I say that a thing has a certain activity, I mean that it goes on in a certain way, and this is the very same as saying that it has a certain quality. I should, then, no more speak of "activities *towards* things" than of "*qualities* towards things". At the same time, I should recognise no more of a logical distinction between *things* and qualities than between subjects and predicates—a matter which I touched on in my article. Thus I could refer to good as a quality or as a sort of thing or as a way of going on, considering as I do that any treatment of these as different types of entities leads to insoluble problems. Now good, on this view, will have relations, and it is possible that there are certain relations that all goods have and certain relations that only goods have. (Corresponding facts would, I take it, be admitted in the case of men.) And, while this is no reason for holding a relational view of good, it opens the way to such a view. All we can do, having recognised certain types of distinction, is to try not to overlook them in any given case. Taking the case of "inquiry", we see at once that this expression has a primarily relational sense, and the same is true of the expression "scientific *interest*". Yet, observing that this is one of many competing interests in a mind, we may be able to distinguish *what* is interested from its *being* interested in something. And, in referring to this interested thing as "the scientific spirit", I consider that I am distinguishing it qualitatively from other things in the same region. But, once such a quality had been distinguished, there would be no harm in using the term "inquiry" to refer both to the possession of the quality and to the possession of those relations which such things always have.

The same applies to love, appreciation, artistic creation and other goods; where a certain "spirit" exists, there are also certain special ways of interacting with surrounding things. In connection with my treatment of love as the first-recognised good, Hope saddles me with the view that its goodness resides in the fact that it promotes the child's "fundamental biological urges and needs". There was, of course, no suggestion of a "biological ethic" in what I said. In associating the word "good" with love rather than with hate, the child is adopting the usage with which he is presented. Admittedly the usage is not without its obscurities and confusions, but it is sufficiently definite in most cases to enable the child to make a qualitative distinction, along with his recognition of authority. This, however, provides only a first rough indication of a field and, as I said, by no means ensures that the child will go on to have a developed theory. What can assist him to do so is his later experience of other sorts of goods and, above all, his encountering of the theories of the great moralists, for, although these contain much of a mandatory character, they also exhibit considerable insight into "ways of life", into the "spirit" which animates various movements. And, in so far as they do so, they can give *him* an insight into the conditions of his own life, can lead him to a more coherent view of mental and social realities. He is not, then, tied to his early teaching, important though that may be, but has the continual stimulation of new facts and new theories. This description may apply to only a few cases, but, if it applies to any, progress in ethical science is possible. The vital question is whether anything but a qualitative ethics can give us a coherent view of the facts and enable us to see what even confused theories are aiming at. I do not think there can be a coherent view which does not recognise a qualitative distinction, similar in the various cases, between science and obscurantism, between art and philistinism, between the productive and the consumptive spirit, between love and hate, between freedom and servility, and recognise also relations of assistance among the various goods. And the sort of confirmation that can be obtained in the case of those who reject these contentions is the demonstration of incoherence in their own views.

I have, I think, brought out a fundamental inconsistency in Hope's argument, as between his Freudian and his Benthamite material. This might be accidental; he might be able to uphold a relational view in one or the other way, while dropping what did not fit in. It seems to me, indeed, that the Benthamite material could not be dropped, that any relational view of ethics is bound up with a unitary view of the "person"—though if, as I have suggested, there are logical objections to any doctrine of the unitary, this would only mean that incoherence would break out on a wider scale. But it is in the attempt to make his relational view specific, in his treatment of "approval", that Hope most decidedly reaches an impasse. Rejecting the contention that, on a relational view, the good must be equated with the demanded (a contention which he attributes to me, though I explicitly treated this equation as only one *example* of a relational view), he goes on to say: "Demands, attitudes, feelings, all types of emotional reactions would be involved, and any of them might be what we refer to when we characterise something as good." Actually there are various types of "emotional reaction" which may be involved in demanding itself, as any economist would recognise. But the contention that *any* type of emotional reaction might be the determinant of our attribution of "goodness" to things leads us to look more closely at the nature of the determination; and, apart from the fact that the emotion of sorrow, e.g., can scarcely be held to generate judgments of goodness, we find that the notion of that "on the occasion of which" joy is felt (and which is accordingly judged good in that "reference") is an obscure one, that it can be made precise only as the "object" of joy (what is enjoyed), and that that means as what is *demanded* by joy—and so in other cases. Thus Hope has provided no alternative to "demandedness", and he certainly gives no indication of how "a large number of attitudes to things some of which might be in direct conflict with others" can possibly "constitute a relation *sui generis*".

It is hard also to follow him in his treatment of ethics as concerned with only a *part* of our attributions of goodness to things,

THE NATURE OF ETHICS (1943) 351

viz., that in which emotional relations of approval and disapproval are involved. But, whatever he means here by "approval", he can be forced, I consider, to take up one of two attitudes—either to treat it as equivalent to demanding, or to treat it as recognition of objective goodness. In what way, except as judgment of the occurrence of a quality, can approving be distinguished from demanding? There can be no distinction on the side of the approved; it, like the demanded, is something whose existence or continuance we desire. (If it were suggested that the approved is what we desire in the way of human behaviour, that would make it just a species of the demanded and would indicate no reason for separating consideration of it from that of other objects of demand or for speaking of a special attitude of "approval".) But, if the distinction is on the mental side, that will only mean that we are considering the demands of some particular sentiment, not that we have got away from "demanding" to something else, "approving"; and, as before, distinction between what demands in one case and what demands in another does not require a separate theory of each demander—their interrelations might be very important. I hold, then, that there is no steady ground on which Hope can rest except the recognition of objective goodness, that in his very use of the term "approval" he is implicitly conceding what he has denied. A distinction, however, should be made here. It would appear from what I have argued above that I should take "approval" to mean the recognition of a certain spirit in human activities. But it is obvious that there are other usages of the term; and the point would be that they are various compromises between the ethical meaning and "demanding", and that only by distinguishing that meaning can we take a coherent view of the whole set of usages.

In conclusion, I should like to express a certain impatience with the recurrent contention that what I, in my inquiries into ethics, find to be good are simply those things which I "favour" or "support"—impatience, i.e., with the ridiculous over-working of the conception of support. The scientific question is how things themselves work; and whatever may be the relations of assistance and of resistance among forms of human behaviour, they do not depend on conscious choice. Such choice is incidental to them; and, in general, choice plays little part in human life.

# 24
# ETHICS AND ADVOCACY (1944)[1]

In replying ("The Nature of Ethics", *A.J.P.P.*, June, 1943),[2] to Mr A. D. Hope's discussion of my article, "The Meaning of Good", I suggested, though I did not expressly state, that the "normative" view of ethics would never be got rid of. I do not find it altogether surprising, then, that I myself should be accused of upholding "norms"—though I think it unfortunate that Mr Prior should ignore so much of the argument of my original article (giving a general impression, with no exact quotation) and should make no mention at all of the supplementary discussion, in which, incidentally, I denied the possibility of a consistent ethical theory of a "relational" kind. I hope, however, in this rejoinder, to be able to develop some fresh material without excessive citation of "what I actually said".

Little need be said about Prior's logic, which appears to be a doctrine of elementary predicates (perhaps even of concepts), the subjects of each of which are its "material exemplifications". The position, whatever it is, is simply assumed, and no comment is made on my contention, in "The Meaning of Good", that subjects and predicates are not distinct classes of terms—that, in particular, "goods" and "good" are the same term, and that Moore's denial of this is bound up with his relativism (his preceptualist view of good). There is, at any rate, nothing in my article to justify the assertion that I make good "synonymous" with a group of other predicates belonging to the things I call good. Even where, as in definition, a complex term XY is *coextensive* with the term A, I should certainly not call A and XY synonymous, since that would suggest, to say the least, that the relation was between words instead of between terms (sorts of things).

Linguistic, of course, is one of the main sources of contemporary confusion, operating, as it does, as a substitute at once for philosophy and for a real theory of language. In this connection, I did not

---
[1] Reply to A. N. Prior, "The Meaning of Good" (*A.J.P.P.*, December, 1944), which commented critically on "The Meaning of Good" (above).
[2] v. s., p.268.

admit in the article, and do not admit now, that my "choice" of a meaning for good "is at least in part a linguistic one". I certainly said that people of my way of thinking would have to explain their "usage", but, since I immediately went on to say that they would point out in terms of it the *errors* of other thinkers, it should have been clear that I was presenting the matter as a question of things and not of conventions. I mentioned, of course, the fact that economists and moralists use the same *word* with different meanings; and I should speak of a relativistic conception of good as a usage, in the sense that it combined incompatible meanings. Thus a person who asserted that he was aware of that distinction and was avoiding that confusion might be said to be "explaining his usage", but he would not be "choosing" or "recommending" anything except concentration on something that *is* referred to in an existing usage, with excision of something else that does not really belong to it.

It does, of course, constantly happen that false beliefs and confused thinking affect usage, that a person who believes that X is Y when actually it is not, thinks he has *told us* that A is Y when he says it is X, or that this unwarranted conclusion is *conveyed* by that statement among a group of people who share the false belief (who "take for granted", as groups constantly do, what is not the case). But it does not follow that a person who recognises the incompatibility of X and Y should, when confronted with this "usage", decide to refrain from talking about X, or should conclude that the persons who have fallen into this confusion know nothing about X. What he can do instead is to try to disentangle the real subject (and the recognised truths about it) from the false accretions—and by so doing he may hope to open the way to fresh discoveries on the subject. This is the attitude I have taken up to the ethical views I have criticised, whereas Prior, it seems to me, has simply *assumed* that the subject as I see it does not exist (and that I could not have learned about that subject even from confused views). At any rate, his argument is weighted from the start in favour of a "relational" view (without adding anything to what I have said in analysis of that type of position) and the first two of the possibilities which, he considers, remain when arbitrariness is ruled out, amount to nothing more than that. As to his third possibility, it is not clear to me how recognition of "inescapable deficiencies of all human language" could lead in the direction of a theological view of the matter; if theology is any sort of doctrine and not just incantation, it, with all other doctrines, will be undermined by that recognition—which, however, is itself a doctrine. The third possibility, then, does not exist, even though some theologians may be prepared to argue sophistically that contradictions don't matter, that they are merely a sign of the "imperfection" of our apprehension of ultimate reality.

It should be understood, of course, in connection with the question of "disentangling" that no thinker is suddenly confronted with this as a task—as who should say, "Ah, there is confusion here! Let me see how much that is positive will be left when I have removed it." His thinking has all the time been affected, on the one side, by the assumptions of his fellows and, on the other, by the impact of the facts (from which issues the commonplace that no two persons have exactly the same usages). And the serious student of ethics in particular will be concerned to get a coherent view of a certain objective field; only so can he be said to be studying (wrestling with problems) and not just memorising formulae dictated by his teachers. Now clearly, in doing so, he may make discoveries—he may find, e.g., that good has characters and relations other than, and even opposed to, those he had been told it had—but a new discovery does not constitute a new usage, and to pretend that it does (that a person who rejects previous views of good is really talking about a different thing) is simply to erect a barrier to discovery. It may be that most people treat the assertion "X is good" as a recommendation, but they do not treat it only as that, and so the possibility is not excluded of someone's finding out that it is not that at all, that the recommendation and the characterisation spring from different sources and that it is confused thinking to combine them, however widespread the confusion may be. But this discovery (as I take it to be) is conditioned by an interest in the subject and not by an abstract objection to relativism; it is interest in the subject that leads to the recognition of ethical relativism, not the recognition of relativism to the setting up of a new subject.

Prior gives a quite inaccurate account of what I "state" in this connection. I am not certain whether he takes me to be arguing that, having first discovered the amalgamation of quality and relation in notions like "the absolutely desirable" or "intrinsic

ETHICS AND ADVOCACY (1944)  355

value", one is then faced with the choice of coming down on the relational or on the qualitative side. I admit that I have expressed myself in one passage in "The Meaning of Good", in a way that lends itself to that misunderstanding. Also, as I explained in "The Nature of Ethics", I carelessly gave the impression, in that passage, that I consider it possible to take a consistently relational view *of ethics*—though, as I further explained, I think it quite possible to give a scientific account of relations (of demanding or whatever it may be). But I neither stated nor suggested that a qualitative treatment of moral "predicates" is one in which they are defined "in such an unambiguously descriptive way that no one will imagine that we are exhorting, prescribing, or advocating any policy when we are using them". As I said towards the end of the article, while I recognise the scientific importance of definition, I do not consider that ethical terms (good, in particular) have to be defined before ethical science can proceed. But, whether an assertion is a definition or not, it can always be misunderstood and, so far from attempting to rule out misunderstanding in the "alternative" I adopted, I said explicitly that "people simply will not be persuaded that, when we say 'X is good', we are not urging them to promote X or to exhibit activities of the character X". Presumably Prior was blind to this statement because it did not accord with the interpretation of my position he was otherwise led to give in terms of his own assumptions; that is just another illustration of the possible misunderstanding of any exposition of any subject. But I think I did something in the article to convey my view that the progress of ethics (as of any other science) consists of a growth of understanding in some people, and neither requires, nor can be expected to get, understanding from everyone—that there will always be people who attach a mandatory character to goodness, and who will have a poorer knowledge, on that account, of goods themselves.

I recognise, then, that when I say "X is good" some people will think I am urging them to promote X. But if I were to confine myself to saying what could not be misunderstood, I should never say anything at all; and since, at the same time, I have maintained as emphatically as I could that it is a misunderstanding, I do not think that the effect of some of my statements on careless readers can be taken as showing that I am surreptitiously urging a particular policy on them. It is not, Prior says, "in accordance with the professional ethics of the disinterested theorist to give his demands, or the demands of his movement, greater weight than they would otherwise have by suggesting that they are somehow also descriptions". And he adds that this is precisely the form of "cheating" I objected to in Moore. But that is taking things the wrong way round; what I objected to was the suggestion that any description could of itself convey an *obligation* (or be imperative). I maintained, on the contrary, that any concrete characterisation would be an inducement only to some people, so that it "is more convenient, if there are objects one wishes above all to promote, dogmatically to call them good and let it be 'understood' that a certain obligatoriness attaches to them on that account". And when, in this way, the giving of a certain description to a thing is taken to be somehow also a direction to us to promote it, the effect, as I suggested, is to make the description itself obscure and confused. The contention that good is the *proper* object of pursuit reduces either to the identity "good is good", the question of pursuit being irrelevant, or to the assertion of a *universal* object of pursuit, the question of its qualities being irrelevant. In maintaining that that assertion is false, that there is no universal object of pursuit and hence no description that is a universal recommendation, I have at least warned readers against any confidence-trick. But this leaves me free to maintain that there are descriptions which the admixture of recommendation confuses, and that they (more exactly, *things* of those kinds) are the concern of the science of ethics.

I said it would be necessary for the ethical theorist to show how these confusions arise and persist—and I offered at least a partial explanation. But Prior, as I have remarked above, seems simply to assume that recommendation cannot be detached from assertions of goodness, that "good" is always a relative term, and thus that if anyone calls things good without qualification he is using "suggestion" on his hearers—what is suggested being that their objects are the same as his, when in fact specification (complete statement) might show that they are not. And on this basis—the linking of good with pursuit, and the recognition of *diversity* of pursuits—it must be denied that good is a descriptive term at all. (There is, of course, the view that the diversity is only superficial, that "rational" consideration of our aims will show that there is "ultimately" a single object, the good, which we are all pursuing. I consider that, on this view also, "good" is deprived of any definite content, and there are other objections to the philosophy of reconciliation—but for the present I shall take diversity of interests as admitted.) I have denied that it is possible to work out a consistently relational view of goodness; and, in that connection, it would be interesting to know what Prior means by saying that certain things are "considered desirable" by a person or in a movement. It would certainly be a curious way of saying that they are *desired*; but, if more than that is meant, there would be some difficulty in showing that a quality is not being covertly introduced.

Now Prior's contention is that I have covertly introduced a relation (supporting), since the things I call "good" are the things I support (or the things supported by "my" movement). This view depends on an interpretation of my conclusions, not on an examination of my argument, though, in attempting to show that it is false (that I do not support the things I call "good"), I shall try to bring out fresh points regarding the conception of "support". But first of all I want to say something about the special question of *inquiry*. Prior's suggestion that, to determine the various goods, I "enumerate the other activities which support that of disinterested theorising" is another piece of interpretation and is not justified by anything in my article. But certainly inquiry is the good which I find myself most frequently taking as an example, and there may be special reasons for that choice. The question is, then, whether the inquirer who attributes goodness to inquiry does not thereby incur the suspicion of advocacy (of "boosting" his own activities), while he who takes the opposite view (who does not, at least, see any goodness in inquiry *as such*) escapes that imputation.

Clearly, some of the activities which the ethical theorist is concerned with will be activities in which he himself engages, and it would not be surprising if he had a special interest in the activity of inquiring; he might, then, have a tendency to bring it into a field to which it did not belong or to give it a prominence to which it was not entitled. And this might be regarded as a "moralist's fallacy", comparable to the "psychologist's fallacy" pointed out by William James—the inclination of the psychologist to believe that his knowledge of the agent's operations is possessed by the agent himself. Indeed, a confusion of the latter type is quite common in moral theory—the belief that, when the agent is "acting well", he must *know* that he is acting well, that no activity can be good unless it is *undertaken* as good or for the sake of its goodness. It may be said, no doubt, that the moralist's predisposition to this sort of view is not a sufficient reason for our rejecting it—there are solider arguments against the notion of a "self-evaluating" activity. But, taking it to be a confused view, we cannot treat as a parallel case the attribution of an ethical character to inquiry in general. For, whatever the theorist's inclinations may be, he has raised an issue which must be discussed in its own terms and not in terms of his inclinations.

Once more, if it is *assumed* that there is no issue, no objective goodness but only preferences, the assertion that inquiry is good may be translated into the assertion that inquiry is "preferable to non-inquiry, and this again may be understood as an attempt to "suggest" that inquiry holds the same place in all systems of preferences or "scale of values"—a suggestion whose effectiveness would depend, as I myself indicated, on people's uncertainty about their "values". The operation of a person's own preferences in the use of the confused notion of "the preferable" could then be studied as part of the subject-matter of a positive theory of preferences. But, if there is an issue, the fact that the theorist has interests which may distort his view of it has no place in the discussion of the issue itself; it is a condition of inquiry in general, and it is only *after* the acceptance of certain views of the subject as facts that evidence of any specific distortion can be given. Indeed, if the fact that it is an inquirer who holds the view were a reason for calling in question the attribution of an ethical character to inquiry, it would be a reason for questioning *any* view about inquiry—however, that is of minor importance compared with the point that, since interests are operative in all inquiry, any view at all could be discounted in this manner. Without setting any view above criticism, we can say that the general consideration that "we may be wrong" forms no part of the discussion of any specific assertion; so, in this special case, the connection which Prior supposes to exist between my inquiring interest and my views about inquiry has no place in a discussion of those views, though it is a question to which attention might be turned if it had been demonstrated independently that my views are false or confused.

The position is, then, that even if it were true that I support inquiry and the other things I regard as good, that would do nothing to show that my views are false or, again, that I cannot legitimately mean more by "good" than "supported by me". But what could be meant by saying that I support inquiry? If it were only that I *engage* in inquiry, then since every student of ethics can be described as engaged in study, his view of the ethical character of study would be suspect since he "supports" it, and we should have to turn to non-students to get an unbiassed view! There is, in fact, no field of study whatever within which there are not *some* features of the inquirer's activity, but this sort of participation in a field is not ordinarily held to prejudice discussion—nor, again, is it commonly called "support". Yet I do not think it can fairly be inferred from my article that I have any other relation to inquiry (apart from inquiring into it) than that of engaging in it. In particular, I cannot fairly be represented as setting up inquiry as an object of pursuit. Of course, we speak of "pursuing inquiries", but that merely means engaging in them, not having them as *ends*. At the conclusion of my discussion, "The Nature of Ethics", I spoke of "the ridiculous overworking of the conception of support" and depreciated the place of *choice* in human life; another way of putting the matter would be to say that a great many writers (particularly, moralists) speak as if the specifying and pursuing of ends (things to be brought about) were the outstanding feature of human conduct, instead of being an occasional and minor occurrence. (We quite often know what we are going to do, but that is quite different from *deciding* to do it.)

There is nothing paradoxical, then, in a statement by anyone engaged in inquiry that he does not take inquiry as an end. Having the habit of inquiring he may at certain times have the choice between different lines of inquiry and decide to follow one of them; but he did not form the habit by deciding to acquire it, and he exercises it, for the most part, without thinking about it at all—his thoughts being concentrated on his subject. And, apart from the particular case of inquiry, there is a general question to be raised regarding the treatment of habits or activities as ends—viz., what is it that chooses or pursues them? Surely, it could only be previously existing habits or activities. Prior speaks of things that we

(W. H. C. Eddy[3] and I) support; but what are "we"? Pure individuals, extensionless centres of force to which various pursuits become somehow attached? If it were true that we support inquiry and the rest, it would be some specific activity in us (perhaps, the inquiring activity itself) that did the supporting. But does inquiry, or does any other activity, pursue inquiry as an objective? Inquiry goes on—not as a matter of policy but as a matter of habit. As I have argued in earlier articles in the *A.J.P.P.* (e.g., "Determinism and Ethics", December, 1928; "Realism versus Relativism in Ethics", March, 1933),[4] goods do not come about by being chosen; and anyone who confusedly takes them as ends will have very poor success in securing them. The main point is that, where choice takes place, it is activities that choose; and while it would be absurd to speak of inquiry choosing to inquire, there is no ground for treating it as the aim of any other activity—or as an object of "my" policy in particular.

I have said, of course, that goods support or assist one another, but this is a question not of policy (choice) but of causality. The activity of inquiry in one mind or group causes the continuance of that activity (or some other good activity) in another; by its natural operation it removes hindrances and provides materials. It might even be said to cause the activity to spring up in another mind or group, provided the capacity was there—though here it might be contended that unless the "capacity" existed as a spontaneous, even if comparatively undeveloped, activity, "communication" would not take place, that education can only be of the nascently inquiring. Now it is undeniable that inquirers can learn to expect the extension of inquiry under certain conditions, also that in the course of these communications certain "rules" (things to be remembered, things to be avoided, etc.) come to be formulated, and further, that the existence and modes of operation of forces hostile to inquiry come to be recognised. But it is still inquiry that is the agent in all this, and, if it forms a policy, it is not itself the *object* of that policy; and, in particular, it will be weakened unless it sits loosely to its rules and, for the most part, forgets about them. This, I think, will be admitted by many with regard to education, and it should not be hard for these people to admit it with regard

---

[3] In "Ethics and Politics" (*A.J.P.P.*, September, 1944).
[4] v. s., pp. 222,3 and 245.

to cultural communication in general. Policy, as we may put it, has to play second fiddle to spontaneity, and goods continue because of their own character—and emphatically *not* because they are wanted. (I find it curious that Prior should describe this part of my position as "a re-statement of Kant's criterion of non-contradictoriness". I have acknowledged, in "Determinism and Ethics", a certain connection between my view and that put forward by Socrates in *Republic* Book I. But whereas Kant is concerned with what can be *willed*, I am talking about how certain things actually go on. And while I say that evils are found opposing other evils, I see nothing "contradictory" in that situation. Prior's substitution of "truthfulness" for inquiry, in the same passage, is further indicative of his inability to avoid giving a preceptual twist to my views. The recognition of the goodness of inquiry is not the laying down of a rule, and inquiry could assist its own continuance even if truthfulness didn't. At the same time, it is conceivable that telling the truth to an enemy of inquiry—or is it an enemy of truthfulness?—would do no harm to the cause of inquiry in the long run, even if it was immediately fatal to the truth-teller. Socrates at his trial is a case in point.)

Prior's statement, then, that the things Eddy and I call "good" are those we consider ourselves to be supporting, and count upon being supported by, when we are disinterestedly theorising, is false because it brings in considerations of policy and pursuit where they do not belong (where I certainly do not "consider" they belong), and thus entirely misinterprets the contention that good activities, in or out of us, support one another. Even where there is a question of a policy of a movement (say, a scientific movement), the things aimed at are always externals, "useful" things (e.g., the provision of apparatus) and not things that could be described in the same terms as scientific activity itself—and, even so, the policy will be both temporary and elastic. Similarly, one might speak of persons engaged in common work as "supporting" one another, but that would not mean that they regarded one another as "good"—at least, in the same sense as that in which the work was good. At any rate, the way in which goods support one another is not the reason for their being called "good" and signifies nothing in the way of policy or recommendation. And this brings me to the final sense in which I might be said to support inquiry (or anything else I regard as good), viz., that I advocate it, that I try to induce people to engage in it. Such advocacy Prior takes to be implicit, though unacknowledged, in my use of the term "good", and, if I can show that that is not so, I shall consider that I have drawn a definite line between the good and the supported.

How, then, I would ask, can one recommend inquiry; what inducement can be held out to people to engage in it? I could scarcely expect people to be moved by my statement that inquiry is good, if they took this to mean only that I *wanted* them to inquire. In order to be influenced in this direction they would have to think that inquiry carried with it something that *they* wanted. In other words, my advocacy would consist in bringing out a causal connection, which they had overlooked, between the activity of inquiry and some object of theirs, in showing the "usefulness" of inquiry to them. Now, if I persuaded them in this way that they should engage in inquiry, I should be doubly deceiving them—first, in that there is *no* object which is uniformly promoted by inquiry, no external thing to which it can be subordinated, and, secondly, in that people cannot become inquirers by simply wanting to, that the spirit of inquiry cannot be so induced. In fact, there is no inducement to inquiry; inquiry develops by the interplay of inquiring minds (including, as I said in connection with education, nascently inquiring minds) and in no other way. Believing this, I can say that I do not advise people to engage in inquiry or tell them that it will serve their purposes, and can trace the taking as recommendation of my assertion that inquiry is good to that obsession with ends (with "results" as contrasted with activities) which, as embodying false theory, I have also criticised. Inquiry spreads (as far as it does so) by its own natural operation, and taking its extension as an aim, *trying* to extend it, is a sign of weakness and confusion. Policies have force only within a "morality" or way of living, and not as between different ways of living. Of course, there is in society an intermingling of movements and moralities, and no person or movement is "given over" to goodness; but still it is the business of the theorist to distinguish the divergent tendencies, not to run them all together.

It is obvious on the face of it that there can be no inducement to disinterestedness, no interest which it can be shown to serve. The fact remains that moralists do appeal to people to be disinterested, to be good, even (in some cases) to be critical. What I take to be the significance of this is that there is a real disinterestedness to which interest pays lip-service, that there is a real solidarity in goodness and that this is imitated by the spurious solidarity of "social unity"—partly because the real thing is useful (produces things that nothing else could produce) and partly as the best way of keeping the real thing in check. At the same time, because the other is spurious (because there are always cracks in the unity), it can never wholly eliminate goodness. This opposition, I suggest, between interest and disinterestedness, between convention and criticism, is what alone makes intelligible the confusion of moral terms and the persistence of relativism. And in this struggle propaganda (advocacy) is a mark of non-goodness, while it is a mark of goodness simply to insist on the facts, to expound and expose, let the results be what they may. The special importance of positive ethics here lies in its rejection of the conception of absolute right (of the imperative or mandatory), as against which it emphasises the quality, goodness. And it is on absolute right that moralistic ethics, the spurious science consecrated to social unity, takes its stand. Such a linking between conflicts in doctrine and conflicts in the field with which the doctrines are concerned will, of course, be peculiar to ethics, but it is only so, I urge, that the questions can be settled.

## 25

## THE ONE GOOD (1945)[1]

While Mr A. N. Prior admits having misinterpreted my position on certain points, he seems to attach little weight to what I regard as the major points in my "Ethics and Advocacy" and so, in my judgment, he goes off into side-lines. Of course, if he sees no force in my distinction between the "real" and the "spurious" solidarity, he will not be inclined to pursue the hypothesis that in the conflict and confusion between those two lies the explanation of the confused state of ethical theorising. But at least he should give me credit for thinking that the distinction is sound, for thinking that, in however summary a manner and with whatever barriers to "getting it across", I am presenting *what is*.

In fact, in taking my position to rest here on a "postulate", Prior would seem to be resurrecting the charge of "recommendation" of which he had previously absolved me; if I am not now directly making demands of other persons, I am making demands of the facts—holding that they *have* to be of such and such kinds—and this would, incidentally, involve making demands of persons, viz., that they should see the facts in that way. But even at the beginning, in speaking of the "morality" of which my writings form a part, Prior shows that he has not really given up thinking of me as advocating something. He could do so, indeed, only if he admitted with me that ethics is just as positive a subject, just as definite a field of study, as physics; failing that, it can only be a variable matter, depending on people's choices, usages, postulates, and what I in particular write on what I call ethics will be merely a presentation of "my" ethics, of the usages, and eventually of the ways of behaving, which I prefer.

The main point of my fairly detailed remarks on inquiry was to show that consideration of "my morality" (or my adherences) was irrelevant to consideration of the actual content of my argument, that inquiry is a subject, and that, even if a man in discussing that

---

[1] Reply to A. N. Prior, "The Subject of Ethics" (*A.J.P.P.*, December, 1945), which commented critically on "Ethics and Advocacy" (above).

subject is himself inquiring, it is obstruction of discussion to turn attention to his activity and away from what he says. Even if he regards "devotion to truth" as having characters, and relations to other devotions, not recognised in common opinion, he is not to be understood as laying claim to a specially high degree of such devotion; and neither his devotion nor his backslidings *as his* have anything to do with the question. But, further, even if the subject under discussion were "adherences", and if a man in what he said about adherences showed in some measure his own adherences, it would still be a side-tracking of discussion to reply to what he said by commenting on what he revealed about himself.

What I have said, then, is that there is a subject *good*, and that what Prior takes as different ways of using a word are different misapprehensions of this subject. And this could be expressed by saying that there is only one thing that is "meant by" good, however confusedly some people may apprehend it. In the same way I should say that there is only one thing that is meant by *mind*, and that, even if some people define it relationally as "what knows", it is *it* that they are thus wrongly defining. Prior speaks as if it were in some quite accidental or arbitrary way that an "inconsistent usage", in which quality and relation were run together, had sprung up in common speech and thought, and as if some persons, seeing the inconsistency, then decided equally arbitrarily that in their "usage" it would be simply the quality or simply the relation that was referred to. But if it can be shown, as I think it can, that the common usage distorts a real subject and that the distortion arises quite naturally in the conditions under which the subject exists, the removal of the distortion will also not be a matter of simple "choice" but will follow a definite line—which will not be the relational one.

At any rate, I do not think Prior has had much success in showing what a "consistent relativist" could say. If an "ethical sentence" is not merely to convey information as to the object desired by the speaker, but also to be an appeal to the hearer's emotions or will, it can only be because the element of "incantation" is also informative. Failing that, how could it possibly influence the hearer? No one, presumably, would say that "X is good" influences a person towards X more than is done by "X is bad", simply because he likes the *sound* "good" better than he likes the sound "bad". The influence would depend on his associating the former with certain activities or "ends" and the latter with certain others. Similarly, if a man were influenced in different ways (or influenced at all) by "Revolution! Rah!" and "Revolution! Bah!", it would be because the monosyllables conveyed to him something of the speakers' attitudes to revolution—this, of course, impinging on his own previous attitudes to revolution and to the speakers. In other words, the supposed incantation is charged with unstated "values"; they are its "meaning". I have acknowledged, of course, that there is a great deal of ambiguity and confusion in such appeals; but always there must be something positive, and always, I contend, when disentanglement has taken place, good will be found to be part of that positive content.

To show that there is one type of activity which has been the "real" subject of all moral theories whatever, would obviously be an immense undertaking. Nevertheless, that is what I believe to be the case; and I do not decide to call the special forms of that general type "good" because they proceed best without recommendation or because they all hang together or make up a single "morality"—or for any other reason than that I think they *are* good. At the same time, I think that Socrates and others, into whatever moralistic confusions they occasionally fall, have seen truly that goods do not conflict with one another. Prior speaks again, in this connection, of disinterested inquiry "contributing to its own destruction". The first question to be raised here is that of "contributing". If an X attacks and destroys a Y only because it *is* Y (so that, if it had not been Y, it would not have been destroyed), is that any ground for saying that it contributed to its own destruction? To say that goods co-operate and propagate themselves in special ways is not to say that nothing is inimical to them and that they cannot be destroyed; but being destroyed by what is opposed to goodness is not being destroyed by goodness. However, Prior seems to be suggesting cases in which, but for Y, there would not have been an X to attack and destroy it—and that brings us to the second question, what is and what is not "disinterested" inquiry.

I take it that the "atom bomb" is an example of the weapons which are furnished by inquiry to destructiveness—weapons the use of which may destroy civilisation and thus inquiry itself. It seems to me quite possible that we have entered a period of cultural degeneration, that we are approaching one of Vico's "new barbarisms". But while that in itself does not mean the end of civilisation, I should maintain that far more potent forces than "scientific weapons" are at the back of the decline of culture. And what is particularly to the point is that "scientific advance" has been largely bound up with the decline of inquiry, that modern science does not exemplify disinterested inquiry. Its spirit has been "practical", it has been concerned with "getting things done", with facilitating transformations and translations, not just with finding out what is the case and with the "criticism of categories" that that involves. It has served "society", i.e., that false solidarity of group interests of which I previously spoke; it has not been disinterested *or philosophical*. And while I should have expected Prior to take a less simple view of science, to see how far it merely imitates inquiry, I also find a certain simplicity in his theory of "disinterested destructiveness". He gives his case away, I think, in his reference to despair; despair is not a disinterested but an egoistic attitude, an elevation of the particular above the general—which is the weakness of all "spurious" creeds.

Now it cannot be said that theology escapes this charge; in so far as it is a doctrine of a universe or system of things, it is "solidarist"—it tries, like the egoist or the patriot, to set up something whose value resides in its "unity" and not just in its character. But in so far as it criticises lesser unities, in so far as it opposes "the world" and "scientific" optimism, it is a closer imitation of the real thing than other views are. Taking "original sin" as signifying the worthlessness of the individual, we can regard it as making some approach to the recognition of those *causes* which, as I suggested (following Croce) in "The Meaning of Good", are the real subject of history—or of culture, or of ethics. And theology (or religion) may be closely connected with those "myths" which, on Vico's view, are the first approach to an understanding of culture.

But while a positive view of ethics may develop in this way and may continue to find more in common with theology than with melioristic science, it is not theological and it has not even that long-range optimism which goes with any belief in a "system" of things. When I argue that goodness cannot be eliminated by the "spurious solidarity of social unity", I take this to be a matter of fact; I take it that goodness (but likewise evil, and likewise pretence) is coeval with society. But I certainly do not take society to be eternal—though I see no possibility of fruitful inquiry into the conditions either of its ending or of its beginning. And I cannot see, in this connection, how Prior, in order to believe in a "solid personality", can accept E. M. Forster's doctrine of necessary fictions. Forster, it appears, considers that although the assumptions that men are immortal and that society is eternal are both false, "both of them must be accepted as true if men are to go on eating and working and loving". Clearly Forster did go on eating, etc.; equally clearly he did not accept as true what he had just said to be false.

I am not attempting in these discussions to give more than a sketch of a position. I cannot say just at what point, and with reference to what background of study, linkages would emerge and the position would appear other than arbitrary to hitherto dissenting readers. But I hope I have shown, with regard to Prior's discussion, that he has not established either that goods, as I have presented them, can conflict or that there is more than one meaning of "good". For the rest, the sort of "imitation" I have referred to, the ways in which "interests" masquerade as disinterested (and the consequent confusion affecting the study of disinterestedness), should be obvious to all those who admit that such a thing as disinterestedness exists.

# 26
# MARXIST PHILOSOPHY (1935)[1]

The philosophical doctrines of Karl Marx and his followers have received very little attention in academic circles, and this is naturally so, because they lie outside the main line of philosophical development. They have contributed nothing to the rise of the most important recent philosophy, that of realism, and, while they have certain affinities with pragmatism, they were not responsible for its emergence as a distinctive tendency in the philosophical field. This state of affairs has been partly due, no doubt, to their defective formulation, to the fact that Marx made no consecutive statement of his philosophic views and that it was left to men of inferior intelligence like Engels, or men like Lenin for whom philosophy was of merely incidental interest, to supply the missing doctrines. There is no doubt, also, that, had there been a greater academic interest in Marxist social theory, correspondingly greater attention would have been paid to the philosophy with which it has been combined. But the main obstacle to the close study of Marxist philosophy has been just this mingling of social and philosophical considerations. Since the philosophical material appeared on a casual scrutiny to be of a perfectly familiar Lockian or Hegelian type, the professional philosopher has seen no point in trying to disentangle it from the peculiar sociological setting which the Marxists gave it.

The philosopher, however, has to admit that *philosophising* at any rate is a social activity and that the existence of a philosophical tradition is a social phenomenon. And it becomes increasingly important for the philosopher, in order to maintain an independent interest in philosophy as against other social interests, to be able to show not merely that philosophy is not social theory but what is the connection between the two. It is not only the orthodox Marxists who confuse between theory and policy, between what is the case and what is to be done, though it is they

---

[1] A paper read at the University of Melbourne on 22nd January, 1935, to Section J of the Australian and New Zealand Association for the Advancement of Science.

who most elaborately defend this confusion; but, in all countries, powerful social interests, not themselves philosophically competent, endeavour to prevent the promulgation of philosophical doctrines which are offensive to them—and especially of a freethinking philosophy, since every established State supports itself by some sort of fetishism. Thus, in upholding the philosophical interest (the interest, i.e., in philosophical truths as such), the philosopher has to recognise how it is affected by other interests, he has to effect the disentanglement above referred to, even if it takes him temporarily away from purely philosophical questions. He does so, of course, as a philosopher; he has to show what *philosophical* errors are involved in socio-philosophy, whether of the Marxist, the Hegelian or any other variety. But in so doing he also enables the social issues to be cleared up. And, on this question, I am convinced that Marxist philosophy has been an obstacle to the acceptance of Marx's main social views, and that a refutation of the philosophy can only advance the most typically Marxist contributions to science.

It should be understood, at the outset, that the outstanding social doctrine of Marx and Engels, the economic interpretation of history, whatever special difficulties it may present, does not in itself involve a socio-philosophical confusion. As Engels puts it (in his preface to the English translation of the *Communist Manifesto* in 1888), "The 'Manifesto' being our joint production, I consider myself bound to state that the fundamental proposition which forms its nucleus belongs to Marx. That proposition is: that in every historical epoch, the prevailing mode of economic production and exchange, and the social organisation necessarily following from it, form the basis upon which is built up, and from which alone can be explained, the political and intellectual history of that epoch: that consequently the whole history of mankind (since the dissolution of primitive tribal society, holding land in common ownership) has been a history of class struggles, contests between exploiting and exploited, ruling and oppressed classes; that the history of these class struggles forms an evolutionary series in which, nowadays, a stage has been reached where the exploited and oppressed class—the proletariat—cannot attain its emancipation from the sway of the exploiting and ruling class—the bourgeoisie—without, at the same time, and once for all emancipating society at large from all exploitation, oppression, class-distinctions and class-struggles." On this showing, it will be important for those interested in what Eastman calls "social engineering" to know that lasting social changes can come only by a change in the economic structure of society, in its "productive relations", and that they cannot come by means of theorising alone, philosophical or other; it will be important to observe that the prevailing productive relations enter into all social activities. In fact, the general account given of social history may be perfectly sound, and yet philosophical theory will remain unaffected.

But a detailed study of the *Manifesto* itself soon reveals much more questionable matter. "Does it require deep intuition", Marx and Engels ask, "to comprehend that man's ideas, views and conceptions, in a word, man's consciousness, change with every change in the conditions of his material existence, in his social relations and in his social life? What else does the history of ideas prove, than that intellectual production changes its character in proportion as material production is changed? The ruling ideas of each age have ever been the ideas of its ruling class. When people speak of ideas that revolutionise society, they do but express the fact that, within the old society, the elements of a new one have been created, and that the dissolution of the old ideas ever keeps pace with the dissolution of the old conditions of existence." Now, whatever may be said about "ruling ideas", we all know that it is not true that a man's views change with every change in the conditions of his life. Again, if there are dominant social forces, they will undoubtedly act so as to check the spread of views inimical to them; but it is quite another thing to say that they determine the whole intellectual history of the period, that they even successfully repress "heretical" views, let alone prevent them from arising in the first place. Marxists will argue, of course, that along with the ruling forces have to be considered the rising revolutionary forces; but, apart from the question of the relation of these forces in a social complex, it is still not true that the two together completely determine either the origin or the fate of "ideas" (views). However, the main point is that, in any case, an account of how views arise is not an account of their truth, any more than, in general, an account of a thing's origin is an account of the thing; and thus an exposition of the social influences on philosophical thought *is not philosophy* and can settle no philosophical problem. And, while it is suggested by the above quotation, it is made still more evident in Engels's main "philosophical" work, which was approved by Marx (the *Anti-Dühring*, partly translated into English under the title *Landmarks of Scientific Socialism*), that this distinction has not been kept clear. The illogical conception of relative truth, of a truth which is appropriate to a given period or social system or to a particular way of living *within* such a system, is embraced, with very damaging effects on Marxist theory in general.

The theory of relative truth receives its classic refutation in Plato's *Theaetetus*, where it is shown that, in the very formulation of a supposedly relative truth, the relativist is presenting something as an absolute truth. If I say "X is true for me", then I am saying that X's being true for me is an absolute fact; and the same applies to any other attempted formulation of the relative. Every statement that can be made raises an issue of fact, the question is always whether X *is* or *is not* Y, and if such an expression as "true for me" had any meaning at all, it would not mean a special kind of truth, a peculiar way of being the case, but it would mean a certain predicate which might or might not belong, in a matter of fact way, to a given subject. Sometimes "true for me" is used as meaning "believed by me", and in that case the question of fact is raised as to what I believe and what I do not believe—this not affecting the further fact that what I believe is sometimes not true. But, even so, the expression "true for me" is a confused one; it covers an attempt to evade the issue, to claim a kind of *personal* truth for my beliefs, in spite of the facts. The fundamental criticism of such relativism, then, is that in trying to evade the issue of fact, the relativist is himself presenting an issue of fact (a proposition which must be adjudged true or false).

This criticism applies to the arguments of Engels, who, besides confusing questions of fact with questions of our discovering fact, takes the historical character of things (a character which he admits to be absolute) as an argument against their absoluteness. Thus in his *Feuerbach* (Kerr edition, pp. 41, 42) he says: "Truth, which it is the province of philosophy to recognise, was no longer, according to Hegel, a collection of ready-made dogmatic statements, which once discovered must only be thoroughly learned; truth lay now in the process of knowledge itself, in the long historical development of learning, which climbs from lower to ever higher heights of knowledge, without ever reaching the point of so-called absolute truth, where it can go no further, where it has nothing more to look forward to, except to fold its hands in its lap and contemplate the absolute truth already gained." Now there is in the conception of absolute truth nothing at all to suggest that anyone will ever know all truths. But not only does Engels imply in speaking of "the process of knowledge itself" that the recognition of that process is absolutely correct; he also passes over the fact that the "development of learning" takes place by successive assertions that something *is the case* and that we cannot speak of having reached a greater "height of knowledge" without implying that we now know something that we did not know before or about which we were wrong before. The very process in question, then, is a process in assertions, some of which are true, and some false, in a quite unambiguous sense.

Further, there is nothing in the recognition of process to suggest doubts as to absolute truth; in saying that a certain process occurs, we are saying that it absolutely occurs and that one phase of it absolutely gives place to another. Engels goes on to say that the dialectic philosophy he espouses "destroyed all theories of absolute truth, and of an absolute state of humanity corresponding with them. In face of it nothing final, absolute or sacred exists, it assigns mortality indiscriminately, and nothing can exist before it save the unbroken process of coming into existence and passing away, the endless passing from the lower to the higher, the mere reflection of which in the brain of the thinker it is. It has indeed also a conservative side, it recognises the suitability of a given condition of knowledge and society for its time and conditions, but only so far. This conservatism of this philosophical view is relative, its revolutionary character is absolute, the only absolute which it allows to exist." But here again it is clear that Engels is making absolute assertions at every point, and that the fact that nothing lasts for ever does not affect the fact that it absolutely exists, absolutely has or has not a given character, at a given time.

The assertion by Engels that "historicity" is itself absolute is a belated and partial recognition of the absoluteness of the assertions he is making. In his *Anti-Dühring* (*Landmarks*, Part I, ch. VI: "Eternal Truths"), he admits that there are a number of "truths of the last instance"—e.g., "that twice two is four, that the three angles of a triangle are equal to two right angles, that Paris is in France, that a man will die of hunger if he does not receive food"—though they are neither so many nor so important as "realists" like Dühring have supposed. But when Engels goes on to indicate truths of other sorts, he is quite unable to make good his distinction of the absolute from the relative. Thus, he says (p. 121), in the field of living organisms, "the changes and causalities are so complex that not only does the solution to each question bring about the rise of an unlimited number of new questions, but the solution to each of these separate new questions depends upon years, frequently centuries, of investigation and can then be only partially completed." This is quite irrelevant to the question of truth; how long it will take people to find out something, or how many other things they will not then have found out, does not affect the fact that what they do find out is something that is absolutely the case. Again, if "there are frequently discoveries like that of the cell which compel us to entirely revise all hitherto firmly established truth of the last instance in biology and to lay numbers of such truths aside for good and all", and if, on the side of social history, "when the intimate relations existing between a social and a political phenomenon come to be recognised, it is not, as a rule, perceived until the conditions are actually on the way to decay", and even if we could admit that "Knowledge is therefore entirely relative, since it is limited to a given people and a given epoch, and their nature under transitory social and political forms, when it examines relations and forms conclusions"—still this is all concerned with conditions of knowing, how we come to beliefs and how we may be led to give them up, and does not at all affect the question of truth. Incidentally, if only a given people at a given time can know certain things, this is not an argument for the "relativity" of knowing any more than of what is known; it merely shows that knowing has conditions. But it is worth noting that Engels presumes himself to be able to transcend historical limitations and to lay down a historical correlation which is absolute and not relative to his own epoch.

There is not, then, in his attempted distinctions, the slightest indication of what a "relative truth" might be. When he goes on to give a detailed example, the weakness of his theory is completely exposed. "Let us take, for example, the well-known Boyle's law, according to which, the temperature remaining the same, the volume of gas varies as the pressure to which it is subjected. Regnault discovered that this law does not apply in certain cases. If he had been a realist-philosopher he would have

MARXIST PHILOSOPHY (1935) 375

been obliged to say, 'Boyle's law is mutable, therefore it does not possess absolute truth, therefore it is untrue, therefore it is false'. He would thus have made a greater error than that which was latent in Boyle's law, his little particle of truth would have drowned in a flood of error; he would in this way have elaborated his correct result into an error compared with which Boyle's law with its particle of error fastened to it would have appeared as the truth. Regnault, scientist as he was, did not trouble himself with such childish performances. He investigated further and found that Boyle's law is only approximately correct, having no validity in the case of gases which can be made liquid by pressure when the pressure approaches the point where liquefaction sets in. Boyle's law therefore is shown only to be true within specific bounds. But is it absolute, a final truth of last instance within specific bounds? No physicist would say so. He would say that it is correct for certain gases and within certain limits of pressure and temperature, and even then within these somewhat narrow limits he would not exclude the possibility of a still narrower limitation or change in application as the result of further investigation" (pp. 125, 126). To which we could add, "and even then he would not exclude the possibility of a still narrower limitation", and so on until he did not exclude the possibility of there being nothing left of Boyle's law.

This *reductio ad absurdum* is the result of Engels's evasion, of his attempt to hold that Boyle's law both is and is not shown to be "true within specific bounds". But that phrase means nothing. The realist would be right in saying that Boyle's law has been shown to be false; and the most that Engels can say is that something like it is true. Boyle asserts that all gases have the property X; Regnault shows that this is false, but that *all gases within specific bounds* have the property X. In other words, a *different* proposition is true, not relatively but absolutely; it is not that a certain proposition has limited truth but that a limited subject has, absolutely, a certain predicate. And, whatever Engels may say about "further limitation", he must admit, as an absolute fact, that some gases under some conditions have the property X or he must say, as he does not wish to do, that Boyle was quite wrong about gases. Supposing, then, that there is a limitation A to be applied to Boyle's law, i.e., that all A-gases, and only those, are X, then if we believed that *all* gases are X, as Boyle said, we should not, in spite of the falsity of that belief, go wrong in our conclusions so long as all the gases we dealt with in our investigations happened to be A-gases. The false belief would lead to true conclusions as far as we went, and so would be *useful*. That is the most that can be meant by relative or approximate truth, but the fact remains that the conclusions themselves are taken as absolutely true, and the so-called relative truth is, in the same sense, absolutely false.

Lenin, who follows Engels closely in all his theories, equally fails to show how the same theory can find room for absolute and relative truths or how any sense whatever can be attached to the expression "relative truth". Thus he says (*Materialism and Empirio-Criticism*, p. 107) that "from the standpoint of modern materialism, or Marxism, the relative limits of our approximation to the cognition of the objective, absolute truth are historically conditioned; but the existence of this truth is unconditioned, as well as the fact that we are continually approaching it.... Every ideology is historically conditioned, but it is unconditionally true that to every scientific theory (as distinct from religion), there corresponds an objective truth, something absolutely so in nature." But the fact that an "ideology" is historically conditioned tells us nothing as to its truth. Historical conditions, let us say, cause A to believe X; in that case, the discussion of what has affected A is quite distinct from the discussion of X—though, indeed, either discussion can go on only by the making of unqualified assertions of fact. Lenin continues: "You will say that this distinction between relative and absolute truth is indefinite. And I will reply that it is sufficiently indefinite to prevent science from becoming dogmatic, in the bad sense of the word, from becoming dead, frozen, ossified; but it is at the same time sufficiently 'definite' to preclude us from espousing any brand of fideism or agnosticism, from embracing the sophistry and philosophical idealism of the followers of Hume and Kant. Here is a boundary which you have not noticed, and not having noticed it, you have fallen into the mire of reactionary philosophy. It is the boundary between dialectical materialism and relativism." But actually no distinction of any kind has been indicated; it has been said that some things are historically conditioned, and that some things are unconditionally true, but nothing has been said to show that these are not the very same things. The only relevant distinction is that between absolute truth and absolute falsity.

Lenin admits this distinction when he says (p. 104), "If you are not in a position to maintain that the proposition 'Napoleon died on May 5, 1821' is false, then you are practically acknowledging that it is true. If you do not assert that it can be refuted in the future, then you are acknowledging this truth to be eternal." But he still finds it possible to say that whereas, for Bogdanov, "the recognition of the relativity of our knowledge excludes the least admission of absolute truth, for Engels absolute truth is made up of relative truths". He does not attempt to show, however, and he could not show, what relative truths make up the absolute truth "Napoleon died on May 5, 1821", and how they make it up. It is to the credit of Engels and Lenin that they recognise that there are absolute truths, but they become involved in shifts and subterfuges when they try to combine this with the false view that there are relative truths.

A word may here be said about the view of Engels on moral truths; for, though the logical position is precisely the same, the moral question is so frequently raised and is found, in many quarters, so compelling an argument for relativity, that it is worth while showing the hollowness of Engels's arguments in this connection also. "From people to people, from age to age, there have been such changes in the ideas of good and evil that these concepts are contradictory in different periods and among different peoples. But someone may remark, 'Good is still not evil and evil is not good; if good and evil are confused all morality is abolished, and each may do what he will.' When the rhetoric is stripped away this is the opinion of Herr Dühring. But the matter is not to be disposed of so easily. If things were as easy as that there would be no dispute about good and evil. Everybody would know what was good and what was evil. How is it to-day, however? What system of ethics is preached to us to-day?" Having mentioned a number of systems, Christian, bourgeois and proletarian, Engels proceeds: "Which is the true one? No single one of them, regarded as a finality, but that system assuredly possesses the most elements of truth which promises the longest duration, which, existent in the present, is also involved in the revolution of the future, the proletarian" (*Landmarks*, p. 127).

So the greatest truth is possessed by that which is longest believed! No less curious than this type of proof is the inference, from *disagreements* about good and evil, that the distinction between the two is not absolute—in other words, that the disagreement is not about anything at all. It is obvious that Engels himself has no clear conception of morals; indeed, he goes on to show that he thinks of a moral position as expressed in commandments like "Thou shalt not steal". Now, if good means commanded and evil means forbidden, then, since different people command and forbid different things, it will appear that good and evil vary and that the same thing can be both good and evil. But what comes of the "disagreements" referred to? If A says "I command X" and B says "I forbid X", they are making statements which may both be true. It does not appear, then, what Engels could mean by "contradictory" moral concepts or by "an advance made in morals as a whole". In fact, his confusion rests in an ambiguous conception of good—in the relational sense of being wanted or commanded, and also in the sense of a positive quality of certain things. It is the prevalence of this unnoticed ambiguity, this confusion of quality and relation (a confusion which also comes out in Engels's reference to a passage from "lower" to "higher"), that is at the root of relativism in ethics.

We come now to the next important division of our subject. The theory of relative truth is connected in Marxist philosophy with a representational theory of knowledge; it is supposed that "our ideas" correspond to a greater or less degree with the "external reality" which has produced them in our minds. As Dietzgen puts it (quoted by Lenin, p.106), "How can a picture 'conform' with its model? Approximately it can. What picture worth the name does not agree approximately with its object? Every portrait is more or less of a likeness. But to be altogether alike, quite the same as the original—what a monstrous idea! We can only know nature and her parts relatively, since even a part, though only a relation of nature, possesses again the characteristics of the Absolute, the nature of the All-Existence which cannot be exhausted by knowledge." And, as Lenin reminds us (*Materialism and Empirio-Criticism*, p. 195) in his polemic against the symbolists, "Engels speaks neither of symbols nor of hieroglyphs, but of copies, photographs, images, mirror-reflections of things". There is no reason, of course, why this copy-theory should be combined, as Dietzgen combines it, with the perfectly correct admission that we never know "all about" any given thing; and there is nothing in the latter fact to suggest that the knowledge we do have is relative.

MARXIST PHILOSOPHY (1935) 379

But the copy-theory is completely false, as was clearly shown by Berkeley, whom Lenin discusses extensively without noticing this fact. Berkeley argues that, in order to show that "an idea" is a good or bad copy of "an external thing", we should have to know them both and compare them—but, of course, if we can know external things directly, then the whole picture-theory collapses. Actually, this realist line is not the one adopted by Berkeley; he goes on, indeed, to argue that our sensations represent acts of will in minds outside our own, though he certainly claims that we have *some* direct knowledge of acts of that kind, viz., in our own minds. But he has still shown the untenability of a representational theory, and the only way out is to admit a direct knowledge of actual things and to reject the whole theory of ideas.

Engels, whom Lenin here as elsewhere wholeheartedly supports, takes a curious way out of the difficulty. He refers (*Historical Materialism*, pp. 6, 7) to the agnostic who, while admitting that "all our knowledge is based upon the information imparted to us by our senses", asks "How do we know that our senses give us correct information of the objects we perceive through them?" and "proceeds to inform us that, whenever he speaks of objects or their qualities, he does in reality not mean these objects and qualities, of which he cannot know anything for certain, but merely the impressions which they have produced on his senses". (It may be remarked in passing, in accordance with Berkeley's argument, that the agnostic could not even say that "they", viz., what Engels calls "objects", are the causes of the representations or that there are any external causes at all—these points being actually made by Hume.) "Now", Engels goes on, "this line of reasoning is undoubtedly hard to beat by mere argumentation. But before there was argumentation, there was action. *Im Anfang war die That.* And human action had solved the difficulty long before human ingenuity invented it. The proof of the pudding is in the eating. From the moment we turn to our own use these objects, according to the qualities we perceive in them, we put to an infallible test the correctness or otherwise of our sense-perceptions. If these perceptions have been wrong, then our estimate of the use to which an object can be turned must also be wrong, and our attempt must fail. But if we succeed in accomplishing our aim, if we find that the object does agree with our idea of it, and does answer the purpose we intended it for, then that is positive proof that our perception of it and its qualities, *so far,* agree with reality outside ourselves." And Lenin (p. 83) on the above passage, remarks: "The materialist theory, then, the theory of reflection of objects by our mind, is here presented with perfect clearness: things exist outside of us. Our perceptions and representations are their images. The verification of these images, the distinction of true and false images, is given by practice."

But Engels has *not* shown how there could be any verification or falsification, any agreement or disagreement between one known entity (whether we call it "object" or "idea") and another. Either he has to admit direct knowledge of things and thus uproot the representational theory; or he has to take the view of Locke and Berkeley that "our idea" at any given time is just what we "have in mind" at that time—and so, while at a different time we naturally have something different in mind, no question of verification or falsification, and no issue as to something beyond our ideas, arises. That there *are* agreements and disagreements is due to the fact that what we have in mind at any time is that something is the case; i.e., something is taken as *being* an independent occurrence and not as "representing" one. Even if we were aware of something called a "representation", we should be aware of it as occurring, and there would be no question of that occurrence meaning any other occurrence—or of its being less "objective", less the case, than any other occurrence. Thus the Marxists, just like Berkeley, neglect the proposition (the statement of fact) as the object of any knowledge whatever, and, in taking their departure from "ideas", are unable logically to *arrive at* propositions and thus to have any coherent theory.

It is commonly supposed that a "correspondence" or representational theory is required to account for error, but what has been said indicates that it does not do so. If we have an "idea" which is unlike a thing, we are not in error unless we think the idea is *like* the thing, and in that case the thing as much as the idea is an immediate object to the mind; i.e., the position is exactly as when we consider the likeness or unlikeness of two things, and no question of "ideas" arises. Engels is quite right in believing that the explanation of error is to be found in the *practical* character of knowing, i.e., its occurrence as part of our manipulations of things, our *demands* that X should be Y, and the illusory satisfaction of some demands, our satisfaction that X is Y when actually it is not. A subsequent dissatisfaction, a falsified expectation, may then show us that we were mistaken (though, of course, it is also possible for us to have a *second* illusory satisfaction, as well as to be disappointed through supposing that what we wanted has not come to pass when actually it has). But such discoveries would not be possible unless we were dealing all the time with actual things; there could, as has been shown, be no way of "correcting" one idea by another, even if we could regard a corrected idea as any more actual than an uncorrected idea or any more capable of leading us beyond ideas.

Also, the fact that we get our knowledge, or make our mistakes, in the course of our demanding, is no reason for confusing the issues themselves (the propositions asserted) with our activity in raising these issues, as is done by Marx in the celebrated *Theses on Feuerbach*, e.g., in the first when he says that the reality should be conceived as human sense-activity or "praxis", and again in the last—"Philosophers have only interpreted the world differently, but the point is to change it." For, although it may be in acting on things (leaving aside for the moment the question of "the world") that we get our knowledge of them, the *theoretical* point is what is the case, not how we know it or what we are going to do, or have done, about it. It is understood, of course, that there can be a theory of our activities as well as of anything else, but this theory consists of assertions of what we actually do and not of the activities that were needed to *find out* what we actually do. That Marx remained committed to the representational theory with all its defects is shown in his statement, in the preface to the second edition of *Capital*, that on his view, as opposed to Hegel's, "the ideal is nothing else than the material world reflected by the human mind and translated into forms of thought". What these "forms of thought" can be except assertions of what is actually the case in the "material world" Marx does not indicate, but no more than Engels could he make a bridge between "thought" and "matter" once they had been separated.

Lenin, as we saw, speaks approvingly of Engels's criterion of "practice", but he too is unable to show how we can "find" that an object does or does not agree with our idea of it unless we have a way of knowing the object otherwise than by having an idea of it—in which case the "idea" becomes simply a different object, and just as much of a thing as the former. In trying to make the bridge, indeed, Lenin offers a variety of explanations, without appearing to be aware of their variety. He recognises that we cannot *infer* the existence of what is not "sensation" from the existence of "sensation", but he does not see that the only way out is to *deny* sensation—as copy or representative of "external reality". Hence he adopts a curious *dual* theory of knowledge, whereby we are presented at one and the same time with a sensation and a source of the sensation—though it is not explained how we know which is which, or why, if everything we know is of the form "A reflects B", we should regard B as having any more of an "objective existence" than A.

In considering the theory of Mach, Lenin says (pp. 101, 102): "We ask whether or not objective reality is assumed as given us, when we see red or perceive hard.... If one holds that it is not given, then he is relapsing, together with Mach, into subjectivism and agnosticism.... If one holds that it is given, then a certain philosophical doctrine necessarily follows. Such a doctrine has long since been worked out, namely, materialism. Matter is a philosophic category which refers to the objective reality given to man in his sensations—a reality which is copied, photographed and reflected by our sensations, but which exists independently of them." The doctrine of realism is, however, opposed to both these views; it asserts that we do not "see red or perceive hard" but perceive a red or hard thing, and it denies that "a philosophic category" is either necessary or sufficient to help us over from alleged "sensations" to things. And, as before, if we did perceive a "sensation", we should perceive it as a thing and we should not "assume as given" the substantiality of some other thing which served it as a "source".

Lenin appears not to see the difference between the statements which he juxtaposes (p. 100), "We recognise the objective reality which is given us in experience" (which can only mean that we recognise what we perceive as *things*) and "we recognise an objective and independent source of our sensations"; or again (p. 116) between "Matter is that which, acting upon our sense-organs, produces sensation" and "matter is the objective reality, given to us in sensation". The distinction between the two senses of "sensation", as the *knowing* of a thing and as a *copy* of a thing (a copy which somehow is not itself a thing but is produced in us by a thing), is one of the most important contributions to philosophy made by modern realism; but it is a contribution rendered possible by Berkeley's refusal to accept the "dual" knowledge of Locke, even if he retained the *relative* object, the "idea", instead of the independent object, the thing. In his endeavour to escape Berkeley's devastating criticism, Lenin not only has to equivocate as above but he has to say (p. 93) that "each one of us has observed innumerable times the simple and palpable transformation of the 'thing-in-itself' into the 'thing-for-us'. This transformation is cognition"; i.e., he has to say that we have *observed the uncognised* becoming cognised—a position comparable to that which he attributes (p. 125) to Feuerbach: "Feuerbach recognises the objectivity of natural law, of causality, reflected only approximately by human conceptions of order, law and so forth", i.e., Feuerbach recognises more than he recognises—unless he is more than human! The bridge is still unbuilt.

Similarly, when Lenin says (p. 101) that "in truth the Machians are subjectivists and agnostics, for they do not sufficiently trust the evidence of our sense-organs and are inconsistent in their sensationalism. They do not recognise objective reality as the source of our sensations. They do not see in sensations the true copy of this objective reality, thus coming into direct contradiction with natural science and opening the way to fideism" (the substitution of faith for knowledge), he does not see that, unless he drops all this talk about sources, copies and the like, he himself is closing the door to "objective reality" and opening the door to fideism. For it is only by an act of faith that we can say that "our sensations" *copy* objective reality, and we have as much (and as little) right to say with Berkeley that mind is the source of our sensations as to say that it is matter; we could not in fact say either, because we know the relation "being a source of" (like the relation "copying") only as a relation between perceived things. For this essential part of modern realistic doctrine the way was prepared by Kant, who, in spite of his confused theory of things themselves, recognised causality as a relation holding between phenomena, i.e., the things we perceive, recognised also that it is of such things that laws of nature hold, as against Locke's theory that these laws apply to the *sources* of "ideas", i.e., to something lying behind what we perceive. Yet the Marxists regard Kant as being further removed from an objectivist position than Locke, and Lenin (pp. 163, 164) treats the recognition of the "thing-in-itself" as an inconsistent *concession* on Kant's part to materialism and even to "naive realism". The difficulty is not solved by denying "a *radical* difference between the thing-in-itself and the phenomenon", and leaving a *relative* difference on the lines of the dual theory of knowledge, but by denying any distinction whatever and maintaining that what Kant calls "phenomena" *are* things themselves and that the conditions under which they fall are conditions of existence and not mere conditions of cognition.

The case is parallel to Marx's misinterpretation of Hegel, in the preface above referred to, where it is made to appear that Hegel regarded nature as reflecting "ideas" in the Lockian sense—though certainly the notion of reflection disfigures the Hegelian theory as it does the Marxist. This running back to Locke, which confuses all the Marxist accounts of the history of philosophy, is due not merely to Marx's undue pre-occupation with the "philosophers" of the French enlightenment who followed Locke, but also to the fact that the dual theory of knowledge goes with a dual theory of reality, a theory of self-subsistence as opposed to relative existence, of "matter" as an ultimate reality or object of faith—an animistic theory whereby, as Eastman indicates (in his excellent pamphlet, *The Last Stand of Dialectical Materialism*), the Marxists were able to persuade themselves that the universe was on their side—in short, an idealist doctrine, since idealism consists in recognising some Absolute (some bearer of capitals), whether we proceed to call it Mind or Matter or The Great Unknown. (It should be noted that Eastman regards the animistic character of Marxism as coming out in its taking a characteristic of the human mind, viz., *purposive action*, as what is ultimate in things. But the position is logically the same, however we describe the "ultimate reality"; because any ultimate must be taken as the "animating principle" of what is not ultimate, and our recognition of what *is* ultimate guarantees that we are "in tune with" it.)

It is to Lenin's credit that he brings these questions into sharp relief, and makes it impossible for anyone styling himself a Marxist to evade the logical issues. Thus he continually insists, following Engels, that there are two and only two fundamental tendencies in philosophy, materialism and idealism, and that any serious thinker must choose his side. "Starting from sensations", he says (p. 99), "it is theoretically possible to follow the line of subjectivism which leads to solipsism ('bodies are complexes or combinations of sensations'), or to follow the line of objectivism which leads to materialism (sensations are images of objects in the external world). The first viewpoint gives us agnosticism, and if we push it a little further, subjective idealism—for which there cannot be any objective truth. The second viewpoint gives us materialism, for which the recognition of the objective truth is essential." So (p. 20) he derides Valentinov, who considers kinship with Berkeley's views "no crime", with the remark "To confound two irreconcilable fundamental divisions in philosophy—really, what 'crime' is there?" In effect he agrees with Hume that Berkeley's arguments "admit of no answer and produce no conviction"—no conviction, i.e., in one who has chosen the materialist, the proletarian, side. But, of course, it is not true that the arguments of Berkeley admit of no answer (apart from the dogmatic assertion, "Matter exists"); it is not true that it is "theoretically possible" to proceed from the recognition of sensations to solipsism or agnosticism or the denial of objective truth; for the recognition of anything is the recognition of the objective truth of certain propositions, of actual facts, it is the recognition of complex occurrences, and only this understanding of the proposition, which Berkeley like any other philosopher has to use, can solve the philosophical problem—it cannot be solved by the postulation of any philosophical "essence", whether mind or matter.

That is the position of realism; if there are sensations, they exist objectively or as a matter of fact; if there are minds they exist as a matter of fact or have objective reality; and nothing can "exist more than", more objectively than, more essentially than, anything else. "Engels", says Lenin (p. 14), "sees this fundamental distinction" between materialists and idealists, "that while to the materialists nature is primary and spirit secondary, to the idealists the reverse is the case". To the realist, however, no such distinction between primary and secondary reality is possible, and minds are as "natural" as stones and trees. One thing that may possibly be meant by saying that (to take the more usual formulation) matter is prior to mind, is that other things existed at a time when minds did not exist. On that line Lenin (p. 60) quotes from Feuerbach the statement that "Natural science necessarily shows us, at least in its present state, that there was a time when conditions were not fit for the existence of man, when nature, the earth, was not yet the object of the human eye and mind, when, consequently, nature was absolutely devoid of any trace of a human being." But natural science could not show us anything of the kind unless it had been recognised, prior to that demonstration, that minds and non-minds exist equally *now*. No amount of natural science can affect the logical fact that at any time there exist a heterogeneity of things, and so we are no nearer discovering what the mysterious "matter" or primary reality is.

In answer to the contention that modern science is bringing about the "disappearance" of matter (i.e., its disappearance from physical theory—though, in any case, science is not competent to settle a logical question), Lenin says (p. 220) that "the sole 'property' of matter—with the recognition of which materialism is vitally concerned—is the property of being *objective reality*, of existing outside of our cognition". But objective reality, existence independently of being known, is characteristic of minds as of other things, and so, as far as Lenin has shown, *mind* might be matter. Moreover, he had previously quoted with approval, from Engels's criticism of Dühring (*Landmarks*, p. 66), the contention that "The unity of the universe does not consist in its existence, although its existence is a presumption of its unity, since it must first exist before it can be a unit. Existence beyond the boundary line of our horizon is an open question. The real unity of the universe consists in its materiality, and this is established, not by a pair of juggling phrases but by means of a long and difficult development of philosophy and natural science." The fact is that Engels and Lenin cannot say what "materiality" is, i.e., what is their primary reality; they can only say, arbitrarily, that it is not mind. A doctrine of a primary reality certainly leads to a monism (or doctrine of "the unity of the universe"), but, in doing so, it makes science impossible.

This was the position established by Parmenides, the first avowed monist, in the fifth century, B.C. He showed that, if we accept such an all-inclusive reality, we must deny everything else. A monist must deny all change and all differentiation; the One can have no history and no parts. For to say that it has a part is to assert the existence of the situation "X is a part of the One", to assert, i.e., the equal presence of X and the One in this situation and thus to take the One as simply one thing among others and no longer the totality of things. It is not true, as Burnet suggests, that a solution may be found by passing from a corporeal monism to an incorporeal monism; the One, however it may be characterised (strictly speaking it cannot be characterised at all, and thus the position of Parmenides, like that of Berkeley, can be refuted by a consideration of the plurality involved in the proposition—in any assertion or theory), is incompatible with history and plurality; and the only resort is the assertion of a thoroughgoing pluralism, the denial of a "universe" or totality of things, and the recognition of the existence anywhere and at any time of a heterogeneity of things, things of various characters of which "materiality", if it is a character at all (i.e., if it does mean more than existence), is only one.

Monism, then, fails as a philosophical theory, whether the One is regarded, with Hegel, as mental or, with the Marxists, as material; in any case, it commits us to a denial of history and the facts of experience, and renders meaningless whatever character is attributed to it. But, like Hegel, the Marxists have proposed to preserve both the facts and "the unity of the universe" by introducing the contradiction between them into the "universe" itself; they give it a history by making "contradiction" the actual moving-force of its development. Thus we have the "dialectic", which Marx said he had freed from the mystification of Hegel, but which is as much of a mystification in the one theory as in the other. Dühring is right, of course, notwithstanding Engels's castigation of him, in holding that there can be no contradiction in reality. If two propositions contradict one another, that indicates that one of the two is false, that in one of them what is asserted *is not the case*; and it is only by means of ambiguity or plain error that either Hegelians or Marxists have made it appear that contradictories can both be actual facts.

Engels attacks Dühring's statement that "there are no contradictions in things" by saying: "This statement will have for people of average common sense the same self-evident truth as to say that straight cannot be crooked nor crooked straight. But the differential calculus shows in spite of all the protests of common sense that under certain conditions straight and crooked are identical, and reaches thereby a conclusion which is not in harmony with the commonsense view of the absurdity of there being any identity between straight and crooked" (*Landmarks*, p. 150). The calculus is certainly a curious instrument in the hands of Engels; but the most that could be meant by saying that it shows that "under certain conditions straight and crooked are identical" is that *some straight things are crooked*. Now, if this is true, it means that the commonsense view that "straight cannot be crooked", i.e., *no straight things are crooked*, is false; it does not mean that straightness and crookedness are at once compatible and incompatible. Neither calculus or anything else will enable Engels to prove this, which would be a real contradiction.

But the outstanding example, to which Engels immediately goes on, is that of motion. "Motion is itself a contradiction since simple mechanical movement from place to place can only accomplish itself by a body being at one and the same moment in one place and simultaneously in another place, by being in one and the same place and yet not there. And motion is just the continuous establishing and dissolving the contradiction" (p. 151). Again this is a mere misstatement (besides introducing the fresh mystery of "dissolving" a contradiction, which appears to mean getting back to commonsense consistency, with the suggestion that there is something not quite right about a contradiction after all). There is a sense in which it may be said that a thing is in two places at the same time, if its stretch covers both places, but there is no sense in which it can be said that a thing is both at a place and not there. If we seriously mean either assertion, we do not mean the other. Engels falls into the old Pythagorean confusion about "moments" as minimum times at which something can happen; actually, moments are the boundaries of durations, and while we can say that a thing is at a place *up to* a certain moment and is not there *from* that moment (in which case, of course, there is no contradiction), we cannot say that it is at a place at a moment—it is just the contradiction that would then arise that forces us to the other view, and the forcing of this conclusion, i.e., of the recognition of the real nature of continuity, is the important outcome of Zeno's "dialectic". In the same way, in his remarks on differentiation and integration, Engels commits himself to the conception of the "infinitesimally small", i.e., that which both has and has not magnitude, and remains ignorant of the mathematical theory of limits which settles the whole question in a positive and non-contradictory way. The fact is that, just as in Zeno's paradoxes, the contradiction is between the rationalist assumption of the elementary, unitary or primary, and the empirical recognition of historical facts; and the solution is to *reject* rationalist assumptions and not attempt to combine opposing views in a single theory—just as in the attempt to combine "truths of the last instance" and "relative truths".

Indeed, it is impossible to be thorough-going with this theory of contradictions, for when the upholder of common sense says that the "dialectic" theory is *false*, the dialectician has to meet him with perfectly straightforward contradiction and say that it is *true* and that the commonsense view is false. Thus Bernstein (cited by Plekhanov, *Fundamental Problems of Marxism*, p. 111) is right when he rejects the formula "Yes is No and No is Yes", and Plekhanov is wrong when he supports it, even with all the authority of Heraclitus (who does not deserve the honour), Hegel and Marx. Plekhanov follows Engels on motion, and he deals in a similar way with the question of becoming. Now if we imagine that, between a thing's being X and its (previously) not being X, there is a period when it is becoming X, then not only shall we have to say that in this period it is neither X nor not X (which also means that it is both) but we shall be faced with the problem of how the transition is made between the period of absence of X and that in which its absence is its presence (the period of its "prabsence", as we might say), and we shall have to invent a further intervening period, and so on. In actual fact, then, we have to reject such intervening periods altogether, and to recognise, as before, that up to a point the quality was absent and from that point it was present. The difficulty of where to draw the line, as in Plekhanov's example of when a man has grown a beard, is quite irrelevant here; because as regards any given amount of hair, there is a point up to which it is not present and from which it is present; and how much hair we call "a beard" is a linguistic, not a logical question. There is no greater logical difficulty in dealing with the contention of Engels (*Landmarks*, p. 43) that it is impossible "to fix the precise moment of death, for physiology shows that death is not a single and sudden event but a very slow process". Physiology could not show this unless it could say when a body is dead and when it is not dead, and, if such statements can be correctly made, then there is a moment up to which it is not dead and from which it is dead. There may be a phase of life which regularly ends at that point, a process which we can call "dying", but even so there will still be a point of death. It is interesting to note, then, that Engels cannot even state his paradoxes coherently.

Lenin, as usual, goes to the root of the matter and brings up (p. 325) the Hegelian contention that the proposition itself involves a contradiction. "One's first impression about the judgment", Hegel is quoted as saying (in the "Logic" from the *Encyclopædia of the Philosophical Sciences*), "is the *independence* of the two extremes, the subject and the predicate." However, Hegel goes on, "it shows a strange want of observation in the logic-books, that in none of them is the fact stated that in *every* judgment there is such a statement made as the *individual* is the *general*, or, still more definitely, *the subject is the predicate* (for instance, God is absolute spirit). No doubt the notions of individuality, universality, subject and predicate, are also quite different, but it remains none the less true in general that every judgment is really a statement of identity." Lenin rightly maintains that the dialectic would have no foundation if it could not be shown in this way that contradiction runs through everything, though he does not observe that in that case nothing is left of even those few absolute truths which Engels and he distinguish from relative truths.

But the attempt to show that the proposition itself is contradictory misses the point that contradiction can only be between propositions, and betrays the fact that some "essence" prior to the proposition (and thus "unspeakable") has been postulated. As regards the proposition itself, if we say, as we do, that subject and predicate are distinct, we can also say that they are connected; there is no contradiction in that. But if we say that they are distinct and also not distinct, we are talking nonsense. There is in fact no identity in the case (except that of the "proposed" situation) just as there is no "is of identity"—though, if there were, it would still be impossible to amalgamate it with another "is of distinction", and to take the proposition in either sense, just as we liked. In making an assertion, then, we are not identifying different notions; we are saying that a thing of a certain sort is at the same time of a certain other sort—and there is nothing paradoxical about that. (Incidentally, Lenin hardly helps his case by speaking of the "transformation" of the particular into the general, which could only mean that something particular and not general came to be general and not particular. Such mishaps are bound to befall the "materialist" when he tries to work with "notions".)

The whole position being erroneous, then, all the further examples of "contradictions" are bound to be erroneous too.

In speaking (*Landmarks*, p. 98) of "the contradiction between the innumerable mass of germs which nature produces in such prodigality and the slight number which can manage to reach maturity", Engels indicates no contradiction whatever; the only thing contradicted is the expectation (if anyone has it) that all germs will reach maturity, i.e., a person so expecting would simply be wrong. When we speak of a struggle for existence or of any other struggle, we imply that a result which would be reached if a given factor were not present in the situation, will not be reached since it is present; but again there is no contradiction in that. And similarly with the alleged contradictions, of which so much is heard, in social affairs. What is shown is not progress by contradictions, not the "negation of negation" (of which Engels gives so many laughable examples), but simple cause and effect, the operation of different factors in the social situation, in the ways in which such factors do operate and in accordance with the other factors with which they come in contact—matters which, if they are known at all, are known as unqualified facts.

Engels asserts (*Landmarks*, p. 183) that "the productive forces of the modern capitalistic mode of production as well as the system of distribution based upon it are in glaring contradiction to the mode of production itself and to such a degree that a revolution in the modes of production and distribution must take place which will abolish all class differences or the whole of modern society will fall". But there is still no contradiction here. Engels recognises as a fact the present coexistence of a number of social forces; he maintains that they cannot continue to coexist—a conclusion he can have reached only by specific consideration of social processes, of how the forces in question do work; and he considers that the outcome will be of one or other of two forms, thus showing uncertainty as to the existence or mode of operation of certain further forces. All this is positive, not "dialectical", theory. So when Marx (*Capital*; quoted by Engels, p. 163) declares that "Capitalism becomes an impediment to the methods of production developed with and under it. The concentration of the means of production and the organisation of labour reach a point where they come into collision with their capitalist covering. It is broken. The hour of capitalist private property strikes. The expropriators are expropriated", he is asserting that recognisable social forces operate in recognisable ways; he is making a social prediction, drawing a conclusion from given premises; he is not exhibiting the "negation of negation", not showing, i.e., that all processes are divisible into three phases of which the first and third share some character not possessed by the second. And even if that were the case, it would not show (as Engels himself naively indicates) that there is only one way of "negating the negation", only one possible third phase after a given first and second; and it most emphatically would not show that the third is the first "raised to a higher power", a Hegelism which means nothing at all as a description of an actual occurrence.

In fact, any specific prediction must be based on the operation of specific forces and has no basis in any general conception of "the universe", of a whole reality which somehow manages to reach "higher" and "higher" forms. The history of society is the history of certain specific activities going on in a certain environment which in turn is further environed, and so on. This pluralistic position does not show that correct prediction is impossible. Our predictions must be based not only a knowledge of certain "general laws" but on the recognition of certain "collocations", and we are capable of being wrong about each of these—about the way in which things we know act, and about what other things they will come in contact with. For there is no contradiction in the fact that the same thing will act differently under different conditions, though we can know this only by recognising such forms of action, by believing that they (absolutely) take place—and, of course, by acting on them ourselves. And this brings out the point that we are also capable of being *right* about the facts relevant to a certain prediction. The general possibility of error or ignorance, then, is nothing against our predicting; we do predict, sometimes rightly, and we cannot help doing so. Thus if we find, as a fact, that capitalism brings about conditions which will themselves bring about the end of capitalism, we do so by observation of social activities and not of "the unity of the universe"; we do so, indeed, whether we realise it or not, by taking a pluralistic or commonsense view of the operation of things. And we do so none the less if we find activities of our own to be part of the conditions referred to.

Here we may briefly mention the views of Engels on freedom. "Freedom", he says (*Landmarks*, p. 147), "does not consist in an imaginary independence of natural laws but in a knowledge of these laws and in the possibility thence derived of applying them intelligently to given ends." But he does not tell us on what law the *applying* is dependent. Again in *Feuerbach* (pp. 95, 96) he says that, when materialism has turned the dialectic right side up, it "became reduced to knowledge of the universal laws of motion—as well of the outer world as of the thought of man—two sets of laws which are identical as far as matter is concerned but which differ as regards expression, in so far as the mind of man can employ them consciously, while, in nature and, up to now, in human history, for the most part they accomplish themselves unconsciously in the form of external necessity, through an endless succession of apparent accidents". But what difference it makes to a law when it is "employed consciously" (or how it can be differently "expressed"—or "reflected") is something that Engels does not and cannot explain—the fact being that minds are different sorts of things from non-minds and thus act in different ways, though equally deterministically, while at the same time they have features in common with various other things and thus also act in *common* ways. Such ways of acting are not inferable from or reducible to "universal laws of motion", even under the special condition of being "consciously employed".

It should be evident that, in spite of the confusions into which the leading Marxist philosophers fall, their doctrines contain much that is sound. They do recognise the causal determination of things, they reject the view that things other than minds exist in dependence on minds, and, above all, they recognise that all things are events or processes, interacting with other processes. But the advantages of this historical position are lost through the conception of the ultimate reality, "matter", and of a moving totality of things; and the development on this basis of a theory of "dialectic" which was applied to the workings of society has been a serious hindrance to the theoretical consolidation of the sound social observations which the Marxist school has made and which place that school, with all its defects, far in advance of any other body of social thinkers. Again, the doctrine of relative truth (especially in the form of the vicious conception of "reflection") has done untold harm to the study of scientific and artistic activity. The confusion which these doctrines have wrought comes out most strikingly, however, in the teleological conception of society which is inherent in the treatment of social history as part of a postulated "universal history". On this assumption, the doctrine that the proletarian movement has "history" on its side comes to mean that it has the *universe* on its side—a doctrine which, in spite of the Marxist theophobia (a phobia which leads Lenin, in particular, to scent out God in every view to which he is opposed), is of an essentially theological or, as Eastman says, an animistic character. Whereas what should be meant is that it has *society*, or the more permanent features of society, on its side—a position which, as has been seen, could be arrived at only by social observation and not by philosophy.

It may be argued, in this connection, that such a faith in the cooperation of ultimate powers will induce an element of fanaticism without which far-reaching social changes cannot be brought about; that the belief that things are working with them, and that they possess a "truth" from which their enemies are debarred, will kindle and keep alight men's revolutionary ardour. No one else, indeed, has stressed so much as the Marxists the fact that society does not proceed by sweet reasonableness, but they would strongly oppose the supposition that an effective social movement must be definitely anti-intellectualist in character; and it seems to me to be a false view. I should rather contend, in line with what I consider to be the only sound theory of ethics, that, as a good way of life is one in which productive forces fight for their continuance and extension and in which they are allied in their scientific, artistic and industrial manifestations (in the progress of what may be broadly called culture or civilisation), so the development of a pluralistic or "free-thinking" philosophy must harmonise with the general movement for a producer's society, and the latter can only gain from the removal of philosophical errors, the rejection of monistic and teleological conceptions. "Dialectic", like any other theory postulating an ultimate reality, is necessarily authoritarian or "fideist", to use Lenin's term; and it is already sufficiently obvious that the conception of "contradictions", of something which can both be and not be, is admirably adapted to the purposes of an unscrupulous and corrupt leadership. The struggle against the corruption of the movement for social revolution, for the establishment of a society of producers, is thus, in my view, linked with the struggle against "dialectic".

And here a concluding point may be made. Recognising the falsity of the theory of relative truth, recognising that theory can progress only by the raising of specific issues, by the asking of the quite unambiguous question, "Is it true?", we can still see that there is a connection between a man's social views and his philosophical views, and that any fetishism, of matter, mind or anything else, is connected with the acceptance of some authority, some established social power as representative of "the nature of things". The element of fetishism in the philosophy we have examined, then, may well be bound up with the fact of its development in a capitalistic society, and the persistence of that element may be taken as indicating a constant danger of reaction. Indeed, recent events in the Communist movement show that this is more than a possibility; the cult of Stalin, the fetishism of "Socialism in one country", the neglect of real historical processes in the blind belief that "history is on our side", with the collapse of the Communist International in the face of Hitler as its most striking consequence—these are among the more and less important indications of a movement away from a producers' society. But they are not a growth of the immediate past alone. The neglect of the real history of philosophy in favour of a fancied culmination in "materialism", the attempted fixing for all time of the philosophical errors of Engels, the ranking of all the works of the masters as "sacred books"—these are phenomena which, in the case especially of so able a social thinker as Lenin, must give us pause and must show us once for all the untenability of any single-line conception of social or philosophical progress.

It will be a sign of renewed progress, then, when we see revolutionists divesting themselves of the idealistic elements in their philosophy and embracing a consistent realism. Meanwhile, it is the philosopher's business to be realistic, to attack idealism wherever he finds it, to consider constantly *what is the case*. In so doing, he will find himself co-operating with those, be they few or many, who take a realistic view of society. His rejection of idealism will, of course, preserve him from any cheaply optimistic expectation of support, and, as we have seen, he would be utterly unphilosophical if he acquiesced in an idealistic movement in the hope that it would give opportunities for being realistic later on—here or nowhere is his reality. But he will be strengthened in his task if he finds his activity to be part of a producers' movement, and he may even find a measure of encouragement in recent setbacks to that movement in that he will no longer be tempted to think that it can roll on without him but will rather see his intellectual levelling as an integral part of social levelling.[2]

---

[2] (v. s., p. 186.)

# 27
# MARXIST ETHICS (1937)

That Marxism is a *Metaphysic*, a doctrine of guiding principles, a mingling of logic and ethics to the detriment of both, is shown by its conception of the advance of things to "higher" and "higher" levels, its belief in a world which, as Eastman puts it,[1] is evolving "by its own inevitable dialectic" toward something "higher", toward something "more magnificent". There is dispute as to whether Marx and Engels *intended* to dispense with philosophy and ethics in favour of their science of society, though, indeed, it is only by an implicit recognition of positive truth and positive goodness that even the term "higher" can appear to have any meaning. But it may be questioned in the first place, whether they can have any logical or ethical theory, whether any instrumentalism, treating truth and goodness as alike relative, alike approximate realisations of purpose, can stand examination—if only into its own truth. No doubt, it may be called a philosophy, in that it suggests answers to certain philosophic problems, but the question is whether it can ever be stated consistently.

The nature of the guiding principles, and of the relation which social theory can be supposed to have to philosophy and ethics, is indicated by Engels in the following way. The developments in science and the social struggles of the early part of the nineteenth century, he argues,[2] "made imperative a new examination of all past history, and then it was seen that *all* past history was the history of class struggles, that these warring classes of society are always the product of the modes of production and exchange, in a word, of the *economic* conditions of their time; that therefore the economic structure of society always forms the real basis from which, in the last analysis, is to be explained the whole

---

[1] Max Eastman, *Marx, Lenin and the Science of Revolution*, pp. 87,8. The particular references, as is indicated in the same author's *Last Stand of Dialictical Materialism* (p. 24), are to Marx's *Civil War in France* (p. 34, Postgate's edition) and to Engels's *Anti-Dühring* (p. 32, translation by Emile Burns; Moscow, 1934.)

[2] *Anti-Dühring*, pp. 32,4. Many other passages from Marx and Engels could, of course, be cited in this connection.

superstructure of legal and political institutions, as well as of religious, philosophical and other conceptions of each historical period". It might be considered that this economic interpretation applies only to the genesis of philosophical and ethical theories and has no bearing on their truth, that it is not in itself a philosophical or ethical theory, or any substitute for one—though, even so, one might question the interpretation so long as "the last analysis" was not forthcoming. But Engels would permit of no such distinction; for him the truth of the conceptions precisely resides in their relation to the basis. As he says elsewhere (*Feuerbach*, Kerr edition, pp. 6–8), in discussing "the revolutionary side of Hegel's philosophy", its "great foundation thought" (of the world as made up of processes in which "there is carried out in the end a progressive development"), "has, particularly since the time of Hegel, so dominated the thoughts of the mass of men that, generally speaking, it is now hardly denied. And if one proceeds steadily in his investigations from this historic point, then a stop is put, once and for all, to the demand for final solutions and for eternal truths; one is firmly conscious of the necessary limitations of all acquired knowledge, of its hypothetical nature, *owing to the circumstances under which it has been gained*" (my italics). And he goes on to say that: "One cannot be imposed upon any longer by the inflated insubstantial antitheses of the older metaphysics of true and false, good and evil, identical and differentiated, necessary and accidental; one knows that these antitheses have only a relative significance, that that which is recognised as true now, has its concealed and later-developing false side, just as that which is recognised as false, its true side, by virtue of which it can later on prevail as the truth; that so-called necessity is made up of the merely accidental, and that the acknowledged accidental is the form behind which necessity conceals itself and so on."

It is clear enough that Engels does not consider that this doctrine of his "has its concealed and later-developing false side", but is putting it forward as absolutely true; otherwise, anything might transpire, even the reinstatement of the "older metaphysics", in the further development of thought. But this is only an illustration of the impossibility of making anything of the "relative significance" of any antithesis or conditioned view; if it is not to remain utterly vague, if its "limitations" are to be indicated, an absolute, not a relative, statement must be made. It appears also that, on this view, there will be a confounding not merely of logic and ethics but of all theories whatsoever; they will all rank as expressions of the basis, and even if (as is not the case) there could still be distinctions of degree, it would only be degrees of expressiveness, and what was legal and what political, what religious and what philosophical, would not appear.

There is no ground, then, for Sidney Hook's distinction between the philosophies of Hegel and Marx in that while, for the former, "values were objectively grounded in the nature of things so that he could delude himself into believing that his philosophy was disinterested and free from any presuppositions", the latter "denied that any philosophy as normative inquiry could be disinterested and frankly avowed his own presuppositions and bias" (*From Hegel to Marx*, p. 26). The difference is only in the norms selected, in the things chosen as "most expressive", and, while the one choice is as arbitrary as the other, the expression is supposed to be real in either case. This becomes still clearer as Hook proceeds. "When Marx speaks of philosophy he is referring to ethical, political or social philosophy[3] and the metaphysical disguises in which they often masquerade. That is why he speaks of philosophical method as criticism [throughout his Critique of Hegel's *Rechtsphilosophie*]. It is a criticism which reveals the values and attitudes, the starting point and secret wishes of our thought. It is a sociology of values investigating the social roots and conditions of what human beings desire. It is not an axiology of values deducing what human beings *ought* to do from self-evident first principles. Philosophy, then, is a criticism of standpoints and methods in the light of the conditions under which they emerge and the purposes which they serve." But Hegel's *Phenomenology* is precisely a criticism of standpoints in so far as they serve the purpose of organising experience, and

[3] What should be said is that for Marx, philosophy *is* social. "The modern conception of philosophy as an analysis of the fundamental categories of space, time, implication, etc.", Hook tells us, "would have been regarded by Marx, at least, as no part of philosophy proper but as problems in the logic of science". Engels, however, in the *Anti-Dühring*, treats them as problems of the dialectic philosophy. The view that this is a "deviation" from Marx's views is cogently refuted by Eastman (*Last Stand*). But, apart from that, Hook himself says, on the very next page, that "against those who would restrict criticism to a consideration of technical philosophy, Marx argues that since *every philosophy* has its material presuppositions, a truly radical criticism must involve changing the material conditions which are at its basis" (my italics). And it is perfectly clear from Hook's account of the "Theses of Feuerbach", later in the book, that Marx is presenting his social view of philosophy, not his view of social philosophy.

his *Logic* is an exposition of the various organising principles or categories as progressive representations of "the Idea". And it is as such representations also that the various institutions and conditions of society appear in his ethical and historical works. Even, therefore, if Marx's class theory is sounder socially, there is no difference on the philosophical side, no difference in "objectivity"; the difference is only in what the two force on philosophy as "higher", more expressive of reality. The common error lies in the treatment of philosophy as normative, of truth as relative, as degree of adequacy, and the doctrine of "class ideologies" is in no better case than any other relativistic theory.

What "light", we may ask, do their conditions and purposes cast on standpoints and methods? Is anything more in question than the fact that they have these conditions and purposes? And is this not a matter of objective truth—A brings about B, X does not bring about Y? The question is evaded by the introduction of "needs". "The new philosophy will triumph, not merely because it represents objective truth in the Pickwickian sense in which truth is relevant to ultimate questions of value, but because it fulfils the *needs* of human beings and the social conditions which generate those needs" (p. 27). In Marx's own words, "Theory becomes realised in a people only in so far as it is the realisation of its needs". This, however, does not at all affect the question of objective truth, not in a "Pickwickian" sense but in the straightforward sense of what is the case. If Marx means that a people thinks what it needs to think, still it does think that and think it true. If he means that it thinks that something is what it needs, again the question is whether that *is* what it needs. And, if the latter is the meaning, it becomes pointless to say that "Each class develops an ideology which it holds to be objectively true, and around which it seeks to rally society at large"; for there would be nothing to hinder *all* ideologies from being objectively true, though there might be something to hinder all classes from having their needs satisfied. But, if the former is the meaning, there need be no conflict between classes except a difference of opinion. It would appear that it is by a confusion of the two meanings that ideology is being substituted for truth, relativism for positive philosophy.

The philosophy of "needs" secures readiest acceptance in its ethical application, since relative theories have always prevailed in this field and positive ethics receives little recognition even now. It is not surprising that under those circumstances there is a widespread doubt whether there is such a subject as ethics. But, in Marx's case, the doubt as to whether his views permitted of ethics could too readily be extended to a doubt of the possibility of his having a philosophy, and Hook maintains that it is wrong to say that he had no place for any ethics in his philosophy of social activity. "For Marx no social life is possible without human consciousness. And there is no characteristically *human* consciousness without ethical ideals of some kind. But Marx went on to inquire what the source of these ideals is, when, why and where they change, and what provided relative justification of any ideal in the present.... Against the abstract morality of Kant and Christ, Marx held that ethics represents a series of demands, not a series of demonstrations or intuitions. His ethics is a class ethics. The ethics which were opposed to it were also, he maintained, class ethics. Peel their pseudological husk away and the kernel will be found to be a concrete class need. It is inevitable that each class consider its ethical demands as absolute: it is not inevitable that it pretend that these demands are impartial or universal. Behind class rights are class needs" (p. 51).

Once more the question of objective truth is covered over in a flood of words, but Hook's verbal dexterity fails to make good the claim that Marx has an ethics. What, we may ask, can Hook possibly mean by a class "considering its ethical demands as absolute"? How does it know which are its ethical demands? Are they those which have binding force? In that case Hook is saying that a class considers that those of its demands which have binding force have binding force. There is no evidence that there is any such species of demands, or that "ideals" are different from any other object of demand; in fact, without the recognition of a *quality* of goodness, there can be no distinction between the ethical and the non-ethical.[4] But if there is such a character of things, then the question whether a certain thing is good will be a question of

---

[4] Cf. Hook, p. 58: "The natural object (as distinct from thing), the esthetic object, the ethical object, the economic object, are in a sense *objectifications* of human purpose." Not only can Hook not show how, for Marx, these types of object can be distinguished, but he quite fails to show, as against Eastman, that Marx distinguishes the natural object from the thing. In the second thesis on Feuerbach (Hook, p. 281), Marx says: "The question whether human thought can achieve objective truth is not a question of theory but a *practical* question." This would not be so if the thing were different from the "natural object" (what we use).

fact, of objective truth, no matter what anybody demands or what class he belongs to. The use of expressions like "ideals" enables Marxists, in Eastman's phrase, to "straddle the issue", to adhere to their relativism while at the same time *suggesting* a positive quality which ethical objects have.

It is to be understood that the "abstract ethics", to which exception is taken, is of a relativist character, and that Marxism rightly draws attention to the weakness of the attempt to erect "absolutes" of duty or interest, to specify what is "absolutely commanded" or "absolutely desirable". But, because of the relativism in Marxism itself, the exposure can never be thorough, and we find not only fundamental ambiguities, but traces of the very doctrines that have been rejected, running right through Marxist discussions of ethics. The issues are particularly well illustrated in a passage in the *Anti-Dühring* (pp. 108, 109),[5] in which the doctrine of eternal moral truths is attacked. "The conceptions of good and bad", says Engels, "have varied so much from nation to nation and from age to age that they have often been in direct contradiction to each other. But all the same, someone may object, good is not bad and bad is not good; if good is confused with bad, there is an end to all morality, and everyone can do or leave undone whatever he cares. This is also, stripped of his oracular phrases, Herr Dühring's opinion. But the matter cannot be so simply disposed of. If it was such an easy business there would certainly be no dispute at all over good and bad; everyone would know what was good and what was bad." And, having shown that this is not so by pointing to the three types of moral theory held by "the three classes of modern Society, the feudal aristocracy, the bourgeoisie and the proletariat", Engels triumphantly concludes that "men, consciously or unconsciously, derive their moral ideas in the last resort from the practical relations on which their class position is based—from the economic relations in which they carry on production and exchange"; and, while none of the class moralities has "absolute validity", the proletarian is awarded the palm as that which "contains the maximum of durable elements" and so "represents the future".

---

[5] I discussed the passage briefly in my article, "Marxist Philosophy"; *A.J.P.P.*, March, 1935. The reference there was to the Kerr edition, entitled *Landmarks of Scientific Socialism* (translation by Austin Lewis): v. s., pp. 298,9.

MARXIST ETHICS (1937) 403

It is, of course, a piece of effrontery on Engels's part to suggest that the drawing of an absolute distinction between good and bad implies that it is "easy" to determine what is good and what is bad. Men distinguished absolutely between flat and round, but did not find it easy to establish the roundness of the earth. It was, however, just because they made a definite, and not a relative, distinction, that they were able to dispute about the earth's shape. But Engels seems to imply that the fact that men disagree about goodness means that they are talking about different things, that their class position (or, more generally, their economic position) determines not merely what they consider to be good but what they mean by good. On this view, all the "theories" would be on different subjects, and there would be no reason for calling them all "moral" theories. But, in that case also, there would be no reason why they should not all be eternally true, even if they are not eternally believed—why X should not always be what the bourgeoisie means by "good" (whatever that may be) and Y always be what the proletariat means by "good". If, however, the theories are on the same question—so that there really are disagreements—if it is merely that economic relations lead men to attach the definite predicate, good, to different subjects, then, as was noted above, this account of the genesis of ethical beliefs does not affect the question of ethical truths at all (and cannot, incidentally, determine whether they are or are not "eternal"). It can never be *evidence* for the proposition "Y is good" to say "I believe it is, because I am a proletarian"—or, again, to say that people are going to believe it in the future. But, even if it were, it would be evidence for an ethical fact.

Engels's "straddling of the issue", then, seems to take the form of arguing that there are ethical theories but no ethical facts. We can come closer to the crux of the matter by considering the contention attributed to an objector that, if good is confused with bad, everyone can do as he pleases. This has force only if by "good" is meant what is to be done and by "bad" what is not to be done; otherwise, even if good and bad were qualitatively distinguished, a person might do what he pleased, and, if they were not, he might regulate his conduct by some other distinction. Now, no one will deny that policies, demands, "needs", vary with conditions of life—and it might readily be admitted that there are no eternal needs. That this is Engels's own line of argument is shown by the example he proceeds to give, that the moral law, "Thou shalt not steal", must exist in all societies in which there is private property, but that "in a society in which the motive for stealing has been done away with... the teacher of morals would be laughed at who tried solemnly to proclaim the eternal truth: Thou shalt not steal!" In other words, the assertion that stealing is bad is a form of exhortation, and, where there is no need to steal, there is no need to exhort people not to steal. But what is "moral" about all this, what distinguishes moral "needs" from other needs, moral "truths" from other truths? The fact is that the term "need" covertly conveys the suggestion of living *better*, that, along with the amalgamation of logic and ethics (and the sciences generally), goes an attempt to get the advantages of the independent recognition of positive goodness.

This is made still clearer as Engels proceeds. Rejecting the "dogma" of an eternal moral law, while himself maintaining the dogma of a "last analysis" according to which moral theories are the product of the economic stage of society, he says: "And as society has hitherto moved in class antagonisms, morality was always a class morality; it has either justified the domination and the interests of the ruling class, or, as soon as the oppressed class has become powerful enough, it has represented the revolt against this domination and the future interests of the oppressed. *That in this process there has on the whole been progress in morality, as in all other branches of human knowledge, cannot be doubted.* But we have not yet passed beyond class morality. A *really human morality* which transcends class antagonisms and their legacies in thought becomes possible only at a stage of society which has not only overcome class contradictions but has even forgotten them in practical life" (my italics). What, on a relative theory, can be meant by "progress in morality"? Does it mean a change in approvals which can itself be approved, the emergence of more demandable demands, more necessary needs? And is there not implied here an absolute necessity by which relative necessities are to be measured? This is, in fact, the position; those needs have greatest force which come nearest to "historic necessity". Progress consists in advance towards a postulated Absolute, reality's, or, on the Marxist theory, Society's, realisation of itself, the establishment of *true society* (Socialism), of the true condition of humanity. "Scientific Socialism" reveals itself as Hegelian metaphysics, with the substitution of Society for the Idea. But since, short of the attainment of the Absolute, we are left with the merely comparative, with degrees of adequacy, it must always be purely arbitrary to say whether and what progress has been made. The recognition of progress, in fact, depends on an implicit admission of a positive goodness which runs counter to the whole theory of "needs" or any other moral relativism.

The Marxists, however, do not see the ambiguity of their position, but remain committed to an unscientific ethics of an evolutionist and rationalist character. The confusions of evolutionary ethics have been forcibly demonstrated by Moore, who shows, in *Principia Ethica*, that its supporters not merely hold both that "better" simply means "more evolved" (or *later*) and that evolution is producing something better, but actually take the former as a *reason* for holding the latter. But what makes it particularly hard for the Marxists to see these confusions is the complicating factor of their Hegelian rationalism, of their taking the later as nearer to the true or rational conditions of affairs.[6] This is the "scientific" basis of their optimism. From a scientific standpoint, says Engels (*Anti-Dühring*, p. 170), the "appeal to morality and justice does not help us an inch further; to economic science, moral indignation, however justifiable, cannot serve as an argument, but only as a symptom. The task of economic science is rather to show the social abuses[7] which are now developing as necessary consequences of the existing mode of production, but at the same time also as the indications of its imminent dissolution; and to reveal, within the already dissolving economic form of motion, the elements of the future new organisation of production and exchange which will put an end to those abuses." Or again, as Kautsky has it (*Ethics and the Materialist Conception of History*; Kerr edition, p. 201): "It was the materialist conception of history which has first completely deposed the moral ideal as the directing factor of social evolution, and has taught us to deduce our social aims solely from the knowledge of the material foundations." And he goes on to speak (p. 206) of the "splendid vistas" of peace, freedom and industry, which "are won from sober economic considerations

---

[6] Cf. Marx, *Capital* (Moore and Aveling translation; Glaisher, 1918, p.51): "The religious reflex of the real world can, in any case, only then finally vanish, when the practical relations of everyday life offer to man none but *perfectly intelligible and reasonable relations* with regard to his fellowmen and to nature" (my italics).
[7] wrongs (Lewis); evils (Eastman).

and not from intoxication through the moral ideals of freedom, equality and fraternity, justice, humanity!"

The process of "deducing" social aims from economic facts is a highly mysterious one. The recognition of a cause, of a necessary and sufficient condition of the occurrence of a phenomenon in a certain field, of what *differentiates* its occurrence from its non-occurrence is equally relevant to the aim of bringing about the phenomenon and to that of preventing it. The assumption is, in fact, that the "material foundations" have their own aims, that they have the "task" of overcoming their own evils. It is because of this assumption that the Marxists treat popular moral notions as merely epiphenomenal, while at the same time they do not rise above the level of such popular notions (ideals, indignation, altruism—as in Kautsky's equating of "the moral law" with "the social impulse"). They have no conception of the specific field of ethical science (or of any other specific field) because of their devotion to an ethico-logic, because, for them, facts of any description are facts of *advance*.[8]

This ethico-logic, this metaphysic or rationalism, is nowhere more evident than in Marx's "Theses on Feuerbach". The first thesis practically sums up the whole position. "The chief defect of all previous materialism—including Feuerbach's—is that the object, reality, sensibility, is conceived only in the form of the object or as conception, but not as human sensory activity, practice [*Praxis*], not subjectively. That is why it happened that the *active* side [of the object], in opposition to materialism, was developed by idealism—but only abstractly, for idealism, naturally, does not know real, sensory activity as such. Feuerbach wants to recognise

---

[8] Cf. Eastman (*Marx, Lenin*, p. 87): "It is easy to scorn your own ideals, treating them as mere signs of a crisis in the evolution of material forces, when you have already confided the attainment of your ideals to those material forces." Again (*Last Stand*, p. 13): "If you do not read your purpose to change the world into the world itself, you cannot be at the same time realistic and purposive. You cannot be a 'materialist' and strive toward an ideal unless you conceive matter itself as striving toward your ideal." And (in comment on Hook's contention that "The purpose of Marx's intellectual activity was the overthrow of the existing order"), "you couldn't overthrow a fence-post, could you... without knowing something... that the man who was trying to stop you would want to know too? It is the need to eliminate the alternative, to make sure of the victory of your effort—a need dictated, remember, by the nature of animistic thinking, not by the nature of revolutionary men—that gives rise to this whole prodigious effort to keep up the bluff that Marxian economics in so far as it is any good is not straight science" (*Last Stand*, p. 30)—i.e., concerned with fact, not "purpose".

MARXIST ETHICS (1937) 407

sensory objects which are really differentiated from objects of thought, but he does not conceive human activity itself as an objective activity. Consequently in the *Essence of Christianity*, he regards only the theoretical attitude as the truly human one, while practice is conceived and fixed only in its dirty-Jewish[9] form. Hence he does not grasp the significance of 'revolutionary', of practical, critical, activity" (Hook pp. 273,4).

The phrase rendered by Hook as "in the form of the object or as conception" is given by Eastman (*Last Stand*, p. 8) as "under the form of object or of *contemplation*",[10] which certainly seems to make better sense. The point is, in any case, that the older materialists conceived reality (which, of course, for them is *material* reality) as an "-ed", while the theory of the "-ing" was developed by idealism as an account of the activity of *spiritual* reality (Hook's interpolated phrase "of the object" showing that he misses this point). Thus, while the idealist theory can only be "abstract" because reality after all *is* material, what materialists have to do is to recognise the "-ing", the activity, in material reality itself. And this is done by identifying sensory activity with the sensible object, by identifying the object with practice, and, in fact, with *revolutionary* activity. The sensory world has to be taken, Marx says, as a historical product. "Even the objects of the simplest 'sensory certainty' are given through social development, industry and commercial relations. The cherry tree like almost all fruit trees was transplanted to our zone, as is well known, through commerce; it was only *by virtue of* this action of a determinate society at a determinate time that it was given to 'the sensory certainty' of Feuerbach" (quoted by Hook, p. 295, from *The German Ideology*). The relativism of this, the confusion of what a thing is with what it is "through", need not be stressed. What is important is that the truth of anything is taken as its place in the development of reality towards "rationality", towards the realisation of its true nature.

[9] commercial, "profit and loss"; practice as getting on, making money. The expression troubles Hook, who solemnly remarks (p. 278) that, although Marx was free of anti-Semitic prejudice (!), "he unfortunately was not over-sensitive to using the term 'Jew', often with unsavoury adjectives, as an epithet of abuse". Marx, of all men, was surely aware that money-grubbing is not a peculiarly Jewish trait. But the point is that it is a popular accusation, a means whereby people cover up their own commercialism. (Cf. *Ulysses*, p. 34: "A merchant, Stephen said, is one who buys cheap and sells dear, jew or gentile, is he not?")
[10] My italics. The word in the original German text is *Anschauung*.

This is confirmed by the tenth and eleventh theses (Hook, pp. 300, 303). "The standpoint of the old materialism is 'civic society'; the standpoint of the new materialism is *human* society or socialised humanity." "Philosophers have only *interpreted* the world differently: the point is, however, to *change* it." Reality is revolution, and revolution is the achievement of a rational state of affairs—of Socialism. It is extraordinary that Hook should occupy space in wondering whether Marx was a "true Socialist"; he might easily differ from the school so described in his estimate of what *was* the truly human or rational condition of things, the choice being quite arbitrary in any case, but the logical position is the same. It may be said, also, that Marx differs from Hegel in that, while the Hegelian Absolute is a "result" which is never arrived at, Socialism is taken to be realisable *in time*. Marx would, in fact, be more consistent if he regarded history as a progressive socialising of things, without any suggestion of reaching Socialism or "perfectly reasonable relations"; his positive views of society collide here with his metaphysics. Hook takes a more Hegelian line in giving (pp. 306,7) what he considers to be the sense of the final (eleventh) thesis: "The very fact that philosophy is an activity in a world of space, time and incompatible interests, makes it clear that its goals cannot be absolute truth or absolute justice. But the fact that action is thoughtful makes it possible to achieve beliefs which are *truer*, the fact that thought leads to action makes it possible to achieve a world which is *more just.*" Here we have comparativism *in excelsis*, with no possibility of showing what beliefs are (truly) truer. But the real outcome of the theses is that not only would Marx not distinguish "truer" from "more just", but that he could not distinguish either of them from *later*.

It is worthy of note that, in spite of Marx's rejection of the individualistic outlook of "contemplative materialism" (ninth thesis), a rejection which Hook (p. 303) expresses by saying that his "conception of man pointed to the necessity (!) of a direct collective control of all social institutions which influenced man", his own outlook is distinctly individualistic in character. This is, indeed, only another example of his Hegelianism, for while Hegel's most useful work may be said to lie in his rejection of social atomism and his recognition of institutions, his philosophy remains a philosophy of *consciousness*, and in this too Marx followed him, identifying the rationalising of things with their "coming to consciousness".

MARXIST ETHICS (1937) 409

The very fact that man is chosen as the subject of history is indicative of individualism. "History does nothing; it 'possesses no colossal riches'; it 'fights no fight'. It is rather man—real, living man—who acts, possesses and fights in everything. It is by no means 'History' which uses man as a means to carry out its ends as if it were a person apart; rather History is nothing but the activity of man in pursuit of his ends" (quoted by Hook, p. 38, from *The Holy Family*). This is the language of individualistic utilitarianism. One would expect a materialist theory, even in the form of a theory of men and not of institutions, to take its departure from what men do, not what they think or seek, but the Marxists can never get away from their talk of wills, ends, needs.

Thus Engels (*Feuerbach*, p. 105) says: "Men make their own history in that each follows his own desired ends independent of results, and the results of these many wills acting in different directions and their manifold effects upon the world constitute history. It depends, therefore, upon what the great majority of individuals intend"—which is still individualism, just as in the case of Hook's "collective control". Going on, then, to inquire into the "impelling forces" behind historical change, Engels remarks (p. 108) that "we cannot consider so much the motives of single individuals, however pre-eminent, as those which set in motion great masses, entire nations, and again, whole classes of people in each nation". And these forces, it need hardly be said, are found (p. 114) in "the economic conditions of the life of society", the prime function of which is "the production of the necessities of existence"—i.e., of the existence of *men*, not of organisations.[11] It is a remarkable fact that when, as by Kautsky, the materialist conception of history is taken as applying Darwinian principles to society, the question is always of the survival or otherwise of persons, of the needs of "life"; and even the class struggle is taken as the struggle for existence of the persons composing the classes, and not of rival forms of activity, which might occur in the same person, and the survival or non-survival of which is, in any

[11] Cf. Engels, *Socialism, Utopian and Scientific*; opening of § III (Aveling's translation). "The materialist conception of history starts from the proposition that the production *of the means to support human life* and, next to production, the exchange of things produced, is the basis of all social structure." The phrase I have italicised does not appear in Burns's translation of the corresponding passage in the *Anti-Dühring* (p. 300).

case, quite a different matter from the survival or non-survival of persons. Any of the elements in culture—Science, Art, Industry itself—no doubt operates through persons, but its "needs", in the sense of conditions necessary for its continuance, its "ends", as the effects its continuance will produce on its surroundings, its interactions generally with other things so that it does or does not "survive", are not dependent on anyone's knowledge of them—any more than, as Marx points out (Preface to *Critique of Political Economy*), a man's own history is dependent on what he thinks of himself. It will not be denied that Marx gives some account of this social struggle, that his doctrine has helped towards a positive theory of organisations; but his humanistic starting-point has prevented the working out, by orthodox Marxists at least, of such a truly materialist conception of history.

It may be said, however, that it is not so much the individualism of this position as its rationalism, the conception of a *true* state or outcome of things, with the connected conception of reality, society, humanity, advancing *as a whole*, that prevents the working out of a necessarily pluralistic theory of the struggle of organisations. This total movement Marx attempts to account for in terms of the Hegelian "negation of negation". Thus he says in *The Holy Family* (quoted by F. Mehring, *Karl Marx: The Story of His Life*, English translation, p. 103): "Because the abstraction of all humanity, even the appearance of humanity, is practically complete in the fully developed proletariat, because the living conditions of the proletariat represent the focal point of all inhuman conditions in contemporary society, because the human being is lost in the proletariat, but has won a theoretical consciousness of loss and is compelled by unavoidable and absolutely compulsory need—the practical expression of necessity—to revolt against this inhumanity, the proletariat can and must emancipate itself. However, it cannot emancipate itself without abolishing the conditions which give it life, and it cannot abolish these conditions without abolishing all those inhuman conditions of social life which are summed up in its own situation." Such rhetorical playing with the notions "human" and "inhuman" (and, according to Eastman, apart from empty rhetoric of this kind, no proof is given anywhere in *Capital* of the "necessity" of Socialism) is a poor substitute for an account of the interactions of social movements, proletarian and otherwise, and an estimate of their outcome in positive terms.

It is somewhat surprising that Marx should immediately go on to say: "It is not a question of what this or that proletarian, or even the proletariat as a whole, may imagine for the moment to be the aim. *It is a question of what the proletariat actually is* and what it will be compelled to do historically as a result of this being. The aim and the historical action of the proletariat are laid down in advance irrevocably and obviously, in its own situation in life, and in the whole organisation of contemporary bourgeois society" (my italics). No doubt there is much here of the sort that has been criticised. But if Marx could have stuck to the view that what a thing is is prior to its aims, it would have meant a complete recasting of Socialist theory. The doctrine of the primacy of "needs", of history as "man's" pursuit of his "ends", would have had to be abandoned; it would have been seen that needs are the needs of already existing activities (viz., what is required to keep them going), that things (human beings or social institutions) have their own ways of working even if they have *no* ends, though, of course, they will always have effects, and that the working-class movement exists positively as a form of activity now, and not relatively as a movement "for" Socialism, and would retain its good features (assuming that it has these) even if Socialism never came about at all. That is not to say that it is inherently impossible, from a knowledge of this and other movements, to predict that Socialism, a society of producers without capitalist property, will come about, but only that it will come about, if at all, from the nature of the movements and not of their "aims", and that absence of proof (or even disproof) of its coming about would not nullify the movements.[12]

---

[12] Eastman, with his theory of what is "possible" but not "necessary", and his connected conception of "social engineering", considers it a merit on Lenin's part, a sign of his being "a scientist and not a priest", that he ignored the appeal of the more orthodox Plekhanov to what, on Marx's view, the proletariat itself "is historically bound to accomplish", and persisted in his doctrine of the bringing of "socialist consciousness" to the working-class movement *from without* by a body of professional revolutionists (cf. *Marx, Lenin,* Part II, ch. IV). Eastman has recently written (*Harper's Magazine*, February, 1937) of "The End of Socialism in Russia". But what he presumably does not see is that the present degradation of Russia is the *outcome* of "social engineering", of "applying" theory to social movements so as to make them go right, of the fact that those who "brought Socialism" to the working-class movement which they presumed to treat as their material, were *not* part of the movement or, more generally, were not producers—not scientists but metaphysicians; as he himself is, in being a voluntarist, a dealer in "possibilities".

The upholding of a utilitarian ethics, an ethics of "ends", has prevented Marxists generally from appreciating the work of Georges Sorel, who, admittedly on a Marxist basis but with a deliberate avoidance of Marxist orthodoxy, has developed an "ethics of the producers". Sorel agrees with Marx that the development of the working-class movement has resulted from the bringing together of the workers in the capitalist factory. But the "heroic values" there engendered are directly opposed to the "consumers' ethics" of the capitalists, the ethics of profit or return, and thus to the tedious preaching of class "interests" and to the theory and practice of "social engineering". Developing the "values" of initiative, emulation, care for exactitude and rejection of the notion of "reward", the factory worker becomes assimilated to the scientist, the artist, the warrior—the types of *disinterested* activity. Sorel rejects the philanthropic "ethics" of Christianity precisely because it is concerned with returns and has no conception of a system of *production*, and a system of rights connected therewith. This is in line with the criticism of the philanthropic Utopians, in *The Communist Manifesto*, because they conceive history as the carrying out of their social plans and the working class only as the most suffering class. But we have seen how near Marx himself came, in *The Holy Family*, to the latter conception and how deeply utilitarianism is embedded in his whole work. And the latter-day Marxists, of the Leninist school, are little enough concerned with craftsmanship or "care for exactitude"; they regard exactitude (combined, of course, with "flexibility") as residing solely in their own dialectical "science", while the masses are moved to revolution not by productive traditions but by desperation ("increasing misery").

It may be noticed that the "values" of the productive movement appear as attitudes of the individual producer. It is to be understood that participation in a movement will affect the character of the participants, but this does not mean that the movement can be summed up in, or expressed as a resultant of, their attitudes. On the contrary, any serious study of society must recognise the way in which individuals are "caught up" in movements, the extraordinary extent to which social developments can raise or lower individual "potential"—including the capacity for thinking and the making of decisions. This is, it may be said, not markedly different from the above-quoted views of Engels. But the point

MARXIST ETHICS (1937) 413

is that it can be developed only by abandoning the doctrine of "ends", whether of individuals or of movements. And, with whatever Bergsonian confusions Sorel may express his departure from such rationalistic doctrines, his main concern is with movements as they are in themselves.

As a result of a preliminary investigation of the three highest achievements of the mind (science, religion, art), he says, "we are led to believe that it is possible to distinguish in every complex body of knowledge a clear and an obscure region, and to say that the latter is perhaps the more important. The mistake made by superficial people consists in the statement that this second part must disappear with the progress of enlightenment, and that eventually everything will be explained rationally in terms of the *little science* (*Reflections on Violence*; Hulme's translation, p. 159)—a view which, as we have seen, would convict Marx of "superficiality" in certain parts of his doctrine, at least. And Sorel goes on to distinguish, in ethics, the clearly expressible part "which has reference to the equitable relations between men" from the obscure part "which has reference to sexual relationships", in legislation, the "scientific" region of contracts from the "mysterious" region of the family, and, in economics, the simplicity of questions of exchange from the complexity presented by the facts of production. ("Ethics", in the first distinction here, is used in the sense of custom.) "Nobody denies", he adds, "that production is the fundamental part of any economic system; this is a truth which plays a great part in Marxism, and which has been acknowledged even by authors who have been unable to understand its importance."

In fact, the "irrational", as opposed to the "rational" or calculable, is what things are, which must be prior to their adjustments. The "consumers'" view, that production is "for the sake of" consumption, cannot account for the development of production itself. The common ethical notions of disinterestedness and of things which are "for their own sake" are approaches to the conception of the independence of production, whether scientific, artistic or industrial. The truth of the "economic interpretation" is that society is production and that consumption is only incidental to its history. And, in general, a doctrine of what things are "for" is idealism, not materialism. The science of ethics, in particular, deals with what goods are, and the view that they are productive activities, while it owes much to Marx, could not have been developed without a shedding of Marx's rationalism and an independent reference to production itself. A full account of Sorel's ethics would require a separate study, in which consideration would have to be given to what he owed to Proudhon and to the French syndicalist movement, as well as to Marx. Enough has been said here, perhaps, to show that Sorel has not only helped to detach Marx's positive contributions to social science from his metaphysic of "true society" (whereas the orthodox Marxists remain in hopeless entanglement), but has opened up the science of ethics itself.

# 28
# THE SERVILE STATE (1943)

The prognostications of Hilaire Belloc in *The Servile State*[1] were not taken very seriously by the Socialists to whom they were, in the main, addressed; and, in the period between the two wars, they must have seemed to many to have lost such point as they had ever had. Even then, of course, there were thinkers who associated the actual establishment of servile conditions with attempts at Collectivism. But for the most part Socialism was still felt to be a liberating force, and the tendency to enslavement was regarded as coming from avowedly anti-Socialist quarters. At the present time, however, the danger of regimentation must be acknowledged to have grown enormously, and at least a strong case can be made out for the view that propaganda of a "Socialist" colour has largely contributed to the decline of the sentiment of liberty. Under these circumstances it is interesting, and may be important, to return to Belloc's analysis and consider its relation to the contemporary situation.

There is, indeed, much in the book which remains as unconvincing as it was thirty years ago. The doctrine of the Distributive State, and the account of its growth from an originally servile civilisation and its decay at the beginning of the modern period, are marked by preconception and partisanship. And although the discussion of Collectivism might be little affected even if the references to Distributivism were completely excised, still it is coloured by the same sort of assumptions, by an undue emphasis, in particular, on property and legality. The emphasis on property leads to a "class" theory which brings Belloc close to the commonly accepted interpretation of Marxism—to a division of society into two sets of individuals,[2] the propertied and the propertyless, as opposed to a distinction of functions (of ways of living and forms

---

[1] First published in October, 1912. References here are to the third impression, October, 1913.
[2] Cf. the disabilities imposed in Russia (for a period at least) on persons "of bourgeois origin". Consideration of what justification for such procedures could be found in Marx does not fall within the scope of this article.

of organisation) which may operate variously in the same individuals. And the emphasis on legality affects the whole argument of the book.

This may be illustrated from the fundamental definition given on p. 16: "That arrangement of society in which so considerable a number of the families and individuals are constrained by positive law to labour for the advantage of other families and individuals as to stamp the whole community with the mark of such labour we call The Servile State." No doubt formal enactment is important; and the "social" legislation whose inception in England was a principle stimulus to this book, was of great political significance. Nevertheless, Belloc's formulation obscures the fact that actual legislation is neither a necessary nor a sufficient determinant of political reality. On the one hand, a law may not be enforceable (as witness attempts in various parts of the world at various times legislatively to abolish strikes); on the other hand, people's social situation may prevent their doing what they are legally "free" to do. This was recognised, in Socialist propaganda, in the application of the term "wage-slavery" to the condition of workers in present-day society, even in the absence of that legal compulsion to labour for a master of which Belloc speaks (p. 3). The usage may be a bad one; the differences between the position of wage-workers and that of slaves may be vastly more important than the resemblances, and particularly the differences in respect of possibilities of *organised* action. But it implies the truth that "status" is not simply a matter of law.

The illustration is an important one in several respects. Clearly, as Belloc argues, the contention that a servile status with security is preferable to wage-labour with insecurity is no sort of proof that the latter also is servile. That the worker is subject to disabilities (disfranchisements) is undeniable; it is equally undeniable that he has certain enfranchisements. Some measure of servitude, an inequality of franchise, the existence of privilege, may be inseparable from society as such. But, in any case, the antithesis of political freedom and economic power is a false one; and it is false, too, to say that the worker cannot have political freedom while economic inequality exists. Here the Marxian doctrine (largely followed by Belloc) of the proletariat or propertyless class is particularly misleading. The divorce of the worker from certain forms of property ("capitalist" property) does not imply his "dehumanisation", his divorce from enterprise, his lack of all control of the processes of production. If he had no such control, he would have no political freedom, no power of agitation, no influence whatever on the progress of events—he would really be a slave. That some workers under some conditions would prefer security to such rights (powers of enterprise) as they now possess may well be true. But that enterprise, such as it is, has the social force of property, and any analysis which concentrates on the legal possession of certain movables can only obscure the issues.

The distinction between the worker and the slave, then, is in terms of enterprise (of rights, of a "movement"), which is at once political and economic. But it is also moral. And here it is remarkable to find Belloc professing, in his inquiry, to "keep strictly to the economic aspect of the case. Only when that is established and when the modern tendency to the re-establishment of slavery is clear, are we free to discuss the advantages and disadvantages of the revolution through which we are passing" (pp. 19, 20).[3] No doubt it does not advance discussion of events to say that some of them "ought to be" and others "ought not to be". But to regard that as moral characterisation is to treat the moral characters of things as not really belonging to them, to take their "advantages" and "disadvantages" not as inherent in their operation but as annexed to them from without—and what would be the force of such judgments *after* the facts had been ascertained is not at all apparent. It is impossible, however, to discuss social processes except in terms of ways of living or forms of enterprise, and that *is* moral characterisation. To know, in particular, that servitude is bad is to know something of its mode of developing and what will help and what hinder it.

Belloc, indeed, does not succeed in avoiding moral considerations; for example, in the fifth Section, he has a good deal to say about the "moral strain" (tension) involved in the divergence between the professions of capitalism and its actual procedures. But in his proposal to postpone moral questions he again exhibits affinity with Marxism, particularly as expounded by Engels. In what precise sense economics can be said to be primary and other

[3] It is perhaps less remarkable to find James Burnham, in *The Managerial Revolution*, similarly professing to avoid moral issues and to deal only with the actual trend of affairs.

aspects of culture (including morals) secondary is a question of great difficulty for the student of Marxism—it may, indeed, be impossible to give *any* clear sense to this doctrine. But at least it has been a commonplace of Socialist propaganda (as it is of current propaganda of "social improvement") that material conditions have first to be put in order and "higher" things can thereafter be attended to. And the view that material things come first is certainly that taken by Engels—most strikingly in his speech at Marx's funeral (contained in *Karl Marx, Man, Thinker, and Revolutionist*, edited by D. Ryazanoff; English translation published by Martin Lawrence in 1927).

Marx, said Engels, "discovered the simple fact (heretofore hidden beneath ideological excrescences) that human beings must have food and drink, clothing and shelter, *first of all*, before they can interest themselves in politics, science, art, religion, and the like. This implies that the production of the immediately requisite material means of subsistence, and therewith the extant economic developmental phase of a nation or an epoch, constitute the foundations upon which the State institutions, the legal outlooks, the artistic and even the religious ideas, of those concerned, have been built up. It implies that these latter must be explained out of the former, whereas the former have been explained as issuing from the latter" (pp. 43,4; my italics). This, of course, is glaringly false. It is not the case that the winning of subsistence is antecedent to cultural ideas and activities; it is, for the most part, bound up with them and is frequently postponed or subordinated to them (i.e., men risk their subsistence for the sake of their "ideas"). If moral forces exist in the society at all, they must (as they obviously do) affect economic exchanges and the whole system of production, and any economic theory which puts them out of consideration will be defective on that account. In fact, the attitude of "putting the economic first" leads straight to that servility whose growth Belloc undoubtedly deplores.

It can be said, then, that while Belloc recognises moral factors in society and indeed considers them of very great importance, his procedure is such as to obscure them. One considerable influence, in his view, making for the establishment of the Servile State, is the desire of the masses themselves for "security and sufficiency". Under capitalism, with its general condition of "political freedom" but restriction to the few of property in the means of production, the many have neither security nor sufficiency; and, seeing no way back to the Distributive State in which the wide diffusion of property gave "economic freedom" and thus such security as is possible to men, they are to a large extent prepared to accept a servile status on the understanding that their material wants will be provided for. This, of course, is only one of the facts recognised by Belloc as leading towards slavery. But the important moral fact which he, with his insistence on property, passes over, is that the desire for security and sufficiency is the very mark of the servile mentality.

No one will deny that certain materials are required for any way of life whatever; but a way of life which sought to have its materials *secured* for it would be poor and unenterprising. Here we may advert to Sorel's distinction[4] between the outlook of the consumer (emphasising ends, things to be secured) and that of the producer (emphasising activities, a way of life, a morality). Excising the utilitarian part of Marxism and drawing upon the work of Proudhon, Sorel takes the social importance of the "working-class movement" to reside in its development of the productive spirit—a development which depends on "expropriation" and can only be retarded by proprietary sentiments. Naturally, Sorel would not claim that the continuance of this spirit is *secured* by existing social divisions, but would regard it as possible for the workers' movement to degenerate—as indeed it has done. If it were true (though Belloc gives no real evidence for it) that already in 1912 the mass of workers were concerned above all with security, that would imply the breakdown of workers' enterprise; and it is certainly against that enterprise that "social service" legislation was and is directed. But, while it flourished, it was bound up with the "propertyless" condition of the workers, with their *lack* of security. And in general it can be said that movements enlivening society and advancing freedom have to engage in constant struggle for the materials they require, and lose their independent and creative spirit under "protection".

The producer's mentality was never, of course, characteristic of the Labour movement, or even the Socialist movement, as a whole. Belloc draws attention, in the eighth Section, to the type of "Socialist" (now in the ascendant) whose real interest is in social

[4] In *Reflections on Violence*. (Cf. my article, "Marxist Ethics"; *A.J.P.P.*, June, 1937: v. s., pp. 325–7.)

regulation and not in social equality. And closely akin to him is the "sentimental Socialist" who seeks to "abolish poverty", for whom, that is to say, the worker is defined negatively, by what he is deprived of, instead of by his positive participation in certain forms of organisation and activity—a kind of view which, as we have noted, appears in Marxism, in spite of Marx's criticism (e.g., in *The Communist Manifesto*) of social philanthropy. But in arguing that even the sincere and revolutionary Collectivist is forced in the same direction, that he "finds the current of his demand canalised" (p. 125) since the road to confiscation is checked and barred while the way to "securing human conditions for the proletariat" is open (viz., by sacrificing freedom, by accepting a position of legal servitude, with security, under the capitalist), Belloc again misses a vital point. That is that by taking Socialism *as an end*, by seeking an established condition of society in which workers' disabilities would be done away with, the Collectivist is already manifesting a servile outlook[5]—and the same applies to the Distributivist "solution" of capitalist instability. To aim at a stable society is to attempt to do away with the conditions under which free activities are possible, and the well-intentioned reformer *always* produces results which he did not anticipate, helps on tendencies to which he is avowedly opposed.

This leads us to consideration of the actual experiment in "collectivisation" which we have witnessed, viz., in the Russian system. It is no reproach to Belloc that he did not anticipate Bolshevism. The fact remains that he was wrong in holding that the Socialist movement would be only a factor contributing to the enslavement of the workers to the existing capitalist class, and would fail to realise Collectivism in the sense of "the placing of the means of production in the hands of the political officers of the community" (definition given on p. 5). It is not, of course, in any literal sense that one can speak of the rulers of Russia as officers "of the community", but their regime is of the character of State Socialism, and the workers are slaves of the State (to the admiration of the Fabian lovers of regulation of whom Belloc spoke) and not of capitalistic owners. No doubt this result has come about in a curious way; the monopoly of enterprise by

---

[5] The view of Bernstein (though his position is less clearly and forcefully developed than Sorel's) is also in point here—that it is the movement, not the end, that matters.

the ruling party was achieved in the *name* of the workers and was marked in its early stages by sincere attempts at devolution of control. No doubt, also, the ruling group is, in some sense, a capitalist class—as the privileged controller of industry. Still, the system was established through confiscation; and it is part of the criticism of Socialist theory that the attempt to establish a Socialist order leads to this new kind of privilege and not, as Belloc supposed, to the mere strengthening of the old privileged class through the agency of the State. This new type of regimented State could have come about in the first instance only with the aid of Socialist propaganda, though, once the example had been given, a similar kind of political control could be brought about by other means. In fact, it could not come again by the same means, since the consolidation of the ruling order has been marked by the gradual disappearance of the revolutionary side of Socialist ideology and the dominance of an ideology of "security and sufficiency", which has been reflected in the ideology of the Labour movement everywhere, the result being that it now *seeks* only what Belloc said it was effecting—a State-guaranteed provision for the people's wants.

Granted that this line of development could scarcely have been anticipated, it should be noted again that what principally distorted Belloc's view was his concentration on property (on legal title to materials) as against the notion of *control*—in terms of which, as we saw, the formal propertylessness of the workers is offset by their power of organising their own industrial and political activities. And here again the antithesis of the economic and the political is misleading. The lesson of Bolshevism is that political monopoly ("dictatorship") is a major economic force, that the monopoly of industrial enterprise which it carries with it, does not require to be supplemented by formal property rights—may, indeed, operate all the more effectively without them. As Burnham puts it (though the view is not original to him), "the concept of 'the separation of ownership and control' has no sociological or historical meaning. Ownership *means* control. . . . If ownership and control are in reality separated, then ownership has changed hands to the 'control', and the separated ownership is a meaningless fiction."[6]

---

[6] *The Managerial Revolution*, English edition, May, 1942; pp. 87,8. (Cf. the statement on p. 69 that the State, in managerial society, "will, if we wish to put it that way, be

It is unfortunate that Burnham, while he clearly delineates certain of the characters of the new ruling class, comes down on the side of management rather than direction (of the internal rather than the external relations of enterprises) as its main distinguishing feature. This involves an underestimation of the importance of *political* monopoly, of centralised direction by "the party". No doubt the technicians are of importance to the party and may influence its policy; but to treat them as the rulers is to ignore important conditions both of the rise and of the continuance of totalitarian regimes—and indeed to ignore essential features of any industrial society. And the point is specially important because Burnham discerns in the capitalist countries (with particular reference to the United States) the growth of the same "managerial" tendencies as have come to fruition in Russia and Germany. We may, I think, properly apply the term "servile" to those States which are marked by the suppression of all political opposition and thus of all independent enterprise. But in other States the managerial and bureaucratic stratum seems to be less closely linked with the really directing class, to occupy a middle ("mediating") position between it and the masses, and the system, in the absence of "the party", is reminiscent of the state of affairs anticipated by Belloc rather than of totalitarianism—with the important proviso that, so long as there are competing parties, the workers will have *some* political power.

It can scarcely be denied, however, even if we reject the "managerial" diagnosis, that the capitalist countries are moving in the direction of regimentation and that the *ideology* of servility is rapidly gaining ground. The process has, of course, been greatly accelerated by the war; this might, indeed, if we abstract from particular national aims and consider the whole society of predatory nations, be described as the "purpose" of the war. Naive persons believe, because one side is opposed to freedom, that the other side must be in favour of it. But freedom consorts ill not merely with regimentation "in the national cause" but with the avowed aims of the "liberating" belligerents. Even if the *word* freedom is used, "freedom from want" and "freedom from fear" are simply the *sufficiency* and *security*, the desire for which marks the servile

the 'property' of the managers. And that will be quite enough to place them in the position of ruling class.")

mentality. And it is this which gives appositeness to Belloc's analysis, even though, as we have seen, he takes these aims not to be servile in themselves but only to make for servility in their collision with existing economic trends. The decline of liberalism could not be more clearly marked than by the association of the name with the advocacy of regimentation, of the "protective" State.

The propagandist character of these formulae should not, of course, be lost sight of. They are partly retrospective and defensive—it has to be made out that the responsibility for war and insecurity rests upon certain particular nations and movements, the subjection of which can thus inaugurate an epoch of peace and security. In this aspect the "security" propaganda, like Wilsonism and the doctrine of "making the world safe for democracy" in the last war, implies no real intention of removing disabilities; its function is that of silencing, or of justifying to the public at large the steps taken to silence, demands for political independence at the present time. But that is not its only aspect. There *is* the real intention of permanently reducing political independence and extending the powers of the State, and this, as Belloc saw, has to be combined with promises of "benefits" in return for the surrender of rights. The expectation of such benefits is of course delusive; there is no system which can abolish insecurity and guarantee sufficiency. But, by the time that is realised, it will not be possible to have back for the asking the rights that have been surrendered in the name of solidarity. Solidarist conceptions, of course, have always been widely accepted, but in ordinary times their influence is checked by independent movements. In time of war, however, the doctrine of "national service" gains enormous force, which can be turned to the establishing, for peace-time, of a corresponding doctrine of service to the community. Thus war, by undermining political independence, gives impetus to the movement in the direction of the "social service" (or servile) State.

It has been argued that, even if the provision of absolute security and sufficiency is impossible, it is still a reasonable policy to "get as much of them as we can". But here it has to be emphasised, first, that no reliance can be placed on the State or any other earthly Providence. As already indicated, the States in question all have their share of responsibility for the "insecurity" which it is proposed to remove; their mode of operation *includes* war and oppression. And those persons who expect "sufficiency" to be provided for them, will find themselves worse off in relying on what the State deems sufficient than in making their own organised efforts for the provision of the materials they require; they will soon find (as indeed they could see already if they wanted to) that State provision will be hedged about with all sorts of qualifications and restrictions, so that, except for those who will themselves embrace bureaucratic careers, their last state will be worse than their first. But the second and more vital point is that the pursuit of security and sufficiency is itself a low aim, that the maintenance of a high level of culture depends on the existence of a plurality of movements which take their chance in the social struggle, instead of having their place and their resources assigned to them from a supposedly all-embracing point of view. Croce, in "History as the Story of Liberty", has particularly emphasised the way in which liberty (and, with it, culture) declines under conditions of fancied security and is reborn in adversity. On this view both liberty and servility are features of society at any stage, but at least the *ordering* of society is antipathetic to liberty.

The absurdity of the pretences of the advocates of a "planned society" should be noted here. It is assumed that the agents of centralised control are capable of fitting every form of social activity into a general scheme. Even in war-time, when many activities are willingly abandoned or curtailed, the anomalies and confusions of directed work are only too apparent. But this will be nothing to the chaotic condition of affairs if the fuller activities of peace-time are to be similarly directed. There is no one who is competent to make provision for all departments and aspects of social life. But if the decline in liberty, the progressive abandonment of the voluntary principle, has been such as to prevent the recrudescence of independent movements, if the desire for security has really taken possession of the mass of the people so that "planning" is inevitable, it can only take the form of the subordination of social life to certain narrow interests, interests, especially, of a commercial kind. That is the direction in which the propaganda of "public utility" and "service of the community" is working. And it is because the Labour movement is so thoroughly devoted to these interests (is, indeed, their standard-bearer) that it can be said, as a movement of "emancipation" or social regeneration, to have failed—in fact, to have made good Belloc's description of it (with special reference to its Socialist side) as working towards slavery.

Contemporary Labour propaganda (with few and uninfluential exceptions) is imbued with the fallacy that what opposes Fascism must be supporting freedom—as if two tyrannies could not conflict. Hence it upholds solidarity, is in favour of the regimentation of strikers and the imprisonment of dissidents (or those suspected of dissidence), and is indifferent to free discussion. In taking this line it ignores the fact that solidarity can only mean the maintenance of present privileges, and that a struggle "for freedom" can proceed only *from* freedom and not through enslavement. And planners in general miss or conceal the fact that planning can advance only *what can be planned for*—and that is not culture but commerce. The particular importance of discussion at the present time lies in the fact that there are different possible outcomes of the war (including a negotiated as against an oppressive peace), and the sinking of opposition "in the interests of all" means an artificial "unity" in which some special interest (and the outcome which it prefers) is favoured. That this will in any case be the commercial interest is hardly to be doubted; but planning will make assurance doubly sure.

These considerations are specially appropriate to the question of planning for education. The conclusion that this can only mean commercialising education is confirmed by observation of present facts, as well as by considerations of the propaganda of the planners. That people's education, for the time being, should be directed by reference to the assistance they can give in the prosecution of the war, will appear plausible to many, though it makes the assumption of identity of interest which has been criticised above—in other words, though it passes over the fact that the kind of society that will emerge from the war will depend in part on the kind of educational and other social activities that have been carried on while it lasted. In fact, it is perfectly clear that the same conceptions of utility and "service of the community" that inform the present regulations will, if our planners have their way, continue to dominate education in the future. Here, as in other planning, there is the pretence at exact measurement of capacity (a pretence which has the support of the tribe of "mental measurers"), there is the fitting of people into their appropriate pigeonholes—a procedure which has the effect of killing the natural interest in learning and encouraging a narrowly professional careerism. These measures are taken under such demagogic slogans as "equal opportunity for all", but such formulae betray the commercial mentality of their users. The real educational question is not of the provision of a career to individuals, of the supplying of education to them as a commodity, but of the maintenance of a tradition of learning, the continuance of the learned way of life—however few or many may participate in it. To attempt to postpone that task to the service of the State is to manifest a deplorably low level of culture.

It must indeed be allowed that, apart from any special planning, the level of culture, the social status of learning, has been falling; and this cultural decline can be closely correlated with the encroachments of "Science" on education. There is not, of course, any scientific field in which disinterested inquiry cannot be pursued; nevertheless, it is practical considerations (e.g., "the needs of industry") that have very largely determined the problems to which scientists have addressed themselves, and it is certainly on account of their practicality that scientific studies have gained ground in the schools. But this is the sort of practicality which takes "social unity" (i.e., established interests) for granted. There is in fact a direct opposition between the "practical" and the critical outlooks, and it is only the study of, and absorption in, ways of life (the study of "the humanities") that can promote criticism.[7] The naïveté of scientists, trying to "get things done" and ignoring the whole range of the literature of social and political criticism, imagining, for example, that social conclusions (in the crude form of precepts) can be drawn from biological premises, is a sufficiently well-marked phenomenon of our times. It might well be argued that the contemporary scientist (whose affinity with the managerial stratum has been emphasised by Burnham) is the typical exponent of a servile ideology. Or, if this description could be applied more aptly to the psychologist, who has introduced a factitious "exactness" into the field of humane studies, at least the propagation of "scientific methods" has gone hand in hand with the overlaying of freedom and culture by Philistinism.

Now the importance of all this for the lover of freedom is that, exemplifying the adverse conditions which can overtake culture, it

---

[7] In saying that this is necessary I do not, of course, say that it is sufficient.

enables him to see more precisely how regeneration comes about. One condition of this recovery is the sharpening of the issues which occurs when servility is gaining ground, the demonstration of the mischievous character of conceptions which had seemed harmless or even admirable—conceptions of "service" or of "the development of personality", the whole mass of philanthropic ideas. Their implications become clearer, and hitherto unawakened minds begin to see into what a morass they are being led, while more fully developed thinkers come to realise what opportunities of criticism they have missed, what are the vulnerable points on which they might have directed their fire. But this leads on to the second condition of recovery—the realisation by these thinkers of their own shortcomings, of their failure to develop the resources of their own fields of study. Thus the adverse conditions under which humane studies, and especially classical studies, may be expected to labour for a considerable time, may lead to their renewal in a more critical form—one in which they may shed their pedantry and appear at once as the true form of scientific thinking and as the vehicle of an intellectual *opposition*. In fact, the two outstanding features of any movement upholding a liberal culture will be intellectualism and opposition.

The intellectualist attitude is especially important in the field of social study, for it is there that the notion of objectivity, of the recognition by the inquirer of the ways of working of things themselves, is weakest. It is quite commonly assumed by teachers in the social sciences, not merely by the uninstructed public, that these are "practical" subjects, the very conception of which involves reference to some purpose (the realisation of "welfare", or whatever it may be), and that it is misleading—to the Marxist it is "reactionary"—to treat them as mere matter of fact. We have noted, indeed, that even the inquiries of the physical scientist are dominated by "practical" considerations, that he treats things from the point of view of what can be done with them. Up to a point this does not affect the objectivity of his inquiries; but it implies a false division of things into users and used, the counterposing of a voluntaristic to a mechanistic realm, and, while in the end it leads to false conceptions of "nature", it confirms the attitude of those who, from a different starting-point, take a voluntaristic view of society. All this may help to explain why the scientist not merely fails to subject established interests to scrutiny but shows no conception of the difficulties of social study and is ready to make pronouncements in that field without having the preliminary training which he would consider essential in the field of his own special study.

The vital point here is that there are *no* "practical" subjects, that social study, like any other study, consists in finding out what is the case, how the things studied actually do work. Of course, people have policies, to which the things they study are relevant. But, while this is equally the case whether these things are human or non-human, while, again, the operation of policies is itself the subject of study, it is part of the findings of that study that what people are doing is very different from what they think they are doing, and that the attitude of "trying" is far from dominating human behaviour—and, in particular, that the activity of study itself is an independent force, having its own "laws" or ways of working, and not depending for its existence on being chosen, either "for its own sake" or for some ulterior purpose. In fact, any *attempted* subordination of study to other purposes is an attack on study itself; and the principle anti-theoretical attitude at the present time is meliorism, the setting up of "betterment" as the guide to social theory and practice.

The confusions inherent in this doctrine have already been partly indicated. The main point is that it represents as a question of degree what can only be a question of kind. Any scheme of social improvement must be such as to advance certain *specific* tendencies and could be treated as "of benefit to all" only in terms of some quite indefinite conception of "benefit". Goodness does not admit of degrees; and if we raise the question of its extension over a wider field, the advancement, let us say, of inquiry as one particular good, it is obvious that these are interests to which this will be a hindrance. Not only so, but such advances can never be settled and secure. It is only in the struggle with evils that goods exist, and the attempt to eliminate evils, as Croce points out (*op. cit.*, English translation, p. 62), could lead, at its most successful, only to a drab existence which would emphatically be evil. Liberty "has lived and always will live...a perilous and fighting life". It is the permanence of this struggle, with its ups and downs, that meliorism ignores.

The scientific student of society, then, will not be concerned with reform. What he will be concerned with is opposition—what he will be above all concerned to reject is "social unity". And he will reject it not merely as a description of present conditions but as a conception of a future society. The doctrine of history as struggle is at once the liberal and the scientific part of Marxism; the doctrine of Socialism as something to be established ("classless society") is its servile part. The point is not merely the drabness that might result from attempts to eliminate social struggles, but the impossibility of eliminating them—and, therewith, the loss of independence and vigour that can result from the spreading of the *belief* that they can be eliminated. The belief (in spite of evidence) in the present existence of a society without "classes", i.e., without distinction and opposition among ways of living, has, more than anything else, facilitated acceptance of the view that insecurity and oppression (brought under the single head of "Fascism") can be done away with. But this view is not merely unscientific, in that it treats such social phenomena as accidental, as having a source essentially alien to society, as arising from the peculiar "wickedness" of a particular individual or group (and all the more unscientific in that there could be no possible safeguard against the repetition of such "accidents"); it is also indicative of a failure in responsibility, of a desire to be relieved of troublesome problems—in a word, of servility.

How far the process of social regimentation and cultural degeneration will go it is, I think, impossible to say. What can be said is that so long as there are rights of opposition (so long, e.g., as we are not subjected to a one-party system), culture will still have a front to fight on. And here independent institutions are of special importance—institutions, i.e., which are not merely nominally autonomous but have a *doctrine* of independence; Universities, trade unions, etc., which will resist being treated as servants of the State, or in which, at the worst, a resistant minority will remain. For the measure of freedom in any community is the extent of opposition to the ruling order, of criticism of the ruling ideas; and belief in established freedom, or in State-guaranteed "benefits", is a mark of the abandonment of liberty. The servile State is the unopposed State.

# 29
# FREUDIANISM AND SOCIETY (1940)[1]

The first two volumes issued in this series were *A General Selection from the Works of Sigmund Freud*, and *Love, Hate and Reparation* by Melanie Klein and Joan Riviere. The fourth volume, here reviewed along with a work by R. Money-Kyrle, consists of part of Freud's *Thoughts for the Times on War and Death* (first published in 1915), a selection, amounting to about two-thirds of the original, from *Civilisation and its Discontents* (1929), and an open letter to Albert Einstein, *Why War?* (published in 1933 along with the letter of Einstein's to which it was a reply). The first of these was written before Freud had developed his theory of aggression as "an innate, independent instinctual disposition in man", but, like the others, it insists on our seeing human nature as it is, noting the anti-cultural tendencies within it, if the threats to culture are to be effectively grappled with.

These writings suffer from the defects of all Freud's "metapsychological" work. The delusion that social problems are to be settled in psychological terms seems, indeed, to affect all contemporary psychologists, and might best be met by the independent development of social theory. But the magnitude of Freud's contribution to knowledge in his earlier work would suggest that it was of some importance, both for social and for psychological theory, to attempt to disentangle what is sound from what is unsound in his doctrines.

At the very outset, in discussing the "disillusionment" occasioned by the war, Freud says (p. 3): "We had expected the great ruling powers among the white nations upon whom the leadership of the human species has fallen, who were known to have cultivated world-wide interests, to whose creative powers were due our technical advances in the direction of dominating nature, as well as the artistic and scientific acquisitions of the mind—peoples

---

[1] A review of: *Superstition and Society*, by R. Money-Kyrle, and *Civilisation, War and Death — Selections from three works by Sigmund Freud*. Edited by John Rickman. *Psycho-analytical Epitomes*, Nos. 3 and 4. The Hogarth Press and the Institute of Psycho-analysis, 1939.

such as these we had expected to succeed in finding another way of settling misunderstandings and conflicts of interest. Within each of these nations there prevailed high standards of accepted custom for the individual, to which his manner of life was bound to conform if he desired a share in communal privileges. These ordinances, frequently too stringent, exacted a great deal from him, much self-restraint, much renunciation of instinctual gratification. He was especially forbidden to make use of the immense advantages to be gained by the practice of lying and deception in the competition with his fellow-men." Hence he might easily be disillusioned when he found the warring state permitting itself "every such misdeed, every such act of violence, as would disgrace the individual man", and it was not astonishing "that this relaxation of all the moral ties between the greater units of mankind should have had a seducing influence on the morality of individuals" (p. 5). While Freud goes on to argue that this disillusionment is not justified (as it could scarcely be, unless a state had instincts to renounce), we can see some of the defects of his outlook even in his statement of the problem. He does, indeed, make a certain distinction between the state and the nation, but even so his "greater unit" is altogether too unitary. Over and above the distinction between legality and morality there is the fact that many conflicting "standards" are operative in society, and the further fact that culture (as represented in "artistic and scientific acquisitions") is not something established by the leading interests but something that has to fight its way against them. But, while no account is taken of the variety and the conflict of the institutions which may be said to constitute a civilisation, it is in regard to the other "unit", the individual on whom civilisation is supposed to impinge, that Freud is most seriously in error; it is his individualism that wrecks his social theory. The civilisation, which here appears as external to the individual, is nowhere represented except as relations among individuals, and is estimated by the kind of individual who exists in it—by the extent to which his instincts are suppressed or are transmuted in the direction of "altruism". The individual is always the agent—or the patient of other individual agents; there is no sense of him as a "vehicle" of social forces, as a member of movements which are just as real, just as definite as he is, and which are the true subject of social science. Hence, on the one hand, Freud has to come down to exhortation ("a little more truthfulness and upright dealing on all sides"), and, on the other hand, he can make nothing of the social facts from which the argument began ("why the national units should disdain, detest, abhor one another, even when they are at peace, is indeed a mystery"). The mystery might have been reduced if he had considered the ways of living, the "causes", in which men are caught up, and had not sought the original springs of action within the individual man.

It might be argued that *Civilisation and its Discontents* ("Das Unbehagen in der Kultur"), in particular, is an attempt to show how social arrangements impinge on the "individual", but the point is that, unless we treat a person otherwise than as a unit, unless we consider the activities which pass *through* him (in which he participates without being either *the* agent or *the* patient), we cannot even give an account of the activities which go on within him. And here we may particularly criticise Freud's use of the notion of "happiness", e.g., in dealing (pp. 28,9) with the problem "what the behaviour of men themselves reveals as the purpose and object of their lives, what they demand and wish to attain in it. The answer to this can hardly be in doubt: they seek happiness, they want to become happy and remain so". As has been indicated, unless a man had his springs of action entirely within himself (on which atomic theory there could be no such thing as human intercourse), his behaviour would not reveal what was peculiarly the purpose and object of *his* life, even if what it revealed was a purpose at all. And, as regards men's seeking happiness, if this is not the uninformative identity that they seek what they seek, if it is contended that they have one governing objective (perhaps describable as surcease from agitation), that is simply false. Here Freud might have learned something from Nietzsche (*The Will to Power*, p. 704): "It is very obvious that the ultimate and smallest 'individuals' cannot be understood in the sense of metaphysical individuals or atoms; their sphere of power is continually shifting its ground: but with all these changes, can it be said that any of them strives after happiness?"—and again (ibid., 930): "A man does *not* strive after 'happiness'; one must be an Englishman to be able to believe that a man is always seeking his own advantage", or, more succinctly, in *The Twilight of the Idols*: "Man does not aspire to happiness; only the Englishman does that"—the Englishman here being taken as the supreme individualist, the Benthamite man.

The point can be even better illustrated from the obituary article on Freud by Ernest Jones, in the current number of the *International Journal of Psycho-analysis* (Vol. XXI, Part I, p. 16). "Even pure 'unhappiness' is now a medico-psychological problem. As a result of all this innumerable people now consult physicians who used either to suffer their troubles as best they could or to seek some form of consolation. I should be surprised to hear that Oscar Wilde ever sought medical advice for his mental condition, still less Dr. Johnson, Schopenhauer or Dean Swift; nor does Herr Hitler. Yet these, and thousands of others, would probably have had a happier life had they done so." Can anyone seriously doubt that Hitler would not have *wanted* to lead a happier life, to engage in the activities which a physician might have shown him had been thwarted in his earlier days, that he would consider the activities in which he is now engaged to be vastly more important? And is it not at least arguable that a man who "suffers his troubles as best he can" will be a better worker in a movement than one who runs to a doctor to get relief? More generally, can "heroic values", can heroism and devotion, be reduced to, or at all accounted for in terms of, the pursuit of happiness? The "medico-psychological" approach prevents the Freudians from getting more than a glimpse of these problems, and involves them ("unconsciously", no doubt) in the use of a scale of importance which falsifies the social facts.

Equally, of course, it falsifies the "personal" facts. Even apart from a man's participation in movements, there is no one end ("satisfaction", "gratification" or whatever it may be called) which he seeks; various activities are going on within him, each of which may have its own objective, but each of which, prior to any question of seeking, has its own character. It is precisely from this point of view, taking what things *are* as fundamental, that we can see how such an activity may be a constituent in a wider movement (one passing through many persons) which has *its* own character. And it is only loosely that, recognising the *conatus* of such activities, their tendency to persist, we could speak of their "seeking" their own continuance. Strictly we should speak of their seeking something other than themselves, something the securing of which may or may not be necessary, and may or may not be sufficient, for their continuance. But, in regard to those that do continue, while it is idle to speak of their continuance as their "satisfaction", it is thoroughly misleading to speak of them as contributing to the satisfaction of a total "self" or as affording it some consolation for the ills of the world and the flesh. No doubt there is an economy of activities, no doubt we can distinguish between a more and a less coherent "life"—and certainly Freud has contributed notably to this region of theory. But, whatever their interrelations, an irreducible plurality of activities (and of "aims") has still to be recognised. It is true that bodily ills and social oppression may interfere with the work of the scientist and the artist; it is not true that this work is a moderately successful attempt at "transferring the instinctual aims into such directions that they cannot be frustrated by the outer world" (p. 32), i.e., at overcoming such ills. For one thing the materials on which scientist and artist work are as "outer" as anything can be; but so, likewise, are their "workings"—thinking and creating (more exactly, what thinks and what creates) exist in exactly the same sense (and in the same "world") as the things they deal with, and do not have a bogey existence which falls short of "reality". There may, again, among *appreciators* of art, whom Freud finds (p. 33) to be further removed from "reality" than artists, be some who are seeking escape from the hardness of life—though such people would actually be *bad* appreciators. But, if the continued exercise of an aesthetic interest in things is to be spoken of as satisfaction or enjoyment, it is certainly a real enjoyment, and the statement (p. 34) that the influence of art "is not strong enough to make us forget real misery" is a confused one. The point is that different mental activities are seeking different objects, and, while it will be interesting to consider how the frustration of one may affect the operation of others, the argument will not be advanced by calling some of the objects real and others not real. The view that aesthetic appreciation is "pleasure in illusion" is not, of course, peculiar to Freud, but, in any case, it is easily met; when, e.g., we appreciate drama we are getting insight into human nature—a perfectly real thing—and if, instead, we are interested in the puppets, then, while our interest is not aesthetic, it is still interest in something real. Of course, if we "identify ourselves" with the characters, we may quite properly be said to be enjoying a "phantasy-pleasure", but this attitude is possible in relation to any material whatever and has nothing specially to do with art. It appears, then, that Freud quite arbitrarily distinguishes certain pains and pleasures as the "real" ones—or, if not arbitrarily, at least unwarrantably—basing his procedure on a supposedly biological conception of fundamental drives and aims, in relation to which actual history can only appear a "mystery".

Freud asserts (p. 39) that "the word 'culture' describes the sum of the achievements and institutions which differentiate our lives from those of our animal forebears and serve two purposes, namely, that of protecting humanity against nature and of regulating the relations of human beings among themselves". It is no wonder he is in difficulties about beauty, of which he says (p. 36) that "the necessity of it for cultural purposes is not apparent, and yet civilisation could not do without it". But not only has he to admit that certain institutions do not protect and regulate, but, in regard to what is protected and regulated, he cannot show what purpose *it* serves—it simply goes on, or fails to go on. The same, then, may be said of institutions or forms of activity; social science is precisely the account of their interrelations, their changes, their continuance or cessation, and, incidentally, of their effects, but there is no point in calling these effects their "purposes". Whether culture is or is not in some special sense "autonomous", at least we can say of it (as we might say of a single person) that it does not serve any purpose. And to the assertion (p. 9) that "civilisation is the fruit of renunciation of instinctual satisfaction" we can retort that it could as easily be called the fruit of instinctual satisfaction, that we have no right to consider the renouncing tendencies any less *original* than the tendencies renounced, that only the recognition of competing tendencies at any stage we like to consider can account for the occurrence of "renunciation" or any other change in ways of acting. It is important enough to show that there can be "substitution", that energy can be carried over from one activity to another, but this does not entitle Freud to say (p. 47) that, in making its restrictions, culture "obtains a great part of the energy it needs by subtracting it from sexuality", as if the energy *belonged* to sexuality; for, unless there were independent non-sexual activities from the beginning, the transference of energy could not take place. Thus, recognising the multiplicity of forms of activity in any man and any society, however primitive, we have no need to attempt the derivation of beauty from "the realms of sexual sensation"; and we can see immediately the falsity of the assertion (p. 36) that "the love of beauty is a perfect example of a feeling with an inhibited aim". For the love of beauty is concerned with things just as definite, and brings about just as definite results, as sexuality does.

Freud does make concessions, inadequate though they are on account of his individualism and biologism, to multiplicity; he recognises aggressiveness as part of men's instinctual endowment, and uses it (p. 51) to fill out his account of civilisation. "The existence of this tendency to aggression which we can detect in ourselves and rightly presume to be present in others is the factor that disturbs our relations with our neighbours and makes it necessary for culture to institute its high demands. Civilised society is perpetually menaced with disintegration through this primary hostility of men towards one another. Their interests in their common work would not hold them together; the passions of instinct are stronger than reasoned interests. Culture has to call up every possible reinforcement in order to erect barriers against the aggressive instincts of men and hold their manifestations in check by reaction-formations in men's minds. Hence its system of methods by which mankind is to be driven to identifications and aim-inhibited love-relationships; hence the restrictions on sexual life; and hence, too, its ideal command to love one's neighbour as oneself, which is really justified by the fact that nothing is so completely at variance with original human nature as this." In fact (p. 52), "if civilisation requires sacrifices, not only of sexuality but also of the aggressive tendencies in mankind, we can better understand why it should be so hard for men to feel happy in it". Here we may argue that the recognition by civilised men of the command "to love one's neighbour as oneself" is by no means so extensive as Freud suggests; even taking it as his personalistic account of the sense of justice (equality before the law), we have to admit that there are considerable restrictions on the social operation of this principle. But the main point is that men, as social, *are* held together in common work (however little they may be "interested" in or aware of this fact), that common work is just as "original" as aggressiveness or sexuality. Freud seems to think that some *inducement* must be held out to men to work together; this bringing together, which is opposed by aggression and which is characteristic of culture, he takes to be the work of Eros, "which aims at binding together single human individuals, then families, then tribes, races, nations, into one great unity, that of humanity" (p. 55). "These masses of men", he adds, "must be bound to one another libidinally; necessity alone, the advantages of common work, would not hold them together." But, as before, it is not a question of "advantages", which in any case could be seen only after the fact; it is the common work itself that holds them together (or is their being together), whatever "libidinal" attachments may be developed on this basis. Freud's conclusion (p. 56) that the evolution of culture is "the struggle between Eros and Death, between the instincts of life and the instincts of destruction", so that "the evolution of civilisation may be simply described as the struggle of the human species *for existence*" (my italics), leaves us wondering why unification is required for survival, and indicates a low view of culture. The real cultural struggle is not for the survival of men but between different institutions or ways of living, which may pass out of existence even if human society continues. Or, supposing it could in fact be shown that unless, e.g., science progresses, the human race will perish, still, if the progress *is* made, it will be the scientific advance, and not the continuance of humanity, which will constitute the gain for culture.

Curiously, while Freud passes over these essential distinctions (among ways of living), his postulate of unification being in harmony with his tendency to theoretical simplification, he may also be said to make unjustifiable distinctions. He himself admits (p. 53) that he had to modify his initial distinction between ego instincts and object instincts, derived from the rough distinction of "hunger and love" as fundamental motives, of which "hunger would serve to represent those instincts which aim at preservation of the individual", while "love seeks for objects; its chief function, which is favoured in every way by nature, is preservation of the species". Rejecting the teleological view (which is not good biology but bad philosophy), observing that no mode of action could be *described* in terms of what it preserves, we can easily see that, as far as effects are concerned, the very same action could assist the preservation both of the individual and of the species. And, in the further working out of their theories, the Freudians have been conspicuously successful in indicating linkages between alimentation and sexuality. That is not to say, however, that there is any justification for unifying all such tendencies under the heading of a "libido" which can invest the ego as well as objects outside it. We may say, in fact, that it is just such forced unification that leads to the search for an equally arbitrary differentiating factor. If we take our departure from the plurality of mental tendencies (allowing that there may be "exchanges" between them), we find that each of them has things which it supports and things which it opposes, i.e., each of them is both "erotic" and "aggressive". (The view that any thwarted tendency becomes aggressive would settle the controversy among analysts, mentioned on p. 71, as to the relation between thwarting and "guilt".) We may even argue that the distinction between ego, id and super-ego is a distinction, not among mental "instances" or organisations, but among possible ways of acting of the same mental tendency (the same passion, as we may put it in default of any more neutral term). The comparative rigidity of Freudian doctrine, its failure to take account of the variety of mental and social qualities, is due not merely to its biological and general "scientific" starting-point, but also to its cognitionalism—its treatment of mental processes in terms of their *objects*, leaving a variety of objects over against an unqualified ego, and, in the end, emptying life of all content. This may seem a curious charge in view of the fact that Freud has above all upheld the existence of the "unconscious"—but the question here is always what it is unconscious *of*, what can be revealed as its true or original object; as if passions could not, in the course of their history, have any number of objects, and as if they did not have their own qualities, even when they had *no* objects. There is, no doubt, a real and important problem of "fixation", but it cannot be solved on a cognitionalist basis; and social theory, too, suffers from fixation, when culture is treated as having an object and not as *being* certain forms of activity.

If aggression is not a separate passion but a way in which various passions work, then, as suggested above, there will be no difficulty in reconciling the view that guilt is engendered by the thwarting of any "instinctual gratification" with Freud's identification of guilt with suppressed aggression—for the suppression of the passion which has become aggressive will at the same time be the suppression of its aggressiveness. It is important also to observe that Freud's theory of guilt as a present-day phenomenon does not require, and even weighs against, acceptance of the doctrine of the "original sin" which he first presented in *Totem and Taboo*

FREUDIANISM AND SOCIETY (1940) 439

and repeats here. In reply to the supposed objection, "Either it is not true that guilt is evoked by suppressed aggressiveness or else the whole story about the father-murder is a romance, and primeval man did not kill his father any more often than people do nowadays", he points out (p. 65) that the *remorse* of the murderer "clearly presupposes that *conscience*, the capacity for feelings of guilt, was already in existence before the deed"; and goes on to say: "This remorse was the result of the very earliest primal ambivalence of feelings toward the father: the sons hated him, but they loved him too; after their hate against him had been satisfied by their aggressive acts, their love came to expression in their remorse about the deed", and set up the punishing super-ego "by identification with the father". Hence (pp. 66,7) "it is not really a decisive matter whether one has killed one's father or abstained from the deed; one must feel guilty in either case, for guilt is the expression of the conflict of ambivalence, the eternal struggle between Eros and the destructive or death instinct. This conflict is engendered as soon as man is confronted with the task of living with his fellows", and, expressing itself first as the Oedipus complex when man is living in a family, it develops into a general feeling of guilt in relation to a wider communal life. "Since culture obeys an inner erotic impulse which bids it bind mankind into a closely knit mass, it can achieve this aim only by means of its vigilance in fomenting an ever-increasing sense of guilt. That which began in relation to the father ends in relation to the community." There is nothing in all this to suggest that the sense of guilt started from a particular *act*, an "occasion which was also the inception of culture" (p. 69). It would rather appear that, while the opposing passions must in any case have found outlet in many acts, the killing of the father might as easily be a phantasy in the case of primitive men as in the case of present-day men. As we have seen, man is *not* confronted with the task of living with his fellows, but is social all along; and, within society, he is involved in conflicts among social tendencies, among his personal tendencies, and between social and personal tendencies. It is a common experience to feel that one has "fallen short" in relation to some "cause" or movement, has been weakly "egoistic". But it is only if egoism ("omnipotence") is taken to be a person's essential character—in which case, as we observed, there would not *be* society—that culture could be supposed to involve "an ever-increasing sense of guilt". On the contrary, responsible participation in a productive movement is marked by a diminution in the sense of guilt, by a rising above "personal" values, and any movement which intensifies feelings of guilt is thereby shown to be anti-progressive.

It is not surprising that Freud thinks little of ethics, since he treats it not as the theory of the varieties of "common work" but as the laying down of precepts ("the ethical standards of the cultural super-ego"), particularly that we should "love our neighbours as ourselves"—precepts which it is impossible to fulfil, and which are therefore a poor defence against aggressiveness. Freud (p. 78) thinks it "unquestionable that an actual change in men's attitude to property would be of more help in this direction than any ethical commands; but among the Socialists this proposal is obscured by new idealistic expectations disregarding human nature, which detract from its value in actual practice". What Freud does not grasp here is that Socialism is a theory not of human nature but of society, of the laws of social working—though it certainly can be argued that Marx makes the opposite error to Freud's, reducing the psychical to the social instead of the social to the psychical. But, whatever the monistic features of Marxism, it gives some recognition at least to the plurality of movements and so can provide some *criticism* of the "enthusiastic partiality", against which Freud (p. 79) has endeavoured to guard himself, for "our civilisation"—as if our civilisation had to be praised or depreciated *in a lump*. Also Marxism would replace the view (p. 80) "that the judgments of value made by mankind are immediately determined by their desires for happiness" by the sounder view that they are determined by the movements in which men participate—though it should be noted that neither view would be evidence for or against the truth of any such judgment. If there is such a thing as value (if we really are judging something to be the case when we pass a "judgment of value"), then it will not matter whether, in passing it, we are "propping up our illusions"; the issue of fact will still have to be discussed objectively. Thus the judgment that something is required for a certain movement, the judgment that a certain movement advances science or art or any other constituent of culture, even the judgment that a certain state of affairs will bring me what I want, all raise just as positive issues as any that Freud has treated of, and are subject to the very same powers of criticism in us. In short, the question "How do we come to regard certain things as good?" is subsequent, not prior, to the question "What things *are* good?" And it is quite apparent that Freud regards the operation of "Eros" as good—though in so doing, as has been indicated, he impoverishes ethics by making the question merely one of "libidinal" unification instead of *specific* co-operative activities, the extension of which is progress and their restriction reaction. Devotion to the cause of science, e.g., is not devotion to one's fellow-scientists, and the family attachment of the Freudians in particular has been an obstacle to their progress.

In the letter to Einstein we find the same emphasis on unification, the same untenable theory of the establishment of community by the coming together of originally separate individuals. In discussing the relation between right and violence in society, Freud contends that "to start with, brute force was the factor which, in small communities, decided points of ownership and the question which man's will was to prevail". And, allowing that "with the coming of weapons, superior brains began to oust brute force", still, "under primitive conditions, it is superior force—brute violence, or violence backed by arms—that lords it everywhere". The passage from this violence to law depended on "a single verity; that the superiority of one strong man can be overborne by an alliance of many weaklings; that *l'union fait la force*. Brute force is overcome by union, the allied might of scattered units makes good its right against the isolated giant. Thus we may define 'right' as the might of a community"—the passage has been made from individual to communal violence. The mark of this community is "the suppression of brute force by the transfer of power to a larger combination, founded on the community of sentiments linking up its members". But, in actual fact, there are always "elements of unequal power" in the group, culminating in its division into rulers and ruled, struggling respectively for privileges and for equal rights. Violence is found also in the struggle between groups; and, at the present time (1933), while the League of Nations is an interesting experiment, there is no body with the authority to exercise a central control over consenting members—which would be the "one sure way of ending war". It appears, then, that "any effort to replace brute force by the might of an ideal is, under present conditions, doomed to fail. Our logic is at fault if we ignore the fact that right is founded on brute force and even today needs violence to maintain it."

In the view thus presented (pp. 84–90) there is at least a recognition of social division, though in terms of power and aggression rather than of forms of activity. We are reminded of Vico's treatment of the heroic age, or the passage from the heroic to the political age, as a struggle between patricians and plebeians, wherein "against one aristocratic privilege after another there was successfully asserted some democratic right" (Flint, *Vico*, p. 222). Vico also held the questionable theory of the family as preceding the wider community, but for him it was a question of the coming together of a number of heads of families (*patres*) to form a social authority, not, as with Freud, the banding together of brothers. The principle point is that *justice* was Vico's leading conception, that the whole process could be described as a development of justice, i.e., in social terms. It is quite apparent that, even in the smallest community, brute force cannot be the decisive factor—unless there is "moral force", unless there are established ways of working, there is not a community. (We might also argue, with Engels, that "the coming of weapons" implies a type of social organisation capable of producing them.) This does not mean that there cannot be violent individuals, but only that there cannot be a system (or group) in which individual violence is dominant. And, as before, the doctrine of the alliance of primarily separate individuals is untenable; the community of sentiments on which their forceful union is said to be founded, could only itself be founded on preceding joint activities. It may well be that only with a division between patricians and plebeians would rights be *formulated*, but in any condition of society there must be regular ways of working (including avoidances); and "right", in this broad sense, is not "founded on brute force"—nor, again, is it founded on "identification", on the socialising of unsocial units.

The defects of Freud's individualism may be finally indicated from his remarks (p. 94) on the question raised by Einstein of the abuse of authority. He says: "That men are divided into leaders and the led is but another manifestation of their inborn and irremediable inequality. The second class constitutes the vast majority; they need a high command to make decisions for them, to which decisions they usually bow without demur. In this context we would point out that man should be at greater pains than heretofore to form a superior class of independent thinkers, unamenable to intimidation and fervent in the quest of truth, whose function it would be to guide the masses dependent on their lead. There is no need to point out how little the rule of politicians and the Church's ban on liberty of thought encourage such a new creation. The ideal conditions would obviously be found in a community where every man subordinated his instinctive life to the dictates of reason." But, as things are, he concludes, such a hope of subduing the "war-impulse" is utterly utopian. Now here, first of all, we find the commonplace insistence on personal differences as a basis of social inequality. But social equality is a matter not of the endowment of individuals but of the primacy of the movement, the setting of the common form of activity above personal considerations; and even when (as in science) a highly endowed participant can stimulate others, there need be no *office* of leader. Again, the well-intentioned "forming" of a guiding class, however fervent they may be, cannot be regarded as a possible means of solving social problems; the point of departure must always be existing "ways of living". And, thirdly, one may wonder what a life subordinated to the "dictates of reason" would be like, or what these dictates themselves could be. If "reason" is to enforce a particular hierarchy of tendencies, it must itself have particular objects; in other words, what is called "reason" is merely certain ruling passions, and *other* passions could (and do) carry out the same function, determine what is "reasonable", in other cases. It appears, in fact, that Freud's thinking is deeply imbued with the rationalistic utilitarianism which is so marked a feature of nineteenth century thought, with fixed ideas of mental and social priority, which have prevented him from working out the consequences of his own recognition of the "unconscious", and have landed him in simplification, in the denial of real distinctions, whether among types of mental processes or between the psychical and the social.

We find in the work of the Freudians generally this rationalistic apparatus—the setting up of *units*, the identification of things which are merely connected, or as frequently in Freud, the reversal of relations (e.g., on p. 44, the supposition that it was when the need for genital satisfaction became permanent that the male "acquired a motive" for keeping his sexual objects near him, and so families were founded)—the outstanding example, of course, being the view that individuals form society instead of society forming individuals. (Even if the two were taken as coordinate phenomena, it would have to be admitted that individualism, with the conception of personal advantage, was a late growth.) In the other work under review (the third in the series of *Epitomes*) these defects are very well marked; indeed, Money-Kyrle is considerably less cautious than Freud in his views of what can be done to improve society. He proposes the establishment of a "psycho-analytical anthropology", since the psychologist and the social anthropologist need each other's help. Thus the former may learn from the latter (p. 2) that the "latency period, in which sexual impulses are in abeyance, between the age of five and puberty" is not a "general developmental character", since in certain tribes "the sex instinct ripens from infancy to adolescence without a break". (Whether such a period *is* universal "among civilised peoples" is a question which the Freudians might well reconsider.) And the latter may help the former (p. 3) in bringing out the *unconscious* motives of the customs and beliefs with which anthropology concerns itself. (As before, it is assumed that they *have* a motive, that the *fons et origo* of institutions is to be found in the individual mind.) Thus (pp. 3, 4) "anthropologists and psycho-analysts need each other's help. Indeed, the sociology of the future will be, I think, the product of their combined labour. This sociology will expose the reciprocal relations between culture, character and education; the factors determining whether groups will diverge or converge, compete or co-operate, and so on. It will give us the power to control our social destiny, not blindly as in the past, or short-sightedly as at present, but with a clear vision of our path ahead. Moreover, with greater knowledge of ourselves and of our social structure, our social aims are likely to become less divergent. Some divergence of politics is, of course, inevitable; but the more obviously irrational policies, by-products perhaps of the psychoses of their authors, will not find much support in a more enlightened age." Certainly, Money-Kyrle at once admits that "many calamities may await our culture" before this goal is attained; but his conclusion (pp. 151, 153) is that, through the scientific co-operation he proposes, we may hope "to formulate laws of sociology, which would give to man, what he has never had before, the power to mould the character of future generations according to his will", and, while this mastery of means might be supposed to leave the aims uncertain, "we have good reason to suppose that in the sphere of morals both the area and the intensity of the conflict will decrease concurrently with an increase in our power to make our hopes prevail. For, on the one hand, a deeper understanding of our own psychology will automatically decrease psychological disease, and therefore also those extreme ideals (e.g., fanatical militarism, asceticism, etc.) which are themselves among the symptoms of disease. And, in the second place, this greater understanding of ourselves will bring greater sympathy with, and therefore tolerance of, the residual deviations of ideal that will no doubt remain. Thus we may hope that one day the infant science of psycho-analytical anthropology will perform the Herculean task—which has so far defeated the philosophies and religions of the world—of giving *homo sapiens* the wisdom that his name implies. Once he acquires this, a rational society, in the political and economic sense, will come almost of its own accord."

The question here is that of "application", of how the infant science (as Rickman puts it in his Preface, with reference to psychology) "can help mankind". We are to find out laws of sociology in order to *change* society; we are to learn how societies or certain types of society invariably work in order that we may introduce our particular variations into them. In other words, we are to "use" laws that we know, and in so doing obey laws that we do not know! It is not merely that (as Freud himself to a considerable extent realised), in finding out laws, we are finding out what *cannot* be helped. What, more particularly, the partisans of "scientific" helpfulness do not grasp is that theories occur as features of social movements, not as independent forces, that they are indices of what we are doing rather than guides for our future conduct. To say this, as was previously pointed out, is not to say that such theories are false, but, at least, the adherents of the movement of which "helpfulness" is a slogan, are not entitled to regard themselves as above the battle or on the side of pure *sapientia*; they are pursuing a particular line of policy under the pretence that it is universal, i.e., that it alone is "truly" pursuable; they are using the formal notion of agreement as if it were something specific on which we could agree. For that is what Money-Kyrle's rather shaky treatment of the means-and-ends problem amounts to: if we learn to agree, we are bound to be agreeing on something—an entirely helpless position in relation to actual social trends. In default of a positive doctrine of social movements and of those activities extension of which would constitute progress (as against the banal dictum that "moral judgments are notoriously subjective"), he cannot show that there is anything wrong with such "extreme ideals" as fanatical militarism and asceticism; he can only appeal to prejudice. And it is just such uncritical views, it is just such illusions as that of moulding humanity, that philosophy exists to criticise.

We have already noted that the conception of rationality is an outstanding feature of the ideology of the movement here being examined, and Money-Kyrle employs it constantly. It would appear that rational behaviour is that in which we know what we are doing, whereas (p. 8) "irrational behaviour has an unconscious basis, and is unintelligible until this basis is explained". For example (p. 71), the compulsive avoidances of the obsessional neurotic resemble taboos in having "no conscious motive". Now what would be meant by having a conscious motive? Presumably, to say that I have a conscious motive for avoiding X is to say that I avoid it because it is Y. But why do I avoid Y? Because it is Z? It is obvious that at some point the chain of "reasons" must stop—that, e.g., no more can be said than that I do avoid Y. Or, at least, while it might be said that I avoid Y because I am a certain sort of person, because I (or I and others) live in a certain way, this is not, properly speaking, to give a *reason* for the avoidance of Y, but only to state more exactly what form of activity it is that avoids Y. More generally, whatever I may know about what I am doing, there are always things I do not know about it; an action is never "fully intended", but always in some measure *does itself*; and so the conscious is always based on the unconscious, reasons on the "irrational". The only escape from this position would be to set up some *identity*—the self-knowing or the essentially avoidable—from which particular cognitions or avoidances would be derived; but actually such derivations are always sophistical, and the rationalist is found to be upholding particular views or policies *without reason*, while endeavouring to put them above criticism by calling them "rational".

A particular example of the operation of "identity" in these doctrines is to be found in the Freudian ethics, where, as we have noted, goodness takes the form of altruism or, more exactly, of *unification* with others. The position is very curiously illustrated in a point made by Money-Kyrle (p. 70, n. 1) in support of his view that morals are always felt as having a sanction, as imposed on us by commandment: "As Kant has pointed out, people who *behave well* because they like doing so, *because they genuinely sympathise with others*, are not moral. If such behaviour should ever become general, morals will have been outgrown and have become superfluous" (my italics). The view that "benevolence is the whole of virtue" is so distinctly not Kant's that, having distinguished the duty of beneficence from natural inclination to bring about satisfaction in others, he immediately goes on (*Fundamental Principles of the Metaphysic of Morals*, First Section) to consider the conditions under which securing one's own happiness is a duty. And, whatever difficulties the distinction between will and inclination may involve, he is most emphatically opposed to the view that morality is imposed on men by *external* command. What has led Money-Kyrle to make this misleading statement is his obsession with his own narrow views; and, it may be added, since he admits that there is such a thing as "behaving well", he implies that, even if "morals" were outgrown, ethics would not be.

More important, however, in identity-theorising is the doctrine of substance, of an inner nature from which all characters are derived—a doctrine we have already encountered in the view that the individual has his springs of action within himself. Strictly speaking this involves a denial of interaction and of all history; the question is just what particular compromise with the facts will be made. The compromise made by the Freudians is to take the earliest experiences as imposing on the original disposition modifications which are decisive for the rest of life. It is, of course, a sufficiently plausible view that a thing's disposition contains all its possible lines of development, and that some of these possibilities are eliminated at each stage. But actual development is conditioned by both character and circumstances, and is not a function of either. It may be true that only things of the sort X ever become Y, but also true that this happens only when an X comes under the influence of C. There is, then, no more sense in saying that the acquired character Y was *in* the original character X than in saying that it was in C; to say that it was there "potentially" is only a way of denying the fact in question, that, when X is subjected to C, *something new* appears. Thus it is a plain fact of human history that many types of activity do not arise at all until later life, and to say that their potentiality, their basis, that out of which they come, must have been present in infancy is really to deny interaction. *Certain* ways of acting must, of course, be common to the various stages, or we could not speak of them as stages in the history of the same being; and what happens to one way of acting at an early stage may have an important influence on its later manifestations. But it is a far cry from this to the description of work, war and religion (p. 141) as "products of infantile neurosis", to the contention (p. 124) that the extreme helplessness and long duration of man's infancy are "ultimately responsible for his neurotic anxiety and his animism—or habit of projecting his own infantile feelings upon his environment—and that his animism, in particular his tendency to rediscover the good and bad parents of his unconscious phantasy in the persons of his leaders and his enemies, is responsible both for his co-operative and competitive tendencies, for his social solidarity, and for his proneness to war". These extraordinary claims would imply that infants make society; actually, they are born into society, into a set of interrelated social movements or institutions, which largely determine their history—and, by being brought into new movements, the adult can develop activities of which no trace could be found in the infant. And as regards tendencies (passions) which may be said to exist throughout life, the object or outlet which they first found may influence later seekings, but that is not to say that *it* is still being sought. To make such *identifications* is to involve oneself in confusions as to actual connections and influences. We may be able, as suggested on p. 110, to connect the development of language with the infant's scream (and that, again, with his helplessness), but that does not give us a theory of language as a social phenomenon. Faced with a new situation, a person has to "express himself" in some way, and the gesture he finds most appropriate may well be one which he had used in relation to earlier situations; but this is not to say that the new situation "means" the old—otherwise, language would not develop, and infants would really be and remain "psychotics". If they are not, it is because they are engaged from the beginning in co-operative activities, because they belong to society and are not self-centred atoms. In fact, the "helplessness" of the human infant should itself be treated as a social phenomenon, as *engendered* by society, as the thing that makes him educable (fit for social living) and not as either the basis of or a fetter upon social development.

As with language, so with Mythology, with Exogamy, Totemism and Taboo, with Animism, Magic and Religion—dealt with by Money-Kyrle in chapters II, III and IV, where he presents, in spite of the brevity of his exposition, a good deal of interesting material and raises many important questions—all these are phenomena of adult social life, they are ways of dealing with situations which may bear a certain resemblance to infantile situations (infants also being in society) but are not reducible to them. In connection with mythology, Money-Kyrle remarks (p. 20) that "the most archaic myths are so much concerned with the improprieties of gods that they can hardly have been composed by legislators, as Aristotle thought, to edify mankind". But what might appear to a later age as improper and requiring to be softened down or explained away, might be quite a natural form of expression in an earlier, "heroic" age. In any case the question is not so much of edifying as of warning men against "Ὕβρις not to "set themselves up" against the gods, that is to say, against social laws. Here we are brought back to Vico's theory, in which, having begun with various forms of interpretation of myths, he finally concentrated on the social interpretation "since, he appears to have thought, the earliest nations were too much intent upon themselves, too much immersed in their hard and difficult life, to speculate in abstraction from social matters. Hence he found reflected in mythology the institutions, inventions, social cleavages, class-struggles, travels and warfare of primitive nations" (Croce, *The Philosophy of Giambattista Vico*; trans. Collingwood, pp. 160,1). Croce goes on to say that Vico set up another important principle, "namely, that indecent meanings were inserted in myths at a late and corrupt period when men interpreted early customs in the light of their own, or tried to justify their own lusts by fancying that the gods had set them the example". It is to be remembered that the manners of an earlier age, even when cruder, may be less indecent than those of a later age. The main point, however, is that the elaboration of myths is bound to involve the introduction of more and more psychical material, which would tend to obscure the fact that the original meaning was not psychical but social. Such elaboration, of course, might well be in terms of the peculiarities of an individual's upbringing and even of his infantile experiences; psycho-analysis has done very much towards establishing such connections, and could do still more if it distinguished the social foundation from the psychic variants. And here it is curious that Money-Kyrle, in discussing demons and vampires in his chapter on Animism, makes no mention of Jones's remarkable work, *On the Nightmare*. (It is curious also that Jones himself, though he mentions, on p. 151), "the oral-sadistic attitude towards the mother's breast"—a matter also touched on by Money-Kyrle—does not see that this is the situation in terms of which coherence can be given to his whole discussion, since it is a situation to which the notions of riding or flying and of the reversal of roles can be referred back, and particularly to his philological excursus on "the MR root", since this root can be taken to express the combination of sucking and biting.)

In the section on Totemism in ch. III, Money-Kyrle shows that recent anthropological work would tend to cast doubt on the theory expounded by Freud in *Totem and Taboo*, not only in regard to the very existence of the "cyclopean family" (dominated by a single father), but in regard to whether certain races ever had a totemic system. While Money-Kyrle thinks there might possibly have been a process (extending over many generations and involving father-killings at various times) in which the cyclopean family alternated with the exogamic clan, he is impressed (pp. 64, 5) by the difficulty of explaining "the survivals of the taboos and rituals thousands of years after the last cyclopean father is supposed to have been slain". As he points out later (p. 121): "The most primitive communities we know of are gerontocratic: a man enjoys prestige in proportion to his age. There are no single chiefs to represent the primal father. But the clan is cemented by common taboos, common rites, and a common veneration for its old men and its ancestral totem. The autocratic primal father is replaced by an endo-psychic force—the super-ego, which is identified with the old men and with the ghosts of ancestors still living in the totem species." Now, if what we find in such communities is always *patres* as the social authority, there is no great obstacle to the rejection of the whole theory of the primal father and the primal sin—to regarding the notion of father-murder as an individualistic modification of a revolt against the *patres* or, more generally, against social law—with all the calamities that this would involve. (Here again Vico's theory is of some interest; he considers that, with the rise of the plebeians, there was a secondary development of myth in which their desire for the overthrow of the patricians was represented. Cf. H. P. Adams, *Life and Writings of Giambattista Vico*, p. 188) As already pointed out, psychical material is constantly being introduced into myths, and much contamination of this kind may be expected to appear in the myths of present-day peoples who, though they are called "primitive", should perhaps rather be regarded as having degenerated from an earlier "heroic" level. It should also be emphasised that Freud's conception of the super-ego is too individualistic, not merely in that it is taken as something established *within* the individual mind, but in the giving of too much weight to the influence of the parents in its formation. For the parents are living in society, and the Freudians themselves have had to admit that the restrictions imposed by the parents on the child are largely representative of general *social* prohibitions. The point is that the "censored" passion encounters these prohibitions in many different forms, and, without taking any one of them as *the* prohibition or regarding the earliest as necessarily the most important, we can still find in some cases, as the psycho-analysts have notably done, peculiarities of upbringing, and even a "primal scene", having a severe effect on later development—though not a finally decisive one, or analysis itself would be impossible. (It may be interesting to remark here on the fact that Vico plays a large part in the inspiration of *Finnegans Wake*, of which I take the "primal scene" to be the theme.)

In line with the above argument it is necessary to reject, at least in the form given to it by the Freudians, the doctrine of the "group ideal", which is one of the conceptions by which they try to smuggle the social into their individualistic theory. "The basis of the group-ideal is, of course, the super-ego, the parental authority incorporated by the child in the early period", says Money-Kyrle (p. 138). But the process of incorporation is continued with reference to respected and authoritative figures. "Such persons already embody our super-egos; indeed it is a condition of our acceptance of their ideals that they should do so. Thus the group-ideal is a late incorporation superimposed upon the earlier super-ego. In a sense, it is an outer layer of the super-ego; but, unlike the core, it is conscious and within limits flexible." On the next page, however, after suggesting as a first approximation that infantile experience is responsible for temperament, as mental foundation, and the group ideal for character, as superstructure, Money-Kyrle remarks that "the mind develops as a whole like a plant, not in sections like a house. What the infantile situation determines, therefore, is not so much a part of the resultant personality as a given range of potential personalities, which is progressively limited by later influences, and in particular by the group ideal". Apart from the criticism already passed on the doctrine of "potentialities", it is obvious that Money-Kyrle's handling of these questions is very uncertain—as it is throughout this final chapter on "Education and Culture". The prevailing assumption is that experience is prior to activities, instead of being gathered by something already active—an assumption in harmony with the situation of helpless patient confronted by helpful analyst, who himself, however, manifests helplessness in face of recalcitrant social facts. Thus (p. 126) Money-Kyrle thinks it a striking support of his theory of "temperament" that the Central Australian "lives in a land of frequent famine; yet he never hoards his food", whereas the Normanby Islander "grows up in a land of plenty where famine is unheard of. Yet his life is dominated by the desire to collect the biggest possible hoard of food"—where what seems strange from the individualist point of view is perfectly obvious from the social point of view, and the suggestion (p. 127) that the "mere" abolition of capitalism might not affect the relative proportion of these two types, is seen to be unfounded. But the weakness of Money-Kyrle's position appears most plainly in his second last paragraph. "The utopian sociologist in general still misunderstands his problem. His fiery eloquence may change a group ideal and through it the economic and political structure of society. But unless temperamental potentialities exist that are appropriate to the new structure, it cannot possibly succeed. If not, his only course is to resign himself to a far slower but more fundamental attack upon the society he disapproves of, and, by modifying the infantile situation, seek to mould temperament to fit his utopian dream. In other words, he must first become an enlightened educationalist." Again, if there is any order in the case, Money-Kyrle has it the wrong way round; there is more to be said for the view that change of structure causes than for the view that it is caused by change of "temperament" and "ideal". But, strictly speaking, change of social structure *is* change of ways of acting, and issues from existing ways of acting (movements). It is the height of political *naïveté* to imagine that those who have not power to change the social structure directly, still have power to change the "infantile situation".

It has been noted that Money-Kyrle raises doubts about the doctrines of *Totem and Taboo*, as does Jones, in the obituary article referred to, about the "death-instinct". But it is still apparent that, from the point of view of theoretical progress, the Freudians are unduly bound by Freud's prejudices and limitations. It may be that the renegades from the movement have taken up positions inferior to Freud's, but, if the Freudians had *helped* them to develop their criticisms, if the movement made provision for thorough-going criticism and had no qualms about saying "Freud is wrong", it (like other movements one could name) would be getting ahead much faster. One is tempted to suggest that the Freudians are terrified of being accused of "father-murder". But the cause lies deeper than that; it is that they, like Freud, are working within the system of nineteenth century "science" and within a social stratum (chiefly medical) to which individualism has a compelling appeal.

# 30
# THE FREUDIAN REVOLUTION (1953)[1]

Freudianism, like Darwinism, may be called revolutionary in that it not merely introduces fresh conceptions into a particular field of inquiry but in some measure affects all our thinking, bringing about a general revaluation of ideas. It is true, of course, that, after the first shock, such influences are hard to sustain and readily collapse into vulgarisations; this is illustrated in the extent to which the catch-phrase "wishful thinking" has replaced study and understanding of the Freudian doctrine of the wish, and vulgar notions of "the struggle for existence" provide a parallel case. But one important feature of Freudianism is that it explains this very fact, that it exhibits the protection of customary views by a pretended assimilation of new ones as conforming to a regular mechanism of defence.

Vulgar notions of Freudianism as a general sexualising of human activities or as a clarion call against "repression" have some countenance in the work of Freud himself—in the doctrine of the "libido" as the single source or reservoir of mental energies and in the treatment of the repressed as the real person, the repressing factors being imposed or "introjected". But there is much in Freud's important, early works that would caution us against such "wild" interpretations; there is a constant insistence on conflict and on the fact that the conflicting tendencies are alike parts of the person, so that solution is not to be found by mere excision.

It is characteristic of a revolution to be a revaluation—to be a revolution in ideas,[2] not a mere alteration of externals or change of fashion. Fashionable trends in psychology (the interest in gadgets, questionnaires, etc.) betray, as contrasted with Freudianism, a fear of fundamentals. The opposition is between systematic thinking and miscellaneous inquiries; a revolution, as against a relapse, in ideas involving the breaking down of divisions, the discovery of unsuspected connections, the establishment of continuity against

[1] Based on an address given in the University of Sydney on April 8, 1952.
[2] Cf. "Empiricism and Logic", p. 186, above.

a postulated discontinuity. And, in its working out of an objective view of mental life, in its attack on this stronghold of subjectivism or "separatism", the Freudian revolution, like all other revolutions, has an essentially philosophical character. The continuity of the mental and the bodily, of thought and action, the breaking down of divisions between conscious and unconscious, between normal and abnormal—these are Freudian contributions to thought in general, and they illustrate the revolutionary character which Freudianism has in common with Darwinism in their rejection of what has been the greatest obstacle to vigorous and systematic inquiry, the dualism of Man and Nature.

The general revolutionary character of Freudianism, then, lies in its naturalism, in its being a contribution to the natural history of man and mind. But what is important in the specification of that character is not sexuality (in spite of the immense amount of interesting material produced by Freud and his school on the varieties and disguises of sexual impulse) but conationalism as opposed to cognitionalism, the treatment of mind as a set of drives or urges and not as an abstract cogniser, the possessor of little bits of cognised content called "ideas".

Though Freud has played a considerable part in the replacing of associationism, the doctrine of individual ideas with their attractions and repulsions, by a doctrine of interest, of activities which attend to or turn away from various objects, he still finds an associative method, the seeking of the "mental associates" of any given content, to be the most profitable way of investigating mental processes. It may be said, indeed, that Freud's emancipation from cognitionalism, from the associationist doctrines which prevailed in the period of his early studies, was incomplete. But the point is that we take a very different view of the search for associated ideas (for "latent content", etc.) if we regard the association as the work of active interests from that which we take if we think the association is the work of ideas themselves—and, with interests as our guiding principle, we are likely to *find* much relevant material that we should otherwise overlook. The notion of analysis would be pointless without the connected notion of the synthetic force of mental activity.

It is in terms of activity that the notion of disguise or substitution becomes intelligible; we are to think of a mental force as seeking outlet, encountering a barrier on its path, spreading sideways along associative lines, and then finding a way out in the general direction of its original pressure. And that these conceptions of flowing, damming, etc., are not merely figurative, that there is nothing wrong with a *physical* description of mental processes, is shown or at least corroborated by Freud's account of the bodily symptom—of its functioning, similarly to the "intellectual" response, as part of the language of the emotions. Nevertheless the classical form of analysis, the investigation of mental forces or drives in terms of their objects or cognised materials, has proved particularly fruitful and is not misleading so long as it is understood that the forces and what they are directed towards are not the same thing. It is certainly misleading to speak of *the* analysis or *the* interpretation of a dream or other mental phenomenon involving substitution and disguise; it has to be understood that there is no complete formula for any mental (and equally for any non-mental) situation, that, whatever of its connections are discovered in a particular investigation, others exist as well, and thus that it can have various "interpretations". But this is nothing against the exactness of any given set of discoveries or mass of exposed material; and it is an outstanding merit of the Freudian procedure that it insists on the definiteness of connections, on mental mechanism or determinism in terms of which alone there can be study of human character or a human character to study.

It is with reference to dreams that the various mechanisms of distortion and substitution have been most clearly and fully presented; and while the formula for the dream, "the realisation of a suppressed wish", has been shown to apply to such varied phenomena as forgetting, error, phantasy in general and even symptom-formation, it may still be said to have its classical exemplification in dream-interpretation. It means in fact that the dream is a falsification or lie; it not merely symbolises a successful outlet for tendencies that have hitherto been held in, but it represents such success as having been gained in the past, it turns previous defeats into victories. On this understanding, the aim of analysis is precise dating, is finding just what earlier events are now being symbolically denied. The fact that a suppressed impulse will regularly, and in various ways and directions, have striven to find outlet, permits it still to be maintained that different analyses are possible—there is not one but a whole series of falsifications or spurious successes; but this does not mean that any given one of them cannot be accurately traced from the dream. The Freudian doctrine is not, of course, entirely new; Nietzsche, for example, was expressing the same position in his epigram, "I did this, says Memory, I could not have done this, says Pride, and remains inexorable. Finally, Memory yields". But Freud is the first to have brought out with precision the character and range of the phenomena in question.

Part of the illumination given by Freudianism lies in its assimilation of diverse phenomena, its demonstration of the working of the same laws in such supposedly unconnected cases as dreams, forgetting, slips of the tongue and neurotic symptoms. But its initial impact was all the stronger from the fact that most of these things had been regarded as subject to no law whatever. Freud has illuminated human life and character by rendering intelligible what had been dismissed as accidental and unworthy of scientific consideration—and, once more, he has shown that the assumption of "meaninglessness" is itself part of the process of defence against unpalatable reality. It is, of course, the finding of significance in *dreams* that is the most striking example of Freud's opening up of the psychological field, and the most noteworthy point is that he has done so by emphasis on *activity*, by finding the working of psychical forces in what had been taken to be a mere picture unrolled on the mental screen.

Like all doctrines, Freudianism has its limitations. These are most apparent in the Freudian movement, since no school can quite rise to the inspiration of its founder. But in Freud himself the limitations are connected with the origin of the doctrine in the treatment of nervous disorders. The view that, because a theory has had a practical stimulus to its formation, it should have a practical outcome (an outcome other than *understanding* which is in its own way a part of human practice) is an example of that emphasis on externals against which revolutionary thinking is directed. The notion of "cure" has been one of the factors leading to the postulation of "the" interpretation of a dream or symptom, and in turn to the reinstatement of the division between normal and abnormal and to the ignoring of the universality of conflict. Freud himself avoids the extravagances of those of his followers who "settle" social conflicts in the manner of the consulting-room, who minister to the world as one great patient. But his later works certainly manifest a loss of philosophical force, a growth of "totalism", a lack of recognition of the fact that the denial of discontinuity does not mean the assertion of identity. The continuity of Man and Nature still leaves a distinction between human and non-human problems, does not merge them in one great problem or imply one great solution of all riddles.

The fact remains that Freud's work has given a tremendous impetus to rigorous thinking on human affairs, to the establishment of a real psychological science. His impact on present-day students is inevitably less than that on students of a generation ago; he has come to be taken for granted, to be treated with a certain complacency as contrasted with earlier enthusiasm and denunciation. But it is not true that "we are all Freudians now"; we can be Freudians only by hard thinking, by returning to Freud as a *classic* for the correction of current looseness. And even if no such "back to Freud" movement takes place, the Freudian revolution will not have petered out; Freudianism will remain as one of the determinants of the outlook of all critical thinkers.

# 31
# PSYCHOLOGICAL MORALISM (1953)[1]

This work resembles other productions of the time of its publication, and especially other productions by psychologists, in professing to have a practical purpose, that of finding a way out of the "tragic tangle" in which society has become involved. The psychologist, recognising that "both the failures of the past and the problems of the present and the future are to a large extent psychological in nature", may feel a certain shame at the failures but will also feel challenged by the problems to review the relevant facts and theories "with some hope that such a scrutiny of available data will reveal him, both to himself and to his fellow-men, as one who is not altogether doomed to gape idly and uselessly at the scene of human tragedy, but rather as one who can at least here and there make a promising suggestion or lend a helping hand in the work of salvage and reconstruction" (p. 9).

Flugel follows up this initial statement of the psychologist's responsibility by saying that it "is pretty generally agreed that the problem of rebuilding our tottering society upon a sounder basis is to some extent a moral problem, in the sense that its solution depends upon an appeal to the moral impulses of man", and that, while some knowledge of the origin and nature of these impulses is required if the appeal is to be successful, recent psychology has in fact gained such knowledge of these impulses as it may be possible now to organise and fruitfully apply. With this may be compared the remark in the Preface (p. 5) that "it appears to be pretty generally agreed that the failure of our civilisation to solve so many of its greatest problems, and above all its involvement in two world wars within a quarter of a century, makes it more than ever necessary that we should think seriously about fundamental moral problems"—this book having the particular task (p. 6) of considering "the possible bearings of the recent psychology

---

[1] A review of: *Man, Morals and Society, A Psycho-Analytical Study.* By J. C. Flugel. Duckworth, London, 1945.

of moral motives upon the ethical problems of an admittedly distracted world".

Flugel thinks it possible to make this response to the "urgent demand for a revision of ethical thought" without any "general treatment of the nature and problem of ethics" (and likewise of psychology and psycho-pathology). But, leaving that point aside for the moment, we may note particularly his conception of a problem and its solution—viz., not by finding that something is the case but by determining that something is to be done. This is the very opposite of the attitude of *serious thinking* on moral or other problems, the attitude of disinterested study which not merely stands aloof from practical urgencies but subjects them, and the conceptions in terms of which they are expressed, to rigorous examination. The only thing that could properly be called a failure in our civilisation would be a failure in criticism; and, of course, the serious or critical thinker knows that, whatever ups and downs criticism may have, it has in any case to maintain itself by struggle in an uncritical and "practical" environment, and that there is no question of a "solution" in which that struggle will disappear. But the raising or lowering of critical standards is not apparent to the vulgar, and the doctrine of a conspicuous breakdown or a conspicuous uplifting of civilisation is itself a vulgar view.

But while, without a "general treatment" of ethics, involving a criticism of ethical conceptions, no important contribution to ethical theory can be made, it is only fair to recognise that practicalist confusions have been very much encouraged by the mass of moral theorists, that they have treated ethics as a special kind of science whole propositions have a special kind of truth, practical truth, or a peculiar copula, the practical or preceptual copula. Thus, although Flugel uses when it suits him all the odds and ends of conventional ethics (desirability, rationality, altruism and so forth), although he never could succeed in substituting psychology for ethics, his efforts in that direction are at least attempts to substitute something which can be inquired into for something which, as conventionally conceived, simply blocks inquiry. To that extent, however he may from time to time smuggle in his own precepts, he casts light on the conditions under which *ethics as a science* (i.e., as a positive science, a subject of empirical investigation) can emerge.

Flugel's argument in the first chapter ("Psychology and Morals") is of particular importance here. He is seeking to justify the contention that psychology can contribute to our understanding of "the field of values" by investigating "the motivations underlying values", and, to that end, to discount the objection that psychologists, in professing to make such contributions, are going beyond their province. "Psychology, we are reminded, is a positive, not a normative, discipline, that is, its business is to describe, classify, and (if it can) explain the facts of mental life, just as physics and chemistry deal with the facts of the material universe. Like these latter sciences, it has no concern with values as such; it must take the facts as it finds them and must not presume to pass judgment on their desirability or undesirability" (p. 11). Flugel's remarks that this general position is one with which few if any psychologists would wish to quarrel—and then goes on to a series of considerations which, if they had any force at all, would require its abandonment. But the primary point is this, that if there were the supposed distinction between facts and values, then not only would investigation of facts cast no light on values but there could be no investigation of values at all, and any suggested connection between a fact and a value would be entirely arbitrary—the value would be somehow "annexed"[2] to the fact but would not *belong* to it and might as well be annexed to any other fact. More exactly, if "values" have any content, any positive character, they must be studied by the same methods and in the same situations as other things; they must be found, like minds, in what Flugel calls "the material universe" (as if there could be several universes). i.e., as objective occurrences. It is the dualistic outlook, with the absurd attempt to attach something of one kind of reality to something of another, that has obstructed ethical *study*, while at the same time it permits everyone to "have his fancy".

This is why Flugel does not throw over "values" altogether; he wants to retain a position in which anyone is expert, to be able to insinuate his values at any stage in his investigation of the facts. Thus the considerations by which he hopes to show the

---

[2] In most cases *phrases* in quotation marks are Flugel's even when no page reference is given. But quotation marks round single expressions are generally intended to indicate some extended or uncommon usage the nature of which I think should be clear from the context. The word "annex", of course, is not used by Flugel.

relevance of psychology to moral theory have to be expressed in such a way as to leave an opening for "annexings". His points are (1) that values "happen to be facts of *mental* life", (2) that a distinction must be made between pure and *applied* science, (3) that the distinction between means and ends "is nearly always relative", and (4) that, in the substitution of the psychological for the moral point of view even in the sphere of "intrinsic values", we are replacing moral judgment, "primarily an orectic process", by scientific judgment, "primarily a cognitive process". In these and other ways the psychological is "tending to replace the moral point of view, and there is little doubt that, in so far as the new approach proves effective, the process will continue" (p. 16). But either this is asking science to do something it cannot do or science *does* provide us with "norms". Flugel straddles the issue by saying that science, while it "may never give us ultimate values", may still, as it advances, "be of help in ever higher levels of the hierarchy of values"; but since he immediately goes on (beginning of ch. II) to say that moral action "is action in accordance with values" and that fundamentally "these values are determined by our biological nature and our innate psychological equipment", it is clear that his reservations are merely such as to permit the scientist, with *his* equipment, to give upon occasion directives as well as findings.

On the first point we are faced with the common *-ing* and *-ed* confusion; it is not made clear whether the question is of *what values* or of *what is valued*, and it is quite possible to take the view that, while the former is mental, the latter is not and would not have its character in any way illuminated by psychological investigation. Of course, if it were a question of a definite quality *good*, it might well be held that both what observes goodness and what is good are mental processes, though it still would not follow that the study of the former would cast any light on the latter. But it is clear enough, from the phrases quoted above, that Flugel does not make these distinctions, that for him values exist in the processes which "annex" them to various things (cf. the remark, in the note to p. 111, that, in the last resort, "it can be maintained that all so-called objective values are ultimately subjective in origin, inasmuch as things in the outer world are good or bad only in virtue of our attitude to them") —clear, too, that no amount of investigation of the positive characters of either mental processes or the things they are cognisant of can show what such "annexings" even *mean*. On the other hand, if we do take the positive view, if we consider, in particular, that goods (good things) are a species of mental activities, then psychological science can be of assistance to ethical science (a) by its formulation of general laws of mental process, (b) by bringing out characters of the other mental processes among which good activities exist and with which they interact; but psychological study which was not direct study of good activities could not itself be a substitute for such direct study—it could help ethics only if ethics were an independent study of certain facts.

So, if there were definite things describable as "values", psychology could conceivably indicate conditions under which they come about, but this would imply no distinction between the kind of science that studied them and the kind of science that studied these conditions, and would, in particular, do nothing to justify a distinction between pure and applied science. According to Flugel (p. 12), whereas "pure science is concerned with things as they are, its only aim being knowledge for its own sake, applied science seeks to use this knowledge for the attainment of certain ends, ends which are assumed to be desirable and which therefore imply certain values (over and above the mere values of truth or knowledge). Thus medicine or engineering imply values in a way that physiology or physics do not; they imply that it is desirable to achieve and maintain a person's health or to construct and keep in order a machine." This, of course, is not the case. True propositions of medical science imply further true propositions of medical science, but they do not imply anything in the way of a policy, nor is any such thing inherent in them. If we desire A, and if we *know* that it comes about under conditions B, and if we are able to bring about conditions B, then we are in a position to satisfy our desire; but this does not entitle us to speak of "applied knowledge" or "applied science" as if it were a special *kind* of knowledge or science. Granting, then, that psychological knowledge may be utilised "in the fields of medicine, education, and industry", what is so utilised is "pure" psychology, not "applied" psychology. And if such utilisation is held to require that certain "ends" should be "assumed to be desirable", then, if this is not a psychological assumption (the assumption that certain propositions in the field of psychology are true), either it is an assumption in some other, equally scientific field—but one taken to be continuous with the psychological field—or it is a mere confusion and in no way elucidates the conception of "application".

In fact, continuity is the vital point. The ambiguity of "desirability" (a much-debated matter on which, it need hardly be said, Flugel does not touch) is one of the devices enabling the dualist to jump the chasm between his antithetical realities—or rather to appear to do so without inconsistency. But, as before, there can be no connection between a thing and its supposed "value" unless this is as much one of its characters, part of its "constitution", as any of its other characters. Of course, the thing has various *relations*, but these will also be studied as matters of fact and within continuous situations, and there is still nothing here to support the sort of distinction suggested. The consideration of the relation of desiring or having ends, however, points to another form of discontinuity besides that which is masked by the *annexing* of "values". This is the discontinuity between the agent and the act, between that which applies and that which is applied, between that which annexes and that which is annexed or that *to* which something is annexed. Unless the mind or person is of the same order as the phenomena in which it is taken to be involved and is subject to the same sort of (indeed, to the same) investigations, there can be no way of saying that any acts or processes are *its*, any more than of saying that the "value" of anything is *its* or can be really *assigned* to it. And, while psycho-analysis has done much to support a pluralistic and empirical view of mind, a residual dualism still appears in its individualism—in the conception of unique agency which, not merely in Flugel's work but in the great mass of psychological and sociological literature, appears in conjunction with voluntarism, i.e., in the substitution of such questions as "What are we to do?" ("How shall we *apply* our knowledge?" etc.) for "What are minds and how do they proceed?" The dualistic and discontinuous "agent" is perhaps the greatest barrier to the advance of both psychological and ethical science, and "desirability" is a good example of the confused conceptions by which it is bolstered up.

It will follow from what has been said that nothing is in itself (or in its own nature) an end and nothing is in itself a means. But Flugel's statement that the distinction between means and ends is "nearly always" relative is not (as indeed the reservation itself would show) based on logical considerations. It follows immediately upon the statement that it is the business of ethics to decide what the "higher values" are (so that applied psychology, like other applied sciences, "is concerned with 'means' rather than with 'ends' "), and is the beginning of an attempt to whittle away that concession to ethics. Thus (p. 13): "At best there can only be a few unquestionably intrinsic values at the top of the hierarchy, such as Truth, Goodness, Beauty; or, if we press the matter further, there should strictly speaking be one only, a *summum bonum* or supreme value, to which all the rest are means—and, as we know, moral philosophers are not yet in agreement as to what this supreme value is." There is no real obstacle, then, to psychology's supplying its own supreme values, and indeed the whole of Flugel's book is propaganda for a psychologists' morality, a morality of a weakly humanitarian type but one just as entitled as any other morality to annex its values to facts to which they are actually extrinsic.

Flugel's fourth point, however, is an attempt to have things both ways, to make his peculiar morality prior to morality as such. "The substitution of the psychological for the moral point of view in any matter implies also a change in mental attitude—a change from a relatively emotional attitude to a relatively intellectual one. Scientific judgment is primarily a cognitive process, moral judgment—in this respect like judgment in matters of religion and aesthetics—primarily an orectic process. But with regard to difficult and delicate problems, cognition is often more effective than orexis" (p. 14). Flugel goes on to say that we do not pass moral judgments on inanimate things and scarcely at all nowadays on animals, and adds that "this restriction of moral judgment and the substitution of judgments in terms of psychological insight is rapidly increasing, even in our dealings with fellow human beings, and for much the same reason as elsewhere, namely that it is so often more effective". Among recent examples of this is the attempt in education "to substitute understanding for censure; it is recognised that *it is better* to find out why a pupil is lazy or stupid than to blame or punish him" (p. 15). The phrase I have italicised here (suggesting the question whether this is a scientific or a moral judgment) is not a mere slip; it exposes what is inadroitly covered up in the expression "effective", where the question is clearly not just of having effects but of having "desirable" effects. But, quite apart from this smuggling in of what was supposed to be set aside, the major contrast proposed by Flugel will not stand up. If there is such a thing as "moral judgment" at all, then it is judgment that something is so, and it is just as "cognitive" as any other judgment. But to say that something is cognised, that some proposition is regarded as true, is not to say what are the characters of *that which cognises* and is nothing against its having such characters and relations as are conveyed by "feeling, striving, and wishing". Thus no distinction between types of judgment has been brought out. The underlying point, of course, is that an "orectic" judgment is not a judgment that something is the case but a judgment that something *is to be* the case—and if we admitted such judgments, we certainly could not regard them as helping inquiry; we do not find out what X is by laying down what X is to be. But, in fact, "is to be" judgments, confused as they stand, are always elliptical, and it is the task of criticism to show what are the unstated purposes to be served or what are the forces concerned to *make* an X be Y. Flugel, however, cannot clear the matter up because, as we have seen, his "psychological point of view" is just another moral one, an attempt to annex a particular set of "values" to the facts, a treatment of *science* as saying what "is to be".

The conception of a peculiarly "cognitive" judgment is akin to that of "rationality" in thought and behaviour. Rational cognition is that which knows the reasons for itself; rational action is that in which we at once know what we are doing and why we are doing it. These are to such an extent underlying presuppositions of Flugel's work, he is so far from imagining that they can be questioned, that he nowhere formulates them, let alone discussing them, but it is only in such terms that the distinction between the kinds of judgment or between reasonable and unreasonable procedures is intelligible. In fact, however, there is no such thing as rationality in the required sense. Whatever reasons are found for anything, the point of departure of the reasoning is always something that is simply found (without reasons); whatever we know about processes either in or out of ourselves, we never know "all about" them. The confused doctrine of "ideas", of entities which are just what they are known as because "what they are known as" is precisely their nature or meaning as ideas—confused because the "they" here could have no content or, as it might alternatively be put, because the attempt to assign one would involve an infinite process—is paralleled by the confused doctrine of "conscious action", action which, in carrying it out, we know all about because it is just our awareness of it that *makes* it conscious action. But, apart from formal objections (decisive though they are), the important point is that such self-wrapped entities could not be connected with anything else, could in particular have no transactions with other things, no history intertwined with other histories. The importance of the Freudian theory of the "unconscious" lay not just in its dispelling of formal confusions but in its indication of a concrete, continuing thing with its own characters, no matter how much or how little it might know or be known at any given time; and one condition of the working out of this theory, of the study of the transactions between the continuing mind and its surroundings, was the recognition of its complexity, of its *internal* transactions (including conflict) continuous with its external transactions. The rejection of the conception of the "unitary person" went with the rejection of the "conscious self".

Unfortunately the Freudians, including Freud himself, were unable to maintain this position or to work out the consequences of the initial revolution. The question became one not of the rejection of consciousness or self-awareness (the assertion of the distinction between a thing's own characters and its relations) but of the *restriction* of consciousness to a particular mental region, and the doctrine of "ego, id, and superego" which finally emerged, and which now dominates the work of the Freudian school, was largely a reinstatement of individualistic or atomistic thinking. Almost two-thirds of Flugel's book (chs. IV to XV) is devoted to consideration of "these three main parts or aspects" of the mind, with special emphasis on the superego as "the source of our moral control", i.e., as exercising a mandatory, and especially prohibitory, function. The consideration is not, of course, critical; it is mainly a setting out, in orthodox Freudian fashion, of types of mental conflict or difficulty, leading up to the major problems which "the human race must solve or perish". There is, in particular, no criticism of functional definition, no suggestion of the possibility that the very same thing could function in the various ways taken to be characteristic of the main mental agencies. Thus, even when it is admitted (p. 198) that there can be "righteous indignation" against an "authority", this is taken to indicate "a split in the superego" and not to undermine the whole conception of *the* superego. The argument throughout is dominated by the conception of the individual agent, exemplified in the personification by which the superego is said to "oppress" the ego or the ego to "defend itself" against the superego, and in the acts of the individual, acts of "introjection" and "projection" in particular, by which the superego, the "moral authority", is built up.

Flugel does not appear to find any difficulty in recognising such processes; jumping across barriers, throwing a content out or in—these are just things that the individual can do. But in fact it is only in terms of continuity among lives, of participation in social activities, that they are even conceivable. Just how important is the part played by *authority* in moral life is another question. The main point is that a person's development of moral characters and his recognition of them depend alike on his coming to participate in continuing "ways of life", forms of activity, which do not depend on him either for their existence or for their character. And just as the egoistic treatment of these questions, the postulation of a separate agent with his distinct acts of acceptance and rejection, is unintelligible, so is the treatment of *good*, in particular, as something which "I" select or pursue. It would, in the first instance, be a low moral view which made good *subject to the choice* of something else which was presumably not good; and the alternative is to treat good not as something which this or that person does or pursues but as something which itself operates in characteristic ways, something which may indeed operate within a person but which does so as being of some positive quality or content and not as an empty "agent". If such a positive view is not taken, then the subject "ethics" simply disappears and there is nothing for psychology to illuminate. But if it is a question of types of activity with their distinctive qualities, then we can see not merely that such activities do not stop at the boundaries of a person, that they pass continuously between persons, but that the understanding of them casts light *on psychology*, that the operations of a mind are strikingly illuminated by a knowledge of the "ways of life" among which it exists and develops. It is perhaps just because ethics casts more light on psychology than psychology does on ethics that psychologists are led to *fabricate* an ethics or to make their psychology *stand for* ethics. But at least there will be no coherent theory on the supposition that either moral forces or ethical conceptions are manufactured by "the individual"—or indeed, as seems to be the position of the Freudian school, by the *infant.* The question is of participation, of the ways in which things and persons *belong together* in concrete forms of activity or ways of living.

Religion and punishment (each of which bulks fairly large in Flugel's discussion) are examples of social phenomena which are not accounted for, or even illuminated, by the attribution to the infant mind of processes of "introjection", "projection" and so forth, but which, as features of the life in which that mind is embedded, help to determine the character of its interchanges with its surroundings or exhibit *forms* of such interchange. It is in terms of the social (not the individualist) theory of religion that we can understand its history and its impact on particular minds—in terms, that is, of the distinct departments of social life and of the conditions of keeping them going, of the rites which were originally *part* of the type of activity in question but became separated off as *symbols* of all that they "belonged together" with, of the "spiritual agencies" which became increasingly personified as being *presiding over* the various departments though their objective content was just these "provinces", these continuing forms of social activity, themselves. If "the needs underlying religion" were of "infantile origin" (p. 271), if the "projection of the superego" (ch. XIII, esp. pp. 186 ff.) were relevant to the formation of religious systems, we should expect monotheism to be religion's primitive form. But in fact polytheism is prior to monotheism, just as participation (or social function) is prior to individualism.

It is in these terms too—it is in that precise connection—that we can understand punishment or "sanctions". The question is of resistance to "encroachment" or of the rectification of boundaries, of the bringing together again of things which "belong together" when some breach of their connection has been made. How far sanctions should go, how far the repairing of injuries to the continuity of social processes requires the imposition of penalties on the offender, is a special question. The offender himself may make good the damage, or official custodians of continuity may do so by "making an example" of the offender. The point is, in any case, that the offence itself has involved a loss of participation, a breaking up of established connections, in social life and not merely on the part of a particular offender; and it is natural enough that the situation of the invasion of rights should be met by a certain disfranchisement or curtailment of rights, a loss, greater or less, temporary or permanent, of the privileges of participation. But the set of social phenomena which can be rendered coherent by the notion of disfranchisement or loss of participation, remain unilluminated if the fundamental feature of punishment is taken to be the infliction of *pain*.

The notion of "belonging together" is not, of course, a universal solvent. It is precisely characteristic of primitive thought to *identify* things which are merely associated in social activity and thus (as in magic and fetishism) to treat each thing as embodying the whole power of its province—though this will at least stand comparison with atomistic doctrines of individual entities with their s*eparate* powers. Again, it is impossible to maintain boundaries and avoid encroachment, if only because things and persons belong to different departments of social life or have many "social functions"; and while primitive thought dimly realises this (as in stories of wars among the gods) and tries to counter it (as in the conception of Moira, or proper apportionment, which "governs even the gods"), it cannot really grapple with what this implies—the inevitability of social change, the impossibility of the indefinite continuance of the forms of social (tribal) activity in existence at any time. But this is only to indicate the unsoundness of a totalistic view, not the soundness of an atomistic view. Participation is fundamental alike to a scientific ethics and to the confused ethical conceptions of the *fitting* or proper, the obligatory and the desirable—that which has such characters as make it a proper thing to desire, as enable it to fit into a certain scheme.

The point is that communication is limited, that there will always be forces opposed to it, that there will always be social conflict—conflict, in particular, between an objective and critical attitude to things and a subjective and uncritical attitude. This is something which Flugel with his humanitarian and progressivist outlook cannot admit, and that is why he cannot really get to grips with ethics, why he has to try to turn it into something else. In his summarising chapter (XVI) on "The Psychology of Moral Progress" he takes as "guiding notions concerning the main lines of moral progress and development" (1) from egocentricity to sociality [but it is only to *altruism*], (2) from unconscious to conscious, (3) from autism to realism [i.e., in both cases, to "knowing what we are doing"], (4) from moral inhibition to spontaneous 'goodness', (5) from aggression to tolerance and love, (6) from fear to security, (7) from heteronomy to autonomy, (8) from orectic (moral) judgment to cognitive (psychological) judgment. These are treated in an essentially preceptual and thus subjectivist manner. Autonomy, e.g., is conceived simply as independence of judgment and not as the objectivity, the independent working, the irreducibility to anything else (as Kant half saw), of the subject-matter of ethics itself—the objectivity of goods. Aggression, again, is dealt by precepts and pious hopes; on the one hand, if it is a need like hunger, the most we could do "would be to discourage [how?] the aggressive equivalent of gluttony and to find [how?] the least harmful and destructive channel for the remaining irreducible aggression"; on the other hand, if it "is purely a reaction to frustration, we can, in theory at least, hope to diminish it by reducing [how?] the frequency and intensity of frustration" (p. 249). The appeal is never to the laws of social science; the assumption is always that whatever the right-minded resolutely decide to do has at least a good chance of coming about.

Flugel himself appears to support the second view of the nature of aggression. At any rate, he ends the last chapter ("The Problem of War and Peace") with a clarion call for the turning of aggression into the battle of man against nature and not against his fellow-man. "It has been chiefly in war that they [men] have sought and found the sense of high adventure; and brotherhood in arms has up to now been the supreme form of co-operation. It is only in quite recent times that they have been able to see at all clearly the possibilities and implications of the goal of Progress; and even now they have hardly begun to realise that Progress can be an ideal embracing and inspiring all mankind—an ideal that still calls upon men to be brothers-in-arms, not against their fellows, but against the forces of nature which, in so far as they threaten, restrict, and embitter human life, are the enemies of all. If we wish to be dramatic (and it is perhaps well that we should be so, if we would compete against the lure of war), we can say that the stage is set for the epic struggle of Man versus the Universe—a spectacle surely no less breath-taking in its audacity and splendour than the most famous exploits of purely inter-human warfare" (p. 321). Flugel wonders whether those who have shown heroism in war will also have the courage and the insight to enter on the struggle "in which all mankind can be allied", and, allowing that what is primitive and sinister in human nature might make us doubt whether "such a thing is possible", he concludes that "we can but try". This, however, is a mere setting aside of the theoretical question whether such a thing *is* possible; there is no merit in stopping inquiry in case it should extinguish a particular hope. And, as regards the content of Flugel's hope, it, on the face of it, falsely divides man from nature and begs the question whether there can be any struggle with "the forces of nature" which is not also (or does not involve) a social struggle. Here, as elsewhere, the appeal would be to history, to social facts and not to hopes—or to the dialectic of Engels. And I should say that the appeal would have to be decided against Flugel, unless "human nature" is to be taken as indefinitely variable—unless, indeed, this is what his conception of Progress means—in which case there is no such thing as human nature or as human (psychological and social) science.

Something of the looseness of Flugel's writing will have been apparent from the quotations given above, but there are a number of points that call for special remark. There are such errors in English as "cannot help but", "compensate" in place of "compensate for" (more than once), the projection of something "on to" something else (repeatedly). There is the statement (p. 108) about the 'English School' that it "centres round the pioneer work of Melanie Klein, who developed a play technique which enabled something resembling psycho-analytic treatment as employed with adults to be adapted to the use of very young children of from 2 to 6 years old"—where clearly the "something resembling" is not what is adapted but is the *outcome* of the adaptation in question. With this may be compared the statement (p. 226) that the system of magic and superstition "endeavours, as Freud showed, to prolong infantile 'omnipotence of thought' and is indeed mankind's most desperate and thoroughgoing attempt in this direction, actually seeking to convert wishful thinking into *something like an exact pseudo-science*", and the remark (p. 164), regarding the difficulty, in the present state of psycho-analytic knowledge, of accounting for or predicting reactions to punishment: "All that we can safely say is that, as often happens at a certain stage in the progress of scientific thought, *improved insight has revealed a somewhat bewildering confusion* of factors at work behind familiar phenomena" (my italics in both cases). The constant and irritating use of hedging or modifying expressions reaches its climax in the statements in three successive sentences (pp. 179, 180) that a certain strength "seems to emanate from the loved object", that the superego "seems, as we might be inclined to say, to embrace, attract, and elevate the ego", and that "in mania also the distinction between the ego and the super-ego seems in some way to be obliterated". Again, the spurious relationships "corresponds to", "represents", "reflects", and the vague "is connected with", are regularly introduced as if they were quite specific and important forms of connection. Finally, we may take the following as the best illustration of the personification referred to earlier: "guilt having been removed and the super-ego satisfied by suffering, the ego is free to turn a favourable ear to the solicitations of the id towards forms of gratification that would be unacceptable as long as guilt remained" (p. 159).

Heaviness of style is at least partly accounted for by heaviness of purpose—by the author's meliorism or salvationism. But, concerned though it was with questions of cure, there was nothing in the original or "classical" doctrine of psycho-analysis which required the adoption of a voluntarist or salvationist view. What was striking about it was its objective and determinist treatment of mental facts, and such a treatment, while opposed to the more recent conception of a peculiar "psychic reality", would harmonise with an objective and determinist treatment of ethics. It would have been possible to give a much more detailed exposition and criticism than I have attempted here of Flugel's ethical relativism, particularly in the form of biologism. But this would have been only incidental to the issues on which I have concentrated—the objective character of ethics and the positive conditions of the working out of ethical theory.

# BIBLIOGRAPHY
(In chronological order)

THIS bibliography, although it does not list every one of Professor Anderson's published writings, is intended to include all of his publications in learned journals, and all of those on philosophic, aesthetic, or general educational topics. A number of writings on local issues, generally connected with education, are also included so as to indicate something of the part Professor Anderson has played in the life of Sydney University. A few of Professor Anderson's contributions to politically radical journals are also included; these contain material from which he would now strongly dissent, but they do show one major direction of his interests; they illustrate also methods of criticism akin to those he still follows.

Most of the abbreviations used need no explanation, but (D) after a title indicates a contribution to the discussion of some article in the journal concerned, while (R) and (Rev. Art.) indicate respectively a review and a review article. The journals referred to more than once are given their full title on their first appearance, with the exception of the *Australasian Journal of Psychology and Philosophy*. This is referred to as *A.J.P.P.* for all numbers up to the end of 1946; for later numbers the abbreviation is *A.J.P.* (the name of the journal having been changed in 1947 to the *Australasian Journal of Philosophy*).

1. Propositions and Judgments (D): *Mind*, XXXV, N.S., No. 138; April 1926; pp 237–241.
2. The Truth of Propositions (D): *Mind*, XXXV, N.S., No. 140; October 1926; pp 466–472.
3. The Knower and the Known: *Proceedings of the Aristotelian Society*, 27, 1926-27; pp 61–84.
4. *Familiar Beliefs and Transcendent Reason*, by the Earl of Balfour (R): *A.J.P.P.*, V, 3, Sept. 1927; p 233.
5. Empiricism: *A.J.P.P.*, V, 4, Dec. 1927, pp 241–254.
6. *Reality*, by B. H. Streeter (R): *A.J.P.P.*, V, 4, Dec. 1927; pp 315–316.
7. History and Theory: *The Communist*, a monthly magazine of the Communist Party of Australia, Dec. 1, 1927.
8. The Moral Factor in the Proletarian Revolution: *The Communist*, Feb. 1, 1928.
9. The University Appeal: *Schooling*, XI, 2, April 1928.
10. Another Outbreak of Virtue (D): *A.J.P.P.*, VI, 2, June 1928, pp 151–152,
11. Reformism and Class Consciousness: *The Communist*, May–June 1928.

12. Censorship: *Schooling*, XI, 4, August 1928.
13. *Proceedings of the Sixth International Congress of Philosophy* (R): *A.J.P.P.*, VI, 3, Sept. 1928, pp 223–228.
14. Determinism and Ethics: *A.J.P.P.*, VI, 4, Dec. 1928, pp 241–255.
15. *The Epinomis of Plato*, by J. Harward (R): *A.J.P.P.*, VI, 4, Dec. 1928, pp 312–313.
16. The Non-Existence of Consciousness: *Space, Time and Deity*, by Samuel Alexander (Rev. Art.): *A.J.P.P.*, VII, 1, March 1929, pp 68–73.
17. "Universals" and Occurrences (D): *A.J.P.P.*, VII, 2, June 1929, pp 138–145.
18. Theory and Practice in Morals (D): *A.J.P.P.*, VII, 4, Dec. 1929, pp 297–300.
19. Realism and Some of its Critics: *A.J.P.P.*, VIII, 2, June 1930, pp 113–134.
20. *Moral Law and the Highest Good*, by E. Morris Miller (R): *A.J.P.P.*, VIII, 3, Sept. 1930, pp 235–236.
21. *Metaphysics and Modern Research*, by I. C. Isbyam (R): *A.J.P.P.*, VIII, 3, Sept. 1930, pp 236–237.
22. *Ulysses: Offprint No. 3 of Australian English Association*, 1930, (offprinted from *The Union Recorder* published by Sydney University Union) 12 pp
23. Socrates as an Educator: *Journal of the Institute of Inspectors of Schools*; N.S.W., 12, 3, Nov. 1930, and 13, 1, June 1931.
24. The Conception of a Liberal Education: *Education*, XII, 2, Dec. 1930.
25. *The Book of Diogenes Laertius: Its Spirit and its Method*, by Richard Hope (R): *A.J.P.P.*, IX, 1, March 1931, pp 71–75.
26. Partisanship of the Press: *Honi Soit*, Journal of the Sydney University Students' Representative Council, III, 17, July 22, 1931, p 1.
27. Academic Autonomy: *Honi Soit*, III, 19, August 5, 1931, p 2.
28. Socrates as an Educator: reprinted in *A.J.P.P.*, IX, 3, Sept. 1931, pp 172–184.
29. Education and Politics: published by Angus and Robertson Ltd., Sydney, 1931, 65 pp—a republication of items 9, 12, 23 and 24, the first under the title of "The University and the Public".
30. The Working Class: *Proletariat*, Organ of the Melbourne University Labour Club, I, 1, April 1932, pp 3–6.
31. The Place of Hegel in the History of Philosophy: *A.J.P.P.*, X, 2, June 1932, pp 81–91.
32. Freedom and the Class Struggle: *Proletariat*, I, 2, July 1932, pp 2–6.
33. Freedom of Thought: *Freethought*, Organ of Sydney University Freethought Society, 1, July 1932, pp 1–3.
34. "Life" versus Logic: *Freethought*, 1, July 1932, pp 11–12.
35. Leadership and Spontaneity: published by Sydney University Freethought Society in a pamphlet entitled "Censorship in the

Working-Class Movement" when the article was rejected by *Proletariat*, 1932, p 7.
36. Utilitarianism: *A.J.P.P.*, X, 3, Sept. 1932, pp 161–172.
37. Some Questions in Aesthetics: published by Sydney University Literary Society, Nov. 1932, p 25.
38. Some Obscurantist Fallacies: *Freethought*, 2, Nov. 1932, pp 10–12.
39. Realism versus Relativism in Ethics: *A.J.P.P.*, XI, 1, March 1933, pp 1–11.
40. James Joyce: *Hermes*, University of Sydney Magazine, XXXIX, Michaehnas Term 1933, pp 13–17.
40a. Science and Education: *The Science Journal*, Journal of the Sydney University Science Society, XII, 1, Michaelmas Term 1933, pp 5–8.
41. Freedom of Speech: *The Student*, Organ of the Sydney University Labor Club, 1, Nov. 1933, p 3.
42. The Science of Logic: *The Foundations of Mathematics*, by F. P. Ramsey; *The Province of Logic*, by Richard Robinson; *L'Empirisme dans les Sciences Exactes*, by W. Rivier (Rev. Art.): *A.J.P.P.*, XI, 4, Dec. 1933, pp 308–314.
43. Mind as Feeling: *A.J.P.P.*, XII, 2, June 1934, pp 81–94.
44. Political "Debunking": *Honi Soit*, VI, 17, July 18, 1934, p 3.
45. Virtue: *A.J.P.P.*, XII, 3, Sept. 1934, pp 224–228.
46. Romanticism and Classicism: *Hermes*, XL, Michaelmas Term 1934, pp 7–10.
47. Some Remarks on Academic Freedom (D): *A.J.P.P.*, XII, 4, Dec. 1934, pp 296–298.
48. Marxist Philosophy: *A.J.P.P.*, XIII, 1, March 1935, pp 24–48.
49. The Perfect Wagnerite: *Manuscripts*, 13, May 1935, pp 25–38.
50. Production, Distribution and Exchange: *A.J.P.P.*, XIII, 2, June 1935, pp 136–142.
51. Scepticism and Construction, by Charles A. Campbell (R): *A.J.P.P.* XIII, 2, June 1935, pp 151–156.
52. Educational Reform: *The Union Recorder*, XV, 19, Aug. 8, 1935, pp 180–181.
53. University Reform: *A.J.P.P.*, XIII, 3, Sept. 1935, pp 215–222.
54. Design: *A.J.P.P.*, XIII, 4, Dec. 1935, pp 241–256.
55. The Cogito of Descartes: *A.J.P.P.*, XIV, 1, March 1936, pp 48–68
56. *Sur le Principe du Tiers Exclu*, by M. Barzin and A. Errera (R): *A.J.P.P.*, XIV, 1, March 1936, p 80.
57. The Comic: *Hermes*, XLII, Lent Term 1936, pp 10–12.
58. Social Service: *Freethought*, 3, May 1936, pp 2–7.
59. Psycho-Analysis and Romanticism: *A.J.P.P.*, XIV, 3, Sept 1936, pp 210–215.
60. *Dialectics: The Logic of Marxism and its Critics*, by T. A. Jackson (R): *The Australian Highway*, Journal of the Workers' Educational Association of Australia, XVIII, 12 (New Series), Nov. 10, 1936, pp 191–194:
61. Causality and Logic (D): *A.J.P.P.*, XIV, 4, Dec. 1936, pp 309–313.

62. *Mathématique et Philosophie*, by. R. Wavre; *La Cause et l'Intervalle, ou Ordre et Probabilité*, by E. Dupreel (R): *A.J.P.P.*, XV, 1, March. 1937, pp 77-80.
63. Marxist Ethics: *A.J.P.P.*, XV, 2, June 1937, pp 98-117.
64. Student Interests: *Candide*, New Arts Magazine of the University of Sydney, Trinity Term 1937, pp 21-23.
65. *How We Think*, by John Dewey (R): *A.J.P.P.*, XV, 3, Sept. 1937, pp 224-230.
66. *Logical Positivism and Analysis*, by L. Susan Stebbing (R): *A.J.P.P.*; XV, 3, Sept. 1937, pp 238-240.
67. *Freud and Marx:-A Dialectical Study*, by R. Osborn (R): *The Australian Highway*, XIX, 9 (New Series), Oct. 10, 1937, pp 138-141.
68. *Studies in the History of Ideas*, Volume III (R): *A.J.P.P.*, XV, 4, Dec. 1937, pp 299-307.
69. *A Textbook of Marxist Philosophy* (R): *The Australian Highway*, XX, 1 (New Series), Feb. 10, 1938, pp 13-17.
70. The Problem of Causality: *A.J.P.P.*, XVI, 2, Aug. 1938, pp 127-142.
71. Logic and Ethics (D): *A.J.P.P.*, XVII, 1, May 1939, pp 55-65.
72. The Status of Logic (D): *A.J.P.P.*, XVII, 2, Aug. 1939, pp 164-169.
73. Logic and Experience (D): *A.J.P.P.*, XVII, 3, Dec. 1939, pp 257-272.
74. Freudianism and Society: *Superstition and Society*, by R. Money-Kyrle; *Civilisation, War and Death-Selections from three works by Sigmund Freud*, ed. John Rickman (Rev. Art.): *A.J.P.P.*, XVIII, 1, June 1940, pp 50-77.;
75. *In the Spirit of William James*, by Ralph Barton Perry (R): *A.J.P.P.*, XVIII, 1, June 1940, pp 85-88.
76. *Psychology for Everyone: An Outline of General Psychology*, by W. J. H. Sprott (R): *A.J.P.P.*, XVIII, 2, Sept. 1940; pp 154-159.
77. *Psychology and Psychotherapy*, by William Brown, 4th edition (R): *A.J.P.P.*, XIX, 1, April 1941, pp 94-96.
78. The Banning of Ulysses: *Honi Soit*, XIII, 24, Sept. 25, 1941, p 3.
79. Art and Morality: *A.J.P.P.*, XIX, 3, Dec. 1941, pp 253-266.
80. *From Beast-Machine to Man-Machine*, by Leonora Cohen Rosenfeld (R): *A.J.P.P.*, XIX, 3, Dec. 1941, pp 277-286.
81. Senate Reform Now: *Honi Soit*, Special Edition, XIII, 29, 1941, p 2.
82. The Meaning of Good: *A.J.P.P.*, XX, 2, Sept. 1942, pp 111-140.
83. Academic Freedom: *Honi Soit*, XV, 11; April 16, 1943, p 1.
84. The Nature of Ethics (D): *A.J.P.P.*, XXI, 1; June 1943, pp 26-40.
85. *Education for Democracy*, by J. D. C. Medley (R): *A.J.P.P.*, XXI, 1, June 1943, pp 53-63.
86. Religion in Education: published in a collection of addresses with this title by The New Education Fellowship (N.S.W.), July 1943, pp 25-32.
87. The Servile State: *A.J.P.P.*, XXI, 2 & 3, Dec. 1943, pp 115-132.

88. *Universities in Australia*, by Eric Ashby (R): *A.J.P.P.*, XXI, 2 & 3, Dec. 1943, pp 183–181.
89. *The Regeneration of Civilisation*; by E. H. Burgmann (R): *A.J.P.P.*, XXI, 2 & 3, Dec. 1943, pp 182–184.
90. Decentralised Education: *Honi Soit*, XVI, 10, June 23, 1944, p 1.
91. Education and Practicality (D): *A.J.P.P.*, XXII, 1 & 2, Sept. 1944, pp 108–111.
92. Ethics and Advocacy (D): *A.J.P.P.*, XXII, 3, Dec. 1944, pp 174–187.
93. Introductory Essay to *Prospects of Democracy*, editor, W. H. C. Eddy, published by Consolidated Press, Sydney, 1945, pp 7–12.
94. The One Good (D): *A.J.P.P.*, XXIII, 1–3, Dec. 1945, pp 85–89.
95. Students' Rights: *Heresy* (an independent publication produced by a group of students on the occasion of the banning of *Honi Soit* in 1948), 1, May 12, 1948, p 3.
96. The Politics of Proscription: *Australian Quarterly*, XX, 2, June 1948, pp 7–15.
97. The University and Religion: *Honi Soit*, XXIII, 15, July 12, 1951, p 4.
98. Logic and Dogma: *Honi Soit*, XXIII, 18, Aug. 2, 1951, p 3.
99. Hypotheticals: *A.J.P.*, XXX, 1, May 1952, pp 1–16.
100. Democratic Illusions: *Hermes*, New Issue, 54, 1, 1952, pp 16–18.
101. Literary Criticism: *The Union Recorder*, XXXIII, 7, April 30, 1953, pp 57–58.
102. The Freudian Revolution: *A.J.P.*, XXXI, 2, Aug. 1953, pp 101–106.
103. Psychological Moralism: *Man, Morals and Society*, by J. C. Flugel (Rev. Art.) *A.J.P.*, XXXI, 3, Dec. 1953, pp 188–205.
104. *Psychology and Psychotherapy*, by William Brown, 5th edition (Critical Notice): *A.J.P.*, XXXII, 1, May 1954, pp 48–56.
105. University Development in N.S.W.: *Honi Soit*, XXVI, 22, Oct. 14, 1954, p 5.
106. *Politics and Morals*, by Benedetto Croce, trans. Salvatore J. Castiglione (Critical Notice): *A.J.P.*, XXXII, 3, Dec. 1954, pp 213–222.
107. The Orr Case and Academic Freedom: *The Observer* (Sydney), 10, June 28, 1958, p 293.
108. Realism: *The Australian Highway*, Special Issue entitled "Anderson and Andersonianism", Sept. 1958, pp 53–56.
109. *The Illusion of the Epoch*, by H. B. Acton (Critical Notice): *A.J.P.*, XXXVII, 2, Aug. 1959, pp 156–167.
110. *My Philosophy and Other Essays on the Moral and Political Problems of our Time*, by B. Croce (R): *A.J.P.*, XXXVII, 3, Dec. 1959, pp 255–260.
111. The Place of the Academic in Modern Society: *Honi Soit*, XXXII, 12, Tune 16, 1960, p 5.
112. *Time and Idea: The Theory of History in Giumbattista Vico*, by A. R. Caponigri (Critical Notice): *A.J.P.*, XXXVIII, 2, Aug. 1960, pp 163–172.
113. Classicism: published by Australian Humanities Research Council in its Fourth Annual Report, 1960, pp 19–30.

# BIBLIOGRAPHY 479

114. *Orage and the "New Age" Circle*, by P. Selver (R) : *The Observer* (Sydney), 3, 23, Nov. 1960, pp 30-31.
115. Academic Autonomy and Religion: *Honi Soit*, XXXIII, 17, July 27, 1961, p 4.
116. *The Western Intellectual Tradition: From Leonardo to Hegel* by J. Bronowski and Bruce Mazlish (Rev. Art.): *The Australian Journal of Politics and History*, VII, 2, Nov. 1961, pp 278-284.
117. Religion and the University: *The Australian Highway*, XLII, 3, Nov. 1961, pp 50-54.
118. Relational Arguments: *Studies to Empirical Philosophy*, published by Angus and Robertson Ltd., Sydney, 1962, pp 148-161.
119. Empiricism and Logic: *Studies in Empirical Philosophy*, 1962, pp 162-188.

# INDEX

Absolute Idealism (see also Idealism and Monism), 50, 51f., 75f., 85
Absolute, the, 2f., 4, 17f., 22, 51f., 57, 59f., 65f., 70f., 75f., 101, 102f., 113f., 342, 373, 401, 408
Actuality, 3, 4f., 10f., 222f., 224, 248
Adamson, R., 247
Advocacy, 307f., 323f., 333f., 357, 363
Agreement, method of, 160
Alexander, S., 44, 45ff., 47, 50ff., 74n., 75, 87ff., 89ff., 92ff., 95ff., 100ff., 109ff., 120ff., 136ff., 141ff., 155, 197, 217, 234f., 279n.
Altruism and egoism, 283, 406, 431, 439, 446, 460, 470
Analogy, argument from, 116ff.
Analysis, 220, 233f.
Anytus, 261
Appearances, saving of, 67, 233
Appreciation, 347ff., 434
Aptitudes, psychology of, 264f.
Arguments, non-syllogistic, 188f.
Arguments, validity of (see also Implication), 174f., 181, 186, 188, 193f., 195f., 200f.
Aristotle, 84, 102, 197, 217, 232f., 266, 288, 309f., 449
Arnold, M., 241ff., 242, 243
Art, Socrate's view of, 268
Atomism, 107, 205, 217, 219f., 339, 470
Authority, 69, 276, 278f., 332f., 343, 346, 349, 395f., 442f., 450ff., 467f., 468

Awareness, analysis of, 77f.
Axiom of parallels, 8f.
Axioms, 6ff., 9ff., 190, 233

Bacon, F., 246f.
Bain, A., 288
Barbarism, return to, 252, 367
Beauty, 347f., 435
Beccaria, C. de, 297
Behaviourism, 94n., 140, 302
Being, single way of, see Dualism
Belief, 3f., 5f., 24f., 30, 40, 41f., 68f., 94, 95f., 129f., 142f., 171, 209, 220f., 274, 429
Belloc, H., 415ff.
Bentham, J., 288ff., 289f., 323
Berkeley, G., 13, 14f., 34f., 35ff., 38f., 40f., 52, 55, 77f., 78, 82f., 85f., 101f., 111f., 115f., 118f., 135f., 140f., 205ff., 206, 379f., 383ff., 385
Bernstein, E., 389, 420n.
Bosanquet, B., 100, 147, 149
Boyle's law, 374f.
Bradley, F. H., 17, 18f., 22f., 92f., 100f.
Broad, C. D., 38ff.
Burnet, J., 63, 66, 100, 109, 178, 232, 234, 244n., 254n., 257f., 258, 259, 265f., 386
Burnham, J., 417n., 421, 422, 426
Bury, J. B., 246
Butler, J., 84, 275f., 277, 289f., 291, 310

Calculus of wants, 293f.
Campbell, C. A., 231f., 232n.

# INDEX

Capacities (see also Aptitudes and Potentialities), 248, 264, 285, 286, 425
Cartesianism, 75, 101, 136
Categories, 57, 102n., 103, 105, 106n., 143, 217f., 230, 233, 234f., 255, 400
Causal chains, 168f.
Causality, 55f., 154f., 158f., 217
Causality and precedence, 165
"Causes", formal, material and efficient, 166
Causes, inclining, 157
Causes, plurality of, 158f., 160f., 163, 170
Certainty, 67f., 69f., 128f., 137, 138f., 247, 248
Chesterton, G. K., 264, 291
Class, 188, 189, 225, 232f., 249f., 400f., 409f., 415, 422, 429
Class-relations, 126, 128, 189f., 200ff.
Class, social, 235f., 249f., 311, 397, 399, 401f., 402, 420f.
Classicism opposed to utilitarianism, 239ff., 422f.
Cogito ergo sum, 36, 45, 85, 128ff., 130, 248
Cognition, 31f., 84, 85f., 248, 438, 446, 455, 466f.
Coherence, 25f., 86f.
Complexity, 12, 13f., 15f., 43, 48f., 104f., 121, 123, 124f., 126, 203, 205ff., 207, 211, 335, 467
Complexity, infinite, 159, 161, 170, 192, 207
Compresence, 48f., 77f., 79f., 91f.
Comte, A., 108
Conation, 47f., 84, 85f., 87f., 90, 94f., 277, 455
Concepts, 35, 38, 87, 378

Conditionals, 172, 184
Conduct of life, Berkeley's theory of, 118, 209ff.
Conflict of demands, 97, 293, 295, 307, 345
Conflict, social, see Social conflict
Conjunction and disjunction, 184, 187f., 201f., 202
Connections and distinctions jointly experienced, 13f., 21f., 28, 29f., 104f.
Conscience, 84, 243, 275ff., 285, 312, 439
Consciousness, 33f., 36f., 44f., 46f., 49, 52f., 69f., 85f., 89f., 114f., 346f., 371, 408, 467
Constitutive relations, 39f., 52f., 54, 56, 60f., 66, 67, 91, 92f., 94f.
Contemplation, 46, 79, 81, 136
Continuity, 126, 128, 183, 201, 216, 234f., 269f., 388, 455f., 458, 464f., 468f., 469
Contradiction, 130, 221, 229f., 387ff.
Contradiction, principle of, 6f., 12f., 130f.
Contrapositive, virtual, 163, 183
Co-operation, social, 283f., 336, 394, 471f.
Copula, 3f., 25f., 27f., 116f., 133f., 134, 135, 149f., 221ff., 224, 230, 235n., 460
Correspondence (see also Representationism), 25f., 88f., 141f., 212ff., 213, 377, 380f.
Cosmological argument, 114ff.
"Criterion of truth" rejected, 67ff.
Criticism, 14f., 39f., 50n., 60, 105f., 106n., 152, 232ff., 239, 241, 253ff., 260f., 269ff., 276,

301, 334, 339f., 399n., 399f., 421f., 460
Criticism of the instrument, 14, 103
Crito, 252, 260
Croce, B., 100n., 337, 367, 424, 428, 449
Culture, 236, 239, 241ff., 247, 252, 254ff., 311f., 337, 367, 394, 418, 429, 431f., 435f., 438, 439f., 444, 451

Dawes Hicks, G., 40, 44
Definition, 6, 215, 313, 326f., 328, 337, 352, 355
Deity, see God
Demands, 95f., 291, 293ff., 295f., 299f., 307f., 310, 321, 325ff., 328, 332f., 351f., 356, 401f., 404f.
Democracy, Athenian, 244, 260f.
Dependence, 38f., 39, 112f., 114, 115f., 116, 207f., 393
Descartes, 36f., 45, 79f., 89f., 114f., 128f., 234, 246ff.
Description, see Location and description
Design or contrivance, 111ff.
Determinism, 1, 72f., 154, 157, 271f., 456
Dialectic, 100n., 232f., 268ff., 269, 373, 387ff., 389, 390f., 394f., 397f.
Dietzgen, J., 378
Difference or differentia, 164, 165, 169
Difference, method of, 162, 166f.
Differences, 32, 51f., 58f., 103, 104, 130f., 316
Disagreement, philosophical, 1f., 5
Discourse, 2ff., 4, 17f., 19, 32f., 146, 149f., 153, 197, 314f.

Disinterestedness, 237, 246, 252, 260, 289, 302, 310ff., 311, 362, 366, 368, 399, 413, 426f.
Disjunction, see Conjunction and disjunction
Dispositions, see Capacities
Doubt, 37f., 62f., 68f., 88f., 129f., 138f.
Dualism (see also Reality, levels of), 59f., 103f., 113, 114f., 127, 128f., 211ff., 212f., 226, 234, 455f., 461f., 464f.
Dualism, ethical, 226, 282, 285, 286f., 289, 461
Dualism of active and passive, 84f., 113, 116, 121, 126, 128, 167, 209, 210f., 249, 304f.
Duhring, E., 372, 373, 377, 386, 387, 402n.
Duty (see also Obligation), 98, 285, 302, 320, 338, 402, 447

Eastman, M., 371, 384, 394f., 397, 397n., 401n., 402, 407f., 410, 411n.
Eclecticism, 101, 172f.
Economic interpretation of history (see also Materialism, historical), 370f., 398f., 402, 405, 413
Eddy, W. H. C., 361f.
Education (see also Socrates), 239f., 241f., 251, 258ff., 284f., 360ff., 425ff.
Education and politics, 255, 257, 259, 269f., 425ff.
Education, classical and utilitarian views of, 239f., 242, 248, 252
Education in Aristotle, 266
Education in Plato, 257f., 264, 266

Educational institutions, 236, 241f., 251, 252, 265
Egalitarianism, 236f., 237, 249
Eleatics, 59ff., 107ff., 114ff.
Emotions, see Feelings or emotions
Empiricism, 1ff., 64, 104, 114, 204ff., 388
Empiricism and realism, 1, 31f., 59f., 60, 66, 76, 211
"Empiricism", English, 12, 101, 104, 113
End (see also Good as end rejected, Means and ends, Purpose), 63, 242f., 275, 288, 302ff., 303, 321ff., 359f., 464
Engels, 370ff., 397ff., 417, 442, 472
Enjoyment, Alexander's theory of, 46ff., 80ff., 92ff., 120ff., 136ff., xii
Entities, inferred, 13, 14ff., 34ff., 59, 64f., 174, 205, 235
Epiphenomenalism, 108f., 142, 143, 164, 406
Epistemological approach to philosophy criticised, 1f., 31, 50f., 51, 66, 74, , 204, 215, 247
Error, 23f., 34f., 44f., 48f., 51f., 88f., 94f., 171, 216f., 268f., 341, 375f., 394, 395f., 456
Essence (see also Natures), 13f., 32, 35, 36f., 75, 107f., 128f., 132f., 136f., 139f., 247, 249, 385
Ethic of the consumer, 310, 412, 413, 419
Ethic of the producer, 237f., 310, 311, 412f., 419
Ethics, 15f., 69ff., 70f., 226, 228ff., 244, 252, 265, 266, 272ff., 289f., 313ff., 339ff., 350ff., 355ff., 378f., 397ff., 440f., 446, 460ff.
Ethics, metaphysical, 270, 287, 312, 338, 340f., 397, 399
Ethics, positive not normative, 271ff., 272f., 274f., 286f., 339f., 341, 343, 352, 364, 400f., 461
Ethics, relational view of, 69, 97, 302f., 306, 310, 313, 322, 328, 335f., 340ff., 349f., 350f., 352ff., 355ff., 365, 376ff., 400ff.
Euclid, 8ff.
Euthyphro, 71, 304
Evolutionary ethics, 249, 324, 405ff.
Exhortation, 226, 278, 279f., 280, 335, 336f., 404, 432
Existence, 4f., 38f., 47f., 57f., 59f., 86f., 113, 114f., 117f., 119f., 134f., 142f., 154f., 178ff., 207f., 272, 286, 324f., 369, 371f., 386f.
Existence, conditions of, 4, 109, 116, 126, 127f., 154
"Existence" theory of propositions, 175f., 197
Explanation, 3f., 62f., 65f., 127f., 134f., 204f., 257ff., 266, 301, 397
Extension, see Class and Class-relations
Extension and intension, 192, 202
"External World", 137, 212, 254, 385, 393, 434, 462

Fact, matters of, 2f., 18f., 23, 24f., 28, 49f., 56, 67, 69f., 137, 138f., 150f., 152, 153f., 204, 205f., 206f., 210f., 219, 220f., 222f., 226f., 272, 321, 371f.,

INDEX 485

372f., 385, 426f., 427f., 440, 460f., 463f., 464f.
Facts, atomic, 219
Faculties, 2f., 14, 88, 115, 116, 269, 275, 277
Faculty, moral, 275ff., 312
Faith, 75, 102n., 126f., 383, 384f., 394
False belief, see Error
Feeling as distinguishing-mark of the mental, 46f., 109ff.
Feelings or emotions, 22, 44f., 81f., 85f., 91f., 93f., 140f., 227ff., 229f., 276, 314f., 321f., 350, 456, 466f.
Ferenczi, 95
Fetishism, 145, 370, 395f., 470
Feuerbach, L., 142f., 250, 383, 385, 406, 407
Fichte, J. G., 103
Field in connection with hypotheticals, 181ff.
Field in the theory of causality and of classification, 158, 163, 165
Field or range in connection with "angular arguments", 193, 200
Flugel, J. C., 459ff.
Form (as contrasted with matter), 101f., 169, 172, 178, 188, 192, 220, 226, 232, 235, 237
"Form of the good", 60, 112, 147, 267, 303, 306
Forms, theory of, 60f., 62, 147f., 265, 269
Forster, E. M., 368
Fox, A. C., 50ff., 52ff., 54f.
Freedom as initiative or enterprise, 155, 311, 337, 417f., 419f.
Freedom, metaphysical (see also Dual-ism of active and passive),
72ff., 155, 240, 249, 271, 287, 305f., 311, 393, 428, 464
Freedom, political, 406, 416ff., 417, 418, 420, 422
Freud, 46, 47, 78, 87, 89, 95, 101, 109, 142, 284, 285, 345, 346, 348, 430ff., 431f., 434f., 450f., 454ff., 467
Freudianism and ethics, 335f., 342, 346, 440f., 446, 460, 466ff.

Geometries, non-Euclidean, 9ff.
Geometry, 5ff., 178f.
Gilson, E., 128
God, 113ff., 125ff., 208, 260, 394
Good (see also Ethics), 215, 217f., 260f., 267, 277f., 299, 302f., 309ff., 320, 328, 330, 335, 336ff., 340f., 347f., 352, 353f., 356, 374f., 402f., 428, 441, 468
Good as a quality, 62, 71, 72f., 320ff., 325, 326f., 337f., 348f., 462f.
Good as end rejected (see also End), 274f., 281f., 289f., 291, 294, 302ff., 308ff., 320ff., 322, 337, 338, 355, 359
Good as non-natural rejected, 308, 328ff., 335
Good, alleged indefinability of, 308, 310, 313, 325ff., 328, 343
Good, how defined, 337
Goodness, degrees of, 249, 331f., 428
Goods mutually supporting, 72, 284f., 286f., 308, 337, 360f., 361
Gorgias, 59f., 64, 66f., 261
Green, T. H., 12, 100

Happiness, 246, 250f., 289ff., 309, 338, 432ff., 433, 447
Hedonism, 322f., 344
Hegel, G. W. F., 99ff., 100f., 103, 234, 254, 342, 387, 390, 398f., 399, 408f.
Hellenism and Hebraism, 243ff.
Helvetius, C. A., 292n.
Heraclitus, 60, 66, 97, 102, 245f., 253, 389
Historical view of things, see Reality as historical
Hook, S., 142, 399n., 399ff., 407n., 407, 408f.
Hope, A. D., 339n., 341, 342ff.
"Humane" studies, 251f., 254, 426
Humanitarianism, 252, 465, 470
Hume, D., 12f., 32f., 54, 84f., 87f., 103f., 112f., 113, 127, 135f., 158, 205f., 385f.
Hunter, T. A., 50n., 70, 71ff.
Huxley, T. H., 240
Hypotheses, destroying or removing of, 67, 232f., 237, 254f., 269f.
Hypotheses, falsification of, 178, 179f., 233n.
Hypotheses, saving of, 73, 233f.
Hypotheses, verification of, 159, 160, 162f., 220
Hypothesis, place of in discourse or inquiry, 4f., 9f., 15f., 67, 145f., 162, 178ff., 262, 269f.
Hypotheticals, 172, 174, 184ff.
Hypotheticals, problem of contradicting, 184f.

Idealism, 3f., 23f., 31f., 50, 51f., 74f., 78, 109f., 137f., 146, 376f., 384, 406f., 413
Idealist fallacy, 152
Ideals, 2, 3f., 13, 16f., 63f., 64, 148, 267f., 271, 273, 286, 401f., 406, 445f., 446, 451f., 470
Ideas, 34f., 36, 38f., 85f., 87, 88f., 104, 105f., 124f., 126f., 132f., 371f., 379, 466f.
Ideas in Berkeley's doctrine, 34f., 39, 82f., 85f., 104f., 118f., 128f., 135f., 205ff., 379f., 385
Identity, 22f., 31, 36f., 45f., 55, 108f., 129f., 132f., 144f., 174, 197f., 246, 249f., 387f., 390f., 445, 446ff.
Identity in difference, 31, 32, 51, 99, 103, 104ff., 130f., 135
Ideologies, 102n., 311, 370f., 376f., 397, 400f., 402, 417, 446
Imperatives, 224ff., 226, 342
Implication, 4, 5f., 11f., 29f., 54f., 69, 86f., 132f., 156, 174f., 183f., 200f., 216
Implication, material, 183
Inclinations, 275ff., 277f., 447
Independence of issues or of truths, 17f., 18, 19, 23f., 29, 37, 51f., 56ff., 75f., 101, 102f., 109, 121, 153, 372, 375
Indeterminism, see Freedom, metaphysical
Individualism, 145, 336, 408, 409f., 410, 431f., 436, 442f., 444, 451f., 453, 464, 469
Inducement, 279f., 280, 286f., 312, 356, 362f., 436
Induction, 159, 247
Infinite regress, 28f., 55f., 65f., 89n., 108, 115f., 147f., 153
-ing and -ed, 45f., 77, 78f., 407, 462
Inquiry, 4f., 12, 28, 86f., 97f., 145f., 164f., 202f., 217, 224,

230, 233ff., 240, 268, 306f., 338, 348f., 357ff., 362f., 364, 426f.
Instrumentalism, 103, 107, 233f., 236, 247, 249, 255, 304, 397, 426
Intellectualism, 73, 90, 241f., 427f.
Interaction, 73ff., 118ff., 122ff., 123, 126ff., 128ff., 157, 168, 202, 210f., 250, 277ff., 304, 410, 447
Interests, operation of, in judging, 22f., 29, 46f., 87f., 91f., 94f., 274ff.
Interests, social or moral, 241f., 260, 287f., 289f., 292, 294, 297–299, 307, 369f., 412f., 424f.
Introspection, 15f., 81f., 140f., 346
Intuition, 247, 275, 309, 326, 329f., 343f., 346
Intuitionism, 289ff., 299
"Is" and "ought", 63, 157, 226, 243f., 249, 271ff., 320, 332, 416
"Is", attempts to distinguish kinds of, 3, 30, 114, 119, 135, 174, 191, 220, 390
Issue, form of, 172ff.
Issues, 1f., 23f., 49, 102f., 107f., 137f., 172f., 174f., 179f., 187f., 203f., 214f., 220, 227, 228f., 237f., 314f., 370f., 384f., 395f., 440f.

James, W., 13, 43n., 45, 46, 78, 89, 92, 100, 109, 357
James-Lange theory of emotions, 93f.
Jones, E., 433, 450, 453
Joyce, J., xxii, xxiii

"Judgment" (see also Objectivism), 246, 253, 254
Judgments, 17f., 19f., 43f., 274f., 276, 390, 465
Judgments, moral or ethical, 70, 226, 274ff., 292, 314, 316ff., 321, 329f., 340, 345, 377, 404, 440f., 446, 462, 465ff.
"Justice", political and ethical, 329, 332, 442

Kant, I., 57, 101, 103, 104f., 106f., 109f., 114f., 155, 234f., 289f., 304f., 341, 361, 383f., 401, 447, 471
Kautsky, K., 405f., 409f.
Knowledge and opinion, 262, 263
Knowledge, realist view of, 14f., 31f., 37, 44, 51, 75f., 86, 135, 140f., 152f., 208, 378, 380, 385
Knowledge, "relativity" of, 39, 374, 377
Knowledge, "storehouse" theory of, 90n., 218n.
Knowledge, "the problem" of, 103, 105, 248

La Mettrie, J. de, 250
Language, 26f., 70, 77, 218n., 228, 242, 246, 334f., 448
Language, learned and vulgar, 246n., 246f., 454f.
Laurie, Ii., 50n., 57
Law, 156, 240, 296ff., 416f., 428, 445f., 471
Laws, 257f., 267, 269
Laws of nature, in Mill and in Berkeley, 55, 158, 168, 208ff.
Legislator, utilitarian view of the, 293ff.
Leibniz, G. W., 5f., 104f., 139f.

Lenin, V. I., 265, 369, 376, 377f., 378, 379, 381f., 385, 390f., 395, 397n., 411n.
Liberal education, 239ff., 261, 265, 268, 425
Linguistic philosophy, 265, 352f.
Location and description (see also Subject and predicate), 42, 48, 87, 88, 92f., 108, 140, 148f., 174, 176, 177, 196, 201, 213, 214, 217f., 229
Locke, J., 14f., 36f., 80f., 102f., 104, 111f., 115f., 205f., 211, 216, 234, 237, 380f., 383f.
Logic as understood by Bacon and Descartes, 246
Logic of events (or situational logic), 49, 50f., 59, 61, 67f., 73f., 75f., 83, 104, 109f., 111, 136, 142, 148, 155, 204, 213, 217, 234, 312
Logic, predicative, 135f., 147, 175f., 186ff., 189, 190, 213, 217, 221, 224
Logic, "proofs" in, 155f.
Logical forms, 173ff., 185f., 190f., 193, 196, 224f.
Logical types, 229ff.
Loughnan, H. B., 156

Mach, E., 382
Marvin, W. T., 31, 52
Marx, K., 109, 141, 250f., 369ff., 397ff., 418, 420, 440
Marxism, 144, 235f., 310, 369f., 371, 376f., 384, 387, 397, 402f., 413f., 415ff., 417, 419, 420, 429, 440
Materialism, 1f., 142f., 235f., 382f., 384ff., 385, 386, 393, 406ff., 408ff.
Materialism, historical, 101n., 370, 379ff., 395f., 406, 413

Mathematical truth, 5, 216f., 254, 269
Mathematics, 11f., 205, 216, 220, 302, 321
Matter, 14f., 109f., 115f., 126f., 143f., 235, 249, 381f., 383ff., 410
McDougall, W., 90, 91f., 280
Meaning, 19, 26f., 27, 73, 191, 320f., 332f., 335f., 347f., 353, 397ff., 421, 449
Meaninglessness, 230f., 231, 457
Means and ends (see also End), 116, 119, 271, 284f., 292, 298, 323f., 325, 329, 409, 445f., 462, 464
Mehring, 410
Meinong, A., 44
Meletus, 261
Meliorism, 236, 242, 249, 251, 367f., 404, 407, 418, 428, 444, 473
Meno, 261, 263
Mentality, 84, 86, 90, 93, 121f., 137, 144, 236, 419, 423, 426
Merrylees, W. A., 50n., 61, 62f., 64, 65, 146n., 146f., 148, 151
Method, 132, 133f., 231f., 237, 247f., 255
Method of difference, direct and in-direct, 166
Method, Cartesian, and actual inquiry, 138f., 247f.
Milesians, 301
Mill, J. S., 101f., 158f., 159, 160, 166f., 168ff., 170f., 321ff., 322
Miller, E. Morris, 50n., 57, 58ff.
Miller, E. V., 50n., 67ff.
Mind, knowledge of, 14f., 15, 32f., 54, 55f., 77f., 86f., 103f., 118f., 137f., 140, 141f., 207, 247, 346f., 379, 451, 455f.

INDEX 489

Mind, objective, in Hegel, 106f., 252, 253
Mind, pluralistic view of, 37, 48, 79, 84, 85f., 107f., 144, 276, 278, 348, 360, 430ff., 436, 443, 464
Mind, threefold division of, 84f., 90
Mind, unitary view of, 15, 37, 108, 275, 346f., 348, 349, 360, 434, 467
Modals, 174, 185, 221ff.
Modern science, 107, 247, 257, 301, 367, 386
Modernism, 246f., 249, 251, 253
Money-Kyrle, R., 430, 444ff.
Monism (see also Absolute Idealism), 51, 52f., 59f., 60, 61ff., 76ff., 107f., 109f., 114f., 386f., 387
Montague, W. P., 31
Moore, G. E., 40, 45n., 69, 113, 120, 275, 282, 306, 308, 310, 313f., 316ff., 321ff., 327ff., 339, 340ff., 341, 347, 405
Moral codes, 71, 72f., 306f., 311, 313, 314
Moral faculty see faculty, moral
Moral judgment, see Judgments, moral or ethical
"Moralist's fallacy", 357
Morals and ethics, distinction between, 312ff., 332, 446
Mores, 307f., 308
Morgan, C. Lloyd, 77
Motives, 84f., 89f., 93f., 276ff., 348

Naturalism, 1, 101, 340, 341, 455
Naturalistic fallacy, 324f., 327ff., 344f.
Natures (see also Essence), 32f., 33, 36f., 40, 44, 48f., 51, 55f.,
67, 85, 97f., 107f., 111, 113f., 122, 125f., 126, 128, 129f., 139f., 143, 150, 205, 211, 219, 221f.
Necessary truths, 4f., 6, 132f., 133, 173, 221
Necessity (see also Modals), 4f., 10f., 130f., 149, 161, 206ff., 222f., 224f., 398, 404
Necessity and sufficiency, 156, 157, 161f., 165f., 167, 406
"Needs", 349, 400f., 403, 411ff., 469
Nietzsche, 432, 457
Norms, 271ff., 272, 276, 315, 316, 328, 339, 341, 352, 399f., 462ff.

Objectivism, 172, 233, 244ff., 245f., 251, 253, 347, 382, 385ff., 453
Objectivity, 19, 22, 98, 109, 208, 316ff., 321, 339f., 380, 383, 400ff., 427f., 471
Obligation (see also Duty, "Is" and "ought"), 226, 275, 285, 287f., 303ff., 326, 356
Ontological argument, 113f., 114, 134f., 138f.
Opinion (see also Belief), 66f., 252, 262, 263f., 267ff.
Order, 126, 151, 230, 269, 295f., 297, 299f., 309, 421f.
Owen, R., 250f.

Paley, W., 112
Parallelism, psycho-physical, 83f., 141f.
Parmenides (see also Eleatics), 59, 60f., 61, 62f., 146, 147, 386
Participation, 61ff.
Particulars, 63, 64f., 148f., 151f., 159, 205f., 219ff.

Percepts, 35, 38, 87
Perfection, 61f., 126f., 132f.,
  134, 152, 259f.
Phaedo, 61, 63, 65, 146, 148,
  263, 265, 268
Philosophic theme, the, 172
Philosophical retrogression,
  102f., 107, 109, 233f., 253
Philosophy as systematic, 73ff.,
  99, 101ff., 154ff., 216ff., 230ff.,
  234, 237ff.
Philosophy in education, 259f.,
  265ff., 267
Physiologism, 91
Plato, 59, 60f., 62f., 65, 99f.,
  147, 216, 246, 254, 257ff.,
  372
Plato's earlier dialogues, 257f.
Plato's later dialogues, 99, 146,
  234, 235n., 257f., 258
Pleasure (see also Utilitarianism),
  97, 207, 210, 266, 290ff., 299,
  321f., 326, 344, 434f.
Plekhanov, G., 389
Pluralism, 1ff., 47ff., 51, 108,
  109ff., 112, 114ff., 121, 125ff.,
  348, 387
Pluralistic view of mind, see Mind,
  pluralistic view of
Plurality of causes, see Causes,
  plurality of
Policy and ethics, 69, 281, 303f.,
  306, 316, 354, 359f., 423f.,
  426, 445f.
Positivism, 1, 101, 107
"Possibilities" in hypotheticals,
  181ff.
Possibility (see also Modals), 18f.,
  129, 130f., 182f., 206ff., 222,
  467f.
Potentialities (see also
  Capacities), 108, 149, 150,
  168, 452f.

Practicalism, 231, 233f., 238,
  244, 246ff., 366, 426ff., 456,
  457f.
Pragmatism, 87, 101, 108, 369,
  379
Predicate, see Subject and
  predicate
Predicates, ethical, 227f., 228,
  314f., 324, 326ff., 328, 332,
  461f.
Priestley, J., 292n.
"Principles", 5f., 12f., 16f., 71,
  72f., 84f., 101, 113, 127f.,
  135f., 186, 204, 250f., 251,
  261, 263f., 400
Prior, A. N., 352ff., 354ff.
Problems, 99f., 108f., 164, 168,
  169f., 239, 255, 259, 459f.
Progress, 101, 102f., 108, 109f.,
  235, 249f., 337f., 395f., 404,
  405f., 437, 440, 446, 453, 471f.
Progressivism, 246, 248f., 470
Property, 296ff., 386, 411, 415,
  417, 421ff., 440f.
Proposition, the, 2, 3ff., 13, 14ff.,
  31f., 37, 44f., 47, 48f., 51f., 60,
  61f., 68f., 109f., 111f., 142f.,
  146, 174, 213, 214, 215ff.,
  272, 276, 313, 340, 385, 390
Proposition treated as
  symmetrical relation, 149f.,
  150, 174, 178f., 211
Propositional functions, 180f.
Propositions, analytic, 6f., 220f.
Propositions, false, 18, 25, 28,
  95, 129, 131f., 138ff., 178,
  214, 215ff., 387f.
Propositions, forms of, 17f., 51f.,
  173ff., 174, 175, 179f., 189f.,
  192, 200f., 205, 214
Propositions, truth of, 18ff., 19f.,
  20, 23ff., 25f., 28f., 65, 86f.,
  131f., 148ff., 275, 460f., 463

Propositions, universal, see
  Universal propositions
Protagoras, 267
Proudhon, P. J., 414, 419
Psycho-analysis, 81, 86, 92, 95,
  100, 444, 445, 449f., 464, 472,
  473
"Psychologist's fallacy", 45, 357
Psychology, 15f., 45, 79f., 86f.,
  93, 94, 107, 108, 109f., 135f.,
  142f., 281, 445, 454, 457,
  459ff., 460, 462, 463, 465, 468
Purpose, 4, 26f., 38, 73f., 109f.,
  126f., 132, 172, 242, 362, 379,
  397, 399, 406n., 422f., 432f.,
  435, 466
Pythagoreans, 59, 60f., 67, 97f.,
  102f., 107f., 113f., 245, 247,
  388

Qualities and relations, 33f., 36,
  46f., 48f., 52, 53f., 61, 68, 70,
  72f., 82f., 83, 89, 90ff., 131,
  153f., 188, 202f., 205ff., 218,
  315, 325f., 336f., 340ff., 341f.,
  348, 349, 354, 365, 378, 400
Quality, degrees of, see Goodness,
  degrees of
Quantification of the predicate,
  151, 173f., 187
Quantities, arguments involving,
  189, 190, 192

"Rationalisation", 262, 345
Rationalism, 1, 3f., 6, 15, 31f.,
  32, 59, 60f., 64, 66f., 75, 102f.,
  107, 108, 109f., 111, 113f.,
  128, 129f., 132, 135f., 139f.,
  144, 145f., 165f., 204f., 211,
  233, 406, 410f., 414
Rationality, 2, 12, 15, 59, 67,
  86f., 97, 128, 130, 134, 204,
  247, 407, 446, 460, 466f.

Realism, 1f., 23f., 31f., 33, 38f.,
  39, 50f., 51, 100f., 208ff., 213,
  233, 301ff., 369, 382f., 385,
  395, 470
Reality as historical, 58f., 59, 65,
  100f., 104, 109f., 226, 245,
  249, 266, 301, 303f., 304, 372,
  379, 407
Reality, levels of, 1f., 2, 59, 64,
  67, 79, 105f., 106n., 113, 156,
  206, 210, 212, 215, 216, 228,
  230, 235, 269, 271, 304
Reason, faculty of (see also
  Faculties), 2f., 13, 84, 87, 91,
  98, 105, 278, 280f., 300
Reid, 135
Relations (see also Qualities and
  relations), 31f., 33f., 37, 46f.,
  48f., 52, 53f., 55f., 57f., 75f.,
  79f., 94f., 105f., 124f., 139f.,
  143, 144f., 163, 186ff., 206f.,
  340, 464f., 466
Relations not mind-imposed (see
  also Connections and
  distinctions jointly
  experienced), 13f., 48f.
Relative truth, see Truth, absolute
  not relative
Relativism, 66, 67f., 70, 92f.,
  106n., 119f., 230, 301ff., 302,
  304, 308, 313, 325, 330f.,
  342f., 352, 354, 363, 372ff.,
  400, 402ff., 405
Relativism, ethical, see Ethics,
  relational view of
Relativity, theory of, 9f., 39, 66f.,
  78f., 136
Reminiscence, doctrine of, 89n.,
  263
Representationism (see also
  Correspondence), 102, 105,
  111, 207f., 208, 211f., 219,
  230, 345, 378

Republic, 71, 232, 258, 260, 265f., 266ff., 283, 284, 288, 328, 332, 361
Responsibility, 278f.
Right, 30, 106n., 243, 260, 285, 297, 298, 306ff., 312, 314, 315ff., 363
Rights, 298f., 401, 417, 423, 441f., 469
Romanticism, 109f., 245f., 253
Ross, W. D., 341
Russell, B. A. W'V, 8ff., 113ff., 219, 229
Ryle, G., 216ff., 227ff., 231f., 234

Sanctions, 245, 292ff., 293, 294, 313, 447, 469
Scepticism, 19, 20f., 24f., 29f., 67f., 101f., 111, 112f., 115f., 119f., 126f., 304f., 311
Schiller, F. C. S., 17ff., 22ff.
Science and philosophy, 5, 12, 66f., 109f., 156, 230f., 231ff., 257, 367
Science, "applied", 6, 247, 272, 302, 393, 462, 463f.
Science, empirical nature of, 3, 5f., 8, 9f., 15f., 68, 69f., 104, 106, 107f., 170f., 230f., 240f., 271ff., 301f., 331, 337, 339f., 414, 426, 461ff., 465f.
Scott, J. W., 21
Security and sufficiency, 418, 421ff., 423f.
Self-knowledge, 14, 31f., 36f., 37f., 45, 76, 79f., 85, 118f., 135f., 141, 248f.
Sense-knowledge, 2f., 12f., 39f., 41ff., 58, 90, 92, 197ff., 199, 208, 215, 219, 227, 379
Sense-objects, 12f., 34f., 37ff., 44, 48, 86, 116, 152f., 205f., 210f., 381f., 384f., 406f.

Shaftesbury, Earl of, 84
Sidgwick, H., 290f., 292n., 344, 347
Situational logic, see Logic of events
Smith, N. Kemp, 112ff.
Social atomism, 339, 408, 431ff., 441f., 448, 464, 468f.
Social conflict, 234f., 252, 299f., 307, 311, 370, 403f., 408f., 428, 431, 436, 439, 441, 445, 449, 457, 470
Social forces or movements, 144, 241, 243, 251, 290, 291, 294, 295, 299f., 306, 308, 311, 315, 318, 319, 337, 338f., 343f., 371, 391f., 394, 410f., 417, 431f., 435, 445, 446f., 448
Social theory, nature of, 102n., 251, 254, 369f., 397, 428, 430, 431, 438f., 469
Social unity, doctrine of, 240, 307, 311, 316, 362, 363, 367, 368, 392, 426f., 429f.
Socialism, 395, 404f., 408, 411f., 415ff., 420ff., 429, 440
Socrates, 2f., 60f., 63, 66, 69, 70f., 84f., 89n., 99f., 113f., 126f., 134f., 146, 147f., 152, 213, 244n., 244f., 252, 257ff., 283, 288, 301, 304f., 306, 328, 340f., 361, 366f.
Sophists, 66f., 70f., 89n., 146, 246, 260, 261, 264, 267f., 301, 306
Sorel, G., 236, 237, 310, 311, 412ff., 419
Space and Time, 15, 48ff., 57ff., 76ff., 106ff., 109ff., 149f., 217, 399n.
Space-Time, 39f., 50f., 75, 83f., 234

Spatio-temporality of things (see also Reality as historical), 16, 83, 105, 117, 128, 155, 204f., 206, 227ff., 231, 245
Spencer, H., 240
Spinoza, B. de, 61, 79, 114
Stekel, W., 94n.
Stephen, L., 112
Subject and predicate, their distinction and relation, 133, 134f., 148ff., 149f., 151, 173ff., 187, 196, 197f., 201, 214f., 218f., 227, 327f., 329f., 332, 348, 352, 389, 390
"Subject-object" relation, 32f., 37, 44, 48, 52, 53, 78f., 85, 128, 135, 136f., 138, 379, 381
Subjectivism, 139, 141, 172, 233, 244f., 245, 256, 382f., 384f., 455f., 469, 471
Sublimation, 284
Super-ego, 345, 438, 450f., 451ff., 467, 469, 473f.
Syllogism, 5, 7, 148, 176, 177ff., 179, 180, 186ff., 188, 247

Teleology, 61f., 71f., 103f., 107, 108f., 114f., 308
Theaetetus, 90n., 146, 147, 263, 372
Theology, 106, 109, 111, 112, 240, 354, 367f.
"Third man" argument, 18, 63, 147
Thought (or thinking), 10f., 84f., 103, 104f., 109f., 111f., 116f., 126f., 131f., 136f., 141f., 143, 144f., 241f., 263, 267f., 301f., 381, 443
Tocqueville, A. de, 237
Totality (see also Monism), 3, 17f., 19, 20f., 22f., 99f., 101f., 105, 107, 108f., 122f., 123, 125f., 386, 393
Tradition and education, 236ff., 239ff., 262ff., 426
Transference, 284ff.
Transitiveness of relations, 165f., 186ff.
Truth, 1ff., 3ff., 6ff., 17f., 22, 23f., 51f., 59f., 87f., 90f., 98f., 109f., 129f., 154, 172f., 180f., 216f., 220f., 233, 274f., 372f., 383f., 393f., 400ff., 443, 465f.
Truth, absolute not relative, 4, 17f., 24f., 51f., 69f., 148, 153, 371ff., 372, 395, 398, 407
Truth, coherence theory of, 25, 87f.
Truth, correspondence theory of, 24, 25, 87f., 88, 90n.
Truth, degrees or kinds of, 1f., 3, 4f., 5, 8, 23f., 25, 30, 66f., 68, 69f., 146f., 173, 204f., 215, 219, 221f., 271f., 344, 460

Ultimates, 16f., 59f., 61, 66, 67f., 69, 73f., 75, 107f., 113f., 171, 204f., 205, 207, 216f., 233, 245f., 302ff., 393, 394
Unconscious, the, 44, 47, 78, 86, 346, 348, 438, 467
Universal propositions, 6, 149, 152, 159, 162, 176, 185f., 217, 220f., 222
Universals (see also Forms, theory of), 61f., 76, 146, 148f., 330
Universities (see also Educational institutions), 241f., 429
Unspeakability, 2, 13, 15, 65, 390
Usage, linguistic, 218n., 245, 315, 319, 326ff., 332, 334f., 349, 351, 352f., 353, 364

Utilitarianism, 72, 101, 104, 237, 248ff., 249f., 288ff., 310, 321f., 409, 412f., 443f.
Utility, 72, 73, 248, 288f., 293, 299f., 424f.

Validity and invalidity, see Arguments and Implication
Values (see also Judgments, moral or ethical), 16, 28, 157, 226, 237, 272f., 330f., 358f., 399f., 412f., 440f., 461ff., 466
Verifiability of all propositions, 227
Verification (see also Hypotheses, verification of), 69f., 160f., 162, 178, 228f., 380f.
Vico, G. B., 366, 442, 449, 451

Voluntarism, 123, 236, 251f., 427f., 464, 473

Watson, J. B., 334f.
Ways of life, 252, 263f., 264, 265, 298, 299, 311, 317, 337f., 343, 345, 349, 362, 372, 394, 415, 417, 426, 429, 468f.
Welfare, 251f., 252, 293, 299, 308, 311f., 321, 427f.
Will, 47, 156, 304f., 409, 444, 447
Wish, 47f., 87f., 89f., 454, 456
Wittgenstein, L., 219

Zeno (see also Eleatics), 60, 61f., 64f., 388

www.ingramcontent.com/pod-product-compliance
Lightning Source LLC
Chambersburg PA
CBHW040252170426
43191CB00019B/2382